FOUR FUNDAMENTAL QUESTIONS

AN INTRODUCTION TO PHILOSOPHY

RICHARD BILSKER
College of Southern Maryland

Kendall Hunt
publishing company

Cover images © Shutterstock, Inc.

Kendall Hunt
publishing company

www.kendallhunt.com
Send all inquiries to:
4050 Westmark Drive
Dubuque, IA 52004-1840

ISBN 978-0-7575-8675-0

Printed in the United States of America
10 9 8 7 6 5 4 3 2 1

CONTENTS

PART THREE: "WHAT CAN I KNOW?" 247

PART FOUR: "WHAT SHOULD I DO AND WHO SHOULD I BE? 371

PART ONE

"WHO OR WHAT AM I?"

Katha Upanishad

The philosophical texts of Hinduism are amongst the oldest philosophical writings, dating back as far as 1500 BCE. The Upanishads *are not the oldest of the Hindu texts, but various* Upanishads *date to as early as sixth century BCE. The word "Upanishad" means, approximately, "sit down to learn." Our selection is from the* Katha Upanishad, *which is a middle-period* Upanishad *probably composed after the development of Buddhism and Jainism, which got their starts in either the sixth or fifth centuries BCE.*

In this selection, Nachiketas meets Yama, the god of death. In it, Yama offers Nachiketas three wishes. One of the wishes he chooses is to know about life and death. Yama first resists and offers alternatives. Nachiketas is persistent and Yama relents. In the dialogue with death, Nachiketas learns about the nature of the self and how to avoid the cycle of rebirth. He learns that he has to live his life in such a way that his true self, the atman, can be revealed (the path of the good, or of wisdom), and that he must learn to not be attached to the material world, the body, or desires (the path of the pleasant, or of ignorance).

In Part IV of Four Fundamental Questions, *you will find a selection from the* Bhagavad Gita, *a later Hindu text that shows how the view of self we see here in the* Katha Upanishad *is related to the Hindu view of ethics.*

PART ONE

Chapter I

1

Vajasravasa, desiring rewards, performed the Visvajit sacrifice, in which he gave away all his property. He had a son named Nachiketa.

2—3

When the gifts were being distributed, faith entered into the heart of Nachiketa, who was still a boy. He said to himself: Joyless, surely, are the worlds to which he goes who gives away cows no longer able to drink, to eat, to give milk, or to calve.

4

He said to his father: Father! To whom will you give me? He said this a second and a third time. Then his father replied: Unto death I will give you.

5

Among many I am the first; or among many I am the middlemost. But certainly I am never the last. What purpose of the King of Death will my father serve today by thus giving me away to him?

6

Nachiketa said: Look back and see how it was with those who came before us and observe how it is with those who are now with us. A mortal ripens like corn and like corn he springs up again.

7

Verily, like fire a brahmin guest enters a house; the householder pacifies him by giving him water and a seat. Bring him water. O King of Death!

8

The brahmin who dwells in a house, fasting, destroys that foolish householder's hopes and expectations, the reward of his intercourse with pious people, the merit of his kindly speech, the good results of his sacrifices and beneficial deeds and his cattle and children as well.

9

Yama said: O Brahmin, salutations to you! You are a venerable guest and have dwelt in my house three nights without eating; therefore choose now three boons, one for each night, O Brahmin! May all be well with me!

10

Nachiketa said: O Death, may Gautama, my father, be calm, cheerful and free from anger toward me! May he recognise me and greet me when I shall have been sent home by you! This I choose as the first of the three boons.

11

Yama said: Through my favour, your father, Auddilaki Aruni, will recognise you and be again toward you as he was before. After having seen you freed from the jaws of death, he will sleep peacefully at night and bear no anger against you.

12—13

Nachiketa said: In the Heavenly World there is no fear whatsoever. You, O Death, are not there and no one is afraid of old age. Leaving behind both hunger and thirst and out of the reach of sorrow, all rejoice in Heaven.

You know, O Death, the Fire—sacrifice, which leads to Heaven. Explain it to me, for I am full of faith. The inhabitants of Heaven attain immortality. This I ask as my second boon.

14

Yama said: I know well the Fire—sacrifice, which leads to Heaven and I will explain it to you. Listen to me. Know this Fire to be the means of attaining Heaven. It is the support of the universe; it is hidden in the hearts of the wise.

15

Yama then told him about the Fire, which is the source of the worlds and what bricks were to be gathered for the altar and how many and how the sacrificial fire was to be lighted. Nachiketa, too, repeated all this as it had been told him. Then Yama, being pleased with him, spoke again.

16

High—souled Death, being well pleased, said to Nachiketa: I will now give you another boon: this fire shall be named after you. Take also from me this many—coloured chain.

17

He who has performed three times this Nachiketa sacrifice, having been instructed by the three and also has performed his three duties, overcomes birth and death. Having known this Fire born of Brahman, omniscient, luminous and adorable and realised it, he attains supreme peace.

18

He who, having known the three, has performed three times the Nachiketa sacrifice, throws off, even here, the chains of death, overcomes grief and rejoices in Heaven.

19

This, O Nachiketa, is your Fire—sacrifice, which leads to Heaven and which you have chosen as your second boon. People will call this Fire by your name. Now, O Nachiketa, choose the third boon.

20

Nachiketa said: There is this doubt about a man when he is dead: Some say that he exists; others, that he does not. This I should like to know, taught by you. This is the third of my boons.

21

Yama said: On this subject even the gods formerly had their doubts. It is not easy to understand: the nature of Atman is subtle. Choose another boon, O Nachiketa! Do not press me. Release me from that boon.

22

Nachiketa said: O Death, even the gods have their doubts about this subject; and you have declared it to be not easy to understand. But another teacher like you cannot be found and surely no other boon is comparable to this.

23

Yama said: Choose sons and grandsons who shall live a hundred years; choose elephants, horses, herds of cattle and gold. Choose a vast domain on earth; live here as many years as you desires.

24

If you deem any other boon equal to that, choose it; choose wealth and a long life. Be the king, O Nachiketa, of the wide earth. I will make you the enjoyer of all desires.

25

Whatever desires are difficult to satisfy in this world of mortals, choose them as you wish: these fair maidens, with their chariots and musical instruments—men cannot obtain them. I give them to you and they shall wait upon you. But do not ask me about death.

26

Nachiketa said: But, O Death, these endure only till tomorrow. Furthermore, they exhaust the vigour of all the sense organs. Even the longest life is short indeed. Keep your horses, dances and songs for yourself.

27

Wealth can never make a man happy. Moreover, since I have beheld you, I shall certainly obtain wealth; I shall also live as long as you rule. Therefore no boon will be accepted by me but the one that I have asked.

29

Tell me, O Death, of that Great Hereafter about which a man has his doubts.

Chapter II

1

Yama said: The good is one thing; the pleasant, another. Both of these, serving different needs, bind a man. It goes well with him who, of the two, takes the good; but he who chooses the pleasant misses the end.

2

Both the good and the pleasant present themselves to a man. The calm soul examines them well and discriminates. Yea, he prefers the good to the pleasant; but the fool chooses the pleasant out of greed and avarice.

3

O Nachiketa, after pondering well the pleasures that are or seem to he delightful, you have renounced them all. You have not taken the road abounding in wealth, where many men sink.

4

Wide apart and leading to different ends are these two: ignorance and what is known as Knowledge. I regard you, O Nachiketa, to be one who desires Knowledge; for even many pleasures could not tempt you away.

5

Fools dwelling in darkness, but thinking themselves wise and erudite, go round and round, by various tortuous paths, like the blind led by the blind.

6

The Hereafter never reveals itself to a person devoid of discrimination, heedless and perplexed by the delusion of wealth. "This world alone exists," he thinks, "and there is no other." Again and again he comes under my sway.

7

Many there are who do not even hear of Atman; though hearing of Him, many do not comprehend. Wonderful is the expounder and rare the hearer; rare indeed is the experiencer of Atman taught by an able preceptor.

8

Atman, when taught by an inferior person, is not easily comprehended, because It is diversely regarded by disputants. But when It is taught by him who has become one with Atman, there can remain no more doubt about It. Atman is subtler than the subtlest and not to be known through argument.

9

This Knowledge cannot be attained by reasoning. Atman become easy of comprehension, O dearest, when taught by another. You have attained this Knowledge now. You are, indeed, a man of true resolve. May we always have an inquirer like you!

10

Yama said: I know that the treasure resulting from action is not eternal; for what is eternal cannot be obtained by the non—eternal. Yet I have performed the Nachiketa sacrifice with the help of non—eternal things and attained this position which is only relatively eternal.

11

The fulfilment of desires, the foundation of the universe, the rewards of sacrifices, the shore where there is no fear, that which adorable and great, the wide abode and the goal—all this you have seen; and being wise, you have with firm resolve discarded everything.

12

The wise man who, by means of concentration on the Self, realises that ancient, effulgent One, who is hard to be seen, unmanifest, hidden and who dwells in the buddhi and rests in the body—he, indeed, leaves joy and sorrow far behind.

13

The mortal who has heard this and comprehended it well, who has separated that Atman, the very soul of dharma, from all physical objects and has realised the subtle essence, rejoices because he has obtained that which is the cause of rejoicing. The Abode of Brahman, I believe, is open for Nachiketa.

14

Nachiketa said: That which you see as other than righteousness and unrighteousness, other than all this cause and effect, other than what has been and what is to be—tell me That.

15

Yama said: The goal which all the Vedas declare, which all austerities aim at and which men desire when they lead the life of continence, I will tell you briefly: it is Om.

16

This syllable Om is indeed Brahman. This syllable is the Highest. Whosoever knows this syllable obtains all that he desires.

17

This is the best support; this is the highest support. Whosoever knows this support is adored in the world of Brahma.

18

The knowing Self is not born; It does not die. It has not sprung from anything; nothing has sprung from It. Birthless, eternal, everlasting and ancient, It is not killed when the body is killed.

19

If the killer thinks he kills and if the killed man thinks he is killed, neither of these apprehends aright. The Self kills not, nor is It killed.

20

Atman, smaller than the small, greater than the great, is hidden in the hearts of all living creatures. A man who is free from desires beholds the majesty of the Self through tranquillity of the senses and the mind and becomes free from grief.

21

Though sitting still, It travels far; though lying down, It goes everywhere. Who but myself can know that luminous Atman who rejoices and rejoices not?

22

The wise man, having realised Atman as dwelling within impermanent bodies but Itself bodiless, vast and all—pervading, does not grieve.

23

This Atman cannot be attained by the study of the Vedas, or by intelligence, or by much hearing of sacred books. It is attained by him alone whom It chooses. To such a one Atman reveals Its own form.

24

He who has not first turn away from wickedness, who is not tranquil and subdued and whose mind is not at peace, cannot attain Atman. It is realised only through the Knowledge of Reality.

25

Who, then, knows where He is—He to whom Brahmins and kshattriyas are mere food and death itself a condiment?

Chapter III

1

Two there are who dwell within the body, in the intellect, the supreme akasa of the heart, enjoying the sure rewards of their own actions. The knowers of Brahman describe them as light and shade, as do those householders who have offered oblations in the Five Fires and also those who have thrice performed the Nachiketa sacrifice.

2

We know how to perform the Nachiketa sacrifice, which is the bridge for sacrificers; and we know also that supreme, imperishable Brahman, which is sought by those who wish to cross over to the shore where there is no fear.

3

Know the atman to be the master of the chariot; the body, chariot; the intellect, the charioteer; and the mind, the reins.

4

The senses, they say, are the horses; the objects, the roads. The wise call the atman—united with the body, the senses and the mind—the enjoyer.

5

If the buddhi, being related to a mind that is always distracted, loses its discriminations, then the senses become uncontrolled, like the vicious horses of a charioteer.

6

But if the buddhi, being related to a mind that is always restrained, possesses discrimination, then the senses come under control, like the good horses of a charioteer.

7

If the buddhi, being related to a distracted mind, loses its discrimination and therefore always remains impure, then the embodied soul never attains the goal, but enters into the round of births.

8

But if the buddhi, being related to a mind that is restrained, possesses discrimination and therefore always remains pure, then the embodied soul attains that goal from which he is not born again.

9

A man who has discrimination for his charioteer and holds the reins of the mind firmly, reaches the end of the road; and that is the supreme position of Vishnu.

10—11

Beyond the senses are the objects; beyond the objects is the mind; beyond the mind, the intellect; beyond the intellect, the Great Atman; beyond the Great Atman, the Unmanifest; beyond the Unmanifest, the Purusha. Beyond the Purusha there is nothing: this is the end, the Supreme Goal.

12

That Self hidden in all beings does not shine forth; but It is seen by subtle seers through their one—pointed and subtle intellects.

13

The wise man should merge his speech in his mind and his mind in his intellect. He should merge his intellect in the Cosmic Mind and the Cosmic Mind in the Tranquil Self.

14

Arise! Awake! Approach the great and learn. Like the sharp edge of a razor is that path, so the wise say—hard to tread and difficult to cross.

15

Having realised Atman, which is soundless, intangible, formless, undecaying and likewise tasteless, eternal and odourless; having realised That which is without beginning and end, beyond the Great and unchanging—one is freed from the jaws of death.

16

The wise man who has heard and related the eternal story of Nachiketa, told by Death, is adored in the world of Brahman.

17

And he who, practising self—control, recites the supreme secret in an assembly of Brahmins or at a after—death ceremony obtains thereby infinite rewards. Yea, he obtains infinite rewards.

PART TWO

Chapter I

1

Yama said: The self—existent Supreme Lord inflicted an injury upon the sense—organs in creating them with outgoing tendencies; therefore a man perceives only outer objects with them and not the inner Self. But a calm person, wishing for Immortality, beholds the inner Self with his eyes closed.

2

Children pursue outer pleasures and fall into the net of widespread death; but calm souls, having known what is unshakable Immortality, do not covet any uncertain thing in this world.

3

It is through Atman that one knows form, taste, smell, sounds, touches and carnal pleasures. Is there anything that remains unknown to Atman? This, verily, is That.

4

It is through Atman that one perceives all objects in sleep or in the waking state. Having realised the vast, all—pervading Atman, the calm soul does not grieve.

5

He who knows the individual soul, the experiencer of the fruits of action, as Atman, always near and the Lord of the past and the future, will not conceal himself from others. This, verily, is That.

6

He verily knows Brahman who knows the First—born, the offspring of austerity, created prior to the waters and dwelling, with the elements, in the cave of the heart. This, verily, is That.

7

He verily knows Brahman who knows Aditi, the soul of all deities, who was born in the form of Prana, who was created with the elements and who, entering into the heart, abides therein. This, verily, is That.

8

Agni, hidden in the two fire—sticks and well guarded—like a child in the womb, by its mother—is worshipped day after day by men who are awake and by those who offer oblations in the sacrifices. This, verily, is That.

9

Whence the sun rises and whither it goes to set, in whom all the devas are contained and whom none can ever pass beyond—This, verily, is That.

10

What is here, the same is there and what is there, the same is here. He goes from death to death who sees any difference here.

11

By the mind alone is Brahman to be realised; then one does not see in It any multiplicity whatsoever. He goes from death to death who sees multiplicity in It. This, verily, is That.

12

The Purusha, of the size of a thumb, dwells in the body. He is the Lord of the past and the future. After knowing Him, one does not conceal oneself any more. This, verily, is That.

13

The Purusha, of the size of a thumb, is like a flame without smoke. The Lord of the past and the future, He is the same today and tomorrow. This, verily, is That.

14

The sages realise that indescribable Supreme Joy as "This is That." How can I realise It? Is It self—luminous? Does It shine brightly, or not?

15

The sun does not shine there, nor the moon and the stars, nor these lightnings—not to speak of this fire. He shining, everything shines after Him. By His light all this is lighted.

Chapter III

6

Having understood that the senses have their separate origin and that they are distinct from Atman and also that their rising and setting belong to them alone, a wise man grieves no more.

7

Beyond the senses is the mind, beyond the mind is the intellect, higher than the intellect is the Great Atman, higher than the Great Atman is the Unmanifest.

8

Beyond the Unmanifest is the Person, all—pervading and imperceptible. Having realised Him, the embodied self becomes liberated and attains Immortality.

9

His form is not an object of vision; no one beholds Him with the eye. One can know Him when He is revealed by the intellect free from doubt and by constant meditation. Those who know this become immortal.

10

When the five instruments of knowledge stand still, together with the mind and when the intellect does not move, that is called the Supreme State.

11

This, the firm Control of the senses, is what is called yoga. One must then be vigilant; for yoga can be both beneficial and injurious.

12

Atman cannot be attained by speech, by the mind, or by the eye. How can It be realised in any other way than by the affirmation of him who says: "He is"?

13

He is to be realised first as Existence limited by upadhis and then in His true transcendental nature. Of these two aspects, Atman realised as Existence leads the knower to the realisation of His true nature.

14

When all the desires that dwell in the heart fall away, then the mortal becomes immortal and here attains Brahman.

15

When all the ties of the heart are severed here on earth, then the mortal becomes immortal. This much alone is the teaching.

16

There are one hundred and one arteries of the heart, one of which pierces the crown of the head. Going upward by it, a man at death attains immortality. But when his prana passes out by other arteries, going in different directions, then he is reborn in the world.

17

The Purusha, not larger than a thumb, the inner Self, always dwells in the hearts of men. Let a man separate Him from his body with steadiness, as one separates the tender stalk from a blade of grass. Let him know that Self as the Bright, as the Immortal—yea, as the Bright, as the Immortal.

18

Having received this wisdom taught by the King of Death and the entire process of yoga, Nachiketa became free from impurities and death and attained Brahman. Thus it will be also with any other who knows, in this manner, the inmost Self.

End of Katha Upanishad

DISCUSSION QUESTIONS

1. Explain the difference between the two paths Yama discusses with Nachiketas.

2. One of the suggestions Yama makes is the practice of yoga. What is the role of yoga here?

3. The atman is described in a very different manner than the Judeo-Christian conception of a soul. What are some of the main differences? Explain.

The Non-Existence of Individuality

Ed. by E.J. Thomas

In "Non-Existence of Individuality," we find the Buddhist doctrine of No-Self. Buddhism formed around the teachings of Siddhartha Gautama, more commonly known as Buddha. It is difficult to place the exact dates of his life, but it was either the sixth or fifth century BCE. The text here, usually referred to as "Questions of Milinda," was probably composed between 100 BCE and 200 CE. King Milinda was a Greek warrior-king (Menander I of Bactria) who came to rule what is now India and Pakistan. It appears that Menander converted to Buddhism after conversations with the monk Nagasena.

In the dialogue, Nagasena argues that "Nagasena" is just a word, shorthand that does not refer to anything. Nagasena uses an analogy with a chariot to demonstrate his point. The chariot cannot be identified with any part of it. The word "chariot" is shorthand you can use instead of saying "all of these parts arranged in this manner." There is no one thing that is the chariot and there is no one thing that is the self. This view is called "anatman," which translates as "no atman." This is part of the Buddhist rejection of Hindu philosophy.

We will encounter Buddhism again in other sections of Four Fundamental Questions. *In Part III, there is a selection on knowledge. There is a discussion of the Buddhist view of life in Part IV.*

XXII

The denial of the individual in the following is not the denial of a fact of existence, but of the theory which was then and is still held, that there is some permanent entity behind the passing phenomena, which gives unity to what we call the individual. Our own theory of the soul, which has come down from Plato, has much in common with the ātman-theory opposed by Nāgasena. In one respect both Plato and Nāgasena make the same logical point. If you infer an entity behind an individual man, you must also logically infer it behind every individual thing, such as a chariot. Nāgasena rejects both entities, and Plato equally logically accepts both. His solution is not identical with the Indian view, but it is an acceptance of the view that it is more than the constituent parts which makes a thing what it is. In each thing—a bed, is Plato's example—he assumes "the existence of some one Form, which includes the numerous particular things to which we apply the same name" (Rep. X).

Now king Milinda approached the elder Nāgasena, and, having approached, he exchanged friendly greetings with him, and after the customary salutations he sat down at one side. And the elder Nāgasena returned the greeting, whereby he won the heart of king Milinda. Then king Milinda said to Nāgasena, "How is your reverence known, what is your name?" "O king, I am known as Nāgasena, my fellow brethren address me as Nāgasena, but whether parents give the name Nāgasena, or Sūrasena, or Vīrasena, or Sīhasena, nevertheless, O king, Nāgasena and so on is a term, appellation, designation, a mere name, for in this matter the individual does not exist."

So king Milinda said, "Let the five hundred Greeks and eighty thousand brethren hear me. Thus says this Nāgasena, that in this matter the individual does not exist; is it a wise thing to approve of this?" Then king Milinda said to Nāgasena, "If, reverend Nāgasena, the individual does not exist, who then gives you your robes, bowls, dwellings, and medicines necessary for the sick? Who enjoys them? Who keeps the commandments? Who practises meditation? Who realizes Nirvana of great fruit? Who destroys life? Who takes what is not given? Who indulges in evil lusts? Who speaks untruth? Who drinks intoxicants? Who commits the five crimes[1] that bring their fruit even in this life? Therefore there is no good, no bad, there is no doer of good or evil deeds, and no one who causes them to be done. There is no fruit or ripening of the fruit of good and bad actions. If, reverend Nāgasena, any one were to kill you, he would not be guilty of taking life, nor have you even a teacher, or instructor, or ordination. When you say that your fellow brethren call you Nāgasena, who in this matter is Nāgasena? Can it be, reverend sir, that Nāgasena is the hair[2]?" "No, O king." "Is he the hair of the body?" "No, O king." "Is Nāgasena the nails, teeth, skin, flesh, sinews, bones, marrow, kidneys, heart, liver, abdomen, spleen, lungs, intestines, mesentery, stomach, excrement, bile, phlegm, pus, blood, sweat, fat, tears, serum, saliva, mucus, lubricating fluid, urine, or brain in the head?" "No, O king." "Can the body be Nāgasena?" "No, O king." "Or the sensations, the perceptions, the predispositions [elements of the mental and moral character], or the consciousness?" "No, O king." "Then, reverend sir, is Nāgasena the body, sensations, perceptions, predispositions, and consciousness combined?" "No, O king." "Well, reverend sir, is Nāgasena anything else than these five?" "No, O king."

"Reverend sir, I ask and ask you, and do not perceive Nāgasena. Is Nāgasena anything but a mere word? Who is Nāgasena in this matter? You are uttering a falsehood: there is no Nāgasena."

Then the elder Nāgasena said to king Milinda, "You, O king, are of noble birth and very delicately nurtured; when you walk at midday with your feet on the hot ground and burning gravel, treading the hard pebbles and stones, your feet hurt, your body is wearied, your mind is afflicted, and the consciousness arises that your body is pained. Now, did you come on foot, or in a carriage?" "I did not come on foot, reverend sir, I came in a chariot." "If your majesty came in a chariot, explain to me what a chariot is. Can the chariot-pole be the chariot, O king?" "No, reverend sir." "Is the axle the chariot?" "No, reverend sir." "Are the wheels, or the frame, or the banner-staff, or the yoke, or the reins, or the goad, the chariot?" "No, reverend sir." "Then, O king, is the chariot all these parts?" "No, reverend sir." "Well, O king, is the chariot anything else than these?" "No, reverend sir." "O king, I ask and ask you, and do not perceive a chariot. Is 'chariot' anything but a mere word? What is a chariot in this matter? Your majesty is uttering a falsehood: there is no chariot. You are the first king in all India: of whom are you afraid in uttering a falsehood? Let the five hundred Greeks and eighty thousand brethren hear me. Thus says this king Milinda, that he came in a chariot, but when he is asked, 'If your majesty came in a chariot, explain to me what a chariot is,' he does not produce a chariot; is it a wise thing to approve of this?"

At these words the five hundred Greeks applauded the elder Nāgasena, and said to king Milinda, "Now let your majesty talk if you can."

So king Milinda said to the elder Nāgasena, "I utter no falsehood, reverend Nāgasena: resulting from the chariot-pole, the axle, the wheels, the frame, the banner-pole, there is that which goes under the term, designation, and name of chariot." "Well does your majesty understand what a chariot is, and even so, resulting from my hair, and so on [the thirty-two parts of the body, and the other groups of elements], there is that which goes under the term, designation, and name of Nāgasena. But in the strict sense there is no individual in the matter. And it was said by the sister Vajirā, O king, in the presence of the Lord:

For just as when its parts are joined,
A chariot, as 'tis termed, exists,
So when the khandhas are combined,
A being then exists, we say.

"Wonderful, reverend Nāgasena, marvellous, reverend Nāgasena, most excellently have the intricate questions been answered. If the Buddha were to stand here, he would applaud. Well done, well done, Nāgasena, excellently have the intricate questions been answered." (*Questions of Milinda*, 25 ff.)

ENDNOTES

1 The first five of the six great crimes mentioned in the Jewel Discourse, see p. 101.

2 This list is the Formula of the thirty-two parts of the body, a subject of meditation for realizing the doctrine of the impermanence of things. It occurs in the first section of the Miscellaneous Collection of Discourses.

DISCUSSION QUESTIONS

1. Explain how the chariot analogy is supposed to work.

2. Compare the Buddhist view of anatman to the Hindu conception found in the *Katha Upanishad*. Which position do you think is better argued? Why? Explain.

Phaedo

By Plato
Translated by Benjamin Jowett

Phaedo *is one of the middle period dialogues by Plato (428/7–348/7 BCE). The setting of this dialogue is the prison where Socrates (470–399 BCE) is awaiting his execution, but it was probably written many years after Socrates' death. Most scholars believe there is no reason to think that the words Plato puts in Socrates' mouth in* Phaedo *represent the actual ideas of Socrates. Socrates never wrote anything, as far as we know.*

The opening frame of the dialogue is Echecrates asking Phaedo if he was there when Socrates died. Phaedo replies that he was present, and then he relates the discussions that took place that day. Socrates is conversing with his friends Simmias and Cebes, and they resolve to discuss whether the soul is immortal or not as they await the signal that Socrates needs to drink the hemlock and end his life. Socrates offers three arguments in favor of the conclusion that the soul is immortal. The first is the argument from opposites. From the general premise that everything comes from its opposite and the specific premise that life and death are opposites, he concludes that as death comes from life, the opposite must also be true. A second argument comes from Plato's Theory of Recollection, which can be found in the dialogue Meno. *The Theory of Recollection states that we don't learn things in life, but rather we recollect them from a time before we were embodied. Plato offers this as a way to explain how we can come to understand perfect abstract concepts like equality or justice which we cannot experience through our senses. In* Phaedo, *this view is recalled as evidence that we must have existed before we born. Simmias and Cebes point out that is only half of what is needed—you also need that we live after bodily death. So, Socrates offers another argument, which is an analogy argument. Plato believed that objects in the material world are imperfect, temporary, and divisible; but that the intelligible world is perfect, eternal, unchanging, and indivisible (more on Plato's view of reality can be found in Part II of* Four Fundamental Questions*). He argues that the soul is more like the intelligible and that the body is more like the material. So, he concludes, by analogy, that if the soul is more like the intelligible, it must be immortal even if the body is not. Plato's view on the soul makes him a dualist on the topic, because he believes in two kinds of things, bodies and souls. Plato is also a rationalist about knowledge, since he thinks that the only path to knowledge is through reason, as opposed to sensory experience. Plato's view of knowledge will be considered in Part III of* Four Fundamental Questions.

PERSONS OF THE DIALOGUE:

Phaedo, who is the narrator of the dialogue to Echecrates of Phlius.

Socrates, Apollodorus, Simmias, Cebes, Crito and an Attendant of the Prison.

SCENE: The Prison of Socrates.

PLACE OF THE NARRATION: Phlius.

ECHECRATES: Were you yourself, Phaedo, in the prison with Socrates on the day when he drank the poison?

PHAEDO: Yes, Echecrates, I was.

ECHECRATES: I should so like to hear about his death. What did he say in his last hours? We were informed that he died by taking poison, but no one knew anything more; for no Phliasian ever goes to Athens now, and it is a long time since any stranger from Athens has found his way hither; so that we had no clear account.

PHAEDO: Did you not hear of the proceedings at the trial?

ECHECRATES: What was the manner of his death, Phaedo? What was said or done? And which of his friends were with him? Or did the authorities forbid them to be present—so that he had no friends near him when he died?

PHAEDO: No; there were several of them with him.

ECHECRATES: Well, and what did you talk about?

PHAEDO: I will begin at the beginning, and endeavour to repeat the entire conversation. On the previous days we had been in the habit of assembling early in the morning at the court in which the trial took place, and which is not far from the prison. There we used to wait talking with one another until the opening of the doors (for they were not opened very early); then we went in and generally passed the day with Socrates. On the last morning we assembled sooner than usual, having heard on the day before when we quitted the prison in the evening that the sacred ship had come from Delos, and so we arranged to meet very early at the accustomed place. On our arrival the jailer who answered the door, instead of admitting us, came out and told us to stay until he called us. 'For the Eleven,' he said, 'are now with Socrates; they are taking off his chains, and giving orders that he is to die to-day.' He soon returned and said that we might come in. On entering we found Socrates just released from chains, and Xanthippe, whom you know, sitting by him, and holding his child in her arms. When she saw us she uttered a cry and said, as women will: 'O Socrates, this is the last time that either you will converse with your friends, or they with you.' Socrates turned to Crito and said: 'Crito, let some one take her home.' Some of Crito's people accordingly led her away, crying out and beating herself. And when she was gone, Socrates, sitting up on the couch, bent and rubbed his leg, saying, as he was rubbing: How singular is the thing called pleasure, and how curiously related to pain, which might be thought to be the opposite of it; for they are never present to a man at the same instant, and yet he who pursues either is generally compelled to take the other; their bodies are two, but they are joined by a single head.

And I cannot help thinking that if Aesop had remembered them, he would have made a fable about God trying to reconcile their strife, and how, when he could not, he fastened their heads together; and this is the reason why when one comes the other follows, as I know by my own experience now, when after the pain in my leg which was caused by the chain pleasure appears to succeed.

Upon this Cebes said: I am glad, Socrates, that you have mentioned the name of Aesop. For it reminds me of a question which has been asked by many, and was asked of me only the day before yesterday by Evenus the poet—he will be sure to ask it again, and therefore if you would like me to have an answer ready for him, you may as well tell me what I should say to him:—he wanted to know why you, who never before wrote a line of poetry, now that you are in prison are turning Aesop's fables into verse, and also composing that hymn in honour of Apollo.

Tell him, Cebes, he replied, what is the truth—that I had no idea of rivalling him or his poems; to do so, as I knew, would be no easy task. But I wanted to see whether I could purge away a scruple which I felt about the meaning of certain dreams. In the course of my life I have often had intimations in dreams 'that I should compose music.' The same dream came to me sometimes in one form, and sometimes in another, but always saying the same or nearly the same words: 'Cultivate and make music,' said the dream. And hitherto I had imagined that this was only intended to exhort and encourage me in the study of philosophy, which has been the pursuit of my life, and is the noblest and best of music. The dream was bidding me do what I was already doing, in the same way that the competitor in a race is bidden by the spectators to run when he is already running. But I was not certain of this, for the dream might have meant music in the popular sense of the word, and being under sentence of death, and the festival giving me a respite, I thought that it would be safer for me to satisfy the scruple, and, in obedience to the dream, to compose a few verses before I departed. And first I made a hymn in honour of the god of the festival, and then considering that a poet, if he is really to be a poet, should not only put together words, but should invent stories, and that I have no invention, I took some fables of Aesop, which I had ready at hand and which I knew—they were the first I came upon—and turned them into verse. Tell this to Evenus, Cebes, and bid him be of good cheer; say that I would have him come after me if he be a wise man, and not tarry; and that to-day I am likely to be going, for the Athenians say that I must.

Simmias said: What a message for such a man! having been a frequent companion of his I should say that, as far as I know him, he will never take your advice unless he is obliged.

Why, said Socrates,—is not Evenus a philosopher?

I think that he is, said Simmias.

Then he, or any man who has the spirit of philosophy, will be willing to die, but he will not take his own life, for that is held to be unlawful.

Here he changed his position, and put his legs off the couch on to the ground, and during the rest of the conversation he remained sitting.

Why do you say, enquired Cebes, that a man ought not to take his own life, but that the philosopher will be ready to follow the dying?

Socrates replied: And have you, Cebes and Simmias, who are the disciples of Philolaus, never heard him speak of this?

Yes, but his language was obscure, Socrates.

My words, too, are only an echo; but there is no reason why I should not repeat what I have heard: and indeed, as I am going to another place, it is very meet for me to be thinking and talking of the nature of the pilgrimage which I am about to make. What can I do better in the interval between this and the setting of the sun?

Then tell me, Socrates, why is suicide held to be unlawful? as I have certainly heard Philolaus, about whom you were just now asking, affirm when he was staying with us at Thebes: and there are others who say the same, although I have never understood what was meant by any of them.

Do not lose heart, replied Socrates, and the day may come when you will understand. I suppose that you wonder why, when other things which are evil may be good at certain times and to certain persons, death is to be the only exception, and why, when a man is better dead, he is not permitted to be his own benefactor, but must wait for the hand of another.

Very true, said Cebes, laughing gently and speaking in his native Boeotian.

I admit the appearance of inconsistency in what I am saying; but there may not be any real inconsistency after all. There is a doctrine whispered in secret that man is a prisoner who has no right to open the door and run away; this is a great mystery which I do not quite understand. Yet I too believe that the gods are our guardians, and that we are a possession of theirs. Do you not agree?

Yes, I quite agree, said Cebes.

And if one of your own possessions, an ox or an ass, for example, took the liberty of putting himself out of the way when you had given no intimation of your wish that he should die, would you not be angry with him, and would you not punish him if you could?

Certainly, replied Cebes.

Then, if we look at the matter thus, there may be reason in saying that a man should wait, and not take his own life until God summons him, as he is now summoning me.

Yes, Socrates, said Cebes, there seems to be truth in what you say. And yet how can you reconcile this seemingly true belief that God is our guardian and we his possessions, with the willingness to die which we were just now attributing to the philosopher? That the wisest of men should be willing to leave a service in which they are ruled by the gods who are the best of rulers, is not reasonable; for surely no wise man thinks that when set at liberty he can take better care of himself than the gods take of him. A fool may perhaps think so—he may argue that he had better run away from his master, not considering that his duty is to remain to the end, and not to run away from the good, and that there would be no sense in his running away. The wise man will want to be ever with him who is better than himself. Now this,

Socrates, is the reverse of what was just now said; for upon this view the wise man should sorrow and the fool rejoice at passing out of life.

The earnestness of Cebes seemed to please Socrates. Here, said he, turning to us, is a man who is always inquiring, and is not so easily convinced by the first thing which he hears.

And certainly, added Simmias, the objection which he is now making does appear to me to have some force. For what can be the meaning of a truly wise man wanting to fly away and lightly leave a master who is better than himself? And I rather imagine that Cebes is referring to you; he thinks that you are too ready to leave us, and too ready to leave the gods whom you acknowledge to be our good masters.

Yes, replied Socrates; there is reason in what you say. And so you think that I ought to answer your indictment as if I were in a court?

We should like you to do so, said Simmias.

Then I must try to make a more successful defence before you than I did when before the judges. For I am quite ready to admit, Simmias and Cebes, that I ought to be grieved at death, if I were not persuaded in the first place that I am going to other gods who are wise and good (of which I am as certain as I can be of any such matters), and secondly (though I am not so sure of this last) to men departed, better than those whom I leave behind; and therefore I do not grieve as I might have done, for I have good hope that there is yet something remaining for the dead, and as has been said of old, some far better thing for the good than for the evil.

But do you mean to take away your thoughts with you, Socrates? said Simmias. Will you not impart them to us?—for they are a benefit in which we too are entitled to share. Moreover, if you succeed in convincing us, that will be an answer to the charge against yourself.

I will do my best, replied Socrates. But you must first let me hear what Crito wants; he has long been wishing to say something to me.

Only this, Socrates, replied Crito:—the attendant who is to give you the poison has been telling me, and he wants me to tell you, that you are not to talk much, talking, he says, increases heat, and this is apt to interfere with the action of the poison; persons who excite themselves are sometimes obliged to take a second or even a third dose.

Then, said Socrates, let him mind his business and be prepared to give the poison twice or even thrice if necessary; that is all.

I knew quite well what you would say, replied Crito; but I was obliged to satisfy him.

Never mind him, he said.

And now, O my judges, I desire to prove to you that the real philosopher has reason to be of good cheer when he is about to die, and that after death he may hope to obtain the greatest good in the other world. And how this may be, Simmias and Cebes, I will endeavour to explain. For I deem that the true votary of philosophy is likely to be misunderstood by other men; they do not perceive that he is always pursuing death and dying; and if this be so, and he has had the desire of death all his life long, why when his time comes should he repine at that which he has been always pursuing and desiring?

Simmias said laughingly: Though not in a laughing humour, you have made me laugh, Socrates; for I cannot help thinking that the many when they hear your words will say how truly you have described philosophers, and our people at home will likewise say that the life which philosophers desire is in reality death, and that they have found them out to be deserving of the death which they desire.

And they are right, Simmias, in thinking so, with the exception of the words 'they have found them out'; for they have not found out either what is the nature of that death which the true philosopher deserves, or how he deserves or desires death. But enough of them:—let us discuss the matter among ourselves: Do we believe that there is such a thing as death?

To be sure, replied Simmias.

Is it not the separation of soul and body? And to be dead is the completion of this; when the soul exists in herself, and is released from the body and the body is released from the soul, what is this but death?

Just so, he replied.

There is another question, which will probably throw light on our present inquiry if you and I can agree about it:—Ought the philosopher to care about the pleasures—if they are to be called pleasures—of eating and drinking?

Certainly not, answered Simmias.

And what about the pleasures of love—should he care for them?

By no means.

And will he think much of the other ways of indulging the body, for example, the acquisition of costly raiment, or sandals, or other adornments of the body? Instead of caring about them, does he not rather despise anything more than nature needs? What do you say?

I should say that the true philosopher would despise them.

Would you not say that he is entirely concerned with the soul and not with the body? He would like, as far as he can, to get away from the body and to turn to the soul.

Quite true.

In matters of this sort philosophers, above all other men, may be observed in every sort of way to dissever the soul from the communion of the body.

Very true.

Whereas, Simmias, the rest of the world are of opinion that to him who has no sense of pleasure and no part in bodily pleasure, life is not worth having; and that he who is indifferent about them is as good as dead.

That is also true.

What again shall we say of the actual acquirement of knowledge?—is the body, if invited to share in the enquiry, a hinderer or a helper? I mean to say, have sight and hearing any truth in them? Are they not, as the poets are always telling us, inaccurate witnesses? and yet, if even they are inaccurate and indistinct, what is to be said of the other senses?—for you will allow that they are the best of them?

Certainly, he replied.

Then when does the soul attain truth?—for in attempting to consider anything in company with the body she is obviously deceived.

True.

Then must not true existence be revealed to her in thought, if at all?

Yes.

And thought is best when the mind is gathered into herself and none of these things trouble her—neither sounds nor sights nor pain nor any pleasure,—when she takes leave of the body, and has as little as possible to do with it, when she has no bodily sense or desire, but is aspiring after true being?

Certainly.

And in this the philosopher dishonours the body; his soul runs away from his body and desires to be alone and by herself?

That is true.

Well, but there is another thing, Simmias: Is there or is there not an absolute justice?

Assuredly there is.

And an absolute beauty and absolute good?

Of course.

But did you ever behold any of them with your eyes?

Certainly not.

Or did you ever reach them with any other bodily sense?—and I speak not of these alone, but of absolute greatness, and health, and strength, and of the essence or true nature of everything. Has the reality of them ever been perceived by you through the bodily organs? or rather, is not the nearest approach to the knowledge of their several natures made by him who so orders his intellectual vision as to have the most exact conception of the essence of each thing which he considers?

Certainly.

And he attains to the purest knowledge of them who goes to each with the mind alone, not introducing or intruding in the act of thought sight or any other sense together with reason, but with the very light of the mind in her own clearness searches into the very truth of each; he who has got rid, as far as he can, of eyes and ears and, so to speak, of the whole body, these being in his opinion distracting elements which when they infect the soul hinder her from acquiring truth and knowledge—who, if not he, is likely to attain the knowledge of true being?

What you say has a wonderful truth in it, Socrates, replied Simmias.

And when real philosophers consider all these things, will they not be led to make a reflection which they will express in words something like the following? 'Have we not found,' they will say, 'a path of thought which seems to bring us and our argument to the conclusion, that while we are in the body, and while the soul is infected with the evils of the body, our desire will not be satisfied? and our desire is of the truth. For the body is a source of endless trouble to us by reason of the mere requirement of food; and is liable also to diseases which overtake and impede us in the search after true being: it fills us full of loves, and lusts, and fears, and fancies of all kinds, and endless foolery, and in fact, as men say, takes away from us the power of thinking at all. Whence come wars, and fightings, and factions? whence but from the body and the lusts of the body? wars are occasioned by the love of money, and money has to be acquired for the sake and in the service of the body; and by reason of all these impediments we have no time to give to philosophy; and, last and worst of all, even if we are at leisure and betake ourselves to some speculation, the body is always breaking in upon us, causing turmoil and confusion in our enquiries, and so amazing us that we are prevented from seeing the truth. It has been proved to us by experience that if we would have pure knowledge of anything we must be quit of the body—the soul in herself must behold things in themselves: and then we shall attain the wisdom which we desire, and of which we say that we are lovers, not while we live, but after death; for if while in company with the body, the soul cannot have pure knowledge, one of two things follows—either knowledge is not to be attained at all, or, if at all, after death. For then, and not till then, the soul will be parted from the body and exist in herself alone. In this present life, I reckon that we make the nearest approach to knowledge when we have the least possible intercourse or communion with the body, and are not surfeited with the bodily nature, but keep ourselves pure until the hour when God himself is pleased to release us. And thus having got rid of the foolishness of the body we shall be pure and hold converse with the pure, and know of ourselves the clear light everywhere, which is no other than the light of truth.' For the impure are not permitted to approach the pure. These are the sort of words, Simmias, which the true lovers of knowledge cannot help saying to one another, and thinking. You would agree; would you not?

Undoubtedly, Socrates.

But, O my friend, if this is true, there is great reason to hope that, going whither I go, when I have come to the end of my journey, I shall attain that which has been the pursuit of my life. And therefore I go on my way rejoicing, and not I only, but every other man who believes that his mind has been made ready and that he is in a manner purified.

Certainly, replied Simmias.

And what is purification but the separation of the soul from the body, as I was saying before; the habit of the soul gathering and collecting herself into herself from all sides out of the body; the dwelling in her own place alone, as in another life, so also in this, as far as she can;—the release of the soul from the chains of the body?

Very true, he said.

And this separation and release of the soul from the body is termed death?

To be sure, he said.

And the true philosophers, and they only, are ever seeking to release the soul. Is not the separation and release of the soul from the body their especial study?

That is true.

And, as I was saying at first, there would be a ridiculous contradiction in men studying to live as nearly as they can in a state of death, and yet repining when it comes upon them.

Clearly.

And the true philosophers, Simmias, are always occupied in the practice of dying, wherefore also to them least of all men is death terrible. Look at the matter thus:—if they have been in every way the enemies of the body, and are wanting to be alone with the soul, when this desire of theirs is granted, how inconsistent would they be if they trembled and repined, instead of rejoicing at their departure to that place where, when they arrive, they hope to gain that which in life they desired—and this was wisdom—and at the same time to be rid of the company of their enemy. Many a man has been willing to go to the world below animated by the hope of seeing there an earthly love, or wife, or son, and conversing with them.

And will he who is a true lover of wisdom, and is strongly persuaded in like manner that only in the world below he can worthily enjoy her, still repine at death? Will he not depart with joy? Surely he will, O my friend, if he be a true philosopher. For he will have a firm conviction that there and there only, he can find wisdom in her purity. And if this be true, he would be very absurd, as I was saying, if he were afraid of death.

He would, indeed, replied Simmias.

And when you see a man who is repining at the approach of death, is not his reluctance a sufficient proof that he is not a lover of wisdom, but a lover of the body, and probably at the same time a lover of either money or power, or both?

Quite so, he replied.

And is not courage, Simmias, a quality which is specially characteristic of the philosopher?

Certainly.

There is temperance again, which even by the vulgar is supposed to consist in the control and regulation of the passions, and in the sense of superiority to them—is not temperance a virtue belonging to those only who despise the body, and who pass their lives in philosophy?

Most assuredly.

For the courage and temperance of other men, if you will consider them, are really a contradiction.

How so?

Well, he said, you are aware that death is regarded by men in general as a great evil.

Very true, he said.

And do not courageous men face death because they are afraid of yet greater evils?

That is quite true.

Then all but the philosophers are courageous only from fear, and because they are afraid; and yet that a man should be courageous from fear, and because he is a coward, is surely a strange thing.

Very true.

And are not the temperate exactly in the same case? They are temperate because they are intemperate—which might seem to be a contradiction, but is nevertheless the sort of thing which happens with this foolish temperance. For there are pleasures which they are afraid of losing; and in their desire to keep them, they abstain from some pleasures, because they are overcome by others; and although to be conquered by pleasure is called by men intemperance, to them the conquest of pleasure consists in being conquered by pleasure. And that is what I mean by saying that, in a sense, they are made temperate through intemperance.

Such appears to be the case.

Yet the exchange of one fear or pleasure or pain for another fear or pleasure or pain, and of the greater for the less, as if they were coins, is not the exchange of virtue. O my blessed Simmias, is there not one true coin for which all things ought to be exchanged?—and that is wisdom; and only in exchange for this, and in company with this, is anything truly bought or sold, whether courage or temperance or justice. And is not all true virtue the companion of wisdom, no matter what fears or pleasures or other similar goods or evils may or may not attend her? But the virtue which is made up of these goods, when they are severed from wisdom and exchanged with one another, is a shadow of virtue only, nor is there any freedom or health or truth in her; but in the true exchange there is a purging away of all these things, and temperance, and justice, and courage, and wisdom herself are the purgation of them. The founders of the mysteries would appear to have had a real meaning, and were not talking nonsense when they intimated in a figure long ago that he who passes unsanctified and uninitiated into the world below will lie in a slough, but that he who arrives there after initiation and purification will dwell with the gods. For 'many,' as they say in the mysteries, 'are the thyrsus-bearers, but few are the mystics,'—meaning, as I interpret the words, 'the true philosophers.' In the number of whom, during my whole life, I have been seeking, according to my ability, to find a place;—whether I have sought in a right way or not, and whether I have succeeded or not, I shall truly know in a little while, if God will, when I myself arrive in the other world—such is my belief. And therefore I maintain that I am right, Simmias and Cebes, in not grieving or repining at parting from you and my masters in this world, for I believe that I shall equally find good masters and friends in another world. But most men do not believe this saying; if then I succeed in convincing you by my defence better than I did the Athenian judges, it will be well.

Cebes answered: I agree, Socrates, in the greater part of what you say. But in what concerns the soul, men are apt to be incredulous; they fear that when she has left the body her place may be nowhere, and that on the very day of death she may perish and come to an end—immediately on her release from the body, issuing forth dispersed like smoke or air and in her flight vanishing away into nothingness.

If she could only be collected into herself after she has obtained release from the evils of which you are speaking, there would be good reason to hope, Socrates, that what you say is true. But surely it requires a great deal of argument and many proofs to show that when the man is dead his soul yet exists, and has any force or intelligence.

True, Cebes, said Socrates; and shall I suggest that we converse a little of the probabilities of these things?

I am sure, said Cebes, that I should greatly like to know your opinion about them.

I reckon, said Socrates, that no one who heard me now, not even if he were one of my old enemies, the Comic poets, could accuse me of idle talking about matters in which I have no concern:—If you please, then, we will proceed with the inquiry.

Suppose we consider the question whether the souls of men after death are or are not in the world below. There comes into my mind an ancient doctrine which affirms that they go from hence into the other world, and returning hither, are born again from the dead. Now if it be true that the living come from the dead, then our souls must exist in the other world, for if not, how could they have been born again? And this would be conclusive, if there were any real evidence that the living are only born from the dead; but if this is not so, then other arguments will have to be adduced.

Very true, replied Cebes.

Then let us consider the whole question, not in relation to man only, but in relation to animals generally, and to plants, and to everything of which there is generation, and the proof will be easier. Are not all things which have opposites generated out of their opposites? I mean such things as good and evil, just and unjust—and there are innumerable other opposites which are generated out of opposites. And I want to show that in all opposites there is of necessity a similar alternation; I mean to say, for example, that anything which becomes greater must become greater after being less.

True.

And that which becomes less must have been once greater and then have become less.

Yes.

And the weaker is generated from the stronger, and the swifter from the slower.

Very true.

And the worse is from the better, and the more just is from the more unjust.

Of course.

And is this true of all opposites? and are we convinced that all of them are generated out of opposites?

Yes.

And in this universal opposition of all things, are there not also two intermediate processes which are ever going on, from one to the other opposite, and back again; where there is a greater and a less there is also an intermediate process of increase and diminution, and that which grows is said to wax, and that which decays to wane?

Yes, he said.

And there are many other processes, such as division and composition, cooling and heating, which equally involve a passage into and out of one another. And this necessarily holds of all opposites, even though not always expressed in words—they are really generated out of one another, and there is a passing or process from one to the other of them?

Very true, he replied.

Well, and is there not an opposite of life, as sleep is the opposite of waking?

True, he said.

And what is it?

Death, he answered.

And these, if they are opposites, are generated the one from the other, and have there their two intermediate processes also?

Of course.

Now, said Socrates, I will analyze one of the two pairs of opposites which I have mentioned to you, and also its intermediate processes, and you shall analyze the other to me. One of them I term sleep, the other waking. The state of sleep is opposed to the state of waking, and out of sleeping waking is generated, and out of waking, sleeping; and the process of generation is in the one case falling asleep, and in the other waking up.

Do you agree?

I entirely agree.

Then, suppose that you analyze life and death to me in the same manner. Is not death opposed to life?

Yes.

And they are generated one from the other?

Yes.

What is generated from the living?

The dead.

And what from the dead?

I can only say in answer—the living.

Then the living, whether things or persons, Cebes, are generated from the dead?

That is clear, he replied.

Then the inference is that our souls exist in the world below?

That is true.

And one of the two processes or generations is visible—for surely the act of dying is visible?

Surely, he said.

What then is to be the result? Shall we exclude the opposite process? And shall we suppose nature to walk on one leg only? Must we not rather assign to death some corresponding process of generation?

Certainly, he replied.

And what is that process?

Return to life.

And return to life, if there be such a thing, is the birth of the dead into the world of the living?

Quite true.

Then here is a new way by which we arrive at the conclusion that the living come from the dead, just as the dead come from the living; and this, if true, affords a most certain proof that the souls of the dead exist in some place out of which they come again.

Yes, Socrates, he said; the conclusion seems to flow necessarily out of our previous admissions.

And that these admissions were not unfair, Cebes, he said, may be shown, I think, as follows: If generation were in a straight line only, and there were no compensation or circle in nature, no turn or return of elements into their opposites, then you know that all things would at last have the same form and pass into the same state, and there would be no more generation of them.

What do you mean? he said.

A simple thing enough, which I will illustrate by the case of sleep, he replied. You know that if there were no alternation of sleeping and waking, the tale of the sleeping Endymion would in the end have no meaning, because all other things would be asleep, too, and he would not be distinguishable from the rest. Or if there were composition only, and no division of substances, then the chaos of Anaxagoras would come again. And in like manner, my dear Cebes, if all things which partook of life were to die, and after they were dead remained in the form of death, and did not come to life again, all would at last die, and nothing would be alive—what other result could there be? For if the living spring from any other things, and they too die, must not all things at last be swallowed up in death? (But compare Republic.)

There is no escape, Socrates, said Cebes; and to me your argument seems to be absolutely true.

Yes, he said, Cebes, it is and must be so, in my opinion; and we have not been deluded in making these admissions; but I am confident that there truly is such a thing as living again, and that the living spring from the dead, and that the souls of the dead are in existence, and that the good souls have a better portion than the evil.

Cebes added: Your favorite doctrine, Socrates, that knowledge is simply recollection, if true, also necessarily implies a previous time in which we have learned that which we now recollect. But this would be impossible unless our soul had been in some place before existing in the form of man; here then is another proof of the soul's immortality.

But tell me, Cebes, said Simmias, interposing, what arguments are urged in favour of this doctrine of recollection. I am not very sure at the moment that I remember them.

One excellent proof, said Cebes, is afforded by questions. If you put a question to a person in a right way, he will give a true answer of himself, but how could he do this unless there were knowledge and right reason already in him? And this is most clearly shown when he is taken to a diagram or to anything of that sort. (Compare Meno.)

But if, said Socrates, you are still incredulous, Simmias, I would ask you whether you may not agree with me when you look at the matter in another way;—I mean, if you are still incredulous as to whether knowledge is recollection.

Incredulous, I am not, said Simmias; but I want to have this doctrine of recollection brought to my own recollection, and, from what Cebes has said, I am beginning to recollect and be convinced; but I should still like to hear what you were going to say.

This is what I would say, he replied:—We should agree, if I am not mistaken, that what a man recollects he must have known at some previous time.

Very true.

And what is the nature of this knowledge or recollection? I mean to ask, Whether a person who, having seen or heard or in any way perceived anything, knows not only that, but has a conception of something else which is the subject, not of the same but of some other kind of knowledge, may not be fairly said to recollect that of which he has the conception?

What do you mean?

I mean what I may illustrate by the following instance:—The knowledge of a lyre is not the same as the knowledge of a man?

True.

And yet what is the feeling of lovers when they recognize a lyre, or a garment, or anything else which the beloved has been in the habit of using? Do not they, from knowing the lyre, form in the mind's eye an image of the youth to whom the lyre belongs? And this is recollection. In like manner any one who sees Simmias may remember Cebes; and there are endless examples of the same thing.

Endless, indeed, replied Simmias.

And recollection is most commonly a process of recovering that which has been already forgotten through time and inattention.

Very true, he said.

Well; and may you not also from seeing the picture of a horse or a lyre remember a man? and from the picture of Simmias, you may be led to remember Cebes?

True.

Or you may also be led to the recollection of Simmias himself?

Quite so.

And in all these cases, the recollection may be derived from things either like or unlike?

It may be.

And when the recollection is derived from like things, then another consideration is sure to arise, which is—whether the likeness in any degree falls short or not of that which is recollected?

Very true, he said.

And shall we proceed a step further, and affirm that there is such a thing as equality, not of one piece of wood or stone with another, but that, over and above this, there is absolute equality? Shall we say so?

Say so, yes, replied Simmias, and swear to it, with all the confidence in life.

And do we know the nature of this absolute essence?

To be sure, he said.

And whence did we obtain our knowledge? Did we not see equalities of material things, such as pieces of wood and stones, and gather from them the idea of an equality which is different from them? For you will acknowledge that there is a difference. Or look at the matter in another way:—Do not the same pieces of wood or stone appear at one time equal, and at another time unequal?

That is certain.

But are real equals ever unequal? or is the idea of equality the same as of inequality?

Impossible, Socrates.

Then these (so-called) equals are not the same with the idea of equality?

I should say, clearly not, Socrates.

And yet from these equals, although differing from the idea of equality, you conceived and attained that idea?

Very true, he said.

Which might be like, or might be unlike them?

Yes.

But that makes no difference; whenever from seeing one thing you conceived another, whether like or unlike, there must surely have been an act of recollection?

Very true.

But what would you say of equal portions of wood and stone, or other material equals? and what is the impression produced by them? Are they equals in the same sense in which absolute equality is equal? or do they fall short of this perfect equality in a measure?

Yes, he said, in a very great measure too.

And must we not allow, that when I or any one, looking at any object, observes that the thing which he sees aims at being some other thing, but falls short of, and cannot be, that other thing, but is inferior, he who makes this observation must have had a previous knowledge of that to which the other, although similar, was inferior?

Certainly.

And has not this been our own case in the matter of equals and of absolute equality?

Precisely.

Then we must have known equality previously to the time when we first saw the material equals, and reflected that all these apparent equals strive to attain absolute equality, but fall short of it?

Very true.

And we recognize also that this absolute equality has only been known, and can only be known, through the medium of sight or touch, or of some other of the senses, which are all alike in this respect?

Yes, Socrates, as far as the argument is concerned, one of them is the same as the other.

From the senses then is derived the knowledge that all sensible things aim at an absolute equality of which they fall short?

Yes.

Then before we began to see or hear or perceive in any way, we must have had a knowledge of absolute equality, or we could not have referred to that standard the equals which are derived from the senses?—for to that they all aspire, and of that they fall short.

No other inference can be drawn from the previous statements.

And did we not see and hear and have the use of our other senses as soon as we were born?

Certainly.

Then we must have acquired the knowledge of equality at some previous time?

Yes.

That is to say, before we were born, I suppose?

True.

And if we acquired this knowledge before we were born, and were born having the use of it, then we also knew before we were born and at the instant of birth not only the equal or the greater or the less, but all other ideas; for we are not speaking only of equality, but of beauty, goodness, justice, holiness, and of all which we stamp with the name of essence in the dialectical process, both when we ask and when we answer questions. Of all this we may certainly affirm that we acquired the knowledge before birth?

We may.

But if, after having acquired, we have not forgotten what in each case we acquired, then we must always have come into life having knowledge, and shall always continue to know as long as life lasts—for knowing is the acquiring and retaining knowledge and not forgetting. Is not forgetting, Simmias, just the losing of knowledge?

Quite true, Socrates.

But if the knowledge which we acquired before birth was lost by us at birth, and if afterwards by the use of the senses we recovered what we previously knew, will not the process which we call learning be a recovering of the knowledge which is natural to us, and may not this be rightly termed recollection?

Very true.

So much is clear—that when we perceive something, either by the help of sight, or hearing, or some other sense, from that perception we are able to obtain a notion of some other thing like or unlike which is associated with it but has been forgotten. Whence, as I was saying, one of two alternatives follows:—either we had this knowledge at birth, and continued to know through life; or, after birth, those who are said to learn only remember, and learning is simply recollection.

Yes, that is quite true, Socrates.

And which alternative, Simmias, do you prefer? Had we the knowledge at our birth, or did we recollect the things which we knew previously to our birth?

I cannot decide at the moment.

At any rate you can decide whether he who has knowledge will or will not be able to render an account of his knowledge? What do you say?

Certainly, he will.

But do you think that every man is able to give an account of these very matters about which we are speaking?

Would that they could, Socrates, but I rather fear that tomorrow, at this time, there will no longer be any one alive who is able to give an account of them such as ought to be given.

Then you are not of opinion, Simmias, that all men know these things?

Certainly not.

They are in process of recollecting that which they learned before?

Certainly.

But when did our souls acquire this knowledge?—not since we were born as men?

Certainly not.

And therefore, previously?

Yes.

Then, Simmias, our souls must also have existed without bodies before they were in the form of man, and must have had intelligence.

Unless indeed you suppose, Socrates, that these notions are given us at the very moment of birth; for this is the only time which remains.

Yes, my friend, but if so, when do we lose them? for they are not in us when we are born—that is admitted. Do we lose them at the moment of receiving them, or if not at what other time?

No, Socrates, I perceive that I was unconsciously talking nonsense.

Then may we not say, Simmias, that if, as we are always repeating, there is an absolute beauty, and goodness, and an absolute essence of all things; and if to this, which is now discovered to have existed in our former state, we refer all our sensations, and with this compare them, finding these ideas to be pre-existent and our inborn possession—then our souls must have had a prior existence, but if not, there would be no force in the argument? There is the same proof that these ideas must have existed before we were born, as that our souls existed before we were born; and if not the ideas, then not the souls.

Yes, Socrates; I am convinced that there is precisely the same necessity for the one as for the other; and the argument retreats successfully to the position that the existence of the soul before birth cannot be separated from the existence of the essence of which you speak. For there is nothing which to my mind is so patent as that beauty, goodness, and the other notions of which you were just now speaking, have a most real and absolute existence; and I am satisfied with the proof.

Well, but is Cebes equally satisfied? for I must convince him too.

I think, said Simmias, that Cebes is satisfied: although he is the most incredulous of mortals, yet I believe that he is sufficiently convinced of the existence of the soul before birth. But that after death the soul will continue to exist is not yet proven even to my own satisfaction. I cannot get rid of the feeling of the many to which Cebes was referring—the feeling that when the man dies the soul will be dispersed, and that this may be the extinction of her. For admitting that she may have been born elsewhere, and framed out of other elements, and was in existence before entering the human body, why after having entered in and gone out again may she not herself be destroyed and come to an end?

Very true, Simmias, said Cebes; about half of what was required has been proven; to wit, that our souls existed before we were born:—that the soul will exist after death as well as before birth is the other half of which the proof is still wanting, and has to be supplied; when that is given the demonstration will be complete.

But that proof, Simmias and Cebes, has been already given, said Socrates, if you put the two arguments together—I mean this and the former one, in which we admitted that everything living is born of the dead. For if the soul exists before birth, and in coming to life and being born can be born only from death and dying, must she not after death continue to exist, since she has to be born again?—Surely the proof which you desire has been already furnished. Still I suspect that you and Simmias would be glad to probe the argument further. Like children, you are haunted with a fear that when the soul leaves the body, the wind may really blow her away and scatter her; especially if a man should happen to die in a great storm and not when the sky is calm.

Cebes answered with a smile: Then, Socrates, you must argue us out of our fears—and yet, strictly speaking, they are not our fears, but there is a child within us to whom death is a sort of hobgoblin; him too we must persuade not to be afraid when he is alone in the dark.

Socrates said: Let the voice of the charmer be applied daily until you have charmed away the fear.

And where shall we find a good charmer of our fears, Socrates, when you are gone?

Hellas, he replied, is a large place, Cebes, and has many good men, and there are barbarous races not a few: seek for him among them all, far and wide, sparing neither pains nor money; for there is no better way of spending your money. And you must seek among yourselves too; for you will not find others better able to make the search.

The search, replied Cebes, shall certainly be made. And now, if you please, let us return to the point of the argument at which we digressed.

By all means, replied Socrates; what else should I please?

Very good.

Must we not, said Socrates, ask ourselves what that is which, as we imagine, is liable to be scattered, and about which we fear? and what again is that about which we have no fear? And then we may proceed further to enquire whether that which suffers dispersion is or is not of the nature of soul—our hopes and fears as to our own souls will turn upon the answers to these questions.

Very true, he said.

Now the compound or composite may be supposed to be naturally capable, as of being compounded, so also of being dissolved; but that which is uncompounded, and that only, must be, if anything is, indissoluble.

Yes; I should imagine so, said Cebes.

And the uncompounded may be assumed to be the same and unchanging, whereas the compound is always changing and never the same.

I agree, he said.

Then now let us return to the previous discussion. Is that idea or essence, which in the dialectical process we define as essence or true existence—whether essence of equality, beauty, or anything else—are these essences, I say, liable at times to some degree of change? or are they each of them always what they are, having the same simple self-existent and unchanging forms, not admitting of variation at all, or in any way, or at any time?

They must be always the same, Socrates, replied Cebes.

And what would you say of the many beautiful—whether men or horses or garments or any other things which are named by the same names and may be called equal or beautiful,—are they all unchanging and the same always, or quite the reverse? May they not rather be described as almost always changing and hardly ever the same, either with themselves or with one another?

The latter, replied Cebes; they are always in a state of change.

And these you can touch and see and perceive with the senses, but the unchanging things you can only perceive with the mind—they are invisible and are not seen?

That is very true, he said.

Well, then, added Socrates, let us suppose that there are two sorts of existences—one seen, the other unseen.

Let us suppose them.

The seen is the changing, and the unseen is the unchanging?

That may be also supposed.

And, further, is not one part of us body, another part soul?

To be sure.

And to which class is the body more alike and akin?

Clearly to the seen—no one can doubt that.

And is the soul seen or not seen?

Not by man, Socrates.

And what we mean by 'seen' and 'not seen' is that which is or is not visible to the eye of man?

Yes, to the eye of man.

And is the soul seen or not seen?

Not seen.

Unseen then?

Yes.

Then the soul is more like to the unseen, and the body to the seen?

That follows necessarily, Socrates.

And were we not saying long ago that the soul when using the body as an instrument of perception, that is to say, when using the sense of sight or hearing or some other sense (for the meaning of perceiving through the body is perceiving through the senses)—were we not saying that the soul too is then dragged by the body into the region of the changeable, and wanders and is confused; the world spins round her, and she is like a drunkard, when she touches change?

Very true.

But when returning into herself she reflects, then she passes into the other world, the region of purity, and eternity, and immortality, and unchangeableness, which are her kindred, and with them she ever lives, when she is by herself and is not let or hindered; then she ceases from her erring ways, and being in communion with the unchanging is unchanging. And this state of the soul is called wisdom?

That is well and truly said, Socrates, he replied.

And to which class is the soul more nearly alike and akin, as far as may be inferred from this argument, as well as from the preceding one?

I think, Socrates, that, in the opinion of every one who follows the argument, the soul will be infinitely more like the unchangeable—even the most stupid person will not deny that.

And the body is more like the changing?

Yes.

Yet once more consider the matter in another light: When the soul and the body are united, then nature orders the soul to rule and govern, and the body to obey and serve. Now which of these two functions is akin to the divine? and which to the mortal? Does not the divine appear to you to be that which naturally orders and rules, and the mortal to be that which is subject and servant?

True.

And which does the soul resemble?

The soul resembles the divine, and the body the mortal—there can be no doubt of that, Socrates.

Then reflect, Cebes: of all which has been said is not this the conclusion?—that the soul is in the very likeness of the divine, and immortal, and intellectual, and uniform, and indissoluble, and unchangeable; and that the body is in the very likeness of the human, and mortal, and unintellectual, and multiform, and dissoluble, and changeable. Can this, my dear Cebes, be denied?

It cannot.

But if it be true, then is not the body liable to speedy dissolution? And is not the soul almost or altogether indissoluble?

Certainly.

And do you further observe, that after a man is dead, the body, or visible part of him, which is lying in the visible world, and is called a corpse, and would naturally be dissolved and decomposed and dissipated, is not dissolved or decomposed at once, but may remain for a for some time, nay even for a long time, if the constitution be sound at the time of death, and the season of the year favourable? For the body when shrunk and embalmed, as the manner is in Egypt, may remain almost entire through infinite ages; and even in decay, there are still some portions, such as the bones and ligaments, which are practically indestructible:—Do you agree?

Yes.

And is it likely that the soul, which is invisible, in passing to the place of the true Hades, which like her is invisible, and pure, and noble, and on her way to the good and wise God, whither, if God will, my soul is also soon to go,—that the soul, I repeat, if this be her nature and origin, will be blown away and destroyed immediately on quitting the body, as the many say? That can never be, my dear Simmias and Cebes. The truth rather is, that the soul which is pure at departing and draws after her no bodily taint, having never voluntarily during life had connection with the body, which she is ever avoiding, herself gathered into herself;—and making such abstraction her perpetual study—which means that she has been a true disciple of philosophy; and therefore has in fact been always engaged in the practice of dying? For is not philosophy the practice of death?—

Certainly—

That soul, I say, herself invisible, departs to the invisible world—to the divine and immortal and rational: thither arriving, she is secure of bliss and is released from the error and folly of men, their fears and wild passions and all other human ills, and for ever dwells, as they say of the initiated, in company with the gods (compare Apol.). Is not this true, Cebes?

Yes, said Cebes, beyond a doubt.

But the soul which has been polluted, and is impure at the time of her departure, and is the companion and servant of the body always, and is in love with and fascinated by the body and by the desires and pleasures of the body, until she is led to believe that the truth only exists in a bodily form, which a man may touch and see and taste, and use for the purposes of his lusts,—the soul, I mean, accustomed to hate and fear and avoid the intellectual principle, which to the bodily eye is dark and invisible, and can be attained only by philosophy;—do you suppose that such a soul will depart pure and unalloyed?

Impossible, he replied.

She is held fast by the corporeal, which the continual association and constant care of the body have wrought into her nature.

Very true.

And this corporeal element, my friend, is heavy and weighty and earthy, and is that element of sight by which a soul is depressed and dragged down again into the visible world, because she is afraid of the invisible and of the world below—prowling about tombs and sepulchres, near which, as they tell us, are seen certain ghostly apparitions of souls which have not departed pure, but are cloyed with sight and therefore visible.

(Compare Milton, Comus:—

'But when lust,
By unchaste looks, loose gestures, and foul talk,
But most by lewd and lavish act of sin,
Lets in defilement to the inward parts,
The soul grows clotted by contagion,
Imbodies, and imbrutes, till she quite lose,
The divine property of her first being.
Such are those thick and gloomy shadows damp
Oft seen in charnel vaults and sepulchres,
Lingering, and sitting by a new made grave,
As loath to leave the body that it lov'd,
And linked itself by carnal sensuality
To a degenerate and degraded state.')

That is very likely, Socrates.

Yes, that is very likely, Cebes; and these must be the souls, not of the good, but of the evil, which are compelled to wander about such places in payment of the penalty of their former evil way of life; and they continue to wander until through the craving after the corporeal which never leaves them, they are imprisoned finally in another body. And they may be supposed to find their prisons in the same natures which they have had in their former lives.

What natures do you mean, Socrates?

What I mean is that men who have followed after gluttony, and wantonness, and drunkenness, and have had no thought of avoiding them, would pass into asses and animals of that sort. What do you think?

I think such an opinion to be exceedingly probable.

And those who have chosen the portion of injustice, and tyranny, and violence, will pass into wolves, or into hawks and kites;—whither else can we suppose them to go?

Yes, said Cebes; with such natures, beyond question.

And there is no difficulty, he said, in assigning to all of them places answering to their several natures and propensities?

There is not, he said.

Some are happier than others; and the happiest both in themselves and in the place to which they go are those who have practised the civil and social virtues which are called temperance and justice, and are acquired by habit and attention without philosophy and mind. (Compare Republic.)

Why are they the happiest?

Because they may be expected to pass into some gentle and social kind which is like their own, such as bees or wasps or ants, or back again into the form of man, and just and moderate men may be supposed to spring from them.

Very likely.

No one who has not studied philosophy and who is not entirely pure at the time of his departure is allowed to enter the company of the Gods, but the lover of knowledge only. And this is the reason, Simmias and Cebes, why the true votaries of philosophy abstain from all fleshly lusts, and hold out against them and refuse to give themselves up to them,—not because they fear poverty or the ruin of their families, like the lovers of money, and the world in general; nor like the lovers of power and honour, because they dread the dishonour or disgrace of evil deeds.

No, Socrates, that would not become them, said Cebes.

No indeed, he replied; and therefore they who have any care of their own souls, and do not merely live moulding and fashioning the body, say farewell to all this; they will not walk in the ways of the blind: and when philosophy offers them purification and release from evil, they feel that they ought not to resist her influence, and whither she leads they turn and follow.

What do you mean, Socrates?

I will tell you, he said. The lovers of knowledge are conscious that the soul was simply fastened and glued to the body—until philosophy received her, she could only view real existence through the bars of a prison, not in and through herself; she was wallowing in the mire of every sort of ignorance; and by reason of lust had become the principal accomplice in her own captivity. This was her original state; and then, as I was saying, and as the lovers of knowledge are well aware, philosophy, seeing how terrible was her confinement, of which she was to herself the cause, received and gently comforted her and sought to release her, pointing out that the eye and the ear and the other senses are full of deception, and persuading her to retire from them, and abstain from all but the necessary use of them, and be gathered up and collected into herself, bidding her trust in herself and her own pure apprehension of pure existence, and to mistrust whatever comes to her through other channels and is subject to variation; for such things are visible and tangible, but what she sees in her own nature is intelligible and invisible. And the soul of the true philosopher thinks that she ought not to resist this deliverance, and therefore abstains from pleasures and desires and pains and fears, as far as she is able; reflecting that when a man has great joys or sorrows or fears or desires, he suffers from them, not merely the sort of evil which might be anticipated—as for example, the loss of his health or property which he has sacrificed to his lusts—but an evil greater far, which is the greatest and worst of all evils, and one of which he never thinks.

What is it, Socrates? said Cebes.

The evil is that when the feeling of pleasure or pain is most intense, every soul of man imagines the objects of this intense feeling to be then plainest and truest: but this is not so, they are really the things of sight.

Very true.

And is not this the state in which the soul is most enthralled by the body?

How so?

Why, because each pleasure and pain is a sort of nail which nails and rivets the soul to the body, until she becomes like the body, and believes that to be true which the body affirms to be true; and from agreeing with the body and having the same delights she is obliged to have the same habits and haunts, and is not likely ever to be pure at her departure to the world below, but is always infected by the body; and so she sinks into another body and there germinates and grows, and has therefore no part in the communion of the divine and pure and simple.

Most true, Socrates, answered Cebes.

And this, Cebes, is the reason why the true lovers of knowledge are temperate and brave; and not for the reason which the world gives.

Certainly not.

Certainly not! The soul of a philosopher will reason in quite another way; she will not ask philosophy to release her in order that when released she may deliver herself up again to the thraldom of pleasures and pains, doing a work only to be undone again, weaving instead of unweaving her Penelope's web. But she will calm passion, and follow reason, and dwell in the contemplation of her, beholding the true and divine (which is not matter of opinion), and thence deriving nourishment. Thus she seeks to live while she lives, and after death she hopes to go to her own kindred and to that which is like her, and to be freed from human ills. Never fear, Simmias and Cebes, that a soul which has been thus nurtured and has had these pursuits, will at her departure from the body be scattered and blown away by the winds and be nowhere and nothing.

When Socrates had done speaking, for a considerable time there was silence; he himself appeared to be meditating, as most of us were, on what had been said; only Cebes and Simmias spoke a few words to one another. And Socrates observing them asked what they thought of the argument, and whether there was anything wanting? For, said he, there are many points still open to suspicion and attack, if any one were disposed to sift the matter thoroughly. Should you be considering some other matter I say no more, but if you are still in doubt do not hesitate to say exactly what you think, and let us have anything better which you can suggest; and if you think that I can be of any use, allow me to help you.

Simmias said: I must confess, Socrates, that doubts did arise in our minds, and each of us was urging and inciting the other to put the question which we wanted to have answered and which neither of us liked to ask, fearing that our importunity might be troublesome under present at such a time.

Socrates replied with a smile: O Simmias, what are you saying? I am not very likely to persuade other men that I do not regard my present situation as a misfortune, if I cannot even persuade you that I am no worse off now than at any other time in my life. Will you not allow that I have as much of the spirit of prophecy in me as the swans? For they, when they perceive that they must die, having sung all their life long, do then sing more lustily than ever, rejoicing in the thought that they are about to go away to the god whose ministers they are. But men, because they are themselves afraid of death, slanderously affirm of the swans that they sing a lament at the last, not considering that no bird sings when cold, or hungry, or in pain, not even the nightingale, nor the swallow, nor yet the hoopoe; which are said indeed to tune a lay of sorrow, although I do not believe this to be true of them any more than of the swans. But because they are sacred to Apollo, they have the gift of prophecy, and anticipate the good things of another world, wherefore they sing and rejoice in that day more than they ever did before. And I too, believing myself to be the consecrated servant of the same God, and the fellow-servant of the swans, and thinking that I have received from my master gifts of prophecy which are not inferior to theirs, would not go out of life less merrily than the swans. Never mind then, if this be your only objection, but speak and ask anything which you like, while the eleven magistrates of Athens allow.

Very good, Socrates, said Simmias; then I will tell you my difficulty, and Cebes will tell you his. I feel myself, (and I daresay that you have the same feeling), how hard or rather impossible is the attainment of any certainty about questions such as these in the present life. And yet I should deem him a coward who did not prove what is said about them to the uttermost, or whose heart failed him before he had examined them on every side. For he should persevere until he has achieved one of two things: either he should discover, or be taught the truth about them; or, if this be impossible, I would have him take the best and most irrefragable of human theories, and let this be the raft upon which he sails through life—not without risk, as I admit, if he cannot find some word of God which will more surely and safely carry him. And now, as you bid me, I will venture to question you, and then I shall not have to reproach myself hereafter with not having said at the time what I think. For when I consider the matter, either alone or with Cebes, the argument does certainly appear to me, Socrates, to be not sufficient.

Socrates answered: I dare say, my friend, that you may be right, but I should like to know in what respect the argument is insufficient.

In this respect, replied Simmias:—Suppose a person to use the same argument about harmony and the lyre—might he not say that harmony is a thing invisible, incorporeal, perfect, divine, existing in the lyre which is harmonized, but that the lyre and the strings are matter and material, composite, earthy, and akin to mortality? And when some one breaks the lyre, or cuts and rends the strings, then he who takes this view would argue as you do, and on the same analogy, that the harmony survives and has not perished—you cannot imagine, he would say, that the lyre without the strings, and the broken strings themselves which are mortal remain, and yet that the harmony, which is of heavenly and immortal nature and kindred, has perished—perished before the mortal. The harmony must still be somewhere, and the wood and strings will decay before anything can happen to that. The thought, Socrates, must have occurred to your own mind that such is our conception of the soul; and that when the body is in a manner strung and held together by the elements of hot and cold, wet and dry, then the soul is the harmony or due proportionate admixture of them. But if so, whenever the strings of the body are unduly loosened or overstrained through disease or other injury, then the soul, though most divine, like other harmonies of music or of works of art, of course perishes at once, although the material remains of the body may last for a considerable time, until they are either decayed or burnt. And if any one maintains that the soul, being the harmony of the elements of the body, is first to perish in that which is called death, how shall we answer him?

Socrates looked fixedly at us as his manner was, and said with a smile: Simmias has reason on his side; and why does not some one of you who is better able than myself answer him? for there is force in his attack upon me. But perhaps, before we answer him, we had better also hear what Cebes has to say that we may gain time for reflection, and when they have both spoken, we may either assent to them, if there is truth in what they say, or if not, we will maintain our position. Please to tell me then, Cebes, he said, what was the difficulty which troubled you?

Cebes said: I will tell you. My feeling is that the argument is where it was, and open to the same objections which were urged before; for I am ready to admit that the existence of the soul before entering into the bodily form has been very ingeniously, and, if I may say so, quite sufficiently proven; but the existence of the soul after death is still, in my judgment, unproven. Now my objection is not the same as that of Simmias; for I am not disposed to deny that the soul is stronger and more lasting than the body, being of opinion that in all such respects the soul very far excels the body. Well, then, says the argument to me, why do you remain unconvinced?—When you see that the weaker continues in existence after the man is dead, will you not admit that the more lasting must also survive during the same period of time? Now I will ask you to consider whether the objection, which, like Simmias, I will express in a figure, is of any weight. The analogy which I will adduce is that of an old weaver, who dies, and after his death somebody says:—He is not dead, he must be alive;—see, there is the coat which he himself wove and wore, and which remains whole and undecayed. And then he proceeds to ask of some one who is incredulous, whether a man lasts longer, or the coat which is in use and wear; and when he is answered that a man lasts far longer, thinks that he has thus certainly demonstrated the survival of the man, who is the more lasting, because the less lasting remains. But that, Simmias, as I would beg you to remark, is a mistake; any one can see that he who talks thus is talking nonsense. For the truth is, that the weaver aforesaid, having woven and worn many such coats, outlived several of them, and was outlived by the last; but a man is not therefore proved to be slighter and weaker than a coat. Now the relation of the body to the soul may be expressed in a similar figure; and any one may very fairly say in like manner that the soul is lasting, and the body weak and short-lived in comparison. He may argue in like manner that every soul wears out many bodies, especially if a man live many years. While he is alive the body deliquesces and decays, and the soul always weaves another garment and repairs the waste. But of course, whenever the soul perishes, she must have on her last garment, and this will survive her; and then at length, when the soul is dead, the body will show its native weakness, and quickly decompose and pass away. I would therefore rather not rely on the argument from superior strength to prove the continued existence of the soul after death. For granting even more than you affirm to be possible, and acknowledging not only that the soul existed before birth, but also that the souls of some exist, and will continue to exist after death, and will be born and die again and again, and that there is a natural strength in the soul which will hold out and be born many times—nevertheless, we may be still inclined to think that she will weary in the labours of successive births, and may at last succumb in one of her deaths and utterly perish; and this death and dissolution of the body which brings destruction to the soul may be unknown to any of us, for no one of us can have had any experience of it: and if so, then I maintain that he who is confident about death has but a foolish confidence, unless he is able to prove that the soul is altogether immortal and imperishable. But if he cannot prove the soul's immortality, he who is about to die will always have reason to fear that when the body is disunited, the soul also may utterly perish.

All of us, as we afterwards remarked to one another, had an unpleasant feeling at hearing what they said. When we had been so firmly convinced before, now to have our faith shaken seemed to introduce a confusion and uncertainty, not only into the previous argument, but into any future one; either we were incapable of forming a judgment, or there were no grounds of belief.

ECHECRATES: There I feel with you—by heaven I do, Phaedo, and when you were speaking, I was beginning to ask myself the same question: What argument can I ever trust again? For what could be more convincing than the argument of Socrates, which has now fallen into discredit? That the soul is a harmony is a doctrine which has always had a wonderful attraction for me, and, when mentioned, came back to me at once, as my own original conviction. And now I must begin again and find another argument which will assure me that when the man is dead the soul survives. Tell me, I implore you, how did Socrates proceed? Did he appear to share the unpleasant feeling which you mention? or did he calmly meet the attack? And did he answer forcibly or feebly? Narrate what passed as exactly as you can.

PHAEDO: Often, Echecrates, I have wondered at Socrates, but never more than on that occasion. That he should be able to answer was nothing, but what astonished me was, first, the gentle and pleasant and approving manner in which he received the words of the young men, and then his quick sense of the wound which had been inflicted by the argument, and the readiness with which he healed it. He might be compared to a general rallying his defeated and broken army, urging them to accompany him and return to the field of argument.

ECHECRATES: What followed?

PHAEDO: You shall hear, for I was close to him on his right hand, seated on a sort of stool, and he on a couch which was a good deal higher. He stroked my head, and pressed the hair upon my neck—he had a way of playing with my hair; and then he said: To-morrow, Phaedo, I suppose that these fair locks of yours will be severed.

Yes, Socrates, I suppose that they will, I replied.

Not so, if you will take my advice.

What shall I do with them? I said.

To-day, he replied, and not to-morrow, if this argument dies and we cannot bring it to life again, you and I will both shave our locks; and if I were you, and the argument got away from me, and I could not hold my ground against Simmias and Cebes, I would myself take an oath, like the Argives, not to wear hair any more until I had renewed the conflict and defeated them.

Yes, I said, but Heracles himself is said not to be a match for two.

Summon me then, he said, and I will be your Iolaus until the sun goes down.

I summon you rather, I rejoined, not as Heracles summoning Iolaus, but as Iolaus might summon Heracles.

That will do as well, he said. But first let us take care that we avoid a danger.

Of what nature? I said.

Lest we become misologists, he replied, no worse thing can happen to a man than this. For as there are misanthropists or haters of men, there are also misologists or haters of ideas, and both spring from the same cause, which is ignorance of the world. Misanthropy arises out of the too great confidence of inexperience;—you trust a man and think him altogether true and sound and faithful, and then in a little while he turns out to be false and knavish; and then another and another, and when this has happened several times to a man, especially when it happens among those whom he deems to be his own most trusted and familiar friends, and he has often quarreled with them, he at last hates all men, and believes that no one has any good in him at all. You must have observed this trait of character?

I have.

And is not the feeling discreditable? Is it not obvious that such an one having to deal with other men, was clearly without any experience of human nature; for experience would have taught him the true state of the case, that few are the good and few the evil, and that the great majority are in the interval between them.

What do you mean? I said.

I mean, he replied, as you might say of the very large and very small, that nothing is more uncommon than a very large or very small man; and this applies generally to all extremes, whether of great and small, or swift and slow, or fair and foul, or black and white: and whether the instances you select be men or dogs or anything else, few are the extremes, but many are in the mean between them. Did you never observe this?

Yes, I said, I have.

And do you not imagine, he said, that if there were a competition in evil, the worst would be found to be very few?

Yes, that is very likely, I said.

Yes, that is very likely, he replied; although in this respect arguments are unlike men—there I was led on by you to say more than I had intended; but the point of comparison was, that when a simple man who has no skill in dialectics believes an argument to be true which he afterwards imagines to be false, whether really false or not, and then another and another, he has no longer any faith left, and great disputers, as you know, come to think at last that they have grown to be the wisest of mankind; for they alone perceive the utter unsoundness and instability of all arguments, or indeed, of all things, which, like the currents in the Euripus, are going up and down in never-ceasing ebb and flow.

That is quite true, I said.

Yes, Phaedo, he replied, and how melancholy, if there be such a thing as truth or certainty or possibility of knowledge—that a man should have lighted upon some argument or other which at first seemed true and then turned out to be false, and instead of blaming himself and his own want of wit, because he is annoyed, should at last be too glad to transfer the blame from himself to arguments in general: and for ever afterwards should hate and revile them, and lose truth and the knowledge of realities.

Yes, indeed, I said; that is very melancholy.

Let us then, in the first place, he said, be careful of allowing or of admitting into our souls the notion that there is no health or soundness in any arguments at all. Rather say that we have not yet attained to soundness in ourselves, and that we must struggle manfully and do our best to gain health of mind—you and all other men having regard to the whole of your future life, and I myself in the prospect of death. For at this moment I am sensible that I have not the temper of a philosopher; like the vulgar, I am only a partisan. Now the partisan, when he is engaged in a dispute, cares nothing about the rights of the question, but is anxious only to convince his hearers of his own assertions. And the difference between him and me at the present moment is merely this—that whereas he seeks to convince his hearers that what he says is true, I am rather seeking to convince myself; to convince my hearers is a secondary matter with me. And do but see how much I gain by the argument. For if what I say is true, then I do well to be persuaded of the truth, but if there be nothing after death, still, during the short time that remains, I shall not distress my friends with lamentations, and my ignorance will not last, but will die with me, and therefore no harm will be done. This is the state of mind, Simmias and Cebes, in which I approach the argument. And I would ask you to be thinking of the truth and not of Socrates: agree with me, if I seem to you to be speaking the truth; or if not, withstand me might and main, that I may not deceive you as well as myself in my enthusiasm, and like the bee, leave my sting in you before I die.

And now let us proceed, he said. And first of all let me be sure that I have in my mind what you were saying. Simmias, if I remember rightly, has fears and misgivings whether the soul, although a fairer and diviner thing than the body, being as she is in the form of harmony, may not perish first. On the other hand, Cebes appeared to grant that the soul was more lasting than the body, but he said that no one could know whether the soul, after having worn out many bodies, might not perish herself and leave her last body behind her; and that this is death, which is the destruction not of the body but of the soul, for in the body the work of destruction is ever going on. Are not these, Simmias and Cebes, the points which we have to consider?

They both agreed to this statement of them.

He proceeded: And did you deny the force of the whole preceding argument, or of a part only?

Of a part only, they replied.

And what did you think, he said, of that part of the argument in which we said that knowledge was recollection, and hence inferred that the soul must have previously existed somewhere else before she was enclosed in the body?

Cebes said that he had been wonderfully impressed by that part of the argument, and that his conviction remained absolutely unshaken. Simmias agreed, and added that he himself could hardly imagine the possibility of his ever thinking differently.

But, rejoined Socrates, you will have to think differently, my Theban friend, if you still maintain that harmony is a compound, and that the soul is a harmony which is made out of strings set in the frame of the body; for you will surely never allow yourself to say that a harmony is prior to the elements which compose it.

Never, Socrates.

But do you not see that this is what you imply when you say that the soul existed before she took the form and body of man, and was made up of elements which as yet had no existence? For harmony is not like the soul, as you suppose; but first the lyre, and the strings, and the sounds exist in a state of discord, and then harmony is made last of all, and perishes first. And how can such a notion of the soul as this agree with the other?

Not at all, replied Simmias.

And yet, he said, there surely ought to be harmony in a discourse of which harmony is the theme.

There ought, replied Simmias.

But there is no harmony, he said, in the two propositions that knowledge is recollection, and that the soul is a harmony. Which of them will you retain?

I think, he replied, that I have a much stronger faith, Socrates, in the first of the two, which has been fully demonstrated to me, than in the latter, which has not been demonstrated at all, but rests only on probable and plausible grounds; and is therefore believed by the many. I know too well that these arguments from probabilities are impostors, and unless great caution is observed in the use of them, they are apt to be deceptive—in geometry, and in other things too. But the doctrine of knowledge and recollection has been proven to me on trustworthy grounds; and the proof was that the soul must have existed before she came into the body, because to her belongs the essence of which the very name implies existence. Having, as I am convinced, rightly accepted this conclusion, and on sufficient grounds, I must, as I suppose, cease to argue or allow others to argue that the soul is a harmony.

Let me put the matter, Simmias, he said, in another point of view: Do you imagine that a harmony or any other composition can be in a state other than that of the elements, out of which it is compounded?

Certainly not.

Or do or suffer anything other than they do or suffer?

He agreed.

Then a harmony does not, properly speaking, lead the parts or elements which make up the harmony, but only follows them.

He assented.

For harmony cannot possibly have any motion, or sound, or other quality which is opposed to its parts.

That would be impossible, he replied.

And does not the nature of every harmony depend upon the manner in which the elements are harmonized?

I do not understand you, he said.

I mean to say that a harmony admits of degrees, and is more of a harmony, and more completely a harmony, when more truly and fully harmonized, to any extent which is possible; and less of a harmony, and less completely a harmony, when less truly and fully harmonized.

True.

But does the soul admit of degrees? or is one soul in the very least degree more or less, or more or less completely, a soul than another?

Not in the least.

Yet surely of two souls, one is said to have intelligence and virtue, and to be good, and the other to have folly and vice, and to be an evil soul: and this is said truly?

Yes, truly.

But what will those who maintain the soul to be a harmony say of this presence of virtue and vice in the soul?—will they say that here is another harmony, and another discord, and that the virtuous soul is harmonized, and herself being a harmony has another harmony within her, and that the vicious soul is inharmonical and has no harmony within her?

I cannot tell, replied Simmias; but I suppose that something of the sort would be asserted by those who say that the soul is a harmony.

And we have already admitted that no soul is more a soul than another; which is equivalent to admitting that harmony is not more or less harmony, or more or less completely a harmony?

Quite true.

And that which is not more or less a harmony is not more or less harmonized?

True.

And that which is not more or less harmonized cannot have more or less of harmony, but only an equal harmony?

Yes, an equal harmony.

Then one soul not being more or less absolutely a soul than another, is not more or less harmonized?

Exactly.

And therefore has neither more nor less of discord, nor yet of harmony?

She has not.

And having neither more nor less of harmony or of discord, one soul has no more vice or virtue than another, if vice be discord and virtue harmony?

Not at all more.

Or speaking more correctly, Simmias, the soul, if she is a harmony, will never have any vice; because a harmony, being absolutely a harmony, has no part in the inharmonical.

No.

And therefore a soul which is absolutely a soul has no vice?

How can she have, if the previous argument holds?

Then, if all souls are equally by their nature souls, all souls of all living creatures will be equally good?

I agree with you, Socrates, he said.

And can all this be true, think you? he said; for these are the consequences which seem to follow from the assumption that the soul is a harmony?

It cannot be true.

Once more, he said, what ruler is there of the elements of human nature other than the soul, and especially the wise soul? Do you know of any?

Indeed, I do not.

And is the soul in agreement with the affections of the body? or is she at variance with them? For example, when the body is hot and thirsty, does not the soul incline us against drinking? and when the body is hungry, against eating? And this is only one instance out of ten thousand of the opposition of the soul to the things of the body.

Very true.

But we have already acknowledged that the soul, being a harmony, can never utter a note at variance with the tensions and relaxations and vibrations and other affections of the strings out of which she is composed; she can only follow, she cannot lead them?

It must be so, he replied.

And yet do we not now discover the soul to be doing the exact opposite—leading the elements of which she is believed to be composed; almost always opposing and coercing them in all sorts of ways throughout life, sometimes more violently with the pains of medicine and gymnastic; then again more gently; now threatening, now admonishing the desires, passions, fears, as if talking to a thing which is not herself, as Homer in the Odyssee represents Odysseus doing in the words—

'He beat his breast, and thus reproached his heart: Endure, my heart; far worse hast thou endured!'

Do you think that Homer wrote this under the idea that the soul is a harmony capable of being led by the affections of the body, and not rather of a nature which should lead and master them—herself a far diviner thing than any harmony?

Yes, Socrates, I quite think so.

Then, my friend, we can never be right in saying that the soul is a harmony, for we should contradict the divine Homer, and contradict ourselves.

True, he said.

Thus much, said Socrates, of Harmonia, your Theban goddess, who has graciously yielded to us; but what shall I say, Cebes, to her husband Cadmus, and how shall I make peace with him?

I think that you will discover a way of propitiating him, said Cebes; I am sure that you have put the argument with Harmonia in a manner that I could never have expected. For when Simmias was mentioning his difficulty, I quite imagined that no answer could be given to him, and therefore I was surprised at finding that his argument could not sustain the first onset of yours, and not impossibly the other, whom you call Cadmus, may share a similar fate.

Nay, my good friend, said Socrates, let us not boast, lest some evil eye should put to flight the word which I am about to speak. That, however, may be left in the hands of those above, while I draw near in Homeric fashion, and try the mettle of your words. Here lies the point:—You want to have it proven to you that the soul is imperishable and immortal, and the philosopher who is confident in death appears to you to have but a vain and foolish confidence, if he believes that he will fare better in the world below than one who has led another sort of life, unless he can prove this; and you say that the demonstration of the strength and divinity of the soul, and of her existence prior to our becoming men, does not necessarily imply her immortality. Admitting the soul to be longlived, and to have known and done much in a former state, still she is not on that account immortal; and her entrance into the human form may be a sort of disease which is the beginning of dissolution, and may at last, after the toils of life are over, end in that which is called death. And whether the soul enters into the body once only or many times, does not, as you say, make any difference in the fears of individuals. For any man, who is not devoid of sense, must fear, if he has no knowledge and can give no account of the soul's immortality. This, or something like this, I suspect to be your notion, Cebes; and I designedly recur to it in order that nothing may escape us, and that you may, if you wish, add or subtract anything.

But, said Cebes, as far as I see at present, I have nothing to add or subtract: I mean what you say that I mean.

Socrates paused awhile, and seemed to be absorbed in reflection. At length he said: You are raising a tremendous question, Cebes, involving the whole nature of generation and corruption, about which, if you like, I will give you my own experience; and if anything which I say is likely to avail towards the solution of your difficulty you may make use of it.

I should very much like, said Cebes, to hear what you have to say.

Then I will tell you, said Socrates. When I was young, Cebes, I had a prodigious desire to know that department of philosophy which is called the investigation of nature; to know the causes of things, and why a thing is and is created or destroyed appeared to me to be a lofty profession; and I was always agitating myself with the consideration of questions such as these:—Is the growth of animals the result of some decay which the hot and cold principle contracts, as some have said? Is the blood the element with which we think, or the air, or the fire? or perhaps nothing of the kind—but the brain may be the originating power of the perceptions of hearing and sight and smell, and memory and opinion may come from them, and science may be based on memory and opinion when they have attained fixity. And then I went on to examine the corruption of them, and then to the things of heaven and earth, and at last I concluded myself to be utterly and absolutely incapable of these enquiries, as I will satisfactorily prove to you. For I was fascinated by them to such a degree that my eyes grew blind to things which I had seemed to myself, and also to others, to know quite well; I forgot what I had before thought self-evident truths; e.g. such a fact as that the growth of man is the result of eating and drinking; for when by the digestion of food flesh is added to flesh and bone to bone, and whenever there is an aggregation of congenial elements, the lesser bulk becomes larger and the small man great. Was not that a reasonable notion?

Yes, said Cebes, I think so.

Well; but let me tell you something more. There was a time when I thought that I understood the meaning of greater and less pretty well; and when I saw a great man standing by a little one, I fancied that one was taller than the other by a head; or one horse would appear to be greater than another horse: and still more clearly did I seem to perceive that ten is two more than eight, and that two cubits are more than one, because two is the double of one.

And what is now your notion of such matters? said Cebes.

I should be far enough from imagining, he replied, that I knew the cause of any of them, by heaven I should; for I cannot satisfy myself that, when one is added to one, the one to which the addition is made becomes two, or that the two units added together make two by reason of the addition. I cannot understand how, when separated from the other, each of them was one and not two, and now, when they are brought together, the mere juxtaposition or meeting of them should be the cause of their becoming two: neither can I understand how the division of one is the way to make two; for then a different cause would produce the same effect,—as in the former instance the addition and juxtaposition of one to one was the cause of two, in this the separation and subtraction of one from the other would be the cause. Nor am I any longer satisfied that I understand the reason why one or anything else is either generated or destroyed or is at all, but I have in my mind some confused notion of a new method, and can never admit the other.

Then I heard some one reading, as he said, from a book of Anaxagoras, that mind was the disposer and cause of all, and I was delighted at this notion, which appeared quite admirable, and I said to myself: If mind is the disposer, mind will dispose all for the best, and put each particular in the best place; and I argued that if any one desired to find out the cause of the generation or destruction or existence of anything, he must find out what state of being or doing or suffering was best for that thing, and therefore a man had only to consider the best for himself and others, and then he would also know the worse, since the same science comprehended both. And I rejoiced to think that I had found in Anaxagoras a teacher of the causes of existence such as I desired, and I imagined that he would tell me first whether the earth is flat or round; and whichever was true, he would proceed to explain the cause and the necessity of this being so, and then he would teach me the nature of the best and show that this was best; and if he said that the earth was in the centre, he would further explain that this position was the best, and I should be satisfied with the explanation given, and not want any other sort of cause. And I thought that I would then go on and ask him about the sun and moon and stars, and that he would explain to me their comparative swiftness, and their returnings and various states, active and passive, and how all of them were for the best. For I could not imagine that when he spoke of mind as the disposer of them, he would give any other account of their being as they are, except that this was best; and I thought that when he had explained to me in detail the cause of each and the cause of all, he would go on to explain to me what was best for each and what was good for all. These hopes I would not have sold for a large sum of money, and I seized the books and read them as fast as I could in my eagerness to know the better and the worse.

What expectations I had formed, and how grievously was I disappointed! As I proceeded, I found my philosopher altogether forsaking mind or any other principle of order, but having recourse to air, and ether, and water, and other eccentricities. I might compare him to a person who began by maintaining generally that mind is the cause of the actions of Socrates, but who, when he endeavoured to explain the causes of my several actions in detail, went on to show that I sit here because my body is made up of bones and muscles; and the bones, as he would say, are hard and have joints which divide them, and the muscles are elastic, and they cover the bones, which have also a covering or environment of flesh and skin which contains them; and as the bones are lifted at their joints by the contraction or relaxation of the muscles, I am able to bend my limbs, and this is why I am sitting here in a curved posture—that is what he would say, and he would have a similar explanation of my talking to you, which he would attribute to sound, and air, and hearing, and he would assign ten thousand other causes of the same sort, forgetting to mention the true cause, which is, that the Athenians have thought fit to condemn me, and accordingly I have thought it better and more right to remain here and undergo my sentence; for I am inclined to think that these muscles and bones of mine would have gone off long ago to Megara or Boeotia—by the dog they would, if they had been moved only by their own idea of what was best, and if I had not chosen the better and nobler part, instead of playing truant and running away, of enduring any punishment which the state inflicts. There is surely a strange confusion of causes and conditions in all this.

It may be said, indeed, that without bones and muscles and the other parts of the body I cannot execute my purposes. But to say that I do as I do because of them, and that this is the way in which mind acts, and not from the choice of the best, is a very careless and idle mode of speaking. I wonder that they cannot distinguish the cause from the condition, which the many, feeling about in the dark, are always mistaking and misnaming. And thus one man makes a vortex all round and steadies the earth by the heaven; another gives the air as a support to the earth, which is a sort of broad trough. Any power which in arranging them as they are arranges them for the best never enters into their minds; and instead of finding any superior strength in it, they rather expect to discover another Atlas of the world who is stronger and more everlasting and more containing than the good;—of the obligatory and containing power of the good they think nothing; and yet this is the principle which I would fain learn if any one would teach me.

But as I have failed either to discover myself, or to learn of any one else, the nature of the best, I will exhibit to you, if you like, what I have found to be the second best mode of enquiring into the cause.

I should very much like to hear, he replied.

Socrates proceeded:—I thought that as I had failed in the contemplation of true existence, I ought to be careful that I did not lose the eye of my soul; as people may injure their bodily eye by observing and gazing on the sun during an eclipse, unless they take the precaution of only looking at the image reflected in the water, or in some similar medium. So in my own case, I was afraid that my soul might be blinded altogether if I looked at things with my eyes or tried to apprehend them by the help of the senses. And I thought that I had better have recourse to the world of mind and seek there the truth of existence. I dare say that the simile is not perfect—for I am very far from admitting that he who contemplates existences through the medium of thought, sees them only 'through a glass darkly,' any more than he who considers them in action and operation. However, this was the method which I adopted: I first assumed some principle which I judged to be the strongest, and then I affirmed as true whatever seemed to agree with this, whether relating to the cause or to anything else; and that which disagreed I regarded as untrue. But I should like to explain my meaning more clearly, as I do not think that you as yet understand me.

No indeed, replied Cebes, not very well.

There is nothing new, he said, in what I am about to tell you; but only what I have been always and everywhere repeating in the previous discussion and on other occasions: I want to show you the nature of that cause which has occupied my thoughts. I shall have to go back to those familiar words which are in the mouth of every one, and first of all assume that there is an absolute beauty and goodness and greatness, and the like; grant me this, and I hope to be able to show you the nature of the cause, and to prove the immortality of the soul.

Cebes said: You may proceed at once with the proof, for I grant you this.

Well, he said, then I should like to know whether you agree with me in the next step; for I cannot help thinking, if there be anything beautiful other than absolute beauty should there be such, that it can be beautiful only in as far as it partakes of absolute beauty—and I should say the same of everything. Do you agree in this notion of the cause?

Yes, he said, I agree.

He proceeded: I know nothing and can understand nothing of any other of those wise causes which are alleged; and if a person says to me that the bloom of colour, or form, or any such thing is a source of beauty, I leave all that, which is only confusing to me, and simply and singly, and perhaps foolishly, hold and am assured in my own mind that nothing makes a thing beautiful but the presence and participation of beauty in whatever way or manner obtained; for as to the manner I am uncertain, but I stoutly contend that by beauty all beautiful things become beautiful. This appears to me to be the safest answer which I can give, either to myself or to another, and to this I cling, in the persuasion that this principle will never be overthrown, and that to myself or to any one who asks the question, I may safely reply, That by beauty beautiful things become beautiful. Do you not agree with me?

I do.

And that by greatness only great things become great and greater greater, and by smallness the less become less?

True.

Then if a person were to remark that A is taller by a head than B, and B less by a head than A, you would refuse to admit his statement, and would stoutly contend that what you mean is only that the greater is greater by, and by reason of, greatness, and the less is less only by, and by reason of, smallness; and thus you would avoid the danger of saying that the greater is greater and the less less by the measure of the head, which is the same in both, and would also avoid the monstrous absurdity of supposing that the greater man is greater by reason of the head, which is small. You would be afraid to draw such an inference, would you not?

Indeed, I should, said Cebes, laughing.

In like manner you would be afraid to say that ten exceeded eight by, and by reason of, two; but would say by, and by reason of, number; or you would say that two cubits exceed one cubit not by a half, but by magnitude?-for there is the same liability to error in all these cases.

Very true, he said.

Again, would you not be cautious of affirming that the addition of one to one, or the division of one, is the cause of two? And you would loudly asseverate that you know of no way in which anything comes into existence except by participation in its own proper essence, and consequently, as far as you know, the only cause of two is the participation in duality—this is the way to make two, and the participation in one is the way to make one. You would say: I will let alone puzzles of division and addition—wiser heads than mine may answer them; inexperienced as I am, and ready to start, as the proverb says, at my own shadow, I cannot afford to give up the sure ground of a principle. And if any one assails you there, you would not mind him, or answer him, until you had seen whether the consequences which follow agree with one another or not, and when you are further required to give an explanation of this principle, you would go on to assume a higher principle, and a higher, until you found a resting-place in the best of the higher; but you would not confuse the principle and the consequences in your reasoning, like the Eristics—at least if you wanted to discover real existence. Not that this confusion signifies to them, who never care or think about the matter at all, for they have the wit to be well pleased with themselves however great may be the turmoil of their ideas. But you, if you are a philosopher, will certainly do as I say.

What you say is most true, said Simmias and Cebes, both speaking at once.

ECHECRATES: Yes, Phaedo; and I do not wonder at their assenting. Any one who has the least sense will acknowledge the wonderful clearness of Socrates' reasoning.

PHAEDO: Certainly, Echecrates; and such was the feeling of the whole company at the time.

ECHECRATES: Yes, and equally of ourselves, who were not of the company, and are now listening to your recital. But what followed?

PHAEDO: After all this had been admitted, and they had that ideas exist, and that other things participate in them and derive their names from them, Socrates, if I remember rightly, said:—

This is your way of speaking; and yet when you say that Simmias is greater than Socrates and less than Phaedo, do you not predicate of Simmias both greatness and smallness?

Yes, I do.

But still you allow that Simmias does not really exceed Socrates, as the words may seem to imply, because he is Simmias, but by reason of the size which he has; just as Simmias does not exceed Socrates because he is Simmias, any more than because Socrates is Socrates, but because he has smallness when compared with the greatness of Simmias?

True.

And if Phaedo exceeds him in size, this is not because Phaedo is Phaedo, but because Phaedo has greatness relatively to Simmias, who is comparatively smaller?

That is true.

And therefore Simmias is said to be great, and is also said to be small, because he is in a mean between them, exceeding the smallness of the one by his greatness, and allowing the greatness of the other to exceed his smallness. He added, laughing, I am speaking like a book, but I believe that what I am saying is true.

Simmias assented.

I speak as I do because I want you to agree with me in thinking, not only that absolute greatness will never be great and also small, but that greatness in us or in the concrete will never admit the small or admit of being exceeded: instead of this, one of two things will happen, either the greater will fly or retire before the opposite, which is the less, or at the approach of the less has already ceased to exist; but will not, if allowing or admitting of smallness, be changed by that; even as I, having received and admitted smallness when compared with Simmias, remain just as I was, and am the same small person. And as the idea of greatness cannot condescend ever to be or become small, in like manner the smallness in us cannot be or become great; nor can any other opposite which remains the same ever be or become its own opposite, but either passes away or perishes in the change.

That, replied Cebes, is quite my notion.

Hereupon one of the company, though I do not exactly remember which of them, said: In heaven's name, is not this the direct contrary of what was admitted before—that out of the greater came the less and out of the less the greater, and that opposites were simply generated from opposites; but now this principle seems to be utterly denied.

Socrates inclined his head to the speaker and listened. I like your courage, he said, in reminding us of this. But you do not observe that there is a difference in the two cases. For then we were speaking of opposites in the concrete, and now of the essential opposite which, as is affirmed, neither in us nor in nature can ever be at variance with itself: then, my friend, we were speaking of things in which opposites are inherent and which are called after them, but now about the opposites which are inherent in them and which give their name to them; and these essential opposites will never, as we maintain, admit of generation into or out of one another. At the same time, turning to Cebes, he said: Are you at all disconcerted, Cebes, at our friend's objection?

No, I do not feel so, said Cebes; and yet I cannot deny that I am often disturbed by objections.

Then we are agreed after all, said Socrates, that the opposite will never in any case be opposed to itself?

To that we are quite agreed, he replied.

Yet once more let me ask you to consider the question from another point of view, and see whether you agree with me:—There is a thing which you term heat, and another thing which you term cold?

Certainly.

But are they the same as fire and snow?

Most assuredly not.

Heat is a thing different from fire, and cold is not the same with snow?

Yes.

And yet you will surely admit, that when snow, as was before said, is under the influence of heat, they will not remain snow and heat; but at the advance of the heat, the snow will either retire or perish?

Very true, he replied.

And the fire too at the advance of the cold will either retire or perish; and when the fire is under the influence of the cold, they will not remain as before, fire and cold.

That is true, he said.

And in some cases the name of the idea is not only attached to the idea in an eternal connection, but anything else which, not being the idea, exists only in the form of the idea, may also lay claim to it. I will try to make this clearer by an example:—The odd number is always called by the name of odd?

Very true.

But is this the only thing which is called odd? Are there not other things which have their own name, and yet are called odd, because, although not the same as oddness, they are never without oddness?—that is what I mean to ask—whether numbers such as the number three are not of the class of odd. And there are many other examples: would you not say, for example, that three may be called by its proper name, and also be called odd, which is not the same with three? and this may be said not only of three but also of five, and of every alternate number—each of them without being oddness is odd, and in the same way two and four, and the other series of alternate numbers, has every number even, without being evenness. Do you agree?

Of course.

Then now mark the point at which I am aiming:—not only do essential opposites exclude one another, but also concrete things, which, although not in themselves opposed, contain opposites; these, I say, likewise reject the idea which is opposed to that which is contained in them, and when it approaches them they either perish or withdraw. For example; Will not the number three endure annihilation or anything sooner than be converted into an even number, while remaining three?

Very true, said Cebes.

And yet, he said, the number two is certainly not opposed to the number three?

It is not.

Then not only do opposite ideas repel the advance of one another, but also there are other natures which repel the approach of opposites.

Very true, he said.

Suppose, he said, that we endeavour, if possible, to determine what these are.

By all means.

Are they not, Cebes, such as compel the things of which they have possession, not only to take their own form, but also the form of some opposite?

What do you mean?

I mean, as I was just now saying, and as I am sure that you know, that those things which are possessed by the number three must not only be three in number, but must also be odd.

Quite true.

And on this oddness, of which the number three has the impress, the opposite idea will never intrude?

No.

And this impress was given by the odd principle?

Yes.

And to the odd is opposed the even?

True.

Then the idea of the even number will never arrive at three?

No.

Then three has no part in the even?

None.

Then the triad or number three is uneven?

Very true.

To return then to my distinction of natures which are not opposed, and yet do not admit opposites—as, in the instance given, three, although not opposed to the even, does not any the more admit of the even, but always brings the opposite into play on the other side; or as two does not receive the odd, or fire the cold—from these examples (and there are many more of them) perhaps you may be able to arrive at the general conclusion, that not only opposites will not receive opposites, but also that nothing which brings the opposite will admit the opposite of that which it brings, in that to which it is brought. And here let me recapitulate—for there is no harm in repetition. The number five will not admit the nature of the even, any more than ten, which is the double of five, will admit the nature of the odd. The double has another opposite, and is not strictly opposed to the odd, but nevertheless rejects the odd altogether. Nor again will parts in the ratio 3:2, nor any fraction in which there is a half, nor again in which there is a third, admit the notion of the whole, although they are not opposed to the whole: You will agree?

Yes, he said, I entirely agree and go along with you in that.

And now, he said, let us begin again; and do not you answer my question in the words in which I ask it: let me have not the old safe answer of which I spoke at first, but another equally safe, of which the truth will be inferred by you from what has been just said. I mean that if any one asks you 'what that is, of which the inherence makes the body hot,' you will reply not heat (this is what I call the safe and stupid answer), but fire, a far superior answer, which we are now in a condition to give. Or if any one asks you 'why a body is diseased,' you will not say from disease, but from fever; and instead of saying that oddness is the cause of odd numbers, you will say that the monad is the cause of them: and so of things in general, as I dare say that you will understand sufficiently without my adducing any further examples.

Yes, he said, I quite understand you.

Tell me, then, what is that of which the inherence will render the body alive?

The soul, he replied.

And is this always the case?

Yes, he said, of course.

Then whatever the soul possesses, to that she comes bearing life?

Yes, certainly.

And is there any opposite to life?

There is, he said.

And what is that?

Death.

Then the soul, as has been acknowledged, will never receive the opposite of what she brings.

Impossible, replied Cebes.

And now, he said, what did we just now call that principle which repels the even?

The odd.

And that principle which repels the musical, or the just?

The unmusical, he said, and the unjust.

And what do we call the principle which does not admit of death?

The immortal, he said.

And does the soul admit of death?

No.

Then the soul is immortal?

Yes, he said.

And may we say that this has been proven?

Yes, abundantly proven, Socrates, he replied.

Supposing that the odd were imperishable, must not three be imperishable?

Of course.

And if that which is cold were imperishable, when the warm principle came attacking the snow, must not the snow have retired whole and unmelted—for it could never have perished, nor could it have remained and admitted the heat?

True, he said.

Again, if the uncooling or warm principle were imperishable, the fire when assailed by cold would not have perished or have been extinguished, but would have gone away unaffected?

Certainly, he said.

And the same may be said of the immortal: if the immortal is also imperishable, the soul when attacked by death cannot perish; for the preceding argument shows that the soul will not admit of death, or ever be dead, any more than three or the odd number will admit of the even, or fire or the heat in the fire, of the cold. Yet a person may say: 'But although the odd will not become even at the approach of the even, why may not the odd perish and the even take the place of the odd?' Now to him who makes this objection, we cannot answer that the odd principle is imperishable; for this has not been acknowledged, but if this had been acknowledged, there would have been no difficulty in contending that at the approach of the even the odd principle and the number three took their departure; and the same argument would have held good of fire and heat and any other thing.

Very true.

And the same may be said of the immortal: if the immortal is also imperishable, then the soul will be imperishable as well as immortal; but if not, some other proof of her imperishableness will have to be given.

No other proof is needed, he said; for if the immortal, being eternal, is liable to perish, then nothing is imperishable.

Yes, replied Socrates, and yet all men will agree that God, and the essential form of life, and the immortal in general, will never perish.

Yes, all men, he said—that is true; and what is more, gods, if I am not mistaken, as well as men.

Seeing then that the immortal is indestructible, must not the soul, if she is immortal, be also imperishable?

Most certainly.

Then when death attacks a man, the mortal portion of him may be supposed to die, but the immortal retires at the approach of death and is preserved safe and sound?

True.

Then, Cebes, beyond question, the soul is immortal and imperishable, and our souls will truly exist in another world!

I am convinced, Socrates, said Cebes, and have nothing more to object; but if my friend Simmias, or any one else, has any further objection to make, he had better speak out, and not keep silence, since I do not know to what other season he can defer the discussion, if there is anything which he wants to say or to have said.

But I have nothing more to say, replied Simmias; nor can I see any reason for doubt after what has been said. But I still feel and cannot help feeling uncertain in my own mind, when I think of the greatness of the subject and the feebleness of man.

Yes, Simmias, replied Socrates, that is well said: and I may add that first principles, even if they appear certain, should be carefully considered; and when they are satisfactorily ascertained, then, with a sort of hesitating confidence in human reason, you may, I think, follow the course of the argument; and if that be plain and clear, there will be no need for any further enquiry.

Very true.

But then, O my friends, he said, if the soul is really immortal, what care should be taken of her, not only in respect of the portion of time which is called life, but of eternity! And the danger of neglecting her from this point of view does indeed appear to be awful. If death had only been the end of all, the wicked would have had a good bargain in dying, for they would have been happily quit not only of their body, but of their own evil together with their souls. But now, inasmuch as the soul is manifestly immortal, there is no release or salvation from evil except the attainment of the highest virtue and wisdom. For the soul when on her progress to the world below takes nothing with her but nurture and education; and these are said greatly to benefit or greatly to injure the departed, at the very beginning of his journey thither.

Me already, as the tragic poet would say, the voice of fate calls. Soon I must drink the poison; and I think that I had better repair to the bath first, in order that the women may not have the trouble of washing my body after I am dead.

When he had done speaking, Crito said: And have you any commands for us, Socrates—anything to say about your children, or any other matter in which we can serve you?

Nothing particular, Crito, he replied: only, as I have always told you, take care of yourselves; that is a service which you may be ever rendering to me and mine and to all of us, whether you promise to do so or not. But if you have no thought for yourselves, and care not to walk according to the rule which I have prescribed for you, not now for the first time, however much you may profess or promise at the moment, it will be of no avail.

We will do our best, said Crito: And in what way shall we bury you?

In any way that you like; but you must get hold of me, and take care that I do not run away from you. Then he turned to us, and added with a smile:—I cannot make Crito believe that I am the same Socrates who have been talking and conducting the argument; he fancies that I am the other Socrates whom he will soon see, a dead body—and he asks, How shall he bury me? And though I have spoken many words in the endeavour to show that when I have drunk the poison I shall leave you and go to the joys of the blessed,—these words of mine, with which I was comforting you and myself, have had, as I perceive, no effect upon Crito. And therefore I want you to be surety for me to him now, as at the trial he was surety to the judges for me: but let the promise be of another sort; for he was surety for me to the judges that I would remain, and you must be my surety to him that I shall not remain, but go away and depart; and then he will suffer less at my death, and not be grieved when he sees my body being burned or buried. I would not have him sorrow at my hard lot, or say at the burial, Thus we lay out Socrates, or, Thus we follow him to the grave or bury him; for false words are not only evil in themselves, but they infect the soul with evil. Be of good cheer, then, my dear Crito, and say that you are burying my body only, and do with that whatever is usual, and what you think best.

When he had spoken these words, he arose and went into a chamber to bathe; Crito followed him and told us to wait. So we remained behind, talking and thinking of the subject of discourse, and also of the greatness of our sorrow; he was like a father of whom we were being bereaved, and we were about to pass the rest of our lives as orphans. When he had taken the bath his children were brought to him—(he had two young sons and an elder one); and the women of his family also came, and he talked to them and gave them a few directions in the presence of Crito; then he dismissed them and returned to us.

Now the hour of sunset was near, for a good deal of time had passed while he was within. When he came out, he sat down with us again after his bath, but not much was said. Soon the jailer, who was the servant of the Eleven, entered and stood by him, saying:—To you, Socrates, whom I know to be the noblest and gentlest and best of all who ever came to this place, I will not impute the angry feelings of other men, who rage and swear at me, when, in obedience to the authorities, I bid them drink the poison—indeed, I am sure that you will not be angry with me; for others, as you are aware, and not I, are to blame. And so fare you well, and try to bear lightly what must needs be—you know my errand. Then bursting into tears he turned away and went out.

Socrates looked at him and said: I return your good wishes, and will do as you bid. Then turning to us, he said, How charming the man is: since I have been in prison he has always been coming to see me, and at times he would talk to me, and was as good to me as could be, and now see how generously he sorrows on my account. We must do as he says, Crito; and therefore let the cup be brought, if the poison is prepared: if not, let the attendant prepare some.

Yet, said Crito, the sun is still upon the hill-tops, and I know that many a one has taken the draught late, and after the announcement has been made to him, he has eaten and drunk, and enjoyed the society of his beloved; do not hurry—there is time enough.

Socrates said: Yes, Crito, and they of whom you speak are right in so acting, for they think that they will be gainers by the delay; but I am right in not following their example, for I do not think that I should gain anything by drinking the poison a little later; I should only be ridiculous in my own eyes for sparing and saving a life which is already forfeit. Please then to do as I say, and not to refuse me.

Crito made a sign to the servant, who was standing by; and he went out, and having been absent for some time, returned with the jailer carrying the cup of poison. Socrates said: You, my good friend, who are experienced in these matters, shall give me directions how I am to proceed. The man answered: You have only to walk about until your legs are heavy, and then to lie down, and the poison will act. At the same time he handed the cup to Socrates, who in the easiest and gentlest manner, without the least fear or change of colour or feature, looking at the man with all his eyes, Echecrates, as his manner was, took the cup and said: What do you say about making a libation out of this cup to any god? May I, or not? The man answered: We only prepare, Socrates, just so much as we deem enough. I understand, he said: but I may and must ask the gods to prosper my journey from this to the other world—even so—and so be it according to my prayer. Then raising the cup to his lips, quite readily and cheerfully he drank off the poison. And hitherto most of us had been able to control our sorrow; but now when we saw him drinking, and saw too that he had finished the draught, we could no longer forbear, and in spite of myself my own tears were flowing fast; so that I covered my face and wept, not for him, but at the thought of my own calamity in having to part from such a friend. Nor was I the first; for Crito, when he found himself unable to restrain his tears, had got up, and I followed; and at that moment, Apollodorus, who had been weeping all the time, broke out in a loud and passionate cry which made cowards of us all. Socrates alone retained his calmness: What is this strange outcry? he said. I sent away the women mainly in order that they might not misbehave in this way, for I have been told that a man should die in peace. Be quiet, then, and have patience. When we heard his words we were ashamed, and refrained our tears; and he walked about until, as he said, his legs began to fail, and then he lay on his back, according to the directions, and the man who gave him the poison now and then looked at his feet and legs; and after a while he pressed his foot hard, and asked him if he could feel; and he said, No; and then his leg, and so upwards and upwards, and showed us that he was cold and stiff. And he felt them himself, and said: When the poison reaches the heart, that will be the end. He was beginning to grow cold about the groin, when he uncovered his face, for he had covered himself up, and said—they were his last words—he said: Crito, I owe a cock to Asclepius; will you remember to pay the debt? The debt shall be paid, said Crito; is there anything else? There was no answer to this question; but in a minute or two a movement was heard, and the attendants uncovered him; his eyes were set, and Crito closed his eyes and mouth.

Such was the end, Echecrates, of our friend; concerning whom I may truly say, that of all the men of his time whom I have known, he was the wisest and justest and best.

DISCUSSION QUESTIONS

1. Which of the arguments in favor of a separable immortal soul do you find most convincing? Why? Explain.

2. How does Plato's view compare to the view found in the *Katha Upanishad*?

3. How are Plato's dualism and rationalism related in his arguments in the *Phaedo*? Explain.

Discourse on Method

By René Descartes

René Descartes (1596–1650) is often referred to as the "Father of Modern Philosophy." Descartes wrote works on optics, music, and mathematics, as well as philosophy. He is credited with inventing analytic geometry and the coordinates used in analytic geometry are still called Cartesian coordinates.

Our selections here come from Discourse on Method *(first published in 1637) and* The Passions of the Soul *(first published in 1649). Like Plato, Descartes was a rationalist and a dualist. Unlike Plato, Descartes wanted to explain* how *the mind and body interact. In our selection from Part V of the* Discourse, *Descartes explains how he thinks the mind acts on (or through) the body. He also argues for the position that humans are unique because we can reason, as opposed to other animals which are essentially machines. The second selection comes from Part I of the later work,* The Passions of the Soul. *Here, we get more detail on the relation of mind (or soul) to the body and the differences between the two. Eventually, in the later parts of this selection, you see his argument for the pineal gland (in the brain) as the seat of the soul. This is problematic for two reasons. First, is this gland, mind-stuff, or body stuff? If it's mind-stuff, how can it be in the brain? If it is body-stuff, how does* it *interact with the soul? Second, it turns out that the function of the pineal gland is different than what Descartes claims. In humans, it seems to regulate hormone levels up through puberty and calcifies in adults. In fact, humans can function without it entirely. This makes it unlikely to do what Descartes ascribes to it. In Part III of* Fundamental Questions, *we will consider some of Descartes' thoughts on knowledge, as laid out in his book* Meditations on First Philosophy.

• • •

I had explained all these matters in some detail in the Treatise which I formerly intended to publish. And afterwards I had shown there, what must be the fabric of the nerves and muscles of the human body in order that the animal spirits therein contained should have the power to move the members, just as the heads of animals, a little while after decapitation, are still observed to move and bite the earth, notwithstanding that they are no longer animate; what changes are necessary in the brain to cause wakefulness, sleep and dreams; how light, sounds, smells, tastes, heat and all other qualities pertaining to external objects are able to imprint on it various ideas by the intervention of the senses; how hunger, thirst and other internal affections can also convey their impressions upon it; what should be regarded as the 'common sense' by which these ideas are received, and what is meant by the memory which retains them, by the fancy which can change them in diverse ways and out of them constitute new ideas, and which, by the same means, distributing the animal spirits through the muscles, can cause the members of such a body to move in as many diverse ways, and in a manner as suitable to the objects which present themselves to its senses and to its internal passions, as can happen in our own case apart from the direction of our free will. And this will not seem strange to those, who, knowing how many different *automata* or moving machines can be made by the industry of man, without employing in so doing more than a very few parts in comparison with the great multitude of bones, muscles, nerves, arteries, veins, or other parts that are found in the body of each animal. From this aspect the body is regarded as a machine which, having been made by the hands of God, is incomparably better arranged, and possesses in itself movements which are much more admirable, than any of those which can be invented by man. Here I specially stopped to show that if there had been such machines, possessing the organs and outward form of a monkey or some other animal without reason, we should not have had any means of ascertaining that they were not of the same nature as those animals. On the other hand, if there were machines which bore a resemblance to our body and imitated our actions as far as it was morally possible to do so, we should always have two very certain tests by which to recognise that, for all that, they were not real men. The first is, that they could never use speech or other signs as we do when placing our thoughts on record for the benefit of others. For we can easily understand a machine's being constituted so that it can utter words, and even emit some responses to action on it of a corporeal kind, which brings about a change in its organs; for instance, if it is touched in a particular part it may ask what we wish to say to it; if in another part it may exclaim that it is being hurt, and so on. But it never happens that it arranges its speech in various ways, in order to reply appropriately to everything that may be said in its presence, as even the lowest type of man can do. And the second difference is, that although machines can perform certain things as well as or perhaps better than any of us can do, they infallibly fall short in others, by the which means we may discover that they did not act from knowledge, but only from the disposition of their organs. For while reason is a universal instrument which can serve for all contingencies, these organs have need of some special adaptation for every particular action. From this it follows that it is morally impossible that there should be sufficient diversity in any machine to allow it to act in all the events of life in the same way as our reason causes us to act.

By these two methods we may also recognise the difference that exists between men and brutes. For it is a very remarkable fact that there are none so depraved and stupid, without even excepting idiots, that they cannot arrange different words together, forming of them a statement by which they make known their thoughts; while, on the other hand, there is no other animal, however perfect and fortunately circumstanced it may be, which can do the same. It is not the want of organs that brings this to pass, for it is evident that magpies and parrots are able to utter words just like ourselves, and yet they cannot speak as we do, that is, so as to give evidence that they think of what they say. On the other hand, men who, being born deaf and dumb, are in the same degree, or even more than the brutes, destitute of the organs which serve the others for talking, are in the habit of themselves inventing certain signs by which they make themselves understood by those who, being usually in their company, have leisure to learn their language. And this does not merely show that the brutes have less reason than men, but that they have none at all, since it is clear that very little is required in order to be able to talk. And when we notice the inequality that exists between animals of the same species, as well as between men, and observe that some are more capable of receiving instruction than others, it is not credible that a monkey or a parrot, selected as the most perfect of its species, should not in these matters equal the stupidest child to be found, or at least a child whose mind is clouded, unless in the case of the brute the soul were of an entirely different nature from ours. And we ought not to confound speech with natural movements which betray passions and may be imitated by machines as well as be manifested by animals; nor must we think, as did some of the ancients, that brutes talk, although we do not understand their language. For if this were true, since they have many organs which are allied to our own, they could communicate their thoughts to us just as easily as to those of their own race. It is also a very remarkable fact that although there are many animals which exhibit more dexterity than we do in some of their actions, we at the same time observe that they do not manifest any dexterity at all in many others. Hence the fact that they do better than we do, does not prove that they are endowed with mind, for in this case they would have more reason than any of us, and would surpass us in all other things. It rather shows that they have no reason at all, and that it is nature which acts in them according to the disposition of their organs, just as a clock, which is only composed of wheels and weights is able to tell the hours and measure the time more correctly than we can do with all our wisdom.

I had described after this the rational soul and shown that it could not be in any way derived from the power of matter, like the other things of which I had spoken, but that it must be expressly created. I showed, too, that it is not sufficient that it should be lodged in the human body like a pilot in his ship, unless perhaps for the moving of its members, but that it is necessary that it should also be joined and united more closely to the body in order to have sensations and appetites similar to our own, and thus to form a true man. In conclusion, I have here enlarged a little on the subject of the soul, because it is one of the greatest importance. For next to the error of those who deny God, which I think I have already sufficiently refuted, there is none which is more effectual in leading feeble spirits from the straight path of virtue, than to imagine that the soul of the brute is of the same nature as our own, and that in consequence, after this life we have nothing to fear or to hope for, any more than the flies and ants. As a matter of fact, when one comes to know how greatly they differ, we understand much better the reasons which go to prove that our soul is in its nature entirely independent of body, and in consequence that it is not liable to die with it. And then, inasmuch as we observe no other causes capable of destroying it, we are naturally inclined to judge that it is immortal.

The Passions of the Soul

By René Descartes

•••

ARTICLE II.

That in order to understand the passions of the soul its functions must be distinguished from those of body.

Next I note also that we do not observe the existence of any subject which more immediately acts upon our soul than the body to which it is joined, and that we must consequently consider that what in the soul is a passion is in the body commonly speaking an action; so that there is no better means of arriving at a knowledge of our passions than to examine the difference which exists between soul and body in order to know to which of the two we must attribute each one of the functions which are within us.

ARTICLE III.

What rule we must follow to bring about this result.

As to this we shall not find much difficulty if we realise that all that we experience as being in us, and that to observation may exist in wholly inanimate bodies, must be attributed to our body alone; and, on the other hand, that all that which is in us and which we cannot in any way conceive as possibly pertaining to a body, must be attributed to our soul.

ARTICLE IV.

That the heat and movement of the members proceed from the body, the thoughts from the soul.

Thus because we have no conception of the body as thinking in any way, we have reason to believe that every kind of thought which exists in us belongs to the soul; and because we do not doubt there being inanimate bodies which can move in as many as or in more diverse modes than can ours, and which have as much heat or more (experience demonstrates this to us in flame, which of itself has much more heat and movement than any of our members), we must believe that all the heat and all the movements which are in us pertain only to body, inasmuch as they do not depend on thought at all.

ARTICLE V.

That it is an error to believe that the soul supplies the movement and heat to body.

By this means we shall avoid a very considerable error into which many have fallen; so much so that I am of opinion that this is the primary cause which has prevented our being able hitherto satisfactorily to explain the passions and the other properties of the soul. It arises from the fact that from observing that all dead bodies are devoid of heat and consequently of movement, it has been thought that it was the absence of soul which caused these movements and this heat to cease; and thus, without any reason, it was thought that our natural heat and all the movements of our body depend on the soul: while in fact we ought on the contrary to believe that the soul quits us on death only because this heat ceases, and the organs which serve to move the body disintegrate.

ARTICLE VI.

The difference that exists between a living body and a dead body.

In order, then, that we may avoid this error, let us consider that death never comes to pass by reason of the soul, but only because some one of the principal parts of the body decays; and we may judge that the body of a living man differs from that of a dead man just as does a watch or other automaton (i.e. a machine that moves of itself), when it is wound up and contains in itself the corporeal principle of those movements for which it is designed along with all that is requisite for its action, from the same watch or other machine when it is broken and when the principle of its movement ceases to act.

ARTICLE VII.

A brief explanation of the parts of the body and some of its functions.

In order to render this more intelligible, I shall here explain in a few words the whole method in which the bodily machine is composed. There is no one who does not already know that there are in us a heart, a brain, a stomach, muscles, nerves, arteries, veins, and such things. We also know that the food that we eat descends into the stomach and bowels where its juice, passing into the liver and into all the veins, mingles with, and thereby increases the quantity of the blood which they contain. Those who have acquired even the minimum of medical knowledge further know how the heart is composed, and how all the blood in the veins can easily flow from the vena cava into its right side and from thence pass into the lung by the vessel which we term the arterial vein, and then return from the lung into the left side of the heart, by the vessel called the venous artery, and finally pass from there into the great artery, whose branches spread throughout all the body. Likewise all those whom the authority of the ancients has not entirely blinded, and who have chosen to open their eyes for the purpose of investigating the opinion of Harvey regarding the circulation of the blood, do not doubt that all the veins and arteries of the body are like streams by which the blood ceaselessly flows with great swiftness, taking its course from the right cavity of the heart by the arterial vein whose branches are spread over the whole of the lung, and joined to that of the venous artery by which it passes from the lung into the left side of the heart; from these, again, it goes into the great artery whose branches, spread throughout all the rest of the body, are united to the branches of the vein, which branches once more carry the same blood into the right cavity of the heart. Thus these two cavities are like sluices through each of which all the blood passes in the course of each circuit which it makes in the body. We further know that all the movements of the members depend on the muscles, and that these muscles are so mutually related one to another that when the one is contracted it draws toward itself the part of the body to which it is attached, which causes the opposite muscle at the same time to become elongated; then if at another time it happens that this last contracts, it causes the former to become elongated and it draws back to itself the part to which they are attached. We know finally that all these movements of the muscles, as also all the senses, depend on the nerves, which resemble small filaments, or little tubes, which all proceed from the brain, and thus contain like it a certain very subtle air or wind which is called the animal spirits.

•••

ARTICLE XVII.

What the functions of the soul are.

After having thus considered all the functions which pertain to the body alone, it is easy to recognise that there is nothing in us which we ought to attribute to our soul excepting our thoughts, which are mainly of two sorts, the one being the actions of the soul, and the other its passions. Those which I call its actions are all our desires, because we find by experience that they proceed directly from our soul, and appear to depend on it alone: while, on the other hand, we may usually term one's passions all those kinds of perception or forms of knowledge which are found in us, because it is often not our soul which makes them what they are, and because it always receives them from the things which are represented by them.

•••

ARTICLE XXX.

That the soul is united to all the portions of the body conjointly.

But in order to understand all these things more perfectly, we must know that the soul is really joined to the whole body, and that we cannot, properly speaking, say that it exists in any one of its parts to the exclusion of the others, because it is one and in some manner indivisible, owing to the disposition of its organs, which are so related to one another that when any one of them is removed, that renders the whole body defective; and because it is of a nature which has no relation to extension, nor dimensions, nor other properties of the matter of which the body is composed, but only to the whole conglomerate of its organs, as appears from the fact that we could not in any way conceive of the half or the third of a soul, nor of the space it occupies, and because it does not become smaller owing to the cutting off of some portion of the body, but separates itself from it entirely when the union of its assembled organs is dissolved.

ARTICLE XXXI.

That there is a small gland in the brain in which the soul exercises its functions more particularly than in the other parts.

It is likewise necessary to know that although the soul is joined to the whole body, there is yet in that a certain part in which it exercises its functions more particularly than in all the others; and it is usually believed that this part is the brain, or possibly the heart: the brain, because it is with it that the organs of sense are connected, and the heart because it is apparently in it that we experience the passions. But, in examining the matter with care, it seems as though I had clearly ascertained that the part of the body in which the soul exercises its functions immediately is in nowise the heart, nor the whole of the brain, but merely the most inward of all its parts, to wit, a certain very small gland which is situated in the middle of its substance and so suspended above the duct whereby the animal spirits in its anterior cavities have communication with those in the posterior, that the slightest movements which take place in it may alter very greatly the course of these spirits; and reciprocally that the smallest changes which occur in the course of the spirits may do much to change the movements of this gland.

ARTICLE XXXII.

How we know that this gland is the main seat of the soul.

The reason which persuades me that the soul cannot have any other seat in all the body than this gland wherein to exercise its functions immediately, is that I reflect that the other parts of our brain are all of them double, just as we have two eyes, two hands, two ears, and finally all the organs of our outside senses are double; and inasmuch as we have but one solitary and simple thought of one particular thing at one and the same moment, it must necessarily be the case that there must somewhere be a place where the two images which come to us by the two eyes, where the two other impressions which proceed from a single object by means of the double organs of the other senses, can unite before arriving at the soul, in order that they may not represent to it two objects instead of one. And it is easy to apprehend how these images or other impressions might unite in this gland by the intermission of the spirits which fill the cavities of the brain; but there is no other place in the body where they can be thus united unless they are so in this gland.

ARTICLE XXXIII.

That the seat of the passions is not in the heart.

As to the opinion of those who think that the soul receives its passions in the heart, it is not of much consideration, for it is only founded on the fact that the passions cause us to feel some change taking place there; and it is easy to see that this change is not felt in the heart excepting through the medium of a small nerve which descends from the brain towards it, just as pain is felt as in the foot by means of the nerves of the foot, and the stars are perceived as in the heavens by means of their light and of the optic nerves; so that it is not more necessary that our soul should exercise its functions immediately in the heart, in order to feel its passions there, than it is necessary for the soul to be in the heavens in order to see the stars there.

ARTICLE XXXIV.

How the soul and the body act on one another.

Let us then conceive here that the soul has its principal seat in the little gland which exists in the middle of the brain, from whence it radiates forth through all the remainder of the body by means of the animal spirits, nerves, and even the blood, which, participating in the impressions of the spirits, can carry them by the arteries into all the members. And recollecting what has been said above about the machine of our body, i.e. that the little filaments of our nerves are so distributed in all its parts, that on the occasion of the diverse movements which are there excited by sensible objects, they open in diverse ways the pores of the brain, which causes the animal spirits contained in these cavities to enter in diverse ways into the muscles, by which means they can move the members in all the different ways in which they are capable of being moved; and also that all the other causes which are capable of moving the spirits in diverse ways suffice to conduct them into diverse muscles; let us here add that the small gland which is the main seat of the soul is so suspended between the cavities which contain the spirits that it can be moved by them in as many different ways as there are sensible diversities in the object, but that it may also be moved in diverse ways by the soul, whose nature is such that it receives in itself as many diverse impressions, that is to say, that it possesses as many diverse perceptions as there are diverse movements in this gland. Reciprocally, likewise, the machine of the body is so formed that from the simple fact that this gland is diversely moved by the soul, or by such other cause, whatever it is, it thrusts the spirits which surround it towards the pores of the brain, which conduct them by the nerves into the muscles, by which means it causes them to move the limbs.

DISCUSSION QUESTIONS

1. Compare Descartes' view to the ideas in Hinduism and Buddhism. Which view do you think Descartes' ideas have more in common with? Explain.

2. Plato and Descartes are both rationalists and dualists. Which set of arguments for dualism do you find most convincing, Plato's or Descartes'? Why? Explain.

3. Explain and evaluate Descartes' argument for the position that humans are qualitatively different from other animals.

An Essay Concerning Human Understanding

By John Locke

John Locke (1632–1704) is one of the most influential philosophers of the late 17th century. In two years, 1689–1690, Locke published three works of lasting importance: A Letter Concerning Toleration *(1689, which was followed by two more letters in 1690 and 1692),* The Second Treatise on Government *(1689), and* An Essay Concerning Human Understanding *(1690). In the Letter, Locke argues for religious toleration (though not for atheists).* The Second Treatise *establishes the groundwork for modern capitalism within a framework of private property and natural rights, using a social contract model. Its influence on the* Declaration of Independence *is well-documented. The* Essay *was published in four books. Book I is a rejection of the theory of innate ideas, which was championed by rationalists such as Descartes. An innate idea would be one we are born with. Chapters I–VII of Book II contain his view on where ideas come from. Although Locke is a dualist like Descartes, Locke is not a rationalist. Locke is an empiricist. He thinks that all knowledge comes through the senses. An excerpt of this discussion will be found in Part III of* Four Fundamental Questions.

Later, in Chapter XXVII of Book II, he explains his conception of what constitutes identity of self. It is this argument that is presented here. The problem Locke is attempting to solve here is what makes us the same over time. Is it material substance, our bodies, or is it immaterial substance, our minds? Is it substance at all? Locke concludes that only the same consciousness, regardless of substance, can make the same person. He also considers some puzzles that might arise from this view. Sometimes when reading this it is easy to forget that it was published in 1690.

BOOK II
CHAPTER XXVII
OF IDENTITY AND DIVERSITY

• • •

3. Identity of modes and relations.

All other things being but modes or relations ultimately terminated in substances, the identity and diversity of each particular existence of them too will be by the same way determined: only as to things whose existence is in succession, such as are the actions of finite beings, v. g. MOTION and THOUGHT, both which consist in a continued train of succession, concerning THEIR diversity there can be no question: because each perishing the moment it begins, they cannot exist in different times, or in different places, as permanent beings can at different times exist in distant places; and therefore no motion or thought, considered as at different times, can be the same, each part thereof having a different beginning of existence.

4. Principium Individuationis.

From what has been said, it is easy to discover what is so much inquired after, the PRINCIPIUM INDIVIDUATIONIS; and that, it is plain, is existence itself; which determines a being of any sort to a particular time and place, incommunicable to two beings of the same kind. This, though it seems easier to conceive in simple substances or modes; yet, when reflected on, is not more difficult in compound ones, if care be taken to what it is applied: v.g. let us suppose an atom, i.e. a continued body under one immutable superficies, existing in a determined time and place; it is evident, that, considered in any instant of its existence, it is in that instant the same with itself. For, being at that instant what it is, and nothing else, it is the same, and so must continue as long as its existence is continued; for so long it will be the same, and no other. In like manner, if two or more atoms be joined together into the same mass, every one of those atoms will be the same, by the foregoing rule: and whilst they exist united together, the mass, consisting of the same atoms, must be the same mass, or the same body, let the parts be ever so differently jumbled. But if one of these atoms be taken away, or one new one added, it is no longer the same mass or the same body. In the state of living creatures, their identity depends not on a mass of the same particles, but on something else. For in them the variation of great parcels of matter alters not the identity: an oak growing from a plant to a great tree, and then lopped, is still the same oak; and a colt grown up to a horse, sometimes fat, sometimes lean, is all the while the same horse: though, in both these cases, there may be a manifest change of the parts; so that truly they are not either of them the same masses of matter, though they be truly one of them the same oak, and the other the same horse. The reason whereof is, that, in these two cases—a MASS OF MATTER and a LIVING BODY—identity is not applied to the same thing.

• • •

7. The Identity of Man.

This also shows wherein the identity of the same MAN consists; *viz.* in nothing but a participation of the same continued life, by constantly fleeting particles of matter, in succession vitally united to the same organized body. He that shall place the identity of man in anything else, but, like that of other animals, in one fitly organized body, taken in any one instant, and from thence continued, under one organization of life, in several successively fleeting particles of matter united to it, will find it hard to make an embryo, one of years, mad and sober, the SAME man, by any supposition, that will not make it possible for Seth, Ismael, Socrates, Pilate, St. Austin, and Caesar Borgia, to be the same man. For if the identity of SOUL ALONE makes the same MAN; and there be nothing in the nature of matter why the same individual spirit may not be united to different bodies, it will be possible that those men, living in distant ages, and of different tempers, may have been the same man: which way of speaking must be from a very strange use of the word man, applied to an idea out of which body and shape are excluded. And that way of speaking would agree yet worse with the notions of those philosophers who allow of transmigration, and are of opinion that the souls of men may, for their miscarriages, be detruded into the bodies of beasts, as fit habitations, with organs suited to the satisfaction of their brutal inclinations. But yet I think nobody, could he be sure that the SOUL of Heliogabalus were in one of his hogs, would yet say that hog were a MAN or Heliogabalus.

8. Idea of Identity suited to the Idea it is applied to.

It is not therefore unity of substance that comprehends all sorts of identity, or will determine it in every case; but to conceive and judge of it aright, we must consider what idea the word it is applied to stands for: it being one thing to be the same SUBSTANCE, another the same MAN, and a third the same PERSON, if PERSON, MAN, and SUBSTANCE, are three names standing for three different ideas;—for such as is the idea belonging to that name, such must be the identity; which, if it had been a little more carefully attended to, would possibly have prevented a great deal of that confusion which often occurs about this matter, with no small seeming difficulties, especially concerning PERSONAL identity, which therefore we shall in the next place a little consider.

9. Same man.

An animal is a living organized body; and consequently the same animal, as we have observed, is the same continued LIFE communicated to different particles of matter, as they happen successively to be united to that organized living body. And whatever is talked of other definitions, ingenious observation puts it past doubt, that the idea in our minds, of which the sound man in our mouths is the sign, is nothing else but of an animal of such a certain form. Since I think I may be confident, that, whoever should see a creature of his own shape or make, though it had no more reason all its life than a cat or a parrot, would call him still a MAN; or whoever should hear a cat or a parrot discourse, reason, and philosophize, would call or think it nothing but a CAT or a PARROT; and say, the one was a dull irrational man, and the other a very intelligent rational parrot.

10. Same man.

For I presume it is not the idea of a thinking or rational being alone that makes the IDEA OF A MAN in most people's sense: but of a body, so and so shaped, joined to it; and if that be the idea of a man, the same successive body not shifted all at once, must, as well as the same immaterial spirit, go to the making of the same man.

11. Personal Identity.

This being premised, to find wherein personal identity consists, we must consider what PERSON stands for;—which, I think, is a thinking intelligent being, that has reason and reflection, and can consider itself as itself, the same thinking thing, in different times and places; which it does only by that consciousness which is inseparable from thinking, and, as it seems to me, essential to it: it being impossible for any one to perceive without PERCEIVING that he does perceive. When we see, hear, smell, taste, feel, meditate, or will anything, we know that we do so. Thus it is always as to our present sensations and perceptions: and by this every one is to himself that which he calls SELF:—it not being considered, in this case, whether the same self be continued in the same or divers substances. For, since consciousness always accompanies thinking, and it is that which makes every one to be what he calls self, and thereby distinguishes himself from all other thinking things, in this alone consists personal identity, i.e. the sameness of a rational being: and as far as this consciousness can be extended backwards to any past action or thought, so far reaches the identity of that person; it is the same self now it was then; and it is by the same self with this present one that now reflects on it, that that action was done.

12. Consciousness makes personal Identity.

But it is further inquired, whether it be the same identical substance. This few would think they had reason to doubt of, if these perceptions, with their consciousness, always remained present in the mind, whereby the same thinking thing would be always consciously present, and, as would be thought, evidently the same to itself. But that which seems to make the difficulty is this, that this consciousness being interrupted always by forgetfulness, there being no moment of our lives wherein we have the whole train of all our past actions before our eyes in one view, but even the best memories losing the sight of one part whilst they are viewing another; and we sometimes, and that the greatest part of our lives, not reflecting on our past selves, being intent on our present thoughts, and in sound sleep having no thoughts at all, or at least none with that consciousness which remarks our waking thoughts,—I say, in all these cases, our consciousness being interrupted, and we losing the sight of our past selves, doubts are raised whether we are the same thinking thing, i.e. the same SUBSTANCE or no. Which, however reasonable or unreasonable, concerns not PERSONAL identity at all. The question being what makes the same person; and not whether it be the same identical substance, which always thinks in the same person, which, in this case, matters not at all: different substances, by the same consciousness (where they do partake in it) being united into one person, as well as different bodies by the same life are united into one animal, whose identity is preserved in that change of substances by the unity of one continued life. For, it being the same consciousness that makes a man be himself to himself, personal identity depends on that only, whether it be annexed solely to one individual substance, or can be continued in a succession of several substances. For as far as any intelligent being CAN repeat the idea of any past action with the same consciousness it had of it at first, and with the same consciousness it has of any present action; so far it is the same personal self. For it is by the consciousness it has of its present thoughts and actions, that it is SELF TO ITSELF now, and so will be the same self, as far as the same consciousness can extend to actions past or to come; and would be by distance of time, or change of substance, no more two persons, than a man be two men by wearing other clothes to-day than he did yesterday, with a long or a short sleep between: the same consciousness uniting those distant actions into the same person, whatever substances contributed to their production.

13. Personal Identity in Change of Substance.

That this is so, we have some kind of evidence in our very bodies, all whose particles, whilst vitally united to this same thinking conscious self, so that WE FEEL when they are touched, and are affected by, and conscious of good or harm that happens to them, are a part of ourselves; i.e. of our thinking conscious self. Thus, the limbs of his body are to every one a part of himself; he sympathizes and is concerned for them. Cut off a hand, and thereby separate it from that consciousness he had of its heat, cold, and other affections, and it is then no longer a part of that which is himself, any more than the remotest part of matter. Thus, we see the SUBSTANCE whereof personal self consisted at one time may be varied at another, without the change of personal identity; there being no question about the same person, though the limbs which but now were a part of it, be cut off.

14. Personality in Change of Substance.

But the question is, Whether if the same substance which thinks be changed, it can be the same person; or, remaining the same, it can be different persons?

And to this I answer: First, This can be no question at all to those who place thought in a purely material animal constitution, void of an immaterial substance. For, whether their supposition be true or no, it is plain they conceive personal identity preserved in something else than identity of substance; as animal identity is preserved in identity of life, and not of substance. And therefore those who place thinking in an immaterial substance only, before they can come to deal with these men, must show why personal identity cannot be preserved in the change of immaterial substances, or variety of particular immaterial substances, as well as animal identity is preserved in the change of material substances, or variety of particular bodies: unless they will say, it is one immaterial spirit that makes the same life in brutes, as it is one immaterial spirit that makes the same person in men; which the Cartesians at least will not admit, for fear of making brutes thinking things too.

15. Whether in Change of thinking Substances there can be one Person.

But next, as to the first part of the question, Whether, if the same thinking substance (supposing immaterial substances only to think) be changed, it can be the same person? I answer, that cannot be resolved but by those who know there can what kind of substances they are that do think; and whether the consciousness of past actions can be transferred from one thinking substance to another. I grant were the same consciousness the same individual action it could not: but it being a present representation of a past action, why it may not be possible, that that may be represented to the mind to have been which really never was, will remain to be shown. And therefore how far the consciousness of past actions is annexed to any individual agent, so that another cannot possibly have it, will be hard for us to determine, till we know what kind of action it is that cannot be done without a reflex act of perception accompanying it, and how performed by thinking substances, who cannot think without being conscious of it. But that which we call the same consciousness, not being the same individual act, why one intellectual substance may not have represented to it, as done by itself, what IT never did, and was perhaps done by some other agent—why, I say, such a representation may not possibly be without reality of matter of fact, as well as several representations in dreams are, which yet whilst dreaming we take for true—will be difficult to conclude from the nature of things. And that it never is so, will by us, till we have clearer views of the nature of thinking substances, be best resolved into the goodness of God; who, as far as the happiness or misery of any of his sensible creatures is concerned in it, will not, by a fatal error of theirs, transfer from one to another that consciousness which draws reward or punishment with it. How far this may be an argument against those who would place thinking in a system of fleeting animal spirits, I leave to be considered. But yet, to return to the question before us, it must be allowed, that, if the same consciousness (which, as has been shown, is quite a different thing from the same numerical figure or motion in body) can be transferred from one thinking substance to another, it will be possible that two thinking substances may make but one person. For the same consciousness being preserved, whether in the same or different substances, the personal identity is preserved.

16. Whether, the same immaterial Substance remaining, there can be two Persons.

As to the second part of the question, Whether the same immaterial substance remaining, there may be two distinct persons; which question seems to me to be built on this,—Whether the same immaterial being, being conscious of the action of its past duration, may be wholly stripped of all the consciousness of its past existence, and lose it beyond the power of ever retrieving it again: and so as it were beginning a new account from a new period, have a consciousness that CANNOT reach beyond this new state. All those who hold pre-existence are evidently of this mind; since they allow the soul to have no remaining consciousness of what it did in that pre-existent state, either wholly separate from body, or informing any other body; and if they should not, it is plain experience would be against them. So that personal identity, reaching no further than consciousness reaches, a pre-existent spirit not having continued so many ages in a state of silence, must needs make different persons. Suppose a Christian Platonist or a Pythagorean should, upon God's having ended all his works of creation the seventh day, think his soul hath existed ever since; and should imagine it has revolved in several human bodies; as I once met with one, who was persuaded his had been the SOUL of Socrates (how reasonably I will not dispute; this I know, that in the post he filled, which was no inconsiderable one, he passed for a very rational man, and the press has shown that he wanted not parts or learning;)—would any one say, that he, being not conscious of any of Socrates's actions or thoughts, could be the same PERSON with Socrates? Let any one reflect upon himself, and conclude that he has in himself an immaterial spirit, which is that which thinks in him, and, in the constant change of his body keeps him the same: and is that which he calls HIMSELF: let his also suppose it to be the same soul that was in Nestor or Thersites, at the siege of Troy, (for souls being, as far as we know anything of them, in their nature indifferent to any parcel of matter, the supposition has no apparent absurdity in it,) which it may have been, as well as it is now the soul of any other man: but he now having no consciousness of any of the actions either of Nestor or Thersites, does or can he conceive himself the same person with either of them? Can he be concerned in either of their actions? attribute them to himself, or think them his own more than the actions of any other men that ever existed? So that this consciousness, not reaching to any of the actions of either of those men, he is no more one SELF with either of them than of the soul of immaterial spirit that now informs him had been created, and began to exist, when it began to inform his present body; though it were never so true, that the same SPIRIT that informed Nestor's or Thersites' body were numerically the same that now informs his. For this would no more make him the same person with Nestor, than if some of the particles of smaller that were once a part of Nestor were now a part of this man the same immaterial substance, without the same consciousness, no more making the same person, by being united to any body, than the same particle of matter, without consciousness, united to any body, makes the same person. But let him once find himself conscious of any of the actions of Nestor, he then finds himself the same person with Nestor.

17. The body, as well as the soul, goes to the making of a Man.

And thus may we be able, without any difficulty, to conceive the same person at the resurrection, though in a body not exactly in make or parts the same which he had here,—the same consciousness going along with the soul that inhabits it. But yet the soul alone, in the change of bodies, would scarce to any one but to him that makes the soul the man, be enough to make the same man. For should the soul of a prince, carrying with it the consciousness of the prince's past life, enter and inform the body of a cobbler, as soon as deserted by his own soul, every one sees he would be the same PERSON with the prince, accountable only for the prince's actions: but who would say it was the same MAN? The body too goes to the making the man, and would, I guess, to everybody determine the man in this case, wherein the soul, with all its princely thoughts about it, would not make another man: but he would be the same cobbler to every one besides himself. I know that, in the ordinary way of speaking, the same person, and the same man, stand for one and the same thing. And indeed every one will always have a liberty to speak as he pleases, and to apply what articulate sounds to what ideas he thinks fit, and change them as often as he pleases. But yet, when we will inquire what makes the same SPIRIT, MAN, or PERSON, we must fix the ideas of spirit, man, or person in our minds; and having resolved with ourselves what we mean by them, it will not be hard to determine, in either of them, or the like, when it is the same, and when not.

18. Consciousness alone unites actions into the same Person.

But though the same immaterial substance or soul does not alone, wherever it be, and in whatsoever state, make the same MAN; yet it is plain, consciousness, as far as ever it can be extended—should it be to ages past—unites existences and actions very remote in time into the same PERSON, as well as it does the existences and actions of the immediately preceding moment: so that whatever has the consciousness of present and past actions, is the same person to whom they both belong. Had I the same consciousness that I saw the ark and Noah's flood, as that I saw an overflowing of the Thames last winter, or as that I write now, I could no more doubt that I who write this now, that saw the Thames overflowed last winter, and that viewed the flood at the general deluge, was the same SELF,—place that self in what SUBSTANCE you please—than that I who write this am the same MYSELF now whilst I write (whether I consist of all the same substance material or immaterial, or no) that I was yesterday. For as to this point of being the same self, it matters not whether this present self be made up of the same or other substances—I being as much concerned, and as justly accountable for any action that was done a thousand years since, appropriated to me now by this self-consciousness, as I am for what I did the last moment.

19. Self depends on Consciousness, not on Substance.

SELF is that conscious thinking thing,—whatever substance made up of, (whether spiritual or material, simple or compounded, it matters not)—which is sensible or conscious of pleasure and pain, capable of happiness or misery, and so is concerned for itself, as far as that consciousness extends. Thus every one finds that, whilst comprehended under that consciousness, the little finger is as much a part of himself as what is most so. Upon separation of this little finger, should this consciousness go along with the little finger, and leave the rest of the body, it is evident the little finger would be the person, the same body. As in this case it is the consciousness that goes along with the substance, when one part is separate from another, which makes the same person, and constitutes this inseparable self: so it is in reference to substances remote in time. That with which the consciousness of this present thinking thing CAN join itself, makes the same person, and is one self with it, and with nothing else; and so attributes to itself, and owns all the actions of that thing, as its own, as far as that consciousness reaches, and no further; as every one who reflects will perceive.

20. Persons, not Substances, the Objects of Reward and Punishment.

In this personal identity is founded all the right and justice of reward and punishment; happiness and misery being that for which every one is concerned for HIMSELF, and not mattering what becomes of any SUBSTANCE, not joined to, or affected with that consciousness. For, as it is evident in the instance I gave but now, if the consciousness went along with the little finger when it was cut off, that would be the same self which was concerned for the whole body yesterday, as making part of itself, whose actions then it cannot but admit as its own now. Though, if the same body should still live, and immediately from the separation of the little finger have its own peculiar consciousness, whereof the little finger knew nothing, it would not at all be concerned for it, as a part of itself, or could own any of its actions, or have any of them imputed to him.

21. Which shows wherein Personal identity consists.

This may show us wherein personal identity consists: not in the identity of substance, but, as I have said, in the identity of consciousness, wherein if Socrates and the present mayor of Queenborough agree, they are the same person: if the same Socrates waking and sleeping do not partake of the same consciousness, Socrates waking and sleeping is not the same person. And to punish Socrates waking for what sleeping Socrates thought, and waking Socrates was never conscious of, would be no more of right, than to punish one twin for what his brother-twin did, whereof he knew nothing, because their outsides were so like, that they could not be distinguished; for such twins have been seen.

22. Absolute oblivion separates what is thus forgotten from the person, but not from the man.

But yet possibly it will still be objected,—Suppose I wholly lose the memory of some parts of my life, beyond a possibility of retrieving them, so that perhaps I shall never be conscious of them again; yet am I not the same person that did those actions, had those thoughts that I once was conscious of, though I have now forgot them? To which I answer, that we must here take notice what the word _I_ is applied to; which, in this case, is the MAN only. And the same man being presumed to be the same person, I is easily here supposed to stand also for the same person. But if it be possible for the same man to have distinct incommunicable consciousness at different times, it is past doubt the same man would at different times make different persons; which, we see, is the sense of mankind in the solemnest declaration of their opinions, human laws not punishing the mad man for the sober man's actions, nor the sober man for what the mad man did,—thereby making them two persons: which is somewhat explained by our way of speaking in English when we say such an one is 'not himself,' or is 'beside himself'; in which phrases it is insinuated, as if those who now, or at least first used them, thought that self was changed; the selfsame person was no longer in that man.

23. Difference between Identity of Man and of Person.

But yet it is hard to conceive that Socrates, the same individual man, should be two persons. To help us a little in this, we must consider what is meant by Socrates, or the same individual MAN.

First, it must be either the same individual, immaterial, thinking substance; in short, the same numerical soul, and nothing else.

Secondly, or the same animal, without any regard to an immaterial soul.

Thirdly, or the same immaterial spirit united to the same animal.

Now, take which of these suppositions you please, it is impossible to make personal identity to consist in anything but consciousness; or reach any further than that does.

For, by the first of them, it must be allowed possible that a man born of different women, and in distant times, may be the same man. A way of speaking which, whoever admits, must allow it possible for the same man to be two distinct persons, as any two that have lived in different ages without the knowledge of one another's thoughts.

By the second and third, Socrates, in this life and after it, cannot be the same man any way, but by the same consciousness; and so making human identity to consist in the same thing wherein we place personal identity, there will be difficulty to allow the same man to be the same person. But then they who place human identity in consciousness only, and not in something else, must consider how they will make the infant Socrates the same man with Socrates after the resurrection. But whatsoever to some men makes a man, and consequently the same individual man, wherein perhaps few are agreed, personal identity can by us be placed in nothing but consciousness, (which is that alone which makes what we call SELF,) without involving us in great absurdities.

24. But is not a man drunk and sober the same person? why else is he punished for the fact he commits when drunk, though he be never afterwards conscious of it? Just as much the same person as a man that walks, and does other things in his sleep, is the same person, and is answerable for any mischief he shall do in it. Human laws punish both, with a justice suitable to THEIR way of knowledge;—because, in these cases, they cannot distinguish certainly what is real, what counterfeit: and so the ignorance in drunkenness or sleep is not admitted as a plea. But in the Great Day, wherein the secrets of all hearts shall be laid open, it may be reasonable to think, no one shall be made to answer for what he knows nothing of; but shall receive his doom, his conscience accusing or excusing him.

25. Consciousness alone unites remote existences into one Person.

Nothing but consciousness can unite remote existences into the same person: the identity of substance will not do it; for whatever substance there is, however framed, without consciousness there is no person: and a carcass may be a person, as well as any sort of substance be so, without consciousness.

Could we suppose two distinct incommunicable consciousnesses acting the same body, the one constantly by day, the other by night; and, on the other side, the same consciousness, acting by intervals, two distinct bodies: I ask, in the first case, whether the day and the night—man would not be two as distinct persons as Socrates and Plato? And whether, in the second case, there would not be one person in two distinct bodies, as much as one man is the same in two distinct clothings? Nor is it at all material to say, that this same, and this distinct consciousness, in the cases above mentioned, is owing to the same and distinct immaterial substances, bringing it with them to those bodies; which, whether true or no, alters not the case: since it is evident the personal identity would equally be determined by the consciousness, whether that consciousness were annexed to some individual immaterial substance or no. For, granting that the thinking substance in man must be necessarily supposed immaterial, it is evident that immaterial thinking thing may sometimes part with its past consciousness, and be restored to it again: as appears in the forgetfulness men often have of their past actions; and the mind many times recovers the memory of a past consciousness, which it had lost for twenty years together. Make these intervals of memory and forgetfulness to take their turns regularly by day and night, and you have two persons with the same immaterial spirit, as much as in the former instance two persons with the same body. So that self is not determined by identity or diversity of substance, which it cannot be sure of, but only by identity of consciousness.

26. Not the substance with which the consciousness may be united.

Indeed it may conceive the substance whereof it is now made up to have existed formerly, united in the same conscious being: but, consciousness removed, that substance is no more itself, or makes no more a part of it, than any other substance; as is evident in the instance we have already given of a limb cut off, of whose heat, or cold, or other affections, having no longer any consciousness, it is no more of a man's self than any other matter of the universe. In like manner it will be in reference to any immaterial substance, which is void of that consciousness whereby I am myself to myself: so that I cannot upon recollection join with that present consciousness whereby I am now myself, it is, in that part of its existence, no more MYSELF than any other immaterial being. For, whatsoever any substance has thought or done, which I cannot recollect, and by my consciousness make my own thought and action, it will no more belong to me, whether a part of me thought or did it, than if it had been thought or done by any other immaterial being anywhere existing.

27. Consciousness unites substances, material or spiritual, with the same personality.

I agree, the more probable opinion is, that this consciousness is annexed to, and the affection of, one individual immaterial substance.

But let men, according to their diverse hypotheses, resolve of that as they please. This every intelligent being, sensible of happiness or misery, must grant—that there is something that is HIMSELF, that he is concerned for, and would have happy; that this self has existed in a continued duration more than one instant, and therefore it is possible may exist, as it has done, months and years to come, without any certain bounds to be set to its duration; and may be the same self, by the same consciousness continued on for the future. And thus, by this consciousness he finds himself to be the same self which did such and such an action some years since, by which he comes to be happy or miserable now. In all which account of self, the same numerical SUBSTANCE is not considered a making the same self; but the same continued CONSCIOUSNESS, in which several substances may have been united, and again separated from it, which, whilst they continued in a vital union with that wherein this consciousness then resided, made a part of that same self. Thus any part of our bodies, vitally united to that which is conscious in us, makes a part of ourselves: but upon separation from the vital union by which that consciousness is communicated, that which a moment since was part of ourselves, is now no more so than a part of another man's self is a part of me: and it is not impossible but in a little time may become a real part of another person. And so we have the same numerical substance become a part of two different persons; and the same person preserved under the change of various substances. Could we suppose any spirit wholly stripped of all its memory of consciousness of past actions, as we find our minds always are of a great part of ours, and sometimes of them all; the union or separation of such a spiritual substance would make no variation of personal identity, any more than that of any particle of matter does. Any substance vitally united to the present thinking being is a part of that very same self which now is; anything united to it by a consciousness of former actions, makes also a part of the same self, which is the same both then and now.

28. Person a forensic Term.

PERSON, as I take it, is the name for this self. Wherever a man finds what he calls himself, there, I think, another may say is the same person. It is a forensic term, appropriating actions and their merit; and so belongs only to intelligent agents, capable of a law, and happiness, and misery. This personality extends itself beyond present existence to what is past, only by consciousness,—whereby it becomes concerned and accountable; owns and imputes to itself past actions, just upon the same ground and for the same reason as it does the present. All which is founded in a concern for happiness, the unavoidable concomitant of consciousness; that which is conscious of pleasure and pain, desiring that that self that is conscious should be happy. And therefore whatever past actions it cannot reconcile or APPROPRIATE to that present self by consciousness, it can be no more concerned in than if they had never been done: and to receive pleasure or pain, i.e. reward or punishment, on the account of any such action, is all one as to be made happy or miserable in its first being, without any demerit at all. For, supposing a MAN punished now for what he had done in another life, whereof he could be made to have no consciousness at all, what difference is there between that punishment and being CREATED miserable? And therefore, conformable to this, the apostle tells us, that, at the great day, when every one shall 'receive according to his doings, the secrets of all hearts shall be laid open.' The sentence shall be justified by the consciousness all persons shall have, that THEY THEMSELVES, in what bodies soever they appear, or what substances soever that consciousness adheres to, are the SAME that committed those actions, and deserve that punishment for them.

•••

30. The Difficulty from ill Use of Names.

To conclude: Whatever substance begins to exist, it must, during its existence, necessarily be the same: whatever compositions of substances begin to exist, during the union of those substances, the concrete must be the same: whatsoever mode begins to exist, during its existence it is the same: and so if the composition be of distinct substances and different modes, the same rule holds. Whereby it will appear, that the difficulty or obscurity that has been about this matter rather rises from the names ill-used, than from any obscurity in things themselves. For whatever makes the specific idea to which the name is applied, if that idea be steadily kept to, the distinction of anything into the same and divers will easily be conceived, and there can arise no doubt about it.

31. Continuance of that which we have made to be our complex idea of man makes the same man.

For, supposing a rational spirit be the idea of a MAN, it is easy to know what is the same man, *viz.* the same spirit—whether separate or in a body—will be the SAME MAN. Supposing a rational spirit vitally united to a body of a certain conformation of parts to make a man; whilst that rational spirit, with that vital conformation of parts, though continued in a fleeting successive body, remains, it will be the SAME MAN. But if to any one the idea of a man be but the vital union of parts in a certain shape; as long as that vital union and shape remain in a concrete, no otherwise the same but by a continued succession of fleeting particles, it will be the SAME MAN. For, whatever be the composition whereof the complex idea is made, whenever existence makes it one particular thing under any denomination, THE SAME EXISTENCE CONTINUED preserves it the SAME individual under the same denomination.

DISCUSSION QUESTIONS

1. Compare Locke's view to Descartes'. Which view do you think is better argued? Explain.

2. Explain the distinction Locke makes between the terms "man" and "person." Why does he make this distinction?

3. Why does Locke consider persons, as opposed to substances, to be the proper recipient of reward and punishment? Explain.

A Treatise of Human Nature

By David Hume

Like John Locke, David Hume (1711–1776) was an Empiricist. Hume's version of Empiricism will be evident in the selection found in Part III of Four Fundamental Questions. *Hume was better known during his lifetime for his four-volume History of England (published in six volumes, 1754–1762), written while he was librarian to Edinburgh Faculty of Advocates, than he was for his philosophical writings. Hume was never awarded a teaching position. Hume wrote extensively on many philosophical topics including ethics, knowledge, politics, art and aesthetics, and religion. Some of Hume's thoughts on ethics are in Part IV of* Fundamental Questions.

Our selection here is from his first major work, A Treatise on Human Nature, *which was first published in three books in 1739–1740. "Of Personal Identity" is Book I, Part IV, section vi of the* Treatise. *Hume rejects Locke's association of identity with consciousness. Instead, Hume rejects that the concept of self is a genuine one at all. In order for an idea to be genuine, using Hume's criteria, it must be traceable back to what he calls an "impression." An impression is an immediate object of sensation, as opposed to a memory, imagination, or reflection, which is a mediated object of consciousness. For Hume, we cannot have an impression of something called a self.*

BOOK I, PART IV
SECT. VI. OF PERSONAL IDENTITY

There are some philosophers who imagine we are every moment intimately conscious of what we call our SELF; that we feel its existence and its continuance in existence; and are certain, beyond the evidence of a demonstration, both o its perfect identity and simplicity. The strongest sensation, the most violent passion, say they, instead of distracting us from this view, only fix it the more intensely, and make us consider their influence on self either by their pain or pleasure. To attempt a farther proof of this were to weaken its evidence; since no proof can be derived from any fact, of which we are so intimately conscious; nor is there any thing, of which we can be certain, if we doubt of this.

Unluckily all these positive assertions are contrary to that very experience, which is pleaded for them, nor have we any idea of self, after the manner it is here explained. For from what impression coued this idea be derived? This question it is impossible to answer without a manifest contradiction and absurdity; and yet it is a question, which must necessarily be answered, if we would have the idea of self pass for clear and intelligible, It must be some one impression, that gives rise to every real idea. But self or person is not any one impression, but that to which our several impressions and ideas are supposed to have a reference. If any impression gives rise to the idea of self, that impression must continue invariably the same, through the whole course of our lives; since self is supposed to exist after that manner. But there is no impression constant and invariable. Pain and pleasure, grief and joy, passions and sensations succeed each other, and never all exist at the same time. It cannot, therefore, be from any of these impressions, or from any other, that the idea of self is derived; and consequently there is no such idea.

But farther, what must become of all our particular perceptions upon this hypothesis? All these are different, and distinguishable, and separable from each other, and may be separately considered, and may exist separately, and have no Deed of tiny thing to support their existence. After what manner, therefore, do they belong to self; and how are they connected with it? For my part, when I enter most intimately into what I call myself, I always stumble on some particular perception or other, of heat or cold, light or shade, love or hatred, pain or pleasure. I never can catch myself at any time without a perception, and never can observe any thing but the perception. When my perceptions are removed for any time, as by sound sleep; so long am I insensible of myself, and may truly be said not to exist. And were all my perceptions removed by death, and coued I neither think, nor feel, nor see, nor love, nor hate after the dissolution of my body, I should be entirely annihilated, nor do I conceive what is farther requisite to make me a perfect non-entity. If any one, upon serious and unprejudiced reflection thinks he has a different notion of himself, I must confess I call reason no longer with him. All I can allow him is, that he may be in the right as well as I, and that we are essentially different in this particular. He may, perhaps, perceive something simple and continued, which he calls himself; though I am certain there is no such principle in me.

But setting aside some metaphysicians of this kind, I may venture to affirm of the rest of mankind, that they are nothing but a bundle or collection of different perceptions, which succeed each other with an inconceivable rapidity, and are in a perpetual flux and movement. Our eyes cannot turn in their sockets without varying our perceptions. Our thought is still more variable than our sight; and all our other senses and faculties contribute to this change; nor is there any single power of the soul, which remains unalterably the same, perhaps for one moment. The mind is a .kind of theatre, where several perceptions successively make their appearance; pass, re-pass, glide away, and mingle in an infinite variety of postures and situations. There is properly no simplicity in it at one time, nor identity in different; whatever natural propension we may have to imagine that simplicity and identity. The comparison of the theatre must not mislead us. They are the successive perceptions only, that constitute the mind; nor have we the most distant notion of the place, where these scenes are represented, or of the materials, of which it is composed.

What then gives us so great a propension to ascribe an identity to these successive perceptions, and to suppose ourselves possest of an invariable and uninterrupted existence through the whole course of our lives? In order to answer this question, we must distinguish betwixt personal identity, as it regards our thought or imagination, and as it regards our passions or the concern we take in ourselves. The first is our present subject; and to explain it perfectly we must take the matter pretty deep, and account for that identity, which we attribute to plants and animals; there being a great analogy betwixt it, and the identity of a self or person.

We have a distinct idea of an object, that remains invariable and uninterrupted through a supposed variation of time; and this idea we call that of identity or sameness. We have also a distinct idea of several different objects existing in succession, and connected together by a close relation; and this to an accurate view affords as perfect a notion of diversity, as if there was no manner of relation among the objects. But though these two ideas of identity, and a succession of related objects be in themselves perfectly distinct, and even contrary, yet it is certain, that in our common way of thinking they are generally confounded with each other. That action of the imagination, by which we consider the uninterrupted and invariable object, and that by which we reflect on the succession of related objects, are almost the same to the feeling, nor is there much more effort of thought required in the latter case than in the former. The relation facilitates the transition of the mind from one object to another, and renders its passage as smooth as if it contemplated one continued object. This resemblance is the cause of the confusion and mistake, and makes us substitute the notion of identity, instead of that of related objects. However at one instant we may consider the related succession as variable or interrupted, we are sure the next to ascribe to it a perfect identity, and regard it as enviable and uninterrupted. Our propensity to this mistake is so great from the resemblance above-mentioned, that we fall into it before we are aware; and though we incessantly correct ourselves by reflection, and return to a more accurate method of thinking, yet we cannot long sustain our philosophy, or take off this biass from the imagination. Our last resource is to yield to it, and boldly assert that these different related objects are in effect the same, however interrupted and variable. In order to justify to ourselves this absurdity, we often feign some new and unintelligible principle, that connects the objects together, and prevents their interruption or variation. Thus we feign the continued existence of the perceptions of our senses, to remove the interruption: and run into the notion of a soul, and self, and substance, to disguise the variation. But we may farther observe, that where we do not give rise to such a fiction, our propension to confound identity with relation is so great, that we are apt to imagine[1] something unknown and mysterious, connecting the parts, beside their relation; and this I take to be the case with regard to the identity we ascribe to plants and vegetables. And even when this does not take place, we still feel a propensity to confound these ideas, though we are not able fully to satisfy ourselves in that particular, nor find any thing invariable and uninterrupted to justify our notion of identity.

Thus the controversy concerning identity is not merely a dispute of words. For when we attribute identity, in an improper sense, to variable or interrupted objects, our mistake is not confined to the expression, but is commonly attended with a fiction, either of something invariable and uninterrupted, or of something mysterious and inexplicable, or at least with a propensity to such fictions. What will suffice to prove this hypothesis to the satisfaction of every fair enquirer, is to shew from daily experience and observation, that the objects, which are variable or interrupted, and yet are supposed to continue the same, are such only as consist of a succession of parts, connected together by resemblance, contiguity, or causation. For as such a succession answers evidently to our notion of diversity, it can only be by mistake we ascribe to it an identity; and as the relation of parts, which leads us into this mistake, is really nothing but a quality, which produces an association of ideas, and an easy transition of the imagination from one to another, it can only be from the resemblance, which this act of the mind bears to that, by which we contemplate one continued object, that the error arises. Our chief business, then, must be to prove, that all objects, to which we ascribe identity, without observing their invariableness and uninterruptedness, are such as consist of a succession of related objects.

In order to this, suppose any mass of matter, of which the parts are contiguous and connected, to be placed before us; it is plain we must attribute a perfect identity to this mass, provided all the parts continue uninterruptedly and invariably the same, whatever motion or change of place we may observe either in the whole or in any of the parts. But supposing some very small or inconsiderable part to be added to the mass, or subtracted from it; though this absolutely destroys the identity of the whole, strictly speaking; yet as we seldom think so accurately, we scruple not to pronounce a mass of matter the same, where we find so trivial an alteration. The passage of the thought from the object before the change to the object after it, is so smooth and easy, that we scarce perceive the transition, and are apt to imagine, that it is nothing but a continued survey of the same object.

There is a very remarkable circumstance, that attends this experiment; which is, that though the change of any considerable part in a mass of matter destroys the identity of the whole, let we must measure the greatness of the part, not absolutely, but by its proportion to the whole. The addition or diminution of a mountain would not be sufficient to produce a diversity in a planet: though the change of a very few inches would be able to destroy the identity of some bodies. It will be impossible to account for this, but by reflecting that objects operate upon the mind, and break or interrupt the continuity of its actions not according to their real greatness, but according to their proportion to each other: And therefore, since this interruption makes an object cease to appear the same, it must be the uninterrupted progress o the thought, which constitutes the imperfect identity.

This may be confirmed by another phenomenon. A change in any considerable part of a body destroys its identity; but it is remarkable, that where the change is produced gradually and insensibly we are less apt to ascribe to it the same effect. The reason can plainly be no other, than that the mind, in following the successive changes of the body, feels an easy passage from the surveying its condition in one moment to the viewing of it in another, and at no particular time perceives any interruption in its actions. From which continued perception, it ascribes a continued existence and identity to the object.

But whatever precaution we may use in introducing the changes gradually, and making them proportionable to the whole, it is certain, that where the changes are at last observed to become considerable, we make a scruple of ascribing identity to such different objects. There is, however, another artifice, by which we may induce the imagination to advance a step farther; and that is, by producing a reference of the parts to each other, and a combination to some common end or purpose. A ship, of which a considerable part has been changed by frequent reparations, is still considered as the same; nor does the difference of the materials hinder us from ascribing an identity to it. The common end, in which the parts conspire, is the same under all their variations, and affords an easy transition of the imagination from one situation of the body to another.

But this is still more remarkable, when we add a sympathy of parts to their common end, and suppose that they bear to each other, the reciprocal relation of cause and effect in all their actions and operations. This is the case with all animals and vegetables; where not only the several parts have a reference to some general purpose, but also a mutual dependence on, and connexion with each other. The effect of so strong a relation is, that though every one must allow, that in a very few years both vegetables and animals endure a total change, yet we still attribute identity to them, while their form, size, and substance are entirely altered. An oak, that grows from a small plant to a large tree, is still the same oak; though there be not one particle of matter, or figure of its parts the same. An infant becomes a man-, and is sometimes fat, sometimes lean, without any change in his identity.

We may also consider the two following phaenomena, which are remarkable in their kind. The first is, that though we commonly be able to distinguish pretty exactly betwixt numerical and specific identity, yet it sometimes happens, that we confound them, and in our thinking and reasoning employ the one for the other. Thus a man, who bears a noise, that is frequently interrupted and renewed, says, it is still the same noise; though it is evident the sounds have only a specific identity or resemblance, and there is nothing numerically the same, but the cause, which produced them. In like manner it may be said without breach of the propriety of language, that such a church, which was formerly of brick, fell to ruin, and that the parish rebuilt the same church of free-stone, and according to modern architecture. Here neither the form nor materials are the same, nor is there any thing common to the two objects, but their relation to the inhabitants of the parish; and yet this alone is sufficient to make us denominate them the same. But we must observe, that in these cases the first object is in a manner annihilated before the second comes into existence; by which means, we are never presented in any one point of time with the idea of difference and multiplicity: and for that reason are less scrupulous in calling them the same.

Secondly, We may remark, that though in a succession of related objects, it be in a manner requisite, that the change of parts be not sudden nor entire, in order to preserve the identity, yet where the objects are in their nature changeable and inconstant, we admit of a more sudden transition, than would otherwise be consistent with that relation. Thus as the nature of a river consists in the motion and change of parts; though in less than four and twenty hours these be totally altered; this hinders not the river from continuing the same during several ages. What is natural and essential to any thing is, in a manner, expected; and what is expected makes less impression, and appears of less moment, than what is unusual and extraordinary. A considerable change of the former kind seems really less to the imagination, than the most trivial alteration of the latter; and by breaking less the continuity of the thought, has less influence in destroying the identity.

We now proceed to explain the nature of personal identity, which has become so great a question ill philosophy, especially of late years in England, where all the abstruser sciences are studyed with a peculiar ardour and application. And here it is evident, the same method of reasoning must be continued which has so successfully explained the identity of plants, and animals, and ships, and houses, and of all the compounded and changeable productions either of art or nature. The identity, which we ascribe to the mind of man, is only a fictitious one, and of a like kind with that which we ascribe to vegetables and animal bodies. It cannot, therefore, have a different origin, but must proceed from a like operation of the imagination upon like objects.

But lest this argument should not convince the reader; though in my opinion perfectly decisive; let him weigh the following reasoning, which is still closer and more immediate. It is evident, that the identity, which we attribute to the human mind, however perfect we may imagine it to be, is not able to run the several different perceptions into one, and make them lose their characters of distinction and difference, which are essential to them. It is still true, that every distinct perception, which enters into the composition of the mind, is a distinct existence, and is different, and distinguishable, and separable from every other perception, either contemporary or successive. But, as, notwithstanding this distinction and separability, we suppose the whole train of perceptions to be united by identity, a question naturally arises concerning this relation of identity; whether it be something that really binds our several perceptions together, or only associates their ideas in the imagination. That is, in other words, whether in pronouncing concerning the identity of a person, we observe some real bond among his perceptions, or only feel one among the ideas we form of them. This question we might easily decide, if we would recollect what has been already proud at large, that the understanding never observes any real connexion among objects, and that even the union of cause and effect, when strictly examined, resolves itself into a customary association of ideas. For from thence it evidently follows, that identity is nothing really belonging to these different perceptions, and uniting them together; but is merely a quality, which we attribute to them, because of the union of their ideas in the imagination, when we reflect upon them. Now the only qualities, which can give ideas an union in the imagination, are these three relations above-mentioned. There are the uniting principles in the ideal world, and without them every distinct object is separable by the mind, and may be separately considered, and appears not to have any more connexion with any other object, than if disjoined by the greatest difference and remoteness. It is, therefore, on some of these three relations of resemblance, contiguity and causation, that identity depends; and as the very essence of these relations consists in their producing an easy transition of ideas; it follows, that our notions of personal identity, proceed entirely from the smooth and uninterrupted progress of the thought along a train of connected ideas, according to the principles above-explained.

The only question, therefore, which remains, is, by what relations this uninterrupted progress of our thought is produced, when we consider the successive existence of a mind or thinking person. And here it is evident we must confine ourselves to resemblance and causation, and must drop contiguity, which has little or no influence in the present case.

To begin with resemblance; suppose we coued see clearly into the breast of another, and observe that succession of perceptions, which constitutes his mind or thinking principle, and suppose that he always preserves the memory of a considerable part of past perceptions; it is evident that nothing coued more contribute to the bestowing a relation on this succession amidst all its variations. For what is the memory but a faculty, by which we raise up the images of past perceptions? And as an image necessarily resembles its object, must not the frequent placing of these resembling perceptions in the chain of thought, convey the imagination more easily from one link to another, and make the whole seem like the continuance of one object? In this particular, then, the memory not only discovers the identity, but also contributes to its production, by producing the relation of resemblance among the perceptions. The case is the same whether we consider ourselves or others.

As to causation; we may observe, that the true idea of the human mind, is to consider it as a system of different perceptions or different existences, which are linked together by the relation of cause and effect, and mutually produce, destroy, influence, and modify each other. Our impressions give rise to their correspondent ideas; said these ideas in their turn produce other impressions. One thought chaces another, and draws after it a third, by which it is expelled in its turn. In this respect, I cannot compare the soul more properly to any thing than to a republic or commonwealth, in which the several members are united by the reciprocal ties of government and subordination, and give rise to other persons, who propagate the same republic in the incessant changes of its parts. And as the same individual republic may not only change its members, but also its laws and constitutions; in like manner the same person may vary his character and disposition, as well as his impressions and ideas, without losing his identity. Whatever changes he endures, his several parts are still connected by the relation of causation. And in this view our identity with regard to the passions serves to corroborate that with regard to the imagination, by the making our distant perceptions influence each other, and by giving us a present concern for our past or future pains or pleasures.

As a memory alone acquaints us with the continuance and extent of this succession of perceptions, it is to be considered, upon that account chiefly, as the source of personal identity. Had we no memory, we never should have any notion of causation, nor consequently of that chain of causes and effects, which constitute our self or person. But having once acquired this notion of causation from the memory, we can extend the same chain of causes, and consequently the identity of car persons beyond our memory, and can comprehend times, and circumstances, and actions, which we have entirely forgot, but suppose in general to have existed. For how few of our past actions are there, of which we have any memory? Who can tell me, for instance, what were his thoughts and actions on the 1st of January 1715, the 11th of March 1719, and the 3rd of August 1733? Or will he affirm, because he has entirely forgot the incidents of these days, that the present self is not the same person with the self of that time; and by that means overturn all the most established notions of personal identity? In this view, therefore, memory does not so much produce as discover personal identity, by shewing us the relation of cause and effect among our different perceptions. It will be incumbent on those, who affirm that memory produces entirely our personal identity, to give a reason why we cm thus extend our identity beyond our memory.

The whole of this doctrine leads us to a conclusion, which is of great importance in the present affair, *viz.* That all the nice and subtile questions concerning personal identity can never possibly be decided, and are to be regarded rather as gramatical than as philosophical difficulties. Identity depends on the relations of ideas; and these relations produce identity, by means of that easy transition they occasion. But as the relations, and the easiness of the transition may diminish by insensible degrees, we have no just standard, by which we can decide any dispute concerning the time, when they acquire or lose a title to the name of identity. All the disputes concerning the identity of connected objects are merely verbal, except so far as the relation of parts gives rise to some fiction or imaginary principle of union, as we have already observed.

What I have said concerning the first origin and uncertainty of our notion of identity, as applied to the human mind, may be extended with little or no variation to that of simplicity. An object, whose different co-existent parts are bound together by a close relation, operates upon the imagination after much the same manner as one perfectly simple and indivisible and requires not a much greater stretch of thought in order to its conception. From this similarity of operation we attribute a simplicity to it, and feign a principle of union as the support of this simplicity, and the center of all the different parts and qualities of the object.

Thus we have finished our examination of the several systems of philosophy, both of the intellectual and natural world; and in our miscellaneous way of reasoning have been led into several topics; which will either illustrate and confirm some preceding part of this discourse, or prepare the way for our following opinions. It is now time to return to a more close examination of our subject, and to proceed in the accurate anatomy of human nature, having fully explained the nature of our judgment and understandings.

ENDNOTE

1 If the reader is desirous to see how a great genius may be influencd by these seemingly trivial principles of the imagination, as well as the mere vulgar, let him read my Lord SHAFTSBURYS reasonings concerning the uniting principle of the universe, and the identity of plants and animals. See his MORALISTS: or, PHILOSOPHICAL RHAPSODY.

DISCUSSION QUESTIONS

1. Compare Hume's view to Locke's. Which view do you think is better argued? Explain.

2. Hume's view is very different from the rationalist accounts in Plato and Descartes. What are the main differences?

3. Many consider Hume's ideas on identity in the *Treatise* to be reminiscent of the account in the Buddhist scriptures (there is no evidence, though, that Hume had knowledge of Buddhism). What are the similarities between Hume's view and the one in the "Non-Existence of Individuality" earlier in *Four Fundamental Questions*?

The Self

By George Herbert Mead

George Herbert Mead (1863–1931) was a philosopher, psychologist, and sociologist, who taught at the University of Chicago from 1894 until his death. He studied philosophy at Harvard with William James (1842–1910), whose view on truth is included in Part III of Four Fundamental Questions, *and psychology with Wilhelm Wundt (1832–1920) in Leipzig, who was a pioneer in physiological psychology. Mead's philosophical outlook was influenced by the pragmatism of both William James and John Dewey (1859–1952), with whom he was a colleague at the University of Michigan, and then later at University of Chicago. One of the main ideas of pragmatism is that truth is instrumental, or in other words, what works is what's true. The founder of the movement was the philosopher and mathematician, Charles Sanders Peirce (1839–1914), who taught at Johns Hopkins University.*

The excerpt here, "The Self and the Organism" is Chapter 18 of Mead's book, Mind, Self, and Society, *which was published posthumously in 1934. The view that is developed here is often called "the social construction of the self." Mead, like Locke and the Empiricists, rejects innate ideas. In Mead's view the self is constructed in the process of interacting with the world, especially other people. He also believes that our personalities may be multiple because of all the different roles we play in life.*

PART III

18. The Self and the Organism

In our statement of the development of intelligence we have already suggested that the language process is essential for the development of the self. The self has a character which is different from that of the physiological organism proper. The self is something which has a development; it is not initially there, at birth, but arises in the process of social experience and activity, that is, develops in the given individual as a result of his relations to that process as a whole and to other individuals within that process. The intelligence of the lower forms of animal life, like a great deal of human intelligence, does not involve a self. In our habitual actions, for example, in our moving about in a world that is simply there and to which we are so adjusted that no thinking is involved, there is a certain amount of sensuous experience such as persons have when they are just waking up, a bare thereness of the world. Such characters about us may exist in experience without taking their place in relationship to the self. One must, of course, under those conditions, distinguish between the experience that immediately takes place and our own organization of it into the experience of the self. One says upon analysis that a certain item had its place in his experience, in the experience of his self. We do inevitably tend at a certain level of sophistication to organize all experience into that of a self. We do so intimately identify our experiences, especially our affective experiences, with the self that it takes a moment's abstraction to realize that pain and pleasure can be there without being the experience of the self. Similarly, we normally organize our memories upon the string of our self. If we date things we always date them from the point of view of our past experiences. We frequently have memories that we cannot date, that we cannot place. A picture comes before us suddenly and we are at a loss to explain when that experience originally took place. We remember perfectly distinctly the picture, but we do not have it definitely placed, and until we can place it in terms of our past experience we are not satisfied. Nevertheless, I think it is obvious when one comes to consider it that the self is not necessarily involved in the life of the organism, nor involved in what we term our sensuous experience, that is, experience in a world about us for which we have habitual reactions.

We can distinguish very definitely between the self and the body. The body can be there and can operate in a very intelligent fashion without there being a self involved in the experience. The self has the characteristic that it is an object to itself, and that characteristic distinguishes it from other objects and from the body. It is perfectly true that the eye can see the foot, but it does not see the body as a whole. We cannot see our backs; we can feel certain portions of them, if we are agile, but we cannot get an experience of our whole body. There are, of course, experiences which are somewhat vague and difficult of location, but the bodily experiences are for us organized about a self. The foot and hand belong to the self. We can see our feet, especially if we look at them from the wrong end of an opera glass, as strange things which we have difficulty in recognizing as our own. The parts of the body are quite distinguishable from the self. We can lose parts of the body without any serious invasion of the self. The mere ability to experience different parts of the body is not different from the experience of a table. The table presents a different feel from what the hand does when one hand feels another, but it is an experience of something with which we come definitely into contact. The body does not experience itself as a whole, in the sense in which the self in some way enters into the experience of the self.

It is the characteristic of the self as an object to itself that I want to bring out. This characteristic is represented in the word "self," which is a reflexive, and indicates that which can be both subject and object. This type of object is essentially different from other objects, and in the past it has been distinguished as conscious, a term which indicates an experience with, an experience of one's self. It was assumed that consciousness in some way carried this capacity of being an object to itself. In giving a behavioristic statement of consciousness we have to look for some sort of experience in which the physical organism can become an object to itself.[1]

When one is running to get away from someone who is chasing him, he is entirely occupied in this action, and his experience may be swallowed up in the objects about him, so that he has, at the time being, no consciousness of self at all. We must be, of course, very completely occupied to have that take place, but we can, I think, recognize that sort of a possible experience in which the self does not enter. We can, perhps, get some light on that situation through those experiences in very intense action there appear in the experience of the individual, back of this intense action, memories and anticipations. Tolstoi as an officer in the war gives an account of having pictures of his past experience in the midst of his most intense action. There are also the pictures that flash into a person's mind when he is drowning. In such instances there is a contrast between an experience that is absolutely wound up in outside activity in which the self as an object does not enter, and an activity of memory and imagination in which the self is the principal of object. The self is then entirely distinguishable from an organism that is surrounded by things and acts with reference to things, including parts of its own body. These latter may be objects like other objects, but they are just objects out there in the field, and they do not involve a self that is an object to the organism. This is, I think, frequently overlooked. It is that fact which makes our anthropomorphic reconstructions of animal life so fallacious. How can an individual get outside himself (experientially) in such a way as to become an object to himself? This is the essential psychological problem of selfhood or of self-consciousness; and its solution is to be found by referring to the process of social conduct or activity in which the given person or individual is implicated. The apparatus of reason would not be complete unless it swept itself into its own analysis of the field of experience; or unless the individual brought himself into the same experiential field as that of the other individual selves in relation to whom he acts in any given social situation. Reason cannot become impersonal unless it takes an objective, non-affective attitude toward itself; otherwise we have just consciousness, not *self*-consciousness. And it is necessary to rational conduct that the individual should thus take an objective, impersonal attitude toward himself, that he should become an object to himself. For the individual organism is obviously an essential and important fact or constituent element of the empirical situation in which it acts; and without taking objective account of itself as such, it cannot act intelligently, or rationally.

The individual experiences himself as such, not directly, but only indirectly, from the particular standpoints of other individual members of the same social group, or from the generalized standpoint of the social group as a whole to which he belongs. For he enters his own experience as a self or individual, not directly or immediately, not by becoming a subject to himself, but only in so far as he first becomes an object to himself just as other individuals are objects to him or in his experience; and he becomes an object to himself only by taking the attitudes of other individuals toward himself within a social environment or context of experience and behavior in which both he and they are involved.

The importance of what we term "communication" lies in the fact that it provides a form of behavior in which the organism or the individual may become an object to himself. It is that sort of communication which we have been discussing—not communication in the sense of the cluck of the hen to the chickens, or the bark of a wolf to the pack, or the lowing of a cow, but communication in the sense of significant symbols, communication which is directed not only to others but also to the individual himself. So far as that type of communication is a part of behavior it at least introduces a self. Of course, one may hear without listening; one may see things that he does not realize; do things that he is not really aware of. But it is where one does respond to that which he addresses to another and where that response of his own becomes a part of his conduct, where he not only hears himself but responds to himself, talks and replies to himself as truly as the other person replies to him, that we have behavior in which the individuals become objects to themselves.

Such a self is not, I would say, primarily the physiological organism. The physiological organism is essential to it,[2] but we are at least able to think of a self without it. Persons who believe in immortality, or believe in ghosts, or in the possibility of the self leaving the body, assume a self which is quite distinguishable from the body. How successfully they can hold these conceptions is an open question, but we do, as a fact, separate the self and the organism. It is fair to say that the beginning of the self as an object, so far as we can see, is to be found in the experiences of people that lead to the conception of a "double." Primitive people assume that there is a double, located presumably in the diaphragm, that leaves the body temporarily in sleep and completely in death. It can be enticed out of the body of one's enemy and perhaps killed. It is represented in infancy by the imaginary playmates which children set up, and through which they come to control their experiences in their play.

The self, as that which can be an object to itself, is essentially a social structure, and it arises in social experience. After a self has arisen, it in a certain sense provides for itself its social experiences, and so we can conceive of an absolutely solitary self. But it is impossible to conceive of a self arising outside of social experience. When it has arisen we can think of a person in solitary confinement for the rest of his life, but who still has himself as a companion, and is able to think and to converse with himself as he had communicated with others. That process to which I have just referred, of responding to one's self as another responds to it, taking part in one's own conversation with others, being aware of what one is saying and using that awareness of what one is saying to determine what one is going to say thereafter—that is a process with which we are all familiar. We are continually following up our own address to other persons by an understanding of what we are saying, and using that understanding in the direction of our continued speech. We are finding out what we are going to say, what we are going to do, by saying and doing, and in the process we are continually controlling the process itself. In the conversation of gestures what we say calls out a certain response in another and that in turn changes our own action, so that we shift from what we started to do because of the reply the other makes. The conversation of gestures is the beginning of communication. The individual comes to carry on a conversation of gestures with himself. He says something, and that calls out a certain reply in himself which makes him change what he was going to say. One starts to say something, we will presume an unpleasant something, but when he starts to say it he realizes it is cruel. The effect on himself of what he is saying checks him; there is here a conversation of gestures between the individual and himself. We mean by significant speech that the action is one that affects the individual himself, and that the effect upon the individual himself is part of the intelligent carrying-out of the conversation with others. Now we, so to speak, amputate that social phase and dispense with it for the time being, so that one is talking to one's self as one would talk to another person.[3]

This process of abstraction cannot be carried on indefinitely. One inevitably seeks an audience, has to pour himself out to somebody. In reflective intelligence one thinks to act, and to act solely so that this action remains a part of a social process. Thinking becomes preparatory to social action. The very process of thinking is, of course, simply an inner conversation that goes on, but it is a conversation of gestures which in its completion implies the expression of that which one thinks to an audience. One separates the significance of what he is saying to others from the actual speech and gets it ready before saying it. He thinks it out, and perhaps writes it in the form of a book; but it is still a part of social intercourse in which one is addressing other persons and at the same time addressing one's self, and in which one controls the address to other persons by the response made to one's own gesture. That the person should be responding to himself is necessary to the self, and it is this sort of social conduct which provides behavior within which that self appears. I know of no other form of behavior than the linguistic in which the individual is an object to himself, and, so far as I can see, the individual is not a self in the reflexive sense unless he is an object to himself. It is this fact that gives a critical importance to communication, since this is a type of behavior in which the individual does so respond to himself.

We realize in everyday conduct and experience that an individual does not mean a great deal of what he is doing and saying. We frequently say that such an individual is not himself. We come away from an interview with a realization that we have left out important things, that there are parts of the self that did not get into what was said. What determines the amount of the self that gets into communication is the social experience itself. Of course, a good deal of the self does not need to get expression. We carry on a whole series of different relationships to different people. We are one thing to one man and another thing to another. There are parts of the self which exist only for the self in relationship to itself. We divide ourselves up in all sorts of different selves with reference to our acquaintances. We discuss politics with one and religion with another. There are all sorts of different selves answering to all sorts of different social reactions. It is the social process itself that is responsible for the appearance of the self; it is not there as a self apart from this type of experience.

A multiple personality is in a certain sense normal, as I have just pointed out. There is usually an organization of the whole self with reference to the community to which we belong, and the situation in which we find ourselves. What the society is, whether we are living with people of the present, people of our own imaginations, people of the past, varies, of course, with different individuals. Normally, within the sort of community as a whole to which we belong, there is a unified self, but that may be broken up. To a person who is somewhat unstable nervously and in whom there is a line of cleavage, certain activities become impossible, and that set of activities may separate and evolve another self. Two separate "me's" and "I's," two different selves, result, and that is the condition under which there is a tendency to break up the personality. There is an account of a professor of education who disappeared, was lost to the community, and later turned up in a logging camp in the West. He freed himself of his occupation and turned to the woods where he felt, if you like, more at home. The pathological side of it was the forgetting, the leaving out of the rest of the self. This result involved getting rid of certain bodily memories which would identify the individual to himself. We often recognize the lines of cleavage that run through us. We would be glad to forget certain things, get rid of things the self is bound up with in past experiences. What we have here is a situation in which there can be different selves, and it is dependent upon the set of social reactions that is involved as to which self we are going to be. If we can forget everything involved in one set of activities, obviously we relinquish that part of the self. Take a person who is unstable, get him occupied by speech, and at the same time get his eye on something you are writing so that he is carrying on two separate lines of communication, and if you go about it in the right way you can get those two currents going so that they do not run into each other. You can get two entirely different sets of activities going on. You can bring about in that way the dissociation of a person's self. It is a process of setting up two sorts of communication which separate the behavior of the individual. For one individual it is this thing said and heard, and for the other individual there exists only that which he sees written. You must, of course, keep one experience out of the field of the other. Dissociations are apt to take place when an event leads to emotional upheavals. That which is separated goes on in its own way.

The unity and structure of the complete self reflects the unity and structure of the social process as a whole; and each of the elementary selves of which it is composed reflects the unity and structure of one of the various aspects of that process in which the individual is implicated. In other words, the various elementary selves which constitute, or are organized into, a complete self are the various aspects of the structure of that complete self answering to the various aspects of the structure of the social process as a whole; the structure of the complete self is thus a reflection of the complete social process. The organization and unification of a social group is identical with the organization and unification of any one of the selves arising within the social process in which that group is engaged, or which it is carrying on.[4]

The phenomenon of dissociation of personality is caused by a breaking up of the complete, unitary self into the component selves of which it is composed, and which respectively correspond to different aspects of the social process in which the person is involved, and within which his complete or unitary self has arisen; these aspects being the different social groups to which he belongs within that process.

ENDNOTES

1 Man's behavior is such in his social group that he is able to become an object to himself, a fact which constitutes him a more advanced product of evolutionary development than are the lower animals. Fundamentally it is this social fact—and not his alleged possession of a soul or mind with which he, as an individual, has been mysteriously and supernaturally endowed, and with which the lower animals have not been endowed—that differentiates him from them.

2*a*) All social interrelations and interactions are rooted in a certain common socio-physiological endowment of every individual involved in them. These physiological bases of social behavior—which have their ultimate seat or locus in the lower part of the individual's central nervous system—are the bases of such behavior, precisely because they in themselves are also social; that is, because they consist in drives or instincts or behavior tendencies, on the part of the given individual, which he cannot carry out or give overt expression and satisfaction to without the co-operative aid of one or more other individuals. The physiological processes of behavior of which they are the mechanisms are processes which necessarily involve more than one individual, processes in which other individuals besides the given individual are perforce implicated. Examples of the fundamental social relations to which these physiological bases of social behavior give rise are those between the sexes (expressing the reproductive instinct), between parent and child (expressing the parental instinct), and between neighbors (expressing the gregarious instinct). These relatively simple and rudimentary physiological mechanisms or tendencies of individual human behavior, besides constituting the physiological bases of all human social behavior, are also the fundamental biological materials of human nature; so that when we refer to human nature, we are referring to something which is essentially social.

b) Sexually and parentally, as well as in its attacks and defenses, the activities of the physiological organism are social in that the acts begun within the organism require their completion in the actions of others. . . . But while the pattern of the individual act may be said to be in these cases social, it is only so in so far as the organism seeks for the stimuli in the attitudes and characters of other forms for the completion of its own responses, and by its behavior tends to maintain the other as a part of its own environment. The actual behavior of the other or the others is not initiated in the individual form as a part of its own pattern of behavior (MS).

3 It is generally recognized that the specifically social expressions of intelligence, or the exercise of what is often called "social intelligence," depend upon the given individual's ability to take the rôles of, or "put himself in the place of," the other individuals implicated with him in given social situations; and upon his consequent sensitivity to their attitudes toward himself and toward one another. These specifically social expressions of intelligence, of course, acquire unique significance in terms of our view that the whole nature of intelligence is social to the

very core—that this putting of one's self in the places of others, this taking by one's self of their rôles or attitudes, is not merely one of the various aspects or expressions of intelligence or of intelligent behavior, but is the very essence of its character. Spearman's "X factor" in intelligence—the unknown factor which, according to him, intelligence contains—is simply (if our social theory of intelligence is correct) this ability of the intelligent individual to take the attitude of the other, or the attitudes of others, thus realizing the significations or grasping the meanings of the symbóls or gestures in terms of which thinking proceeds; and thus being able to carry on with himself the internal conversation with these symbols or gestures which thinking involves.

4 The unity of the mind is not identical with the unity of the self. The unity of the self is constituted by the unity of the entire relational pattern of social behavior and experience in which the individual is implicated, and which is reflected in the structure of the self; but many of the aspects or features of this entire pattern do not enter into consciousness, so that the unity of the mind is in a sense an abstraction from the more inclusive unity of the self.

DISCUSSION QUESTIONS

1. Compare Mead's view to Hume's. Which view do you think is better argued? Explain.

2. How is Mead's view different from rationalist views like Plato and Descartes? Explain.

3. Do you think Mead is right about the idea of multiple personalities? Why or why not?

4. To what extent do you think our selves are shaped by other people? Explain.

Of Our Spiritual Strivings

By W.E.B Du Bois

A founding member of the NAACP (National Association for the Advancement of Colored People) in 1909, a philosopher, sociologist, and historian, W.E.B. Du Bois (1868–1963), was a prominent African American intellectual of the first half of the 20th century. He graduated in 1895 from Harvard with a Ph.D., the first African American to do so. After his graduation, he published many works in diverse areas, including sociology, history, and criminology. He was politically active most of his life, and was questioned by the House Un-American Activities Committee (HUAC) of the U.S. Congress and was surveilled by the F.B.I. as someone with socialist leanings. His philosophical ideas were influenced by his studies at Harvard with William James.

Our essay, "Of Our Spiritual Strivings" is from his 1903 collection of essays, The Souls of Black Folk. *The essays in this book include topics on history, sociology, and education. "Of Our Spiritual Strivings" is a plea for "work, culture, liberty . . . not singly, but together." There is also autobiographical material at the beginning of the essay, discussing his childhood in Great Barrington, Massachusetts.*

Between me and the other world there is ever an unasked question: unasked by some through feelings of delicacy; by others through the difficulty of rightly framing it. All, nevertheless, flutter round it. They approach me in a half-hesitant sort of way, eye me curiously or compassionately, and then, instead of saying directly, How does it feel to be a problem? they say, I know an excellent colored man in my town; or, I fought at Mechanicsville; or, Do not these Southern outrages make your blood boil? At these I smile, or am interested, or reduce the boiling to a simmer, as the occasion may require. To the real question, How does it feel to be a problem? I answer seldom a word.

And yet, being a problem is a strange experience,—peculiar even for one who has never been anything else, save perhaps in babyhood and in Europe. It is in the early days of rollicking boyhood that the revelation first bursts upon one, all in a day, as it were. I remember well when the shadow swept across me. I was a little thing, away up in the hills of New England, where the dark Housatonic winds between Hoosac and Taghkanic to the sea. In a wee wooden schoolhouse, something put it into the boys' and girls' heads to buy gorgeous visiting-cards—ten cents a package—and exchange. The exchange was merry, till one girl, a tall newcomer, refused my card,—refused it peremptorily, with a glance. Then it dawned upon me with a certain suddenness that I was different from the others; or like, mayhap, in heart and life and longing, but shut out from their world by a vast veil. I had thereafter no desire to tear down that veil, to creep through; I held all beyond it in common contempt, and lived above it in a region of blue sky and great wandering shadows. That sky was bluest when I could beat my mates at examination-time, or beat them at a foot-race, or even beat their stringy heads. Alas, with the years all this fine contempt began to fade; for the words I longed for, and all their dazzling opportunities, were theirs, not mine. But they should not keep these prizes, I said; some, all, I would wrest from them. Just how I would do it I could never decide: by reading law, by healing the sick, by telling the wonderful tales that swam in my head,—some way. With other black boys the strife was not so fiercely sunny: their youth shrunk into tasteless sycophancy, or into silent hatred of the pale world about them and mocking distrust of everything white; or wasted itself in a bitter cry, Why did God make me an outcast and a stranger in mine own house? The shades of the prison-house closed round about us all: walls strait and stubborn to the whitest, but relentlessly narrow, tall, and unscalable to sons of night who must plod darkly on in resignation, or beat unavailing palms against the stone, or steadily, half hopelessly, watch the streak of blue above.

After the Egyptian and Indian, the Greek and Roman, the Teuton and Mongolian, the Negro is a sort of seventh son, born with a veil, and gifted with second-sight in this American world,—a world which yields him no true self-consciousness, but only lets him see himself through the revelation of the other world. It is a peculiar sensation, this double-consciousness, this sense of always looking at one's self through the eyes of others, of measuring one's soul by the tape of a world that looks on in amused contempt and pity. One ever feels his twoness,—an American, a Negro; two souls, two thoughts, two unreconciled strivings; two warring ideals in one dark body, whose dogged strength alone keeps it from being torn asunder.

The history of the American Negro is the history of this strife,—this longing to attain self-conscious manhood, to merge his double self into a better and truer self. In this merging he wishes neither of the older selves to be lost. He would not Africanize America, for America has too much to teach the world and Africa. He would not bleach his Negro soul in a flood of white Americanism, for he knows that Negro blood has a message for the world. He simply wishes to make it possible for a man to be both a Negro and an American, without being cursed and spit upon by his fellows, without having the doors of Opportunity closed roughly in his face.

This, then, is the end of his striving: to be a co-worker in the kingdom of culture, to escape both death and isolation, to husband and use his best powers and his latent genius. These powers of body and mind have in the past been strangely wasted, dispersed, or forgotten. The shadow of a mighty Negro past flits through the tale of Ethiopia the Shadowy and of Egypt the Sphinx. Through history, the powers of single black men flash here and there like falling stars, and die sometimes before the world has rightly gauged their brightness. Here in America, in the few days since Emancipation, the black man's turning hither and thither in hesitant and doubtful striving has often made his very strength to lose effectiveness, to seem like absence of power, like weakness. And yet it is not weakness,—it is the contradiction of double aims. The double-aimed struggle of the black artisan—on the one hand to escape white contempt for a nation of mere hewers of wood and drawers of water, and on the other hand to plough and nail and dig for a poverty-stricken horde—could only result in making him a poor craftsman, for he had but half a heart in either cause. By the poverty and ignorance of his people, the Negro minister or doctor was tempted toward quackery and demagogy; and by the criticism of the other world, toward ideals that made him ashamed of his lowly tasks. The would-be black savant was confronted by the paradox that the knowledge his people needed was a twice-told tale to his white neighbors, while the knowledge which would teach the white world was Greek to his own flesh and blood. The innate love of harmony and beauty that set the ruder souls of his people a-dancing and a-singing raised but confusion and doubt in the soul of the black artist; for the beauty revealed to him was the soul-beauty of a race which his larger audience despised, and he could not articulate the message of another people. This waste of double aims, this seeking to satisfy two unreconciled ideals, has wrought sad havoc with the courage and faith and deeds of ten thousand thousand people,—has sent them often wooing false gods and invoking false means of salvation, and at times has even seemed about to make them ashamed of themselves.

Away back in the days of bondage they thought to see in one divine event the end of all doubt and disappointment; few men ever worshipped Freedom with half such unquestioning faith as did the American Negro for two centuries. To him, so far as he thought and dreamed, slavery was indeed the sum of all villainies, the cause of all sorrow, the root of all prejudice; Emancipation was the key to a promised land of sweeter beauty than ever stretched before the eyes of wearied Israelites. In song and exhortation swelled one refrain—Liberty; in his tears and curses the God he implored had Freedom in his right hand. At last it came,—suddenly, fearfully, like a dream. With one wild carnival of blood and passion came the message in his own plaintive cadences:—

"Shout, O children!
Shout, you're free!
For God has bought your liberty!"

Years have passed away since then,—ten, twenty, forty; forty years of national life, forty years of renewal and development, and yet the swarthy spectre sits in its accustomed seat at the Nation's feast. In vain do we cry to this our vastest social problem:—

"Take any shape but that, and my firm nerves
Shall never tremble!"

The Nation has not yet found peace from its sins; the freedman has not yet found in freedom his promised land. Whatever of good may have come in these years of change, the shadow of a deep disappointment rests upon the Negro people,—a disappointment all the more bitter because the unattained ideal was unbounded save by the simple ignorance of a lowly people.

The first decade was merely a prolongation of the vain search for freedom, the boon that seemed ever barely to elude their grasp,—like a tantalizing will-o'-the-wisp, maddening and misleading the headless host. The holocaust of war, the terrors of the Ku-Klux Klan, the lies of carpet-baggers, the disorganization of industry, and the contradictory advice of friends and foes, left the bewildered serf with no new watchword beyond the old cry for freedom. As the time flew, however, he began to grasp a new idea. The ideal of liberty demanded for its attainment powerful means, and these the Fifteenth Amendment gave him. The ballot, which before he had looked upon as a visible sign of freedom, he now regarded as the chief means of gaining and perfecting the liberty with which war had partially endowed him. And why not? Had not votes made war and emancipated millions? Had not votes enfranchised the freedmen? Was anything impossible to a power that had done all this? A million black men started with renewed zeal to vote themselves into the kingdom. So the decade flew away, the revolution of 1876 came, and left the half-free serf weary, wondering, but still inspired. Slowly but steadily, in the following years, a new vision began gradually to replace the dream of political power,—a powerful movement, the rise of another ideal to guide the unguided, another pillar of fire by night after a clouded day. It was the ideal of "book-learning"; the curiosity, born of compulsory ignorance, to know and test the power of the cabalistic letters of the white man, the longing to know. Here at last seemed to have been discovered the mountain path to Canaan; longer than the highway of Emancipation and law, steep and rugged, but straight, leading to heights high enough to overlook life.

Up the new path the advance guard toiled, slowly, heavily, doggedly; only those who have watched and guided the faltering feet, the misty minds, the dull understandings, of the dark pupils of these schools know how faithfully, how piteously, this people strove to learn. It was weary work. The cold statistician wrote down the inches of progress here and there, noted also where here and there a foot had slipped or some one had fallen. To the tired climbers, the horizon was ever dark, the mists were often cold, the Canaan was always dim and far away. If, however, the vistas disclosed as yet no goal, no resting-place, little but flattery and criticism, the journey at least gave leisure for reflection and self-examination; it changed the child of Emancipation to the youth with dawning self-consciousness, self-realization, self-respect. In those sombre forests of his striving his own soul rose before him, and he saw himself,—darkly as through a veil; and yet he saw in himself some faint revelation of his power, of his mission. He began to have a dim feeling that, to attain his place in the world, he must be himself, and not another. For the first time he sought to analyze the burden he bore upon his back, that dead-weight of social degradation partially masked behind a half-named Negro problem. He felt his poverty; without a cent, without a home, without land, tools, or savings, he had entered into competition with rich, landed, skilled neighbors. To be a poor man is hard, but to be a poor race in a land of dollars is the very bottom of hardships. He felt the weight of his ignorance,—not simply of letters, but of life, of business, of the humanities; the accumulated sloth and shirking and awkwardness of decades and centuries shackled his hands and feet. Nor was his burden all poverty and ignorance. The red stain of bastardy, which two centuries of systematic legal defilement of Negro women had stamped upon his race, meant not only the loss of ancient African chastity, but also the hereditary weight of a mass of corruption from white adulterers, threatening almost the obliteration of the Negro home.

A people thus handicapped ought not to be asked to race with the world, but rather allowed to give all its time and thought to its own social problems. But alas! while sociologists gleefully count his bastards and his prostitutes, the very soul of the toiling, sweating black man is darkened by the shadow of a vast despair. Men call the shadow prejudice, and learnedly explain it as the natural defence of culture against barbarism, learning against ignorance, purity against crime, the "higher" against the "lower" races. To which the Negro cries Amen! and swears that to so much of this strange prejudice as is founded on just homage to civilization, culture, righteousness, and progress, he humbly bows and meekly does obeisance. But before that nameless prejudice that leaps beyond all this he stands helpless, dismayed, and well-nigh speechless; before that personal disrespect and mockery, the ridicule and systematic humiliation, the distortion of fact and wanton license of fancy, the cynical ignoring of the better and the boisterous welcoming of the worse, the all-pervading desire to inculcate disdain for everything black, from Toussaint to the devil,—before this there rises a sickening despair that would disarm and discourage any nation save that black host to whom "discouragement" is an unwritten word.

But the facing of so vast a prejudice could not but bring the inevitable self-questioning, self-disparagement, and lowering of ideals which ever accompany repression and breed in an atmosphere of contempt and hate. Whisperings and portents came home upon the four winds: Lo! we are diseased and dying, cried the dark hosts; we cannot write, our voting is vain; what need of education, since we must always cook and serve? And the Nation echoed and enforced this self-criticism, saying: Be content to be servants, and nothing more; what need of higher culture for half-men? Away with the black man's ballot, by force or fraud,—and behold the suicide of a race! Nevertheless, out of the evil came something of good,—the more careful adjustment of education to real life, the clearer perception of the Negroes' social responsibilities, and the sobering realization of the meaning of progress.

So dawned the time of Sturm und Drang: storm and stress to-day rocks our little boat on the mad waters of the world-sea; there is within and without the sound of conflict, the burning of body and rending of soul; inspiration strives with doubt, and faith with vain questionings. The bright ideals of the past,—physical freedom, political power, the training of brains and the training of hands,—all these in turn have waxed and waned, until even the last grows dim and overcast. Are they all wrong,—all false? No, not that, but each alone was over-simple and incomplete,—the dreams of a credulous race-childhood, or the fond imaginings of the other world which does not know and does not want to know our power. To be really true, all these ideals must be melted and welded into one. The training of the schools we need to-day more than ever,—the training of deft hands, quick eyes and ears, and above all the broader, deeper, higher culture of gifted minds and pure hearts. The power of the ballot we need in sheer self-defence,—else what shall save us from a second slavery? Freedom, too, the long-sought, we still seek,—the freedom of life and limb, the freedom to work and think, the freedom to love and aspire. Work, culture, liberty,—all these we need, not singly but together, not successively but together, each growing and aiding each, and all striving toward that vaster ideal that swims before the Negro people, the ideal of human brotherhood, gained through the unifying ideal of Race; the ideal of fostering and developing the traits and talents of the Negro, not in opposition to or contempt for other races, but rather in large conformity to the greater ideals of the American Republic, in order that some day on American soil two world-races may give each to each those characteristics both so sadly lack. We the darker ones come even now not altogether empty-handed: there are to-day no truer exponents of the pure human spirit of the Declaration of Independence than the American Negroes; there is no true American music but the wild sweet melodies of the Negro slave; the American fairy tales and folklore are Indian and African; and, all in all, we black men seem the sole oasis of simple faith and reverence in a dusty desert of dollars and smartness. Will America be poorer if she replace her brutal dyspeptic blundering with light-hearted but determined Negro humility? or her coarse and cruel wit with loving jovial good-humor? or her vulgar music with the soul of the Sorrow Songs?

Merely a concrete test of the underlying principles of the great republic is the Negro Problem, and the spiritual striving of the freedmen's sons is the travail of souls whose burden is almost beyond the measure of their strength, but who bear it in the name of an historic race, in the name of this the land of their fathers' fathers, and in the name of human opportunity.

And now what I have briefly sketched in large outline let me on coming pages tell again in many ways, with loving emphasis and deeper detail, **that men may listen to the striving in the souls of black folk.**

DISCUSSION QUESTIONS

1. What does Du Bois mean by "the veil" and "double-consciousness"?

2. Mead and Du Bois were both students of William James. What similarities do you find in their views of the self? Explain.

3. To what extent do you think race and/or ethnicity shape who we are? Why? Explain.

4. In the middle of the essay, Du Bois says "[t]his, then, is the end of his striving: to be a co-worker in the kingdom of culture." Explain what he means.

Existentialism

By Jean-Paul Sartre

French philosopher Jean-Paul Sartre (1905–1980) may be the most read philosopher of the 20th century. Sartre wrote short stories, novels, plays, essays, literary criticism, cultural criticism and biographies. Although there were many writers before Sartre who were concerned with the existential condition, he is the one that was branded an Existentialist. The roots of this kind of philosophy can be found in the Russian novelist Fyodor Dostoyevsky (1821–1881), the Danish philosopher Søren Kierkegaard (1813–1855), German philosophers Friedrich Nietzsche (1844–1900) and Martin Heidegger (1889–1976), and others. Some of Nietzsche's views can be found in Parts II and IV of Four Fundamental Questions. *Sartre's most read books are the short novel* Nausea *(1938), the play No Exit (1944), and his monumental treatise,* Being and Nothingness *(1943). In 1964, Sartre was awarded the Nobel Prize for Literature, but refused to accept it.*

Our selection is from Existentialism Is a Humanism, *a book published in 1946, based on a lecture Sartre delivered after the war in 1945. This is at once a defense of Existentialism as a philosophy and an explanation of some of the core ideas from* Being and Nothingness. *First, Sartre defends Existentialism from popular criticisms of the time: that it leads to quietism (the idea that you shouldn't do anything because it has already been determined, so maybe I'm not* supposed *to do anything), that it is overly pessimistic, and that it demeans the human condition. Yet, at the same time, he tells us that his view also recognizes the human condition as one that unavoidably contains anguish, forlornness, and despair. Anguish comes from the fact that we are totally responsible for our choices—there are no excuses. Forlornness derives from the fact that we have no one to ask for help; ultimately, we have to make the choice alone without guidelines or excuses. Despair comes from the fact that we cannot depend on anyone to finish your work for you (now, or after your death), or even to pick you up at the train station, but you have to act as if they will. To Sartre, these actually give us dignity—we are radically free in choosing our actions and are totally responsible for our choices—we make a difference. We make ourselves.*

I should like on this occasion to defend existentialism against some charges which have been brought against it.

First, it has been charged with inviting people to remain in a kind of desperate quietism because, since no solutions are possible, we should have to consider action in this world as quite impossible. We should then end up in a philosophy of contemplation; and since contemplation is a luxury, we come in the end to a bourgeois philosophy. The communists in particular have made these charges.

From *Existentialism* by Jean-Paul Sartre, translated by Bernard Frechtman, 1947. Reprinted by permission of the Philosophical Library, New York.

On the other hand, we have been charged with dwelling on human degradation, with pointing up everywhere the sordid, shady, and slimy, and neglecting the gracious and beautiful, the bright side of human nature; for example, according to Mlle. Mercier, a Catholic critic, with forgetting the smile of the child. Both sides charge us with, having ignored human solidarity, with considering man as an isolated being. The communists say that the main reason for this is that we take pure subjectivity, the *Cartesian I think,* as our starting point; in other words, the moment in which man becomes fully aware of what it means to him to be an isolated being; as a result, we are unable to return to a state of solidarity with the men who are not ourselves, a state which we can never reach in the *cogito.*

From the Christian standpoint, we are charged with denying the reality and seriousness of human undertakings, since, if we reject God's commandments and the eternal verities, there no longer remains anything but pure caprice, with everyone permitted to do as he pleases and incapable, from his own point of view, of condemning the points of view and acts of others.

I shall try today to answer these different charges. Many people are going to be surprised at what is said here about humanism. We shall try to see in what sense it is to be understood. In any case, what can be said from the very, beginning is that by existentialism we mean a doctrine which makes human life possible and, in addition, declares that every truth and every action implies a human setting and a human subjectivity.

As is generally known, the basic charge against us is that we put the emphasis on the dark side of human life. Someone recently told me of a lady who, when she let slip a vulgar word in a moment of irritation, excused herself by saying, "I guess I'm becoming an existentialist." Consequently, existentialism is regarded as something ugly; that is why we are said to be naturalists; and if we are, it is rather surprising that in this day and age we cause so much more alarm and scandal than does naturalism, properly so called. The kind of person who can take in his stride such a novel as Zola's *The Earth* is disgusted as soon as he starts reading an existentialist novel; the kind of person who is resigned to the wisdom of the ages—which is pretty sad—finds us even sadder. Yet, what can be more disillusioning than saying "true charity begins at home" or "a scoundrel will always return evil for good"?

We know the commonplace remarks made when this subject comes up, remarks which always add up to the same thing: we shouldn't struggle against the powers-that-be; we shouldn't resist authority; we shouldn't try to rise above our station; any action which doesn't conform to authority is romantic; any effort not based on past experience is doomed to failure; experience shows that man's bent is always toward trouble, that there must be a strong hand to hold him in check, if not, there will be anarchy. There are still people who go on mumbling these melancholy old saws, the people who say, "It's only human!" whenever a more or less repugnant act is pointed out to them, the people who glut themselves on *chansons réalistes;* these are the people who accuse existentialism of being too gloomy, and to such an extent that I wonder whether they are complaining about it, not for its pessimism, but much rather its optimism. Can it be that what really scares them in the doctrine I shall try to present here is that it leaves to man a possibility of choice? To answer this question, we must re-examine it on a strictly philosophical plane. What is meant by the term *existentialism?*

Most people who use the word would be rather embarrassed if they had to explain it, since, now that the word is all the rage, even the work of a musician or painter is being called existentialist. A gossip columnist in *Clartés* signs himself *The Existentialist,* so that by this time the word has been so stretched and has taken on so broad a meaning, that it no longer means anything at all. It seems that for want of an advance-guard doctrine analogous to surrealism, the kind of people who are eager for scandal and flurry turn to this philosophy which in other respects does not at all serve their purposes in this sphere.

Actually, it is the least scandalous, the most austere of doctrines. It is intended strictly for śpecialists and philosophers. Yet it can be defined easily. What complicates matters is that there are two kinds of existentialist; first, those who are Christian, among whom I would include Jaspers and Gabriel Marcel, both Catholic; and on the other hand the atheistic existentialists, among whom I class Heidegger, and then the French existentialists and myself. What they have in common is that they think that existence precedes essence, or, if you prefer, that subjectivity must be the starting point.

Just what does that mean? Let us consider some object that is manufactured, for example, a book or a paper-cutter: here is an object which has been made by an artisan whose inspiration came from a concept. He referred to the concept of what a paper-cutter is and likewise to a known method of production, which is part of the concept, something which is, by and large, a routine. Thus, the paper-cutter is at once an object produced in a certain way and, on the other hand, one having a specific use; and one can not postulate a man who produces a paper-cutter but does not know what it is used for. Therefore, let us say that, for the paper-cutter, essence—that is, the ensemble of both the production routines and the properties which enable it to be both produced and defined—precedes existence. Thus, the presence of the paper-cutter or book in front of me is determined. Therefore, we have here a technical view of the world whereby it can be said that production precedes existence.

When we conceive God as the Creator, He is generally thought of as a superior sort of artisan. Whatever doctrine we may be considering, whether one like that of Descartes or that of Leibnitz, we always grant that will more or less follows understanding or, at the very least, accompanies it, and that when God creates He knows exactly what He is creating. Thus, the concept of man in the mind of God is comparable to the concept of paper-cutter in the mind of the manufacturer, and, following certain techniques and a conception, God produces man, just as the artisan, following a definition and a technique, makes a paper-cutter. Thus, the individual man is the realization of a certain concept in the divine intelligence.

In the eighteenth century, the atheism of the *philosophes* discarded the idea of God, but not so much for the notion that essence precedes existence. To a certain extent, this idea is found everywhere; we find it in Diderot, in Voltaire, and even in Kant. Man has a human nature; this human nature, which is the concept of the human, is found in all men, which means that each man is a particular example of a universal concept, man. In Kant, the result of this universality is that the wild-man, the natural man, as well as the bourgeois, are circumscribed by the same definition and have the same basic qualities. Thus, here too the essence of man precedes the historical existence that we find in nature.

Atheistic existentialism, which I represent, is more coherent. It states that if God does not exist, there is at least one being in whom existence precedes essence, a being who exists before he can be defined by any concept, and that this being is man, or, as Heidegger says, human reality. What is meant here by saying that existence precedes essence? It means that, first of all, man exists, turns up, appears on the scene, and, only afterwards, defines himself. If man, as the existentialist conceives him, is indefinable, it is because at first he is nothing. Only afterward will he be something, and he himself will have made what he will be. Thus, there is no human nature, since there is no God to conceive it. Not only is man what he conceives himself to be, but he is also only what he wills himself to be after this thrust toward existence.

Man is nothing else but what he makes of himself. Such is the first principle of existentialism. It is also what is called subjectivity, the name we are labeled with when charges are brought against us. But what do we mean by this, if not that man has a greater dignity than a stone or table? For we mean that man first exists, that is, that man first of all is the being who hurls himself toward a future and who is conscious of imagining himself as being in the future. Man is at the start a plan which is aware of itself, rather than a patch of moss, a piece of garbage, or a cauliflower; nothing exists prior to this plan; there is nothing in heaven; man will be what he will have planned to be. Not what he will want to be. Because by the word "will" we generally mean a conscious decision, which is subsequent to what we have already made of ourselves. I may want to belong to a political party, write a book, get married; but all that is only a manifestation of an earlier, more spontaneous choice that is called "will." But if existence really does precede essence, man is responsible for what he is. Thus, existentialism's first move is to make every man aware of what he is and to make the full responsibility of his existence rest on him. And when we say that a man is responsible for himself, we do not only mean that he is responsible for his own individuality, but that he is responsible for all men.

The word subjectivism has two meanings, and our opponents play on the two. Subjectivism means, on the one hand, that an individual chooses and makes himself; and, on the other, that it is impossible for man to transcend human subjectivity. The second of these is the essential meaning of existentialism. When we say that man chooses his own self, we mean that every one of us does likewise; but we also mean by that that in making this choice he also chooses all men. In fact, in creating the man that we want to be, there is not a single one of our acts which does not at the same time create an image of man as we think he ought to be. To choose to be this or that is to affirm at the same time the value of what we choose, because we can never choose evil. We always choose the good, and nothing can be good for us without being good for all.

If, on the other hand, existence precedes essence, and if we grant that we exist and fashion our image at one and the same time, the image is valid for everybody and for our whole age. Thus, our responsibility is much greater than we might have supposed, because it involves all mankind. If I am a workingman and choose to join a Christian trade-union rather than be a communist, and if by being a member I want to show that the best thing for man is resignation, that the kingdom of man is not of this world, I am not only involving my own case—I want to be resigned for everyone. As a result, my action has involved all humanity. To take a more individual matter, if I want to marry, to have children; even if this marriage depends solely on my own circumstances or passion or wish, I am involving all humanity in monogamy and not merely myself. Therefore, I am responsible for myself and for everyone else. I am creating a certain image of man of my own choosing. In choosing myself, I choose man.

This helps us understand what the actual content is of such rather grandiloquent words as anguish, forlornness, despair. As you will see, it's all quite simple.

First, what is meant by anguish? The existentialists say at once that man is anguish. What that means is this: the man who involves himself and who realizes that he is not only the person he chooses to be, but also a lawmaker who is, at the same time, choosing all mankind as well as himself, can not help escape the feeling of his total and deep responsibility. Of course, there are many people who are not anxious; but we claim that they are hiding their anxiety, that they are fleeing from it. Certainly, many people believe that when they do something, they themselves are the only ones involved, and when someone says to them, "What if everyone acted that way?" they shrug their shoulders and answer, "Everyone doesn't act that way." But really, one should always ask himself, "What would happen if everybody looked at things that way?" There is no escaping this disturbing thought except by a kind of double-dealing. A man who lies and makes excuses for himself by saying "not everybody does that," is someone with an uneasy conscience, because the act of lying implies that a universal value is conferred upon the lie.

Anguish is evident even when it conceals itself. This is the anguish that Kierkegaard called the anguish of Abraham. You know the story: an angel has ordered Abraham to sacrifice his son; if it really were an angel who has come and said, "You are Abraham, you shall sacrifice your son," everything would be all right. But everyone might first wonder, "Is it really an angel, and am I really Abraham? What proof do I have?"

There was a madwoman who had hallucinations; someone used to speak to her on the telephone and give her orders. Her doctor asked her, "Who is it who talks to you?" She answered, "He says it's God." What proof did she really have that it was God? If an angel comes to me, what proof is there that it's an angel? And if I hear voices, what proof is there that they come from heaven and not from hell, or from the subconscious, or a pathological condition? What proves that they are addressed to me? What proof is there that I have been appointed to impose my choice and my conception of man on humanity? I'll never find any proof or sign to convince me of that. If a voice addresses me, it is always for me to decide that this is the angel's voice; if I consider that such an act is a good one, it is I who will choose to say that it is good rather than bad.

Now, I'm not being singled out as an Abraham, and yet at every moment I'm obliged to perform exemplary acts. For every man, everything happens as if all mankind had its eyes fixed on him and were guiding itself by what he does. And every man ought to say to himself, "Am I really the kind of man who has the right to act in such a way that humanity might guide itself by my actions?" And if he does not say that to himself, he is masking his anguish.

There is no question here of the kind of anguish which would lead to quietism, to inaction. It is a matter of a simple sort of anguish that anybody who has had responsibilities is familiar with. For example, when a military officer takes the responsibility for an attack and sends a certain number of men to death, he chooses to do so, and in the main he alone makes the choice. Doubtless, orders come from above, but they are too broad; he interprets them, and on this interpretation depend the lives of ten or fourteen or twenty men. In making a decision he can not help having a certain anguish. All leaders know this anguish. That doesn't keep them from acting; on the contrary, it is the very condition of their action. For it implies that they envisage a number of possibilities, and when they choose one, they realize that it has value only because it is chosen. We shall see that this kind of anguish, which is the kind that existentialism describes, is explained, in addition, by a direct responsibility to the other men whom it involves. It is not a curtain separating us from action, but is part of action itself.

When we speak of forlornness, a term Heidegger was fond of, we mean only that God does not exist and that we have to face all the consequences of this. The existentialist is strongly opposed to a certain kind of secular ethics which would like to abolish God with the least possible expense. About 1880, some French teachers tried to set up a secular ethics which went something like this: God is a useless and costly hypothesis; we are discarding it; but, meanwhile, in order for there to be an ethics, a society, a civilization, it is essential that certain values be taken seriously and that they be considered as having an *a priori* existence. It must be obligatory, *a priori,* to be honest, not to lie, not to beat your wife, to have children, etc., etc. So we're going to try a little device which will make it possible to show that values exist all the same, inscribed in a heaven of ideas, though otherwise God does not exist. In other words—and this, I believe, is the tendency of everything called reformism in France—nothing will be changed if God does not exist. We shall find ourselves with the same norms of honesty, progress, and humanism, and we shall have made of God an outdated hypothesis which will peacefully die off by itself.

The existentialist, on the contrary, thinks it very distressing that God does not exist, because all possibility of finding values in a heaven of ideas disappears along with Him; there can no longer be an *a priori* Good, since there is no infinite and perfect consciousness to think it. Nowhere is it written that the Good exists, that we must be honest, that we must not lie; because the fact is we are on a plane where there are only men. Dostoievsky said, "If God didn't exist, everything would be possible." That is the very starting point of existentialism. Indeed, everything is permissible if God does not exist, and as a result man is forlorn, because neither within him nor without does he find anything to cling to. He can't start making excuses for himself.

If existence really does precede essence, there is no explaining things away by reference to a fixed and given human nature. In other words, there is no determinism, man is free, man is freedom. On the other hand, if God does not exist, we find no values or commands to turn to which legitimize our conduct. So, in the bright realm of values, we have no excuse behind us, nor justification before us. We are alone, with no excuses.

That is the idea I shall try to convey when I say that man is condemned to be free. Condemned, because he did not create himself, yet, in other respects is free; because, once thrown into the world, he is responsible for everything he does. The existentialist does not believe in the power of passion. He will never agree that a sweeping passion is a ravaging torrent which fatally leads a man to certain acts and is therefore an excuse. He thinks that man is responsible for his passion.

The existentialist does not think that man is going to help himself by finding in the world some omen by which to orient himself. Because he thinks that man will interpret the omen to suit himself. Therefore, he thinks that man, with no support and no aid, is condemned every moment to invent man. Ponge, in a very fine article, has said, "Man is the future of man." That's exactly it. But if it is taken to mean that this future is recorded in heaven, that God sees it, then it is false, because it would really no longer be a future. If it is taken to mean that, whatever a man may be, there is a future to be forged, a virgin future before him, then this remark is sound. But then we are forlorn.

To give you an example which will enable you to understand forlornness better, I shall cite the case of one of my students who came to see me under the following circumstances: his father was on bad terms with his mother, and, moreover, was inclined to be a collaborationist; his older brother had been killed in the German offensive of 1940, and the young man, with somewhat immature but generous feelings, wanted to avenge him. His mother lived alone with him, very much upset by the half-treason of her husband and the death of her older son; the boy was her only consolation.

The boy was faced with the choice of leaving for England and joining the Free French Forces—that is, leaving his mother behind—or remaining with his mother and helping her to carry on. He was fully aware that the woman lived only for him and that his going-off—and perhaps his death—would plunge her into despair. He was also aware that every act that he did for his mother's sake was a sure thing, in the sense that it was helping her to carry on, whereas every effort he made toward going off and fighting was an uncertain move which might run aground and prove completely useless; for example, on his way to England he might, while passing through Spain, be detained indefinitely in a Spanish camp; he might reach England or Algiers and be stuck in an office at a desk job. As a result, he was faced with two very different kinds of action: one, concrete, immediate, but concerning only one individual; the other concerned an incomparably vaster group, a national collectivity, but for that very reason was dubious, and might be interrupted en route. And, at the same time, he was wavering between two kinds of ethics. On the one hand, an ethics of sympathy, of personal devotion; on the other, a broader ethics, but one whose efficacy was more dubious. He had to choose between the two.

Who could help him choose? Christian doctrine? No. Christian doctrine says, "Be charitable, love your neighbor, take the more rugged path, etc., etc." But which is the more rugged path? Whom should he love as a brother? The fighting man or his mother? Which does the greater good, the vague act of fighting in a group, or the concrete one of helping a particular human being to go on living? Who can decide *a priori?* Nobody. No book of ethics can tell him. The Kantian ethics says, "Never treat any person as a means, but as an end." Very well, if I stay with my mother, I'll treat her as an end and not as a means; but by virtue of this very fact, I'm running the risk of treating the people around me who are fighting, as means; and, conversely, if I go to join those who are fighting, I'll be treating them as an end, and, by doing that, I run the risk of treating my mother as a means.

If values are vague, and if they are always too broad for the concrete and specific case that we are considering, the only thing left for us is to trust our instincts. That's what this young man tried to do; and when I saw him, he said, "In the end, feeling is what counts. I ought to choose whichever pushes me in one direction. If I feel that I love my mother enough to sacrifice everything else for her—my desire for vengeance, for action, for adventure—then I'll stay with her. If, on the contrary, I feel that my love for my mother isn't enough, I'll leave."

But how is the value of a feeling determined? What gives his feeling for his mother value? Precisely the fact that he remained with her. I may say that I like so-and-so well enough to sacrifice a certain amount of money for him, but I may say so only if I've done it. I may say "I love my mother well enough to remain with her" if I have remained with her. The only way to determine the value of this affection is, precisely, to perform an act which confirms and defines it. But, since I require this affection to justify my act, I find myself caught in a vicious circle.

On the other hand, Gide has well said that a mock feeling and a true feeling are almost indistinguishable; to decide that I love my mother and will remain with her, or to remain with her by putting on an act, amount somewhat to the same thing. In other words, the feeling is formed by the acts one performs; so, I can not refer to it in order to act upon it. Which means that I can neither seek within myself the true condition which will impel me to act, nor apply to a system of ethics for concepts which will permit me to act. You will say, "At least, he did go to a teacher for advice." But if you seek advice from a priest, for example, you have chosen this priest; you already knew, more or less, just about what advice he was going to give you. In other words, choosing your adviser is involving yourself. The proof of this is that if you are a Christian, you will say, "Consult a priest." But some priests are collaborating, some are just marking time, some are resisting. Which to choose? If the young man chooses a priest who is resisting or collaborating, he has already decided on the kind of advice he's going to get. Therefore, in coming to see me he knew the answer I was going to give him, and I had only one answer to give: "You're free, choose, that is, invent." No general ethics can show you what is to be done; there are no omens in the world. The Catholics will reply, "But there are." Granted—but, in any case, I myself choose the meaning they have.

When I was a prisoner, I knew a rather remarkable young man who was a Jesuit. He had entered the Jesuit order in the following way: he had had a number of very bad breaks; in childhood, his father died, leaving him in poverty, and he was a scholarship student at a religious institution where he was constantly made to feel that he was being kept out of charity; then, he failed to get any of the honors and distinctions that children like; later on, at about eighteen, he bungled a love affair; finally, at twenty-two, he failed in military training, a childish enough matter, but it was the last straw.

This young fellow might well have felt that he had botched everything. It was a sign of something, but of what? He might have taken refuge in bitterness or despair. But he very wisely looked upon all this as a sign that he was not made for secular triumphs, and that only the triumphs of religion, holiness, and faith were open to him. He saw the hand of God in all this, and so he entered the order. Who can help seeing that he alone decided what the sign meant?

Some other interpretation might have been drawn from this series of setbacks; for example, that he might have done better to turn carpenter or revolutionist. Therefore, he is fully responsible for the interpretation. Forlornness implies that we ourselves choose our being. Forlornness and anguish go together.

As for despair, the term has a very simple meaning. It means that we shall confine ourselves to reckoning only with what depends upon our will, or on the ensemble of probabilities which make our action possible. When we want something, we always have to reckon with probabilities. I may be counting on the arrival of a friend. The friend is coming by rail or street-car; this supposes that the train will arrive on schedule, or that the street-car will not jump the track. I am left in the realm of possibility; but possibilities are to be reckoned with only to the point where my action comports with the ensemble of these possibilities, and no further. The moment the possibilities I am considering are not rigorously involved by my action, I ought to disengage myself from them, because no God, no scheme, can adapt the world and its possibilities to my will. When Descartes said, "Conquer yourself rather than the world," he meant essentially the same thing.

The Marxists to whom I have spoken reply, "You can rely on the support of others in your action, which obviously has certain limits because you're not going to live forever. That means: rely on both what others are doing elsewhere to help you, in China, in Russia, and what they will do later on, after your death, to carry on the action and lead it to its fulfillment, which will be the revolution. You even *have* to rely upon that, otherwise you're immoral." I reply at once that I will always rely on fellow-fighters insofar as these comrades are involved with me in a common struggle, in the unity of a party or a group in which I can more or less make my weight felt; that is, one whose ranks I am in as a fighter and whose movements I am aware of at every moment. In such a situation, relying on the unity and will of the party is exactly like counting on the fact that the train will arrive on time or that the car won't jump the track. But, given that man is free and that there is no human nature for me to depend on, I can not count on men whom I do not know by relying on human goodness or man's concern for the good of society. I don't know what will become of the Russian revolution; I may make an example of it to the extent that at the present time it is apparent that the proletariat plays a part in Russia that it plays in no other nation. But I can't swear that this will inevitably lead to a triumph of the proletariat. I've got to limit myself to what I see.

Given that men are free and that tomorrow they will freely decide what man will be, I can not be sure that, after my death, fellow-fighters will carry on my work to bring it to its maximum perfection. Tomorrow, after my death, some men may decide to set up Fascism, and the others may be cowardly and muddled enough to let them do it. Fascism will then be the human reality, so much the worse for us.

Actually, things will be as man will have decided they are to be. Does that mean that I should abandon myself to quietism? No. First, I should involve myself; then, act on the old saw, "Nothing ventured, nothing gained." Nor does it mean that I shouldn't belong to a party, but rather that I shall have no illusions and shall do what I can. For example, suppose I ask myself, "Will socialization, as such, ever come about?" I know nothing about it. All I know is that I'm going to do everything in my power to bring it about. Beyond that, I can't count on anything. Quietism is the attitude of people who say, "Let others do what I can't do." The doctrine I am presenting is the very opposite of quietism, since it declares, "There is no reality except in action." Moreover, it goes further, since it adds, "Man is nothing else than his plan; he exists only to the extent that he fulfills himself; he is therefore nothing else than the ensemble of his acts, nothing else than his life."

According to this, we can understand why our doctrine horrifies certain people. Because often the only way they can bear their wretchedness is to think, "Circumstances have been against me. What I've been and done doesn't show my true worth. To be sure, I've had no great love, no great friendship, but that's because I haven't met a man or woman who was worthy. The books I've written haven't been very good because I haven't had the proper leisure. I haven't had children to devote myself to because I didn't find a man with whom I could have spent my life. So there remains within me, unused and quite viable, a host of propensities, inclinations, possibilities, that one wouldn't guess from the mere series of things I've done."

Now, for the existentialist there is really no love other than one which manifests itself in a person's being in love. There is no genius other than one which is expressed in works of art; the genius of Proust is the sum of Proust's works; the genius of Racine is his series of tragedies. Outside of that, there is nothing. Why say that Racine could have written another tragedy, when he didn't write it? A man is involved in life, leaves his impress on it, and outside of that there is nothing. To be sure, this may seem a harsh thought to someone whose life hasn't been a success. But, on the other hand, it prompts people to understand that reality alone is what counts, that dreams, expectations, and hopes warrant no more than to define a man as a disappointed dream, as miscarried hopes, as vain expectations. In other words, to define him negatively and not positively. However, when we say, "You are nothing else than your life," that does not imply that the artist will be judged solely on the basis of his works of art; a thousand other things will contribute toward summing him up. What we mean is that a man is nothing else than a series of undertakings, that he is the sum, the organization, the ensemble of the relationships which make up these undertakings.

When all is said and done, what we are accused of, at bottom, is not our pessimism, but an optimistic toughness. If people throw up to us our works of fiction in which we write about people who are soft, weak, cowardly, and sometimes even downright bad, it's not because these people are soft, weak, cowardly, or bad; because if we were to say, as Zola did, that they are that way because of heredity, the workings of environment, society, because of biological or psychological determinism, people would be reassured. They would say, "Well, that's what we're like, no one can do anything about it." But when the existentialist writes about a coward, he says that this coward is responsible for his cowardice. He's not like that because he has a cowardly heart or lung or brain; he's not like that on account of his physiological make-up; but he's like that because he has made himself a coward by his acts. There's no such thing as a cowardly constitution; there are nervous constitutions; there is poor blood, as the common people say, or strong constitutions. But the man whose blood is poor is not a coward on that account, for what makes cowardice is the act of renouncing or yielding. A constitution is not an act; the coward is defined on the basis of the acts he performs. People feel, in a vague sort of way, that this coward we're talking about is guilty of being a coward, and the thought frightens them. What people would like is that a coward or a hero be born that way.

• • •

What the existentialist says is that the coward makes himself cowardly, that the hero makes himself heroic. There's always a possibility for the coward not to be cowardly any more and for the hero to stop being heroic. What counts is total involvement; some one particular action or set of circumstances, is not total involvement.

Thus, I think we nave answered a number of the charges concerning existentialism. You see that it can not be taken for a philosophy of quietism, since it defines man in terms of action; nor for a pessimistic description of man—there is no doctrine more optimistic, since man's destiny is within himself; nor for an attempt to discourage man from acting, since it tells him that the only hope is in his acting and that action is the only thing that enables a man to live. Consequently, we are dealing here with an ethics of action and involvement.

• • •

I've been reproached for asking whether existentialism is humanistic. It's been said, "But you said in *Nausea* that the humanists were all wrong. You made fun of a certain kind of humanist. Why come back to it now?" Actually, the word humanism has two very different meanings. By humanism one can mean a theory which takes man as an end and as a higher value. Humanism in this sense can be found in Cocteau's tale

Around the World in Eighty Hours when a character, because he is flying over some mountains in an airplane, declares, "Man is simply amazing." That means that I, who did not build the airplanes, shall personally benefit from these particular inventions, and that I, as man, shall personally consider myself responsible for, and honored by, acts of a few particular men. This would imply that we ascribe a value to man on the basis of the highest deeds of certain men. This humanism is absurd, because only the dog or the horse would be able to make such an over-all judgment about man, which they are careful not to do, at least to my knowledge.

But it can not be granted that a man may make a judgment about man. Existentialism spares him from any such judgment. The existentialist will never consider man as an end because he is always in the making. Nor should we believe that there is a mankind to which we might set up a cult in the manner of Auguste Comte. The cult of mankind ends in the self-enclosed humanism of Comte, and, let it be said, of fascism. This kind of humanism we can do without.

But there is another meaning of humanism. Fundamentally it is this: man is constantly outside of himself; in projecting himself, in losing himself outside of himself, he makes for man's existing; and, on the other hand, it is by pursuing transcendent goals that he is able to exist; man, being this state of passing-beyond, and seizing upon things only as they bear upon this passing-beyond, is at the heart, at the center of this passing-beyond. There is no universe other than a human universe, the universe of human subjectivity. This connection between transcendency, as a constituent element of man—not in the sense that God is transcendent, but in the sense of passing beyond—and subjectivity, in the sense that man is not closed in on himself but is always present in a human universe, is what we call existentialism humanism. Humanism, because we remind man that there is no law-maker other than himself, and that in his forlornness he will decide by himself; because we point out that man will fulfill himself as man, not in turning toward himself, but in seeking outside of himself a goal which is just this liberation, just this particular fulfillment.

From these few reflections it is evident that nothing is more unjust than the objections that have been raised against us. Existentialism is nothing else than an attempt to draw all the consequences of a coherent atheistic position. It isn't trying to plunge man into despair at all. But if one calls every attitude of unbelief despair, like the Christians, then the word is not being used in its original sense. Existentialism isn't so atheistic that it wears itself out showing that God doesn't exist. Rather, it declares that even if God did exist, that would change nothing. There you've got our point of view. Not that we believe that God exists, but we think that the problem of His existence is not the issue. In this sense existentialism is optimistic, a doctrine of action, and it is plain dishonesty for Christians to make no distinction between their own despair and ours and then to call us despairing.

DISCUSSION QUESTIONS

1. Explain what Sartre means when he says "existence precedes essence."

2. What is the example of the anguish of Abraham supposed to show? Explain.

3. What is the example of the student seeking Sartre's advice supposed to show?

4. Explain what Sartre means when he says we are "condemned to be free."

5. Explain what Sartre means when he says we are "responsible for all men" through our choices.

6. Do you think Sartre's view of the self is compatible with Mead's view? If so, how? If not, why not? Explain.

Borges and I

By Jorge Luis Borges

Argentinean writer Jorge Luis Borges (1899–1986) is most famous for his short stories. As he aged and began losing his sight, his stories became shorter and more compact. He also wrote philosophical essays, literary criticism, poetry, and did translations of other authors. His works are often concerned with the nature of time, or of reality. Some of his short pieces are book reviews of works that don't exist.

Included here are two short pieces written in the 1950s about the nature of the self. "Borges and I" explores the nature of identity between a writer and what is written, how the author changes while writing, and the relation between private and public personae. The "I" refers to the writer, and "Borges" refers to the attributed author. The second piece, "Everything and Nothing" is a fable about what made a certain 17th century playwright so great and what conversation he might have with God in the afterlife.

It's to the other man, to Borges, that things happen. I walk along the streets of Buenos Aires, stopping now and then—perhaps out of habit—to look at the arch of an old entranceway or a grillwork gate; of Borges I get news through the mail and glimpse his name among a committee of professors or in a dictionary of biography. I have a taste for hourglasses, maps, eighteenth-century typography, the roots of words, the smell of coffee, and Stevenson's prose; the other man shares these likes, but in a showy way that turns them into stagy mannerisms. It would be an exaggeration to say that we are on bad terms; I live, I let myself live, so that Borges can weave his tales and poems, and those tales and poems are my justification. It is not hard for me to admit that he has managed to write a few worthwhile pages, but these pages cannot save me, perhaps because what is good no longer belongs to anyone—not even the other man—but rather to speech or tradition. In any case, I am fated to become lost once and for all, and only some moment of myself will survive in the other man. Little by little, I have been surrendering everything to him, even though I have evidence of his stubborn habit of falsification and exaggerating. Spinoza held that all things try to keep on being themselves; a stone wants to be a stone and the tiger, a tiger. I shall remain in Borges, not in myself (if it is so that I am someone), but I recognize myself less in his books than in those of others or than in the laborious tuning of a guitar. Years ago, I tried ridding myself of him and I went from myths of the outlying slums of the city to games with time and infinity, but those games are now part of Borges and I will have to turn to other things. And so, my life is a running away, and I lose everything and everything is left to oblivion or to the other man.

Which of us is writing this page I don't know.

Everything and Nothing

By Jorge Luis Borges

There was no one in him; behind his face (which even through the bad paintings of those times resembles no other) and his words, which were copious, fantastic and stormy, there was only a bit of coldness, a dream dreamt by no one. At first he thought that all people were like him, but the astonishment of a friend to whom he had begun to speak of this emptiness showed him his error and made him feel always that an individual should not differ in outward appearance. Once he thought that in books he would find a cure for his ill and thus he learned the small Latin and less Greek a contemporary would speak of; later he considered that what he sought might well be found in an elemental rite of humanity, and let himself be initiated by Anne Hathaway one long June afternoon. At the age of twenty-odd years he went to London. Instinctively he had already become proficient in the habit of simulating that he was someone, so that others would not discover his condition as no one; in London he found the profession to which he was predestined, that of the actor, who on a stage plays at being another before a gathering of people who play at taking him for that other person. His histrionic tasks brought him a singular satisfaction, perhaps the first he had ever known; but once—the last verse had been acclaimed and the last dead man withdrawn from the stage, the hated flavour of unreality returned to him. He ceased to be Ferrex or Tamberlane and became no one again. Thus hounded, he took to imagining other heroes and other tragic fables. And so, while his flesh fulfilled its destiny as flesh in the taverns and brothels of London, the soul that inhabited him was Caesar, who disregards the augur's admonition, and Juliet. who abhors the lark, and Macbeth, who converses on the plain with the witches who are also Fates. No one has ever been so many men as this man who like the Egyptian Proteus could exhaust all the guises of reality. At times he would leave a confession hidden away in some corner of his work, certain that it would not be deciphered; Richard affirms that in his person he plays the part of many and Iago claims with curious words 'I am not what I am'. The fundamental identity of existing, dreaming and acting inspired famous passages of his.

For twenty years he persisted in that controlled hallucination, but one morning he was suddenly gripped by the tedium and the terror of being so many kings who die by the sword and so many suffering lovers who converge, diverge and melodiously expire. That very day he arranged to sell his theatre. Within. . a week he had returned to his native village, where he recovered the trees and rivers of his childhood and did not relate them to the others his muse had celebrated, illustrious with mythological allusions and Latin terms. He had to be 'someone: he was a retired impresario who had made his fortune and concerned himself with loans, lawsuits and petty usury. It was in this character that he dictated the arid will and testament known to us, from which he deliberately excluded all traces of pathos or literature. His friends from London would visit his retreat and for them he would take up again his role as poet.

History adds that before or after dying he found himself in the presence of God and told Him: 'I who have been so many men in vain want to be one and myself.' The voice of the Lord answered from a whirlwind: 'Neither am I anyone; I have dreamt the world as you dreamt your work, my Shakespeare, and among the forms in my dream are you, who like myself are many and no one.'

DISCUSSION QUESTIONS

1. Compare these two short pieces to the views of the self in Mead and Du Bois.

2. In "Borges and I" he makes reference to the Dutch philosopher Spinoza (1632–1677). Why do you think he does this? Explain.

3. Explain what it means when Borges opens "Everything and Nothing" like this: "[t]here was no one in him; behind his face."

PART TWO

"WHAT IS REAL?"

The Republic

By Plato
Translated by Benjamin Jowett

Plato's Republic, *like* Phaedo *from Part I of* Four Fundamental Questions, *is a middle-period dialogue, though it is considered to have been written later than* Phaedo. *The* Republic *is one of the longer works by Plato. In the opening books of the* Republic, *there is a discussion of the nature of justice—what is a just person? Eventually, the character Socrates suggests that they need to look at the state before they look at the person because larger things are easier to see than smaller ones. The state is clearly larger than the individual and the adjective "just" can be applied to either one. The middle books of the dialogue comprise a discussion of the nature of the just state. There is also a discussion of the reasons that other forms of governance are less than ideal. Toward the end, the analogy is brought back to the person and the parts of the state and the parts of the soul are aligned. Finally, justice is defined as a harmony of the parts.*

Our selection, Book VII of the Republic, *is usually referred to as the "Allegory of the Cave." In the allegory, Plato compares ordinary humans to people who have lived their entire lives in a cave, with no knowledge of the outside world (or even that there is an outside world). One who leads a prisoner out of the cave is like the philosopher who moves the ordinary person out of their ordinary way of thinking. The everyday world is as pale a comparison to the world of ideas as the inside of the cave is to the world outside the cave. In other words, what we take to be real on a daily basis is not what is* really *real.*

BOOK VII

Socrates – GLAUCON

And now, I said, let me show in a figure how far our nature is enlightened or unenlightened:—Behold! human beings living in a underground den, which has a mouth open towards the light and reaching all along the den; here they have been from their childhood, and have their legs and necks chained so that they cannot move, and can only see before them, being prevented by the chains from turning round their heads. Above and behind them a fire is blazing at a distance, and between the fire and the prisoners there is a raised way; and you will see, if you look, a low wall built along the way, like the screen which marionette players have in front of them, over which they show the puppets.

I see.

And do you see, I said, men passing along the wall carrying all sorts of vessels, and statues and figures of animals made of wood and stone and various materials, which appear over the wall? Some of them are talking, others silent.

You have shown me a strange image, and they are strange prisoners.

Like ourselves, I replied; and they see only their own shadows, or the shadows of one another, which the fire throws on the opposite wall of the cave?

True, he said; how could they see anything but the shadows if they were never allowed to move their heads?

And of the objects which are being carried in like manner they would only see the shadows?

Yes, he said.

And if they were able to converse with one another, would they not suppose that they were naming what was actually before them?

Very true.

And suppose further that the prison had an echo which came from the other side, would they not be sure to fancy when one of the passers-by spoke that the voice which they heard came from the passing shadow?

No question, he replied.

To them, I said, the truth would be literally nothing but the shadows of the images.

That is certain.

And now look again, and see what will naturally follow it' the prisoners are released and disabused of their error. At first, when any of them is liberated and compelled suddenly to stand up and turn his neck round and walk and look towards the light, he will suffer sharp pains; the glare will distress him, and he will be unable to see the realities of which in his former state he had seen the shadows; and then conceive some one saying to him, that what he saw before was an illusion, but that now, when he is approaching nearer to being and his eye is turned towards more real existence, he has a clearer vision,—what will be his reply? And you may further imagine that his instructor is pointing to the objects as they pass and requiring him to name them,—will he not be perplexed? Will he not fancy that the shadows which he formerly saw are truer than the objects which are now shown to him?

Far truer.

And if he is compelled to look straight at the light, will he not have a pain in his eyes which will make him turn away to take and take in the objects of vision which he can see, and which he will conceive to be in reality clearer than the things which are now being shown to him?

True, he now

And suppose once more, that he is reluctantly dragged up a steep and rugged ascent, and held fast until he 's forced into the presence of the sun himself, is he not likely to be pained and irritated? When he approaches the light his eyes will be dazzled, and he will not be able to see anything at all of what are now called realities.

Not all in a moment, he said.

He will require to grow accustomed to the sight of the upper world. And first he will see the shadows best, next the reflections of men and other objects in the water, and then the objects themselves; then he will gaze upon the light of the moon and the stars and the spangled heaven; and he will see the sky and the stars by night better than the sun or the light of the sun by day?

Certainly.

Last of he will be able to see the sun, and not mere reflections of him in the water, but he will see him in his own proper place, and not in another; and he will contemplate him as he is.

Certainly.

He will then proceed to argue that this is he who gives the season and the years, and is the guardian of all that is in the visible world, and in a certain way the cause of all things which he and his fellows have been accustomed to behold?

Clearly, he said, he would first see the sun and then reason about him.

And when he remembered his old habitation, and the wisdom of the den and his fellow-prisoners, do you not suppose that he would felicitate himself on the change, and pity them?

Certainly, he would.

And if they were in the habit of conferring honours among themselves on those who were quickest to observe the passing shadows and to remark which of them went before, and which followed after, and which were together; and who were therefore best able to draw conclusions as to the future, do you think that he would care for such honours and glories, or envy the possessors of them? Would he not say with Homer.

Better to be the poor servant of a poor master, and to endure anything, rather than think as they do and live after their manner?

Yes, he said, I think that he would rather suffer anything than entertain these false notions and live in this miserable manner.

Imagine once more, I said, such an one coming suddenly out of the sun to be replaced in his old situation; would he not be certain to have his eyes full of darkness?

To be sure, he said.

And if there were a contest, and he had to compete in measuring the shadows with the prisoners who had never moved out of the den, while his sight was still weak, and before his eyes had become steady (and the time which would be needed to acquire this new habit of sight might be very considerable) would he not be ridiculous? Men would say of him that up he went and down he came without his eyes; and that it was better not even to think of ascending; and if any one tried to loose another and lead him up to the light, let them only catch the offender, and they would put him to death.

No question, he said.

This entire allegory, I said, you may now append, dear Glaucon, to the previous argument; the prison-house is the world of sight, the light of the fire is the sun, and you will not misapprehend me if you interpret the journey upwards to be the ascent of the soul into the intellectual world according to my poor belief, which, at your desire, I have expressed whether rightly or wrongly God knows. But, whether true or false, my opinion is that in the world of knowledge the idea of good appears last of all, and is seen only with an effort; and, when seen, is also inferred to be the universal author of all things beautiful and right, parent of light and of the lord of light in this visible world, and the immediate source of reason and truth in the intellectual; and that this is the power upon which he who would act rationally, either in public or private life must have his eye fixed.

I agree, he said, as far as I am able to understand you.

Moreover, I said, you must not wonder that those who attain to this beatific vision are unwilling to descend to human affairs; for their souls are ever hastening into the upper world where they desire to dwell; which desire of theirs is very natural, if our allegory may be trusted.

Yes, very natural.

And is there anything surprising in one who passes from divine contemplations to the evil state of man, misbehaving himself in a ridiculous manner; if, while his eyes are blinking and before he has become accustomed to the surrounding darkness, he is compelled to fight in courts of law, or in other places, about the images or the shadows of images of justice, and is endeavouring to meet the conceptions of those who have never yet seen absolute justice?

Anything but surprising, he replied.

Any one who has common sense will remember that the bewilderments of the eyes are of two kinds, and arise from two causes, either from coming out of the light or from going into the light, which is true of the mind's eye, quite as much as of the bodily eye; and he who remembers this when he sees any one whose vision is perplexed and weak, will not be too ready to laugh; he will first ask whether that soul of man has come out of the brighter light, and is unable to see because unaccustomed to the dark, or having turned from darkness to the day is dazzled by excess of light. And he will count the one happy in his condition and state of being, and he will pity the other; or, if he have a mind to laugh at the soul which comes from below into the light, there will be more reason in this than in the laugh which greets him who returns from above out of the light into the den.

That, he said, is a very just distinction.

But then, if I am right, certain professors of education must be wrong when they say that they can put a knowledge into the soul which was not there before, like sight into blind eyes.

They undoubtedly say this, he replied.

Whereas, our argument shows that the power and capacity of learning exists in the soul already; and that just as the eye was unable to turn from darkness to light without the whole body, so too the instrument of knowledge can only by the movement of the whole soul be turned from the world of becoming into that of being, and learn by degrees to endure the sight of being, and of the brightest and best of being, or in other words, of the good.

Very true.

And must there not be some art which will effect conversion in the easiest and quickest manner; not implanting the faculty of sight, for that exists already, but has been turned in the wrong direction, and is looking away from the truth?

Yes, he said, such an art may be presumed.

And whereas the other so-called virtues of the soul seem to be akin to bodily qualities, for even when they are not originally innate they can be implanted later by habit and exercise, the of wisdom more than anything else contains a divine element which always remains, and by this conversion is rendered useful and profitable; or, on the other hand, hurtful and useless. Did you never observe the narrow intelligence flashing from the keen eye of a clever rogue—how eager he is, how clearly his paltry soul sees the way to his end; he is the reverse of blind, but his keen eyesight is forced into the service of evil, and he is mischievous in proportion to his cleverness.

Very true, he said.

But what if there had been a circumcision of such natures in the days of their youth; and they had been severed from those sensual pleasures, such as eating and drinking, which, like leaden weights, were attached to them at their birth, and which drag them down and turn the vision of their souls upon the things that are below—if, I say, they had been released from these impediments and turned in the opposite direction, the very same faculty in them would have seen the truth as keenly as they see what their eyes are turned to now.

Very likely.

Yes, I said; and there is another thing which is likely. or rather a necessary inference from what has preceded, that neither the uneducated and uninformed of the truth, nor yet those who never make an end of their education, will be able ministers of State; not the former, because they have no single aim of duty which is the rule of all their actions, private as well as public; nor the latter, because they will not act at all except upon compulsion, fancying that they are already dwelling apart in the islands of the blest.

Very true, he replied.

Then, I said, the business of us who are the founders of the State will be to compel the best minds to attain that knowledge which we have already shown to be the greatest of all-they must continue to ascend until they arrive at the good; but when they have ascended and seen enough we must not allow them to do as they do now.

What do you mean?

I mean that they remain in the upper world: but this must not be allowed; they must be made to descend again among the prisoners in the den, and partake of their labours and honours, whether they are worth having or not.

But is not this unjust? he said; ought we to give them a worse life, when they might have a better?

You have again forgotten, my friend, I said, the intention of the legislator, who did not aim at making any one class in the State happy above the rest; the happiness was to be in the whole State, and he held the citizens together by persuasion and necessity, making them benefactors of the State, and therefore benefactors of one another; to this end he created them, not to please themselves, but to be his instruments in binding up the State.

True, he said, I had forgotten.

Observe, Glaucon, that there will be no injustice in compelling our philosophers to have a care and providence of others; we shall explain to them that in other States, men of their class are not obliged to share in the toils of politics: and this is reasonable, for they grow up at their own sweet will, and the government would rather not have them. Being self-taught, they cannot be expected to show any gratitude for a culture which they have never received. But we have brought you into the world to be rulers of the hive, kings of yourselves and of the other citizens, and have educated you far better and more perfectly than they have been educated, and you are better able to share in the double duty. Wherefore each of you, when his turn comes, must go down to the general underground abode, and get the habit of seeing in the dark. When you have acquired the habit, you will see ten thousand times better than the inhabitants of the den, and you will know what the several images are, and what they represent, because you have seen the beautiful and just and good in their truth. And thus our State which is also yours will be a reality, and not a dream only, and will be administered in a spirit unlike that of other States, in which men fight with one another about shadows only and are distracted in the struggle for power, which in their eyes is a great good. Whereas the truth is that the State in which the rulers are most reluctant to govern is always the best and most quietly governed, and the State in which they are most eager, the worst.

Quite true, he replied.

And will our pupils, when they hear this, refuse to take their turn at the toils of State, when they are allowed to spend the greater part of their time with one another in the heavenly light?

Impossible, he answered; for they are just men, and the commands which we impose upon them are just; there can be no doubt that every one of them will take office as a stern necessity, and not after the fashion of our present rulers of State.

Yes, my friend, I said; and there lies the point. You must contrive for your future rulers another and a better life than that of a ruler, and then you may have a well-ordered State; for only in the State which offers this, will they rule who are truly rich, not in silver and gold, but in virtue and wisdom, which are the true blessings of life. Whereas if they go to the administration of public affairs, poor and hungering after the' own private advantage, thinking that hence they are to snatch the chief good, order there can never be; for they will be fighting about office, and the civil and domestic broils which thus arise will be the ruin of the rulers themselves and of the whole State.

Most true, he replied.

And the only life which looks down upon the life of political ambition is that of true philosophy. Do you know of any other?

Indeed, I do not, he said.

And those who govern ought not to be lovers of the task? For, if they are, there will be rival lovers, and they will fight.

No question.

Who then are those whom we shall compel to be guardians? Surely they will be the men who are wisest about affairs of State, and by whom the State is best administered, and who at the same time have other honours and another and a better life than that of politics?

They are the men, and I will choose them, he replied.

And now shall we consider in what way such guardians will be produced, and how they are to be brought from darkness to light,—as some are said to have ascended from the world below to the gods?

By all means, he replied.

The process, I said, is not the turning over of an oyster-shell, but the turning round of a soul passing from a day which is little better than night to the true day of being, that is, the ascent from below, which we affirm to be true philosophy?

DISCUSSION QUESTIONS

1. In the allegory, Socrates argues that the individual prisoner that returns to the cave and could no longer easily see in the dark would be chastised, or possibly killed. Why does he suppose this? Explain.

2. What does the Sun represent in the allegory? Explain.

3. The view in the *Phaedo* talks about perfect realities, and these are at the root of the allegory in the *Republic*. Explain Plato's view by combining these two excerpts.

THE TAO TE CHING

By Lao Tzu
Translated by Lin Yutang

The Tao te Ching *is a classical work of Chinese philosophy, usually attributed to Lao Tzu. It is debated among scholars when Lao Tzu lived, and even* whether *he lived. Most believe he lived in fourth century BCE, but some make him a contemporary of Confucius and place him in the sixth century BCE. The title can be translated as* The Book of the Way of Virtue, *but it is usually left untranslated. The book, as it has come down to us, is in 81 short chapters, grouped in two parts (1–37, 38–81), though it is not clear that this is a division that goes back to the original. Part I of the* Tao te Ching *is primarily concerned with describing reality, and Part II is more concerned with ethical and social philosophy, though both topics occur throughout the text. Followers of this kind of philosophy have come to be known as Taoists, and some devotional practices have arisen around this text and other Taoist texts. To many, this makes Taoism a religion, but this depends on your definition of what constitutes a religion. In Part III of* Four Fundamental Questions, *you will find an excerpt from Chuang Tzu which contains a Taoist perspective on knowledge.*

Included here are more than 50 chapters of the Tao te Ching, *comprising most of the book's discussion of the nature of reality. The chapters are not dependent on each other in the sense that later chapters here do not depend on the earlier ones. They do not need to be read in any particular order. The chapters read more like poetry than they do like a philosophical essay. A big part of the Taoist view on reality can be found in Chapter 1: the idea that you cannot talk about the Tao (ultimate reality). For this reason, much of the discussion in the* Tao te Ching *is in the form of metaphorical language and analogy arguments. Themes you will find in the book are often paradoxical: that everything contains its opposite (illustrated by the yin-yang symbol) or that the Tao accomplishes much by not doing anything (actionless action). The Tao is also likened to water, because it flows and all flows from it.*

1.1 The Tao the can be told of Is not the Absolute Tao; The Names that can be given Are not Absolute Names.

1.2 The Nameless is the origin of Heaven and Earth; The Named is the Mother of All Things.

1.3 Therefore: Oftentimes, one strips oneself of passion In order to see the Secret of Life; Oftentimes, one regards life with passion, In order to see its manifest forms.

1.4 These two (the Secret and its manifestations) Are (in their nature) the same; They are given different names When they become manifest.

1.5 They may both be called the Cosmic Mystery: Reaching from the Mystery into the Deeper Mystery Is the Gate to the Secret of All Life.

2.1 When the people of the Earth all know beauty as beauty, There arises (the recognition of) ugliness.

2.2 When the people of the Earth all know the good as good, There arises (the recognition of) evil.

2.3 Therefore: Being and non-being interdepend in growth; Difficult and easy interdepend in completion; Long and short interdepend in contrast;

2.4 High and low interdepend in position; Tones and voice interdepend in harmony; Front and behind interdepend in company.

2.5 Therefore the Sage: Manages affairs without action; Preaches the doctrine without words;

2.6 All things take their rise, but he does not turn away from them; He gives them life, but does not take possession of them; He acts, but does not appropriate;

2.7 Accomplishes, but claims no credit. It is because he lays claim to no credit That the credit cannot be taken away from him.

3.1 Exalt not the wise, So that the people shall not scheme and contend;

3.2 Prize not rare objects, So that the people shall not steal;

3.3 Shut out from site the things of desire, So that the people's hearts shall not be disturbed.

3.4 Therefore in the government of the Sage: He keeps empty their hearts Makes full their bellies, Discourages their ambitions, Strengthens their frames;

3.5 So that the people may be innocent of knowledge and desires. And the cunning ones shall not presume to interfere.

3.6 By action without deeds May all live in peace.

• • •

7.1 The universe is everlasting.

7.2 The reason the universe is everlasting Is that it does not live for Self. Therefore it can long endure.

7.3 Therefore the Sage puts himself last, And finds himself in the foremost place;

7.4 Regards his body as accidental, And his body is thereby preserved.

7.5 Is it not because he does not live for Self That his Self is realized?

8.1 The best of men is like water; Water benefits all things And does not compete with them. It dwells in (the lowly) places that all disdain—Wherein it comes near to the Tao.

8.2 In his dwelling, (the Sage) loves the (lowly) earth; In his heart, he loves what is profound; In his relations with others, he loves kindness; In his words, he loves sincerity;

8.3 In government, he loves peace; In business affairs, he loves ability; In his actions, he loves choosing the right time.

8.4 It is because he does not contend That he is without reproach.

9.1 Stretch (a bow) to the very full, And you will wish you had stopped in time.

9.2 Temper a (sword-edge) to its very sharpest, And the edge will not last long.

9.3 When gold and jade fill your hall, You will not be able to keep them safe.

9.4 To be proud with wealth and honor Is to sow seeds of one's own downfall.

9.5 Retire when your work is done, Such is Heaven's way.

• • •

11.1 Thirty spokes unite around the nave; From their not-being (loss of their individuality) Arises the utility of the wheel.

11.2 Mold clay into a vessel; From its not-being (in the vessel's hollow) Arises the utility of the vessel.

11.3 Cut out doors and windows in the house (-wall), From their not-being (empty space) arises the utility of the house.

11.4 Therefore by the existence of things we profit. And by the non-existence of things we are served.

12.1 The five colors blind the eyes of man; The five musical notes deafen the ears of man; The five flavors dull the taste of man;

12.2 Horse-racing, hunting and chasing madden the minds of man; Rare, valuable goods keep their owners awake at night.

12.3 Therefore the Sage: Provides for the belly and not the eye. Hence, he rejects the one and accepts the other.

13.1 "Favor and disgrace cause one dismay; What we value and what we fear are within our Self."

13.2 What does this mean: "Favor and disgrace cause one dismay?" Those who receive a favor from above Are dismayed when they receive it, And dismayed when they lose it.

13.3 What does this mean: "What we value and what we fear are within our Self?" We have fears because we have a self. When we do not regard that self as self, What have we to fear?

13.4 Therefore he who values the world as his self May then be entrusted with the government of the world; And he who loves the world as his self—The world may then be entrusted to his care.

14.1 Looked at, but cannot be seen—That is called the Invisible (yi). Listened to, but cannot be heard—That is called the Inaudible (hsi). Grasped at, but cannot be touched—That is called the Intangible (wei).

14.2 These three elude our inquiries And hence blend and become One.

14.3 Not by its rising, is there light, Nor by its sinking, is there darkness. Unceasing, continuous, It cannot be defined, And reverts again to the realm of nothingness.

14.4 That is why it is called the Form of the Formless, The Image of Nothingness. That is why it is called the Elusive: Meet it and you do not see its face; Follow it and you do not see its back.

14.5 —

15.1 The wise ones of old had subtle wisdom and depth of understanding, So profound that they could not be understood.

15.2 And because they could not be understood, Perforce must they be so described: Cautious, like crossing a wintry stream, Irresolute, like one fearing danger all around, Grave, like one acting as guest,

15.3 Self-effacing, like ice beginning to melt, Genuine, like a piece of undressed wood, Open-minded, like a valley, And mixing freely, like murky water.

15.4 Who can find repose in a muddy world? By lying still, it becomes clear. Who can maintain his calm for long? By activity, it comes back to life.

15.5 He who embraces this Tao Guards against being over-full. Because he guards against being over-full, He is beyond wearing out and renewal.

16.1 Attain the utmost in Passivity, Hold firm to the basis of Quietude.

16.2 The myriad things take shape and rise to activity, But I watch them fall back to their repose. Like vegetation that luxuriantly grows But returns to the root (soil) from which it springs.

16.3 To return to the root is Repose; It is called going back to one's Destiny. Going back to one's Destiny is to find the Eternal Law. To know the Eternal Law is Enlightenment. And not to know the Eternal Law Is to court disaster.

16.4 He who knows the Eternal Law is tolerant; Being tolerant, he is impartial; Being impartial, he is kingly; Being kingly, he is in accord with Nature; Being in accord with Nature, he is in accord with Tao;

16.5 Being in accord with Tao, he is eternal, And his whole life is preserved from harm.

• • •

20.1 Banish learning, and vexations end. Between "Ah!" and "Ough!" How much difference is there? Between "good" and "evil" How much difference is there?"

20.2 That which men fear Is indeed to be feared; But, alas, distant yet is the dawn (of awakening)!

20.3 The people of the world are merry-making, As if partaking of the sacrificial feasts, As if mounting the terrace in spring; I alone am mild, like one unemployed, Like a new-born babe that cannot yet smile, Unattached, like one without a home.

20.4 The people of the world have enough and to spare, But I am like one left out, My heart must be that of a fool, Being muddled, nebulous!

20.5 The vulgar are knowing, luminous; I alone am dull, confused. The vulgar are clever, self-assured; I alone, depressed. Patient as the sea, Adrift, seemingly aimless.

20.6 The people of the world all have a purpose; I alone appear stubborn and uncouth. I alone differ from the other people, And value drawing sustenance from the Mother.

• • •

22.1 To yield is to be preserved whole. To be bent is to become straight. To be hollow is to be filled. To be tattered is to be renewed. To be in want is to possess. To have plenty is to be confused.

22.2 Therefore the Sage embraces the One, And becomes the model of the world.

22.3 He does not reveal himself, And is therefore luminous. He does not justify himself, And is therefore far-famed. He does not boast of himself, And therefore people give him credit. He does not pride himself, And is therefore the chief among men.

22.4 —

22.5 Is it not indeed true, as the ancients say, "To yield is to be preserved whole?" Thus he is preserved and the world does him homage.

23.1 Nature says few words: Hence it is that a squall lasts not a whole morning. A rainstorm continues not a whole day.

23.2 Where do they come from? From Nature. Even Nature does not last long (in its utterances), How much less should human beings?

23.3 Therefore it is that: He who follows the Tao is identified with the Tao. He who follows Character (Teh) is identified with Character. He who abandons (Tao) is identified with abandonment (of Tao).

23.4 He who is identified with Tao—Tao is also glad to welcome him. He who is identified with character—Character is also glad to welcome him. He who is identified with abandonment—Abandonment is also glad to welcome him.

23.5 He who has not enough faith Will not be able to command faith from others.

24.1 He who stands on tiptoe does not stand (firm); He who strains his strides does not walk (well);

24.2 He who reveals himself is not luminous; He who justifies himself is not far-famed;

24.3 He who boasts of himself is not given credit; He who prides himself is not chief among men.

24.4 These in the eyes of Tao Are called "the dregs and tumors of Virtue," Which are things of disgust. Therefore the man of Tao spurns them.

25.1 Before the Heaven and Earth existed There was something nebulous: Silent, isolated, Standing alone, changing not, Eternally revolving without fail, Worthy to be the Mother of All Things.

25.2 I do not know its name And address it as Tao. If forced to give it a name, I shall call it "Great".

25.3 Being great implies reaching out in space, Reaching out in space implies far-reaching, Far-reaching implies reversion to the original point.

25.4 Therefore: Tao is Great, The Heaven is great, The Earth is great, The King is also great. There are the Great Four in the universe, And the King is one of them.

25.5 Man models himself after the Earth; The Earth models itself after Heaven; The Heaven models itself after Tao; Tao models itself after nature.

• • •

29.1 There are those who will conquer the world And make of it (what they conceive or desire). I see that they will not succeed.

29.2 (For) the world is God's own Vessel It cannot be made (by human interference). He who makes it spoils it. He who holds it loses it.

29.3 For: Some things go forward, Some things follow behind; some blow hot, And some blow cold; Some are strong, And some are weak; Some may break, And some may fall.

29.4 Hence the Sage eschews excess, eschews extravagance, Eschews pride.

30.1 He who by Tao purposes to help the ruler of men Will oppose all conquest by force of arms. For such things are wont to rebound.

30.2 Where armies are, thorns and brambles grow. The raising of a great host Is followed by a year of dearth.

30.3 Therefore a good general effects his purpose and stops. He dares not rely upon the strength of arms;

30.4 Effects his purpose and does not glory in it; Effects his purpose and does not boast of it; Effects his purpose and does not take pride in it; Effects his purpose as a regrettable necessity; Effects his purpose but does not love violence.

30.5 (For) things age after reaching their prime. That (violence) would be against the Tao. And he who is against the Tao perishes young.

• • •

32.1 Tao is absolute and has no name. Though the uncarved wood is small, It cannot be employed (used as vessel) by anyone.

32.2 If kings and barons can keep (this unspoiled nature), The whole world shall yield them lordship of their own accord.

32.3 The Heaven and Earth join, And the sweet rain falls, Beyond the command of men, Yet evenly upon all.

32.4 Then human civilization arose and there were names. Since there were names, It were well one knew where to stop. He who knows where to stop May be exempt from danger.

32.5 Tao in the world May be compared to rivers that run into the sea.

33.1 He who knows others is learned; He who knows himself is wise.

33.2 He who conquers others has power of muscles; He who conquers himself is strong.

33.3 He who is contented is rich. He who id determined has strength of will.

33.4 He who does not lose his center endures. He who dies yet (his power) remains has long life.

• • •

37.1 The Tao never does, Yet through it everything is done.

37.2 If princes and dukes can keep the Tao, the world will of its own accord be reformed. When reformed and rising to action, Let it be restrained by the Nameless pristine simplicity. The Nameless pristine simplicity Is stripped of desire (for contention).

37.3 By stripping of desire quiescence is achieved, And the world arrives at peace of its own accord.

38.1 The man of superior character is not (conscious of his) character. Hence he has character. The man of inferior character (is intent on) not losing character. Hence he is devoid of character.

38.2 The man of superior character never acts, Nor ever (does so) with an ulterior motive. The man of inferior character acts, And (does so) with an ulterior motive.

38.3 The man of superior kindness acts, But (does so) without an ulterior motive. The man of superior justice acts, And (does so) with an ulterior motive. (But when) the man of superior li acts and finds no response, He rolls up his sleeves to force it on others.

38.4 Therefore: After Tao is lost, then (arises the doctrine of) humanity. After humanity is lost, then (arises the doctrine of) justice. After justice is lost, then (arises the doctrine of) li. Now li is the thinning out of loyalty and honesty of heart. And the beginning of chaos.

38.5 The prophets are the flowering of Tao And the origin of folly.

38.6 Therefore the noble man dwells in the heavy (base), And not in the thinning (end). He dwells in the fruit, And not in the flowering (expression). Therefore he rejects the one and accepts the other.

• • •

40.1 Reversion is the action of Tao. Gentleness is the function of Tao.

40.2 The things of this world come from Being, And Being (comes) from Non-being.

41.1 When the highest type of men hear the Tao (truth), they try hard to live in accordance with it. When the mediocre type hear the Tao, they seem to be aware and yet unaware of it.

41.2 When the lowest type hear the Tao, They break into loud laughter—If it were not laughed at, it would not be Tao.

41.3 Therefore there is the established saying: "Who understands Tao seems dull of comprehension; Who is advance in Tao seems to slip backwards; Who moves on the even Tao (Path) seems to go up and down."

41.4 Superior character appears like a hollow (valley); Sheer white appears like tarnished; Great character appears like infirm; Pure worth appears like contaminated. Great space has no corners; Great talent takes long to mature; Great music is faintly heard; Great form has no contour;

41.5 And Tao is hidden without a name. It is this Tao that is adept at lending (its power) and bringing fulfillment.

42.1 Out of Tao, One is born; Out of One, Two; Out of Two, Three; Out of Three, the created universe.

42.2 The created universe carries the yin at its back and the yang in front; Through the union of the pervading principles it reaches harmony.

42.3 To be "orphaned," "lonely" and "unworthy" is what men hate most. Yet the princes and dukes call themselves by such names.

42.4 For sometimes things are benefited by being taken away from, And suffer by being added to.

42.5 Others have taught this maxim, Which I shall teach also: "The violent man shall die a violent death." This I shall regard as my spiritual teacher.

43.1 The softest substance of the world Goes through the hardest. That-which-is-without-form penetrates that-which-has-no-crevice; Through this I know the benefit of taking no action.

43.2 The teaching without words And the benefit of taking no action Are without compare in the universe.

44.1 Fame or one's own self, which does one love more? One's own self or material goods, which has more worth? Loss (of self) or possession (of goods), which is the greater evil?

44.2 Therefore: he who loves most spends most, He who hoards much loses much.

44.3 The contented man meets no disgrace; Who know when to stop runs into no danger—He can long endure.

45.1 The highest perfection is like imperfection, And its use is never impaired. The greatest abundance seems meager, And its use will never fail. What s most straight appears devious,

45.2 The greatest skill appears clumsiness; The greatest eloquence seems like stuttering.

45.3 Movement overcomes cold, (But) keeping still overcomes heat. Who is calm and quiet becomes the guide for the universe.

46.1 When the world lives in accord with Tao, Racing horses are turned back to haul refuse carts. When the world lives not in accord with Tao, Cavalry abounds in the countryside.

46.2 There is no greater curse than the lack of contentment. No greater sin than the desire for possession.

46.3 Therefore he who is contented with contentment shall be always content.

47.1 Without stepping outside one's doors, One can know what is happening in the world, Without looking out of one's windows, One can see the Tao of heaven. The farther one pursues knowledge, The less one knows.

47.2 Therefore the Sage knows without running about, Understands without seeing, Accomplishes without doing.

48.1 The student of knowledge (aims at) learning day by day; The student of Tao (aims at) losing day by day. By continual losing One reaches doing nothing (laissez-faire).

48.2 He who conquers the world often does so by doing nothing.

48.3 When one is compelled to do something, The world is already beyond his conquering.

49.1 The Sage has no decided opinions and feelings, But regards the people's opinions and feelings as his own.

49.2 The good ones I declare good; The bad ones I also declare good. That is the goodness of Virtue.

49.3 The honest ones I believe; The liars I also believe; That is the faith of Virtue.

49.4 The Sage dwells in the world peacefully, harmoniously. The people of the world are brought into a community of heart, And the Sage regards them all as his own children.

50.1 Out of life, death enters.

50.2 The companions (organs) of life are thirteen; The companions (organs) of death are (also) thirteen. What send man to death in this life are also (these) thirteen. How is it so? Because of the intense activity of multiplying life.

50.3 It has been said that the who is a good preserver of hi life Meets no tigers or wild buffaloes on land, Is not vulnerable to weapons in the field of battle.

50.4 The horns of the wild buffalo are powerless against him. How is it so? Because he is beyond death.

51.1 Tao gives them birth, Teh (character) fosters them. The material world gives them form. The circumstances of the moment complete them. Therefore all things of the universe worship Tao and exalt Teh.

51.2 Tao is worshipped and Teh is exalted Without anyone's order but is so of its own accord. Therefore Tao gives them birth, Teh fosters them, Makes them grow, develops them, Gives them a harbor, a place to dwell in peace, Feeds them and shelter them.

51.3 It gives them birth and does not own them, Acts (helps) and does not appropriate them, Is superior, and does not control them.—This is the Mystic Virtue.

52.1 There was a beginning of the universe Which may be regarded as the Mother of the Universe. From the Mother, we may know her sons. After knowing the sons, keep to the Mother.

52.2 Thus one's whole life may be preserved from harm.

52.3 Stop its apertures, Close its doors, And one's whole life is without toil.

52.4 Open its apertures, Be busy about its affairs, And one's whole life is beyond redemption.

52.5 He who can see the small is clear-sighted; He who stays by gentility is strong.

52.6 Use the light, And return to clear-sightedness—Thus cause not yourself later distress.—This is to rest in the Absolute.

53.1 If I were possessed of Austere Knowledge, Walking on the Main Path (Tao), I would avoid the by-paths.

53.2 The Main path is easy to walk on, Yet people love the small by-paths.

53.3 The (official) courts are spic and span, (While) the fields go untilled, And the (people's) granaries are very low.

53.4 (Yet) clad in embroidered gowns, And carrying find swords, Surfeited with good food and drinks, (They are) splitting with wealth and possessions.—This is to lead the world toward brigandage. Is this not corruption of Tao?

• • •

55.1 Who is rich in character Is like a child. No poisonous insects sting him, No wild beasts attack him, And no birds of prey pounce upon him. His bones are soft, his sinews tender, yet his grip is strong.

55.2 Not knowing the union of male and female, yet his organs are complete, Which means his vigor is unspoiled.

55.3 Crying the whole day, yet his voice never runs hoarse, Which means his (natural) harmony is perfect. To know harmony is to be in accord with the eternal, (And) to know eternity is called discerning.

55.4 (But) to improve upon life is called an ill-omen; To let go the emotions through impulse is called assertiveness.

55.5 (For) things age after reaching their prime; That (assertiveness) would be against Tao. And he who is against Tao perishes young.

56.1 He who knows does not speak; He who speaks does not know.

56.2 Fill up its apertures, Close its doors, Dull its edges, Untie its tangles, Soften its light, Submerge its turmoil,—This is the Mystic Unity.

56.3 Then love and hatred cannot touch him. Profit and loss cannot reach him. Honor and disgrace cannot affect him. Therefore is he always the honored one of the world.

57.1 Rule a kingdom by the Normal. Fight a battle by (abnormal) tactics of surprise. Win the world by doing nothing. How do I know it is so? Through this:—

57.2 The more prohibitions there are, The poorer the people become. The more sharp weapons there are, The greater the chaos in the state.

57.3 The more skills of technique, The more cunning things are produced. The greater the number of statutes, The greater the number of thieves and brigands.

57.4 Therefore the sage says: I do nothing and the people are reformed of themselves. I love quietude and the people are righteous of themselves.

57.5 I deal in no business and the people grow rich by themselves. I have no desires and the people are simple and honest by themselves.

58.1 When the government is lazy and dull, Its people are unspoiled; When the government is efficient and smart, Its people are discontented.

58.2 Disaster is the avenue of fortune, (And) fortune is the concealment for disaster.

58.3 Who would be able to know its ultimate results? (As it is), there would never be the normal. But the normal would (immediately) revert to the deceitful. And the good revert to the sinister. Thus long has mankind gone astray!

58.4 Therefore the Sage is square (has firm principles), but not cutting (sharp-cornered), Has integrity but does not hurt (others), Is straight, but not high-handed, Bright, but not dazzling.

59.1 In managing human affairs, there is no better rule than to be sparing.

59.2 To be sparing is to forestall; To forestall is to be prepared and strengthened; To be prepared and strengthened is to be ever-victorious; To be ever-victorious is to have infinite capacity; He who has infinite capacity is fit to rule a country,

59.3 And the Mother (principle) of a ruling country can long endure.

59.4 This is to be firmly rooted, to have deep strength, The road to immortality and enduring vision.

• • •

61.1 A big country (should be like) the delta low-regions, Being the concourse of the world, (And) the Female of the world. The Female overcomes the Male by quietude, And achieves the lowly position by quietude.

61.2 Therefore if a big country places itself below a small country It absorbs the small country. (And) if a small country places itself below a big country, It absorbs the big country.

61.3 Therefore some place themselves low to absorb (others), Some are (naturally) low and absorb (others).

61.4 What a big country wants is but to shelter others, And what a small country wants is but to be able to come in and be sheltered.

61.5 Thus (considering) that both may have what they want, A big country ought to place itself low.

• • •

63.1 Accomplish do-nothing. Attend to no-affairs. Taste the flavorless.

63.2 Whether it is big or small, many or few, Requite hatred with virtue.

63.3 Deal with the difficult while yet it is easy; Deal wit the big while yet it is small.

63.4 The difficult (problems) of the world Must be dealt with while they are yet easy; The great (problems) of the world Must be dealt with while they are yet small.

63.5 Therefore the Sage by never dealing with great (problems) Accomplishes greatness.

63.6 He who lightly makes a promise Will find it often hard to keep his faith.

63.7 He who makes light of many things Will encounter many difficulties. Hence even the Sage regards things as difficult, And for that reason never meets with difficulties.

64.1 That which lies still is easy to hold; That which is not yet manifest is easy to forestall; That which is brittle (like ice) easily melts; That which is minute easily scatters.

64.2 Deal with a thing before it is there; Check disorder before it is rife.

64.3 A tree with a full span's girth begins from a tiny sprout; A nine-storied terrace begins with a clod of earth. A journey of a thousand li beings at one's feet.

64.4 He who acts, spoils; He who grasps, lets slip. Because the Sage does not act, he does not spoil, Because he does not grasp, he does not let slip.

64.5 The affairs of men are often spoiled within an ace of completion. By being careful at the end as at the beginning Failure is averted.

64.6 Therefore the Sage desires to have no desire, And values not objects difficult to obtain. Learns that which is unlearned, And restores what the multitude have lost. That he may assist in the course of Nature And not presume to interfere.

65.1 The ancients who knew how to follow the Tao Aimed not to enlighten the people. But to keep them ignorant.

65.2 The reason it is difficult for the people to leave in peace Is because of too much knowledge. Those who seek to rule a country by knowledge Are the nation's curse. Those who seek not to rule a country by knowledge Are the nation's blessing.

65.3 Those who know these two (principles) Also know the ancient standard, And to know always the ancient standard Is called the Mystic Virtue.

65.4 When the Mystic Virtue becomes clear, far-reaching, And things revert back (to their source) Then and then only emerges the Grand Harmony.

66.1 How did the great rivers and seas become the Lords of the ravines? By being good at keeping low. That was how they became Lords of the Ravines.

66.2 Therefore in order to be the chief among the people, One must speak like their inferiors. In order to be foremost among the people, One must walk behind them.

66.3 Thus it is that the Sage stays above, And the people do not feel his weight; Walks in front, And the people do not wish him harm. Then the people of the world are glad to uphold him forever.

66.4 Because he does not contend, No one in the world can contend against him.

67.1 All the world says: my teaching (Tao) greatly resembles folly. Because it is great; therefore it resembles folly. If it did not resemble folly, It would have long ago become petty indeed!

67.2 I have Three Treasures; Guard them and keep them safe: the first is Love. The second is, Never too much. The third is, Never be the first in the world.

67.3 Through Love, one has no fear; Through not doing too much, one has amplitude (of reserve power); Through not presuming to be the first in the world, One can develop one's talent and let it mature.

67.4 If one forsakes love and fearlessness, forsakes restraint and reserve power, forsakes following behind and rushes in front, He is doomed!

67.5 For love is victorious in attack, And invulnerable in defense. Heaven arms with love Those it would not see destroyed.

68.1 The brave soldier is not violent; The good fighter does not lose his temper;

68.2 The great conqueror does not fight (on small issues); The good user of men places himself below others.

68.3 This is the virtue of not-contending, Is called the capacity to use men, Is reaching to the height of being Mated to Heaven, to what was of old.

69.1 There is the maxim of military strategists; I dare not be the first to invade, but rather be the invaded. Dare not press forward an inch, but rather retreat a foot.

69.2 That is, to march without formations, To roll up the sleeves, To charge not in frontal attacks, To arm without weapons.

69.3 There is no greater catastrophe than to underestimate the enemy.

69.4 To underestimate the enemy might entail the loss of my treasures. Therefore when two equally matched armies meet, It is the man of sorrow who wins.

• • •

71.1 Who knows that he does not know is the highest; Who (pretends to) know what he does not know is sick-minded. And who recognizes sick-mindedness as sick-mindedness is not sick-minded.

71.2 The Sage is not sick-minded. Because he recognizes sick-mindedness as sick-mindness, Therefore he is not sick-minded.

72.1 When people have no fear of force, Then (as is the common practice) great force descends upon them.

72.2 Despise not their dwellings, Dislike not their progeny. Because you do not dislike them, You will not be disliked yourself.

72.3 Therefore the Sage knows himself, but does not show himself, Loves himself, but does not exalt himself. Therefore he rejects the one (force) and accepts the other (gentility).

73.1 Who is brave in daring (you) kill, Who is brave in not daring (you) let live.

73.2 In these two, There is some advantage and some disadvantage. (Even if) Heaven dislikes certain people, Who would know (who are to be killed and) why? Therefore even the Sage regards it as a difficult question.

73.3 Heaven's Way (Tao) is good at conquest without strife, Rewarding (vice and virtue) without words, Making its appearance without call, Achieving results without obvious design.

73.4 The heaven's net is broad and wide. With big meshes, yet letting nothing slip through.

74.1 The people are not afraid of death; Why threaten them with death?

74.2 Supposing that the people are afraid of death, And we can seize and kill the unruly, Who would dare to do so?

74.3 Often it happens that the executioner is killed. And to take the place of the executioner Is like handling the hatchet for the master carpenter. He who handles the hatchet for the master carpenter seldom escapes injury to his hands.

75.1 When people are hungry, It is because their rulers eat too much tax-grain.

75.2 Therefore the unruliness of hungry people Is due to the interference of their rulers. That is why they are unruly.

75.3 The people are not afraid of death, Because they are anxious to make a living. That is why they are not afraid of death. It is those who interfere not with their living That are wise in exalting life.

76.1 When man is born, he is tender and weak; At death, he is hard and stiff.

76.2 When the things and plants are alive, they are soft and supple; When they are dead, they are brittle and dry.

76.3 Therefore hardness and stiffness are the companions of death, And softness and gentleness are the companions of life.

76.4 Therefore when an army is headstrong, it will lose in a battle. When a tree is hard, it will be cut down.

76.5 The big and strong belong underneath. The gentle and weak belong at the top.

77.1 The Tao (way) of Heaven, Is it not like the bending of a bow? The top comes down and the bottom-end goes up, The extra (length) is shortened, the insufficient (width) is expanded.

77.2 It is the way of Heaven to take away from those that have too much And give to those that have not enough. Not so with man's way: He takes from those that have not And gives it as tribute to those that have too much.

77.3 Who can have enough and to spare to give to the entire world? Only the man of Tao.

77.4 Therefore the Sage acts, but does not possess, Accomplishes but lays claim to no credit, Because he has no wish to seem superior.

78.1 There is nothing weaker than water But none is superior to it in overcoming the hard, For which there is no substitute.

78.2 That weakness overcomes strength And gentleness overcomes rigidity, No one does not know; No one can put into practice.

78.3 Therefore the Sage says: "Who receives unto himself the calumny of the world Is the preserver of the state. Who bears himself the sins of the world Is king of the world." Straight words seem crooked.

79.1 Patching up a great hatred is sure to leave some hatred behind. How can this be regarded as satisfactory?

79.2 Therefore the Sage holds the left tally, And does not put the guilt on the other party.

79.3 The virtuous man is for patching up; The vicious is for fixing guilt.

79.4 But "the way of Heaven is impartial; It sides only with the good man."

80.1 (Let there be) a small country with a small population, Where the supply of goods are tenfold or hundredfold, more than they can use. Let the people value their lives and not migrate far.

80.2 Though there be boats and carriages, None be there to ride them. Though there be armor and weapons, No occasion to display them.

80.3 Let the people again tie ropes for reckoning, Let them enjoy their food, Beautify their clothing, Be satisfied with their homes, Delight in their customs.

80.4 The neighboring settlements overlook one another So that they can hear the barking of dogs and crowing of cocks of their neighbors, And the people till the end of their days shall never have been outside their country.

81.1 True words are not fine-sounding; Fine-sounding words are not true.

81.2 A good man does not argue; he who argues is not a good man.

81.3 The wise one does not know many things; He who knows many things is not wise.

81.4 The Sage does not accumulate (for himself). He lives for other people, And grows richer himself; He gives to other people, And has greater abundance.

81.5 The Tao of Heaven Blesses, but does not harm. The Way of the Sage Accomplishes, but does not contend.

DISCUSSION QUESTIONS

1. Given that we cannot talk about the Tao, how can there be 81 chapters in the *Tao te Ching*? Explain.

2. Compare the view of reality found here with the one found in Plato's allegory of the cave. Which one makes more sense to you? Why? Explain.

3. Pick your favorite five of the chapters included here. Explain what the ideas mean and why you like them.

On the Nature of Things

By Lucretius

Titus Lucretius Carus (99–55 BCE), usually referred to as Lucretius, was an Epicurean philosopher. Epicureanism is named for Epicurus (341–270), a Greek philosopher. The Epicurean belief system includes a way of life based on avoiding pain and seeking simple pleasures. There is a selection by Epicurus himself in Part IV of Four Fundamental Questions. *Epicureanism also has a view of reality called atomism. Atomism originated in Greece around the time of Socrates. Its founders were the philosophers Democritus (c. 460–370 BCE) and his mentor Leucippus (c. first half of the fifth century BCE). The basic atomist view is that all of reality is made of atoms, which are the very small building blocks of nature, and the void, which is the space through which atoms can move. The philosophy of early atomists only survives in fragments.*

The poem, On the Nature of Things, *contains Lucretius's full Epicurean view. Book I, which our selection comes from, is the basic atomistic part of the philosophy. Contained here are arguments for the view that there are atoms, that there cannot be anything but atoms and void, and that the atoms are eternal. The view is a mechanistic one. Lucretius uses the word "seed" in his poem, instead of the word "atom."*

BOOK I

• • •

For I will essay to discourse to you of the most high system of heaven and the gods and will open up the first beginnings of things, out of which nature gives birth to all things and increase and nourishment, and into which nature likewise dissolves them back after their destruction. These we are accustomed in explaining their reason to call matter and begetting bodies of things and to name seeds of things and also to term first bodies, because from them as first elements all things are.

When human life to view lay foully prostrate upon earth crushed down under the weight of religion, who showed her head from the quarters of heaven with hideous aspect lowering upon mortals, a man of Greece[1] ventured first to lift up his mortal eyes to her face and first to withstand her to her face. Him neither story of gods nor thunderbolts nor heaven with threatening roar could quell: they only chafed the more the eager courage of his soul, filling him with desire to be the first to burst the fast bars of nature's portals. Therefore the living force of his soul gained the day: on he passed far beyond the flaming walls of the world and traversed throughout in mind and spirit the immeasurable universe; whence he returns a conqueror to tell us what can, what cannot come into being; in short on what principle each thing has its powers defined, its deepset boundary mark. Therefore religion is put under foot and trampled upon in turn; us his victory brings level with heaven.

• • •

This terror then and darkness of mind must be dispelled not by the rays of the sun, and glittering shafts of day, but by the aspect and the law of nature the warp of whose design we shall begin with this first principle, nothing is ever gotten out of nothing by divine power. Fear in sooth holds so in check all mortals, because they see many operations go on in earth and heaven, the causes of which they can in no way understand, believing them therefore to be done by power divine. For these reasons when we shall have seen that nothing can be produced from nothing, we shall then more correctly ascertain that which we are seeking, both the elements out of which every thing can be produced and the manner in which all things are done without the hand of the gods.

If things came from nothing, any kind might be born of any thing, nothing would require seed. Men for instance might rise out of the sea, the scaly race out of the earth, and birds might burst out of the sky; horned and other herds, every kind of wild beasts would haunt with changing brood tilth and wilderness alike. Nor would the same fruits keep constant to trees, but would change; any tree might bear any fruit. For if there were not begetting bodies for each, how could things have a fixed unvarying mother? But in fact because things are all produced from fixed seeds, each thing is born and goes forth into the borders of light out of that in which resides its matter and first bodies; and for this reason all things cannot be gotten out of all things, because in particular things resides a distinct power. Again why do we see the rose put forth in spring, corn in the season of heat, vines yielding at the call of autumn, if not because, when the fixed seeds of things have streamed together at the proper time, whatever is born discloses itself, while the due seasons are there and the quickened earth brings its weakly products in safety forth into the borders of light? But if they came from nothing, they would rise up suddenly at uncertain periods and unsuitable times of year, inasmuch as there would be no first-beginnings to be kept from a begetting union by the unpropitious season. No nor would time be required for the growth of things after the meeting of the seed, if they could increase out of nothing. Little babies would at once grow into men and trees in a moment would rise and spring out of the ground. But none of these events it is plain ever comes to pass, since all things grow step by step at a fixed time, as is natural, since they all grow from a fixed seed and in growing preserve their kind; so that you may be sure that all things increase in size and are fed out of their own matter. Furthermore without fixed seasons of rain the earth is unable to put forth its gladdening produce, nor again if kept from food could the nature of living things continue its kind and sustain life; so that you may hold with greater truth that many bodies are common to many things, as we see letters common to different words, than that any thing could come into being without first-beginnings. Again why could not nature have produced men of such a size and strength as to be able to wade on foot across the sea and rend great mountains with their hands and outlive many generations of living men, if not because an unchanging matter has been assigned for begetting things and what can arise out of this matter is fixed? We must admit therefore that nothing can come from nothing, since things require seed before they can severally be born and be brought out into the buxom fields of air. Lastly since we see that tilled grounds surpass unfilled and yield a better produce by the labour of hands, we may infer that there are in the earth first-beginnings of things which by turning up the fruitful clods with the share and labouring the soil of the earth we stimulate to rise. But if there were not such, you would see all things without any labour of ours spontaneously come forth in much greater perfection.

Moreover nature dissolves every thing back into its first bodies and does not annihilate things. For if aught were mortal in all its parts alike, the thing in a moment would be snatched away to destruction from before our eyes; since no force would be needed to produce disruption among its parts and undo their fastenings. Whereas in fact, as all things consist of an imperishable seed, nature suffers the destruction of nothing to be seen, until a force has encountered it sufficient to dash things to pieces by a blow or to pierce through the void places within them and break them up. Again if time, whenever it makes away with things through age, utterly destroys them eating up all their matter, out of what does Venus bring back into the light of life the race of living things each after its kind, or, when they are brought back, out of what does earth manifold in works give them nourishment and increase, furnishing them with food each after its kind? Out of what do its own native fountains and extraneous rivers from far and wide keep full the sea? Out of what does ether feed the stars? For infinite time gone by and lapse of days must have eaten up all things which are of mortal body. Now if in that period of time gone by those things have existed, of which this sum of things is composed and recruited, they are possessed no doubt of an imperishable body, and cannot therefore any of them return to nothing. Again the same force and cause would destroy all things without distinction, unless everlasting matter held them together, matter more or less closely linked in mutual entanglement: a touch in sooth would be sufficient cause of death, inasmuch as any amount of force must of course undo the texture of things in which no parts at all were of an everlasting body. But in fact, because the fastenings of first-beginnings one with the other are unlike and matter is everlasting, things continue with body uninjured, until a force is found to encounter them strong enough to overpower the texture of each. A thing therefore never returns to nothing, but all things after disruption go back into the first bodies of matter. Lastly rains die, when father ether has tumbled them into the lap of mother earth; but then goodly crops spring up and boughs are green with leaves upon the trees, trees themselves grow and are laden with fruit; by them in turn our race and the race of wild beasts are fed, by them we see glad towns teem with children and the leafy forests ring on all sides with the song of new birds; through them cattle wearied with their load of fat lay their bodies down about the glad pastures and the white milky stream pours from the distended udders; through them a new brood with weakly limbs frisks and gambols over the soft grass, rapt in their young hearts with the pure new milk. None of the things therefore which seem to be lost is utterly lost, since nature replenishes one thing out of another and does not suffer any thing to be begotten, before she has been recruited by the death of some other.

Now mark me: since I have taught that things cannot be born from nothing, cannot when begotten be brought back to nothing, that you may not haply yet begin in any shape to mistrust my words, because the first-beginnings of things cannot be seen by the eyes, take moreover this list of bodies which you must yourself admit are in the number of things and cannot be seen. First of all the force of the wind when aroused beats on the harbours and whelms huge ships and scatters clouds; sometimes in swift whirling eddy it scours the plains and straws them with large trees and scourges the mountain summits with forest-rending blasts: so fiercely does the wind rave with a shrill howling and rage with threatening roar. Winds therefore sure enough are unseen bodies which sweep the seas, the lands, ay and the clouds of heaven, tormenting them and catching them up in sudden whirls. On they stream and spread destruction abroad in just the same way as the soft liquid nature of water, when all at once it is borne along in an overflowing stream, and a great downfall of water from the high hills augments it with copious rains, flinging together fragments of forests and entire trees; nor can the strong bridges sustain the sudden force of coming water: in such wise turbid with much rain the river dashes upon the piers with mighty force: makes havoc with loud noise and rolls under its eddies huge stones: wherever aught opposes its waves, down it dashes it. In this way then must the blasts of wind as well move on, and when they like a mighty stream have borne down in any direction, they push things before them and throw them down with repeated assaults, sometimes catch them up in curling eddy and carry them away in swift-circling whirl. Wherefore once and again I say winds are unseen bodies, since in their works and ways they are found to rival great rivers which are of a visible body. Then again we perceive the different smells of things, yet never see them coming to our nostrils; nor do we behold heats nor can we observe cold with the eyes nor are we used to see voices. Yet all these things must consist of a bodily nature, since they are able to move the senses; for nothing but body can touch and be touched. Again clothes hung up on a shore which waves break upon become moist, and then get dry if spread out in the sun. Yet is has not been seen in what way the moisture of water has sunk into them nor again in what way this has been dispelled by heat. The moisture therefore is dispersed into small particles which the eyes are quite unable to see. Again after the revolution of many of the sun's years a ring on the finger is thinned on the under side by wearing, the dripping from the eaves hollows a stone, the bent ploughshare of iron imperceptibly decreases in the fields, and we behold the stone-paved streets worn down by the feet of the multitude; the brass statues too at the gates show their right hands to be wasted by the touch of the numerous passers by who greet them. These things then we see are lessened, since they have been thus worn down; but what bodies depart at any given time the nature of vision has jealously shut out our seeing. Lastly the bodies which time and nature add to things by little and little, constraining them to grow in due measure, no exertion of the eyesight can behold; and so too wherever things grow old by age and decay, and when rocks hanging over the sea are eaten away by the gnawing salt spray, you cannot see what they lose at any given moment. Nature therefore works by unseen bodies.

And yet all things are not on all sides jammed together and kept in by body: there is also void in things. To have learned this will be good for you on many accounts; it will not suffer you to wander in doubt and be to seek in the sum of things and distrustful of our words. If there were not void, things could not move at all; for that which is the property of body, to let and hinder, would be present to all things at all times; nothing therefore could go on, since no other thing would be the first to give way. But in fact throughout seas and lands and the heights of heaven we see before our eyes many things move in many ways for various reasons, which things, if there were no void, I need not say would lack and want restless motion: they never would have been begotten at all since matter jammed on all sides would have been at rest. Again however solid things are thought to be, you may yet learn from this that they are of rare body: in rocks and caverns the moisture of water oozes through and all things weep with abundant drops; food distributes itself through the whole body of living things; trees grow and yield fruit in season, because food is diffused through the whole from the very roots over the stem and all the boughs. Voices pass through walls and fly through houses shut, stiffening frost pierces to the bones. Now if there are no void parts, by what way can the bodies severally pass? You would see it to be quite impossible. Once more, why do we see one thing surpass another in weight though not larger in size? For if there is just as much body in a ball of wool as there is in a lump of lead, it is natural it should weigh the same, since the property of body is to weigh all things downwards, while on the contrary the nature of void is ever without weight. Therefore when a thing is just as large, yet is found to be lighter, it proves sure enough that it has more of void in it; while on the other hand that which is heavier shows that there is in it more of body and that it contains within it much less of void. Therefore that which we are seeking with keen reason exists sure enough, mixed up in things; and we call it void.

• • •

All nature then, as it exists by itself, is founded on two things: there are bodies and there is void in which these bodies are placed and through which they move about. For that body exists by itself the general feeling of mankind declares; and unless at the very first belief in this be firmly grounded, there will be nothing to which we can appeal on hidden things in order to prove anything by reasoning of mind. Then again, if room and space which we call void did not exist, bodies could not be placed anywhere nor move about at all to any side; as we have demonstrated to you a little before. Moreover there is nothing which you can affirm to be at once separate from all body and quite distinct from void, which would so to say count as the discovery of a third nature. For whatever shall exist, this of itself must be something or other. Now if it shall admit of touch in however slight and small a measure, it will, be it with a large or be it with a little addition, provided it do exist, increase the amount of body and join the sum. But if it shall be intangible and unable to hinder any thing from passing through it on any side, this you are to know will be that which we call empty void. Again whatever shall exist by itself, will either do something or will itself suffer by the action of other things, or will be of such a nature as things are able to exist and go on in. But no thing can do and suffer without body, nor aught furnish room except void and vacancy. Therefore beside void and bodies no third nature taken by itself can be left in the number of things, either such as to fall at any time under the ken of our senses or such as any one can grasp by the reason of his mind.

For whatever things are named, you will either find to be properties linked to these two things or you will see to be accidents of these things. That is a property which can in no case be disjoined and separated without utter destruction accompanying the severance, such as the weight of a stone, the heat of fire, the fluidity of water. Slavery on the other hand, poverty and riches, liberty, war, concord, and all other things which may come and go while the nature of the thing remains unharmed, these we are wont, as it is right we should, to call accidents. Time also exists not by itself, but simply from the things which happen the sense apprehends what has been done in time past, as well as what is present and what is to follow after. And we must admit that no one feels time by itself abstracted from the motion and calm rest of things.

• • •

Bodies again are partly first-beginnings of things, partly those which are formed of a union of first-beginnings. But those which are first-beginnings of things no force can quench: they are sure to have the better by their solid body. Although it seems difficult to believe that aught can be found among things with a solid body. For the lightning of heaven passes through the walls of houses, as well as noise and voices; iron grows red-hot in the fire and stones burn with fierce heat and burst asunder; the hardness of gold is broken up and dissolved by heat; the ice of brass melts vanquished by the flame; warmth and piercing cold ooze through silver, since we have felt both, as we held cups with the hand in due fashion and the water was poured down into them. So universally there is found to be nothing solid in things. But yet because true reason and the nature of things constrains, attend until we make clear in a few verses that there are such things as consist of solid and everlasting body, which we teach are seeds of things and first-beginnings, out of which the whole sum of things which now exists has been produced.

First of all then since there has been found to exist a two-fold and widely dissimilar nature of two things, that is to say of body and of place in which things severally go on, each of the two must exist for and by itself and quite unmixed. For wherever there is empty space which we call void, there body is not; wherever again body maintains itself, there empty void no wise exists. First bodies therefore are solid and without void. Again since there is void in things begotten, solid matter must exist about this void, and no thing can be proved by true reason to conceal in its body and have within it void, unless you choose to allow that that which holds it in is solid. Again that can be nothing but a union of matter which can keep in the void of things. Matter therefore, which consists of a solid body, may be everlasting, though all things else are dissolved. Moreover if there were no empty void, the universe would be solid; unless on the other hand there were certain bodies to fill up whatever places they occupied, the existing universe would be empty and void space. Therefore sure enough body and void are marked off in alternate layers, since the universe is neither of a perfect fullness nor a perfect void. There are therefore certain bodies which can vary void space with full. These can neither be broken in pieces by the stroke of blows from without nor have their texture undone by aught piercing to their core nor give way before any other kind of assault; as we have proved to you a little before. For without void nothing seems to admit of being crushed in or broken up or split in two by cutting, or of taking in wet or permeating cold or penetrating fire, by which all things are destroyed. And the more anything contains within it of void, the more thoroughly it gives way to the assault of these things. Therefore if first bodies are as I have shown solid and without void, they must be everlasting. Again unless matter had been eternal, all things before this would have utterly returned to nothing and whatever things we see would have been born anew from nothing. But since I have proved above that nothing can be produced from nothing, and that what is begotten cannot be recalled to nothing, first-beginnings must be of an imperishable body into which all things can be dissolved at their last hour, that there may be a supply of matter for the reproduction of things. Therefore first-beginnings are of solid singleness, and in no other way can they have been preserved through ages during infinite time past in order to reproduce things.

Again if nature had set no limit to the breaking of things, by this time the bodies of matter would have been so far reduced by the breaking of past ages that nothing could within a fixed time be conceived out of them and reach its utmost growth of being. For we see that anything is more quickly destroyed than again renewed; and therefore that which the long, the infinite duration of all bygone time had broken up demolished and destroyed, could never be reproduced in all remaining time. But now sure enough a fixed limit to their breaking has been set, since we see each thing renewed, and at the same time definite periods fixed for things each after its kind to reach the flower of their age. Moreover while the bodies of matter are most solid, it may yet be explained in what way all things which are formed soft, as air, water, earth, fires, are so formed and by what force they severally go on, since once for all there is void mixed up in things. But on the other hand if the first-beginnings of things be soft, it cannot be explained out of what enduring basalt and iron can be produced; for their whole nature will utterly lack a first foundation to begin with.

First-beginnings therefore are strong in solid singleness, and by a denser combination of these all things can be closely packed and exhibit enduring strength.

•••

But since I have taught that most solid bodies of matter fly about for ever unvanquished through all time, mark now, let us unfold whether there is or is not any limit to their sum; likewise let us clearly see whether that which has been found to be void, or room and space, in which things severally go on, is all of it altogether finite or stretches without limits and to an unfathomable depth.

Well then the existing universe is bounded in none of its dimensions; for then it must have had an outside. Again it is seen that there can be an outside of nothing, unless there be something beyond to bound it, so that that is seen, farther than which the nature of this our sense does not follow the thing. Now since we must admit that there is nothing outside the sum, it has no outside, and therefore is without end and limit. And it matters not in which of its regions you take your stand; so invariably, whatever position any one has taken up, he leaves the universe just as infinite as before in all directions. Again if for the moment all existing space be held to be bounded, supposing a man runs forward to its outside borders, and stands on the utmost verge and then throws a winged javelin, do you choose that when hurled with vigorous force it shall advance to the point to which it has been sent and fly to a distance, or do you decide that something can get in its way and stop it? for you must admit and adopt one of the two suppositions; either of which shuts you out from all escape and compels you to grant that the universe stretches without end. For whether there is something to get in its way and prevent its coming whither it was sent and placing itself in the point intended, or whether it is carried forward, in either case it has not started from the end. In this way I will go on and, wherever you have placed the outside borders, I will ask what then becomes of the javelin. The result will be that an end can nowhere be fixed, and that the room given for flight will still prolong the power of flight. Lastly one thing is seen by the eyes to end another thing; air bounds off hills, and mountains air, earth limits sea and sea again all lands; the universe however there is nothing outside to end.

Again if all the space of the whole sum were enclosed within fixed borders and were bounded, in that case the store of matter by its solid weights would have streamed together from all sides to the lowest point nor could anything have gone on under the canopy of heaven, no nor would there have been a heaven nor sunlight at all, inasmuch as all matter, settling down through infinite time past, would lie together in a heap. But as it is, sure enough no rest is given to the bodies of the first-beginnings, because there is no lowest point at all, to which they might stream together as it were, and where they might take up their positions. All things are ever going on in ceaseless motion on all sides and bodies of matter stirred to action are supplied from beneath out of infinite space. Therefore the nature of room and the space of the unfathomable void are such as bright thunderbolts cannot race through in their course though gliding on through endless tract of time, no nor lessen one jot the journey that remains to go by all their travel: so huge a room is spread out on all sides for things without any bounds in all directions round.

Again nature keeps the sum of things from setting any limit to itself, since she compels body to be ended by void and void in turn by body, so that either she thus renders the universe infinite by this alternation of the two, or else the one of the two, in case the other does not bound it, with its single nature stretches nevertheless immeasurably. But void I have already proved to be infinite; therefore matter must be infinite: for if void were infinite, and matter finite[7] neither sea nor earth nor the glittering quarters of heaven nor mortal kind nor the holy bodies of the gods could hold their ground one brief passing hour; since forced asunder from its union the store of matter would be dissolved and borne along the mighty void, or rather I should say would never have combined to produce any thing, since scattered abroad it could never have been brought together. For verily not by design did the first-beginnings of things station themselves each in its right place guided by keen intelligence, nor did they bargain sooth to say what motions each should assume, but because many in number and shifting about in many ways throughout the universe they are driven and tormented by blows during infinite time past, after trying motions and unions of every kind at length they fall into arrangements such as those out of which this our sum of things has been formed, and by which too it is preserved through many great years when once it has been thrown into the appropriate motions, and causes the streams to replenish the greedy sea with copious river waters and the earth, fostered by the heat of the sun, to renew its produce, and the race of living things to come up and flourish, and the gliding fires of ether to live: all which these several things could in no wise bring to pass, unless a store of matter could rise up from infinite space, out of which store they are wont to make up in due season whatever has been lost. For as the nature of living things when robbed of food loses its substance and wastes away, thus all things must be broken up, as soon as matter has ceased to be supplied, diverted in any way from its proper course. Nor can blows from without hold together all the sum which has been brought into union. They can, it is true, frequently strike upon and stay a part, until others come and the sum can be completed. At times however they are compelled to rebound and in so doing grant to the first-beginnings of things room and time for flight, to enable them to get clear away from the mass in union. Wherefore again and again I repeat many bodies must rise up; nay for the blows themselves not to fail, there is need of an infinite supply of matter on all sides.

DISCUSSION QUESTIONS

1. The view you find in Lucretius seems to imply that the universe is explainable. This goes against the Taoist view that you cannot talk about it. Which view makes more sense to you? Why? Explain.

2. Plato rejected the view of the ancient atomists. Based on the Plato selections you have read, why might he have done this? Explain.

3. Explain Lucretius's argument for the position that all there is consists of atoms and void.

The Monadology

By Gottfried Wilhelm Leibniz
Translated by Robert Latta

Gottfried Wilhelm Leibniz (1646–1716), was a mathematician, logician, scientist, diplomat, and philosopher. Along with Sir Isaac Newton (1643–1727), he is credited with independently inventing the calculus. Leibniz, like Descartes, was a rationalist. Leibniz did not accept Descartes' pineal gland solution to the interaction problem. Leibniz is also well known for ideas contained in his 1710 book Theodicy. *In* Theodicy, *Leibniz argues that this is the best of all possible worlds and that the origin of evil comes in with human freedom, not from God. The word "theodicy" is now the term used to describe an attempt to explain how evil is possible if God is all-good (omnibenevolent), all-powerful (omnipotent), and all-knowing (omniscient). Leibniz's view is often called Optimism. It is this view that is being parodied in the short novel* Candide *by Voltaire (1694–1778). We will read a short fiction by Voltaire in Part IV of* Four Fundamental Questions.

Monadology *is a short paper from late in Leibniz's life, and was completed in 1714, but not published until 1720. In many ways, it is a summary, with arguments, of his main philosophical ideas. It contains his view of the self, his view on knowledge (which we will talk about in relation to Hume and Kant in Part III of* Four Fundamental Questions*), his proof for God's existence, and his theodicy. His view of reality, as expressed in the* Monadology*, is a kind of atomism. Leibniz's atoms, though, are not material. He calls them "monads" and they are simple substances. He gets around the mind/body problem of Descartes by denying that the monads interact at all.*

---

1. The Monad, of which we shall here speak, is nothing but a simple substance, which enters into compounds. By 'simple' is meant 'without parts.'

2. And there must be simple substances, since there are compounds; for a compound is nothing but a collection or aggregatum of simple things.

3. Now where there are no parts, there can be neither extension nor form [figure] nor divisibility. These Monads are the real atoms of nature and, in a word, the elements of things.

4. No dissolution of these elements need be feared, and there is no conceivable way in which a simple substance can be destroyed by natural means.

5. For the same reason there is no conceivable way in which a simple substance can come into being by natural means, since it cannot be formed by the combination of parts [composition].

6. Thus it may be said that a Monad can only come into being or come to an end all at once; that is to say, it can come into being only by creation and come to an end only by annihilation, while that which is compound comes into being or comes to an end by parts.

7. Further, there is no way of explaining how a Monad can be altered in quality or internally changed by any other created thing; since it is impossible to change the place of anything in it or to conceive in it any internal motion which could be produced, directed, increased or diminished therein, although all this is possible in the case of compounds, in which there are changes among the parts. The Monads have no windows, through which anything could come in or go out. Accidents cannot separate themselves from substances nor go about outside of them, as the 'sensible species' of the Scholastics used to do. Thus neither substance nor accident can come into a Monad from outside.

8. Yet the Monads must have some qualities, otherwise they would not even be existing things. And if simple substances did not differ in quality, there would be absolutely no means of perceiving any change in things. For what is in the compound can come only from the simple elements it contains, and the Monads, if they had no qualities, would be indistinguishable from one another, since they do not differ in quantity. Consequently, space being a plenum, each part of space would always receive, in any motion, exactly the equivalent of what it already had, and no one state of things would be discernible from another.

9. Indeed, each Monad must be different from every other. For in nature there are never two beings which are perfectly alike and in which it is not possible to find an internal difference, or at least a difference founded upon an intrinsic quality [denomination].

10. I assume also as admitted that every created being, and consequently the created Monad, is subject to change, and further that this change is continuous in each.

11. It follows from what has just been said, that the natural changes of the Monads come from an internal principle, since an external cause can have no influence upon their inner being.

12. But, besides the principle of the change, there must be a particular series of changes [*un detail de ce qui change*], which constitutes, so to speak, the specific nature and variety of the simple substances.

13. This particular series of changes should involve a multiplicity in the unit [*unite*] or in that which is simple. For, as every natural change takes place gradually, something changes and something remains unchanged; and consequently a simple substance must be affected and related in many ways, although it has no parts.

14. The passing condition, which involves and represents a multiplicity in the unit [*unite*] or in the simple substance, is nothing but what is called Perception, which is to be distinguished from Apperception or Consciousness, as will afterwards appear. In this matter the Cartesian view is extremely defective, for it treats as non-existent those perceptions of which we are not consciously aware. This has also led them to believe that minds [*esprits*] alone are Monads, and that there are no souls of animals nor other Entelechies. Thus, like the crowd, they have failed to distinguish between a prolonged unconsciousness and absolute death, which has made them fall again into the Scholastic prejudice of souls entirely separate [from bodies], and has even confirmed ill-balanced minds in the opinion that souls are mortal.

15. The activity of the internal principle which produces change or passage from one perception to another may be called Appetition. It is true that desire [*l'appetit*] cannot always fully attain to the whole perception at which it aims, but it always obtains some of it and attains to new perceptions.

16. We have in ourselves experience of a multiplicity in simple substance, when we find that the least thought of which we are conscious involves variety in its object. Thus all those who admit that the soul is a simple substance should admit this multiplicity in the Monad; and M. Bayle ought not to have found any difficulty in this, as he has done in his Dictionary, article 'Rorarius.'

17. Moreover, it must be confessed that perception and that which depends upon it are inexplicable on mechanical grounds, that is to say, by means of figures and motions. And supposing there were a machine, so constructed as to think, feel, and have perception, it might be conceived as increased in size, while keeping the same proportions, so that one might go into it as into a mill. That being so, we should, on examining its interior, find only parts which work one upon another, and never anything by which to explain a perception. Thus it is in a simple substance, and not in a compound or in a machine, that perception must be sought for. Further, nothing but this (namely, perceptions and their changes) can be found in a simple substance. It is also in this alone that all the internal activities of simple substances can consist.

18. All simple substances or created Monads might be called Entelechies, for they have in them a certain perfection (*echousi to enteles*); they have a certain self-sufficiency (*autarkeia*) which makes them the sources of their internal activities and, so to speak, incorporeal automata.

19. If we are to give the name of Soul to everything which has perceptions and desires [*appetits*] in the general sense which I have explained, then all simple substances or created Monads might be called souls; but as feeling [le sentiment] is something more than a bare perception, I think it right that the general name of Monads or Entelechies should suffice for simple substances which have perception only, and that the name of Souls should be given only to those in which perception is more distinct, and is accompanied by memory.

20. For we experience in ourselves a condition in which we remember nothing and have no distinguishable perception; as when we fall into a swoon or when we are overcome with a profound dreamless sleep. In this state the soul does not perceptibly differ from a bare Monad; but as this state is not lasting, and the soul comes out of it, the soul is something more than a bare Monad.

21. And it does not follow that in this state the simple substance is without any perception. That, indeed, cannot be, for the reasons already given; for it cannot perish, and it cannot continue to exist without being affected in some way, and this affection is nothing but its perception. But when there is a great multitude of little perceptions, in which there is nothing distinct, one is stunned; as when one turns continuously round in the same way several times in succession, whence comes a giddiness which may make us swoon, and which keeps us from distinguishing anything. Death can for a time put animals into this condition.

22. And as every present state of a simple substance is naturally a consequence of its preceding state, in such a way that its present is big with its future;

23. And as, on waking from stupor, we are conscious of our perceptions, we must have had perceptions immediately before we awoke, although we were not at all conscious of them; for one perception can in a natural way come only from another perception, as a motion can in a natural way come only from a motion.

24. It thus appears that if we had in our perceptions nothing marked and, so to speak, striking and highly-flavoured, we should always be in a state of stupor. And this is the state in which the bare Monads are.

25. We see also that nature has given heightened perceptions to animals, from the care she has taken to provide them with organs, which collect numerous rays of light, or numerous undulations of the air, in order, by uniting them, to make them have greater effect. Something similar to this takes place in smell, in taste and in touch, and perhaps in a number of other senses, which are unknown to us. And I will explain presently how that which takes place in the soul represents what happens in the bodily organs.

26. Memory provides the soul with a kind of consecutiveness, which resembles [imite] reason, but which is to be distinguished from it. Thus we see that when animals have a perception of something which strikes them and of which they have formerly had a similar perception, they are led, by means of representation in their memory, to expect what was combined with the thing in this previous perception, and they come to have feelings similar to those they had on the former occasion. For instance, when a stick is shown to dogs, they remember the pain it has caused them, and howl and run away.

27. And the strength of the mental image which impresses and moves them comes either from the magnitude or the number of the preceding perceptions. For often a strong impression produces all at once the same effect as a long-formed habit, or as many and oft-repeated ordinary perceptions.

28. In so far as the concatenation of their perceptions is due to the principle of memory alone, men act like the lower animals, resembling the empirical physicians, whose methods are those of mere practice without theory. Indeed, in three-fourths of our actions we are nothing but empirics. For instance, when we expect that there will be daylight to-morrow, we do so empirically, because it has always so happened until now. It is only the astronomer who thinks it on rational grounds.

29. But it is the knowledge of necessary and eternal truths that distinguishes us from the mere animals and gives us Reason and the sciences, raising us to the knowledge of ourselves and of God. And it is this in us that is called the rational soul or mind [*esprit*].

30. It is also through the knowledge of necessary truths, and through their abstract expression, that we rise to acts of reflexion, which make us think of what is called I, and observe that this or that is within us: and thus, thinking of ourselves, we think of being, of substance, of the simple and the compound, of the immaterial, and of God Himself, conceiving that what is limited in us is in Him without limits. And these acts of reflexion furnish the chief objects of our reasonings.

31. Our reasonings are grounded upon two great principles, that of contradiction, in virtue of which we judge false that which involves a contradiction, and true that which is opposed or contradictory to the false;

32. And that of sufficient reason, in virtue of which we hold that there can be no fact real or existing, no statement true, unless there be a sufficient reason, why it should be so and not otherwise, although these reasons usually cannot be known by us.

33. There are also two kinds of truths, those of reasoning and those of fact. Truths of reasoning are necessary and their opposite is impossible: truths of fact are contingent and their opposite is possible. When a truth is necessary, its reason can be found by analysis, resolving it into more simple ideas and truths, until we come to those which are primary.

34. It is thus that in Mathematics speculative Theorems and practical Canons are reduced by analysis to Definitions, Axioms and Postulates.

35. In short, there are simple ideas, of which no definition can be given; there are also axioms and postulates, in a word, primary principles, which cannot be proved, and indeed have no need of proof; and these are identical propositions, whose opposite involves an express contradiction.

36. But there must also be a sufficient reason for contingent truths or truths of fact, that is to say, for the sequence or connexion of the things which are dispersed throughout the universe of created beings, in which the analyzing into particular reasons might go on into endless detail, because of the immense variety of things in nature and the infinite division of bodies. There is an infinity of present and past forms and motions which go to make up the efficient cause of my present writing; and there is an infinity of minute tendencies and dispositions of my soul, which go to make its final cause.

37. And as all this detail again involves other prior or more detailed contingent things, each of which still needs a similar analysis to yield its reason, we are no further forward: and the sufficient or final reason must be outside of the sequence or series of particular contingent things, however infinite this series may be.

38. Thus the final reason of things must be in a necessary substance, in which the variety of particular changes exists only eminently, as in its source; and this substance we call God.

39. Now as this substance is a sufficient reason of all this variety of particulars, which are also connected together throughout; there is only one God, and this God is sufficient.

40. We may also hold that this supreme substance, which is unique, universal and necessary, nothing outside of it being independent of it,—this substance, which is a pure sequence of possible being, must be illimitable and must contain as much reality as is possible.

41. Whence it follows that God is absolutely perfect; for perfection is nothing but amount of positive reality, in the strict sense, leaving out of account the limits or bounds in things which are limited. And where there are no bounds, that is to say in God, perfection is absolutely infinite.

42. It follows also that created beings derive their perfections from the influence of God, but that their imperfections come from their own nature, which is incapable of being without limits. For it is in this that they differ from God. An instance of this original imperfection of created beings may be seen in the natural inertia of bodies.

43. It is farther true that in God there is not only the source of existences but also that of essences, in so far as they are real, that is to say, the source of what is real in the possible. For the understanding of God is the region of eternal truths or of the ideas on which they depend, and without Him there would be nothing real in the possibilities of things, and not only would there be nothing in existence, but nothing would even be possible.

44. For if there is a reality in essences or possibilities, or rather in eternal truths, this reality must needs be founded in something existing and actual, and consequently in the existence of the necessary Being, in whom essence involves existence, or in whom to be possible is to be actual.

45. Thus God alone (or the necessary Being) has this prerogative that He must necessarily exist, if He is possible. And as nothing can interfere with the possibility of that which involves no limits, no negation and consequently no contradiction, this [His possibility] is sufficient of itself to make known the existence of God *a priori*. We have thus proved it, through the reality of eternal truths. But a little while ago we proved it also a posteriori, since there exist contingent beings, which can have their final or sufficient reason only in the necessary Being, which has the reason of its existence in itself.

• • •

47. Thus God alone is the primary unity or original simple substance, of which all created or derivative Monads are products and have their birth, so to speak, through continual fulgurations of the Divinity from moment to moment, limited by the receptivity of the created being, of whose essence it is to have limits.

48. In God there is Power, which is the source of all, also Knowledge, whose content is the variety of the ideas, and finally Will, which makes changes or products according to the principle of the best. These characteristics correspond to what in the created Monads forms the ground or basis, to the faculty of Perception and to the faculty of Appetition. But in God these attributes are absolutely infinite or perfect; and in the created Monads or the Entelechies (or *perfectihabiae*, as Hermolaus Barbarus translated the word) there are only imitations of these attributes, according to the degree of perfection of the Monad.

49. A created thing is said to act outwardly in so far as it has perfection, and to suffer [or be passive, *patir*] in relation to another, in so far as it is imperfect. Thus activity [action] is attributed to a Monad, in so far as it has distinct perceptions, and passivity [passion] in so far as its perceptions are confused.

50. And one created thing is more perfect than another, in this, that there is found in the more perfect that which serves to explain *a priori* what takes place in the less perfect, and it is on this account that the former is said to act upon the latter.

51. But in simple substances the influence of one Monad upon another is only ideal, and it can have its effect only through the mediation of God, in so far as in the ideas of God any Monad rightly claims that God, in regulating the others from the beginning of things, should have regard to it. For since one created Monad cannot have any physical influence upon the inner being of another, it is only by this means that the one can be dependent upon the other.

52. Accordingly, among created things, activities and passivities are mutual. For God, comparing two simple substances, finds in each reasons which oblige Him to adapt the other to it, and consequently what is active in certain respects is passive from another point of view; active in so far as what we distinctly know in it serves to explain [*rendre raison de*] what takes place in another, and passive in so far as the explanation [*raison*] of what takes place in it is to be found in that which is distinctly known in another.

53. Now, as in the Ideas of God there is an infinite number of possible universes, and as only one of them can be actual, there must be a sufficient reason for the choice of God, which leads Him to decide upon one rather than another.

54. And this reason can be found only in the fitness [*convenance*], or in the degrees of perfection, that these worlds possess, since each possible thing has the right to aspire to existence in proportion to the amount of perfection it contains in germ.

55. Thus the actual existence of the best that wisdom makes known to God is due to this, that His goodness makes Him choose it, and His power makes Him produce it.

56. Now this connexion or adaptation of all created things to each and of each to all, means that each simple substance has relations which express all the others, and, consequently, that it is a perpetual living mirror of the universe.

57. And as the same town, looked at from various sides, appears quite different and becomes as it were numerous in aspects [*perspectivement*]; even so, as a result of the infinite number of simple substances, it is as if there were so many different universes, which, nevertheless are nothing but aspects [*perspectives*] of a single universe, according to the special point of view of each Monad.

58. And by this means there is obtained as great variety as possible, along with the greatest possible order; that is to say, it is the way to get as much perfection as possible.

59. Besides, no hypothesis but this (which I venture to call proved) fittingly exalts the greatness of God; and this Monsieur Bayle recognized when, in his Dictionary (article Rorarius), he raised objections to it, in which indeed he was inclined to think that I was attributing too much to God—more than it is possible to attribute. But he was unable to give any reason which could show the impossibility of this universal harmony, according to which every substance exactly expresses all others through the relations it has with them.

60. Further, in what I have just said there may be seen the reasons *a priori* why things could not be otherwise than they are. For God in regulating the whole has had regard to each part, and in particular to each Monad, whose nature being to represent, nothing can confine it to the representing of only one part of things; though it is true that this

representation is merely confused as regards the variety of particular things [*le detail*] in the whole universe, and can be distinct only as regards a small part of things, namely, those which are either nearest or greatest in relation to each of the Monads; otherwise each Monad would be a deity. It is not as regards their object, but as regards the different ways in which they have knowledge of their object, that the Monads are limited. In a confused way they all strive after [*vont a*] the infinite, the whole; but they are limited and differentiated through the degrees of their distinct perceptions.

61. And compounds are in this respect analogous with [*symbolisent avec*] simple substances. For all is a plenum (and thus all matter is connected together) and in the plenum every motion has an effect upon distant bodies in proportion to their distance, so that each body not only is affected by those which are in contact with it and in some way feels the effect of everything that happens to them, but also is mediately affected by bodies adjoining those with which it itself is in immediate contact. Wherefore it follows that this inter-communication of things extends to any distance, however great. And consequently every body feels the effect of all that takes place in the universe, so that he who sees all might read in each what is happening everywhere, and even what has happened or shall happen, observing in the present that which is far off as well in time as in place: sympnoia panta, as Hippocrates said. But a soul can read in itself only that which is there represented distinctly; it cannot all at once unroll everything that is enfolded in it, for its complexity is infinite.

62. Thus, although each created Monad represents the whole universe, it represents more distinctly the body which specially pertains to it, and of which it is the entelechy; and as this body expresses the whole universe through the connexion of all matter in the plenum, the soul also represents the whole universe in representing this body, which belongs to it in a special way.

63. The body belonging to a Monad (which is its entelechy or its soul) constitutes along with the entelechy what may be called a living being, and along with the soul what is called an animal. Now this body of living being or of an animal is always organic; for, as every Monad is, in its own way, a mirror of the universe, and as the universe is ruled according to a perfect order, there must also be order in that which represents it, i.e. in the perceptions of the soul, and consequently there must be order in the body, through which the universe is represented in the soul.

64. Thus the organic body of each living being is a kind of divine machine or natural automaton, which infinitely surpasses all artificial automata. For a machine made by the skill of man is not a machine in each of its parts. For instance, the tooth of a brass wheel has parts or fragments which for us are not artificial products, and which do not have the special characteristics of the machine, for they give no indication of the use for which the wheel was intended. But the machines of nature, namely, living bodies, are still machines in their smallest parts *ad infinitum.* It is this that constitutes the difference between nature and art, that is to say, between the divine art and ours.

65. And the Author of nature has been able to employ this divine and infinitely wonderful power of art, because each portion of matter is not only infinitely divisible, as the ancients observed, but is also actually subdivided without end, each part

into further parts, of which each has some motion of its own; otherwise it would be impossible for each portion of matter to express the whole universe.

66. Whence it appears that in the smallest particle of matter there is a world of creatures, living beings, animals, entelechies, souls.

67. Each portion of matter may be conceived as like a garden full of plants and like a pond full of fishes. But each branch of every plant, each member of every animal, each drop of its liquid parts is also some such garden or pond.

68. And though the earth and the air which are between the plants of the garden, or the water which is between the fish of the pond, be neither plant nor fish; yet they also contain plants and fishes, but mostly so minute as to be imperceptible to us.

69. Thus there is nothing fallow, nothing sterile, nothing dead in the universe, no chaos, no confusion save in appearance, somewhat as it might appear to be in a pond at a distance, in which one would see a confused movement and, as it were, a swarming of fish in the pond, without separately distinguishing the fish themselves.

70. Hence it appears that each living body has a dominant entelechy, which in an animal is the soul; but the members of this living body are full of other living beings, plants, animals, each of which has also its dominant entelechy or soul.

71. But it must not be imagined, as has been done by some who have misunderstood my thought, that each soul has a quantity or portion of matter belonging exclusively to itself or attached to it for ever, and that it consequently owns other inferior living beings, which are devoted for ever to its service. For all bodies are in a perpetual flux like rivers, and parts are entering into them and passing out of them continually.

72. Thus the soul changes its body only by degrees, little by little, so that it is never all at once deprived of all its organs; and there is often metamorphosis in animals, but never metempsychosis or transmigration of souls; nor are there souls entirely separate [from bodies] nor unembodied spirits [*genies sans corps*]. God alone is completely without body.

73. It also follows from this that there never is absolute birth [generation] nor complete death, in the strict sense, consisting in the separation of the soul from the body. What we call births [generations] are developments and growths, while what we call deaths are envelopments and diminutions.

74. Philosophers have been much perplexed about the origin of forms, entelechies, or souls; but nowadays it has become known, through careful studies of plants, insects, and animals, that the organic bodies of nature are never products of chaos or putrefaction, but always come from seeds, in which there was undoubtedly some preformation; and it is held that not only the organic body was already there before conception, but also a soul in this body, and, in short, the animal itself; and that by means of conception this animal has merely been prepared for the great transformation involved in its becoming an animal of another kind. Something like this is indeed seen apart from birth [generation], as when worms become flies and caterpillars become butterflies.

75. The animals, of which some are raised by means of conception to the rank of larger animals, may be called spermatic, but those among them which are not so raised but remain in their own kind (that is, the majority) are born, multiply, and are destroyed like the large animals, and it is only a few chosen ones [elus] that pass to a greater theatre.

76. But this is only half of the truth, and accordingly I hold that if an animal never comes into being by natural means [*naturellement*], no more does it come to an end by natural means; and that not only will there be no birth [generation], but also no complete destruction or death in the strict sense. And these reasonings, made a posteriori and drawn from experience are in perfect agreement with my principles deduced *a priori*, as above.

77. Thus it may be said that not only the soul (mirror of an indestructible universe) is indestructible, but also the animal itself, though its mechanism [machine] may often perish in part and take off or put on an organic slough [*des depouilles organiques*].

78. These principles have given me a way of explaining naturally the union or rather the mutual agreement [*conformite*] of the soul and the organic body. The soul follows its own laws, and the body likewise follows its own laws; and they agree with each other in virtue of the pre-established harmony between all substances, since they are all representations of one and the same universe.

79. Souls act according to the laws of final causes through appetitions, ends, and means. Bodies act according to the laws of efficient causes or motions. And the two realms, that of efficient causes and that of final causes, are in harmony with one another.

80. Descartes recognized that souls cannot impart any force to bodies, because there is always the same quantity of force in matter. Nevertheless he was of opinion that the soul could change the direction of bodies. But that is because in his time it was not known that there is a law of nature which affirms also the conservation of the same total direction in matter. Had Descartes noticed this he would have come upon my system of pre-established harmony.

81. According to this system bodies act as if (to suppose the impossible) there were no souls, and souls act as if there were no bodies, and both act as if each influenced the other.

82. As regards minds [*esprits*] or rational souls, though I find that what I have just been saying is true of all living beings and animals (namely that animals and souls come into being when the world begins and no more come to an end that the world does), yet there is this peculiarity in rational animals, that their spermatic animalcules, so long as they are only spermatic, have merely ordinary or sensuous [sensitive] souls; but when those which are chosen [*elus*], so to speak, attain to human nature through an actual conception, their sensuous souls are raised to the rank of reason and to the prerogative of minds [*esprits*].

83. Among other differences which exist between ordinary souls and minds [*esprits*], some of which differences I have already noted, there is also this: that souls in general are living mirrors or images of the universe of created things, but

that minds are also images of the Deity or Author of nature Himself, capable of knowing the system of the universe, and to some extent of imitating it through architectonic ensamples [*echantillons*], each mind being like a small divinity in its own sphere.

84. It is this that enables spirits [or minds—*esprits*] to enter into a kind of fellowship with God, and brings it about that in relation to them He is not only what an inventor is to his machine (which is the relation of God to other created things), but also what a prince is to his subjects, and, indeed, what a father is to his children.

85. Whence it is easy to conclude that the totality [assemblage] of all spirits [*esprits*] must compose the City of God, that is to say, the most perfect State that is possible, under the most perfect of Monarchs.

86. This City of God, this truly universal monarchy, is a moral world in the natural world, and is the most exalted and most divine among the works of God; and it is in it that the glory of God really consists, for He would have no glory were not His greatness and His goodness known and admired by spirits [*esprits*]. It is also in relation to this divine City that God specially has goodness, while His wisdom and His power are manifested everywhere.

87. As we have shown above that there is a perfect harmony between the two realms in nature, one of efficient, and the other of final causes, we should here notice also another harmony between the physical realm of nature and the moral realm of grace, that is to say, between God, considered as Architect of the mechanism [machine] of the universe and God considered as Monarch of the divine City of spirits [*esprits*].

88. A result of this harmony is that things lead to grace by the very ways of nature, and that this globe, for instance, must be destroyed and renewed by natural means at the very time when the government of spirits requires it, for the punishment of some and the reward of others.

89. It may also be said that God as Architect satisfies in all respects God as Lawgiver, and thus that sins must bear their penalty with them, through the order of nature, and even in virtue of the mechanical structure of things; and similarly that noble actions will attain their rewards by ways which, on the bodily side, are mechanical, although this cannot and ought not always to happen immediately.

90. Finally, under this perfect government no good action would be unrewarded and no bad one unpunished, and all should issue in the well-being of the good, that is to say, of those who are not malcontents in this great state, but who trust in Providence, after having done their duty, and who love and imitate, as is meet, the Author of all good, finding pleasure in the contemplation of His perfections, as is the way of genuine 'pure love,' which takes pleasure in the happiness of the beloved. This it is which leads wise and virtuous people to devote their energies to everything which appears in harmony with the presumptive or antecedent will of God, and yet makes them content with what God actually brings to pass by His secret, consequent and positive [decisive] will, recognizing that if we could sufficiently understand the order of the universe, we should find that it exceeds all the desires of the wisest men,

and that it is impossible to make it better than it is, not only as a whole and in general but also for ourselves in particular, if we are attached, as we ought to be, to the Author of all, not only as to the architect and efficient cause of our being, but as to our master and to the final cause, which ought to be the whole aim of our will, and which can alone make our happiness.

THE END

DISCUSSION QUESTIONS

1. Compare the atomisms of Lucretius and Leibniz. Which view do you think is better argued? Why? Explain.

2. Explain Leibniz's argument for the position that the monads must have all come into existence at once.

3. How does his view of monads function as a premise in his argument for God's existence? Explain.

The Gay Science

By Friedrich Nietzsche

Friedrich Nietzsche (1844–1900) was a philosopher whose writings were all published in the 19th century, but whose influence became great only in the 20th. It is difficult to assess what Nietzsche's philosophy is, because he eschewed the great systems of other 19th century writers like Immanuel Kant (1724–1804), Georg Wilhelm Friedrich Hegel (1770–1831), and Arthur Schopenhauer (1788–1860). He was much influenced by Schopenhauer in his early years, but ultimately rejected Schopenhauer's ideas as too pessimistic, since they called for a denial of the will. Nietzsche instead called for an affirmation of the will, as can be seen in the Nietzsche selection found in Part IV of Four Fundamental Questions. *Nietzsche's writings become increasingly more aphoristic over time. Aphorisms are little nuggetlike thoughts. The early writings are more essaylike. There is no attempt at achieving the internal consistency found in the system-building philosophies of his predecessors.*

The selection here from Nietzsche is three paragraphs, §276, §285, and §341, from his 1882 book The Gay Science. *The title is a reference to the* gaia scienza, *a term in the language Provençal, which referred to the unity of poetry and free spirit in troubadour knights. In fact, there is an appendix of poetry at the end of the book. These selections introduce a few concepts that might make us think differently about reality. In §276 he uses the phrase* cogito, ergo sum, *the phrase coined by Descartes, which means "I think, therefore I am." The other important concept here is* amor fati, *which means love your fate. In §285, we see the introduction of the phrase "eternal recurrence," the idea that history, or time itself, repeats. The most famous passage of the three is §341. Here, he uses the idea of eternal return as a thought experiment: how would you choose to act, if you knew you would repeat that action innumerable times? Many cultures have cyclical views of time, including some Native American tribes, Hindu philosophy, the ancient Greek Pythagoreans, and possibly the ancient Egyptians.*

BOOK IV
SANCTUS JANUARIUS

•••

276

For the New Year. I still live, I still think; I must still live, for I must still think. Sum, ergo cogito: *Cogito, ergo sum.* Today everyone takes the liberty of expressing his wish and his favorite thought: well, I also mean to tell what I have wished for myself today, and what thought first crossed my mind this year-a thought which ought to be the basis, the pledge and the sweetening of all my future life! I want more and more to perceive the necessary characters in things as the beautiful-I shall thus be one of those who beautify things. *Amor fati*: let that henceforth be my love! I do not want to wage war with the ugly. I do not want to accuse, I do not want even to accuse the accusers. Looking aside, let that be my sole negation! And all in all, to sum up: I wish to be at any time hereafter only a yea-sayer!

• • •

285

Excelsior. "Thou wilt never more pray, never more worship, never more repose in infinite trust-thou refusest to stand still and dismiss thy thoughts before an ultimate wisdom, an ultimate virtue, an ultimate power-thou hast no constant guardian and friend in thy seven solitudes-thou livest without the outlook on a mountain that has snow on its head and fire in its heart-there is no I longer any requiter for thee, nor any amender with his finishing touch-there is no longer any reason in that which happens, or any love in that which will happen to thee-there is no longer any resting place for thy weary heart, where it has only to find and no longer to seek, thou art opposed to any kind of ultimate peace, thou desirest the eternal recurrence of war and peace-man of renunciation, wilt thou renounce in all these things? Who will give thee the strength to do so? No one has yet had this strength!"—There is a lake which one day refused to flow away, and threw up a dam at the place where it had hitherto discharged: since then this lake has always risen higher and higher. Perhaps the very renunciation will also furnish us with the strength with which the renunciation itself can be borne; perhaps man will ever rise higher and higher from that point onward, when he no longer goes out into a God.

• • •

341

The Greatest Burden. What if a demon crept after thee into thy loneliest loneliness some day or night, and said to thee: "This life, as thou livest it at present, and hast lived it, thou must live it once more, and also innumerable times; and there will be nothing new in it, but every pain and every joy and every thought and every sigh, and all the unspeakably small and great in thy life must come to thee again, and all in the same series and sequence-and similarly this spider and this moonlight among the trees, and similarly this moment, and I myself. The eternal sand-glass of existence will ever be turned once more, and thou with it, thou speck of dust!"—Wouldst thou not throw thyself down and gnash thy teeth, and curse the demon that so spake? Or hast thou once experienced a tremendous moment in which thou wouldst answer him: "Thou art a God, and never did I hear anything so divine! "If that thought acquired power over thee as thou art, it would transform thee, and perhaps crush thee; the question with regard to all and everything: "Dost thou want this once more, and also for innumerable times?" would lie as the heaviest burden upon thy activity! Or, how wouldst thou have to become favorably inclined to thyself and to life, so as to long for nothing more ardently than for this last eternal sanctioning and sealing?

DISCUSSION QUESTIONS

1. What would it mean to put the idea of *amor fati* into action? Explain.

2. How would you respond to the thought experiment in §341? Why? Explain.

3. Compare the idea that we make ourselves through our actions as it is occurs here and in Sartre's lecture *Existentialism*.

An Introduction to Metaphysics

By Henri Bergson

Some philosophers are famous during their lifetimes and for perpetuity, like Plato or Kant. Others, like Hume and Nietzsche, reach the heights of popularity only after their deaths. Yet others are very popular while alive, and then have interest in their views wane after time. Henri Bergson (1859–1941) was a French philosopher who falls into this third category. Although interest has revived in his work recently, he was not studied as much in the first few decades following his death. He was popular enough to have been awarded the Nobel Prize for literature in 1927. Bergson's interests included biology, psychology, religion, physics, and humor. He was one of the first academics to write a scholarly book on humor; his book Laughter *was published in 1900 and influenced much of 20th century thought on the subject.*

Our selection is from An Introduction to Metaphysics, *a short book published in 1903. In this essay, Bergson makes a distinction between analysis and intuition as modes of acquiring knowledge. Analysis, the technique that is used in science, cannot yield a complete view of reality because it can only approach from the outside. Intuition, on the other hand, gets to the inside. For Bergson, only intuition can provide knowledge of reality. He rejects the kind of mechanistic explanations that were scientifically inspired. One of the key examples in the essay is the difference between clock time (which can be measured quantitatively through analysis) and lived time (which he calls "duration," and is qualitative, instead of quantitative). What is real, for Bergson, is more fluid than fixed.*

A comparison of the definitions of metaphysics and the various concepts of the absolute leads to the discovery that philosophers, in spite of their apparent divergencies, agree in distinguishing two profoundly different ways of knowing a thing. The first implies that we move round the object; the second, that we enter into it. The first depends on the point of view at which we are placed and on the symbols by which we express ourselves. The second neither depends on a point of view nor relies on any symbol. The first kind of knowledge may be said to stop at the *relative;* the second, in those cases where it is possible, to attain the *absolute.*

Consider, for example, the movement of an object in space. My perception of the motion will vary with the point of view, moving or stationary, from which I observe it. My expression of it will vary with the systems of axes, or the points of reference, to which I relate it; that is, with the symbols by which I translate it. For this double reason I call such motion *relative:* in the one case, as in the other, I am placed outside the object itself. But when I speak of an *absolute* movement, I am attributing to the moving object an interior and, so to speak, states of mind; I also imply that I am in sympathy with those states, and that I insert myself in them by an effort of imagination. Then, according as the object is moving or stationary, according as it adopts one movement or another, what I experience will vary. And what I experience will depend neither on the point of view I may take up in regard to the object, since I am inside the object itself, nor on the symbols by which I may translate the motion, since I have rejected all translations in order to possess the original. In short, I shall no longer grasp the movement from without, remaining where I am, but from where it is, from within, as it is in itself. I shall possess an absolute.

Consider, again, a character whose adventures are related to me in a novel. The author may multiply the traits of his hero's character, may make him speak and act as much as he pleases, but all this can never be equivalent to the simple and indivisible feeling which I should experience if I were able for an instant to identify myself with the person of the hero himself. Out of that indivisible feeling, as from a spring, all the words, gestures, and actions of the man would appear to me to flow naturally. They would no longer be accidents which, added to the idea I had already formed of the character, continually enriched that idea, without ever completing it. The character would be given to me all at once, in its entirety, and the thousand incidents which manifest it, instead of adding themselves to the idea and so enriching it, would seem to me, on the contrary, to detach themselves from it, without, however, exhausting it or impoverishing its essence. All the things I am told about the man provide me with so many points of view from which I can observe him. All the traits which describe him, and which can make him known to me only by so many comparisons with persons or things I know already, are signs by which he is expressed more or less symbolically. Symbols and points of view, therefore, place me outside him; they give me only what he has in common with others, and not what belongs to him and to him alone. But that which is properly himself, that which constitutes his essence, cannot be perceived from without, being internal by definition, nor be expressed by symbols, being incommensurable with everything else. Description, history, and analysis leave me here in the relative. Coincidence with the person himself would alone give me the absolute.

It is in this sense, and in this sense only, that *absolute* is synonymous with *perfection*. Were all the photographs of a town, taken from all possible points of view, to go on indefinitely completing one another, they would never be equivalent to the solid town in which we walk about. Were all the translations of a poem into all possible languages to add together their various shades of meaning and, correcting each other by a kind of mutual retouching, to give a more and more faithful image of the poem they translate, they would yet never succeed in rendering the inner meaning of the original. A representation taken from a certain point of view, a translation made with certain symbols, will always remain imperfect in comparison with the object of which a view has been taken, or which the symbols seek to express. But the absolute, which is the object and not its representation, the original and not its translation, is perfect, by being perfectly what it is.

It is doubtless for this reason that the *absolute* has often been identified with the *infinite*. Suppose that I wished to communicate to someone who did not know Greek the extraordinarily simple impression that a passage in Homer makes upon me; I should first give a translation of the lines, I should then comment on my translation, and then develop the commentary; in this way, by piling up explanation on explanation, I might approach nearer and nearer to what I wanted to express; but I should never quite reach it. When you raise your arm, you accomplish a movement of which you have, from within, a simple perception; but for me, watching it from the outside, your arm passes through one point, then through another, and between these two there will be still other points; so that, if I began to count, the operation would go on forever. Viewed from the inside, then, an absolute is a simple thing; but looked at from the outside, that is to say, relatively to other things, it becomes, in relation to these signs which express it, the gold coin for which we never seem able to finish giving small change. Now, that which lends itself at the same time both to an indivisible apprehension and to an inexhaustible enumeration is, by the very definition of the word, an infinite.

It follows from this that an absolute could only be given in an *intuition,* whilst everything else falls within the province of *analysis.* By intuition is meant the kind of *intellectual sympathy* by which one places oneself within an object in order to coincide with what is unique in it and consequently inexpressible. Analysis, on the contrary, is the operation which reduces the object to elements already known, that is, to elements common both to it and other objects. To analyze, therefore, is to express a thing as a function of something other than itself. All analysis is thus a translation, a development into symbols, a representation taken from successive points of view from which we note as many resemblances as possible between the new object which we are studying and others which we believe we know already. In its eternally unsatisfied desire to embrace the object around which it is compelled to turn, analysis multiplies without end the number of its points of view in order to complete its always incomplete representation, and ceaselessly varies its symbols that it may perfect the always imperfect translation. It goes on, therefore, to infinity. But intuition, if intuition is possible, is a simple act.

Now it is easy to see that the ordinary function of positive science is analysis. Positive science works, then, above all, with symbols. Even the most concrete of the natural sciences, those concerned with life, confine themselves to the visible form of living beings, their organs and anatomical elements. They make comparisons between these forms, they reduce the more complex to the more simple; in short, they study the workings of life in what is, so to speak, only its visual symbol. If there exists any means of possessing a reality absolutely instead of knowing it relatively, of placing oneself within it instead of looking at it from outside points of view, of having the intuition instead of making the analysis: in short, of seizing it without any expression, translation, or symbolic representation—metaphysics is that means. *Metaphysics, then, is the science which claims to dispense with symbols.*

There is one reality, at least, which we all seize from within, by intuition and not by simple analysis. It is our own personality in its flowing through time—our self which endures We may sympathize intellectually with nothing else, but we certainly sympathize with our own selves.

When I direct my attention inward to contemplate my own self (supposed for the moment to be inactive), I perceive at first, as a crust solidified on the surface, all the perceptions which come to it from the material world. These perceptions are clear, distinct, juxtaposed or juxtaposable one with another; they tend to group themselves into objects. Next, I notice the memories which more or less adhere to these perceptions and which serve to interpret them. These memories have been detached, as it were, from the depth of my personality, drawn to the surface by the perceptions which resemble them; they rest on the surface of my mind without being absolutely myself. Lastly, I feel the stir of tendencies and motor habits—a crowd of virtual actions, more or less firmly bound to these perceptions and memories. All these clearly defined elements appear more distinct from me, the more distinct they are from each other. Radiating, as they do, from within outwards, they form, collectively, the surface of a sphere which tends to grow larger and lose itself in the exterior world. But if I draw myself in from the periphery towards the center, if I search in the depth of my being that which is most uniformly, most constantly, and most enduringly myself, I find an altogether different thing.

There is, beneath these sharply cut crystals and this frozen surface, a continuous flux which is not comparable to any flux I have ever seen. There is a succession of states, each of which announces that which follows and contains that which precedes it. They can, properly speaking, only be said to form multiple states when I have already passed them and turn back to observe their track. Whilst I was experiencing them they were so solidly organized, so profoundly animated with a common life, that I could not have said where any one of them finished or where another commenced. In reality no one of them begins or ends, but all extend into each other.

This inner life may be compared to the unrolling of a coil, for there is no living being who does not feel himself coming gradually to the end of his role; and to live is to grow old. But it may just as well be compared to a continual rolling up, like that of a thread on a ball, for our past follows us, it swells incessantly with the present that it picks up on its way; and consciousness means memory.

But actually it is neither an unrolling nor a rolling up, for these two similes evoke the idea of lines and surfaces whose parts are homogeneous and superposable on one another. Now, there are no two identical moments in the life of the same conscious being. Take the simplest sensation, suppose it constant, absorb in it the entire personality: the consciousness which will accompany this sensation cannot remain identical with itself for two consecutive moments, because the second moment always contains, over and above the first, the memory that the first has bequeathed to it. A consciousness which could experience two identical moments would be a consciousness without memory. It would die and be born again continually. In what other way could one represent unconsciousness?

It would be better, then, to use as a comparison the myriad-tinted spectrum, with its insensible gradations leading from one shade to another. A current of feeling which passed along the spectrum, assuming in turn the tint of each of its shades, would experience a series of gradual changes, each of which would announce the one to follow and would sum up those which preceded it. Yet even here the successive shades of the spectrum always remain external one to another. They are juxtaposed; they occupy space. But pure duration, on the contrary, excludes all idea of juxtaposition, reciprocal externality, and extension.

Let us, then, rather, imagine an infinitely small elastic body, contracted, if it were possible, to a mathematical point. Let this be drawn out gradually in such a manner that from the point comes a constantly lengthening line. Let us fix our attention not on the line as a line, but on the action by which it is traced. Let us bear in mind that this action, in spite of its duration, is indivisible if accomplished without stopping, that if a stopping-point is inserted, we have two actions instead of one, that each of these separate actions is then the indivisible operation of which we speak, and that it is not the moving action itself which is divisible, but, rather, the stationary line it leaves behind it as its track in space. Finally, let us free ourselves from the space which underlies the movement in order to consider only the movement itself, the act of tension or extension; in short, pure mobility. We shall have this time a more faithful image of the development of our self in duration.

However, even this image is incomplete, and, indeed, every comparison will be insufficient, because the unrolling of our duration resembles in some of its aspects the unity of an advancing movement and in others the multiplicity of expanding states; and, clearly, no metaphor can express one of these two aspects without sacrificing the other. If I use the comparison of the spectrum with its thousand shades, I have before me a thing already made, whilst duration is continually in the making. If I think of an elastic which is being stretched, or of a spring which is extended or relaxed, I forget the richness of color, characteristic of duration that is lived, to see only the simple movement by which consciousness passes from one shade to another. The inner life is all this at once: variety of qualities, continuity of progress, and unity of direction. It cannot be represented by images.

But it is even less possible to represent it by *concepts,* that is by abstract, general, or simple ideas. It is true that no image can reproduce exactly the original feeling I have of the flow of my own conscious life. But it is not even necessary that I should attempt to render it. If a man is incapable of getting for himself the intuition of the constitutive duration of his own being, nothing will ever give it to him, concepts no more than images. Here the single aim of the philosopher should be to promote a certain effort, which in most men is usually fettered by habits of mind more useful to life. Now the image has at least this advantage, that it keeps us in the concrete. No image can replace the intuition of duration, but many diverse images, borrowed from very different orders of things, may, by the convergence of their action, direct consciousness to the precise point where there is a certain intuition to be seized. By choosing images as dissimilar as possible, we shall prevent any one of them from usurping the place of the intuition it is intended to call up, since it would then be driven away at once by its rivals. By providing that, in spite of their differences of aspect, they all require from the mind the same kind of attention, and in some sort the same degree of tension, we shall gradually accustom consciousness to a particular and clearly-defined disposition—that precisely which it must adopt in order to appear to itself as it really is, without any veil. But, then, consciousness must at least consent to make the effort. For it will have been shown nothing: It will simply have been placed in the attitude it must take up in order to make the desired effort, and so come by itself to the intuition. Concepts, on the contrary—especially if they are simple—have the disadvantage of being in reality symbols substituted for the object they symbolize, and demand no effort on our part. Examined closely, each of them, it would be seen, retains only that part of the object which is common to it and to others, and expresses, still more than the image does, a *comparison* between the object and others which resemble it. But as the comparison has made manifest a resemblance, as the resemblance is a property of the object, and as a property has every appearance of being a *part* of the object which possesses it, we easily persuade ourselves that by setting concept beside concept we are reconstructing the whole of the object with its parts, thus obtaining, so to speak, its intellectual equivalent. In this way we believe that we can form a faithful representation of duration by setting in line the concepts of unity, multiplicity, continuity, finite or infinite divisibility, etc. There precisely is the illusion. There also is the danger. Just in so far as abstract ideas can render service to analysis, that is, to the scientific study of the object in its relations to other objects, so far are they incapable of replacing intuition, that is, the metaphysical investigation of what is essential and unique in the object. For, on the one hand, these concepts, laid side by side, never actually give us more than an artificial reconstruction of the object, of which they can only symbolize certain general and, in a way, impersonal aspects; it is therefore useless to believe that with them we can seize a reality of which they present to us the shadow alone. And, on the other hand, besides the illusion there is also a very serious danger. For the concept generalizes at the same time as it abstracts. The concept can only symbolize a particular property by making it common to an infinity of things. It therefore always more or less deforms the property by the extension it gives to it. Replaced in the metaphysical object to which it belongs, a property coincides with the object, or at least molds itself on it, and adopts the same outline. Extracted from the metaphysical object, and presented in a concept, it grows indefinitely larger, and goes beyond the object itself, since henceforth it has to contain it, along with a number of other objects. Thus the different concepts that we form of the properties of a thing inscribe round it so many circles, each much too large and none of them fitting it exactly. And yet, in the thing itself the properties coincided with the thing, and coincided consequently with one another. So that if we are bent on reconstructing the object with concepts, some artifice must be sought whereby this coincidence of the object and its properties can be brought about. For example, we may choose one of the concepts and try, starting from it, to get round to the others. But we shall then soon discover that according as we start from one concept or another, the meeting and combination of the concepts will take place in an altogether different way. According as we start, for example, from unity or from multiplicity, we shall have to conceive differently the multiple unity of duration. Everything will depend on the weight we attribute to this or that concept, and this weight will always be arbitrary, since the concept extracted from the object has no weight, being only the shadow of a body. In this way, as many different *systems* will spring up as there are external points of view from which the reality can be examined, or larger circles in which it can be enclosed. Simple concepts have, then, not only the inconvenience of dividing the concrete unity of the object into so many symbolical expressions; they also divide philosophy into distinct schools, each of which takes its seat, chooses its counters, and carries on with the others a game that will never end. Either metaphysics is only this play of ideas, or else, if it is a serious occupation of the mind, if it is a science and not simply an exercise, it must transcend concepts in order to reach intuition. Certainly, concepts are necessary to it, for all the other sciences work as a rule with concepts, and metaphysics cannot dispense with the other sciences. But it is only truly itself when it goes beyond the concept, or at least when it frees itself from rigid and ready-made concepts in order to create a kind very different from those which we habitually use; I mean supple, mobile, and almost fluid representations, always ready to mold themselves on the fleeting forms of intuition. We shall return later to this important point. Let it suffice us for the moment to have shown that our duration can be presented to us directly in an intuition, that it can be suggested to us indirectly by images, but that it can never—if we confine the word concept to its proper meaning—be enclosed in a conceptual representation.

Let us try for an instant to consider our duration as a multiplicity. It will then be necessary to add that the terms of this multiplicity, instead of being distinct, as they are in any other multiplicity, encroach on one another; and that while we can no doubt, by an effort of imagination, solidify duration once it has elapsed, divide it into juxtaposed portions and count all these portions, yet this operation is accomplished on the frozen memory of the duration, on the stationary trace which the mobility of duration leaves behind it, and not on the duration itself. We must admit, therefore, that if there is a multiplicity here, it bears no resemblance to any other multiplicity we know. Shall we say, then, that duration has unity? Doubtless, a continuity of elements which prolong themselves into one another participates in unity as much as in multiplicity; but this moving, changing, colored, living unity has hardly anything in common with the abstract, motionless, and empty unity which the concept of pure unity circumscribes. Shall we conclude from this that duration must be defined as unity and multiplicity at the same time? But singularly enough, however much I manipulate the two concepts, portion them out, combine them differently, practice on them the most subtle operations of mental chemistry, I never obtain anything which resembles the simple intuition that I have of duration; while, on the contrary, when I replace myself in duration by an effort of intuition, I immediately perceive how it is unity, multiplicity, and many other things besides. These different concepts, then, were only so many standpoints from which we could consider duration. Neither separated nor reunited have they made us penetrate into it.

We do penetrate into it, however, and that can only be by an effort of intuition. In this sense, an inner, absolute knowledge of the duration of the self by the self is possible. But if metaphysics here demands and can obtain an intuition, science has none the less need of an analysis. Now it is a confusion between the function of analysis and that of intuition which gives birth to the discussions between the schools and the conflicts between systems.

DISCUSSION QUESTIONS

1. Does the distinction between analysis and intuition make sense to you? Why or why not?

2. What is the example of walking the streets of the city, as opposed to looking at photographs of the city, supposed to show? Explain.

3. Do you think there is a big difference between clock time and lived time? Why or why not?

4. Compare Bergson to Plato. What are the main differences in their approaches? Explain.

The Simulation Argument: Why the Probability That You Are Living in a Matrix Is Quite High

By Nick Bostrom

Nick Bostrom (b. 1973) is a Swedish philosopher who teaches at the University of Oxford and is director of the Future of Humanity Institute. In 2003 he published a paper, "Are You Living in a Computer Simulation?" in the journal Philosophical Quarterly. *Later that year, he published a shortened version for a popular audience in the* Times Higher Education Supplement, *a publication of the* London Times. *It is the shorter paper, "The Simulation Argument: Why the Probability That You Are Living in a Matrix Is Quite High," that is included here. Early in the article it is made clear that he means a matrix, not* The Matrix. *Although the movie is thought-provoking, that is not the kind of computer simulation he means. He does not think we have enough computer power right now to run this kind of large-scale computer simulation, but he does think we know what it would take. Using some concepts from computer science and philosophy, he thinks that at least one of these propositions is true:*

1. *"The chances that a species at our current level of development can avoid going extinct before becoming technologically mature is negligibly small."*
2. *"Almost no technologically mature civilisations are interested in running computer simulations of minds like ours."*
3. *"You are almost certainly in a simulation."*

He then runs through the possibilities and their implications.

The Matrix got many otherwise not-so-philosophical minds ruminating on the nature of reality. But the scenario depicted in the movie is ridiculous: human brains being kept in tanks by intelligent machines just to produce power.

There is, however, a related scenario that is more plausible and a serious line of reasoning that leads from the possibility of this scenario to a striking conclusion about the world we live in. I call this the simulation argument. Perhaps its most startling lesson is that there is a significant probability that you are living in computer simulation. I mean this literally: if the simulation hypothesis is true, you exist in a virtual reality simulated in a computer built by some advanced civilisation. Your brain, too, is merely a part of that simulation. What grounds could we have for taking this hypothesis seriously? Before getting to the gist of the simulation argument, let us

"The Simulation Argument: Why the Probability that You Are Living in a Matrix is Quite High" by Nick Bostrom from *Times Higher Education Supplement*, May 16, 2003. Original version published in 2001. Reprinted by permission of the author.

consider some of its preliminaries. One of these is the assumption of "substrate independence". This is the idea that conscious minds could in principle be implemented not only on carbon-based biological neurons (such as those inside your head) but also on some other computational substrate such as silicon-based processors.

Of course, the computers we have today are not powerful enough to run the computational processes that take place in your brain. Even if they were, we wouldn't know how to program them to do it. But ultimately, what allows you to have conscious experiences is not the fact that your brain is made of squishy, biological matter but rather that it implements a certain computational architecture. This assumption is quite widely (although not universally) accepted among cognitive scientists and philosophers of mind. For the purposes of this article, we shall take it for granted.

Given substrate independence, it is in principle possible to implement a human mind on a sufficiently fast computer. Doing so would require very powerful hardware that we do not yet have. It would also require advanced programming abilities, or sophisticated ways of making a very detailed scan of a human brain that could then be uploaded to the computer. Although we will not be able to do this in the near future, the difficulty appears to be merely technical. There is no known physical law or material constraint that would prevent a sufficiently technologically advanced civilisation from implementing human minds in computers.

Our second preliminary is that we can estimate, at least roughly, how much computing power it would take to implement a human mind along with a virtual reality that would seem completely realistic for it to interact with. Furthermore, we can establish lower bounds on how powerful the computers of an advanced civilisation could be. Technological futurists have already produced designs for physically possible computers that could be built using advanced molecular manufacturing technology. The upshot of such an analysis is that a technologically mature civilisation that has developed at least those technologies that we already know are physically possible, would be able to build computers powerful enough to run an astronomical number of human-like minds, even if only a tiny fraction of their resources was used for that purpose.

If you are such a simulated mind, there might be no direct observational way for you to tell; the virtual reality that you would be living in would look and feel perfectly real. But all that this shows, so far, is that you could never be completely sure that you are not living in a simulation. This result is only moderately interesting. You could still regard the simulation hypothesis as too improbable to be taken seriously.

Now we get to the core of the simulation argument. This does not purport to demonstrate that you are in a simulation. Instead, it shows that we should accept as true at least one of the following three propositions:

(1) The chances that a species at our current level of development can avoid going extinct before becoming technologically mature is negligibly small

(2) Almost no technologically mature civilisations are interested in running computer simulations of minds like ours

(3) You are almost certainly in a simulation.

Each of these three propositions may be prima facie implausible; yet, if the simulation argument is correct, at least one is true (it does not tell us which).

While the full simulation argument employs some probability theory and formalism, the gist of it can be understood in intuitive terms. Suppose that proposition (1) is false. Then a significant fraction of all species at our level of development eventually becomes technologically mature. Suppose, further, that (2) is false, too. Then some significant fraction of these species that have become technologically mature will use some portion of their computational resources to run computer simulations of minds like ours. But, as we saw earlier, the number of simulated minds that any such technologically mature civilisation could run is astronomically huge.

Therefore, if both (1) and (2) are false, there will be an astronomically huge number of simulated minds like ours. If we work out the numbers, we find that there would be vastly many more such simulated minds than there would be non-simulated minds running on organic brains. In other words, almost all minds like yours, having the kinds of experiences that you have, would be simulated rather than biological. Therefore, by a very weak principle of indifference, you would have to think that you are probably one of these simulated minds rather than one of the exceptional ones that are running on biological neurons.

So if you think that (1) and (2) are both false, you should accept (3). It is not coherent to reject all three propositions. In reality, we do not have much specific information to tell us which of the three propositions might be true. In this situation, it might be reasonable to distribute our credence roughly evenly between the three possibilities, giving each of them a substantial probability.

Let us consider the options in a little more detail. Possibility (1) is relatively straightforward. For example, maybe there is some highly dangerous technology that every sufficiently advanced civilization develops, and which then destroys them. Let us hope that this is not the case.

Possibility (2) requires that there is a strong convergence among all sufficiently advanced civilisations: almost none of them is interested in running computer simulations of minds like ours, and almost none of them contains any relatively wealthy individuals who are interested in doing that and are free to act on their desires. One can imagine various reasons that may lead some civilisations to forgo running simulations, but for (2) to obtain, virtually all civilisations would have to do that. If this were true, it would constitute an interesting constraint on the future evolution of advanced intelligent life.

The third possibility is the philosophically most intriguing. If (3) is correct, you are almost certainly now living in computer simulation that was created by some advanced civilisation. What kind of empirical implications would this have? How should it change the way you live your life?

Your first reaction might think that if (3) is true, then all bets are off, and that one would go crazy if one seriously thought that one was living in a simulation.

To reason thus would be an error. Even if we were in a simulation, the best way to predict what would happen next in our simulation is still the ordinary methods—extrapolation of past trends, scientific modelling, common sense and so on. To a first approximation, if you thought you were in a simulation, you should get on with your life in much the same way as if you were convinced that you are living a non-simulated life at the bottom level of reality.

The simulation hypothesis, however, may have some subtle effects on rational everyday behaviour. To the extent that you think that you understand the motives of the simulators, you can use that understanding to predict what will happen in the simulated world they created. If you think that there is a chance that the simulator of this world happens to be, say, a true-to-faith descendant of some contemporary Christian fundamentalist, you might conjecture that he or she has set up the simulation in such a way that the simulated beings will be rewarded or punished according to Christian moral criteria. An afterlife would, of course, be a real possibility for a simulated creature (who could either be continued in a different simulation after her death or even be "uploaded" into the simulator's universe and perhaps be provided with an artificial body there). Your fate in that afterlife could be made to depend on how you behaved in your present simulated incarnation. Other possible reasons for running simulations include the artistic, scientific or recreational. In the absence of grounds for expecting one kind of simulation rather than another, however, we have to fall back on the ordinary empirical methods for getting about in the world.

If we are in a simulation, is it possible that we could know that for certain? If the simulators don't want us to find out, we probably never will. But if they choose to reveal themselves, they could certainly do so. Maybe a window informing you of the fact would pop up in front of you, or maybe they would "upload" you into their world. Another event that would let us conclude with a very high degree of confidence that we are in a simulation is if we ever reach the point where we are about to switch on our own simulations. If we start running simulations, that would be very strong evidence against (1) and (2). That would leave us with only (3).

DISCUSSION QUESTIONS

1. Compare the view here with Plato's allegory of the cave.

2. Compare what he says about the idea that the third possibility is true to what Nietzsche says about *amor fati*.

3. He wonders if we could tell whether we were in a simulation or not. What are the implications of this? Explain.

Latina Feminist Metaphysics and Genetically Engineered Foods

By Lisa A. Bergin

Lisa Bergin is Visiting Assistant Professor of Philosophy at Hamline University in Minnesota. Her 2009 paper, "Latina Feminist Metaphysics and Genetically Modified Foods," was published in the Journal of Agricultural and Environmental Ethics. *The article begins by exploring one of the common objections to genetically modified (she uses the abbreviation "GM") foods—that "it's gross." She first draws upon the work of Mark Sagoff, who argues that there are at least four senses of the word "natural." Sagoff thinks you need to understand what each one of these mean before you can reject something as "unnatural." Bergin then points out that some of the "grossness" factor comes from the idea of GM foods as "impure." To further consider this, she draws upon the ideas of anthropologist Mary Douglas (1921–2007) on purity. Bergin also discusses Gloria Anzaldua (1942–2004), a poet and cultural critic best known for her semi-autobiographical book,* Borderlands/La Frontera: The New Mestiza. *The idea of the* mestiza *is relevant here because of its allusion to the idea of mixed race. The term* mestizo *originally referred to people who were of both European and Amerindian descent. Anzaldua, herself* mestiza, *discusses her own consciousness of her status. Bergin then considers Nahua philosophy, which goes back to the Aztecs, and contrasts it with ideas like Plato's. After this, she considers purity arguments used by the "pro-biotech" arguments. These industry accounts she contrasts with the work of Maria Lugones, who teaches philosophy and comparative literature at Binghamton University. Bergin also looks at the current debates in biology concerning use of the word "gene." In her conclusions, Bergin notes that we are living in a time where we might need to do genetics, without the concept of a "gene." This shows that by exploring the meanings of concepts, philosophy still has a role to play in considering the nature of reality.*

WHAT DO YOU MEAN, YOU HAVE PUT JELLYFISH IN MY POTATOES? MONSTROUS VEGETABLES AND FRANKENFRUITS

This first portion of the paper is a philosophical exploration of one reason why many find genetically engineered foods disturbing: we may believe that GE food crops are unnatural.[1] My motivation for analyzing this source of discomfort with GE foods

With kind permission from Springer Science+Business Media and the author: "Latina Feminist Metaphysics and Genetically Engineered Foods" by Lisa A. Bergin from *Journal of Agricultural and Environmental Ethics,* Vol. 22, No. 3, pp. 257–271. © Springer Science+Business Media B.V. 2009.

came about after learning about jellyfish DNA being inserted into potato plants so that when the plants need water, they will glow under a special light; about spider genes being inserted into goats so that proteins in the goats' milk can be turned into a silk substitute; about fish genes being spliced into tomatoes to make them more cold tolerant . . . and in each case I thought yuck, gross, disgusting. And I am not alone; my lefty, organically-minded friends have similar reactions and it is not uncommon to see these same attitudes reflected in both mainstream and alternative media's referencing of GE technology as producing "Frankenfoods."

In what follows, I will argue that this attitude toward GE foods is anti-feminist and, hence, inappropriate. This self-critical stance was prompted after reading a blurb from England's Prince Charles, who stated that genetic engineering is "tampering with something very fundamental" and attempting "to redesign nature and re-engineer humanity in our image and not God's image." Note how similar the Prince of Wales's comments were to my own thoughts at the time, thoughts that I had taken to be consistent with my non-religious feminist philosophy. And yet at base my disgust with GEOs like the jellyfish potato derived from the belief that these entities are not natural; that we are tampering with nature's fundamental design. Prince Charles's putting this very same opinion in the context of religious belief forced me to take a closer look at my own thoughts. It set me off thinking about what other things religious leaders and politicians believe are unnatural, or have believed thus in the past: women being educated; women working outside the home; women who did not marry; women who did not have, or want to have, children; gays and lesbians; gays and lesbians who have children; feminists; interracial couples and families; multiracial individuals; the intersexed; transgendered peoples. . . . Just as I question church doctrine concerning what is unnatural, maybe I ought to examine my own thinking about the unnaturalism of GE crops.

So what does it mean for something to be natural? For something to be unnatural? In "Genetic Engineering and the Concept of the Natural," Sagoff (2003) briefly sets out, following Mill's (1998) classification, four separate understandings of naturalness. According to this classification, being natural can mean (1) belonging to the universe (as opposed to being supernatural), (2) having been created by God (as opposed to being the profane creation of humans), (3) being independent of human influence (as opposed to being artificial), and/or (4) being authentic (as opposed to being illusory, superficial, or deceptive). Sagoff goes on to show that not only has the food industry consistently promoted its products as natural in the last three senses, but it has also tied the healthiness and goodness of its products to their naturalness. Therefore, Sagoff argues, it is not surprising that those who find GE foods unnatural would also find them risky given the connections the food industry itself has stressed between what is natural and what is good.

Note that Sagoff does not consider the specific issue that I wish to address here. While he explores the view by consumers that GE foods are suspicious, potentially risky, and therefore undesirable, he does not analyze the reaction of repugnance to these technologies. Nevertheless, his discussion is a useful starting point for my project. In what follows, I will expand on Sagoff's later two conceptions of the natural, again, that being natural means being non-artificial and/or authentic. I will treat separately some understandings that he lumps together under a single heading; I pick out three distinct meanings for *natural*, which Sagoff categorizes under the single heading of non-artificial. In my expanded discussion, I will also be assessing whether or not the differing conceptions of naturalness explain viewing GE potatoes as unnatural, and further, whether or not they explain the disgust reaction.[2]

Natural-as-Naturally Occurring versus Unnatural-as-Synthetic

Sagoff points out that one thing we might mean when we call something natural is that it is not artificial. For example, we commonly mark a distinction between natural foods, whose ingredients are "found in nature" and non-natural foods, which contain human-made, synthesized, artificial ingredients—usually dyes and/or flavors. This explains why we might say that red pistachios are not natural. It does not explain the GE potato example, however; the potato does have an added element of jellyfish, but jellyfish, unlike many red dyes, are not synthetic or artificial additives. Further, this understanding also fails to explain the disgust reaction: we may believe that artificial flavors and colors are unhealthy, but we do not seem to think the foods containing them are gross.

Natural-as-Real versus Unnatural-as-Fake

Sagoff also points out that holding that something is natural can mean that we believe it is not superficial. Accordingly, a slightly different set of understandings of natural and unnatural appears when analyzing the example of one's natural hair coloring versus one's hair coloring after being dyed. These conceptions of the natural and unnatural understand the natural to be real, and the unnatural to be fake, an artifice. Yet, again, the unnatural-as-fake conception does not seem to capture why we would call the jellyfish potato unnatural—these are not imitation, fake, or artificial potatoes (as a plastic potato would be); they aren't trying to be or look like something that they are not or were not. They are real potatoes, albeit modified ones, different in some way from "natural" potatoes. Further, something's being fake or an artifice doesn't seem enough to warrant our reacting to it with disgust.

Natural-as-Unmodified versus Unnatural-as-Modified

Note a common element in the above examples. To create the "unnatural" nut/hair tint, the "natural" pistachios and the "natural" hair color have both been interfered with by human manipulation, corresponding to yet another meaning in Sagoff's categorization: to be natural is to be "absent of the effects of human activity." There is a sense in which GEOs fit this understanding of unnatural—we have a "natural" potato that has been modified by humans. Yet, all agricultural practices include modification; indeed, the manipulation of plant matter by humans is the central practice of fanning. Humans have been modifying plants from the first farmers' saving seeds through to the more modern techniques of hybridization. Given that all agriculture is based on modification, something beyond mere manipulation is necessary to explain why so many find GE foods unnatural.[3] And as with the above two meanings of the concept "unnatural," this current understanding also cannot account for why many have such a strong physical reaction to them. We do not seem to be disturbed by the modifying of the potato per se, by the process of creating the GE potato, we're disturbed by the product, the potato itself.

Natural-as-Normal versus Unnatural-as-Abnormal

Not explored in the above discussion is the fact that GE potatoes differ from so-called natural potatoes in that not only have they been modified, but also they have been altered by the addition of a non-potato element. This leads to another way of thinking about the distinction between natural and unnatural. To be natural is to be true to one's essence, to be a characteristic instance of one's type, to be normal rather than abnormal. In Sagoff's terminology, to be natural is to be authentic or true to one's self. So, perhaps, we can say that a natural potato is a normal potato in that it has the essence of a potato and the GE potato is an unnatural, abnormal potato because its essence is not potato-hood, but jellyfishypotato-hood. This account rests upon a metaphysics that values essences, in which an element is coherent, natural, sensical to the extent that its essential nature is clear, unmixed. In short, it is a metaphysics that values purity. Further, this metaphysics offers a conception of naturalness that can explain my reaction to GE foods as gross and monstrous. It is the combining of the two species that I initially found disturbing, we have mixed together things that nature never intended to be mixed, we have created entities that lack pure essences, we have confused our categories. You want to put *what* in a *potato*?!?

Let us return to the List of the Unnatural. If women are a specific type, defined as associated with the body (and not the mind), with the home, with nurturing capacities, and as having natural affection toward men, then, women who desire higher learning, women who work in public spheres, women who do not want children, lesbians become unnatural/abnormal because they do not fit properly into their category, woman. Women who challenged gender stereotypes and restrictions are/were attempting to combine elements from categories that were supposed to be separate. Similarly, interracial families, multiracial peoples, the intersexed and transgendered folks challenge understandings that categories are distinct and separate from one another; they challenge the understanding that members of those categories are pure instances of the category type, neatly exhibiting the essence necessary for membership.[4] The mixing of elements across categories, the instances of impure beings leads to ascriptions of unnaturalness.

As further evidence that I am on the right track, cases of the unnatural-as-abnormal within human categories have been reacted to with repudiation and disgust. Linda Alcoff in "Mestizo Identity" analyzes examples of such reactions to mixed-race peoples: "[both] oppressed and dominant communities disapproved of open mixing, both fail to acknowledge and accept mixed offspring, and both value a purity for racial identity" (1995, p. 259). The reaction of disgust is seen especially in white supremacist ideology, which understands mixed-race relationships and children as pollution (1995, p. 260).

> Thus, in many cultures today, mixed-race people are treated as the corporeal instantiation of a lack—the lack of an identity that can provide a public status. They (we) are turned away from as if from an unpleasant sight, the sight and mark of an unclean copulation, the product of a taboo, the sign of racial impurity, cultural dilution, colonial aggression, or even emasculation. (1995, p. 260)

In addition, Mary Douglas, in her influential work, *Purity and Danger* (1966), explores cross-cultural examples of human groups' treating ambiguous beings, beings that are exceptions to accepted metaphysical orders, as abominations. So, the unnatural-as-abnormal not only reflects why we might consider GE crops unnatural, it also is consistent with some viewing the abnormality as disturbing, even disgusting.

Further, I posit that with respect to GE foods, the ascription of grossness comes not only from a negative attitude toward mixing up categories long-held to be separate, but also from our unease at the conceptual distance between categories that are being combined. Consider two examples of mixing of non-human categories: horses and donkeys are bred in order to produce mules; cabbages and turnips were bred in order to produce rutabagas. These sorts of mixing involve conceptually similar entities; cabbages and turnips are closely related, both members of the brassica genus.[5] I suppose some may turn their noses up at a rutabaga, not appreciating their sweet, rooty flavor, but I do not know that anyone would do so because they found the idea of mixing cabbages and turnips distasteful. It seems that humans are able to be flexible in our metaphysics.[6] For example, in the cases above we have been able to incorporate two separate essences into a new one. Comparing a rutabaga to a jellyfish-potato, we see that a bit of slight fiddling can be manageable if we conceptualize the original categories as very closely situated within our taxonomies, but we do not like our categories messed with, and as more and more disparate categories are combined, we become more and more uneasy: "potatoes and jellyfish, no way![7]

At this point I have really raised my feminist hackles against myself. The work of feminist philosophers, and especially Latina feminists and other feminists of color, has been absolutely instrumental in showing the flaws with the purity-valuing metaphysics underlying these ascriptions of unnaturalness. And this very metaphysics, I fear, is the conceptual scheme that has been underlying my own initial reaction to the jellyfish potato. To explore this in some more depth, I will use Gloria Anzaldúa's *Borderlands/La Frontera* (1999) as an example of the feminist critique of the above purity-valuing metaphysics. I choose to discuss *Borderlands* because Anzaldúa's metaphors are often agricultural ones, linking up nicely with my topic.

In *Borderlands/La Frontera*, Gloria Anzaldúa explores the emerging of the new *mestiza* consciousness. This philosophical account of the human self stands in contrast to a common view of the self in the tradition of Western philosophy. It has envisioned a new personhood; a self that accords with the facts of her own life better than the idealized self which is centered in the mind, floats above the everyday concerns of specificity, is untroubled by the tumults of the body, is at once anyone and no-one in particular. Anzaldúa finds that she is a very specific self, a willful woman, a Chicana, a lesbian. The theme that runs throughout her exploration of her self is that of the mixing of what have been taken to be opposites. As a Chicana she comes from both indigenous peoples and their European conquerors. As a Texan, living in the Borderlands, her family is both Mexican (when taking a historical view of the geography of her homeland) and American (when taking a more recent view). As a strong-willed girl/woman, and a lesbian, she incorporates both masculine and feminine aspects into her self.

This hybrid self is not without its problems; initially Anzaldúa experiences her self negatively. For example, she is rejected by Americans as Mexican, by Mexicans as American. This dynamic is present especially in negative reactions people have (some of my students included) to her mixed language. She speaks, and in fact writes this text, in a distinctively Chicano language, combining elements of English, various Spanish dialects, Nahuatl, and Chicano slang. She was a willful girl-child who was punished for desiring male activities, goals, and modes of being. In short, she understands herself as a mixed self, in lands and cultures that value purity; she understands her own self as a site of conflict and contradiction due to her lack of purity.

Through embracing the Nahua religion, and especially the Goddess Coatlicue, Anzaldúa transforms the denigration associated with mixture into opportunity and value. In her person, Coatlicue combines seeming opposites; her figure contains both male and female elements, she is beautiful and horrible, she represents both life and death. Anzaldúa uses Coatlicue as a model for a self that can sustain and embrace contraction—further, she challenges that the combining of these elements in fact represents a contradiction. In Anzaldúa's words "*Soy un amasamiento*, I am an act of kneading, of uniting and joining that not only has produced both a creature of darkness and a creature of light, but also a creature that questions the definitions of light and dark and gives them new meanings" (1999, p. 103). It is only if we have a dualist metaphysics that separates reality into distinct, and opposing, elements that the contradictions arise in the first place. At the conclusion of *Borderlands*, (Anzaldúa describes her personal journey as unending), she understands the mixed self as positive for her own life:

> Indigenous like corn, the *mestiza* is a product of crossbreeding, designed for preservation under a variety of conditions. Like an ear of corn—a female seed-bearing organ—the mestiza is tenacious, tightly wrapped in the husks of her culture. Like kernels she clings to the cob; with thick stalks and strong brace roots, she holds tight to the earth—she will survive the crossroads. (1999, p. 103)

Although her multiplicity of self has been denigrated by many around her, Anzaldúa celebrates her hybridity as a force of creativity personally, and a potential source of freedom and power socially. She believes that the valuing of mixed selves will also benefit those of us who have been taken as pure; these folks too are damaged by dualist metaphysics that limit our potential, and that mark us all as different from, better, worse than each other.

As a feminist I have tried to adopt such a rethinking of how we choose to classify and value each other. And yet, the jellyfish potato rears an ugly head in my psyche. Anzaldúa's words help to challenge this reaction to GE foods:

> The *mestizo* and the queer exist at this time and point on the evolutionary continuum for a purpose. We are a blending that proves that all blood is intricately woven together, and that we are spawned out of similar souls. . . . (1999, p. 107) [The *mestiza*] becomes a *nahual*, [a form shifting shaman] able to transform herself into a tree, a coyote, into another person. She learns to transform the small "I" into the total Self (1999, pp. 104–105).

To understand these quotes more fully, it is helpful to consider the philosophy that influences much of Anzaldúa's writing, in particular Nahua metaphysics, epistemology, and aesthetics. I have found James Maffie's work to be particularly helpful in my understanding of Nahua philosophy; what follows is what I have understood from thinking about Maffie's work together with Anzaldúa's.[8]

According to the Nahua tradition, the universe, reality, is *teotl*. Humans are epistemically disadvantaged with respect to understanding *teotl*; our perceptions impede our knowing reality. We perceive reality as made up of static, distinct, and independent elements that we tend to classify and come to understand through marking difference: for example, the male is the opposite of the female. Yet, these perceptions do not accurately reflect reality, for *teotl* is a dynamic life-force, ever changing, ever becoming-and-unbecoming; *teotl* is one, non-separable. When humans perceive the universe incorrectly, we perceive *teotl's nahual*, or mask, not *teotl* itself. Unlike Platonic epistemology, Nahua philosophy does not assert that although knowledge via the senses may be impossible, knowledge is attainable through the mind, when properly divorced from the influences of sense perception. Instead, according to Nahua belief, one comes to know *teotl* not through the mind, but through the heart; we can know *teotl* aesthetically, through performance of song, music, and dance; in so doing, we come to know *teotl* in the sense of being at one with reality.

Returning to GE foods, I can now more clearly state my dilemma. As a feminist, I agree with Anzaldúa's critiques of purity-valuing dualist metaphysics, and their resulting denigration, rather than valuing, of mixed beings. Yet my own reaction to GE crops as monstrous depends upon this very ideology, an ideology that I reject (or at least I thought I had rejected). If I truly value mixed beings, then the jellyfish potato ought not to disturb me for the reasons that it does. Within a Nahua framework, I am already mistaken to think that jellyfish are separate from potatoes in the first place. So, this exploration has helped me to be much more critical of a specific attitude toward GE crops, the attitude that these crops are unnatural, mutant, monstrous Frankenfood. In the end, from this feminist perspective, there is nothing unnatural per se about mixed beings, and thus, the transgenic potato ought not to be viewed as such. In the words of Audre Lorde (1984), feminist environmentalists, when we discount GE foods by calling upon the specter of the unnatural, mixed being, we are yet again using the master's tools to try to dismantle the master's house.

THE MATHEMATICAL COOKBOOKS OF MODERN SCIENCE OFFER A RECIPE FOR RED BANANAS: INGREDIENTS—1. RED 2. BANANA. INSTRUCTIONS—COMBINE

The opponents of GE food biotechnology criticize its use on numerous fronts, arguing, for example, that it has grave economic, social, health, and environmental costs. Conversely, the pro-GE position advocates for the very same technology by arguing in its favor on economic, social, health, and environmental grounds. To reiterate, my purpose in the paper is not to weigh these competing arguments, instead it is to examine where and how the logic of purity is used in arguments for and against GE foods. Above I have criticized a specific attitude toward GE foods that has been exploited by opponents; I argued that the raising of the unnatural specter of the rampaging Frankenfood relies on a purity-loving metaphysics. In this section I turn the tables, examining how the concept of purity informs a particular pro-biotech attitude. To accomplish this new task, I will rely heavily on María Lugones' work in "Purity, Impurity, and Separation."

In this essay, Lugones explores the concepts of purity and impurity as central components of two inconsistent metaphysics (in her words, *logics*). The logic of purity is a metaphysical attitude in which every multiple thing can be (or ought to be able to be) neatly separated into pure unitaries, as one might split an egg into yolk and white (1994, p. 275). Lugones explores what happens when the purity-loving metaphysics apprehends complex individuals.[9] Two examples she offers are the following. First, when this metaphysics comprehends embodied (raced, gendered . . .) needy, passionate beings, these beings can be "split-separated" and the fragmentary parts constituting the whole can be placed on a hierarchy so that the rational mind becomes the central, important component of the self and the remaining parts become transparent, uninteresting, unimportant (1994, pp. 281–283). In another example, the contemplation of the Chicano self, we move from the above control over the self to the control over the other.[10] Here, through Anglo eyes, the complex Chicano self becomes the bifurcated Mexican/American self; the colorful, stereotypical Mexican self that sits alongside the transparent American self. The Mexican/American is assimilated into U.S. culture only as an ornament, not as a participating member and producer of our culture (1994, pp. 286–288). Lugones stresses that control plays a central, motivating role within the purity-loving metaphysics: the whole point of clearly separating the complex individual is to exercise control over ourselves and others.

The above is how things look from the standpoint of the logic of purity; let's turn now to the logic of impurity. According to this logic, there are not pure unitaries that make up complex beings. Multiple beings cannot be separated into fragments nor can these fragments be placed into categories containing pure members. As such, there are no parts to be ranked, highlighted, or effaced. Instead, Lugones suggests that the elements that make up the whole exist in a "curdled state," as when you curdle mayonnaise. Curdled mayonnaise is made up of oil, water, and egg yolk, but once curdled, there is no way to separate these three elements into pure component parts. And yet, in curdling there is a separation, there is yolky oil and oily yolk. Whereas the logic of purity has control as a central motivating force, the logic of impurity is resistant to that control. Lugones explores the being of the ambiguous individual, the mestiza, as embodying, and as generating, this resistance:

> Mestizaje defies control through simultaneously asserting the impure, curdled multiple state and rejecting fragmentation into pure parts. In this play of assertion and rejection, the mestiza is unclassifiable, unmanageable. She as no pure parts to be "had," controlled. (1994, p. 277)

Throughout her examination of these two logics, as in the above examples, Lugones discusses how our understanding of the human self can shift when we shift metaphysics. I intend to draw on her insights concerning *human* individuals in my exploration of attitudes toward non-human individuals, plants. I will examine a number of descriptions of genetic engineering that are aimed at the general public, and offered by the following proponents of genetic engineering: Monsanto, the leading agricultural biotechnology company; BIO, the Biotechnology Industry Organization; and ISAAA, the International Service for the Acquisition of Agri-biotech Applications, a nonprofit organization whose goal, according to their home page, is to "deliver the benefits of new agricultural biotechnologies to the poor in developing countries." In examining the descriptions offered by these supporters of GE foods, I will first explore how their use of the logic of purity misleadingly supports the science, and safety, of genetic engineering. Next, I will suggest that we will have much more accurate results by reframing our views of plants by adopting an impurity-valuing metaphysics.

Plants, Genes, Genetic Engineering and the Logic of Purity

Among the list of links to educational resources for understanding crop biotechnology included on Monsanto's website is a link to the University of Nebraska's Extension Service. The following is their description of genetic engineering from a page entitled "What is Genetic Engineering and How Does it Work?":

> If all cookbooks around the world were written in a single language that everyone knew, recipes could be easily shared with anyone. DNA is a "universal language" in that the genetic code means the same thing in all organisms. This characteristic is critical to the success of genetic engineering. Genes can be transferred across species and still work . . . (Hain et al. 2004).

Along with this description is a diagram portraying a red pigment gene, having been inserted into bacteria, a banana, clover, and a frog, each of which is now red. According to this account, complex organisms can be separated into their simple, pure, component parts, their traits. These discrete units can then be inserted into a new organism to sit alongside their original traits. We excise the red pigment gene from an organism that has it, and when we insert it into a banana, the banana will also become red, but its other traits (aside from those that determine pigment) will remain intact. Because every organism understands the DNA code in the same way, we can turn any living thing red by inserting the red-trait controlling gene into it.

The University of Nebraska text goes on:

> Genetic engineering, also known as transformation, works by obtaining a gene from the genome of one organism and inserting it into the genome of another. This gives the recipient organism the ability to express the trait encoded by that gene. It is like taking a single recipe out of one cookbook and placing it into another cookbook (Hain et al. 2004).

I argue that the logic of purity is being employed in the above metaphor. For example, as one cuts and pastes recipes from one cookbook to another, every remaining page, the cover, the paper on which the book is printed, the other recipes are completely untouched. Perhaps we have only nudged some other recipes a bit forward, or covered up a previously existing recipe. Recall Lugones's metaphor of separating the egg: it appears in the U of N account that we can separate the gene that controls a trait in one species from an individual of that species, cleanly, and then insert it into an individual of another species which will then exhibit that trait.

ISAAA, the nonprofit pro-biotech organization, offers a similar account in their Mentor's Kit, a presentation intended as an overview of biotechnology; here, their description of genetic engineering consists of a definition of the word "gene" and an explanation for how genes are linked to traits. The definition reads that genes are the "basic physical and functional units of heredity which carries [sic] information for the expression of a particular trait." And the explanation: "[a gene] is the one responsible for the expression of a particular trait like the height of plants. That's why there are short plants, and there are tall plants. . . .Through genetic engineering, the gene controlling the expression of a short plant can be transferred into a tall but high yielding plant. The resulting plant will now be a short type but with high yield" (2003). Again we see an account that seems to imply that there is a one-to-one correspondence between genes and traits. Isolate the gene, remove it, insert it a new organism, and presto, that gene's trait emerges there too.

The Biotechnology Industry Organization echoes the University of Nebraska's description DNA as a universal language; in their Guide to Biotechnology, they state that "[a]ll cells speak the same genetic language. The DNA information manual of one cell can be read and implemented by cells from other living things." Indeed, the metaphor of DNA as a universal language appears often in pro-ge descriptions of genetic engineering, although it is not confined to such accounts. Perhaps the most eloquent usage of the metaphor appears in John C. Avis's *The Hope, Hype, and Reality of Genetic Engineering*, his attempt at a balanced account of both the positive and negative features of genetic engineering:

> In nature's nucleic acid alphabets, nucleotides are the four kinds of letters (G, A, T, and C) that, variously ordered, compose every genetic word, sentence,

> paragraph, and chapter in each organism's operations manual. In the genetic engineering trade, scientists edit these tomes, substituting a biochemical letter here, inserting a word or sentence there, transposing paragraphs, duplicating particular passages or sometimes the whole text, and, in general, attempting to tweak or revamp particular instructions in the code" (2004, p. 12).

According to accounts of DNA as the "Esperanto of Biology," not only can we split-separate the traits of plants by split-separating their genes, but also those genes are not context-dependent and, as such, they can be transported into new contexts.[11]

The view that complex beings are compilations of separable units is, according to Lugones, only one component of the purity-loving metaphysics; another important feature is that adopting this split-separation view is intrinsically tied to control. This element of control also appears in the pro-GE accounts examined here. In comparing genetic engineering to traditional breeding methods, Hain et al., from the University of Nebraska, find that a disadvantage of traditional methods is that in using them we can only move genes from pairs that can be mated.

> Genetic engineering, on the other hand, . . . allows the movement of genes between organisms of any species. Therefore, the potential traits that can be used are virtually unlimited. . . .Genetic engineering of plants has some distinct differences from traditional plant breeding. In many cases, these differences provide advantages in developing plants that meet the needs of people (2004).

Further, Monsanto's website states that "Agricultural biotechnology is an extension of . . . traditional plant breeding with one very important difference—it allows for the transfer of a greater variety of genetic information in a more precise, controlled manner." The Biotechnology Industry Organization explanation of genetic engineering cited above ends with the following declaration: "*Specific, precise, predictable.* Those are the words that best describe today's biotechnology" (emphasis in the original). And by the time we get to BIO's response to the question of food safety on their Frequently Asked Questions page, we might begin to feel a bit panicky about giving "nature" any role at all in the creation of our food:

> Indeed, because scientists know more about the changes being made using biotechnology, these foods may be even safer than conventional foods. The precision of biotechnology puts plant developers and regulators are in a better position to address safety that cannot be addressed for products of conventional breeding, which involves the uncontrolled crossing of tens of thousands of uncharacterized genes.

This quote almost begs the reader to throw up their hands in fright: "We can't have that! Those uncontrolled masses, combining willy-nilly! Uncharacterized genes? Who knows what kind of shenanigans they might be getting up to?"

The combined story from these sorts of accounts of crop biotechnology goes as follows: Humans cannot control plants effectively enough through traditional breeding, which relies on sexual reproduction; we have much more control through genetic engineering. The discrete component parts of plants are so nicely simple that we can successfully recombine them together to create better crops (ones that are more nutritious, more pest-resistant, longer lasting after harvest . . .). Using Lugones's perspective, when we look at the gene structure of an organism and see a complex entity that can be separated into distinct, pure parts, and our seeing them in this way is tied to our desire to manipulate those parts for our benefit, we are employing the logic of purity.[12]

Further, by using this metaphysics, we can increase confidence in the safety of our efforts. We put a yummy new recipe in our favorite cookbook and all the other recipes in that cookbook retain their original character. Placing the recipe into a new environment does not, for example, turn it into a recipe for poison, nor does the addition alter any of the neighboring recipes. If I cooked various recipes in the cookbook I could produce a meal, not a stomachache. If the recipe is a good one, then the cookbook is merely improved by an additive process. Not only does the new recipe not affect the integrity of the cookbook, it can hardly affect the integrity of the other things sitting on the shelf in my kitchen near it. Further, if I inadvertently insert a mediocre recipe, it is easy enough to remove, just rip out the page and toss it in the recycling bin. Analogously, the new transorganism's safety is secure—we put a safe trait into a safe organism, and the new transorganism remains safe—for human consumption, for its surrounding environ, for the organism's own viability.

Plants, Genes, Genetic Engineering and the Logic of Impurity

In this section, I will argue that the Logic of Impurity better captures current scientific understanding of genetics. If I am right that it would be more accurate to conceptualize genes, traits, and genetic engineering under the logic of impurity, the above cookbook metaphor must change, and with it, our reassuring control will be called into question. Rather than picturing a one-to-one correspondence between gene and trait, genes and the cells they exist within will now be conceptualized as curdled together, working in consort with one another to produce the traits exhibited by the individual. Now, transporting a gene into another species is less akin to copying a new recipe in a cookbook and more akin to adding a new ingredient into a recipe. This new ingredient will then interact with the other ingredients to produce a result that may or may not be what we are expecting. (I recall the time my partner thought she was adding cornstarch to a stir-fry, but instead added baking soda; rather than thickening her sauce, she made it fizzy, and inedibly salty; she changed the very character of the meal.)

In what ways does the logic of impurity and its metaphor of curdled genes offer a more accurate description of genetics as currently understood by geneticists? To start, a single gene can affect more than one trait of the organism (called pleiotropy), some genes have the ability to modify the expression of other genes (epistasis), and many traits are the product of numerous genes working together. (Rissler and

Mellon 1996, pp. 38, 14). Indeed, Jane Rissler and Margaret Mellon of the Union of Concerned Scientists, confirm that

> "[t]he most desirable traits-yield, drought resistance, nitrogen fixation—are determined by many genes. Nitrogen fixation, for example, requires a complex interplay of dozens of plant and bacterial genes. . . .For traits like yield and drought-resistance, scientists are only beginning to understand the full complement of genes that determine the trait." (1996, p. 14)

Thus, at the very least, there is not always a one-to-one correspondence between genes and traits, but instead, in at least some cases, reproducing traits involves more complicated interactions than simple subtractive and additive functions. More significantly, in their separate surveys of recent genetic research, Evelyn Fox Keller and Barry Commoner (2003) explain that genes on their own cannot faithfully replicate their own sequencing codes. Instead, they rely on the help of a variety of proteins, in the first place, to assist in the faithful replication, and in the second, to correct any improperly replicated nucleotide codes.

Although Keller's work in *The Century of the Gene* summarizes a number of ways in which genes are context-dependent, she begins by explaining how the historical legacy of the search for the gene has wrapped into its very concept that it is both the structural and the functional unit that produces an organism's traits and ensures the stability of those traits appearing in future generations. In other words, even before we knew what it was or how it worked, the gene was the name for *the* mechanism that produces the proteins that make for an organism's traits. And yet, as Keller enumerates, current scientific understandings of genetics hold that genes are not separable units producing proteins, instead they are merely pieces within a dynamic, context-specific process:

> . . . the evidence accruing over recent decades obliges us to think of the gene as (at least) two very different kinds of entities: one, a structural entity—maintained by the molecular machinery of the cell so that it can be faithfully transmitted from generation to generation; and the other, a functional entity that emerges only out of the dynamic interaction between and along a great many players, only one of which is the structural gene from which the original protein sequences are derived. Or, to put it just a little differently, the function of a structural gene depends not only on its sequence but, as well, on its genetic context, on the chromosomal structure in which it is embedded (and which is itself subject to developmental regulation), and on its developmentally specific cytoplasmic and nuclear context (2000, pp. 71–72).

Keller concludes by suggesting that the very concept of the gene may have outlived its productivity for geneticists' and, perhaps more critically, laypeople's understandings of genetics.

Complicating the story of the relationships between genes, proteins, and traits to include genetic contexts, we see that BIO's description of genetic engineering as

"Specific, precise, [and] predictable" is misleading. John Avise, a professor of genetics at the University of Georgia, offers a fuller description of the process of moving genes from one organism to another:

> In many cases, producing a transgenic organism is the technologically easy part. Often the greater challenge is to engineer the transgene so that it functions as intended in its new biological house. Accordingly, much of the research effort put into genetic engineering is directed toward designing and then monitoring transgenes to see that they functions properly at several levels: inside the cell and its metabolic pathways; within the developmental milieu of the organism; and the context of the species' ecological setting. Therein lie some of the greatest challenges for the genetic engineering enterprise (2004, p. 13).

From this brief survey of current scientific understanding of genetics, we see that genes work in consort with their environment, at both the cellular and ecological level. And so, adding a new gene into a plant's genome may have other ramifications, beyond our expectations of adding a single new trait. The new gene will interact with surrounding genes and proteins and together the genome will interact with the wider environment, meaning that the same gene placed into two differing genomes may not work in exactly the same way. If DNA is like a universal language, as many accounts claim, it seems that it is a language that contains vagueness and ambiguity such that the same phrase can be understood differently, depending upon the context the phrase finds itself in.

The interaction among genes and between genes and their environment could explain why pest-resistant GE soybeans can have lower yields than their non-GE cousins: energy used by the plant in producing throughout its physiology the proteins that are fatal to pests cannot be used in the production of seeds. It also might explain the instability of GE crops, why in successive generations, the offspring plants can fail to exhibit the desired trait of the original parent or, in the terminology of the field, the transplanted genes are "silenced."[13] If trans-traits are not securely enmeshed in the dynamic processes occurring within the organism and between the organism and its environment, they may be edited out.

While traditional breeding methods, producing varieties well-suited to local environments, yield the most stable expression of traits, they do not render traits static; plants continue to evolve as the environment changes. This highlights another flaw with conceptualizing plants using the purity-loving metaphysics: it can render hidden the creativity of the plant, as it focuses solely on the creativity of the human controller. Lugones discusses this shift:

> When seen from the logic of curdling, the alteration of the impure to unity is seen as fictitious and as an exercise in domination: the impure are rendered uncreative, ascetic, static, realizers of the contents of the modern subject's imagination. Curdling, in contrast, realizes their against-the-grain creativity, articulates their within-structure-inarticulate powers (1994, p. 286).

Lugones also has a very evocative discussion of her mother's mestizaje approach to the objects in her environ: she rarely uses names for objects, but instead notes them by their position relative to other things or herself; an object is not ruined or changed when broken; "She has always had multiple functions for it, many possibilities. Its multiplicity has always been obvious to her" (1994, p. 278). We see in this passage the connections between rigid versus loose conceptual borders and blocked thinking versus creativity. Valuing an impure metaphysics, we may comprehend the creativity exhibited by the plant as its own resistance to control. That is, we might understand sexual reproduction as the plant's resistance to, or power within, its environment: the very diversity of genes that are exchanged through such reproduction helps to ensure the survival of the species as its environment changes because genetic diversity in its offspring increases the possibility of some of them surviving environmental change. We can also understand the silencing of transgenes as the plant's curdled, interactive, process for expunging genes that fail to fit, that fail to support the plant's fitness in its environment.

Purity and Monoculture; Impurity and Diversity

I want to end my discussion with a final theme that runs through the feminist philosophy that I am here using—both Anzaldúa and Lugones, in their valuing of the resistances and creative power of the hybrid, the ambiguous, the mestiza, the impure, also value diversity. Lugones notes, for example, that "monophilia and purity are cut from the same cloth." (1994, p. 281) And from Anzaldúa's *Borderlands*:

> Jose Vasconcelos, Mexican philosopher, envisaged una raza mestiza. . . . Opposite to the theory of the pure Aryan, and to the policy of racial purity that white America practices, his theory is one of inclusivity. At the confluence of two or more genetic streams, with chromosomes constantly "crossing over," this mixture of races, rather than resulting in an inferior being, provides hybrid progeny, a mutable, more malleable species with a rich gene pool. From this racial, ideological, cultural and biological cross-pollinization, an 'alien' consciousness is presently in the making—a new *mestiza* consciousness. . . . (1999, p. 99)

We should not understand the *raza mestiza* as a melting pot race; the goal is not to combine "separate" races into one homogenous race of humans. Instead, Anzaldúa's and Vasconcelos' vision is a *mestizo* race, a race that continually creates and regenerates diversity of being. Central to valuing mixed-race beings, is a valuing of diversity.

And this valuing of diversity is lacking in current global, GE practices. I will end with two examples. First, the large multi-national seed/chemical/pharmaceutical companies that are investing in GE technology are replacing smaller, more diverse markets. Second, the financial interests of these companies create an atmosphere in which food crop biodiversity is endangered. If you want to make lots of money you will invest in monoculture farming, rather than investing in the preservation of local, diverse crop strains. Thus, the use of GE technology is a partial explanation for why our food gene pool is becoming less and less diverse.

CONCLUSION

What I have tried to accomplish in this paper is to replace a poor reason for being wary of GE food with better reasons for doing so. Both opponents and proponents of biotechnology have relied on a logic of purity; opponents presenting GE foods as monstrous, hybrid beings, directing our attention to them as mixed beings that are dangerous because they are impure. Proponents on the other hand present these same foods as healthful, yet benign beings, directing our attention to them as aggregates of simple, pure unities that are safe because they are additive composites of safe parts. I am suggesting that we move away from a logic of purity and contemplate plants, their genes, and genetic engineering from a metaphysics that values impurity and resistance.

Taking up such a metaphysics will mean that we should be more wary of GE foods than some biotech supporters believe is warranted. Using the logic of impurity reveals complications to the story presented by biotech corporations about the safety of their products; taking up the more complicated story requires that we will have to investigate much more fully the short and long-term consequences of genetic engineering.

Finally, adopting this alternative conceptual scheme might offer a useful tool for the moment we currently find ourselves in, a moment that Evelyn Fox Keller describes as one in which the concept of the gene may no longer be useful. Conceptualizing genes under a logic of impurity could allow us to retain the concept of the gene, and yet hold within our understanding of it that it is curdled within a larger context; genes become identifiable, and yet inseparable elements of their environment. Perhaps this Latina Feminist Metaphysics can be a point along our way to new understandings of how life works.

REFERENCES

Alcoff, L. M. (1995). Mestizo identity. In N. Zack (Ed.), *American mixed race: The culture of microdiversity* (pp. 257–278). New York: Rowman and Littlefield.

Anzaldúa, G. (1999). *Borderlands/la frontera: The new Mestiza*. San Francisco: Aunt Lute.

Avise, J. C. (2004). *The hope, hype, and reality of genetic engineering: Remarkable stories from agriculture, industry, medicine, and the environment*. Oxford: Oxford University Press.

Biotechnology Industry Organization. Biotechnology: A guide to technologies, (n.d.). Retrieved Sep 24, 2008, from http://www.bio.org/speeches/pubs/er/technologycollection.asp.

Biotechnology Industry Organization. Frequently asked questions on agricultural biotechnology, (n.d.). Retrieved Sep 24, 2008, from http://www.bio.Org/foodag/faq.asp#1.

Bowring, F. (2003). *Science, seeds and cyborgs: Biotechnology and the appropriation of life*. London: Verso.

Commoner, B. (2003). Unraveling the DNA myth. *Seedling*, July, 6–12.

Douglas, M. (1966). *Purity and danger*. New York: Routledge.

Finnegan, J., & McElroy, D. (1994). Transgene inactivation: Plants fight back!. *Bio/Technology, 12*, 883–888.

Frye, M. (2005). Categories in distress. In B. Andrew, J. Keller, & L. Schwartzman (Eds.), *Feminist interventions in ethics and politics* (pp. 41–58). New York: Rowman and Littlefield.

Hain, M., Albrecht, J. A., & Golick, D. A. (2004). What is genetic engineering and how does it work? Retrieved Sep 24, 2008, from http://agbiosafety.unl.edu/basic_genetics.shtml.

International Service for the Acquisition of Agri-Biotech Applications. (2003). Mentor's kit. Retrieved Sep 24, 2008, from http://www.isaaa.org/Resources/presentationslides/mentorskit/default.html.

Keller, E. F. (2000). *The Century of the gene*. Cambridge: Harvard University Press.

Leiser, B. (2000). Is homosexuality unnatural? In L. P. Pojman (Ed.), *The moral life* (pp. 698–707). Oxford: Oxford University Press.

Lorde, A. (1984). The master's tools will never dismantle the master's house. In *Sister outsider* (pp. 110–113). Berkeley: Crossing Press.

Lugones, M. (1994). Purity, impurity, and separation. *Signs: journal of women in culture and society, 19*, 275–296.

Maffie, J. (2000). 'Like a painting, we will be erased; like a flower, we will dry up here on earth' Ultimate reality and meaning according to Nahua philosophy in the age of conquest. *Ultimate reality and meaning: interdisciplinary studies in the philosophy of understanding, 23*, 295–318.

Mill, J. S. (1998). *Three essays on religion*. New York: Prometheus Books.

Monsanto. Biotech basics, (n.d.). Retrieved Sep 24, 2008, from *http://www.monsanto.com/responsibility*/youth/educationaloutreach/biotechbasics.asp.

Rissler, J & Mellon, M. (1996). *The ecological risks of engineered crops.* Cambridge: MIT Press.

Sagoff, M. (2003). Genetic engineering and the concept of the natural. In V. V. Gehring (Ed.), *Genetic prospects: Essays on biotechnology, ethics, and public policy* (pp. 11–25). New York: Rowman and Littlefield.

ENDNOTES

1 Note that not everyone has this reaction of disturbance to the idea of genetically engineered foods. When I have given versions of this paper in public forums, some audience members report not having this attitude toward GE foods. However, because many do have the reaction, and because anti-GE organizations make use of it in their campaigns against GE technology, I think it is worth exploring.

2 For another critique of "the unnatural," see Burton Leiser's (2000) "Is Homosexuality Unnatural?" Although not addressing GE food, Leiser's paper coincides with my own thinking about unnaturalness at a number of points—particularly in our

discussions of artificiality and abnormality. Where I discuss the notion of being abnormal as "improperly fitting one's category," Leiser discusses the notion of acting abnormally as "improperly using one's genital organs."

3 Because all agriculture involves genetic modification by humans, others and I prefer the phrase Genetically Engineered (GE) to Genetically Modified (GM), in order to mark a distinction between our newest techniques of genetic manipulations and older ones. Note though that, as John C. Avise (2004) has pointed out, the term engineering does not quite capture what transgenic technicians do: unlike mechanical engineers' designing a physical structure, genetic engineers are producing a structure that will, as an organism, develop and at least attempt to self-replicate and, as part of a species, evolve as time goes on. "The net results are ever-changing and varied responses to genetic manipulations and levels of temporal unpredictability that far surpass what physical engineers encounter." (175).

4 For a recent critique of the metaphysics that I am addressing, see Marilyn Frye's recent work "Categories in Distress" (2005). In this article, not only does she show some of the problems with metaphysics that understand categories as species, sets, and containers, she also offers a variety of very useful reimaginings of categories.

5 Why, if this is the case, would we see the negative connotations of mixed-raced people cited above? How much more similarity than two individuals of the same species could we have? The point here is that this discussion takes place at the metaphysical, conceptual level, rather than the scientific, biological one. Although biologically false, (not to mention thoroughly racist,) Western conceptual schemes historically held whites and people of color in separate categories; indeed, those holding these metaphysics even employed science in their attempts to confirm that Africans, for example, were closer to animals than humans.

6 We shall see soon that some philosophical positions have more flexibility than others.

7 One might counter that the reason this combination is so disturbing to me is not because the *combination* is disturbing, but instead, it is that the *jellyfish* is disturbing. If I find the prospect of eating jellyfish distasteful, I may find the idea of a jellyfish gene in a potato distasteful. I don't dispute this; however, I think that in addition to being disturbed by one portion of the parentage, as it were, I am disturbed as well by the very combination of the two elements of the natural world into one being. Consider the following thought experiment. I can well believe that we may find a genetically engineered cat with tomato genes disturbing, even when we thoroughly enjoy cats and tomatoes on their own (and for those who may find eating cats distasteful, let us suppose that the cat with tomato genes is developed not as food, but as a remarkably red pet).

8 Maffie's analysis of Nahua philosophy centers on the structures of thinking among pre-conquest Nahuatl-speakers (such as the Acolhuans, Texcocans, Tlacopans, Chalcan, Tepanecs, Huexotzincas, Tlaxcaltecs, and Mexicas—known to North Americans as 'Aztecs') (2000, p. 295).

9 Lugones also explores how this metaphysics functions in social worlds, among/between collectivities of individuals.

10 Under the logic of purity Chicanos must be other; their being cannot realize the true selfhood of the rational self because their bodies/ethnicity/race are not allowed transparency.

11 The phrase "Esperanto of Biology" comes from Finn Bowring (2003), in his critique of Crick and Watson's understanding of DNA as the biochemical language understood by all living things.

12 We will have to wait a bit to more clearly see the connection between the story of the clean separation of plants into their component parts and human desire to control the plant. After I have discussed an alternate story we can tell about plants using the logic of impurity, the above will be clearer.

13 See also Finnegan and McElroy (1994) for a survey of organisms' turning off transgenes.

DISCUSSION QUESTIONS

1. Compare the discussion of Anzaldua as *mestiza* in Bergin to the discussion of self in Mead and Du Bois.

2. What are some of the similarities and differences between Nahua philosophy and traditional European philosophies, such as Plato's? Explain.

3. Explain the distinction Bergin makes between the "logic of purity" and the "logic of impurity."

4. Explain the cookbook analogy and Bergin's evaluation of its use.

PART THREE

"WHAT CAN I KNOW?"

The Questions of Mālunkyāputta

Ed. by E.J. Thomas

One of the more famous passages in Buddhism is the "Parable of the Arrow," which is contained here under the name, "The Questions of Malunkyaputta." It can be found in Sutta 63 of the Majjhima-nikaya. *It is hard to date this work, but the current view is that it is older than the Buddhist text we saw in Part I of* Four Fundamental Questions. *In the parable, Malunkyaputta tells Buddha that he will stop studying with him if he does not answer some questions. The questions have to do with whether the world is eternal or not, whether there is life or death, and body/soul relationship. The Buddha tells Malunkyaputta that he never promised to answer these questions, but instead will teach him about suffering. He will not answer Malunkyaputta's questions because they are not relevant to living a good life. The parable points out that if you have been shot by a poisoned arrow, the questions you should be asking involve safely removing the arrow, rather than questions about what kind of wood the arrow is made of. The questions Malunkyaputta wants answered are metaphysical questions, questions about reality, like the ones in Part II of* Four Fundamental Questions. *The Buddhist position seems to be that we should restrict our concerns about knowledge to practical matters analogous to removing the arrow. The knowledge about suffering here will be discussed in the Buddhist selection on the Four Noble Truths in Part IV of* Four Fundamental Questions.

XI

Thus have I heard: The Lord was once dwelling near Sāvatthi, at Jetavana in the park of Anāthapindika. Now the elder Mālunkyāputta had retired from the world, and as he meditated the thought arose: "These theories have been left unexplained by the Lord, set aside, and rejected, whether the world is eternal or not eternal, whether the world is finite or not, whether the soul (life) is the same as the body, or whether the soul is one thing and the body another, whether a Buddha (Tathāgata) exists after death or does not exist after death, whether a Buddha both exists and does not exist after death, and whether a Buddha is non-existent and not non-existent after death—these things the Lord does not explain to me, and that he does not explain them to me does not please me, it does not suit me. I will approach the Lord, and ask about this matter. . . . If the Lord does not explain to me, I will give up the training, and return to a worldly life."

[When Mālunkyāputta had approached and put his questions the Lord replied:] "Now did I, Mālunkyāputta, ever say to you, 'Come, Mālunkyāputta, lead a religious life with me, and I will explain to you whether the world is eternal or not eternal [and so on with the other questions]?'" "You did not, reverend sir." "Anyone,

Mālunkyāputta, who should say 'I will not lead a religious life with the Lord, until the Lord explains to me whether the world is eternal or not eternal [etc.] . . .' that person would die, Mālunkyāputta, without its being explained. It is as if a man had been wounded by an arrow thickly smeared with poison, and his friends, companions, relatives, and kinsmen were to get a surgeon to heal him, and he were to say, 'I will not have this arrow pulled out, until I know by what man I was wounded, whether he is of the warrior caste, or a brahmin, or of the agricultural, or the lowest caste.' Or if he were to say, 'I will not have this arrow pulled out until I know of what name or family the man is . . . or whether he is tall, or short, or of middle height . . . or whether he is black, or dark, or yellowish . . . or whether he comes from such and such a village, or town, or city . . . or until I know whether the bow with which I was wounded was a chāpa or a kodanda, or until I know whether the bow-string was of swallow-wort, or bamboo-fibre, or sinew, or hemp, or of milk-sap tree, or until I know whether the shaft was from a wild or cultivated plant . . . or whether it was feathered from a vulture's wing or a heron's or a hawk's, or a peacock's, or a sithilahanu-bird's . . . or whether it was wrapped round with the sinew of an ox, or of a buffalo, or of a ruru-deer, or of a monkey . . . or until I know whether it was an ordinary arrow, or a razor-arrow, or a vekanda, or an iron arrow or a calf-tooth arrow, or one of a karavīra leaf.' That man would die, Mālunkyāputta, without knowing all this.

"It is not on the view that the world is eternal, Mālunkyāputta, that a religious life depends; it is not on the view that the world is not eternal that a religious life depends. Whether the view is held that the world is eternal, or that the world is not eternal, there is still re-birth, there is old age, there is death, and grief, lamentation, suffering, sorrow, and despair, the destruction of which even in this life I announce. It is not on the view that the world is finite . . . It is not on the view that a Tathāgata exists after death . . . Therefore, Mālunkyāputta, consider as unexplained what I have not explained, and consider as explained what I have explained. And what, Mālunkyāputta, have I not explained? Whether the world is eternal I have not explained, whether the world is not eternal . . . whether a Tathāgata is both non-existent and not nonexistent after death I have not explained. And why, Mālunkyāputta, have I not explained this? Because this, Mālunkyāputta, is not useful, it is not concerned with the principle of a religious life, does not conduce to aversion, absence of passion, cessation, tranquillity, supernatural faculty, perfect knowledge, Nirvana, and therefore I have not explained it.

"And what, Mālunkyāputta, have I explained? Suffering have I explained, the cause of suffering, the destruction of suffering, and the path that leads to the destruction of suffering have I explained. For this, Mālunkyāputta, is useful, this is concerned with the principle of a religious life; this conduces to aversion, absence of passion, cessation, tranquillity, supernatural faculty, perfect knowledge, Nirvana, and therefore have I explained it. Therefore, Mālunkyāputta, consider as unexplained what I have not explained, and consider as explained what I have explained." Thus spoke the Lord, and with joy the elder Mālunkyāputta applauded the words of the Lord. (*Majjh. Nik.* I. 426 ff.)

DISCUSSION QUESTIONS

1. Explain how the parable of the arrow is supposed to work.

2. How often do you think we are like Malunkyaputta? Why? Explain.

3. Malunkyaputta applauds at the end. Why do you think he might have been convinced by the parable? Explain.

The Writings of Chuang Tzu

By Chuang Tzu
Translated by James Legge

Chuang Tzu (370–301 BCE) is usually referred to as the second of the great Taoists. There is some controversy as to whether he actually existed, but not as much as there is about Lao Tzu (see Part II of Four Fundamental Questions*). Chuang Tzu's book is named after himself: The* Chuang Tzu. *Our selection is from Book II, Part I, Section 2 of the* Chuang Tzu. *In these paragraphs we see a skeptical view of knowledge. That is, it seems at bottom, we cannot know which side of a conflict of ideas is correct. Our selection is also called "The Adjustment of Controversies." Like the* Tao te Ching, *the* Chuang Tzu *is not meant to be read sequentially like an essay. Also, it is like the* Tao te Ching *because most arguments are analogical.*

BOOK II – PART I, SECTION II

Khî Wû Lun, or 'The Adjustment of Controversies.'

1. Nan-kwo Tsze-khî was seated, leaning forward on his stool. He was looking up to heaven and breathed gently, seeming to be in a trance, and to have lost all consciousness of any companion. (His disciple), Yen Khang Tsze-yû, who was in attendance and standing before him, said, 'What is this? Can the body be made to become thus like a withered tree, and the mind to become like slaked lime? His appearance as he leans forward on the stool to-day is such as I never saw him have before in the same position.' Tsze-khî said, 'Yen, you do well to ask such a question, I had just now lost myself; but how should you understand it? You may have heard the notes of Man, but have not heard those of Earth; you may have heard the notes of Earth, but have not heard those of Heaven.'

   Tsze-yû said, 'I venture to ask from you a description of all these.' The reply was, 'When the breath of the Great Mass (of nature) comes strongly, it is called Wind. Sometimes it does not come so; but when it does, then from a myriad apertures there issues its excited noise;—have you not heard it in a prolonged gale? Take the projecting bluff of a mountain forest;—in the great trees, a hundred spans round, the apertures and cavities are like the nostrils, or the mouth, or the ears; now square, now round like a cup or a mortar; here like a wet footprint, and there like a large puddle. (The sounds issuing from them are like) those of fretted water, of the arrowy whizz, of the stern command, of the inhaling of the breath, of the shout, of the gruff note, of the deep wail, of the sad and piping note. The first notes are slight, and those that follow deeper, but in harmony with them.

Gentle winds produce a small response; violent winds a great one. When the fierce gusts have passed away, all the apertures are empty (and still);—have you not seen this in the bending and quivering of the branches and leaves?'

Tsze-yû said, 'The notes of Earth then are simply those which come from its myriad apertures; and the notes of Man may just be compared to those which (are brought from the tubes of) bamboo;—allow me to ask about the notes of Heaven.' Tsze-khî replied, 'When (the wind) blows, (the sounds from) the myriad apertures are different, and (its cessation) makes them stop of themselves. Both of these things arise from (the wind and the apertures) themselves:—should there be any other agency that excites them?'

2. Great knowledge is wide and comprehensive; small knowledge is partial and restricted. Great speech is exact and complete; small speech is (merely) so much talk. When we sleep, the soul communicates with (what is external to us); when we awake, the body is set free. Our intercourse with others then leads to various activity, and daily there is the striving of mind with mind. There are hesitancies; deep difficulties; reservations; small apprehensions causing restless distress, and great apprehensions producing endless fears. Where their utterances are like arrows from a bow, we have those who feel it their charge to pronounce what is right and what is wrong; where they are given out like the conditions of a covenant, we have those who maintain their views, determined to overcome. (The weakness of their arguments), like the decay (of things) in autumn and winter, shows the failing (of the minds of some) from day to day; or it is like their water which, once voided, cannot be gathered up again. Then their ideas seem as if fast bound with cords, showing that the mind is become like an old and dry moat, and that it is nigh to death, and cannot be restored to vigour and brightness.

Joy and anger, sadness and pleasure, anticipation and regret, fickleness and fixedness, vehemence and indolence, eagerness and tardiness;—(all these moods), like music from an empty tube, or mushrooms from the warm moisture, day and night succeed to one another and come before us, and we do not know whence they sprout. Let us stop! Let us stop! Can we expect to find out suddenly how they are produced?

If there were not (the views of) another, I should not have mine; if there were not I (with my views), his would be uncalled for:—this is nearly a true statement of the case, but we do not know what it is that makes it be so. It might seem as if there would be a true Governor concerned in it, but we do not find any trace (of his presence and acting). That such an One could act so I believe; but we do not see His form. He has affections, but He has no form.

Given the body, with its hundred parts, its nine openings, and its six viscera, all complete in their places, which do I love the most? Do you love them all equally? or do you love some more than others? Is it not the case that they all perform the part of your servants and waiting women? All of them being such, are they not incompetent to rule one another? or do they take it in turns to be now ruler and now servants? There must be a true Ruler (among them) whether by searching you can find out His character or not, there is neither advantaae nor hurt, so far as the truth of His operation is concerned. When once we have received the bodily form complete, its parts do not fail to perform their functions till the end comes. In conflict with things or in harmony with them, they pursue their course to the end, with the speed of a galloping horse which cannot be stopped;—is it not sad? To be constantly toiling all one's lifetime, without seeing the fruit of one's labour, and to be weary and worn out with his labour, without knowing where he is going to:—is it not a deplorable case? Men may say, 'But it is not death;' yet of what advantage is this? When the body is decomposed, the mind will be the same along with it:—must not the case be pronounced very deplorable? Is the life of man indeed enveloped in such darkness? Is it I alone to whom it appears so? And does it not appear to be so to other men?

3. If we were to follow the judgments of the predetermined mind, who would be left alone and without a teacher? Not only would it be so with those who know the sequences (of knowledge and feeling) and make their own selection among them, but it would be so as well with the stupid and unthinking. For one who has not this determined mind, to have his affirmations and negations is like the case described in the saying, 'He went to Yüeh to-day, and arrived at it yesterday.' It would be making what was not a fact to be a fact. But even the spirit-like Yü could not have known how to do this, and how should one like me be able to do it?

But speech is not like the blowing (of the wind); the speaker has (a meaning in) his words. If, however, what he says, be indeterminate (as from a mind not made up), does he then really speak or not? He thinks that his words are different from the chirpings of fledgelings; but is there any distinction between them or not? But how can the Tâo be so obscured, that there should be 'a True' and 'a False' in it? How can speech be so obscured that there should be 'the Right' and 'the Wrong' about them? Where shall the Tâo go to that it will not be found? Where shall speech be found that it will be inappropriate? Tâo becomes obscured through the small comprehension (of the mind), and speech comes to be obscure through the vain-gloriousness (of the speaker). So it is that we have the contentions between the Literati and the Mohists, the one side affirming what the other denies, and vice versa. If we would decide on their several affirmations and denials, no plan is like bringing the (proper) light (of the mind) to bear on them.

All subjects may be looked at from (two points of view),—from that and from this. If I look at a thing from another's point of view, I do not see it; only as I know it myself, do I know it. Hence it is said, 'That view comes from this; and this view is a consequence of that:'—which is the theory that that view and this—(the opposite views)—produce each the other. Although it be so, there is affirmed now life and now death; now death and now life; now the admissibility of a thing and now its inadmissibility; now its inadmissibility and now its admissibility. (The disputants) now affirm and now deny; now deny and now affirm. Therefore the sagely man does not pursue this method, but views things in the light of (his) Heaven (-ly nature), and hence forms his judgment of what is right.

This view is the same as that, and that view is the same as this. But that view involves both a right and a wrong; and this view involves also a right and a wrong:—are there indeed, or are there not the two views, that and this? They have not found their point of correspondency which is called the pivot of the Tâo. As soon as one finds this pivot, he stands in the centre of the ring (of thought), where he can respond without end to the changing views;—without end to those affirming, and without end to those denying. Therefore I said, 'There is nothing like the proper light (of the mind).'

4. By means of a finger (of my own) to illustrate that the finger (of another) is not a finger is not so good a plan as to illustrate that it is not so by means of what is (acknowledged to be) not a finger; and by means of (what I call) a horse to illustrate that (what another calls) a horse is not so, is not so good a plan as to illustrate that it is not a horse, by means of what is (acknowledged to be) not a horse. (All things in) heaven and earth may be (dealt with as) a finger; (each of) their myriads may be (dealt with as) a horse. Does a thing seem so to me? (I say that) it is so. Does it seem not so to me? (I say that) it is not so. A path is formed by (constant) treading on the ground. A thing is called by its name through the (constant) application of the name to it. How is it so? It is so because it is so. How is it not so? It is not so, because it is not so. Everything has its inherent character and its proper capability. There is nothing which has not these. Therefore, this being so, if we take a stalk of grain and a (large) pillar, a loathsome (leper) and (a beauty like) Hsî Shih, things large and things insecure, things crafty and things strange;—they may in the light of the Tâo all be reduced to the same category (of opinion about them).

It was separation that led to completion; from completion ensued dissolution. But all things, without reoard to their completion and dissolution, may again be comprehended in their unity;—it is only the far reaching in thought who know how to comprehend them in this unity. This being so, let us give up our devotion to our own views, and occupy ourselves with the ordinary views. These ordinary views are grounded on the use of things. (The study of that) use leads to the comprehensive judgment, and that judgment secures the success (of the inquiry). That success gained, we are near (to the object of our search), and there we stop. When we stop, and yet we do not know how it is so, we have what is called the Tâo.

When we toil our spirits and intelligence, obstinately determined (to establish our own view), and do not know the agreement (which underlies it and the views of others), we have what is called 'In the morning three.' What is meant by that 'In the morning three?' A keeper of monkeys, in giving them out their acorns, (once) said, 'In the morning I will give you three (measures) and in the evening four.' This made them all angry, and he said, 'Very well. In the morning I will give you four and in the evening three.' His two proposals were substantially the same, but the result of the one was to make the creatures angry, and of the other to make them pleased:—an illustration of the point I am insisting on. Therefore the sagely man brings together a dispute in its affirmations and denials, and rests in the equal fashioning of Heaven. Both sides of the question are admissible.

•••

6. But here now are some other sayings:—I do not know whether they are of the same character as those which I have already given, or of a different character. Whether they be of the same character or not when looked at along with them, they have a character of their own, which cannot be distinguished from the others. But though this be the case, let me try to explain myself.

There was a beginning. There was a beginning before that beginning. There was a beginning previous to that beginning before there was the beginning.

There was existence; there had been no existence. There was no existence before the beginning of that no existence. There was no existence previous to the no existence before there was the beginning of the no existence. If suddenly there was nonexistence, we do not know whether it was really anything existing, or really not existing. Now I have said what I have said, but I do not know whether what I have said be really anything to the point or not.

Under heaven there is nothing greater than the tip of an autumn down, and the Thâi mountain is small. There is no one more long-lived than a child which dies prematurely, and Phang Tsû did not live out his time. Heaven, Earth, and I were produced together, and all things and I are one. Since they are one, can there be speech about them? But since they are spoken of as one, must there not be room for speech? One and Speech are two; two and one are three. Going on from this (in our enumeration), the most skilful reckoner cannot reach (the end of the necessary numbers), and how much less can ordinary people do so! Therefore from non-existence we proceed to existence till we arrive at three; proceeding from existence to existence, to how many should we reach? Let us abjure such procedure, and simply rest here.

7. The Tâo at first met with no responsive recognition. Speech at first had no constant forms of expression. Because of this there came the demarcations (of different views). Let me describe those demarcations:—they are the Left and the Right; the Relations and their Obligations; Classifications and their Distinctions; Emulations and Contentions. These are what are called 'the Eight Qualities.' Outside the limits of the world of men, the sage occupies his thoughts, but does not discuss about anything; inside those limits he occupies his thoughts, but does not pass any judgments. In the Khun Khiû, which embraces the history of the former kings, the sage indicates his judgments, but does not argue (in vindication

of them). Thus it is that he separates his characters from one another without appearing to do so, and argues without the form of argument. How does he do so? The sage cherishes his views in his own breast, while men generally state theirs argumentatively, to show them to others. Hence we have the saying, 'Disputation is a proof of not seeing clearly.'

The Great Tâo does not admit of being praised. The Great Argument does not require words. Great Benevolence is not (officiously) benevolent. Great Disinterestedness does not vaunt its humility. Great Courage is not seen in stubborn bravery.

The Tâo that is displayed is not the Tâo. Words that are argumentative do not reach the point. Benevolence that is constantly exercised does not accomplish its object. Disinterestedness that vaunts its purity is not genuine. Courage that is most stubborn is ineffectual. These five seem to be round (and complete), but they tend to become square (and immovable). Therefore the knowledge that stops at what it does not know is the greatest. Who knows the argument that needs no words, and the Way that is not to be trodden?

He who is able to know this has what is called 'The Heavenly Treasure-house.' He may pour into it without its being filled; he may pour from it without its being exhausted; and all the while he does not know whence (the supply) comes. This is what is called 'The Store of Light.'

Therefore of old Yâo asked Shun, saying, 'I wish to smite (the rulers of) Tsung, Kwei, and Hsü-âo. Even when standing in my court, I cannot get them out of my mind. How is it so?' Shun replied, 'Those three rulers live (in their little states) as if they were among the mugwort and other brushwood;—how is it that you cannot get them out of your mind? Formerly, ten suns came out together, and all things were illuminated by them;—how much should (your) virtue exceed (all) suns!'

8. Nieh Khüeh asked Wang Î, saying, 'Do you know, Sir, what all creatures agree in approving and affirming?' 'How should I know it?' was the reply. 'Do you know what it is that you do not know?' asked the other again, and he got the same reply. He asked a third time,—'Then are all creatures thus without knowledge?' and Wang Î answered as before, (adding however), 'Notwithstanding, I will try and explain my meaning. How do you know that when I say "I know it," I really (am showing that) I do not know it, and that when I say "I do not know it," I really am showing that I do know it.' And let me ask you some questions:—'If a man sleep in a damp place, he will have a pain in his loins, and half his body will be as if it were dead; but will it be so with an eel? If he be living in a tree, he will be frightened and all in a tremble; but will it be so with a monkey? And does any one of the three know his right place ? Men eat animals that have been fed on grain and grass; deer feed on the thick-set grass; centipedes enjoy small snakes; owls and crows delight in mice; but does any one of the four know the right taste? The dog-headed monkey finds its mate in the female gibbon; the elk

and the axis deer cohabit; and the eel enjoys itself with other fishes. Mâo Tshiang and Lî Kî were accounted by men to be most beautiful, but when fishes saw them, they dived deep in the water from them; when birds, they flew from them aloft; and when deer saw them, they separated and fled away. But did any of these four know which in the world is the right female attraction? As I look at the matter, the first principles of benevolence and rightcousness and the paths of approval and disapproval are inextricably mixed and confused together:—how is it possible that I should know how to discriminate among them?'

Nieh Khüeh said (further), 'Since you, Sir, do not know what is advantageous and what is hurtful, is the Perfect man also in the same way without the knowledge of them?' Wang Î replied, 'The Perfect man is spirit-like. Great lakes might be boiling about him, and he would not feel their heat; the Ho and the Han might be frozen tip, and he would not feel the cold; the hurrying thunderbolts might split the mountains, and the wind shake the ocean, without being able to make him afraid. Being such, he mounts on the clouds of the air, rides on the sun and moon, and rambles at ease beyond the four seas. Neither death nor life makes any change in him, and how much less should the considerations of advantage and injury do so!'

9. Khü Tshiâo-tsze asked Khang-wû Tsze, saying, 'I heard the Master (speaking of such language as the following):—"The sagely man does not occupy himself with worldly affairs. He does not put himself in the way of what is profitable, nor try to avoid what is hurtful; he has no pleasure in seeking (for anything from any one); he does not care to be found in (any established) Way; he speaks without speaking; he does not speak when he speaks; thus finding his enjoyment outside the dust and dirt (of the world)." The Master considered all this to be a shoreless flow of mere words, and I consider it to describe the course of the Mysterious Way.—What do you, Sir, think of it?' Khang-wû Tsze replied, 'The hearing of such words would have perplexed even Hwang-Tî, and how should Khiû be competent to understand them? And you, moreover, are too hasty in forming your estimate (of their meaning). You see the egg, and (immediately) look out for the cock (that is to be hatched from it); you see the bow, and (immediately) look out for the dove (that is to be brought down by it) being roasted. I will try to explain the thing to you in a rough way; do you in the same way listen to me.

'How could any one stand by the side of the sun and moon, and hold under his arm all space and all time? (Such language only means that the sagely man) keeps his mouth shut, and puts aside questions that are uncertain and dark; making his inferior capacities unite with him in honouring (the One Lord). Men in general bustle about and toil; the sagely man seems stupid and to know nothing. He blends ten thousand years together in the one (conception of time); the myriad things all pursue their spontaneous course, and they are all before him as doing so.

'How do I know that the love of life is not a delusion? and that the dislike of death is not like a young person's losing his way, and not knowing that he is (really) going home? Lî Kî was a daughter of the border Warden of Âi. When (the ruler of) the state of Tsin first got possession of her, she wept till the tears wetted all the front of her dress. But when she came to the place of the king, shared with him his luxurious couch, and ate his grain-and-grass-fed meat, then she regretted that she had wept. How do I know that the dead do not repent of their former craving for life?

'Those who dream of (the pleasures of) drinking may in the morning wail and weep; those who dream of wailing and weeping may in the morning be going out to hunt. When they were dreaming they did not know it was a dream; in their dream they may even have tried to interpret it; but when they awoke they knew that it was a dream. And there is the great awaking, after which we shall know that this life was a great dream. All the while, the stupid think they are awake, and with nice discrimination insist on their knowledge; now playing the part of rulers, and now of grooms. Bigoted was that Khiû! He and you are both dreaming. I who say that you are dreaming am dreaming myself. These words seem very strange; but if after ten thousand ages we once meet with a great sage who knows how to explain them, it will be as if we met him (unexpectedly) some morning or evening.

10. 'Since you made me enter into this discussion with you, if you have got the better of me and not I of you, are you indeed right, and I indeed wrong? If I have got the better of you and not you of me, am I indeed right and you indeed wrong? Is the one of us right and the other wrong? are we both right or both wrong? Since we cannot come to a mutual and common understanding, men will certainly continue in darkness on the subject.

'Whom shall I employ to adjudicate in the matter? If I employ one who agrees with you, how can he, agreeing with you, do so correctly? And the same may be said, if I employ one who agrees with me. It will be the same if I employ one who differs from us both or one who agrees with us both. In this way I and you and those others would all not be able to come to a mutual understanding; and shall we then wait for that (great sage)? (We need not do so.) To wait on others to learn how conflicting opinions are changed is simply like not so waiting at all. The harmonising of them is to be found in the invisible operation of Heaven, and by following this on into the unlimited past. It is by this method that we can complete our years (without our minds being disturbed).

'What is meant by harmonising (conflicting opinions) in the invisible operation of Heaven? There is the affirmation and the denial of it; and there is the assertion of an opinion and the rejection of it. If the affirmation be according to the reality of the fact, it is certainly different from the denial of it:—there can be no dispute about that. If the assertion of an opinion be correct, it is certainly different from its rejection:—neither can there be any dispute about that. Let us forget the lapse of time; let us forget the conflict of opinions. Let us make our appeal to the Infinite, and take up our position there.'

11. The Penumbra asked the Shadow, saying, 'Formerly you were walking on, and now you have stopped; formerly you were sitting, and now you have risen up:—how is it that you are so without stability?' The Shadow replied, 'I wait for the movements of something else to do what I do, and that something else on which I wait waits further on another to do as it does. My waiting,—is it for the scales of a snake, or the wings of a cicada? How should I know why I do one thing, or do not do another?

    'Formerly, I, Kwang Kâu, dreamt that I was a butterfly, a butterfly flying about, feeling that it was enjoying itself. I did not know that it was Kâu. Suddenly I awoke, and was myself again, the veritable Kâu. I did not know whether it had formerly been Kâu dreaming that he was a butterfly, or it was now a butterfly dreaming that it was Kâu. But between Kâu and a butterfly there must be a difference. This is a case of what is called the Transformation of Things.'

DISCUSSION QUESTIONS

1. Compare the story of Li Ki here with the Buddhist parable of the arrow. Explain the main similarities and differences.

2. Explain the butterfly passage.

3. How do the ideas here relate to the ideas in the *Tao te Ching*? Explain.

4. Compare the butterfly passage to Borges's two pieces. Explain the main similarities and differences.

Meditations I & II

By René Descartes

As mentioned in Part I of Four Fundamental Questions, *Descartes was a rationalist. Descartes'* Meditations on First Philosophy *was first published in 1641. There are six meditations in the book. In Meditation I, Descartes lays out his criteria for knowledge. Since he had found out that things he believed to be true in the past turned out to be false, he now determines how not to be deceived. He wants to know what cannot be doubted. At the end of the Meditation, he has decided that nothing is indubitable. In Meditation II, Descartes finds one thing that cannot be doubted: that he exists. Using this foothold, Descartes provides a conceptual proof for God's existence in Meditation III. Meditation IV delves deeper into how to tell truth from falsehood. Another argument for God's existence is provided in Meditation V. He derives the ordinary world again in Meditation VI, from the idea that God is not a deceiver.*

Meditations I and II are included here. In Meditation I, using his method of doubting, one by one he eliminates things he thinks are true, if they can be doubted. The material world, his own body, science, and even mathematics are eliminated. Descartes introduces the idea of an evil demon, who could make us think that 2 + 3 = 6, as he said "how do I know that I am not deceived every time that I add two and three." In Meditation II, he utters "I am, I exist." This is the foothold, what he knows for certain. He must exist, he states, because there must be something that exists that is doing the doubting. But what is he? A "thinking thing," is all he is justified in concluding based on Meditation I.

MEDITATION I: OF THE THINGS OF WHICH WE MAY DOUBT

Several years have now elapsed since I first became aware that I had accepted, even from my youth, many false opinions for true, and that consequently what I afterwards based on such principles was highly doubtful; and from that time I was convinced of the necessity of undertaking once in my life to rid myself of all the opinions I had adopted, and of commencing anew the work of building from the foundation, if I desired to establish a firm and abiding superstructure in the sciences. But as this enterprise appeared to me to be one of great magnitude, I waited until I had attained an age so mature as to leave me no hope that at any stage of life more advanced I should be better able to execute my design. On this account, I have delayed so long that I should henceforth consider I was doing wrong were I still to consume in deliberation any of the time that now remains for action. To-day, then, since I have opportunely freed my mind from all cares [and am happily disturbed by no passions], and since I am in the secure possession of leisure in a peaceable retirement, I will at length apply myself earnestly and freely to the general overthrow of all my former opinions. But, to this end, it will not be necessary for me to show that the whole of these are false—a point, perhaps, which I shall never reach; but as even now my reason convinces me that I ought not the less carefully to withhold belief from what is not entirely certain and indubitable, than from what is manifestly false, it will be sufficient to justify the rejection of the whole if I shall find in each some ground for doubt. Nor for this purpose will it be necessary even to deal with each belief individually, which would be truly an endless labour; but, as the removal from below of the foundation necessarily involves the downfall of the whole edifice, I will at once approach the criticism of the principles on which all my former beliefs rested.

All that I have, up to this moment, accepted as possessed of the highest truth and certainty, I received either from or through the senses. I observed, however, that these sometimes misled us; and it is the part of prudence not to place absolute confidence in that by which we have even once been deceived.

But it may be said, perhaps, that, although the senses occasionally mislead us respecting minute objects, and such as are so far removed from us as to be beyond the reach of close observation, there are yet many other of their informations (presentations), of the truth of which it is manifestly impossible to doubt; as for example, that I am in this place, seated by the fire, clothed in a winter dressing-gown, that I hold in my hands this piece of paper, with other intimations of the same nature. But how could I deny that I possess these hands and this body, and withal escape being classed with persons in a state of insanity, whose brains are so disordered and clouded by dark bilious vapours as to cause them pertinaciously to assert that they are monarchs when they are in the greatest poverty; or clothed [in gold] and purple when destitute of any covering; or that their head is made of clay, their body of glass, or that they are gourds? I should certainly be not less insane than they, were I to regulate my procedure according to examples so extravagant.

Though this be true, I must nevertheless here consider that I am a man, and that, consequently, I am in the habit of sleeping, and representing to myself in dreams those same things, or even sometimes others less probable, which the insane think are presented to them in their waking moments. How often have I dreamt that I was in these familiar circumstances—that I was dressed, and occupied this place by the fire, when I was lying undressed in bed? At the present moment, however, I certainly look upon this paper with eyes wide awake; the head which I now move is not asleep; I extend this hand consciously and with express purpose, and I perceive it; the occurrences in sleep are not so distinct as all this. But I cannot forget that, at other times, I have been deceived in sleep by similar illusions; and, attentively considering those cases, I perceive so clearly that there exist no certain marks by which the state of waking can ever be distinguished from sleep, that I feel greatly astonished; and in amazement I almost persuade myself that I am now dreaming.

Let us suppose, then, that we are dreaming, and that all these particulars—namely, the opening of the eyes, the motion of the head, the forth-putting of the hands—are merely illusions; and even that we really possess neither an entire body nor hands such as we see. Nevertheless, it must be admitted at least that the objects which appear to us in sleep are, as it were, painted representations which could not have been formed unless in the likeness of realities; and, therefore, that those general objects, at all events—namely, eyes, a head, hands, and an entire body—are not simply imaginary, but really existent. For, in truth, painters themselves, even when they study to represent sirens and satyrs by forms the most fantastic and extraordinary, cannot bestow upon them natures absolutely new, but can only make a certain medley of the members of different animals; or if they chance to imagine something so novel that nothing at all similar has ever been seen before, and such as is, therefore, purely fictitious and absolutely false, it is at least certain that the colours of which this is composed are real.

And on the same principle, although these general objects, *viz.* [a body], eyes, a head, hands, and the like, be imaginary, we are nevertheless absolutely necessitated to admit the reality at least of some other objects still more simple and universal than these, of which, just as of certain real colours, all those images of things, whether true and real, or false and fantastic, that are found in our consciousness (cogitatio), are formed.

To this class of objects seem to belong corporeal nature in general and its extension; the figure of extended things, their quantity or magnitude, and their number, as also the place in, and the time during, which they exist, and other things of the same sort. We will not, therefore, perhaps reason illegitimately if we conclude from this that physics, astronomy, medicine, and all the other sciences that have for their end the consideration of composite objects, are indeed of a doubtful character; but that arithmetic, geometry, and the other sciences of the same class, which regard merely the simplest and most general objects, and scarcely inquire whether or not these are really existent, contain somewhat that is certain and indubitable: for whether I am awake or dreaming, it remains true that two and three make five, and that a square has but four sides; nor does it seem possible that truths so apparent can ever fall under a suspicion of falsity [or incertitude].

Nevertheless, the belief that there is a God who is all-powerful, and who created me, such as I am, has for a long time, obtained steady possession of my mind. How, then, do I know that he has not arranged that there should be neither earth, nor sky, nor any extended thing, nor figure, nor magnitude, nor place, providing at the same time, however, for [the rise in me of the perceptions of all these objects, and] the persuasion that these do not exist otherwise than as I perceive them? And further, as I sometimes think that others are in error respecting matters of which they believe themselves to possess a perfect knowledge, how do I know that I am not also deceived each time I add together two and three, or number the sides of a square, or form some judgment still more simple, if more simple indeed can be imagined? But perhaps Deity has not been willing that I should be thus deceived, for He is said to be supremely good. If, however, it were repugnant to the goodness of Deity to have created me subject to constant deception, it would seem likewise to be contrary to his goodness to allow me to be occasionally deceived; and yet it is clear that this is permitted. Some, indeed, might perhaps be found who would be disposed rather to deny the existence of a being so powerful than to believe that there is nothing certain. But let us for the present refrain from opposing this opinion, and grant that all which is here said of a Deity is fabulous: nevertheless, in whatever way it be supposed that I reached the state in which I exist, whether by fate, or chance, or by an endless series of antecedents and consequents, or by any other means, it is clear (since to be deceived and to err is a certain defect) that the probability of my being so imperfect as to be the constant victim of deception, will be increased exactly in proportion as the power possessed by the cause, to which they assign my origin, is lessened. To these reasonings I have assuredly nothing to reply, but am constrained at last to avow that there is nothing at all that I formerly believed to be true of which it is impossible to doubt, and that not through thoughtlessness or levity, but from cogent and maturely considered reasons; so that henceforward, if I desire to discover anything certain, I ought not the less carefully to refrain from assenting to those same opinions than to what might be shown to be manifestly false.

But it is not sufficient to have made these observations; care must be taken likewise to keep them in remembrance. For those old and customary opinions perpetually recur—long and familiar usage giving them the right of occupying my mind, even almost against my will, and subduing my belief; nor will I lose the habit of deferring to them and confiding in them so long as I shall consider them to be what in truth they are, *viz.*, opinions to some extent doubtful, as I have already shown, but still highly probable, and such as it is much more reasonable to believe than deny. It is for this reason I am persuaded that I shall not be doing wrong, if, taking an opposite judgment of deliberate design, I become my own deceiver, by supposing, for a time, that all those opinions are entirely false and imaginary, until at length, having thus balanced my old by my new prejudices, my judgment shall no longer be turned aside by perverted usage from the path that may conduct to the perception of truth. For I am assured that, meanwhile, there will arise neither peril nor error from this course, and that I cannot for the present yield too much to distrust, since the end I now seek is not action but knowledge.

I will suppose, then, not that Deity, who is sovereignly good and the fountain of truth, but that some malignant demon, who is at once exceedingly potent and deceitful, has employed all his artifice to deceive me; I will suppose that the sky, the air, the earth, colours, figures, sounds, and all external things, are nothing better than the illusions of dreams, by means of which this being has laid snares for my credulity; I will consider myself as without hands, eyes, flesh, blood, or any of the senses, and as falsely believing that I am possessed of these; I will continue resolutely fixed in this belief, and if indeed by this means it be not in my power to arrive at the knowledge of truth, I shall at least do what is in my power, *viz.* [suspend my judgment], and guard with settled purpose against giving my assent to what is false, and being imposed upon by this deceiver, whatever be his power and artifice.

But this undertaking is arduous, and a certain indolence insensibly leads me back to my ordinary course of life; and just as the captive, who, perchance, was enjoying in his dreams an imaginary liberty, when he begins to suspect that it is but a vision, dreads awakening, and conspires with the agreeable illusions that the deception may be prolonged; so I, of my own accord, fall back into the train of my former beliefs, and fear to arouse myself from my slumber, lest the time of laborious wakefulness that would succeed this quiet rest, in place of bringing any light of day, should prove inadequate to dispel the darkness that will arise from the difficulties that have now been raised.

MEDITATION II: OF THE NATURE OF THE HUMAN MIND; AND THAT IT IS MORE EASILY KNOWN THAN THE BODY

THE Meditation of yesterday has filled my mind with so many doubts, that it is no longer in my power to forget them. Nor do I see, meanwhile, any principle on which they can be resolved; and, just as if I had fallen all of a sudden into very deep water, I am so greatly disconcerted as to be made unable either to plant my feet firmly on the bottom or sustain myself by swimming on the surface. I will, nevertheless, make an effort, and try anew the same path on which I had entered yesterday, that is, proceed by casting aside all that admits of the slightest doubt, not less than if I had discovered it to be absolutely false; and I will continue always in this track until I shall find something that is certain, or at least, if I can do nothing more, until I shall know with certainty that there is nothing certain. Archimedes, that he might transport the entire globe from the place it occupied to another, demanded only a point that was firm and immovable; so also, I shall be entitled to entertain the highest expectations, if I am fortunate enough to discover only one thing that is certain and indubitable.

I suppose, accordingly, that all the things which I see are false (fictitious); I believe that none of those objects which my fallacious memory represents ever existed; I suppose that I possess no senses; I believe that body, figure, extension, motion, and place are merely fictions of my mind. What is there, then, that can be esteemed true? Perhaps this only, that there is absolutely nothing certain.

But how do I know that there is not something different altogether from the objects I have now enumerated, of which it is impossible to entertain the slightest doubt? Is there not a God, or some being, by whatever name I may designate him, who causes these thoughts to arise in my mind? But why suppose such a being, for it may be I myself am capable of producing them? Am I, then, at least not something? But I before denied that I possessed senses or a body; I hesitate, however, for what follows from that? Am I so dependent on the body and the senses that without these I cannot exist? But I had the persuasion that there was absolutely nothing in the world, that there was no sky and no earth, neither minds nor bodies; was I not, therefore, at the same time, persuaded that I did not exist? Far from it; I assuredly existed, since I was persuaded. But there is I know not what being, who is possessed at once of the highest power and the deepest cunning, who is constantly employing all his ingenuity in deceiving me. Doubtless, then, I exist, since I am deceived; and, let him deceive me as he may, he can never bring it about that I am nothing, so long as I shall be conscious that I am something. So that it must, in fine, be maintained, all things being maturely and carefully considered, that this proposition (pronunciatum) I am, I exist, is necessarily true each time it is expressed by me, or conceived in my mind.

But I do not yet know with sufficient clearness what I am, though assured that I am; and hence, in the next place, I must take care, lest perchance I inconsiderately substitute some other object in room of what is properly myself, and thus wander from truth, even in that knowledge (cognition) which I hold to be of all others the most certain and evident. For this reason, I will now consider anew what I formerly believed myself to be, before I entered on the present train of thought; and of my previous opinion I will retrench all that can in the least be invalidated by the grounds of doubt I have adduced, in order that there may at length remain nothing but what is certain and indubitable. What then did I formerly think I was? Undoubtedly I judged that I was a man. But what is a man? Shall I say a rational animal? Assuredly not; for it would be necessary forthwith to inquire into what is meant by animal, and what by rational, and thus, from a single question, I should insensibly glide into others, and these more difficult than the first; nor do I now possess enough of leisure to warrant me in wasting my time amid subtleties of this sort. I prefer here to attend to the thoughts that sprung up of themselves in my mind, and were inspired by my own nature alone, when I applied myself to the consideration of what I was. In the first place, then, I thought that I possessed a countenance, hands, arms, and all the fabric of members that appears in a corpse, and which I called by the name of body. It further occurred to me that I was nourished, that I walked, perceived, and thought, and all those actions I referred to the soul; but what the soul itself was I either did not stay to consider, or, if I did, I imagined that it was something extremely rare and subtile, like wind, or flame, or ether, spread through my grosser parts. As regarded the body, I did not even doubt of its nature, but thought I distinctly knew it, and if I had wished to describe it according to the notions I then entertained, I should have explained myself in this manner: By body I understand all that can be terminated by a certain figure; that can be comprised in a certain place, and so fill a certain space as therefrom to exclude every other body; that can be perceived either by touch, sight, hearing, taste, or smell; that can be moved in different ways, not indeed of itself, but by something foreign to it by which it is touched [and from which it receives the impression]; for the power of self-motion, as likewise that of perceiving and thinking, I held as by no means pertaining to the nature of body; on the contrary, I was somewhat astonished to find such faculties existing in some bodies.

But [as to myself, what can I now say that I am], since I suppose there exists an extremely powerful, and, if I may so speak, malignant being, whose whole endeavours are directed towards deceiving me? Can I affirm that I possess any one of all those attributes of which I have lately spoken as belonging to the nature of body? After attentively considering them in my own mind, I find none of them that can properly be said to belong to myself. To recount them were idle and tedious. Let us pass, then, to the attributes of the soul. The first mentioned were the powers of nutrition and walking; but, if it be true that I have no body, it is true likewise that I am capable neither of walking nor of being nourished. Perception is another attribute of the soul; but perception too is impossible without the body: besides, I have frequently, during sleep, believed that I perceived objects which I afterwards observed I did not in reality perceive. Thinking is another attribute of the soul; and here I discover what properly belongs to myself. This alone is inseparable from me. I am—I exist: this is certain; but how often? As often as I think; for perhaps it would even happen, if I should wholly cease to think, that I should at the same time altogether cease to be. I now admit nothing that is not necessarily true: I am therefore, precisely speaking, only a thinking thing, that is, a mind (mens sive animus), understanding, or reason,—terms whose signification was before unknown to me. I am, however, a real thing, and really existent; but what thing? The answer was, a thinking thing. The question now arises, am I aught besides? I will stimulate my imagination with a view to discover whether I am not still something more than a thinking being. Now it is plain I am not the assemblage of members called the human body; I am not a thin and penetrating air diffused through all these members, or wind, or flame, or vapour, or breath, or any of all the things I can imagine; for I supposed that all these were not, and, without changing the supposition, I find that I still feel assured of my existence.

But it is true, perhaps, that those very things which I suppose to be non-existent, because they are unknown to me, are not in truth different from myself whom I know. This is a point I cannot determine, and do not now enter into any dispute regarding it. I can only judge of things that are known to me: I am conscious that I exist, and I who know that I exist inquire into what I am. It is, however, perfectly certain that the knowledge of my existence, thus precisely taken, is not dependent on things, the existence of which is as yet unknown to me: and consequently it is not dependent on any of the things I can feign in imagination. Moreover, the phrase itself, I frame an image (*effingo*), reminds me of my error; for I should in truth frame one if I were to imagine myself to be anything, since to imagine is nothing more than to contemplate the figure or image of a corporeal thing; but I already know that I exist, and that it is possible at the same time that all those images, and in general all that relates to the nature of body, are merely dreams [or chimeras]. From this I discover that it is not more reasonable to say, I will excite my imagination that I may know more distinctly what I am, than to express myself as follows: I am now awake, and perceive something real; but because my perception is not sufficiently clear, I will of express purpose go to sleep that my dreams may represent to me the object of my perception with more truth and clearness. And, therefore, I know that nothing of all that I can embrace in imagination belongs to the knowledge which I have of myself, and that there is need to recall with the utmost care the mind from this mode of thinking, that it may be able to know its own nature with perfect distinctness.

But what, then, am I? A thinking thing, it has been said. But what is a thinking thing? It is a thing that doubts, understands [conceives], affirms, denies, wills, refuses, that imagines also, and perceives. Assuredly it is not little, if all these properties belong to my nature. But why should they not belong to it? Am I not that very being who now doubts of almost everything; who, for all that, understands and conceives certain things, who affirms one alone as true, and denies the others; who desires to know more of them, and does not wish to be deceived; who imagines many things, sometimes even despite his will; and is likewise percipient of many, as if through the medium of the senses. Is there nothing of all this as true as that I am, even although I should be always dreaming, and although he who gave me being employed all his ingenuity to deceive me? Is there also any one of these attributes that can be properly distinguished from my thought, or that can be said to be separate from myself? For it is of itself so evident that it is I who doubt, I who understand, and I who desire, that it is here unnecessary to add anything by way of rendering it more clear. And I am as certainly the same being who imagines; for, although it may be (as I before supposed) that nothing I imagine is true, still the power of imagination does not cease really to exist in me and to form part of my thoughts. In fine, I am the same being who perceives, that is, who apprehends certain objects as by the organs of sense, since, in truth, I see light, hear a noise, and feel heat. But it will be said that these presentations are false, and that I am dreaming. Let it be so. At all events it is certain that I seem to see light, hear a noise, and feel heat; this cannot be false, and this is what in me is properly called perceiving (sentire), which is nothing else than thinking. From this I begin to know what I am with somewhat greater clearness and distinctness than heretofore.

But, nevertheless, it still seems to me, and I cannot help believing, that corporeal things, whose images are formed by thought [which fall under the senses], and are examined by the same, are known with much greater distinctness than that I know not what part of myself which is not imaginable; although, in truth, it may seem strange to say that I know and comprehend with greater distinctness things whose existence appears to me doubtful, that are unknown, and do not belong to me, than others of whose reality I am persuaded, that are known to me, and appertain to my proper nature; in a word, than myself. But I see clearly what is the state of the case. My mind is apt to wander, and will not yet submit to be restrained within the limits of truth. Let us therefore leave the mind to itself once more, and, according to it every kind of liberty [permit it to consider the objects that appear to it from without], in order that, having afterwards withdrawn it from these gently and opportunely [and fixed it on the consideration of its being and the properties it finds in itself], it may then be the more easily controlled.

Let us now accordingly consider the objects that are commonly thought to be [the most easily, and likewise] the most distinctly known, *viz.*, the bodies we touch and see; not, indeed, bodies in general, for these general notions are usually somewhat more confused, but one body in particular. Take, for example, this piece of wax; it is quite fresh, having been but recently taken from the beehive; it has not yet lost the sweetness of the honey it contained; it still retains somewhat of the odour of the flowers from which it was gathered; its colour, figure, size, are apparent (to the sight); it is hard, cold, easily handled; and sounds when struck upon with the finger. In fine, all that contributes to make a body as distinctly known as possible, is found in the one before us. But, while I am speaking, let it be placed near the fire—what remained of the taste exhales, the smell evaporates, the colour changes, its figure is destroyed, its size increases, it becomes liquid, it grows hot, it can hardly be handled, and, although struck upon, it emits no sound. Does the same wax still remain after this change? It must be admitted that it does remain; no one doubts it, or judges otherwise. What, then, was it I knew with so much distinctness in the piece of wax? Assuredly, it could be nothing of all that I observed by means of the senses, since all the things that fell under taste, smell, sight, touch, and hearing are changed, and yet the same wax remains. It was perhaps what I now think, *viz.*, that this wax was neither the sweetness of honey, the pleasant odour of flowers, the whiteness, the figure, nor the sound, but only a body that a little before appeared to me conspicuous under these forms, and which is now perceived under others. But, to speak precisely, what is it that I imagine when I think of it in this way? Let it be attentively considered, and, retrenching all that does not belong to the wax, let us see what remains. There certainly remains nothing, except something extended, flexible, and movable. But what is meant by flexible and movable? Is it not that I imagine that the piece of wax, being round, is capable of becoming square, or of passing from a square into a triangular figure? Assuredly such is not the case, because I conceive that it admits of an infinity of similar changes; and I am, moreover, unable to compass this infinity by imagination, and consequently this conception which I have of the wax is not the product of the faculty of imagination. But what now is this extension? Is it not also unknown? for it becomes greater when the wax is melted, greater when it is boiled, and greater still when the heat increases; and I should not conceive [clearly and] according to truth, the wax as it is, if I did not suppose that the piece we are considering admitted even of a wider variety of extension than I ever imagined. I must, therefore, admit that I cannot even comprehend by imagination what the piece of wax is, and that it is the mind alone (*mens*, Lat.; *entendement*, F.) which perceives it. I speak of one piece in particular; for, as to wax in general, this is still more evident. But what is the piece of wax that can be perceived only by the [understanding of] mind? It is certainly the same which I see, touch, imagine; and, in fine, it is the same which, from the beginning, I believed it to be. But (and this it is of moment to observe) the perception of it is neither an act of sight, of touch, nor of imagination, and never was either of these, though it might formerly seem so, but is simply an intuition (inspectio) of the mind, which may be imperfect and confused, as it formerly was, or very clear and distinct, as it is at present, according as the attention is more or less directed to the elements which it contains, and of which it is composed.

But, meanwhile, I feel greatly astonished when I observe [the weakness of my mind, and] its proneness to error. For although, without at all giving expression to what I think, I consider all this in my own mind, words yet occasionally impede my progress, and I am almost led into error by the terms of ordinary language. We say, for example, that we see the same wax when it is before us, and not that we judge it to be the same from its retaining the same colour and figure: whence I should forthwith be disposed to conclude that the wax is known by the act of sight, and not by the intuition of the mind alone, were it not for the analogous instance of human beings passing on in the street below, as observed from a window. In this case I do not fail to say that I see the men themselves, just as I say that I see the wax; and yet what do I see from the window beyond hats and cloaks that might cover artificial machines, whose motions might be determined by springs? But I judge that there are human beings from these appearances, and thus I comprehend, by the faculty of judgment alone which is in the mind, what I believed I saw with my eyes.

The man who makes it his aim to rise to knowledge superior to the common, ought to be ashamed to seek occasions of doubting from the vulgar forms of speech: instead, therefore, of doing this, I shall proceed with the matter in hand, and inquire whether I had a clearer and more perfect perception of the piece of wax when I first saw it, and when I thought I knew it by means of the external sense itself, or, at all events, by the common sense (*sensus communis*), as it is called, that is, by the imaginative faculty; or whether I rather apprehend it more clearly at present, after having examined with greater care, both what it is, and in what way it can be known. It would certainly be ridiculous to entertain any doubt on this point. For what, in that first perception, was there distinct? What did I perceive which any animal might not have perceived? But when I distinguish the wax from its exterior forms, and when, as if I had stripped it of its vestments, I consider it quite naked, it is certain, although some error may still be found in my judgment, that I cannot, nevertheless, thus apprehend it without possessing a human mind.

But, finally, what shall I say of the mind itself, that is, of myself? for as yet I do not admit that I am anything but mind. What, then! I who seem to possess so distinct an apprehension of the piece of wax,—do I not know myself, both with greater truth and certitude, and also much more distinctly and clearly? For if I judge that the wax exists because I see it, it assuredly follows, much more evidently, that I myself am or exist, for the same reason: for it is possible that what I see may not in truth be wax, and that I do not even possess eyes with which to see anything; but it cannot be that when I see, or, which comes to the same thing, when I think I see, I myself who think am nothing. So likewise, if I judge that the wax exists because I touch it, it will still also follow that I am; and if I determine that my imagination, or any other cause, whatever it be, persuades me of the existence of the wax, I will still draw the same conclusion. And what is here remarked of the piece of wax is applicable to all the other things that are external to me. And further, if the [notion or] perception of wax appeared to me more precise and distinct, after that not only sight and touch, but many other causes besides, rendered it manifest to my apprehension, with how much greater distinctness must I now know myself, since all the reasons that contribute to the knowledge of the nature of wax, or of any body whatever, manifest still better the nature of my mind? And there are besides so many other things in the mind itself that contribute to the illustration of its nature, that those dependent on the body, to which I have here referred, scarcely merit to be taken into account.

But, in conclusion, I find I have insensibly reverted to the point I desired; for, since it is now manifest to me that bodies themselves are not properly perceived by the senses nor by the faculty of imagination, but by the intellect alone; and since they are not perceived because they are seen and touched, but only because they are understood [or rightly comprehended by thought], I readily discover that there is nothing more easily or clearly apprehended than my own mind. But because it is difficult to rid one's self so promptly of an opinion to which one has been long accustomed, it will be desirable to tarry for some time at this stage, that, by long continued meditation, I may more deeply impress upon my memory this new knowledge.

DISCUSSION QUESTIONS

1. Explain the wax example from Meditation I.

2. What are some ways around the "I am, I exist" argument? Explain.

3. Explain how the excerpt from the *Meditations* is connected to the excerpts in Part I of *Four Fundamental Questions*.

4. Compare how Descartes answers the question "How do I know if I am dreaming?" to the way Chuang Tzu answers.

An Essay Concerning Human Understanding

By John Locke

Locke's view on knowledge, like his view on self, can be found in of Book II of the Essay Concerning Human Understanding. *In this selection, Locke begins by defining terms such as "ideas," "sensation," and "reflection." Once these are defined, Locke argues that sensation and reflection are the only sources of ideas. This is his empiricism, the idea that we are blank slates when we are born. Once ideas are defined, he can distinguish between simple and complex ideas. Then he explains the empirical basis for various ideas. From there he moves on to how we generally tend to name only complex ideas.*

BOOK II: OF IDEAS

CHAPTER I
OF IDEAS IN GENERAL, AND THEIR ORIGINAL

1. Idea is the Object of Thinking.

   Every man being conscious to himself that he thinks; and that which his mind is applied about whilst thinking being the IDEAS that are there, it is past doubt that men have in their minds several ideas,—such as are those expressed by the words whiteness, hardness, sweetness, thinking, motion, man, elephant, army, drunkenness, and others: it is in the first place then to be inquired, HOW HE COMES BY THEM?

   I know it is a received doctrine, that men have native ideas, and original characters, stamped upon their minds in their very first being. This opinion I have at large examined already; and, I suppose what I have said in the foregoing Book will be much more easily admitted, when I have shown whence the understanding may get all the ideas it has; and by what ways and degrees they may come into the mind;—for which I shall appeal to every one's own observation and experience.

2. All Ideas come from Sensation or Reflection.

   Let us then suppose the mind to be, as we say, white paper, void of all characters, without any ideas:—How comes it to be furnished? Whence comes it by that vast store which the busy and boundless fancy of man has painted on it with an almost endless variety? Whence has it all the MATERIALS of reason and knowledge? To this I answer, in one word, from EXPERIENCE. In that all our knowledge is founded; and from that it ultimately derives itself. Our observation employed either, about external sensible objects, or about the internal operations of our minds perceived and reflected on by ourselves, is that which supplies our understandings with all the MATERIALS of thinking. These two are the fountains of knowledge, from whence all the ideas we have, or can naturally have, do spring.

3. The Objects of Sensation one Source of Ideas

First, our Senses, conversant about particular sensible objects, do convey into the mind several distinct perceptions of things, according to those various ways wherein those objects do affect them. And thus we come by those IDEAS we have of yellow, white, heat, cold, soft, hard, bitter, sweet, and all those which we call sensible qualities; which when I say the senses convey into the mind, I mean, they from external objects convey into the mind what produces there those perceptions. This great source of most of the ideas we have, depending wholly upon our senses, and derived by them to the understanding, I call SENSATION.

4. The Operations of our Minds, the other Source of them.

Secondly, the other fountain from which experience furnisheth the understanding with ideas is,—the perception of the operations of our own mind within us, as it is employed about the ideas it has got;—which operations, when the soul comes to reflect on and consider, do furnish the understanding with another set of ideas, which could not be had from things without. And such are perception, thinking, doubting, believing, reasoning, knowing, willing, and all the different actings of our own minds;—which we being conscious of, and observing in ourselves, do from these receive into our understandings as distinct ideas as we do from bodies affecting our senses. This source of ideas every man has wholly in himself; and though it be not sense, as having nothing to do with external objects, yet it is very like it, and might properly enough be called INTERNAL SENSE. But as I call the other Sensation, so I call this REFLECTION, the ideas it affords being such only as the mind gets by reflecting on its own operations within itself. By reflection then, in the following part of this discourse, I would be understood to mean, that notice which the mind takes of its own operations, and the manner of them, by reason whereof there come to be ideas of these operations in the understanding. These two, I say, *viz.* external material things, as the objects of SENSATION, and the operations of our own minds within, as the objects of REFLECTION, are to me the only originals from whence all our ideas take their beginnings. The term OPERATIONS here I use in a large sense, as comprehending not barely the actions of the mind about its ideas, but some sort of passions arising sometimes from them, such as is the satisfaction or uneasiness arising from any thought.

5. All our Ideas are of the one or of the other of these.

The understanding seems to me not to have the least glimmering of any ideas which it doth not receive from one of these two. EXTERNAL OBJECTS furnish the mind with the ideas of sensible qualities, which are all those different perceptions they produce in us; and THE MIND furnishes the understanding with ideas of its own operations.

These, when we have taken a full survey of them, and their several modes, and the compositions made out of them we shall find to contain all our whole stock of ideas; and that we have nothing in our minds which did not come in one of these two ways. Let any one examine his own thoughts, and thoroughly search into his understanding; and then let him tell me, whether all the original ideas he has there, are any other than of the objects of his senses, or of the operations of his mind, considered as objects of his reflection. And how great a mass of knowledge soever he imagines to be lodged there, he will, upon taking a strict view, see that he has not any idea in his mind but what one of these two have imprinted.

• • •

9. The Soul begins to have Ideas when it begins to perceive.

To ask, at what TIME a man has first any ideas, is to ask, when he begins to perceive;—HAVING IDEAS, and PERCEPTION, being the same thing. I know it is an opinion, that the soul always thinks, and that it has the actual perception of ideas in itself constantly, as long as it exists; and that actual thinking is as inseparable from the soul as actual extension is from the body; which if true, to inquire after the beginning of a man's ideas is the same as to inquire after the beginning of his soul. For, by this account, soul and its ideas, as body and its extension, will begin to exist both at the same time.

• • •

11. It is not always conscious of it.

I grant that the soul, in a waking man, is never without thought, because it is the condition of being awake. But whether sleeping without dreaming be not an affection of the whole man, mind as well as body, may be worth a waking man's consideration; it being hard to conceive that anything should think and not be conscious of it. If the soul doth think in a sleeping man without being conscious of it, I ask whether, during such thinking, it has any pleasure or pain, or be capable of happiness or misery? I am sure the man is not; no more than the bed or earth he lies on. For to be happy or miserable without being conscious of it, seems to me utterly inconsistent and impossible. Or if it be possible that the SOUL can, whilst the body is sleeping, have its thinking, enjoyments, and concerns, its pleasures or pain, apart, which the MAN is not conscious of nor partakes in,—it is certain that Socrates asleep and Socrates awake is not the same person; but his soul when he sleeps, and Socrates the man, consisting of body and soul, when he is waking, are two persons: since waking Socrates has no knowledge of, or concernment for that happiness or misery of his soul, which it enjoys alone by itself whilst he sleeps, without perceiving anything of it; no more than he has for the happiness or misery of a man in the Indies, whom he knows not. For, if we take wholly away all consciousness of our actions and sensations, especially of pleasure and pain, and the concernment that accompanies it, it will be hard to know wherein to place personal identity.

12. If a sleeping Man thinks without knowing it, the sleeping and waking Man are two Persons.

The soul, during sound sleep, thinks, say these men. Whilst it thinks and perceives, it is capable certainly of those of delight or trouble, as well as any other perceptions; and IT must necessarily be CONSCIOUS of its own perceptions. But it has all this apart: the sleeping MAN, it is plain, is conscious of nothing of all this. Let us suppose, then, the soul of Castor, while he is sleeping, retired from his body; which is no impossible supposition for the men I have here to do with, who so liberally allow life, without a thinking soul, to all other animals. These men cannot then judge it impossible, or a contradiction, that the body should live without the soul; nor that the soul should subsist and think, or have perception, even perception of happiness or misery, without the body. Let us then, I say, suppose the soul of Castor separated during his sleep from his body, to think apart. Let us suppose, too, that it chooses for its scene of thinking the body of another man, v. g. Pollux, who is sleeping without a soul. For, if Castor's soul can think, whilst Castor is asleep, what Castor is never conscious of, it is no matter what PLACE it chooses to think in. We have here, then, the bodies of two men with only one soul between them, which we will suppose to sleep and wake by turns; and the soul still thinking in the waking man, whereof the sleeping man is never conscious, has never the least perception. I ask, then, whether Castor and Pollux, thus with only one soul between them, which thinks and perceives in one what the other is never conscious of, nor is concerned for, are not two as distinct PERSONS as Castor and Hercules, or as Socrates and Plato were? And whether one of them might not be very happy, and the other very miserable? Just by the same reason, they make the soul and the man two persons, who make the soul think apart what the man is not conscious of. For, I suppose nobody will make identity of persons to consist in the soul's being united to the very same numerical particles of matter. For if that be necessary to identity, it will be impossible, in that constant flux of the particles of our bodies, that any man should be the same person two days, or two moments, together.

• • •

20. No ideas but from Sensation and Reflection, evident, if we observe Children.

I see no reason, therefore, to believe that the soul thinks before the senses have furnished it with ideas to think on; and as those are increased and retained, so it comes, by exercise, to improve its faculty of thinking in the several parts of it; as well as, afterwards, by compounding those ideas, and reflecting on its own operations, it increases its stock, as well as facility in remembering, imagining, reasoning, and other modes of thinking.

• • •

23. A man begins to have ideas when he first has sensation. What sensation is.

If it shall be demanded then, WHEN a man BEGINS to have any ideas, I think the true answer is,—WHEN HE FIRST HAS ANY SENSATION. For, since there appear not to be any ideas in the mind before the senses have conveyed any in, I conceive that ideas in the understanding are coeval with SENSATION; WHICH IS SUCH AN IMPRESSION OR MOTION MADE IN SOME PART OF THE BODY, AS MAKES IT BE TAKEN NOTICE OF IN THE UNDERSTANDING.

24. The Original of all our Knowledge.

The impressions then that are made on our sense by outward objects that are extrinsical to the mind; and its own operations about these impressions, reflected on by itself, as proper objects to be contemplated by it, are, I conceive, the original of all knowledge. Thus the first capacity of human intellect is,—that the mind is fitted to receive the impressions made on it; either through the senses by outward objects, or by its own operations when it reflects on them. This is the first step a man makes towards the discovery of anything, and the groundwork whereon to build all those notions which ever he shall have naturally in this world. All those sublime thoughts which tower above the clouds, and reach as high as heaven itself, take their rise and footing here: in all that great extent wherein the mind wanders, in those remote speculations it may seem to be elevated with, it stirs not one jot beyond those ideas which SENSE or REFLECTION have offered for its contemplation.

25. In the Reception of simple Ideas, the Understanding is for the most part passive.

In this part the understanding is merely passive; and whether or no it will have these beginnings, and as it were materials of knowledge, is not in its own power. For the objects of our senses do, many of them, obtrude their particular ideas upon our minds whether we will or not; and the operations of our minds will not let us be without, at least, some obscure notions of them. No man can be wholly ignorant of what he does when he thinks. These simple ideas, when offered to the mind, the understanding can no more refuse to have, nor alter when they are imprinted, nor blot them out and make new ones itself, than a mirror can refuse, alter, or obliterate the images or ideas which the objects set before it do therein produce. As the bodies that surround us do diversely affect our organs, the mind is forced to receive the impressions; and cannot avoid the perception of those ideas that are annexed to them.

CHAPTER II
OF SIMPLE IDEAS

1. Uncompounded Appearances.

The better to understand the nature, manner, and extent of our knowledge, one thing is carefully to be observed concerning the ideas we have; and that is, that some of them, are SIMPLE and some COMPLEX.

Though the qualities that affect our senses are, in the things themselves, so united and blended, that there is no separation, no distance between them; yet it is plain, the ideas they produce in the mind enter by the senses simple; and unmixed. For, though the sight and touch often take in from the same object, at the same time, different ideas;—as a man sees at once motion and colour; the hand feels softness and warmth in the same piece of wax: yet the simple ideas thus united in the same subject, are as perfectly distinct as those that come in by different senses. The coldness and hardness which a man feels in a piece of ice being as distinct ideas in the mind as the smell and whiteness of a lily; or as the taste of sugar, and smell of a rose. And there is nothing can be plainer to a man than the clear and distinct perception he has of those simple ideas; which, being each in itself uncompounded, contains in it nothing but ONE UNIFORM APPEARANCE, OR CONCEPTION IN THE MIND, and is not distinguishable into different ideas.

2. The Mind can neither make nor destroy them.

These simple ideas, the materials of all our knowledge, are suggested and furnished to the mind only by those two ways above mentioned, *viz.* sensation and reflection. When the understanding is once stored with these simple ideas, it has the power to repeat, compare, and unite them, even to an almost infinite variety, and so can make at pleasure new complex ideas. But it is not in the power of the most exalted wit, or enlarged understanding, by any quickness or variety of thought, to INVENT or FRAME one new simple idea in the mind, not taken in by the ways before mentioned: nor can any force of the understanding DESTROY those that are there. The dominion of man, in this little world of his own understanding being much what the same as it is in the great world of visible things; wherein his power, however managed by art and skill, reaches no farther than to compound and divide the materials that are made to his hand; but can do nothing towards the making the least particle of new matter, or destroying one atom of what is already in being. The same inability will every one find in himself, who shall go about to fashion in his understanding one simple idea, not received in by his senses from external objects, or by reflection from the operations of his own mind about them. I would have any one try to fancy any taste which had never affected his palate; or frame the idea of a scent he had never smelt: and when he can do this, I will also conclude that a blind man hath ideas of colours, and a deaf man true distinct notions of sounds.

CHAPTER III
OF SIMPLE IDEAS OF SENSE

1. Division of simple ideas.

The better to conceive the ideas we receive from sensation, it may not be amiss for us to consider them, in reference to the different ways whereby they make their approaches to our minds, and make themselves perceivable by us.

FIRST, then, There are some which come into our minds BY ONE SENSE ONLY.

SECONDLY, There are others that convey themselves into the mind BY MORE SENSES THAN ONE.

THIRDLY, Others that are had from REFLECTION ONLY.

FOURTHLY, There are some that make themselves way, and are suggested to the mind BY ALL THE WAYS OF SENSATION AND REFLECTION.

• • •

CHAPTER VI
OF SIMPLE IDEAS OF REFLECTION

Simple Ideas are the Operations of Mind about its other Ideas.

The mind receiving the ideas mentioned in the foregoing chapters from without, when it turns its view inward upon itself, and observes its own actions about those ideas it has, takes from thence other ideas, which are as capable to be the objects of its contemplation as any of those it received from foreign things.

The Idea of Perception, and Idea of Willing, we have from Reflection.

The two great and principal actions of the mind, which are most frequently considered, and which are so frequent that every one that pleases may take notice of them in himself, are these two:—

PERCEPTION, or THINKING; and VOLITION, or WILLING.

The power of thinking is called the UNDERSTANDING, and the power of volition is called the WILL; and these two powers or abilities in the mind are denominated faculties.

Of some of the MODES of these simple ideas of reflection, such as are REMEMBRANCE, DISCERNING, REASONING, JUDGING, KNOWLEDGE, FAITH, &c., I shall have occasion to speak hereafter.

• • •

CHAPTER VIII
SOME FURTHER CONSIDERATIONS CONCERNING OUR SIMPLE IDEAS OF SENSATION

1. Positive Ideas from privative causes.

   Concerning the simple ideas of Sensation; it is to be considered,—that whatsoever is so constituted in nature as to be able, by affecting our senses, to cause any perception in the mind, doth thereby produce in the understanding a simple idea; which, whatever be the external cause of it, when it comes to be taken notice of by our discerning faculty, it is by the mind looked on and considered there to be a real positive idea in the understanding, as much as any other whatsoever; though, perhaps, the cause of it be but a privation of the subject.

2. Ideas in the mind distinguished from that in things which gives rise to them.

   Thus the ideas of heat and cold, light and darkness, white and black, motion and rest, are equally clear and positive ideas in the mind; though, perhaps, some of the causes which produce them are barely privations, in those subjects from whence our senses derive those ideas. These the understanding, in its view of them, considers all as distinct positive ideas, without taking notice of the causes that produce them: which is an inquiry not belonging to the idea, as it is in the understanding, but to the nature of the things existing without us. These are two very different things, and carefully to be distinguished; it being one thing to perceive and know the idea of white or black, and quite another to examine what kind of particles they must be, and how ranged in the superficies, to make any object appear white or black.

3. We may have the ideas when we are ignorant of their physical causes.

   A painter or dyer who never inquired into their causes hath the ideas of white and black, and other colours, as clearly, perfectly, and distinctly in his understanding, and perhaps more distinctly, than the philosopher who hath busied himself in considering their natures, and thinks he knows how far either of them is, in its cause, positive or privative; and the idea of black is no less positive in his mind than that of white, however the cause of that colour in the external object may be only a privation.

4. Why a privative cause in nature may occasion a positive idea.

   If it were the design of my present undertaking to inquire into the natural causes and manner of perception, I should offer this as a reason why a privative cause might, in some cases at least, produce a positive idea; *viz.* that all sensation being produced in us only by different degrees and modes of motion in our animal spirits, variously agitated by external objects, the abatement of any former motion must as necessarily produce a new sensation as the variation or increase of it; and so introduce a new idea, which depends only on a different motion of the animal spirits in that organ.

• • •

5. Negative names need not be meaningless.

   But whether this be so or not I will not here determine, but appeal to every one's own experience, whether the shadow of a man, though it consists of nothing but the absence of light (and the more the absence of light is, the more discernible is the shadow) does not, when a man looks on it, cause as clear and positive idea in his mind, as a man himself, though covered over with clear sunshine? And the picture of a shadow is a positive thing. Indeed, we have negative names, to which there be no positive ideas; but they consist wholly in negation of some certain ideas, as SILENCE, INVISIBLE; but these signify not any ideas in the mind but their absence.

6. Whether any ideas are due to causes really private.

   And thus one may truly be said to see darkness. For, supposing a hole perfectly dark, from whence no light is reflected, it is certain one may see the figure of it, or it may be painted; or whether the ink I write with makes any other idea, is a question. The privative causes I have here assigned of positive ideas are according to the common opinion; but, in truth, it will be hard to determine whether there be really any ideas from a privative cause, till it be determined, whether rest be any more a privation than motion.

7. Ideas in the Mind, Qualities in Bodies.

To discover the nature of our IDEAS the better, and to, discourse of them intelligibly, it will be convenient to distinguish them AS THEY ARE IDEAS OR PERCEPTIONS IN OUR MINDS; and AS THEY ARE MODIFICATIONS OF MATTER IN THE BODIES THAT CAUSE SUCH PERCEPTIONS IN US: that so we may not think (as perhaps usually is done) that they are exactly the images and resemblances of something inherent in the subject; most of those of sensation being in the mind no more the likeness of something existing without us, than the names that stand for them are the likeness of our ideas, which yet upon hearing they are apt to excite in us.

8. Our Ideas and the Qualities of Bodies.

Whatsoever the mind perceives IN ITSELF, or is the immediate object of perception, thought, or understanding, that I call IDEA; and the power to produce any idea in our mind, I call QUALITY of the subject wherein that power is. Thus a snowball having the power to produce in us the ideas of white, cold, and round,—the power to produce those ideas in us, as they are in the snowball, I call qualities; and as they are sensations or perceptions in our understandings, I call them ideas; which IDEAS, if I speak of sometimes as in the things themselves, I would be understood to mean those qualities in the objects which produce them in us.

9. Primary Qualities of Bodies.

Concerning these qualities, we, I think, observe these primary ones in bodies that produce simple ideas in us, *viz.* SOLIDITY, EXTENSION, MOTION or REST, NUBMER or FIGURE. These, which I call ORIGINAL or PRIMARY qualities of body, are wholly inseperable from it; and such as in all the alterations and changes it suffers, all the force can be used upon it, it constantly keeps; and such as sense constantly finds in every particle of matter which has bulk enough to be perceived; and the mind finds inseparable from every particle of matter, though less than to make itself singly be perceived by our senses: v.g. Take a grain of wheat, divide it into two parts; each part has still solidity, extension, figure, and mobility: divide it again, and it retains still the same qualities; and so divide it on, till the parts become insensible; they must retain still each of them all those qualities. For division (which is all that a mill, or pestle, or any other body, does upon another, in reducing it to insensible parts) can never take away either solidity, extension, figure, or mobility from any body, but only makes two or more distinct separate masses of matter, of that which was but one before; all which distinct masses, reckoned as so many distinct bodies, after division, make a certain number.

10. [not in early editions]

11. How Bodies produce Ideas in us.

The next thing to be considered is, how bodies operate one upon another; and that is manifestly by impulse, and nothing else. It being impossible to conceive that body should operate on WHAT IT DOES NOT TOUCH (which is all one as to imagine it can operate where it is not), or when it does touch, operate any other way than by motion.

12. By motions, external, and in our organism.

If then external objects be not united to our minds when they produce ideas therein; and yet we perceive these ORIGINAL qualities in such of them as singly fall under our senses, it is evident that some motion must be thence continued by our nerves, or animal spirits, by some parts of our bodies, to the brains or the seat of sensation, there to produce in our minds the particular ideas we have of them. And since the extension, figure, number, and motion of bodies of an observable bigness, maybe perceived at a distance by the sight, it is evident some singly imperceptible bodies must come from them; to the eyes, and thereby convey to the brain some motion; which produces these ideas which we have of them in us.

13. How secondary Qualities produce their ideas.

After the same manner that the ideas of these original qualities are produced in us, we may conceive that the ideas of SECONDARY qualities are also produced, *viz.* by the operation of insensible particles on our senses. For, it being manifest that there are bodies and good store of bodies, each whereof are so small, that we cannot by any of our senses discover either their bulk, figure, or motion,—as is evident in the particles of the air and water, and others extremely smaller than those; perhaps as much smaller than the particles of air and water, as the particles of air and water are smaller than peas or hail-stones;—let us suppose at present that, the different motions and figures, bulk and number, of such particles, affecting the several organs of our senses, produce: in us those different sensations which we have from the colours and smells of bodies; v.g. that a violet, by the impulse of such insensible particles of matter, of peculiar figures and bulks, and in different degrees and modifications of their motions, causes the ideas of the blue colour, and sweet scent of that flower to be produced in our minds. It being no more impossible to conceive that God should annex such ideas to such motions, with which they have no similitude, than that he should annex the idea of pain to the motion of a piece of steel dividing our flesh, with which that idea hath no resemblance.

14. They depend on the primary Qualities.

What I have said concerning colours and smells may be understood also of tastes and sounds, and other the like sensible qualities; which, whatever reality we by mistake attribute to them, are in truth nothing in the objects themselves, but powers to produce various sensations in us; and depend on those primary qualities, *viz.* bulk, figure, texture, and motion of parts and therefore I call them SECONDARY QUALITIES.

15. Ideas of primary Qualities are Resemblances; of secondary, not.

From whence I think it easy to draw this observation,—that the ideas of primary qualities of bodies are resemblances of them, and their patterns do really exist in the bodies themselves, but the ideas produced in us by these secondary qualities have no resemblance of them at all. There is nothing like our ideas, existing in the bodies themselves. They are, in the bodies we denominate from them, only a power to produce those sensations in us: and what is sweet, blue, or warm in idea, is but the certain bulk, figure, and motion of the insensible parts, in the bodies themselves, which we call so.

16. Examples.

Flame is denominated hot and light; snow, white and cold; and manna, white and sweet, from the ideas they produce in us. Which qualities are commonly thought to be the same in those bodies that those ideas are in us, the one the perfect resemblance of the other, as they are in a mirror, and it would by most men be judged very extravagant if one should say otherwise. And yet he that will consider that the same fire that, at one distance produces in us the sensation of warmth, does, at a nearer approach, produce in us the far different sensation of pain, ought to bethink himself what reason he has to say—that this idea of warmth, which was produced in him by the fire, is ACTUALLY IN THE FIRE; and his idea of pain, which the same fire produced in him the same way, is NOT in the fire. Why are whiteness and coldness in snow, and pain not, when it produces the one and the other idea in us; and can do neither, but by the bulk, figure, number, and motion of its solid parts?

17. The ideas of the Primary alone really exist.

The particular bulk, number, figure, and motion of the parts of fire or snow are really in them,—whether any one's senses perceive them or no: and therefore they may be called REAL qualities, because they really exist in those bodies. But light, heat, whiteness, or coldness, are no more really in them than sickness or pain is in manna. Take away the sensation of them; let not the eyes see light or colours, nor the can hear sounds; let the palate not taste, nor the nose smell, and all colours, tastes, odours, and sounds, AS THEY ARE SUCH PARTICULAR IDEAS, vanish and cease, and are reduced to their causes, i.e. bulk, figure, and motion of parts.

18. The secondary exist in things only as modes of the primary.

A piece of manna of a sensible bulk is able to produce in us the idea of a round or square figure; and by being removed from one place to another, the idea of motion. This idea of motion represents it as it really is in manna moving: a circle or square are the same, whether in idea or existence, in the mind or in the manna. And this, both motion and as figure, are really in the manna, whether we take notice of primary, them or no: this everybody is ready to agree to. Besides, manna, by the bulk, figure, texture, and motion of its parts, has a power to produce the sensations of sickness, and sometimes of acute pains or gripings in us. That these ideas of sickness and pain are NOT in the manna, but effects of its operations on us, and are nowhere when we feel them not; this also every one readily agrees to. And yet men are hardly to be brought to think that sweetness and whiteness are not really in manna; which are but the effects of the operations of manna, by the motion, size, and figure of its particles, on the eyes and palate: as the pain and sickness caused by manna are confessedly nothing but the effects of its operations on the stomach and guts, by the size, motion, and figure of its insensible parts, (for by nothing else can a body operate, as has been proved): as if it could not operate on the eyes and palate, and thereby produce in the mind particular distinct ideas, which in itself it has not, as well as we allow it can operate on the guts and stomach, and thereby produce distinct ideas, which in itself it has not. These ideas, being all effects of the operations of manna on several parts of our bodies, by the size, figure, number, and motion of its parts;—why those produced by the eyes and palate should rather be thought to be really in the manna, than those produced by the stomach and guts; or why the pain and sickness, ideas that are the effect of manna, should be thought to be nowhere when they are not felt; and yet the sweetness and whiteness, effects of the same manna on other parts of the body, by ways equally as unknown, should be thought to exist in the manna, when they are not seen or tasted, would need some reason to explain.

• • •

21. Explains how water felt as cold by one hand may be warm to the other.

Ideas being thus distinguished and understood, we may be able to give an account how the same water, at the same time, may produce the idea of cold by one hand and of heat by the other: whereas it is impossible that the same water, if those ideas were really in it, should at the same time be both hot and cold. For, if we imagine WARMTH, as it is in our hands, to be nothing but a certain sort and degree of motion in the minute particles of our nerves or animal spirits, we may understand how it is possible that the same water may, at the same time, produce the sensations of heat in one hand and cold in the other; which yet FIGURE never does, that never producing the idea of a square by one hand which has produced the idea of a globe by another. But if the sensation of heat and cold be nothing but the increase or diminution of the motion of the minute parts of our bodies, caused by the corpuscles of any other body, it is easy to be understood, that if that motion be greater in one hand than in the other; if a body be applied to the two hands, which has in its minute particles a greater motion than in those of one of the hands, and a less than in those of the other, it will increase the motion of the one hand and lessen it in the other; and so cause the different sensations of heat and cold that depend thereon.

• • •

23. Three Sorts of Qualities on Bodies.

The qualities, then, that are in bodies, rightly considered are of three sorts:—

FIRST, The bulk, figure, number, situation, and motion or rest of their solid parts. Those are in them, whether we perceive them or not; and when they are of that size that we can discover them, we have by these an idea of the thing as it is in itself; as is plain in artificial things. These I call PRIMARY QUALITIES.

SECONDLY, The power that is in any body, by reason of its insensible primary qualities, to operate after a peculiar manner on any of our senses, and thereby produce in US the different ideas of several colours, sounds, smells, tastes, &c. These are usually called SENSIBLE QUALITIES.

THIRDLY, The power that is in any body, by reason of the particular constitution of its primary qualities, to make such a change in the bulk, figure, texture, and motion of ANOTHER BODY, as to make it operate on our senses differently from what it did before. Thus the sun has a power to make wax white, and fire to make lead fluid.

The first of these, as has been said, I think may be properly called real, original, or primary qualities; because they are in the things themselves, whether they are perceived or not: and upon their different modifications it is that the secondary qualities depend.

The other two are only powers to act differently upon other things: which powers result from the different modifications of those primary qualities.

24. The first are Resemblances; the second thought to be Resemblances, but are not, the third neither are nor are thought so.

But, though the two latter sorts of qualities are powers barely, and nothing but powers, relating to several other bodies, and resulting from the different modifications of the original qualities, yet they are generally otherwise thought of. For the SECOND sort, *viz.* the powers to produce several ideas in us, by our senses, are looked upon as real qualities in the things thus affecting us: but the THIRD sort are called and esteemed barely powers, v.g. The idea of heat or light, which we receive by our eyes, or touch, from the sun, are commonly thought real qualities existing in the sun, and something more than mere powers in it. But when we consider the sun in reference to wax, which it melts or blanches, we look on the whiteness and softness produced in the wax, not as qualities in the sun, but effects produced by powers in it. Whereas, if rightly considered, these qualities of light and warmth, which are perceptions in me when I am warmed or enlightened by the sun, are no otherwise in the sun, than the changes made in the wax, when it is blanched or melted, are in the sun. They are all of them equally POWERS IN THE SUN, DEPENDING ON ITS PRIMARY QUALITIES; whereby it is able, in the one case, so to alter the bulk, figure, texture, or motion of some of the insensible parts of my eyes or hands, as thereby to produce in me the idea of light or heat; and in the other, it is able so to alter the bulk, figure, texture, or motion of the insensible parts of the wax, as to make them fit to produce in me the distinct ideas of white and fluid.

25. Why the secondary are ordinarily taken for real Qualities and not for bare Powers.

The reason why the one are ordinarily taken for real qualities, and the other only for bare powers, seems to be because the ideas we have of distinct colours, sounds, &c. containing nothing at all in them of bulk, figure, or motion we are not apt to think them the effects of these primary qualities; which appear not, to our senses, to operate in their production, and with which they have not any apparent congruity or conceivable connexion. Hence it is that we are so forward as to imagine, that those ideas are the resemblances of something really existing in the objects themselves since sensation discovers nothing of bulk, figure, or motion of parts in their production; nor can reason show how bodies BY THEIR BULK, FIGURE, AND MOTION, should produce in the mind the ideas of blue or yellow, &c. But, in the other case in the operations of bodies changing the qualities one of another, we plainly discover that the quality produced hath commonly no resemblance with anything in the thing producing it; wherefore we look on it as a bare effect of power. For, through receiving the idea of heat or light from the sun, we are apt to think IT is a perception and resemblance of such a quality in the sun; yet when we see wax, or a fair face, receive change of colour from the sun, we cannot imagine THAT to be the reception or resemblance of anything in the sun, because we find not those different colours in the sun itself. For, our senses being able to observe a likeness or unlikeness of sensible qualities in two different external objects, we forwardly enough conclude the production of any sensible quality in any subject to be an effect of bare power, and not the communication of any quality which was really in the efficient, when we find no such sensible quality in the thing that produced it. But our senses, not being able to discover any unlikeness between the idea produced in us, and the quality of the object producing it, we are apt to imagine that our ideas are resemblances of something in the objects, and not the effects of certain powers placed in the modification of their primary qualities, with which primary qualities the ideas produced in us have no resemblance.

26. Secondary Qualities twofold; first, immediately perceivable; secondly, mediately perceivable.

To conclude. Beside those before-mentioned primary qualities in bodies, *viz.* bulk, figure, extension, number, and motion of their solid parts; all the rest, whereby we take notice of bodies, and distinguish them one from another, are nothing else but several powers in them, depending on those primary qualities; whereby they are fitted, either by immediately operating on our bodies to produce several different ideas in us; or else, by operating on other bodies, so to change their primary qualities as to render them capable of producing ideas in us different from what before they did. The former of these, I think, may be called secondary qualities IMMEDIATELY PERCEIVABLE: the latter, secondary qualities, MEDIATELY PERCEIVABLE.

DISCUSSION QUESTIONS

1. Compare Locke's view to Descartes's. Which view do you think is better argued? Explain.

2. Explain the distinction Locke makes between the terms "simple idea" and "complex ideas." Why does he make this distinction?

3. Why does Locke consider empiricism the right way to view the world? Explain.

A Treatise Concerning the Principles of Human Knowledge

By George Berkeley

George Berkeley (1685–1753) was an Irish philosopher who later became a Bishop in 1734. Like Locke, Berkeley was an empiricist about knowledge. Berkeley's empiricism led him to reject the dualism of Plato, Descartes, and Locke. Berkeley noted that we never actually perceive anything but our own ideas. Berkeley concluded that the only kinds of stuff are ideas and the minds that formulate them. This view is called idealism. For Berkeley, the concept of matter yields a contradiction as you can see in the passage contained here from his major work, A Treatise Concerning the Principles of Knowledge, *which was published in 1710. Berkeley was much affected by the work of Sir Isaac Newton (1643–1727). Berkeley rejects the thoroughgoing materialism of Newton's philosophy. Berkeley was not antiscience. He made many contributions to theories of vision, mathematics, and science. He did not think you needed a concept of matter to do this. What we call things* do *exist for him. They are ideas that combine in orderly ways, and we give them names, but they are nothing but ideas. A famous phrase of his is* esse est percipi *("to be is to be perceived"). Does this mean that things blink in and out of existence when you look away? No, because God doesn't blink. How does he know there is a God? The regularity of nature (that we do not control the color of the sky, for example) is proof for God's existence. So, there is always a mind perceiving things.*

PART I, PARAGRAPHS 1–38

1. It is evident to any one who takes a survey of the objects of human knowledge, that they are either ideas actually imprinted on the senses; or else such as are perceived by attending to the passions and operations of the mind; or lastly, ideas formed by help of memory and imagination—either compounding, dividing, or barely representing those originally perceived in the aforesaid ways. By sight I have the ideas of light and colours, with their several degrees and variations. By touch I perceive hard and soft, heat and cold, motion and resistance, and of all these more and less either as to quantity or degree. Smelling furnishes me with odours; the palate with tastes; and hearing conveys sounds to the mind in all their variety of tone and composition. And as several of these are observed to accompany each other, they come to be marked by one name, and so to be reputed as one thing. Thus, for example a certain colour, taste, smell, figure and consistence having been observed to go together, are accounted one distinct thing, signified by the name apple; other collections of ideas constitute a

stone, a tree, a book, and the like sensible things—which as they are pleasing or disagreeable excite the passions of love, hatred, joy, grief, and so forth.

2. But, besides all that endless variety of ideas or objects of knowledge, there is likewise something which knows or perceives them, and exercises divers operations, as willing, imagining, remembering, about them. This perceiving, active being is what I call mind, spirit, soul, or myself. By which words I do not denote any one of my ideas, but a thing entirely distinct from them, wherein, they exist, or, which is the same thing, whereby they are perceived—for the existence of an idea consists in being perceived.

3. That neither our thoughts, nor passions, nor ideas formed by the imagination, exist without the mind, is what everybody will allow. And it seems no less evident that the various sensations or ideas imprinted on the sense, however blended or combined together (that is, whatever objects they compose), cannot exist otherwise than in a mind perceiving them.—I think an intuitive knowledge may be obtained of this by any one that shall attend to what is meant by the term exists, when applied to sensible things. The table I write on I say exists, that is, I see and feel it; and if I were out of my study I should say it existed—meaning thereby that if I was in my study I might perceive it, or that some other spirit actually does perceive it. There was an odour, that is, it was smelt; there was a sound, that is, it was heard; a colour or figure, and it was perceived by sight or touch. This is all that I can understand by these and the like expressions. For as to what is said of the absolute existence of unthinking things without any relation to their being perceived, that seems perfectly unintelligible. Their esse is percepi, nor is it possible they should have any existence out of the minds or thinking things which perceive them.

4. It is indeed an opinion strangely prevailing amongst men, that houses, mountains, rivers, and in a word all sensible objects, have an existence, natural or real, distinct from their being perceived by the understanding. But, with how great an assurance and acquiescence soever this principle may be entertained in the world, yet whoever shall find in his heart to call it in question may, if I mistake not, perceive it to involve a manifest contradiction. For, what are the fore-mentioned objects but the things we perceive by sense? and what do we perceive besides our own ideas or sensations? and is it not plainly repugnant that any one of these, or any combination of them, should exist unperceived?

5. If we thoroughly examine this tenet it will, perhaps, be found at bottom to depend on the doctrine of abstract ideas. For can there be a nicer strain of abstraction than to distinguish the existence of sensible objects from their being perceived, so as to conceive them existing unperceived? Light and colours, heat and cold, extension and figures—in a word the things we see and feel—what are they but so many sensations, notions, ideas, or impressions on the sense? and is it possible to separate, even in thought, any of these from perception? For my part, I might as easily divide a thing from itself. I may, indeed, divide in my thoughts, or conceive apart from each other, those things which, perhaps I never perceived by sense so divided. Thus, I imagine the trunk of a human body without the limbs, or conceive the smell of a rose

without thinking on the rose itself. So far, I will not deny, I can abstract—if that may properly be called abstraction which extends only to the conceiving separately such objects as it is possible may really exist or be actually perceived asunder. But my conceiving or imagining power does not extend beyond the possibility of real existence or perception. Hence, as it is impossible for me to see or feel anything without an actual sensation of that thing, so is it impossible for me to conceive in my thoughts any sensible thing or object distinct from the sensation or perception of it.

6. Some truths there are so near and obvious to the mind that a man need only open his eyes to see them. Such I take this important one to be, *viz.*, that all the choir of heaven and furniture of the earth, in a word all those bodies which compose the mighty frame of the world, have not any subsistence without a mind, that their being is to be perceived or known; that consequently so long as they are not actually perceived by me, or do not exist in my mind or that of any other created spirit, they must either have no existence at all, or else subsist in the mind of some Eternal Spirit—it being perfectly unintelligible, and involving all the absurdity of abstraction, to attribute to any single part of them an existence independent of a spirit. To be convinced of which, the reader need only reflect, and try to separate in his own thoughts the being of a sensible thing from its being perceived.

7. From what has been said it follows there is not any other Substance than Spirit, or that which perceives. But, for the fuller proof of this point, let it be considered the sensible qualities are colour, figure, motion, smell, taste, etc., i.e. the ideas perceived by sense. Now, for an idea to exist in an unperceiving thing is a manifest contradiction, for to have an idea is all one as to perceive; that therefore wherein colour, figure, and the like qualities exist must perceive them; hence it is clear there can be no unthinking substance or substratum of those ideas.

8. But, say you, though the ideas themselves do not exist without the mind, yet there may be things like them, whereof they are copies or resemblances, which things exist without the mind in an unthinking substance. I answer, an idea can be like nothing but an idea; a colour or figure can be like nothing but another colour or figure. If we look but never so little into our thoughts, we shall find it impossible for us to conceive a likeness except only between our ideas. Again, I ask whether those supposed originals or external things, of which our ideas are the pictures or representations, be themselves perceivable or no? If they are, then they are ideas and we have gained our point; but if you say they are not, I appeal to any one whether it be sense to assert a colour is like something which is invisible; hard or soft, like something which is intangible; and so of the rest.

9. Some there are who make a distinction betwixt primary and secondary qualities. By the former they mean extension, figure, motion, rest, solidity or impenetrability, and number; by the latter they denote all other sensible qualities, as colours, sounds, tastes, and so forth. The ideas we have of these they acknowledge not to be the resemblances of anything existing without the mind, or unperceived, but they will have our ideas of the primary qualities to be patterns or images of things which exist without the mind, in an unthinking substance which they call Matter.

By Matter, therefore, we are to understand an inert, senseless substance, in which extension, figure, and motion do actually subsist. But it is evident from what we have already shown, that extension, figure, and motion are only ideas existing in the mind, and that an idea can be like nothing but another idea, and that consequently neither they nor their archetypes can exist in an unperceiving substance. Hence, it is plain that that the very notion of what is called Matter or corporeal substance, involves a contradiction in it.

10. They who assert that figure, motion, and the rest of the primary or original qualities do exist without the mind in unthinking substances, do at the same time acknowledge that colours, sounds, heat cold, and suchlike secondary qualities, do not—which they tell us are sensations existing in the mind alone, that depend on and are occasioned by the different size, texture, and motion of the minute particles of matter. This they take for an undoubted truth, which they can demonstrate beyond all exception. Now, if it be certain that those original qualities are inseparably united with the other sensible qualities, and not, even in thought, capable of being abstracted from them, it plainly follows that they exist only in the mind. But I desire any one to reflect and try whether he can, by any abstraction of thought, conceive the extension and motion of a body without all other sensible qualities. For my own part, I see evidently that it is not in my power to frame an idea of a body extended and moving, but I must withal give it some colour or other sensible quality which is acknowledged to exist only in the mind. In short, extension, figure, and motion, abstracted from all other qualities, are inconceivable. Where therefore the other sensible qualities are, there must these be also, to wit, in the mind and nowhere else.

11. Again, great and small, swift and slow, are allowed to exist nowhere without the mind, being entirely relative, and changing as the frame or position of the organs of sense varies. The extension therefore which exists without the mind is neither great nor small, the motion neither swift nor slow, that is, they are nothing at all. But, say you, they are extension in general, and motion in general: thus we see how much the tenet of extended movable substances existing without the mind depends on the strange doctrine of abstract ideas. And here I cannot but remark how nearly the vague and indeterminate description of Matter or corporeal substance, which the modern philosophers are run into by their own principles, resembles that antiquated and so much ridiculed notion of materia prima, to be met with in Aristotle and his followers. Without extension solidity cannot be conceived; since therefore it has been shewn that extension exists not in an unthinking substance, the same must also be true of solidity.

12. That number is entirely the creature of the mind, even though the other qualities be allowed to exist without, will be evident to whoever considers that the same thing bears a different denomination of number as the mind views it with different respects. Thus, the same extension is one, or three, or thirty-six, according as the mind considers it with reference to a yard, a foot, or an inch. Number is so visibly relative, and dependent on men's understanding, that it is strange to think how any one should give it an absolute existence without the mind. We say one book, one page, one line, etc.; all these are equally units, though some contain several of the

others. And in each instance, it is plain, the unit relates to some particular combination of ideas arbitrarily put together by the mind.

13. Unity I know some will have to be a simple or uncompounded idea, accompanying all other ideas into the mind. That I have any such idea answering the word unity I do not find; and if I had, methinks I could not miss finding it: on the contrary, it should be the most familiar to my understanding, since it is said to accompany all other ideas, and to be perceived by all the ways of sensation and reflexion. To say no more, it is an abstract idea.

14. I shall farther add, that, after the same manner as modern philosophers prove certain sensible qualities to have no existence in Matter, or without the mind, the same thing may be likewise proved of all other sensible qualities whatsoever. Thus, for instance, it is said that heat and cold are affections only of the mind, and not at all patterns of real beings, existing in the corporeal substances which excite them, for that the same body which appears cold to one hand seems warm to another. Now, why may we not as well argue that figure and extension are not patterns or resemblances of qualities existing in Matter, because to the same eye at different stations, or eyes of a different texture at the same station, they appear various, and cannot therefore be the images of anything settled and determinate without the mind? Again, it is proved that sweetness is not really in the sapid thing, because the thing remaining unaltered the sweetness is changed into bitter, as in case of a fever or otherwise vitiated palate. Is it not as reasonable to say that motion is not without the mind, since if the succession of ideas in the mind become swifter, the motion, it is acknowledged, shall appear slower without any alteration in any external object?

15. In short, let any one consider those arguments which are thought manifestly to prove that colours and taste exist only in the mind, and he shall find they may with equal force be brought to prove the same thing of extension, figure, and motion. Though it must be confessed this method of arguing does not so much prove that there is no extension or colour in an outward object, as that we do not know by sense which is the true extension or colour of the object. But the arguments foregoing plainly shew it to be impossible that any colour or extension at all, or other sensible quality whatsoever, should exist in an unthinking subject without the mind, or in truth, that there should be any such thing as an outward object.

16. But let us examine a little the received opinion.—It is said extension is a mode or accident of Matter, and that Matter is the substratum that supports it. Now I desire that you would explain to me what is meant by Matter's supporting extension. Say you, I have no idea of Matter and therefore cannot explain it. I answer, though you have no positive, yet, if you have any meaning at all, you must at least have a relative idea of Matter; though you know not what it is, yet you must be supposed to know what relation it bears to accidents, and what is meant by its supporting them. It is evident "support" cannot here be taken in its usual or literal sense—as when we say that pillars support a building; in what sense therefore must it be taken?

17. If we inquire into what the most accurate philosophers declare themselves to mean by material substance, we shall find them acknowledge they have no

other meaning annexed to those sounds but the idea of Being in general, together with the relative notion of its supporting accidents. The general idea of Being appeareth to me the most abstract and incomprehensible of all other; and as for its supporting accidents, this, as we have just now observed, cannot be understood in the common sense of those words; it must therefore be taken in some other sense, but what that is they do not explain. So that when I consider the two parts or branches which make the signification of the words material substance, I am convinced there is no distinct meaning annexed to them. But why should we trouble ourselves any farther, in discussing this material substratum or support of figure and motion, and other sensible qualities? Does it not suppose they have an existence without the mind? And is not this a direct repugnancy, and altogether inconceivable?

18. But, though it were possible that solid, figured, movable substances may exist without the mind, corresponding to the ideas we have of bodies, yet how is it possible for us to know this? Either we must know it by sense or by reason. As for our senses, by them we have the knowledge only of our sensations, ideas, or those things that are immediately perceived by sense, call them what you will: but they do not inform us that things exist without the mind, or unperceived, like to those which are perceived. This the materialists themselves acknowledge. It remains therefore that if we have any knowledge at all of external things, it must be by reason, inferring their existence from what is immediately perceived by sense. But what reason can induce us to believe the existence of bodies without the mind, from what we perceive, since the very patrons of Matter themselves do not pretend there is any necessary connexion betwixt them and our ideas? I say it is granted on all hands (and what happens in dreams, phrensies, and the like, puts it beyond dispute) that it is possible we might be affected with all the ideas we have now, though there were no bodies existing without resembling them. Hence, it is evident the supposition of external bodies is not necessary for the producing our ideas; since it is granted they are produced sometimes, and might possibly be produced always in the same order, we see them in at present, without their concurrence.

19. But, though we might possibly have all our sensations without them, yet perhaps it may be thought easier to conceive and explain the manner of their production, by supposing external bodies in their likeness rather than otherwise; and so it might be at least probable there are such things as bodies that excite their ideas in our minds. But neither can this be said; for, though we give the materialists their external bodies, they by their own confession are never the nearer knowing how our ideas are produced; since they own themselves unable to comprehend in what manner body can act upon spirit, or how it is possible it should imprint any idea in the mind. Hence it is evident the production of ideas or sensations in our minds can be no reason why we should suppose Matter or corporeal substances, since that is acknowledged to remain equally inexplicable with or without this supposition. If therefore it were possible for bodies to exist without the mind, yet to hold they do so, must needs be a very precarious opinion; since it is to suppose, without any reason

at all, that God has created innumerable beings that are entirely useless, and serve to no manner of purpose.

20. In short, if there were external bodies, it is impossible we should ever come to know it; and if there were not, we might have the very same reasons to think there were that we have now. Suppose—what no one can deny possible—an intelligence without the help of external bodies, to be affected with the same train of sensations or ideas that you are, imprinted in the same order and with like vividness in his mind. I ask whether that intelligence hath not all the reason to believe the existence of corporeal substances, represented by his ideas, and exciting them in his mind, that you can possibly have for believing the same thing? Of this there can be no question—which one consideration were enough to make any reasonable person suspect the strength of whatever arguments be may think himself to have, for the existence of bodies without the mind.

21. Were it necessary to add any farther proof against the existence of Matter after what has been said, I could instance several of those errors and difficulties (not to mention impieties) which have sprung from that tenet. It has occasioned numberless controversies and disputes in philosophy, and not a few of far greater moment in religion. But I shall not enter into the detail of them in this place, as well because I think arguments a posteriori are unnecessary for confirming what has been, if I mistake not, sufficiently demonstrated a priori, as because I shall hereafter find occasion to speak somewhat of them.

22. I am afraid I have given cause to think I am needlessly prolix in handling this subject. For, to what purpose is it to dilate on that which may be demonstrated with the utmost evidence in a line or two, to any one that is capable of the least reflexion? It is but looking into your own thoughts, and so trying whether you can conceive it possible for a sound, or figure, or motion, or colour to exist without the mind or unperceived. This easy trial may perhaps make you see that what you contend for is a downright contradiction. Insomuch that I am content to put the whole upon this issue:—If you can but conceive it possible for one extended movable substance, or, in general, for any one idea, or anything like an idea, to exist otherwise than in a mind perceiving it, I shall readily give up the cause. And, as for all that compages of external bodies you contend for, I shall grant you its existence, though you cannot either give me any reason why you believe it exists, or assign any use to it when it is supposed to exist. I say, the bare possibility of your opinions being true shall pass for an argument that it is so.

23. But, say you, surely there is nothing easier than for me to imagine trees, for instance, in a park, or books existing in a closet, and nobody by to perceive them. I answer, you may so, there is no difficulty in it; but what is all this, I beseech you, more than framing in your mind certain ideas which you call books and trees, and the same time omitting to frame the idea of any one that may perceive them? But do not you yourself perceive or think of them all the while? This therefore is nothing to the purpose; it only shews you have the power of imagining or forming ideas in your mind: but it does not shew that you can conceive it possible the objects of your

thought may exist without the mind. To make out this, it is necessary that you conceive them existing unconceived or unthought of, which is a manifest repugnancy. When we do our utmost to conceive the existence of external bodies, we are all the while only contemplating our own ideas. But the mind taking no notice of itself, is deluded to think it can and does conceive bodies existing unthought of or without the mind, though at the same time they are apprehended by or exist in itself. A little attention will discover to any one the truth and evidence of what is here said, and make it unnecessary to insist on any other proofs against the existence of material substance.

24. It is very obvious, upon the least inquiry into our thoughts, to know whether it is possible for us to understand what is meant by the absolute existence of sensible objects in themselves, or without the mind. To me it is evident those words mark out either a direct contradiction, or else nothing at all. And to convince others of this, I know no readier or fairer way than to entreat they would calmly attend to their own thoughts; and if by this attention the emptiness or repugnancy of those expressions does appear, surely nothing more is requisite for the conviction. It is on this therefore that I insist, to wit, that the absolute existence of unthinking things are words without a meaning, or which include a contradiction. This is what I repeat and inculcate, and earnestly recommend to the attentive thoughts of the reader.

25. All our ideas, sensations, notions, or the things which we perceive, by whatsoever names they may be distinguished, are visibly inactive—there is nothing of power or agency included in them. So that one idea or object of thought cannot produce or make any alteration in another. To be satisfied of the truth of this, there is nothing else requisite but a bare observation of our ideas. For, since they and every part of them exist only in the mind, it follows that there is nothing in them but what is perceived: but whoever shall attend to his ideas, whether of sense or reflexion, will not perceive in them any power or activity; there is, therefore, no such thing contained in them. A little attention will discover to us that the very being of an idea implies passiveness and inertness in it, insomuch that it is impossible for an idea to do anything, or, strictly speaking, to be the cause of anything: neither can it be the resemblance or pattern of any active being, as is evident from sect. 8. Whence it plainly follows that extension, figure, and motion cannot be the cause of our sensations. To say, therefore, that these are the effects of powers resulting from the configuration, number, motion, and size of corpuscles, must certainly be false.

26. We perceive a continual succession of ideas, some are anew excited, others are changed or totally disappear. There is therefore some cause of these ideas, whereon they depend, and which produces and changes them. That this cause cannot be any quality or idea or combination of ideas, is clear from the preceding section. I must therefore be a substance; but it has been shewn that there is no corporeal or material substance: it remains therefore that the cause of ideas is an incorporeal active substance or Spirit.

27. A spirit is one simple, undivided, active being—as it perceives ideas it is called the understanding, and as it produces or otherwise operates about them it is called

the will. Hence there can be no idea formed of a soul or spirit; for all ideas whatever, being passive and inert (*vide* sect. 25), they cannot represent unto us, by way of image or likeness, that which acts. A little attention will make it plain to any one, that to have an idea which shall be like that active principle of motion and change of ideas is absolutely impossible. Such is the nature of spirit, or that which acts, that it cannot be of itself perceived, but only by the effects which it produceth. If any man shall doubt of the truth of what is here delivered, let him but reflect and try if he can frame the idea of any power or active being, and whether he has ideas of two principal powers, marked by the names will and understanding, distinct from each other as well as from a third idea of Substance or Being in general, with a relative notion of its supporting or being the subject of the aforesaid powers—which is signified by the name soul or spirit. This is what some hold; but, so far as I can see, the words will, soul, spirit, do not stand for different ideas, or, in truth, for any idea at all, but for something which is very different from ideas, and which, being an agent, cannot be like unto, or represented by, any idea whatsoever. Though it must be owned at the same time that we have some notion of soul, spirit, and the operations of the mind: such as willing, loving, hating—inasmuch as we know or understand the meaning of these words.

28. I find I can excite ideas in my mind at pleasure, and vary and shift the scene as oft as I think fit. It is no more than willing, and straightway this or that idea arises in my fancy; and by the same power it is obliterated and makes way for another. This making and unmaking of ideas doth very properly denominate the mind active. Thus much is certain and grounded on experience; but when we think of unthinking agents or of exciting ideas exclusive of volition, we only amuse ourselves with words.

29. But, whatever power I may have over my own thoughts, I find the ideas actually perceived by Sense have not a like dependence on my will. When in broad daylight I open my eyes, it is not in my power to choose whether I shall see or no, or to determine what particular objects shall present themselves to my view; and so likewise as to the hearing and other senses; the ideas imprinted on them are not creatures of my will. There is therefore some other Will or Spirit that produces them.

30. The ideas of Sense are more strong, lively, and distinct than those of the imagination; they have likewise a steadiness, order, and coherence, and are not excited at random, as those which are the effects of human wills often are, but in a regular train or series, the admirable connexion whereof sufficiently testifies the wisdom and benevolence of its Author. Now the set rules or established methods wherein the Mind we depend on excites in us the ideas of sense, are called the laws of nature; and these we learn by experience, which teaches us that such and such ideas are attended with such and such other ideas, in the ordinary course of things.

31. This gives us a sort of foresight which enables us to regulate our actions for the benefit of life. And without this we should be eternally at a loss; we could not know how to act anything that might procure us the least pleasure, or remove the least pain of sense. That food nourishes, sleep refreshes, and fire warms us; that to

sow in the seed-time is the way to reap in the harvest; and in general that to obtain such or such ends, such or such means are conducive—all this we know, not by discovering any necessary connexion between our ideas, but only by the observation of the settled laws of nature, without which we should be all in uncertainty and confusion, and a grown man no more know how to manage himself in the affairs of life than an infant just born.

32. And yet this consistent uniform working, which so evidently displays the goodness and wisdom of that Governing Spirit whose Will constitutes the laws of nature, is so far from leading our thoughts to Him, that it rather sends them wandering after second causes. For, when we perceive certain ideas of Sense constantly followed by other ideas and we know this is not of our own doing, we forthwith attribute power and agency to the ideas themselves, and make one the cause of another, than which nothing can be more absurd and unintelligible. Thus, for example, having observed that when we perceive by sight a certain round luminous figure we at the same time perceive by touch the idea or sensation called heat, we do from thence conclude the sun to be the cause of heat. And in like manner perceiving the motion and collision of bodies to be attended with sound, we are inclined to think the latter the effect of the former.

33. The ideas imprinted on the Senses by the Author of nature are called real things; and those excited in the imagination being less regular, vivid, and constant, are more properly termed ideas, or images of things, which they copy and represent. But then our sensations, be they never so vivid and distinct, are nevertheless ideas, that is, they exist in the mind, or are perceived by it, as truly as the ideas of its own framing. The ideas of Sense are allowed to have more reality in them, that is, to be more strong, orderly, and coherent than the creatures of the mind; but this is no argument that they exist without the mind. They are also less dependent on the spirit, or thinking substance which perceives them, in that they are excited by the will of another and more powerful spirit; yet still they are ideas, and certainly no idea, whether faint or strong, can exist otherwise than in a mind perceiving it.

34. Before we proceed any farther it is necessary we spend some time in answering objections which may probably be made against the principles we have hitherto laid down. In doing of which, if I seem too prolix to those of quick apprehensions, I hope it may be pardoned, since all men do not equally apprehend things of this nature, and I am willing to be understood by every one.

First, then, it will be objected that by the foregoing principles all that is real and substantial in nature is banished out of the world, and instead thereof a chimerical scheme of ideas takes place. All things that exist, exist only in the mind, that is, they are purely notional. What therefore becomes of the sun, moon and stars? What must we think of houses, rivers, mountains, trees, stones; nay, even of our own bodies? Are all these but so many chimeras and illusions on the fancy? To all which, and whatever else of the same sort may be objected, I answer, that by the principles premised we are not deprived of any one thing in nature. Whatever we see, feel, hear, or anywise conceive or understand remains as secure as ever, and is as real as ever. There is a rerum natura, and the distinction between realities and chimeras retains its full force. This is evident from sect. 29, 30, and 33, where we have shewn what is meant by real things in opposition to chimeras or ideas of our own framing; but then they both equally exist in the mind, and in that sense they are alike ideas.

35. I do not argue against the existence of any one thing that we can apprehend either by sense or reflexion. That the things I see with my eyes and touch with my hands do exist, really exist, I make not the least question. The only thing whose existence we deny is that which philosophers call Matter or corporeal substance. And in doing of this there is no damage done to the rest of mankind, who, I dare say, will never miss it. The Atheist indeed will want the colour of an empty name to support his impiety; and the Philosophers may possibly find they have lost a great handle for trifling and disputation.

36. If any man thinks this detracts from the existence or reality of things, he is very far from understanding what hath been premised in the plainest terms I could think of. Take here an abstract of what has been said:—There are spiritual substances, minds, or human souls, which will or excite ideas in themselves at pleasure; but these are faint, weak, and unsteady in respect of others they perceive by sense—which, being impressed upon them according to certain rules or laws of nature, speak themselves the effects of a mind more powerful and wise than human spirits. These latter are said to have more reality in them than the former:—by which is meant that they are more affecting, orderly, and distinct, and that they are not fictions of the mind perceiving them. And in this sense the sun that I see by day is the real sun, and that which I imagine by night is the idea of the former. In the sense here given of reality it is evident that every vegetable, star, mineral, and in general each part of the mundane system, is as much a real being by our principles as by any other. Whether others mean anything by the term reality different from what I do, I entreat them to look into their own thoughts and see.

37. I will be urged that thus much at least is true, to wit, that we take away all corporeal substances. To this my answer is, that if the word substance be taken in the vulgar sense—for a combination of sensible qualities, such as extension, solidity, weight, and the like—this we cannot be accused of taking away: but if it be taken in a philosophic sense—for the support of accidents or qualities without the mind—then indeed I acknowledge that we take it away, if one may be said to take away that which never had any existence, not even in the imagination.

38. But after all, say you, it sounds very harsh to say we eat and drink ideas, and are clothed with ideas. I acknowledge it does so—the word idea not being used in common discourse to signify the several combinations of sensible qualities which are called things; and it is certain that any expression which varies from the familiar use of language will seem harsh and ridiculous. But this doth not concern the truth of the proposition, which in other words is no more than to say, we are fed and clothed with those things which we perceive immediately by our senses. The hardness or softness, the colour, taste, warmth, figure, or suchlike qualities, which

combined together constitute the several sorts of victuals and apparel, have been shewn to exist only in the mind that perceives them; and this is all that is meant by calling them ideas; which word if it was as ordinarily used as thing, would sound no harsher nor more ridiculous than it. I am not for disputing about the propriety, but the truth of the expression. If therefore you agree with me that we eat and drink and are clad with the immediate objects of sense, which cannot exist unperceived or without the mind, I shall readily grant it is more proper or conformable to custom that they should be called things rather than ideas.

DISCUSSION QUESTIONS

1. Compare Berkeley's view to Locke's. What are the main similarities and differences between their versions of empiricism? Explain.

2. Many people find Berkeley's argument disturbing. Where is the flaw in his argument, if there is one? Explain.

3. Why does Berkeley reject the distinction between primary and secondary qualities? Explain.

An Enquiry Concerning Human Understanding

By David Hume

Another empiricist philosopher was Scottish philosopher David Hume, whose view of the self was considered in Part I of Four Fundamental Questions. *There, his view of knowledge was referenced in order to explain his rejection of the idea of a self. Here, we have an excerpt from Hume's later work,* An Enquiry Concerning Human Understanding *(1748). The* Enquiry *is a reworking of some of the ideas from Book I of the* Treatise. *Hume makes a distinction between "matters of fact" and "relations of ideas." Relations of ideas are necessary truths that are demonstratively certain, like the truths of arithmetic and geometry, or statements that are true by definition (their negation leads to a contradiction). Matters of fact are not necessary truths, they are contingent and could have been otherwise (their negation does not lead to a contradiction). This distinction matches up with the distinction made in Leibniz's* Monadology *between "truths of fact" and "truths of reasoning." Hume points out that most things that people claim as knowledge are matters of fact, and are thus not certain. In other words, we know a lot less than we think we do. We draw conclusions about matters of fact, he thinks, because of the relation of cause and effect. Unlike rationalists like Descartes and Leibniz, Hume rejects the notion that causation is something we know for certain as an innate idea. Hume follows Locke's rejection of innate ideas. We don't have experiences of causation. We call things that are constantly conjoined cause and effect, but that is merely custom or habit.*

SECTION IV
SCEPTICAL DOUBTS CONCERNING THE OPERATIONS OF THE UNDERSTANDING

PART I

All the objects of human reason or enquiry may naturally be divided into two kinds, to wit, Relations of Ideas, and Matters of Fact. Of the first kind are the sciences of Geometry, Algebra, and Arithmetic; and in short, every affirmation which is either intuitively or demonstratively certain. That the square of the hypothenuse is equal to the square of the two sides, is a proposition which expresses a relation between these figures. That three times five is equal to the half of thirty, expresses a relation between these numbers. Propositions of this kind are discoverable by the mere operation of thought, without dependence on what is anywhere existent in the universe. Though there never were a circle or triangle in nature, the truths demonstrated by Euclid would for ever retain their certainty and evidence.

Matters of fact, which are the second objects of human reason, are not ascertained in the same manner; nor is our evidence of their truth, however great, of a like nature with the foregoing. The contrary of every matter of fact is still possible; because it can never imply a contradiction, and is conceived by the mind with the same facility and distinctness, as if ever so conformable to reality. That the sun will not rise tomorrow is no less intelligible a proposition, and implies no more contradiction than the affirmation, that it will rise. We should in vain, therefore, attempt to demonstrate its falsehood. Were it demonstratively false, it would imply a contradiction, and could never be distinctly conceived by the mind.

It may, therefore, be a subject worthy of curiosity, to enquire what is the nature of that evidence which assures us of any real existence and matter of fact, beyond the present testimony of our senses, or the records of our memory. This part of philosophy, it is observable, has been little cultivated, either by the ancients or moderns; and therefore our doubts and errors, in the prosecution of so important an enquiry, may be the more excusable; while we march through such difficult paths without any guide or direction. They may even prove useful, by exciting curiosity, and destroying that implicit faith and security, which is the bane of all reasoning and free enquiry. The discovery of defects in the common philosophy, if any such there be, will not, I presume, be a discouragement, but rather an incitement, as is usual, to attempt something more full and satisfactory than has yet been proposed to the public.

All reasonings concerning matter of fact seem to be founded on the relation of Cause and Effect. By means of that relation alone we can go beyond the evidence of our memory and senses. If you were to ask a man, why he believes any matter of fact, which is absent; for instance, that his friend is in the country, or in France; he would give you a reason; and this reason would be some other fact; as a letter received from him, or the knowledge of his former resolutions and promises. A man finding a watch or any other machine in a desert island, would conclude that there had once been men in that island. All our reasonings concerning fact are of the same nature. And here it is constantly supposed that there is a connexion between the present fact and that which is inferred from it. Were there nothing to bind them together, the inference would be entirely precarious. The hearing of an articulate voice and rational discourse in the dark assures us of the presence of some person: Why? because these are the effects of the human make and fabric, and closely connected with it. If we anatomize all the other reasonings of this nature, we shall find that they are founded on the relation of cause and effect, and that this relation is either near or remote, direct or collateral. Heat and light are collateral effects of fire, and the one effect may justly be inferred from the other.

If we would satisfy ourselves, therefore, concerning the nature of that evidence, which assures us of matters of fact, we must enquire how we arrive at the knowledge of cause and effect.

I shall venture to affirm, as a general proposition, which admits of no exception, that the knowledge of this relation is not, in any instance, attained by reasonings a priori; but arises entirely from experience, when we find that any particular objects are constantly conjoined with each other. Let an object be presented to a man of ever so strong natural reason and abilities; if that object be entirely new to him, he will not be able, by the most accurate examination of its sensible qualities, to discover any of its causes or effects. Adam, though his rational faculties be supposed, at the very first, entirely perfect, could not have inferred from the fluidity and transparency of water that it would suffocate him, or from the light and warmth of fire that it would consume him. No object ever discovers, by the qualities which appear to the senses, either the causes which produced it, or the effects which will arise from it; nor can our reason, unassisted by experience, ever draw any inference concerning real existence and matter of fact.

This proposition, that causes and effects are discoverable, not by reason but by experience, will readily be admitted with regard to such objects, as we remember to have once been altogether unknown to us; since we must be conscious of the utter inability, which we then lay under, of foretelling what would arise from them. Present two smooth pieces of marble to a man who has no tincture of natural philosophy; he will never discover that they will adhere together in such a manner as to require great force to separate them in a direct line, while they make so small a resistance to a lateral pressure. Such events, as bear little analogy to the common course of nature, are also readily confessed to be known only by experience; nor does any man imagine that the explosion of gunpowder, or the attraction of a loadstone, could ever be discovered by arguments a priori. In like manner, when an effect is supposed to depend upon an intricate machinery or secret structure of parts, we make no difficulty in attributing all our knowledge of it to experience. Who will assert that he can give the ultimate reason, why milk or bread is proper nourishment for a man, not for a lion or a tiger?

But the same truth may not appear, at first sight, to have the same evidence with regard to events, which have become familiar to us from our first appearance in the world, which bear a close analogy to the whole course of nature, and which are supposed to depend on the simple qualities of objects, without any secret structure of parts. We are apt to imagine that we could discover these effects by the mere operation of our reason, without experience. We fancy, that were we brought on a sudden into this world, we could at first have inferred that one Billiard-ball would communicate motion to another upon impulse; and that we needed not to have waited for the event, in order to pronounce with certainty concerning it. Such is the influence of custom, that, where it is strongest, it not only covers our natural ignorance, but even conceals itself, and seems not to take place, merely because it is found in the highest degree.

But to convince us that all the laws of nature, and all the operations of bodies without exception, are known only by experience, the following reflections may, perhaps, suffice. Were any object presented to us, and were we required to pronounce concerning the effect, which will result from it, without consulting past observation; after what manner, I beseech you, must the mind proceed in this operation? It must invent or imagine some event, which it ascribes to the object as its effect; and it is plain that this invention must be entirely arbitrary. The mind can never possibly find the effect in the supposed cause, by the most accurate scrutiny and examination. For the effect is totally different from the cause, and consequently can never be discovered in it. Motion in the second Billiard-ball is a quite distinct event from motion in the first; nor is there anything in the one to suggest the smallest hint of the other. A stone or piece of metal raised into the air, and left without any support, immediately falls: but to consider the matter a priori, is there anything we discover in this situation which can beget the idea of a downward, rather than an upward, or any other motion, in the stone or metal?

And as the first imagination or invention of a particular effect, in all natural operations, is arbitrary, where we consult not experience; so must we also esteem the supposed tie or connexion between the cause and effect, which binds them together, and renders it impossible that any other effect could result from the operation of that cause. When I see, for instance, a Billiard-ball moving in a straight line towards another; even suppose motion in the second ball should by accident be suggested to me, as the result of their contact or impulse; may I not conceive, that a hundred different events might as well follow from that cause? May not both these balls remain at absolute rest? May not the first ball return in a straight line, or leap off from the second in any line or direction? All these suppositions are consistent and conceivable. Why then should we give the preference to one, which is no more consistent or conceivable than the rest? All our reasonings a priori will never be able to show us any foundation for this preference.

In a word, then, every effect is a distinct event from its cause. It could not, therefore, be discovered in the cause, and the first invention or conception of it, a priori, must be entirely arbitrary. And even after it is suggested, the conjunction of it with the cause must appear equally arbitrary; since there are always many other effects, which, to reason, must seem fully as consistent and natural. In vain, therefore, should we pretend to determine any single event, or infer any cause or effect, without the assistance of observation and experience.

Hence we may discover the reason why no philosopher, who is rational and modest, has ever pretended to assign the ultimate cause of any natural operation, or to show distinctly the action of that power, which produces any single effect in the universe. It is confessed, that the utmost effort of human reason is to reduce the principles, productive of natural phenomena, to a greater simplicity, and to resolve the many particular effects into a few general causes, by means of reasonings from analogy, experience, and observation. But as to the causes of these general causes, we should in vain attempt their discovery; nor shall we ever be able to satisfy ourselves, by any particular explication of them. These ultimate springs and principles are totally shut up from human curiosity and enquiry. Elasticity, gravity, cohesion of parts, communication of motion by impulse; these are probably the ultimate causes and principles which we shall ever discover in nature; and we may esteem ourselves sufficiently happy, if, by accurate enquiry and reasoning, we can trace up the particular phenomena to, or near to, these general principles. The most perfect philosophy of the natural kind only staves off our ignorance a little longer: as perhaps the most perfect philosophy of the moral or metaphysical kind serves only to discover larger portions of it. Thus the observation of human blindness and weakness is the result of all philosophy, and meets us at every turn, in spite of our endeavours to elude or avoid it.

PART II

But we have not yet attained any tolerable satisfaction with regard to the question first proposed. Each solution still gives rise to a new question as difficult as the foregoing, and leads us on to farther enquiries. When it is asked, What is the nature of all our reasonings concerning matter of fact? the proper answer seems to be, that they are founded on the relation of cause and effect. When again it is asked, What is the foundation of all our reasonings and conclusions concerning that relation? it may be replied in one word, Experience. But if we still carry on our sifting humour, and ask, What is the foundation of all conclusions from experience? this implies a new question, which may be of more difficult solution and explication. Philosophers, that give themselves airs of superior wisdom and sufficiency, have a hard task when they encounter persons of inquisitive dispositions, who push them from every corner to which they retreat, and who are sure at last to bring them to some dangerous dilemma. The best expedient to prevent this confusion, is to be modest in our pretensions; and even to discover the difficulty ourselves before it is objected to us. By this means, we may make a kind of merit of our very ignorance.

I shall content myself, in this section, with an easy task, and shall pretend only to give a negative answer to the question here proposed. I say then, that, even after we have experience of the operations of cause and effect, our conclusions from that experience are not founded on reasoning, or any process of the understanding. This answer we must endeavour both to explain and to defend.

It must certainly be allowed, that nature has kept us at a great distance from all her secrets, and has afforded us only the knowledge of a few superficial qualities of objects; while she conceals from us those powers and principles on which the influence of those objects entirely depends. Our senses inform us of the colour, weight, and consistence of bread; but neither sense nor reason can ever inform us of those qualities which fit it for the nourishment and support of a human body. Sight or feeling conveys an idea of the actual motion of bodies; but as to that wonderful force or power, which would carry on a moving body for ever in a continued change of place, and which bodies never lose but by communicating it to others; of this we cannot form the most distant conception. But notwithstanding this ignorance of natural powers[1] and principles, we always presume, when we see like sensible qualities, that they have like secret powers, and expect that effects, similar to those which we have experienced, will follow from them. If a body of like colour and consistence with that bread, which we have formerly eat, be presented to us, we make no scruple of repeating the experiment, and foresee, with certainty, like nourishment and support. Now this is a process of the mind or thought, of which I would willingly know the foundation. It is allowed on all hands that there is no known connexion between the sensible qualities and the secret powers; and consequently, that the mind is not led to form such a conclusion concerning their constant and regular conjunction, by anything which it knows of their nature. As to past Experience, it can be allowed to give direct and certain information of those precise objects only, and that precise period of time, which fell under its cognizance: but why this experience should be extended to future times, and to other objects, which for aught we know, may be only in appearance similar; this is the main question on which I would insist. The bread, which I formerly eat, nourished me; that is, a body of such sensible qualities was, at that time, endued with such secret powers: but does it follow, that other bread must also nourish me at another time, and that like sensible qualities must always be attended with like secret powers? The consequence seems nowise necessary. At least, it must be acknowledged that there is here a consequence drawn by the mind; that there is a certain step taken; a process of thought, and an inference, which wants to be explained. These two propositions are far from being the same. I have found that such an object has always been attended with such an effect, and I foresee, that other objects, which are, in appearance, similar, will be attended with similar effects. I shall allow, if you please, that the one proposition may justly be inferred from the other: I know, in fact, that it always is inferred. But if you insist that the inference is made by a chain of reasoning, I desire you to produce that reasoning. The connexion between these propositions is not intuitive. There is required a medium, which may enable the mind to draw such an inference, if indeed it be drawn by reasoning and argument. What that medium is, I must confess, passes my comprehension; and it is incumbent on those to produce it, who assert that it really exists, and is the origin of all our conclusions concerning matter of fact.

This negative argument must certainly, in process of time, become altogether convincing, if many penetrating and able philosophers shall turn their enquiries this way and no one be ever able to discover any connecting proposition or intermediate step, which supports the understanding in this conclusion. But as the question is yet new, every reader may not trust so far to his own penetration, as to conclude, because an argument escapes his enquiry, that therefore it does not really exist. For this reason it may be requisite to venture upon a more difficult task; and enumerating all the branches of human knowledge, endeavour to show that none of them can afford such an argument.

All reasonings may be divided into two kinds, namely, demonstrative reasoning, or that concerning relations of ideas, and moral reasoning, or that concerning matter of fact and existence. That there are no demonstrative arguments in the case seems evident; since it implies no contradiction that the course of nature may change, and that an object, seemingly like those which we have experienced, may be attended with different or contrary effects. May I not clearly and distinctly conceive that a body, falling from the clouds, and which, in all other respects, resembles snow, has yet the taste of salt or feeling of fire? Is there any more intelligible proposition than to affirm, that all the trees will flourish in December and January, and decay in May and June? Now whatever is intelligible, and can be distinctly conceived, implies no contradiction, and can never be proved false by any demonstrative argument or abstract reasoning a priori.

If we be, therefore, engaged by arguments to put trust in past experience, and make it the standard of our future judgment, these arguments must be probable only, or such as regard matter of fact and real existence according to the division above mentioned. But that there is no argument of this kind, must appear, if our explication of that species of reasoning be admitted as solid and satisfactory. We have said that all arguments concerning existence are founded on the relation of cause and effect; that our knowledge of that relation is derived entirely from experience; and that all our experimental conclusions proceed upon the supposition that the future will be conformable to the past. To endeavour, therefore, the proof of this last supposition by probable arguments, or arguments regarding existence, must be evidently going in a circle, and taking that for granted, which is the very point in question.

In reality, all arguments from experience are founded on the similarity which we discover among natural objects, and by which we are induced to expect effects similar to those which we have found to follow from such objects. And though none but a fool or madman will ever pretend to dispute the authority of experience, or to reject that great guide of human life, it may surely be allowed a philosopher to have so much curiosity at least as to examine the principle of human nature, which gives this mighty authority to experience, and makes us draw advantage from that similarity which nature has placed among different objects. From causes which appear similar we expect similar effects. This is the sum of all our experimental conclusions. Now it seems evident that, if this conclusion were formed by reason, it would be as perfect at first, and upon one instance, as after ever so long a course of experience. But the case is far otherwise. Nothing so like as eggs; yet no one, on account of this appearing similarity, expects the same taste and relish in all of them. It is only after a long course of uniform experiments in any kind, that we attain a firm reliance and security with regard to a particular event. Now where is that process of reasoning which, from one instance, draws a conclusion, so different from that which it infers from a hundred instances that are nowise different from that single one? This question I propose as much for the sake of information, as with an intention of raising difficulties. I cannot find, I cannot imagine any such reasoning. But I keep my mind still open to instruction, if any one will vouchsafe to bestow it on me.

Should it be said that, from a number of uniform experiments, we infer a connexion between the sensible qualities and the secret powers; this, I must confess, seems the same difficulty, couched in different terms. The question still recurs, on what process of argument this inference is founded? Where is the medium, the interposing ideas, which join propositions so very wide of each other? It is confessed that the colour, consistence, and other sensible qualities of bread appear not, of themselves, to have any connexion with the secret powers of nourishment and support. For otherwise we could infer these secret powers from the first appearance of these sensible qualities, without the aid of experience; contrary to the sentiment of all philosophers, and contrary to plain matter of fact. Here, then, is our natural state of ignorance with regard to the powers and influence of all objects. How is this remedied by experience? It only shows us a number of uniform effects, resulting from certain objects, and teaches us that those particular objects, at that particular time, were endowed with such powers and forces. When a new object, endowed with similar sensible qualities, is produced, we expect similar powers and forces, and look for a like effect. From a body of like colour and consistence with bread we expect like nourishment and support. But this surely is a step or progress of the mind, which wants to be explained. When a man says, I have found, in all past instances, such sensible qualities conjoined with such secret powers: And when he says, Similar sensible qualities will always be conjoined with similar secret powers, he is not guilty of a tautology, nor are these propositions in any respect the same. You say that the one proposition is an inference from the other. But you must confess that the inference is not intuitive; neither is it demonstrative: Of what nature is it, then? To say it is experimental, is begging the question. For all inferences from experience suppose, as their foundation, that the future will resemble the past, and that similar powers will be conjoined with similar sensible qualities. If there be any suspicion that the course of nature may change, and that the past may be no rule for the future, all experience becomes useless, and can give rise to no inference or conclusion. It is impossible, therefore, that any arguments from experience can prove this resemblance of the past to the future; since all these arguments are founded on the supposition of that resemblance. Let the course of things be allowed hitherto ever so regular; that alone, without some new argument or inference, proves not that, for the future, it will continue so. In vain do you pretend to have learned the nature of bodies from your past experience. Their secret nature, and consequently all their effects and influence, may change, without any change in their sensible qualities. This happens sometimes, and with regard to some objects: Why may it not happen always, and with regard to all objects? What logic, what process or argument secures you against this supposition? My practice, you say, refutes my doubts. But you mistake the purport of my question. As an agent, I am quite satisfied in the point; but as a philosopher, who has some share of curiosity, I will not say scepticism, I want to learn the foundation of this inference. No reading, no enquiry has yet been able to remove my difficulty, or give me satisfaction in a matter of such importance. Can I do better than propose the difficulty to the public, even though, perhaps, I have small hopes of obtaining a solution? We shall at least, by this means, be sensible of our ignorance, if we do not augment our knowledge.

I must confess that a man is guilty of unpardonable arrogance who concludes, because an argument has escaped his own investigation, that therefore it does not really exist. I must also confess that, though all the learned, for several ages, should have employed themselves in fruitless search upon any subject, it may still, perhaps, be rash to conclude positively that the subject must, therefore, pass all human comprehension. Even though we examine all the sources of our knowledge, and conclude them unfit for such a subject, there may still remain a suspicion, that the enumeration is not complete, or the examination not accurate. But with regard to the present subject, there are some considerations which seem to remove all this accusation of arrogance or suspicion of mistake.

It is certain that the most ignorant and stupid peasants—nay infants, nay even brute beasts—improve by experience, and learn the qualities of natural objects, by observing the effects which result from them. When a child has felt the sensation of pain from touching the flame of a candle, he will be careful not to put his hand near any candle; but will expect a similar effect from a cause which is similar in its sensible qualities and appearance. If you assert, therefore, that the understanding of the child is led into this conclusion by any process of argument or ratiocination, I may justly require you to produce that argument; nor have you any pretence to refuse so equitable a demand. You cannot say that the argument is abstruse, and may possibly escape your enquiry; since you confess that it is obvious to the capacity of a mere infant. If you hesitate, therefore, a moment, or if, after reflection, you produce any intricate or profound argument, you, in a manner, give up the question, and confess that it is not reasoning which engages us to suppose the past resembling the future, and to expect similar effects from causes which are, to appearance, similar. This is the proposition which I intended to enforce in the present section. If I be right, I pretend not to have made any mighty discovery. And if I be wrong, I must acknowledge myself to be indeed a very backward scholar; since I cannot now discover an argument which, it seems, was perfectly familiar to me long before I was out of my cradle.

ENDNOTE

1 The word, Power, is here used in a loose and popular sense. The more accurate explication of it would give additional evidence to this argument. See Sect. 7.

DISCUSSION QUESTIONS

1. Explain Hume's billiard ball example.

2. Explain the differences between Hume's empiricism and the kind found in Locke and Berkeley.

3. Which view of knowledge makes more sense to you, the rationalist position or the empiricist position? Why? Explain.

4. What are the similarities and differences between Hume's skepticism and the skepticism of Chuang Tzu? Explain.

Critique of Pure Reason

By Immanuel Kant

Some consider Immanuel Kant (1724–1804) the most important philosopher of the modern era (others say he was the most important philosopher ever). Kant was a rationalist philosopher for his early career and made many contributions to science, as well. Then he discovered Hume, who Kant claimed "awakened him from his dogmatic slumber." Kant realized that Hume's skepticism really made it necessary to rethink the foundations of his rationalism. Kant then entered what scholars call "the silent decade," during which he did not publish. He emerged in 1781 with the Critique of Pure Reason, *which was followed by two other Critiques, the* Critique of Practical Reason *(1788), which was about moral philosophy, and the* Critique of Judgment *(1790), which is concerned with aesthetic judgment and teleological judgment. We will see Kant's moral philosophy in Part IV of* Four Fundamental Questions.

Our excerpt is the Introduction from the Critique of Pure Reason. *Here, Kant defines his terms and sets his course. He makes a distinction between pure and empirical knowledge. He then argues that there are things we can know before experience (*a priori*), but he does not tie them to the innate ideas of earlier rationalists. Philosophy's job, he says, is to determine what we can know* a priori. *He makes a further distinction between analytic and synthetic judgments. An analytic judgment contains its own truth, but a synthetic one needs to seek confirmation outside. He then draws out the implications of these distinctions and sets the tone for the rest of his work.*

INTRODUCTION

I. Of the difference between Pure and Empirical Knowledge

That all our knowledge begins with experience there can be no doubt. For how is it possible that the faculty of cognition should be awakened into exercise otherwise than by means of objects which affect our senses, and partly of themselves produce representations, partly rouse our powers of understanding into activity, to compare to connect, or to separate these, and so to convert the raw material of our sensuous impressions into a knowledge of objects, which is called experience? In respect of time, therefore, no knowledge of ours is antecedent to experience, but begins with it.

But, though all our knowledge begins with experience, it by no means follows that all arises out of experience. For, on the contrary, it is quite possible that our empirical knowledge is a compound of that which we receive through impressions, and that which the faculty of cognition supplies from itself (sensuous impressions giving merely the occasion), an addition which we cannot distinguish from the original element given by sense, till long practice has made us attentive to, and skilful in separating it. It is, therefore, a question which requires close investigation, and not to be answered at first sight, whether there exists a knowledge altogether independent of experience, and even of all sensuous impressions? Knowledge of this kind is called a priori, in contradistinction to empirical knowledge, which has its sources a posteriori, that is, in experience.

But the expression, "a priori," is not as yet definite enough adequately to indicate the whole meaning of the question above started. For, in speaking of knowledge which has its sources in experience, we are wont to say, that this or that may be known a priori, because we do not derive this knowledge immediately from experience, but from a general rule, which, however, we have itself borrowed from experience. Thus, if a man undermined his house, we say, "he might know a priori that it would have fallen;" that is, he needed not to have waited for the experience that it did actually fall. But still, a priori, he could not know even this much. For, that bodies are heavy, and, consequently, that they fall when their supports are taken away, must have been known to him previously, by means of experience.

By the term "knowledge a priori," therefore, we shall in the sequel understand, not such as is independent of this or that kind of experience, but such as is absolutely so of all experience. Opposed to this is empirical knowledge, or that which is possible only a posteriori, that is, through experience. Knowledge a priori is either pure or impure. Pure knowledge a priori is that with which no empirical element is mixed up. For example, the proposition, "Every change has a cause," is a proposition a priori, but impure, because change is a conception which can only be derived from experience.

II. The Human Intellect, even in an Unphilosophical State, is in Possession of Certain Cognitions "a priori"

The question now is as to a criterion, by which we may securely distinguish a pure from an empirical cognition. Experience no doubt teaches us that this or that object is constituted in such and such a manner, but not that it could not possibly exist otherwise. Now, in the first place, if we have a proposition which contains the idea of necessity in its very conception, it is a if, moreover, it is not derived from any other proposition, unless from one equally involving the idea of necessity, it is absolutely priori. Secondly, an empirical judgement never exhibits strict and absolute, but only assumed and comparative universality (by induction); therefore, the most we can say is—so far as we have hitherto observed, there is no exception to this or that rule. If, on the other hand, a judgement carries with it strict and absolute universality, that is, admits of no possible exception, it is not derived from experience, but is valid absolutely a priori.

Empirical universality is, therefore, only an arbitrary extension of validity, from that which may be predicated of a proposition valid in most cases, to that which is asserted of a proposition which holds good in all; as, for example, in the affirmation, "All bodies are heavy." When, on the contrary, strict universality characterizes a judgement, it necessarily indicates another peculiar source of knowledge, namely, a faculty of cognition a priori. Necessity and strict universality, therefore, are infallible tests for distinguishing pure from empirical knowledge, and are inseparably connected with each other. But as in the use of these criteria the empirical limitation is sometimes more easily detected than the contingency of the judgement, or the unlimited universality which we attach to a judgement is often a more convincing proof than its necessity, it may be advisable to use the criteria separately, each being by itself infallible.

Now, that in the sphere of human cognition we have judgements which are necessary, and in the strictest sense universal, consequently pure a priori, it will be an easy matter to show. If we desire an example from the sciences, we need only take any proposition in mathematics. If we cast our eyes upon the commonest operations of the understanding, the proposition, "Every change must have a cause," will amply serve our purpose. In the latter case, indeed, the conception of a cause so plainly involves the conception of a necessity of connection with an effect, and of a strict universality of the law, that the very notion of a cause would entirely disappear, were we to derive it, like Hume, from a frequent association of what happens with that which precedes; and the habit thence originating of connecting representations—the necessity inherent in the judgement being therefore merely subjective. Besides, without seeking for such examples of principles existing a priori in cognition, we might easily show that such principles are the indispensable basis of the possibility of experience itself, and consequently prove their existence a priori. For whence could our experience itself acquire certainty, if all the rules on which it depends were themselves empirical, and consequently fortuitous? No one, therefore, can admit the validity of the use of such rules as first principles. But, for the present, we may content ourselves with having established the fact, that we do possess and exercise a faculty of pure a priori cognition; and, secondly, with having pointed out the proper tests of such cognition, namely, universality and necessity.

Not only in judgements, however, but even in conceptions, is an a priori origin manifest. For example, if we take away by degrees from our conceptions of a body all that can be referred to mere sensuous experience—colour, hardness or softness, weight, even impenetrability—the body will then vanish; but the space which it occupied still remains, and this it is utterly impossible to annihilate in thought. Again, if we take away, in like manner, from our empirical conception of any object, corporeal or incorporeal, all properties which mere experience has taught us to connect with it, still we cannot think away those through which we cogitate it as substance, or adhering to substance, although our conception of substance is more determined than that of an object. Compelled, therefore, by that necessity with which the conception of substance forces itself upon us, we must confess that it has its seat in our faculty of cognition a priori.

III. Philosophy stands in need of a Science which shall Determine the Possibility, Principles, and Extent of Human Knowledge "a priori"

Of far more importance than all that has been above said, is the consideration that certain of our cognitions rise completely above the sphere of all possible experience, and by means of conceptions, to which there exists in the whole extent of experience no corresponding object, seem to extend the range of our judgements beyond its bounds. And just in this transcendental or supersensible sphere, where experience affords us neither instruction nor guidance, lie the investigations of reason, which, on account of their importance, we consider far preferable to, and as having a far more elevated aim than, all that the understanding can achieve within the sphere of sensuous phenomena. So high a value do we set upon these investigations, that even at the risk of error, we persist in following them out, and permit neither doubt nor disregard nor indifference to restrain us from the pursuit. These unavoidable problems of mere pure reason are God, freedom (of will), and immortality. The science which, with all its preliminaries, has for its especial object the solution of these problems is named metaphysics—a science which is at the very outset dogmatical, that is, it confidently takes upon itself the execution of this task without any previous investigation of the ability or inability of reason for such an undertaking.

Now the safe ground of experience being thus abandoned, it seems nevertheless natural that we should hesitate to erect a building with the cognitions we possess, without knowing whence they come, and on the strength of principles, the origin of which is undiscovered. Instead of thus trying to build without a foundation, it is rather to be expected that we should long ago have put the question, how the understanding can arrive at these a priori cognitions, and what is the extent, validity, and worth which they may possess? We say, "This is natural enough," meaning by the word natural, that which is consistent with a just and reasonable way of thinking; but if we understand by the term, that, which usually happens, nothing indeed could be more natural and more comprehensible than that this investigation should be left long unattempted. For one part of our pure knowledge, the science of mathematics, has been long firmly established, and thus leads us to form flattering expectations with regard to others, though these may be of quite a different nature. Besides, when we get beyond the bounds of experience, we are of course safe from opposition in that quarter; and the charm of widening the range of our knowledge is so great that, unless we are brought to a standstill by some evident contradiction, we hurry on undoubtingly in our course. This, however, may be avoided, if we are sufficiently cautious in the construction of our fictions, which are not the less fictions on that account.

Mathematical science affords us a brilliant example, how far, independently of all experience, we may carry our a priori knowledge. It is true that the mathematician occupies himself with objects and cognitions only in so far as they can be represented by means of intuition. But this circumstance is easily overlooked, because the said intuition can itself be given a priori, and therefore is hardly to be distinguished from a mere pure conception. Deceived by such a proof of the power of reason, we can perceive no limits to the extension of our knowledge. The light dove cleaving in free flight the thin air, whose resistance it feels, might imagine that her movements would be far more free and rapid in airless space. Just in the same way did Plato, abandoning the world of sense because of the narrow limits it sets to the understanding, venture upon the wings of ideas beyond it, into the void space of pure intellect. He did not reflect that he made no real progress by all his efforts; for he met with no resistance which might serve him for a support, as it were, whereon to rest, and on which he might apply his powers, in order to let the intellect acquire momentum for its progress. It is, indeed, the common fate of human reason in speculation, to finish the imposing edifice of thought as rapidly as possible, and then for the first time to begin to examine whether the foundation is a solid one or no. Arrived at this point, all sorts of excuses are sought after, in order to console us for its want of stability, or rather, indeed, to enable us to dispense altogether with so late and dangerous an investigation. But what frees us during the process of building from all apprehension or suspicion, and flatters us into the belief of its solidity, is this. A great part, perhaps the greatest part, of the business of our reason consists in the analysation of the conceptions which we already possess of objects. By this means we gain a multitude of cognitions, which although really nothing more than elucidations or explanations of that which (though in a confused manner) was already thought in our conceptions, are, at least in respect of their form, prized as new introspections; whilst, so far as regards their matter or content, we have really made no addition to our conceptions, but only disinvolved them. But as this process does furnish a real priori knowledge, which has a sure progress and useful results, reason, deceived by this, slips in, without being itself aware of it, assertions of a quite different kind; in which, to given conceptions it adds others, a priori indeed, but entirely foreign to them, without our knowing how it arrives at these, and, indeed, without such a question ever suggesting itself. I shall therefore at once proceed to examine the difference between these two modes of knowledge.

IV. Of the Difference Between Analytical and Synthetical Judgements

In all judgements wherein the relation of a subject to the predicate is cogitated (I mention affirmative judgements only here; the application to negative will be very easy), this relation is possible in two different ways. Either the predicate B belongs to the subject A, as somewhat which is contained (though covertly) in the conception A; or the predicate B lies completely out of the conception A, although it stands in connection with it. In the first instance, I term the judgement analytical, in the second, synthetical. Analytical judgements (affirmative) are therefore those in which the connection of the predicate with the subject is cogitated through identity; those in which this connection is cogitated without identity, are called synthetical judgements. The former may be called explicative, the latter augmentative judgements; because the former add in the predicate nothing to the conception of the subject, but only analyse it into its constituent conceptions, which were thought already in the subject, although in a confused manner; the latter add to our conceptions of the subject a predicate which was not contained in it, and which no analysis could ever have discovered therein. For example, when I say, "All bodies are extended," this is an analytical judgement. For I need not go beyond the conception of body in order to find extension connected with it, but merely analyse the conception, that is, become conscious of the manifold properties which I think in that conception, in order to discover this predicate in it: it is therefore an analytical judgement. On the other hand, when I say, "All bodies are heavy," the predicate is something totally different from that which I think in the mere conception of a body. By the addition of such a predicate, therefore, it becomes a synthetical judgement.

Judgements of experience, as such, are always synthetical. For it would be absurd to think of grounding an analytical judgement on experience, because in forming such a judgement I need not go out of the sphere of my conceptions, and therefore recourse to the testimony of experience is quite unnecessary. That "bodies are extended" is not an empirical judgement, but a proposition which stands firm a priori. For before addressing myself to experience, I already have in my conception all the requisite conditions for the judgement, and I have only to extract the predicate from the conception, according to the principle of contradiction, and thereby at the same time become conscious of the necessity of the judgement, a necessity which I could never learn from experience. On the other hand, though at first I do not at all include the predicate of weight in my conception of body in general, that conception still indicates an object of experience, a part of the totality of experience, to which I can still add other parts; and this I do when I recognize by observation that bodies are heavy. I can cognize beforehand by analysis the conception of body through the characteristics of extension, impenetrability, shape, etc., all which are cogitated in this conception. But now I extend my knowledge, and looking back on experience from which I had derived this conception of body, I find weight at all times connected with the above characteristics, and therefore I synthetically add to my conceptions this as a predicate, and say, "All bodies are heavy." Thus it is experience upon which rests the possibility of the synthesis of the predicate of weight with the conception of body, because both conceptions, although the one is not contained in the other, still belong to one another (only contingently, however), as parts of a whole, namely, of experience, which is itself a synthesis of intuitions.

But to synthetical judgements a priori, such aid is entirely wanting. If I go out of and beyond the conception A, in order to recognize another B as connected with it, what foundation have I to rest on, whereby to render the synthesis possible? I have here no longer the advantage of looking out in the sphere of experience for what I want. Let us take, for example, the proposition, "Everything that happens has a cause." In the conception of "something that happens," I indeed think an existence which a certain time antecedes, and from this I can derive analytical judgements. But the conception of a cause lies quite out of the above conception, and indicates something entirely different from "that which happens," and is consequently not contained in that conception. How then am I able to assert concerning the general conception—"that which happens"—something entirely different from that conception, and to recognize the conception of cause although not contained in it, yet as belonging to it, and even necessarily? what is here the unknown = X, upon which the understanding rests when it believes it has found, out of the conception A a foreign predicate B, which it nevertheless considers to be connected with it? It cannot be experience, because the principle adduced annexes the two representations, cause and effect, to the representation existence, not only with universality, which experience cannot give, but also with the expression of necessity, therefore completely a priori and from pure conceptions. Upon such synthetical, that is augmentative propositions, depends the whole aim of our speculative knowledge a priori; for although analytical judgements are indeed highly important and necessary, they are so, only to arrive at that clearness of conceptions which is requisite for a sure and extended synthesis, and this alone is a real acquisition.

V. In all Theoretical Sciences of Reason, Synthetical Judgements "a priori" are contained as Principles

1. Mathematical judgements are always synthetical. Hitherto this fact, though incontestably true and very important in its consequences, seems to have escaped the analysts of the human mind, nay, to be in complete opposition to all their conjectures. For as it was found that mathematical conclusions all proceed according to the principle of contradiction (which the nature of every apodeictic certainty requires), people became persuaded that the fundamental principles of the science also were recognized and admitted in the same way. But the notion is fallacious; for although a synthetical proposition can certainly be discerned by means of the principle of contradiction, this is possible only when another synthetical proposition precedes, from which the latter is deduced, but never of itself.

   Before all, be it observed, that proper mathematical propositions are always judgements a priori, and not empirical, because they carry along with them the conception of necessity, which cannot be given by experience. If this be demurred to, it matters not; I will then limit my assertion to pure mathematics, the very conception of which implies that it consists of knowledge altogether non-empirical and a priori.

   We might, indeed at first suppose that the proposition $7 + 5 = 12$ is a merely analytical proposition, following (according to the principle of contradiction) from the conception of a sum of seven and five. But if we regard it more narrowly, we find that our conception of the sum of seven and five contains nothing more than the uniting of both sums into one, whereby it cannot at all be cogitated what this single number is which embraces both. The conception of twelve is by no means obtained by merely cogitating the union of seven and five; and we may analyse our conception of such a possible sum as long as we will, still we shall never discover in it the notion of twelve. We must go beyond these conceptions, and have recourse to an intuition which corresponds to one of the two—our five fingers, for example, or like Segner in his Arithmetic five points, and so by degrees, add the units contained in the five given in the intuition, to the conception of seven. For I first take the number 7, and, for the conception of 5 calling in the aid of the fingers of my hand as objects of intuition, I add the units, which I before took together to make up the number 5, gradually now by means of the material image my hand, to the number 7, and by this process, I at length see the number 12 arise. That 7 should be added to 5, I have certainly cogitated in my conception of a sum = 7 + 5, but not that this sum was equal to 12. Arithmetical propositions are therefore always synthetical, of which we may become more clearly convinced by trying large numbers. For it will thus become quite evident that, turn and twist our conceptions as we may, it is impossible, without having recourse to intuition, to arrive at the sum total or product by means of the mere analysis of our conceptions. Just as little is any principle of pure geometry analytical. "A straight line between two points is the shortest," is a synthetical proposition. For my conception of straight contains no notion of quantity, but is merely qualitative. The conception of the shortest is therefore fore wholly an addition, and by no analysis can it be extracted from our conception of a straight line. Intuition must therefore here lend its aid, by means of which, and thus only, our synthesis is possible.

Some few principles preposited by geometricians are, indeed, really analytical, and depend on the principle of contradiction. They serve, however, like identical propositions, as links in the chain of method, not as principles—for example, a = a, the whole is equal to itself, or (a+b) > a, the whole is greater than its part. And yet even these principles themselves, though they derive their validity from pure conceptions, are only admitted in mathematics because they can be presented in intuition. What causes us here commonly to believe that the predicate of such apodeictic judgements is already contained in our conception, and that the judgement is therefore analytical, is merely the equivocal nature of the expression. We must join in thought a certain predicate to a given conception, and this necessity cleaves already to the conception. But the question is, not what we must join in thought to the given conception, but what we really think therein, though only obscurely, and then it becomes manifest that the predicate pertains to these conceptions, necessarily indeed, yet not as thought in the conception itself, but by virtue of an intuition, which must be added to the conception.

2. The science of natural philosophy (physics) contains in itself synthetical judgements a priori, as principles. I shall adduce two propositions. For instance, the proposition, "In all changes of the material world, the quantity of matter remains unchanged"; or, that, "In all communication of motion, action and reaction must always be equal." In both of these, not only is the necessity, and therefore their origin a priori clear, but also that they are synthetical propositions. For in the conception of matter, I do not cogitate its permanency, but merely its presence in space, which it fills. I therefore really go out of and beyond the conception of matter, in order to think on to it something a priori, which I did not think in it. The proposition is therefore not analytical, but synthetical, and nevertheless conceived a priori; and so it is with regard to the other propositions of the pure part of natural philosophy.

3. As to metaphysics, even if we look upon it merely as an attempted science, yet, from the nature of human reason, an indispensable one, we find that it must

contain synthetical propositions a priori. It is not merely the duty of metaphysics to dissect, and thereby analytically to illustrate the conceptions which we form a priori of things; but we seek to widen the range of our a priori knowledge. For this purpose, we must avail ourselves of such principles as add something to the original conception—something not identical with, nor contained in it, and by means of synthetical judgements a priori, leave far behind us the limits of experience; for example, in the proposition, "the world must have a beginning," and such like. Thus metaphysics, according to the proper aim of the science, consists merely of synthetical propositions a priori.

VI. The Universal Problem of Pure Reason

It is extremely advantageous to be able to bring a number of investigations under the formula of a single problem. For in this manner, we not only facilitate our own labour, inasmuch as we define it clearly to ourselves, but also render it more easy for others to decide whether we have done justice to our undertaking. The proper problem of pure reason, then, is contained in the question: "How are synthetical judgements a priori possible?"

That metaphysical science has hitherto remained in so vacillating a state of uncertainty and contradiction, is only to be attributed to the fact that this great problem, and perhaps even the difference between analytical and synthetical judgements, did not sooner suggest itself to philosophers. Upon the solution of this problem, or upon sufficient proof of the impossibility of synthetical knowledge a priori, depends the existence or downfall of the science of metaphysics. Among philosophers, David Hume came the nearest of all to this problem; yet it never acquired in his mind sufficient precision, nor did he regard the question in its universality. On the contrary, he stopped short at the synthetical proposition of the connection of an effect with its cause (principium causalitatis), insisting that such proposition a priori was impossible. According to his conclusions, then, all that we term metaphysical science is a mere delusion, arising from the fancied insight of reason into that which is in truth borrowed from experience, and to which habit has given the appearance of necessity. Against this assertion, destructive to all pure philosophy, he would have been guarded, had he had our problem before his eyes in its universality. For he would then have perceived that, according to his own argument, there likewise could not be any pure mathematical science, which assuredly cannot exist without synthetical propositions a priori—an absurdity from which his good understanding must have saved him.

In the solution of the above problem is at the same time comprehended the possibility of the use of pure reason in the foundation and construction of all sciences which contain theoretical knowledge a priori of objects, that is to say, the answer to the following questions:

How is pure mathematical science possible?
How is pure natural science possible?

Respecting these sciences, as they do certainly exist, it may with propriety be asked, how they are possible?—for that they must be possible is shown by the fact of their really existing.* But as to metaphysics, the miserable progress it has hitherto made, and the fact that of no one system yet brought forward, far as regards its true aim, can it be said that this science really exists, leaves any one at liberty to doubt with reason the very possibility of its existence.

Yet, in a certain sense, this kind of knowledge must unquestionably be looked upon as given; in other words, metaphysics must be considered as really existing, if not as a science, nevertheless as a natural disposition of the human mind (metaphysica naturalis). For human reason, without any instigations imputable to the mere vanity of great knowledge, unceasingly progresses, urged on by its own feeling of need, towards such questions as cannot be answered by any empirical application of reason, or principles derived therefrom; and so there has ever really existed in every man some system of metaphysics. It will always exist, so soon as reason awakes to the exercise of its power of speculation. And now the question arises: "How is metaphysics, as a natural disposition, possible?" In other words, how, from the nature of universal human reason, do those questions arise which pure reason proposes to itself, and which it is impelled by its own feeling of need to answer as well as it can?

But as in all the attempts hitherto made to answer the questions which reason is prompted by its very nature to propose to itself, for example, whether the world had a beginning, or has existed from eternity, it has always met with unavoidable contradictions, we must not rest satisfied with the mere natural disposition of the mind to metaphysics, that is, with the existence of the faculty of pure reason, whence, indeed, some sort of metaphysical system always arises; but it must be possible to arrive at certainty in regard to the question whether we know or do not know the things of which metaphysics treats. We must be able to arrive at a decision on the subjects of its questions, or on the ability or inability of reason to form any judgement respecting them; and therefore either to extend with confidence the bounds of our pure reason, or to set strictly defined and safe limits to its action. This last question, which arises out of the above universal problem, would properly run thus: "How is metaphysics possible as a science?"

Thus, the critique of reason leads at last, naturally and necessarily, to science; and, on the other hand, the dogmatical use of reason without criticism leads to groundless assertions, against which others equally specious can always be set, thus ending unavoidably in scepticism.

Besides, this science cannot be of great and formidable prolixity, because it has not to do with objects of reason, the variety of which is inexhaustible, but merely with Reason herself and her problems; problems which arise out of her own bosom, and are not proposed to her by the nature of outward things, but by her own nature. And when once Reason has previously become able completely to understand her own power in regard to objects which she meets with in experience, it will be easy to determine securely the extent and limits of her attempted application to objects beyond the confines of experience.

We may and must, therefore, regard the attempts hitherto made to establish metaphysical science dogmatically as non-existent. For what of analysis, that is, mere dissection of conceptions, is contained in one or other, is not the aim of, but only a preparation for metaphysics proper, which has for its object the extension, by means of synthesis, of our a priori knowledge. And for this purpose, mere analysis is of course useless, because it only shows what is contained in these conceptions, but not how we arrive, a priori, at them; and this it is her duty to show, in order to be able afterwards to determine their valid use in regard to all objects of experience, to all knowledge in general. But little self-denial, indeed, is needed to give up these pretensions, seeing the undeniable, and in the dogmatic mode of procedure, inevitable contradictions of Reason with herself, have long since ruined the reputation of every system of metaphysics that has appeared up to this time. It will require more firmness to remain undeterred by difficulty from within, and opposition from without, from endeavouring, by a method quite opposed to all those hitherto followed, to further the growth and fruitfulness of a science indispensable to human reason—a science from which every branch it has borne may be cut away, but whose roots remain indestructible.

VII. Idea and Division of a Particular Science, under the Name of a Critique of Pure Reason

From all that has been said, there results the idea of a particular science, which may be called the Critique of Pure Reason. For reason is the faculty which furnishes us with the principles of knowledge a priori. Hence, pure reason is the faculty which contains the principles of cognizing anything absolutely a priori. An organon of pure reason would be a compendium of those principles according to which alone all pure cognitions a priori can be obtained. The completely extended application of such an organon would afford us a system of pure reason. As this, however, is demanding a great deal, and it is yet doubtful whether any extension of our knowledge be here possible, or, if so, in what cases; we can regard a science of the mere criticism of pure reason, its sources and limits, as the propaedeutic to a system of pure reason. Such a science must not be called a doctrine, but only a critique of pure reason; and its use, in regard to speculation, would be only negative, not to enlarge the bounds of, but to purify, our reason, and to shield it against error—which alone is no little gain. I apply the term transcendental to all knowledge which is not so much occupied with objects as with the mode of our cognition of these objects, so far as this mode of cognition is possible a priori. A system of such conceptions would be called transcendental philosophy. But this, again, is still beyond the bounds of our present essay. For as such a science must contain a complete exposition not only of our synthetical a priori, but of our analytical a priori knowledge, it is of too wide a range for our present purpose, because we do not require to carry our analysis any farther than is necessary to understand, in their full extent, the principles of synthesis a priori, with which alone we have to do. This investigation, which we cannot properly call a doctrine, but only a transcendental critique, because it aims not at the enlargement, but at the correction and guidance, of our knowledge, and is to serve as a touchstone of the worth or worthlessness of all knowledge a priori, is the sole object of our present essay. Such a critique is consequently, as far as possible, a preparation for an organon; and if this new organon should be found to fail, at least for a canon of pure reason, according to which the complete system of the philosophy of pure reason, whether it extend or limit the bounds of that reason, might one day be set forth both analytically and synthetically. For that this is possible, nay, that such a system is not of so great extent as to preclude the hope of its ever being completed, is evident. For we have not here to do with the nature of outward objects, which is infinite, but solely with the mind, which judges of the nature of objects, and, again, with the mind only in respect of its cognition a priori. And the object of our investigations, as it is not to be sought without, but, altogether within, ourselves, cannot remain concealed, and in all probability is limited enough to be completely surveyed and fairly estimated, according to its worth or worthlessness. Still less let the reader here expect a critique of books and systems of pure reason; our present object is exclusively a critique of the faculty of pure reason itself. Only when we make this critique our foundation, do we possess a pure touchstone for estimating the philosophical value of ancient and modern writings on this subject; and without this criterion, the incompetent historian or judge decides upon and corrects the groundless assertions of others with his own, which have themselves just as little foundation.

Transcendental philosophy is the idea of a science, for which the Critique of Pure Reason must sketch the whole plan architectonically, that is, from principles, with a full guarantee for the validity and stability of all the parts which enter into the building. It is the system of all the principles of pure reason. If this Critique itself does not assume the title of transcendental philosophy, it is only because, to be a complete system, it ought to contain a full analysis of all human knowledge a priori. Our critique must, indeed, lay before us a complete enumeration of all the radical conceptions which constitute the said pure knowledge. But from the complete analysis of these conceptions themselves, as also from a complete investigation of those derived from them, it abstains with reason; partly because it would be deviating from the end in view to occupy itself with this analysis, since this process is not attended with the difficulty and insecurity to be found in the synthesis, to which our critique is entirely devoted, and partly because it would be inconsistent with the unity of our plan to burden this essay with the vindication of the completeness of such an analysis and deduction, with which, after all, we have at present nothing to do. This completeness of the analysis of these radical conceptions, as well as of the deduction from the conceptions a priori which may be given by the analysis, we can, however, easily attain, provided only that we are in possession of all these radical conceptions, which are to serve as principles of the synthesis, and that in respect of this main purpose nothing is wanting.

To the Critique of Pure Reason, therefore, belongs all that constitutes transcendental philosophy; and it is the complete idea of transcendental philosophy, but still not the science itself; because it only proceeds so far with the analysis as is necessary to the power of judging completely of our synthetical knowledge a priori.

The principal thing we must attend to, in the division of the parts of a science like this, is that no conceptions must enter it which contain aught empirical; in other words, that the knowledge a priori must be completely pure. Hence, although the highest principles and fundamental conceptions of morality are certainly cognitions a priori, yet they do not belong to transcendental philosophy; because, though they certainly do not lay the conceptions of pain, pleasure, desires, inclinations, etc. (which are all of empirical origin), at the foundation of its precepts, yet still into the conception of duty—as an obstacle to be overcome, or as an incitement which should not be made into a motive—these empirical conceptions must necessarily enter, in the construction of a system of pure morality. Transcendental philosophy is consequently a philosophy of the pure and merely speculative reason. For all that is practical, so far as it contains motives, relates to feelings, and these belong to empirical sources of cognition.

If we wish to divide this science from the universal point of view of a science in general, it ought to comprehend, first, a Doctrine of the Elements, and, secondly, a Doctrine of the Method of pure reason. Each of these main divisions will have its subdivisions, the separate reasons for which we cannot here particularize. Only so much seems necessary, by way of introduction of premonition, that there are two sources of human knowledge (which probably spring from a common, but to us unknown root), namely, sense and understanding. By the former, objects are given to us; by the latter, thought. So far as the faculty of sense may contain representations a priori, which form the conditions under which objects are given, in so far it belongs to transcendental philosophy. The transcendental doctrine of sense must form the first part of our science of elements, because the conditions under which alone the objects of human knowledge are given must precede those under which they are thought.

ENDNOTE

* As to the existence of pure natural science, or physics, perhaps many may still express doubts. But we have only to look at the different propositions which are commonly treated of at the commencement of proper (empirical) physical science—those, for example, relating to the permanence of the same quantity of matter, the vis inertiae, the equality of action and reaction, etc.—to be soon convinced that they form a science of pure physics (physica pura, or rationalis), which well deserves to be separately exposed as a special science, in its whole extent, whether that be great or confined.

DISCUSSION QUESTIONS

1. Explain the distinction between pure and empirical knowledge.

2. Explain the analytic/synthetic distinction.

3. How is Kant's view different from rationalists like Descartes and Leibniz? Explain.

4. How is Kant's view different from the empiricist views of Locke, Berkeley, and Hume? Explain.

5. What does Kant mean by "transcendental philosophy" here?

PRAGMATISM

By William James

As mentioned in the discussion of the view of the self by Mead and Du Bois, William James (1842–1910) was a major figure in the development of pragmatism. James started his academic career at Harvard in 1873 teaching anatomy and physiology (he completed an M.D. degree, but never practiced medicine), and then in 1876 he was appointed professor of psychology, before turning to philosophy in 1881 (though he continued to teach psychology). His Principles of Psychology *(1890) was widely used as a textbook for many years. He is better known now for publications of his famed lecture series:* The Varieties of Religious Experience *(1902), delivered at the University of Edinburgh, Scotland, and* Pragmatism *(1907) delivered at Harvard.*

Our selection is "Lecture VI: Pragmatism's Conception of Truth," from Pragmatism. *He wants a theory of truth that is less abstract than either empiricism or rationalism. For James, truth is something that* happens *to an idea as it is verified. If a theory or statement works, if it has "cash value," it is true. If it stops working, it stops being true. If something fits in with what you already believe to be true, it's true. If it doesn't fit in, then you have to reject it, or revise your system.*

• • •

LECTURE VI

I fully expect to see the pragmatist view of truth run through the classic stages of a theory's career. First, you know, a new theory is attacked as absurd; then it is admitted to be true, but obvious and insignificant; finally it is seen to be so important that its adversaries claim that they themselves discovered it. Our doctrine of truth is at present in the first of these three stages, with symptoms of the second stage having begun in certain quarters. I wish that this lecture might help it beyond the first stage in the eyes of many of you.

Truth, as any dictionary will tell you, is a property of certain of our ideas. It means their 'agreement,' as falsity means their disagreement, with 'reality.' Pragmatists and intellectualists both accept this definition as a matter of course. They begin to quarrel only after the question is raised as to what may precisely be meant by the term 'agreement,' and what by the term 'reality,' when reality is taken as something for our ideas to agree with.

In answering these questions the pragmatists are more analytic and painstaking, the intellectualists more offhand and irreflective. The popular notion is that a true idea must copy its reality. Like other popular views, this one follows the analogy of the most usual experience. Our true ideas of sensible things do indeed copy them. Shut your eyes and think of yonder clock on the wall, and you get just such a true picture or copy of its dial. But your idea of its 'works' (unless you are a clock-maker) is much less of a copy, yet it passes muster, for it in no way clashes with the reality. Even tho it should shrink to the mere word 'works,' that word still serves you truly; and when you speak of the 'time-keeping function' of the clock, or of its spring's 'elasticity,' it is hard to see exactly what your ideas can copy.

You perceive that there is a problem here. Where our ideas cannot copy definitely their object, what does agreement with that object mean? Some idealists seem to say that they are true whenever they are what God means that we ought to think about that object. Others hold the copy-view all through, and speak as if our ideas possessed truth just in proportion as they approach to being copies of the Absolute's eternal way of thinking.

These views, you see, invite pragmatistic discussion. But the great assumption of the intellectualists is that truth means essentially an inert static relation. When you've got your true idea of anything, there's an end of the matter. You're in possession; you KNOW; you have fulfilled your thinking destiny. You are where you ought to be mentally; you have obeyed your categorical imperative; and nothing more need follow on that climax of your rational destiny. Epistemologically you are in stable equilibrium.

Pragmatism, on the other hand, asks its usual question. "Grant an idea or belief to be true," it says, "what concrete difference will its being true make in anyone's actual life? How will the truth be realized? What experiences will be different from those which would obtain if the belief were false? What, in short, is the truth's cash-value in experiential terms?"

The moment pragmatism asks this question, it sees the answer: TRUE IDEAS ARE THOSE THAT WE CAN ASSIMILATE, VALIDATE, CORROBORATE AND VERIFY. FALSE IDEAS ARE THOSE THAT WE CANNOT. That is the practical difference it makes to us to have true ideas; that, therefore, is the meaning of truth, for it is all that truth is known-as.

This thesis is what I have to defend. The truth of an idea is not a stagnant property inherent in it. Truth HAPPENS to an idea. It BECOMES true, is MADE true by events. Its verity is in fact an event, a process: the process namely of its verifying itself, its veri-FICATION. Its validity is the process of its valid-ATION.

But what do the words verification and validation themselves pragmatically mean? They again signify certain practical consequences of the verified and validated idea. It is hard to find any one phrase that characterizes these consequences better than the ordinary agreement-formula—just such consequences being what we have in mind whenever we say that our ideas 'agree' with reality. They lead us, namely, through the acts and other ideas which they instigate, into or up to, or towards, other parts of experience with which we feel all the while-such feeling being among our potentialities—that the original ideas remain in agreement. The connexions and transitions come to us from point to point as being progressive, harmonious, satisfactory.

This function of agreeable leading is what we mean by an idea's verification. Such an account is vague and it sounds at first quite trivial, but it has results which it will take the rest of my hour to explain.

Let me begin by reminding you of the fact that the possession of true thoughts means everywhere the possession of invaluable instruments of action; and that our duty to gain truth, so far from being a blank command from out of the blue, or a 'stunt' self-imposed by our intellect, can account for itself by excellent practical reasons.

The importance to human life of having true beliefs about matters of fact is a thing too notorious. We live in a world of realities that can be infinitely useful or infinitely harmful. Ideas that tell us which of them to expect count as the true ideas in all this primary sphere of verification, and the pursuit of such ideas is a primary human duty. The possession of truth, so far from being here an end in itself, is only a preliminary means towards other vital satisfactions. If I am lost in the woods and starved, and find what looks like a cow-path, it is of the utmost importance that I should think of a human habitation at the end of it, for if I do so and follow it, I save myself. The true thought is useful here because the house which is its object is useful. The practical value of true ideas is thus primarily derived from the practical importance of their objects to us. Their objects are, indeed, not important at all times. I may on another occasion have no use for the house; and then my idea of it, however verifiable, will be practically irrelevant, and had better remain latent. Yet since almost any object may some day become temporarily important, the advantage of having a general stock of extra truths, of ideas that shall be true of merely possible situations, is obvious. We store such extra truths away in our memories, and with the overflow we fill our books of reference. Whenever such an extra truth becomes practically relevant to one of our emergencies, it passes from cold-storage to do work in the world, and our belief in it grows active. You can say of it then either that 'it is useful because it is true' or that 'it is true because it is useful.' Both these phrases mean exactly the same thing, namely that here is an idea that gets fulfilled and can be verified. True is the name for whatever idea starts the verification-process, useful is the name for its completed function in experience. True ideas would never have been singled out as such, would never have acquired a class-name, least of all a name suggesting value, unless they had been useful from the outset in this way.

From this simple cue pragmatism gets her general notion of truth as something essentially bound up with the way in which one moment in our experience may lead us towards other moments which it will be worth while to have been led to. Primarily, and on the common-sense level, the truth of a state of mind means this function of A LEADING THAT IS WORTH WHILE. When a moment in our experience, of any kind whatever, inspires us with a thought that is true, that means that sooner or later we dip by that thought's guidance into the particulars of experience again and make advantageous connexion with them. This is a vague enough statement, but I beg you to retain it, for it is essential.

Our experience meanwhile is all shot through with regularities. One bit of it can warn us to get ready for another bit, can 'intend' or be 'significant of' that remoter object. The object's advent is the significance's verification. Truth, in these cases, meaning nothing but eventual verification, is manifestly incompatible with waywardness on our part. Woe to him whose beliefs play fast and loose with the order which realities follow in his experience: they will lead him nowhere or else make false connexions.

By 'realities' or 'objects' here, we mean either things of common sense, sensibly present, or else common-sense relations, such as dates, places, distances, kinds, activities. Following our mental image of a house along the cow-path, we actually come to see the house; we get the image's full verification. SUCH SIMPLY AND FULLY VERIFIED LEADINGS ARE CERTAINLY THE ORIGINALS AND PROTOTYPES OF THE TRUTH-PROCESS. Experience offers indeed other forms of truth-process, but they are all conceivable as being primary verifications arrested, multiplied or substituted one for another.

Take, for instance, yonder object on the wall. You and I consider it to be a 'clock,' altho no one of us has seen the hidden works that make it one. We let our notion pass for true without attempting to verify. If truths mean verification-process essentially, ought we then to call such unverified truths as this abortive? No, for they form the overwhelmingly large number of the truths we live by. Indirect as well as direct verifications pass muster. Where circumstantial evidence is sufficient, we can go without eye-witnessing. Just as we here assume Japan to exist without ever having been there, because it WORKS to do so, everything we know conspiring with the belief, and nothing interfering, so we assume that thing to be a clock. We USE it as a clock, regulating the length of our lecture by it. The verification of the assumption here means its leading to no frustration or contradiction. VerifiABILITY of wheels and weights and pendulum is as good as verification. For one truth-process completed there are a million in our lives that function in this state of nascency. They turn us TOWARDS direct verification; lead us into the SURROUNDINGS of the objects they envisage; and then, if everything runs on harmoniously, we are so sure that verification is possible that we omit it, and are usually justified by all that happens.

Truth lives, in fact, for the most part on a credit system. Our thoughts and beliefs 'pass,' so long as nothing challenges them, just as bank-notes pass so long as nobody refuses them. But this all points to direct face-to-face verifications somewhere, without which the fabric of truth collapses like a financial system with no cash-basis whatever. You accept my verification of one thing, I yours of another. We trade on each other's truth. But beliefs verified concretely by SOMEBODY are the posts of the whole superstructure.

Another great reason—beside economy of time—for waiving complete verification in the usual business of life is that all things exist in kinds and not singly. Our world is found once for all to have that peculiarity. So that when we have once directly verified our ideas about one specimen of a kind, we consider ourselves free to apply them to other specimens without verification. A mind that habitually discerns the kind of thing before it, and acts by the law of the kind immediately, without pausing to verify, will be a 'true' mind in ninety-nine out of a hundred emergencies, proved so by its conduct fitting everything it meets, and getting no refutation.

INDIRECTLY OR ONLY POTENTIALLY VERIFYING PROCESSES MAY THUS BE TRUE AS WELL AS FULL VERIFICATION-PROCESSES. They work as true processes would work, give us the same advantages, and claim our recognition for the same reasons. All this on the common-sense level of, matters of fact, which we are alone considering.

But matters of fact are not our only stock in trade. RELATIONS AMONG PURELY MENTAL IDEAS form another sphere where true and false beliefs obtain, and here the beliefs are absolute, or unconditional. When they are true they bear the name either of definitions or of principles. It is either a principle or a definition that 1 and 1 make 2, that 2 and 1 make 3, and so on; that white differs less from gray than it does from black; that when the cause begins to act the effect also commences. Such propositions hold of all possible 'ones,' of all conceivable 'whites' and 'grays' and 'causes.' The objects here are mental objects. Their relations are perceptually obvious at a glance, and no sense-verification is necessary. Moreover, once true, always true, of those same mental objects. Truth here has an 'eternal' character. If you can find a concrete thing anywhere that is 'one' or 'white' or 'gray,' or an 'effect,' then your principles will everlastingly apply to it. It is but a case of ascertaining the kind, and then applying the law of its kind to the particular object. You are sure to get truth if you can but name the kind rightly, for your mental relations hold good of everything of that kind without exception. If you then, nevertheless, failed to get truth concretely, you would say that you had classed your real objects wrongly.

In this realm of mental relations, truth again is an affair of leading. We relate one abstract idea with another, framing in the end great systems of logical and mathematical truth, under the respective terms of which the sensible facts of experience eventually arrange themselves, so that our eternal truths hold good of realities also. This marriage of fact and theory is endlessly fertile. What we say is here already true in advance of special verification, IF WE HAVE SUBSUMED OUR OBJECTS RIGHTLY. Our ready-made ideal framework for all sorts of possible objects follows from the very structure of our thinking. We can no more play fast and loose with these abstract relations than we can do so with our sense-experiences. They coerce us; we must treat them consistently, whether or not we like the results. The rules of addition apply to our debts as rigorously as to our assets. The hundredth decimal of pi, the ratio of the circumference to its diameter, is predetermined ideally now, tho no one may have computed it. If we should ever need the figure in our dealings with an actual circle we should need to have it given rightly, calculated by the usual rules; for it is the same kind of truth that those rules elsewhere calculate.

Between the coercions of the sensible order and those of the ideal order, our mind is thus wedged tightly. Our ideas must agree with realities, be such realities concrete or abstract, be they facts or be they principles, under penalty of endless inconsistency and frustration. So far, intellectualists can raise no protest. They can only say that we have barely touched the skin of the matter.

Realities mean, then, either concrete facts, or abstract kinds of things and relations perceived intuitively between them. They furthermore and thirdly mean, as things that new ideas of ours must no less take account of, the whole body of other truths already in our possession. But what now does 'agreement' with such three-fold realities mean?—to use again the definition that is current.

Here it is that pragmatism and intellectualism begin to part company. Primarily, no doubt, to agree means to copy, but we saw that the mere word 'clock' would do instead of a mental picture of its works, and that of many realities our ideas can only be symbols and not copies. 'Past time,' 'power,' 'spontaneity'—how can our mind copy such realities?

To 'agree' in the widest sense with a reality, CAN ONLY MEAN TO BE GUIDED EITHER STRAIGHT UP TO IT OR INTO ITS SURROUNDINGS, OR TO BE PUT INTO SUCH WORKING TOUCH WITH IT AS TO HANDLE EITHER IT OR SOMETHING CONNECTED WITH IT BETTER THAN IF WE DISAGREED. Better either intellectually or practically! And often agreement will only mean the negative fact that nothing contradictory from the quarter of that reality comes to interfere with the way in which our ideas guide us elsewhere. To copy a reality is, indeed, one very important way of agreeing with it, but it is far from being essential. The essential thing is the process of being guided. Any idea that helps us to DEAL, whether practically or intellectually, with either the reality or its belongings, that doesn't entangle our progress in frustrations, that FITS, in fact, and adapts our life to the reality's whole setting, will agree sufficiently to meet the requirement. It will hold true of that reality.

Thus, NAMES are just as 'true' or 'false' as definite mental pictures are. They set up similar verification-processes, and lead to fully equivalent practical results.

All human thinking gets discursified; we exchange ideas; we lend and borrow verifications, get them from one another by means of social intercourse. All truth thus gets verbally built out, stored up, and made available for everyone. Hence, we must TALK consistently just as we must THINK consistently: for both in talk and thought we deal with kinds. Names are arbitrary, but once understood they must be kept to. We mustn't now call Abel 'Cain' or Cain 'Abel.' If we do, we ungear ourselves from the whole book of Genesis, and from all its connexions with the universe of speech and fact down to the present time. We throw ourselves out of whatever truth that entire system of speech and fact may embody.

The overwhelming majority of our true ideas admit of no direct or face-to-face verification-those of past history, for example, as of Cain and Abel. The stream of time can be remounted only verbally, or verified indirectly by the present prolongations or effects of what the past harbored. Yet if they agree with these verbalities and effects, we can know that our ideas of the past are true. AS TRUE AS PAST TIME ITSELF WAS, so true was Julius Caesar, so true were antediluvian monsters, all in their proper dates and settings. That past time itself was, is guaranteed by its coherence with everything that's present. True as the present is, the past was also.

Agreement thus turns out to be essentially an affair of leading—leading that is useful because it is into quarters that contain objects that are important. True ideas lead us into useful verbal and conceptual quarters as well as directly up to useful sensible termini. They lead to consistency, stability and flowing human intercourse. They lead away from excentricity and isolation, from foiled and barren thinking. The untrammeled flowing of the leading-process, its general freedom from clash and contradiction, passes for its indirect verification; but all roads lead to Rome, and in the end and eventually, all true processes must lead to the face of directly verifying sensible experiences SOMEWHERE, which somebody's ideas have copied.

Such is the large loose way in which the pragmatist interprets the word agreement. He treats it altogether practically. He lets it cover any process of conduction from a present idea to a future terminus, provided only it run prosperously. It is only thus that 'scientific' ideas, flying as they do beyond common sense, can be said to agree with their realities. It is, as I have already said, as if reality were made of ether, atoms or electrons, but we mustn't think so literally. The term 'energy' doesn't even pretend to stand for anything 'objective.' It is only a way of measuring the surface of phenomena so as to string their changes on a simple formula.

Yet in the choice of these man-made formulas we cannot be capricious with impunity any more than we can be capricious on the common-sense practical level. We must find a theory that will WORK; and that means something extremely difficult; for our theory must mediate between all previous truths and certain new experiences. It must derange common sense and previous belief as little as possible, and it must lead to some sensible terminus or other that can be verified exactly. To 'work' means both these things; and the squeeze is so tight that there is little loose play for any hypothesis. Our theories are wedged and controlled as nothing else is. Yet sometimes alternative theoretic formulas are equally compatible with all the truths we know, and then we choose between them for subjective reasons. We choose the kind of theory to which we are already partial; we follow 'elegance' or 'economy.' Clerk Maxwell somewhere says it would be "poor scientific taste" to choose the more complicated of two equally well-evidenced conceptions; and you will all agree with him. Truth in science is what gives us the maximum possible sum of satisfactions, taste included, but consistency both with previous truth and with novel fact is always the most imperious claimant.

• • •

Our account of truth is an account of truths in the plural, of processes of leading, realized in rebus, and having only this quality in common, that they PAY. They pay by guiding us into or towards some part of a system that dips at numerous points into sense-percepts, which we may copy mentally or not, but with which at any rate we are now in the kind of commerce vaguely designated as verification. Truth for us is simply a collective name for verification-processes, just as health, wealth, strength, etc., are names for other processes connected with life, and also pursued because it pays to pursue them. Truth is MADE, just as health, wealth and strength are made, in the course of experience.

Here rationalism is instantaneously up in arms against us. I can imagine a rationalist to talk as follows:

"Truth is not made," he will say; "it absolutely obtains, being a unique relation that does not wait upon any process, but shoots straight over the head of experience, and hits its reality every time. Our belief that yon thing on the wall is a clock is true already, altho no one in the whole history of the world should verify it. The bare quality of standing in that transcendent relation is what makes any thought true that possesses it, whether or not there be verification. You pragmatists put the cart before the horse in making truth's being reside in verification-processes. These are merely signs of its being, merely our lame ways of ascertaining after the fact, which of our ideas already has possessed the wondrous quality. The quality itself is timeless, like all essences and natures. Thoughts partake of it directly, as they partake of falsity or of irrelevancy. It can't be analyzed away into pragmatic consequences."

The whole plausibility of this rationalist tirade is due to the fact to which we have already paid so much attention. In our world, namely, abounding as it does in things of similar kinds and similarly associated, one verification serves for others of its kind, and one great use of knowing things is to be led not so much to them as to their associates, especially to human talk about them. The quality of truth, obtaining ante rem, pragmatically means, then, the fact that in such a world innumerable ideas work better by their indirect or possible than by their direct and actual verification. Truth ante rem means only verifiability, then; or else it is a case of the stock rationalist trick of treating the NAME of a concrete phenomenal reality as an independent prior entity, and placing it behind the reality as its explanation.

• • •

'The true,' to put it very briefly, is only the expedient in the way of our thinking, just as 'the right' is only the expedient in the way of our behaving. Expedient in almost any fashion; and expedient in the long run and on the whole of course; for what meets expediently all the experience in sight won't necessarily meet all farther experiences equally satisfactorily. Experience, as we know, has ways of BOILING OVER, and making us correct our present formulas.

The 'absolutely' true, meaning what no farther experience will ever alter, is that ideal vanishing-point towards which we imagine that all our temporary truths will some day converge. It runs on all fours with the perfectly wise man, and with the absolutely complete experience; and, if these ideals are ever realized, they will all be realized together. Meanwhile we have to live to-day by what truth we can get to-day, and be ready to-morrow to call it falsehood. Ptolemaic astronomy, euclidean space, aristotelian logic, scholastic metaphysics, were expedient for centuries, but human experience has boiled over those limits, and we now call these things only relatively true, or true within those borders of experience. 'Absolutely' they are false; for we know that those limits were casual, and might have been transcended by past theorists just as they are by present thinkers.

When new experiences lead to retrospective judgments, using the past tense, what these judgments utter WAS true, even tho no past thinker had been led there. We live forwards, a Danish thinker has said, but we understand backwards. The present sheds a backward light on the world's previous processes. They may have been truth-processes for the actors in them. They are not so for one who knows the later revelations of the story.

This regulative notion of a potential better truth to be established later, possibly to be established some day absolutely, and having powers of retroactive legislation, turns its face, like all pragmatist notions, towards concreteness of fact, and towards the future. Like the half-truths, the absolute truth will have to be MADE, made as a relation incidental to the growth of a mass of verification-experience, to which the half-true ideas are all along contributing their quota.

I have already insisted on the fact that truth is made largely out of previous truths. Men's beliefs at any time are so much experience funded. But the beliefs are themselves parts of the sum total of the world's experience, and become matter, therefore, for the next day's funding operations. So far as reality means experienceable reality, both it and the truths men gain about it are everlastingly in process of mutation-mutation towards a definite goal, it may be—but still mutation.

• • •

The most fateful point of difference between being a rationalist and being a pragmatist is now fully in sight. Experience is in mutation, and our psychological ascertainments of truth are in mutation—so much rationalism will allow; but never that either reality itself or truth itself is mutable. Reality stands complete and ready-made from all eternity, rationalism insists, and the agreement of our ideas with it is that unique unanalyzable virtue in them of which she has already told us. As that intrinsic excellence, their truth has nothing to do with our experiences. It adds nothing to the content of experience. It makes no difference to reality itself; it is supervenient, inert, static, a reflexion merely. It doesn't EXIST, it HOLDS or OBTAINS, it belongs to another dimension from that of either facts or fact-relations, belongs, in short, to the epistemological dimension—and with that big word rationalism closes the discussion.

Thus, just as pragmatism faces forward to the future, so does rationalism here again face backward to a past eternity. True to her inveterate habit, rationalism reverts to 'principles,' and thinks that when an abstraction once is named, we own an oracular solution.

• • •

It is quite evident that our obligation to acknowledge truth, so far from being unconditional, is tremendously conditioned. Truth with a big T, and in the singular, claims abstractly to be recognized, of course; but concrete truths in the plural need be recognized only when their recognition is expedient. A truth must always be preferred to a falsehood when both relate to the situation; but when neither does, truth is as little of a duty as falsehood. If you ask me what o'clock it is and I tell you that I live at 95 Irving Street, my answer may indeed be true, but you don't see why it is my duty to give it. A false address would be as much to the purpose.

With this admission that there are conditions that limit the application of the abstract imperative, THE PRAGMATISTIC TREATMENT OF TRUTH SWEEPS BACK UPON US IN ITS FULNESS. Our duty to agree with reality is seen to be grounded in a perfect jungle of concrete expediencies.

When Berkeley had explained what people meant by matter, people thought that he denied matter's existence. When Messrs. Schiller and Dewey now explain what people mean by truth, they are accused of denying ITS existence. These pragmatists destroy all objective standards, critics say, and put foolishness and wisdom on one level. A favorite formula for describing Mr. Schiller's doctrines and mine is that we are persons who think that by saying whatever you find it pleasant to say and calling it truth you fulfil every pragmatistic requirement.

I leave it to you to judge whether this be not an impudent slander. Pent in, as the pragmatist more than anyone else sees himself to be, between the whole body of funded truths squeezed from the past and the coercions of the world of sense about him, who so well as he feels the immense pressure of objective control under which our minds perform their operations? If anyone imagines that this law is lax, let him keep its commandment one day, says Emerson. We have heard much of late of the uses of the imagination in science. It is high time to urge the use of a little imagination in philosophy. The unwillingness of some of our critics to read any but the silliest of possible meanings into our statements is as discreditable to their imaginations as anything I know in recent philosophic history. Schiller says the true is that which 'works.' Thereupon he is treated as one who limits verification to the lowest material utilities. Dewey says truth is what gives 'satisfaction.' He is treated as one who believes in calling everything true which, if it were true, would be pleasant.

Our critics certainly need more imagination of realities. I have honestly tried to stretch my own imagination and to read the best possible meaning into the rationalist conception, but I have to confess that it still completely baffles me. The notion of a reality calling on us to 'agree' with it, and that for no reasons, but simply because its claim is 'unconditional' or 'transcendent,' is one that I can make neither head nor tail of. I try to imagine myself as the sole reality in the world, and then to imagine what more I would 'claim' if I were allowed to. If you suggest the possibility of my claiming that a mind should come into being from out of the void inane and stand and COPY me, I can indeed imagine what the copying might mean, but I can conjure up no motive. What good it would do me to be copied, or what good it would do that mind to copy me, if farther consequences are expressly and in principle ruled out as motives for the claim (as they are by our rationalist authorities) I cannot fathom. When the Irishman's admirers ran him along to the place of banquet in a sedan chair with no bottom, he said, "Faith, if it wasn't for the honor of the thing, I might as well have come on foot." So here: but for the honor of the thing, I might as well have remained uncopied. Copying is one genuine mode of knowing (which for some strange reason our contemporary transcendentalists seem to be tumbling over each other to repudiate); but when we get beyond copying, and fall back on unnamed forms of agreeing that are expressly denied to be either copyings or leadings or fittings, or any other processes pragmatically definable, the WHAT of the 'agreement' claimed becomes as unintelligible as the why of it. Neither content nor motive can be imagine for it. It is an absolutely meaningless abstraction.

• • •

Surely in this field of truth it is the pragmatists and not the rationalists who are the more genuine defenders of the universe's rationality.

DISCUSSION QUESTIONS

1. How does the pragmatist view differ from rationalism and empiricism? Explain.

2. Compare James's position here with Buddha's response to Malunkyaputta. Explain the similarities and differences.

3. Explain what the examples of the clock and Japan are supposed to show.

4. Explain what James says we should do with statements that cannot "admit of no direct face-to-face verification."

A Question of Silence: Feminist Theory and Women's Voices

By Alice Crary

Alice Crary is Associate Professor of Philosophy at the New School for Social Research in New York City. Since the 1970s many philosophers have been calling into question traditional stances on knowledge. One such challenge comes from feminist philosophers who have pointed out what they see as "male bias" in the history of philosophy. In "A Question of Silence: Feminist Theory and Women's Voices," an article published in the journal Philosophy *in 2001, Crary looks at the current state of thinking in feminist theory. She argues that there are insights to be had from feminist critique of the history of philosophy. She is wary, though, of drawing conclusions that argue there are essential differences in men's and women's standpoints. Essentialism is the view that there is one definable set of characteristics that make the thing under discussion what it is. Crary argues that some writers do not articulate well the differences between "sex," which is a biological term referring to hormones, chromosomes, and sex organs (male and female), and "gender" which is a social construction (masculine and feminine). Crary, then, finds feminist critique acceptable, but rejects the theoretical idea that there is a monolithic "women's experience" or "men's experience." She also rejects the antifeminist position. Hers is a middle ground based on the arguments for the positions that have been offered thus far.*

In this paper, I critically examine some recent trends in *feminist epistemology*, the study of whether, and if so, how our knowledge carries a masculine bias. The purpose of my examination is twofold: (i) to expose pitfalls in investigations within feminist epistemology and (ii) to shed light on promising methodologies for such investigations—methodologies that can lead to productive feminist thought and action.

I begin by exploring the point of departure of some feminist theory. Many feminist theories begin as responses to women's concerns about gender bias and then end by putting forward general epistemological claims about how a masculine bias *must* pervade our prevailing theoretical discourses. I will be critical of theories which, in so far as they take this form, might be described as involving a 'philosophical must'. In their insistence that the structure of our body of knowledge must be of a particular character (i.e., one which, in a specified manner, encodes a masculine bias), such theories make *a priori* claims about the structure of knowledge in particular areas. I will argue that this strand of feminist theory—like the putatively 'male' metaphysics which it calls upon itself to replace—ultimately discourages us from directing our attention primarily to an understanding of the role gender plays in the composition of particular bodies of knowledge, and that it thus in the end fails to be genuinely responsive to the concerns it first undertakes to address. I will close by considering two important moments in the development of feminist thought, both of which I believe are best understood from the perspective of a feminism which is free of the general theoretical claims advanced in the strand of feminist theory I want to criticize.

1. A moment of silence

> One of the great powers of feminism is that it goes so far in making the experiences and lives of women intelligible. Trying to make sense of one's own feelings, motivations, desires, ambitions, actions and reactions without taking into account the forces which maintain the subordination of women to men is like trying to explain why a marble stops rolling without taking friction into account. What 'feminist theory' is about, to a great extent, is just identifying those forces (or some range of them or kinds of them) and displaying the mechanics of their applications to women as a group (or caste) and to individual women. The measure of the success of the theory is just how much sense it makes of what did not make sense before.
>
> —Marilyn Frye[1]

Investigations into whether or how knowledge is gendered often take as their point of departure what is described as a condition of *alienation*—women's powerful and often unanalysed sense of alienation from the dominant epistemic or linguistic practices of their society. Women sometimes begin a discussion of these difficult matters by focusing on what they take to be a symptom of this alienation—both their own and that of other women—a symptom which manifests itself, in the first instance, as a sense of unease only vaguely associated with gender identity.[2]

Women's articulations of such a sense of unease are some of the data which feminist thought—at least in its beginning stages—undertakes to organize and clarify.[3] Many accounts of the first awakening of a feeling of need for some kind of feminist theorizing begin with descriptions of a woman's sense of unease and then proceed to characterizations of this sense as linked to her feeling of dislocation between her experience and the resources she has for claiming it.

Some feminist theorists attempt to understand their own and other women's feeling of dislocation by analysing the structure of dominant theoretical discourses. One central topic of concern for feminists has been to uncover and articulate those areas of knowledge in which women's experience—experience which appears to be entirely pertinent to the variety of knowledge in question—has been treated as irrelevant even to the collection of data. Most conspicuous, perhaps, are the areas of women's sexuality and motherhood. In nineteenth-century American medical practice, an almost exclusively male profession found it acceptable to treat disease in women as generally linked to sexual organs. Thus a medical expert might treat a woman for consumption, indigestion or backache (conditions for which male patients received more specific treatments) with a 'medical assault on her sexual organs'.[4] One respected justification for this practice of disregarding women patients' felt symptoms was the widespread view that the ovaries (or other sexual organs) 'give a woman all her characteristics of body and mind'.[5] In this century, theorists have declared the vaginal orgasm a sign of 'sexual maturity'—thereby ignoring women's actual experience of the character of their sexuality. Medical professionals have also instructed patients with assurance and authority about what a healthy, well-adjusted woman will feel during pregnancy—their instruction being primarily related to current social norms and only secondarily to an understanding of what women most often actually go through.[6] In these cases, women's perceptions of the character of their experience are taken as at best tangential, and at worst irrelevant, to the development of properly 'objective' or 'scientific' accounts of matters—matters which are of pressing concern to them as women. It is in reference to cases such as these that feminists have suggested that a woman's feeling of dislocation may be traced in part to her sense that her own perceptions of what she undergoes are abnormal, unnatural or invalid; she may in such cases experience the clash between her own, often submerged, perception of something she underwent and the 'official version' of what should have happened as a kind of alienation or dislocation.[7]

Many feminists have pointed out, further, that even once the marginalization of women's experience in cases such as these is accounted for, women may be written out of theoretical discourses in yet another way. The words or concepts employed within 'official accounts'—although they may appear to be objective or universal—may themselves already encode a gender bias. Simone de Beauvoir, for example, draws attention to a historical pattern in which that which is called 'masculine' is upheld as a norm for all people and that which is identified as 'feminine' is characterized by its lack of certain positive qualities:

The terms *masculine* and *feminine* are used symmetrically only as a matter of form, as on legal papers. In actuality the relation of the two sexes is not quite like that of two electrical poles, for man represents both the positive and the neutral, as is indicated by the common use of *man* to designate human beings in general; whereas woman represents only the negative, defined by limiting criteria, without reciprocity.[8]

Women's experience, even when its relevance is acknowledged, may be portrayed in a way which is intrinsically biased.

Feminist epistemology tends to start by claiming to speak to, and for, the pathos of women's descriptions of their feelings of alienation. It wishes to go on from this starting point and take account of the fact that historically and for the most part, not only have women not generally participated directly in the production of our body of knowledge, but they have also not participated in activities of theorizing about our body of knowledge. They have not taken part in those second-order activities which bequeath to us our image of knowledge.[9] Women have, for the most part, remained theoretically and philosophically mute. Feminist epistemology (or feminist theory more generally) often presents itself as a vehicle through which women can come to find their own voices. It therefore naturally tends to take as its point of departure this sort of discussion of ways in which prevailing theoretical discourses have failed to engage women's voices.

Perceptions (such as those just touched upon) of the historical irrelevance of women's experience to prevailing activities of theory-construction sometimes get coupled with a more general epistemological insight which does not itself turn on feminist preoccupations: *viz.*, that what a person takes from particular experiences is not written into the experiences themselves; that, from early childhood on, over the course of our cultural education, we learn to take experience as bearing on knowledge in many different ways. Feminist theorists have been particularly concerned to further specify the implications of this broad epistemological insight by bringing into relief the manner in which certain sorts of personal characteristics of knowers (such as gender, sexual orientation, race and class) can affect the way in which experience is taken to bear on knowledge. They tend to begin therefore with the following *epistemologically* relatively innocuous perception:[10]

As women, homosexuals, blacks, or members of the working class (etc.) we are socialized in ways which are specific to our 'group' or 'groups'; the manner in which we then incorporate our experience will reflect this difference in socialization.

It is at this point that the particular strain of feminist theory I am concerned with begins to depart from a genuine responsiveness to women's voices. This epistemologically innocuous perception is often taken to support the suspicious—but epistemologically still potentially quite innocuous—claim that instances of androcentrism in discourse constitute evidence that all our discursive practices only reflect ways in which men incorporate their experience.[11] It is in their manner of going on from this already suspicious claim that the feminist arguments I am concerned with diverge most dramatically from responsiveness to things that women say in recounting their experience and become driven by a kind of philosophical insistence. It is characteristic of these arguments to move from this claim (which is consistent with the perception that ways in which we take experience as bearing on knowledge reflect differences in our socialization) directly—and without acknowledging that any philosophically momentous step is being taken—to the following considerably less innocuous claim:

Instances of androcentrism in language and theory constitute evidence that our language and theories—and, ultimately, all of our dominant bodies of knowledge—only reflect distinctly male experience.

Some feminists who present themselves as beginning with the innocuous epistemological insight wind up advocating the claim that our current forms of knowledge are suited only to the task of incorporating the character of 'male experience', and that we currently lack a theoretical discourse at all adequate to the task of incorporating 'female experience'. It is an assumption of this claim that female experience is thoroughly and systematically different from male experience, where this means that women's and men's experience are in a strong sense incommensurable:[12] women and men should be understood as perceiving and inhabiting logically separate 'realities'; 'male' language expresses distinctly male experience to the exclusion of distinctly female experience.[13] This claim thus carries the suggestion that women should establish their own language (now one which would reflect distinctly 'female' experience), and it implies that this project will involve rejecting the concepts, theories and methodologies which have been integral to 'male' theory construction—including the very notions of objectivity, experience and rationality which are themselves thought by some feminist theorists to presuppose a masculine way of knowing the world.[14]

Some theorists go on from this already less than innocuous argument to claim that there can therefore be no such thing as an impersonal theory of knowledge or language. What once looked like the possibility of such a theory must now be given up on the grounds that it illicitly presupposes a gender neutral standpoint from which the theory can encounter its subject-matter. What some theorists see as the necessary intrusion of personal characteristics of the knower into both the structure and content of what is known is taken by them to demonstrate the impossibility of any attempt to construct a theory of what others have thought of as the 'language which we (women and men) share'.

Andrea Nye, e.g., undertakes to demonstrate that the discipline which has traditionally been called 'logic' is grounded on a philosophical confusion (and can therefore, she wants to argue, play only a distorting role in social and philosophical debates).[15] Nye's argument opens with her fairly uncontroversial suggestion that it is possible to give commentaries on the work of major figures in the history of logic which centre, not on evaluating their logical achievements in isolation, but rather on assessing those achievements from within the context of their personal backgrounds, social circumstances, hopes and ambitions. (Nye calls this kind of understanding 'reading'.) She criticizes philosophers of logic for overlooking or obscuring the possibility of this kind of understanding, for assuming that '[a]dvances in logic depend on thought only, unrelated to any personal, political, or economic considerations'.[16] Nye's work is of value in so far as she reminds us that a thinker's presuppositions can surreptitiously inform 'his' logical work and that it is simple-minded to assume that the practical context of logical research cannot influence content. But Nye's criticism goes deeper than a recommendation for a more complete, human understanding of the achievements comprising the history of logic. She laments some philosophers' willingness to allow for the possibility of a discipline which (although it is susceptible of 'readings') is valued philosophically precisely because it allows us to abstract from the social context of thought in order to achieve a clearer view of the workings of thought. She moves from the philosophically innocuous claim that the social circumstances of a logician may influence the character of 'his' work to the hardly innocent conclusion that there can be no such thing as logic—no such thing as a discipline which, although its history can be 'read', can be conceived as the laying out of the conceptual structure of the space of reasons which we share. In what follows, I isolate what I see as confusions in general theoretical arguments like Nye's—arguments which wind up denying the possibility of a space of reasons which women and men can fruitfully cohabit.

2. The nature of the silence

The master's tools will never dismantle the master's house.

—Audré Lorde[17]

I am assuming that an understanding of the sources of women's sense of alienation from dominant linguistic and epistemic practices plays a central role in any satisfactory feminist theory. One sign of the adequacy of such an understanding will be that it occasions self-recognition in the women whose lives it aims to describe—that women may come to recognize it as at least in part a diagnosis of the character of the unease that they in fact feel.[18] Women's articulations of feelings of unease should thus continue, within the development of feminist theory, to be engaged and responded to. Investigations which do not aim primarily for this kind of responsiveness to women's voices will tend to overlook those avenues of thought and action which lead to a form of just and fruitful attention to different women's concrete positions with respect to particular epistemic practices. So, as long as feminist theory continues to aim for the development of lines of thought and action which women can identify as just and fruitful for women, it should continue to measure itself by its responsiveness to women's judgments about what is just and fruitful for women. Although the needs and concerns which women articulate will undoubtedly change as women enrich their senses of what it is to speak as women and for women, those needs and concerns articulated by women, however altered, should remain the primary data to which feminist theory is responsible. It should be taken as a criterion of adequacy of an investigation within feminist theory that it occasions women's greater understanding of the sources of women's pervasive sense of dislocation—where it is a measure of genuine understanding that it enables the development of a coherent and productive feminist politics.

For these reasons I am suspicious of arguments, such as that sketched in the last section, which move from a general epistemological insight—one about the influence of individual characteristics on ways in which experience is taken to bear on knowledge—to the conclusion that all our dominant epistemic practices *must* be thoroughly pervaded by a masculine bias. In their insistence that all our prevailing discourses must have a certain structure (i.e., one which encodes a masculine bias), such arguments lapse into a distinctive metaphysical tone. Enthralled by a picture of the way things must be in the world, they lay down philosophical requirements on what our investigations can reveal about the character of knowledge. These requirements—putting aside worries about their internal coherence—may then serve to distort our perception of the experiences which originally suggested the need for feminist theory. They predispose us to insist that we already know what must be there (within a particular epistemic practice), so we come to feel that we don't have to *look*—or at least not further than a certain point. Within feminist theory, the invisible requirements of a 'philosophical must' can constrain what we see when we look at our lives, every bit as much as can the sorts of requirements imposed on us by our prevailing theoretical discourses. If a tendency to blind us to the character of certain experiences is characteristic of certain classical metaphysical theses, and if it is a dominant tendency of contemporary feminist theory to criticize such blindness in its traditional guises (and view it as a symptom of a masculine theoretical bias), it does not automatically follow that such feminist theory has already, in its gesture of rejecting 'male' metaphysics, succeeded in liberating itself from that metaphysics.

I want to emphasize that, in diagnosing the sources of a tone of metaphysical insistence which rings clearly in certain strands of feminist argument, my aim is to achieve a clearer view of the actual sources of women's sense of alienation. I am not arguing against feminist discoveries of *de facto* masculine bias in linguistic or epistemic practices or social institutions—no matter how systematic or widespread feminist inquiries reveal such bias to be—but only against the claim that such bias *must* be there, even in places we have not yet looked.

i. How 'male' is our language?

Consider how certain strands of feminist theory may encourage us to develop a distorted picture of women's relation to particular linguistic and epistemic practices. Feminist theorists have drawn attention to different ways in which linguistic expressions may encode a masculine bias. 'Exorcising'[19] or eliminating such bias from a particular expression may afford a woman a greater sense of the compatibility between her words and her experiences. She may also find that her first discovery of bias is systematically related to other instances of bias in her forms of thought and speech. Feminist investigations have revealed some of the deeply ingrained ways in which the uses of linguistic expressions encourage what might be called 'masculinist thought'. Once the practice of referring to all people with the expressions 'man' and 'mankind' had been uncovered, feminists uncovered expressions such as 'people and their wives'[20] and 'spousal consent for obtaining an abortion'. But such investigations depend for their possibility on our ability to use expressions in ways which are not 'masculinist'.

Our recognition of the practice of using 'man' to refer to all people as a biased use of language depends on our being able to recognize other uses of 'man' as not biased.

When theorists respond to a woman's sense of 'not being at home in her language' by recommending the wholesale rejection of 'male language',[21] they presuppose that our most basic concepts of objectivity and rationality (which are seen as somehow precipitating the local biased uses of language) can, in the end, simply be rejected. They operate on the assumption that when we have gone deep enough—when we have fully corrected the masculine biases of language—we will wind up with a language which is no longer conceptually akin to our present 'male' language. We will then not merely have readjusted our forms of expression to accommodate certain feminist insights, but we will have, as it were, 'gotten outside of our 'male' skins'.

Even in those cases, however, in which we can achieve a limited analogue of a wholesale rejection of things 'male' in favour of things 'female', such a gesture still will not accomplish what is intended. The affirmation of the negation of a metaphysical thesis tends to issue in another metaphysical thesis—one which participates in the same picture and hence bears the image of its opposing counterpart. The theorists I am concerned to criticize here reflect on traditional metaphysical renderings of our basic everyday concepts of objectivity, rationality and experience—and accept these renderings as successfully representing the structure of these concepts—and then turn on them and want to reject them as fully 'male'. This gesture of rejecting a traditional metaphysics of objectivity, rationality and experience is open to question from the following direction. Given that the theorists who make it want to distance themselves from confused or limiting metaphysical accounts of these concepts, we need to ask whether the gesture suits their purposes.

The worry is that, if our current metaphysical conceptions of rationality, experience and objectivity are understood as presupposing what is 'male' as a norm for all humans, and if we attempt simply to affirm the negation of these traditional metaphysical theses (imagining we are thereby exchanging 'male' basic concepts for 'female' ones), then we end up simply maintaining the structures of that 'male' metaphysics, reflected now in the mirror-image of its antitheses. Mere denial of the validity of what some philosophers have seen as the metaphysical underpinnings of our most basic concepts will not amount to a dismantling of that tradition. In simply denying some of the central tenets of traditional metaphysics, some theorists recognize it as advancing straightforward tenets which can be denied and thereby limit themselves to a space of alternatives whose dimensions are determined by that tradition. Denial of the correctness of a traditional metaphysical thesis in a sense simply rehearses a moment within the tradition.[22] Certain kinds of feminist arguments legitimize traditional ('male') metaphysics in their very attempt to reject it.

ii. Tension between social constructivism and essentialism about gender

The arguments I am concerned with begin with an innocuous general insight about the social context of knowledge. They underline the fact that we are socialized into certain norms and describe ways in which our experience is mediated by these norms. This insight is then often elaborated into the thought that *gender* (as opposed to *sex* which is often taken to be biologically determinative) is socially constructed. This strain of feminist thought is at odds with another feminist position, one which does not take a sociological perspective on gender but rather embraces an essentialist view, a view asserting that women simply experience things differently from men (and vice-versa). Some feminist arguments that explicitly claim to embrace the former sociological perspective and reject the latter essentialist one are nevertheless implicitly committed to some version of the latter. Some theorists have wanted to build on a relatively innocuous version of the sociological insight to go on to argue that our current forms of knowledge are adequate only to the task of incorporating distinctly male experience. As we saw, it is an implicit assumption of this claim that female experience is thoroughly and systematically different from male experience—and this is just what feminists (and others, including various kinds of misogynist thinkers) who are essentialists about gender have hoped to show. This perception of ways in which our experience is mediated by social norms, when it is taken to show that our body of knowledge *must* be thoroughly and systematically pervaded by a masculine bias, thus becomes intertwined with an essentialist position with which it is deeply in tension. (Many feminist theorists whose work is threatened by this tension fail to notice it because they waffle between two senses in which one might understand the claim that 'female experience differs systematically from male experience'. They trade on the ambiguity between saying that women's experience tends to differ in systematic ways from men's experience (because women's and men's experience are both mediated by social norms which differentiate systematically between women and men) and saying that it is constitutive of women's experience and men's experience that they be systematically different (because it is essential to what it is to be a woman and what it is to be a man that each experience things differently).) These kinds of arguments therefore leave themselves open to criticisms that have been made of essentialist arguments about gender. In tacitly assuming that women's and men's experience are essentially different, they suggest that there are some features of women's experience which cannot be influenced by socialization. And they incline toward the suggestion that women's experience (or 'women's intuition') is self-validating: it is unquestionably valid because beyond the reach of any social or individual forces.

Without some independent argument (i.e., an argument for why social differentiation with respect to gender is of an epistemologically privileged kind), this move, which places a fundamental division between women's and men's experience, threatens to make room for further fundamental divisions along lines other than gender—e.g., among groups of women from different backgrounds. It welcomes a splintering of what might be called 'women's reality' into numerous separate 'realities' for women of different races, classes, sexual orientations, ethnicities or religions (each of whom may, on this line of thought, be presumed to inhabit their own self-validating 'reality'). It suggests that there are *a priori* obstacles blocking communication between diverse groups of women as well as between women and men. This strain of feminist theory thus veers toward the conclusion that true communication between persons with significantly different personal characteristics is impossible.

Further, a thesis affirming the metaphysical separation of 'male' and 'female' experience undercuts one of the original insights which motivated feminists to complain about our prevailing theoretical discourses: *viz.*, that they unjustly exclude the voices of women. If it is true that there are essential differences between women's and men's experience, then what feminists lament as the inadequacy of dominant theoretical discourses must be viewed, no longer as a reparable shortcoming of (and therefore a ground of complaint against) these discourses, but rather as an inevitable structural feature. If women's experience and men's experience are fundamentally incommensurable, then we must resign ourselves to the fact that no single set of concepts could serve the purposes of both women and men. Whatever concepts provide a man with the resources to lead a rich and fulfilling life will necessarily obstruct the possibility of such a life for a woman. So women's alienation from 'male' theoretical discourses is not primarily an artifact of their society's attitudes towards women, but rather an undeniable fact rooted in essential differences between the genders.

Leaving aside for the moment its despair at the possibility of formulating any positive conception of human flourishing (i.e., one which could equally inform the lives of women and men), the mere attempt to state this feminist position seems to invite the following worry. In describing this position, we seem to need to grasp some notion of 'women's experience' which is prior to any concepts which could be used to make sense of that experience. We might well wonder what understanding we have of the notion of 'women's experience' if it is taken to refer to a phenomenon which precedes even our very first discursive stammerings.[23]

iii. What 'female thoughts' might not be

A number of recent feminist arguments champion some version of the thought that our prevailing discourses are thoroughly and exclusively 'male'. This thought is typically developed in conjunction with the claim that our most basic logical concepts—such as objectivity, rationality, experience, etc.—reflect exclusively 'male' ways of knowing the world. The idea is that, in order to avoid falling into 'male' ways of thinking, women must 'get outside' 'male' language (language which includes those concepts) by creating a fully 'female' language which reflects 'female' ways of thinking.

It is helpful to consider this sort of argument against the background of a well known critique, developed in Wittgenstein's writings, of a prevalent and very natural view of nonsense. Wittgenstein attacks views on which combinations of words fail to make sense because the thoughts that they (try to) express are taken to be in some way impermissible or illegitimate. He stresses that, in so far as such views represent combinations of words as failing to be proper units of language on account of the nature of thoughts they (endeavour to) impart, they presuppose an understanding of the very combinations of words they portray as nonsensical. These views waver unsteadily between representing certain strings of signs as having senses we can at least vaguely make out and rejecting those same strings of signs as lacking sense. They are at least tacitly committed to drawing on a problematic category of *nonsensical* yet somehow also *intelligible* strings of signs.

Wittgenstein's critique bears directly on the feminist arguments at issue here. It is a presupposition of these arguments that we are in a position to grasp the notion of 'female' thoughts although—situated as we are within a 'male' language—we are not yet in a position fully to articulate *them.*[24] It is at least implicit in them that there are ('female') thoughts which, because of the limits of ('male') language, we are unable fully to say or think. When we formulate these ('female') thoughts in ('male') language, we necessarily fail to give full expression to their ('female') meaning. We are, nonetheless, somehow able to achieve a position from which we can discern what ('female') thoughts these as yet nonsensical sentences would be expressing if they could be properly formulated. Still we recognize that the limits of ('male') language confine us. Try as we might, we can't (as yet) fully express these ('female') thoughts. This way of understanding the significance of certain nonsensical ('female') combinations of words commits its proponents to an understanding of language as having a communicative function over and above that of saying what can be said. The nonsensical ('female') sentence does not express an intelligible thought, yet it imparts a 'meaning' in spite of its senselessness. It show us that there is something it is attempting to say even though it cannot be said—something which is, as of yet, unsayable. It is implicit in such arguments, then, that it is in some sense intelligible to discuss what a nonsensical ('female') thought attempts to express. Theorists who embrace such arguments resemble proponents of the view of nonsense Wittgenstein attacks in that they find themselves committed to a notion of intelligible nonsense. In saying that certain nonsensical ('female') sentences attempt to express things that can't be said, these theorists simultaneously use those ('female') sentences to impart something and deny that that something can be said. They tell us that the sentences are nonsense at the same time that they provide us with an apparently intelligible rendering of what it is the sentences fail to say.[25]

Wittgenstein represents the tendency to be drawn toward adopting this kind of internally inconsistent position as a characteristic, though often disguised, symptom of philosophical scepticism. This suggests an analogy between the epistemological ambitions of the sceptic and those of the feminist theorists I am considering.

Both the traditional philosophical sceptic and a certain kind of feminist theorist aspire to achieve what they conceive as the wholesale rejection of the conceptual resources with which we make sense of the world. The sceptic wants to do so because she is impressed by what she claims is a disastrously important fact about our lives: *viz.*, the fact that our conceptual resources may not be adequate to the task of accommodating our (i.e., women's and men's) experience. She accordingly insists that we should not blindly rely on our everyday ways of making sense of things. A particular kind of feminist theorist also aspires to fully reject our conceptual resources, but for a different reason. She holds that our current resources are inadequate to the task of incorporating women's experience.

There is a significant difference between the sceptic and this theorist. The sceptic tends to admit that we may never be able to articulate her insight fully appropriately or intelligibly. None the less, she holds that we have a grasp of *what* it is she is trying to say about our lives even if the conditions for saying it are never fully met. This theorist, in contrast, thinks that as we gradually develop a 'feminist language' we will better understand what (currently nonsensical) 'female thoughts' attempt to express. At the same time she also holds that right now we can somehow have insight into what such (currently nonsensical) thoughts are trying to say.

Despite this difference, there is a deep similarity between their positions. The feminist theorists I am discussing, like the sceptic, want to reject the very conceptual resources which they need to rely on to underwrite the intelligibility of what they hope to express. They put themselves, together with the sceptic, in a traditional philosophical position of speechlessness in the face of what they want to say, while at the same time insisting that their silence is pregnant with meaning.

iv. Recoiling in the wrong direction

There are important differences between my criticism of certain feminist arguments and charges brought against these same sorts of arguments by critics of *feminism*. One prominent and, for my purposes, representative critic is Janet Radcliffe Richards. Radcliffe Richards worries that women will have given up too much if they relinquish certain 'weapons' which, historically, have been controlled by men. She claims that 'the way to cope with men's treachery is not to outlaw the use of their weapons (especially since women cannot do without these themselves) but to become expert enough in their use to prevent further harm from being done'.[26] Here Radcliffe Richards is moved by her perception that women will continue to be dominated by men unless they come to terms with the 'weapons' which have been used to subordinate them. She is concerned that feminists who want simply to reject 'male tools' will be unsuccessful in their attempts to resist the instruments of their oppression. There is a valid worry somewhere here. But Radcliffe Richards goes on without a pause to declare: 'Women should be so adept in argument that they can see what is happening if men seem to have proved that black is white, instead of being driven into a baffled and furious silence'.[27] A paragraph later, she criticizes the feminist 'who thinks logic is something better ignored'. Radcliffe Richards embraces the idea that argument and logic are 'weapons' that women would be unwise to abandon. She thus buys into a central presupposition of the feminist arguments she wants to oppose: the assumption that there is something intelligible which women might do which would be 'a wholesale rejection of (male) logic or of (male) standards of consistency in argumentation'. She accepts the intelligibility of the recommendation—of someone like Andrea Nye—that women engage in a 'wholesale rejection of (male) logic'. But she chooses not to follow this recommendation on the grounds that it would be a tactical error.

In so far as Radcliffe Richards repudiates a feminist position like Nye's without questioning its presuppositions, her own view ends up incorporating its most problematic features. One might attempt to capture the respective positions of the critic of feminism (e.g., Radcliffe Richards) and the theorist who is a proponent of 'a wholesale rejection of male logic' (e.g., Nye) by relying on the slogan from the work of Audré Lorde: 'the master's tools will never dismantle the master's house'. Adopting the terms of this slogan, we might say that a particular kind of theorist (Nye) thinks 'the master's tools' must all be thrown out, while a certain critic (Radcliffe Richards) thinks that they must all be kept, not as tools to build with, but only as weapons to fight with. The theorist is impressed by her perception that the character of many of our linguistic and epistemic practices has been shaped by their use in 'the master's' regime; she concludes that everything about them must, in the end, be rejected—they are hopelessly tainted. The critic is worried that women will never successfully resist oppression if they do not first learn to fight the adversary on his own terms. She responds that the theorist's plan is 'ridiculous' or 'unreasonable' because 'women cannot do without these [weapons]'. Both theorist and critic see themselves as forced to make a choice between what they see as two equally intelligible courses of action: either to reject all 'the master's tools' (where 'the master's tools' are taken to include not just certain applications of, say, logic, but all of our most basic practices of reason) or to keep them. But neither theorist nor critic is arguing a fully intelligible position in so far as they share the assumption that there is something like a choice to be made along these lines. In embracing Audré Lord's slogan, we are not thereby forced to take the theorist's side in this 'debate'. We are not forced to acknowledge this as a fully coherent debate at all. The slogan can be heard as expressing an epistemologically innocuous (though none the less critically important) feminist perception of the type I touched on above: namely, that certain structures of knowledge and language encode a masculine bias, and that, until we have recognized where and how bias is built into those practices, we will not have identified which are the tools that serve the purpose of the master. If we fail to recognize bias, then we end up trying to dismantle the master's domain with tools which only serve one purpose well, namely that of extending it.[28]

If the slogan is read in this epistemologically uncontentious way, then it seems to redirect our sense of where our central task lies: to discern which 'tools' the 'master's tools' are. On this view, one of the main tasks of feminist thought becomes, not throwing away the bulk of our current conceptual resources, but rather seeing where and how certain masculine biases have become encoded into what now seem to be natural ways of thinking and speaking.

3. Acknowledgment

Look at me! Look at my arm! I have ploughed and planted, and gathered into barns, and no man could head me! And ain't I a woman?

—Sojourner Truth

My criticism of a particular strain of feminist theory is not directed towards feminist discoveries of actual gender bias in our epistemic and linguistic practices. I have attempted, not to take issue with factual claims about the existence of such bias, but rather to diagnose the sources of a line of argument which some theorists have used to explain its existence. I have been concerned to trace the development of a tone of philosophical insistence which resounds within certain feminist arguments and to question a metaphysical claim which such a tone insinuates—the claim that a masculine bias *must* pervade our epistemic practices, even those practices we have not yet examined.

The work of feminist epistemologists should be valued for, among other things, bringing into relief roles that gender and other individual characteristics can play in the acquisition and dissemination of knowledge. Feminist epistemologists have drawn attention to aspects of the social context of knowledge. They have pointed out ways in which our socialization differs according to sex and explored the manner in which these differences are reflected in women's and men's contributions to knowledge in various areas. They have demonstrated that some of our sociological and natural knowledge (knowledge which sometimes strongly reflects society's demeaning attitudes toward women) at times fails to do justice to the character of women's experience. Further, in cataloguing particular ways in which gender biases are encoded in bodies of knowledge, feminist theorists begin to identify patterns. They develop skills for identifying similar kinds of biases in as yet unexamined bodies of knowledge. This is an important contribution of feminist thought. But even the existence of patterns does not warrant the inference to the conclusion that gender bias *must* pervade all forms of knowledge which represent themselves as impersonal—a conclusion which would excuse us from undertaking the kind of detailed investigation of particular practices which best further our understanding of the sources of women's sense of alienation.

• • •

The power of the work of many feminist thinkers is best understood from the perspective of a feminism which does not champion general theoretical claims about how a masculine bias *must* pervade our epistemic and linguistic practices and which does not involve us in an attempt to identify the ('female') thoughts that certain nonsensical sentences try but fail to impart. Many feminist thinkers direct our attention to places in our lives in which we may not have suspected gender bias could reside (e.g., in our use of the word 'woman', or in our failure to project the concept 'harassment' into certain contexts), thereby allowing us to make sense of experiences which, previously, may have been painful and disorienting as well as (perhaps at first only vaguely) unjust. The ways in which gender is at play in our knowledge are as complex as the lives we lead as gendered people. The challenge of feminist thought is one of bringing our attention back to the all too familiar everyday moments which form the fabric of these gendered lives.[40]

ENDNOTES

1 *The Politics of Reality: Essays in Feminist Theory* (Freedom, CA: The Crossing Press, 1983), xi–xii.

2 To take this as a point of departure is *not* to ignore the fact that many women's experience of oppression is anything but vague. Many women suffer the violence of rape, battery, forced prostitution, incest, sexual harassment, forced maternity, etc. Since these horrors are often suffered in isolation, however, they sometimes seem—even to the women who are forced to undergo them—individual, even chosen. A woman may not view her particular experience as, in any significant sense, peculiarly that of a woman. Her original inclination to look to feminism for an understanding of her experience may therefore—even in these violent cases—take the form of a sense of vague unease; that is, a feeling which, for all its force-fulness, none the less presents itself to her only vaguely as one of oppression.

3 Although this sketch of the beginnings of feminism is relatively uncontentious, some philosophers would dispute it. Richard Rorty, e.g., wants to focus exclusively on a moment in the writing of some feminists at which feminist theory views itself, not as an attempt to respond to women's articulations of their needs and concerns, but rather as an attempt to bring women to experience things—things they do not now for the most part experience as severe injustices—as severe injustices. (Rorty is thinking of things such as marital rape which neither the law nor social mores consider egregious wrongs, things which women themselves therefore often do not feel entitled to protest.) For Rorty, feminist theory should be viewed as an attempt to 'create' unease or magnify kinds of unease which are muted. Thus he admires the work of Catharine MacKinnon because he thinks 'she sees feminists as needing to alter the data of moral theory rather than needing to formulate principles which fit pre-existent data better' (*Truth*

and Progress: Philosophical Papers, vol. 3, Cambridge University Press, 1998, 204). Rorty is right that there is a moment within much feminist writing which focuses on the ability of feminist theory to shape women's experiences of certain events. It is, however, difficult to find a major feminist author whose work fails to combine this moment with the moment I begin with (the moment in which feminist theory views itself as responding to women's articulations of their experience of certain things).

4 Barbara Ehrenreich and Deirdre English, *For Her Own Good* (New York: Anchor, 1979), 123.

5 Ibid., 120. This citation is taken from 'Dr. G. L. Austin's 1883 book of advice of "maiden, wife and mother'" (123).

6 Jean Grimshaw discusses both of these cases in *Philosophy and Feminist Thinking* (Minneapolis: University of Minnesota Press, 1986), 76–7.

7 This feminist diagnosis is not undermined by the insight that our experience is mediated by dominant social norms. Although some women may in fact successfully rely on the norms of their society in their attempts to articulate their experience of, e.g., pregnancy, others may become frustrated or confused by their failure to make sense of their experience within the terms of those norms. It is not inconsistent to claim both that women's attempts to understand the character of their experience are mediated by prevailing social norms and also that, in some cases, those norms simply do not do justice to what women in fact experience.

8 Simone de Beauvoir, *The Second Sex*, H. M. Parshley, trans., (New York: Alfred A. Knopf, 1989), xxi, emphasis in the original.

9 This has been the case even where the object of knowledge is woman. We can, e.g., recall questions Virginia Woolf wanted to get us to ponder: 'Have you any notion how many books are written about women in the course of one year? Have you any notion how many are written by men?' (*A Room of One's Own* (Orlando: Harcourt Brace Javanovich, Inc., 1957), 26).

10 I say *epistemologically* innocuous, because this perception is anything but *politically* innocuous. Thoughts about the way gender, sexual orientation, race, class, etc. affect our socialization provoke enormous political resistance (as the history of resistance in the U.S. to various policies of affirmative action aptly demonstrates). *Epistemologically*, however, it is innocuous in the sense of being relatively uncontested. Claims of this form can be traced back as far as Aristotle in the history of Western philosophy. Few philosophers of note have ever claimed that the particular ways in which we are initiated into our society have no bearing on how we conceptualize the world. (I rely on this distinction between what is epistemologically and what is politically innocuous throughout this paper. I am making explicit my disagreement with an unstated assumption of some feminist theory to the effect that only a philosophical position which is *anything but epistemologically innocuous* can avoid being politically innocuous as well—and therefore that only; a form of feminist action connected to a theory which is sufficiently epistemologically radical can hold forth the promise of genuine progress.)

11 I use the term 'androcentrism' here to refer to two phenomena of feminist concern touched on above: 1) the irrelevance of women's perceptions of the character of their experience to certain dominant discourses; 2) the 'male-as-norm-syndrome'—i.e., the upholding of what is 'masculine' as a norm for all people and the identification of the 'feminine' by its lack of positive qualities. The two phenomena may, of course, reinforce each other.

12 Sheila Ruth, e.g., explicitly draws on this assumption. See 'Methodocracy, Misogyny and Bad Faith: The Response of Philosophy', *Men's Studies Modified: The Impact of Feminism on the Academic Disciplines,* D. Spender (ed.) (New York: Pergamon Press, 1981), 47.

13 Liz Stanley and Sue Wise contend that 'women's experiences constitute a different view of reality, an entirely different ontology or way of going about making sense of the world . . . Women sometimes construct and inhabit what is in effect an entirely different social reality' (*Breaking Out: Feminist Consciousness and Feminist Research* (London: Routledge & Kegan Paul, 1983), 117).

14 Both Cora Diamond ('Knowing Tornados and Other Things', *New Literary History* (1991), 1001–16; see 1001–4) and Jean Grimshaw ((op. cit., note 6), esp. ch. 3) are critical of feminist argument which proceed on structurally similar paths to this conclusion.

15 *Words of Power* (New York: Routledge, 1990).

16 Ibid., 3.

17 *Sister Outsider* (The Crossing Press feminist series, 1984), 110–3.

18 Stanley Cavell (part IV of *The Claim of Reason* (Oxford University Press, 1979) and Cora Diamond ('Losing Your Concepts', *Ethics* **98** (January 1988), 255–77)) use the concept of *acknowledgment* to express such forms of self-recognition. In their terms, women's recognition of something about themselves in feminist theory might also be described as their 'acknowledgement' of an image or reflection of themselves in feminist theory—their acknowledgement of such an image as speaking to and for them.

19 In *Gyn/Ecology* (Boston: Beacon Press, 1978), Mary Daly writes about the radical feminist 'journey' which 'involves exorcism of the internal Godfather in his various manifestations'.

20 Ibid., 18.

21 Where 'male language' is not just bits and phrases of our current language which can be corrected the way 'man' can be, but extends beyond concrete examples such as this to what are thought of as the metaphysical underpinnings of the whole of our current language.

22 By employing such a strategy, I want to suggest, some feminist thought runs the risk of simply repeating a traditional philosophical problematic of scepticism. Below (2iii) I argue that the feminist theorist may find herself arriving, together with the sceptic, at a traditional philosophical terminus of muteness in the face of the ineffability of what she wants to say.

23 This strain of feminist theory thus recapitulates a recurring set of problems in philosophy often subsumed under the heading of 'the Given'.

24 It is also a presupposition of such arguments that we are in a position to grasp the notion of 'male language' although—situated as we are within such a language—we as yet have no concept of 'some other kind of language' with which to contrast (and thus to make the relevant sense of) the notion of a 'male language'.

25 Liz Stanley and Sue Wise champion a version of this view of 'feminist thoughts'. In *Breaking Out* (op. cit., note 13), they claim both that 'female' thoughts are accessible to us even though such thoughts must be formulated in a language which is predominantly 'male' and also that 'male language' is language which is not even capable of expressing or rendering intelligible 'female thoughts' (117 and 183). A somewhat more sophisticated version of this view of 'feminist thoughts' is developed in the essays in Part I of Catharine MacKinnon, *Toward a Feminist Theory of the State* (Cambridge, MA: Harvard University Press, 1989).

26 Janet Radcliffe Richards, *The Skeptical Feminist: a Philosophical Enquiry* (Boston: Routledge & Kegan Paul, 1980), 24–5.

27 Ibid., 25.

28 Lorde is concerned with the way the structure of the contemporary Women's Movement mirrors features of the sexist society it hopes to confront. She claims that as women we have been taught to view our differences (along lines of race, class, sexual orientation, etc.) as causes for 'separation and suspicion', and she argues that the Women's Movement will not be in a position to challenge sexism until it takes stock of the way intertwined threads of sexism, classism and homophobia have fuelled its own development.

40 This paper grew out of a set of provocative conversations with James Conant, Cora Diamond and members of a 1991–2 reading group on feminist theory in the Philosophy Department at the University of Pittsburgh. I am grateful to Elizabeth Anderson, Nancy Bauer, Stanley Cavell, James Conant, Cora Diamond, Nathaniel Hupert, John McDowell, Anthony O'Hear, Elijah Millgram, Naomi Scheman, Lisa Shapiro and Jennifer Whiting for helpful comments on earlier drafts.

DISCUSSION QUESTIONS

1. Why does Crary reject the ideas of writers such as Andrea Nye? Explain.

2. How does Crary think that the ideas of Ludwig Wittgenstein (1889–1951) are helpful in combating essentialism? Explain.

3. Why does Crary reject the ideas of writers such as Janet Radcliffe Richards? Explain.

4. Evaluate Crary's position in light of the other writers in Part III of *Four Fundamental Questions*.

PART FOUR

"WHAT SHOULD I DO AND WHO SHOULD I BE?"

Bhagavad Gita

The Bhagavad Gita *is an epic poem of Hinduism, which is a part of the larger epic poem, the* Mahabharata. *It has been dated from as far back as the fifth century BCE and as recent as the first century CE. Many of the ideas, though, are consistent with older texts. The setting for the* Gita *is the battlefield. Arjuna, who is part of the warrior caste, is supposed to fight. He is considering not fighting, even though it is his duty to fight, because some of his cousins are on the opposing side. He is not contemplating running away, but rather laying down his arms. His chariot driver is actually the Hindu god, Krishna, in human form. Krishna tries to get Arjuna to fulfill his* dharma *(duty) and fight. Eventually, Krishna is successful, but not until he has reinforced Arjuna by allowing Arjuna the ability to see him in his divine form.*

Our excerpt is the first two chapters of the Bhagavad Gita. *Chapter 1 sets the stage, as Arjuna expresses his doubt and sinks down in anguish. Chapter 2 contains the first attempts by Krishna to convince Arjuna to do his duty. Krishna explains to Arjuna that the true self cannot be killed on the battlefield. This is the view on* atman *we saw in Part I of* Four Fundamental Questions. *What makes this a duty-based, or deontological, view of ethics is that Krishna is telling Arjuna that what makes an action the right thing to do is the act itself and the intention behind it, not the result. It is the deed, the motive, not the fruit, as Krishna puts it. Krishna also tells Arjuna that he needs to not pay attention to the sense objects that might provide pleasure since that sets us off on the wrong foot. This view can also be seen in our earlier selection from Hinduism in Part I.*

CHAPTER I

Dh*ri*tarâsh*t*ra said

What did my (people) and the Pân*d*avas do, O Sañ*g*aya! when they assembled together on the holy field of Kurukshetra, desirous to do battle?

Sañ*g*aya said:

Seeing the army of the Pân*d*avas drawn up in battle-array[1], the prince Duryodhana approached the preceptor, and spoke (these) words: 'O preceptor! observe this grand army of the sons of Pân*d*u, drawn up in battle-array by your talented pupil, the son of Drupada. In it are heroes (bearing) large bows, the equals of Bhîma and Ar*g*una in battle—(namely), Yuyudhâna, Virâ*t*a, and Drupada, the master of a great car[2], and Dh*ri*sh*t*aketu, *K*ekitâna, and the valiant king of Kâsî, Puru*g*it and Kuntibho*g*a, and that eminent man *S*aibya; the heroic Yudhâmanyu, the valiant Uttamau*g*as, the son of Subhadrâ, and the sons of Draupadî—all masters of great cars. And now, O best of Brâhma*n*as! learn who are most distinguished among us, and are leaders of my army. I will name them to you, in order that you may know them well. Yourself, and Bhîshma, and Kar*n*a, and K*ri*pa the victor of (many) battles; A*s*vatthâman, and Vikar*n*a, and also the son of Somadatta, and many other brave men, who have given up their lives for me, who fight with various weapons, (and are) all dexterous in battle. Thus our army which is protected by Bhîshma is unlimited; while this army of theirs which is protected by Bhîma is very limited. And therefore do ye all, occupying respectively the positions[3] assigned to you, protect Bhîshma[4] only.'

Then his powerful grandsire, Bhîshma, the oldest of the Kauravas, roaring aloud like a lion, blew his conch, (thereby) affording delight to Duryodhana. And then all at once, conchs, and kettledrums, and tabors, and trumpets were played upon; and there was a tumultuous din. Then, too, Mâdhava and the son of Pâ*nd*u (Ar*g*una), seated in a grand chariot to which white steeds were yoked, blew their heavenly conchs. H*r*ishîkesa[5] blew the Pâñ*k*a*g*anya[6], and Dhanañ*g*aya the Devadatta, and Bhîma, (the doer) of fearful deeds, blew the great conch Pau*nd*ra. King Yudhish*th*ira, the son of Kuntî[7], blew the Anantavi*g*aya, and Nakula and Sahadeva (respectively) the Sughosha and Ma*n*ipushpaka. And the king of Kâ*s*î, too, who has an excellent bow, and Sikha*nd*in, the master of a great car, and Dh*r*ish*t*adyumna, Virâ*t*a, and the unconquered Sâtyaki, and Drupada, and the sons of Draupadî, and the son of Subhadrâ, of mighty arms, blew conchs severally from all sides, O king of the earth! That tumultuous din rent the hearts of all (the people) of Dh*r*itarâsh*t*ra's (party), causing reverberations throughout heaven and earth. Then seeing (the people of) Dh*r*itarâsh*t*ra's party regularly marshalled, the son of Pâ*nd*u, whose standard is the ape, raised his bow[8], after the discharge of missiles had commenced, and O king of the earth! spake these words to H*r*ishîkesa: 'O undegraded one! station my chariot between the two armies, while I observe those, who stand here desirous to engage in battle, and with whom, in the labours of this struggle, I must do battle. I will observe those who are assembled here and who are about to engage in battle, wishing to do service in battle[9] to the evil-minded son of Dh*r*itarâsh*t*ra.'

Sañ*g*aya said:

Thus addressed by Gu*d*âkesa[10], O descendant of Bharata[11]! H*r*ishîkesa stationed that excellent chariot between the two armies, in front of Bhîshma and Dro*n*a and of all the kings of the earth, and said O son of P*r*ithâ! look at these assembled Kauravas.' There the son of P*r*ithâ saw in both armies, fathers and grandfathers, preceptors, maternal uncles, brothers, sons[12], grandsons, companions, fathers-in-law, as well as friends. And seeing all those kinsmen standing (there), the son of Kuntî was overcome by excessive pity, and spake thus despondingly.

Ar*g*una said:

Seeing these kinsmen, O K*r*ish*n*a! standing (here) desirous to engage in battle, my limbs droop down; my mouth is quite dried up; a tremor comes on my body; and my hairs stand on end; the Gâ*n*dîva (bow) slips from my hand; my skin burns intensely. I am unable, too, to stand up; my mind whirls round, as it were; O Kesava! I see adverse omens[13]; and I do not perceive any good (to accrue) after killing (my) kinsmen in the battle. I do not wish for victory, O K*r*ish*n*a! nor sovereignty, nor pleasures: what is sovereignty to us, O Govinda! what enjoyments, and even life? Even those, for whose sake we desire sovereignty, enjoyments, and pleasures, are standing here for battle, abandoning life and wealth-preceptors, fathers, sons as well as grandfathers, maternal uncles, fathers-in-law, grandsons, brothers-in-law, as also (other) relatives. These I do not wish to kill, though they kill (me), O destroyer of Madhu[14]! even for the sake of sovereignty over the three worlds, how much less then for this earth (alone)? What joy shall be ours, O Ganârdana! after killing Dh*ri*tarâsh*t*ra's sons? Killing these felons[15] we shall only incur sin. Therefore it is not proper for us to kill our own kinsmen, the sons of Dh*ri*tarâsh*t*ra. For how, O Mâdhava! shall we be happy after killing our own relatives? Although having their consciences corrupted by avarice, they do not see the evils flowing from the extinction of a family, and the sin in treachery to friends, still, O Ganârdana! should not we, who do see the evils flowing from the extinction of a family, learn to refrain from that sin? On the extinction of a family, the eternal rites of families are destroyed[16]. Those rites being destroyed, impiety predominates over the whole family[17]. In consequence of the predominance of impiety, O K*r*ish*n*a! the women of the family become corrupt[18]; and the women becoming corrupt, O descendant of V*r*ish*n*i! intermingling of castes results; that intermingling necessarily leads the family and the destroyers of the family to hell; for when the ceremonies of (offering) the balls of food and water (to them) fail[19], their ancestors fall down (to hell). By these transgressions of the destroyers of families, which occasion interminglings of castes, the eternal rites of castes and rites, of families are subverted. And O Ganârdana! we have heard that men whose family-rites are subverted, must necessarily live in hell. Alas! we are engaged in committing a heinous sin, seeing that we are making efforts for killing our own kinsmen out of greed of the pleasures of sovereignty. If the sons of Dh*ri*tarâsh*t*ra, weapon in hand, should kill me in battle, me weaponless and not defending (myself), that would be better for me.

Sañgaya said:

Having spoken thus, Arguna cast aside his bow together with the arrows, on the battle-field, and sat down in (his) chariot, with a mind agitated by grief.

CHAPTER II

Sañgaya said:

To him, who was thus overcome with pity, and dejected, and whose eyes were full of tears and turbid, the destroyer of Madhu spoke these words.

The Deity said:

How (comes it that) this delusion, O Arguna! which is discarded by the good, which excludes from heaven, and occasions infamy, has overtaken you in this (place of) peril? Be not effeminate, O son of P*r*ithâ! it is not worthy of you. Cast off this base weakness of heart, and arise, O terror of (your) foes!

Arguna said:

How, O destroyer of Madhu! shall I encounter with arrows in the battle Bhîshma and Dro*n*a—both, O destroyer of enemies! entitled to reverence? Not killing (my) preceptors—(men) of great glory—it is better to live even on alms in this world. But killing them, though they are avaricious of worldly goods, I should only enjoy blood-tainted enjoyments. Nor do we know which of the two is better for us-whether that we should vanquish them, or that they should vanquish us. Even those, whom having killed, we do not wish to live—even those sons of Dhr*i*tarâsh*t*ra stand (arrayed) against us. With a heart contaminated by the taint of helplessness[20], with a mind confounded about my duty, I ask you. Tell me what is assuredly good for me. I am your disciple; instruct me, who have thrown myself on your (indulgence). For I do not perceive what is to dispel that grief which will dry up my organs[21] after I shall have obtained a prosperous kingdom on earth without a foe, or even the sovereignty of the gods[22].

Sañgaya said:

Having spoken thus to Hrishîkesa, O terror of (your) foes! Gu*d*âkesa said to Govinda, 'I shall not engage in battle;' and verily remained silent. To him thus desponding between the two armies, O descendant of Bharata! H*r*ishîkesa spoke these words with a slight smile.

The Deity said:

You have grieved for those who deserve no grief, and you talk words of wisdom[23]. Learned men grieve not for the living nor the dead. Never did I not exist, nor you, nor these rulers of men; nor will any one of us ever hereafter cease to be. As, in this body, infancy and youth and old age (come) to the embodied (self)[24], so does the acquisition of another body; a sensible man is not deceived about that The contacts of the senses[25], O son of Kuntî! which produce cold and heat, pleasure and pain, are not permanent, they are ever coming and going. Bear them, O descendant of Bharata! For, O chief of men! that sensible man whom they[26] (pain and pleasure being alike to him) afflict not, he merits immortality. There is no existence for that which is unreal; there is no non-existence for that which is real. And the (correct) conclusion about both[27] is perceived by those who perceive the truth. Know that to be indestructible which pervades all this; the destruction of that inexhaustible (principle) none can bring about. These bodies appertaining to the embodied (self) which is eternal, indestructible, and indefinable, are said[28] to be perishable; therefore do engage in battle, O descendant of Bharata! He who thinks it to be the killer and he who thinks it to be killed, both know nothing. It kills not, is not killed[29]. It is not born, nor does it ever die, nor, having existed, does it exist no more. Unborn, everlasting, unchangeable, and primeval, it is not killed when the body is killed[30]. O son of P*r*ithâ! how can that man who knows it thus to be indestructible, everlasting, unborn, and inexhaustible, how and whom can he kill, whom can he cause to be killed? As a man, casting off old clothes, puts on others and new ones, so the embodied (self) casting off old bodies, goes to others and new ones. Weapons do not divide it (into pieces); fire does not burn it, waters do not moisten it; the wind does not dry it up. It is not divisible; it is not combustible; it is not to be moistened; it is not to be dried up. It is everlasting, all-pervading, stable, firm, and eternal[31]. It is said to be unperceived, to be unthinkable, to be unchangeable. Therefore knowing it to be such, you ought not to grieve, But even if you think that it is constantly born, and constantly dies, still, O you of mighty arms! you ought not to grieve thus. For to one that is born, death is certain; and to one that dies, birth is certain[32]. Therefore about (this) unavoidable thing, you ought not to grieve. The source of things, O descendant of Bharata! is unperceived; their middle state is perceived; and their end again is unperceived. What (occasion is there for any) lamentation regarding them[33]? One looks upon it[34] as a wonder; another similarly speaks of it as a wonder; another too hears of it as a wonder; and even after having heard of it, no one does really know it[35]. This embodied (self), O descendant of Bharata! within every one's body is ever indestructible. Therefore you ought not to grieve for any being. Having regard to your own duty also, you ought not to falter, for there is nothing better for a Kshatriya[36] than a righteous battle. Happy those Kshatriyas, O son of P*ri*thâ! who can find such a battle (to fight)—come of itself[37]—an open door to heaven! But if you will not fight this righteous battle, then you will have abandoned your own duty and your fame, and you will incur sin. All beings, too, will tell of your everlasting infamy; and to one who has been honoured, infamy is (a) greater (evil) than death. (Warriors who are) masters of great cars will think that you abstained from the battle through fear, and having been highly thought of by them, you will fall down to littleness. Your enemies, too, decrying your power, will speak much about you that should not be spoken. And what, indeed, more lamentable than that? Killed, you will obtain heaven; victorious, you will enjoy the earth. Therefore arise, O son of Kuntî! resolved to (engage in) battle. Looking alike on pleasure and pain, on gain and loss, on victory and defeat, then prepare for battle, and thus you will not incur sin. The knowledge here declared to you is that relating to the Sâ<u>n</u>khya,[38]. Now hear that relating to the Yoga. Possessed of this knowledge, O son of P*ri*thâ! you will cast off the bonds of action. In this (path to final emancipation) nothing that is commenced becomes abortive; no obstacles exist; and even a little of this (form of) piety protects one from great danger[39]. There is here[40], O descendant of Kuru! but one state of mind consisting in firm understanding. But the states of mind of those who have no firm understanding are many-branched and endless. The state of mind consisting in firm understanding regarding steady contemplation[41] does not belong to those, O son of P*ri*thâ! who are strongly attached to (worldly) pleasures and power, and whose minds are drawn away by that flowery talk which is full of (ordinances of) specific acts for the attainment of (those) pleasures and (that) power, and which promises birth as the fruit of acts[42]—(that flowery talk) which those unwise ones utter, who are enamoured of Vedic words, who say there is nothing else, who are full of desires, and whose goal is heaven[43]. The Vedas (merely) relate to the effects of the three qualities[44]; do you, O Ar*g*una! rise above those effects of the three qualities, and be free from the pairs of opposites[45], always preserve courage[46], be free from anxiety for new acquisitions or protection of old acquisitions, and be self-controlled[47]. To the instructed Brâhma*n*a, there is in all the Vedas as much utility as in a reservoir of water into which waters flow from all sides[48]. Your business is with action alone; not by any means with fruit. Let not the fruit of action be your motive (to action). Let not your attachment be (fixed) on inaction[49]. Having recourse to devotion, O Dhanañgaya! perform actions, casting off (all) attachment, and being equable in success or ill-success; (such) equability is called devotion. Action, O Dhanañgaya! is far inferior to the devotion of the mind. In that devotion seek shelter. Wretched are those whose motive (to action) is the fruit (of action). He who has obtained devotion in this world casts off both merit and sin[50]. Therefore apply yourself to devotion; devotion in (all) actions is wisdom. The wise who have obtained devotion cast off the fruit of action; and released from the shackles of (repeated)births[51], repair to that seat where there is no unhappiness[52]. When your mind shall have crossed beyond the taint of delusion, then will you become indifferent to all that you have heard or will heard[53]. When your mind, confounded by what you have heard[54], will stand firm and steady in contemplation[55], then will you acquire devotion.

Arguna said:

What are the characteristics, O Kesava! of one whose mind is steady, and who is intent on contemplation? How should one of steady mind speak, how sit, how move?

The Deity said:

When a man, O son of Prithâ! abandons all the desires of his heart, and is pleased in his self only and by his self[56], he is then called one of steady mind. He whose heart is not agitated in the midst of calamities, who has no longing for pleasures, and from whom (the feelings of) affection, fear, and wrath[57] have departed, is called a sage of steady mind. His mind is steady, who, being without attachments anywhere, feels no exultation and no aversion on encountering the various agreeable and disagreeable[58] (things of this world). A man's mind is steady, when he withdraws his senses from (all) objects of sense, as the tortoise (withdraws) its limbs from all sides. Objects of sense draw back from a person who is abstinent; not so the taste (for those objects). But even the taste departs from him, when he has seen the Supreme[59]. The boisterous senses, O son of Kuntî! carry away by force the mind even of a wise man, who exerts himself (for final emancipation). Restraining them all, a man should remain engaged in devotion, making me his only resort. For his mind is steady whose senses are under his control. The man who ponders over objects of sense forms an attachment to them; from (that) attachment is produced desire; and from desire anger is produced[60]; from anger results want of discrimination[61]; from want of discrimination, confusion of the memory; from confusion of the memory, loss of reason; and in consequence of loss of reason. he is utterly ruined. But the self-restrained man who moves among[62] objects with senses under the control of his own self, and free from affection and aversion, obtains tranquillity[63]. When there is tranquillity, all his miseries are destroyed, for the mind of him whose heart is tranquil soon becomes steady. He who is not self-restrained has no steadiness of mind; nor has he who is not self-restrained perseverance[64] in the pursuit of self-knowledge; there is no tranquillity for him who does not persevere in the pursuit of self-knowledge; and whence can there be happiness for one who is not tranquil? For the heart which follows the rambling senses leads away his judgment, as the wind leads a boat astray upon the waters. Therefore, O you of mighty arms! his mind is steady whose senses are restrained on all sides from objects of sense. The self-restrained man is awake, when it is night for all beings; and when all beings are awake, that is the night of the right-seeing sage[65].

He into whom all objects of desire enter, as waters enter the ocean, which, (though) replenished, (still) keeps its position unmoved,-he only obtains tranquillity; not he who desires (those) objects of desire. The man who, casting off all desires, lives free from attachments, who is free from egoism[66], and from (the feeling that this or that is) mine[67], obtains tranquillity. This, O son of P*ri*thâ! is the Brahmic[68] state; attaining to this, one is never deluded; and remaining in it in (one's) last moments, one attains (brahma-nirvâ*n*a) the Brahmic bliss[69].

ENDNOTES

1 Several of these modes of array are described in Manu VII, 187, like a staff, like a wain, like a boar, &c. That of the Pâ*nd*avas, here referred to, appears to have been like the thunderbolt, as to which see Manu VII, 191.

2 This is a literal rendering; the technical meaning is 'a warrior proficient in military science, who can fight single-handed a thousand archers.'

3 The original word means, according to *S*rîdhara, 'the ways of entrance into a Vyûha or phalanx.'

4 Who, as generalissimo, remained in the centre of the army.

5 Literally, according to the commentators, 'lord of the senses of perception.'

6 Schlegel renders the names of these conchs by Gigantea, Theodotes, Arundinea, Triumphatrix, Dulcisona, and Gemmiflorea respectively.

7 So called, par excellence, apparently.

8 I.e. to join in the fight.

9 In the original, several derivatives from the root yudh, meaning 'to fight,' occur with the same frequency as 'battle' here.

10 Generally interpreted 'lord of sleep,' i. e. not indolent. Nîlaka*nth*a also suggests, that it may mean 'of thick hair.'

11 The son of Dushyanta and *S*akuntalâ, after whom India is called 'Bhâratavarsha,' and from whom both Pâ*nd*avas and Kauravas were descended.

12 The words in this list include all standing in similar relationships to those directly signified.

13 Such as the appearance of vultures, cars moving without horses, &c., mentioned in the Bhîshma Parvan II, 17. Cf. Sutta Nipâta, p. 100.

14 A demon of this name.

15 Six classes are mentioned: an incendiary; one who administers poison; one who assaults another—weapon in hand; one who destroys property; one who robs another of his wife; or his fields.

16 I.e. there being none to attend to the 'rites,' women being ineligible.

17 I. e. the surviving members.

18 I. e. either by the mere fact of relationship to such men, or by following their bad example.

19 There being no qualified person to perform them; 'their ancestors'—that is to say, of the 'destroyers of families.'

20 The commentators say that 'heart' here signifies the dispositions which are stated in chapter XVIII infra, p. 126. The feeling. of 'helplessness' is incompatible with what is there stated as the proper disposition for a Kshatriya.
21 I.e. by the heat of vexation; the meaning is, 'which will cause constant vexation of spirit.'
22 I.e. if the means employed are the sinful acts referred to.
23 Scil. regarding family-rites, &c.,. for, says Nîlaka*nth*a, they indicate knowledge of soul as distinct from body.
24 A common word in the Gîtâ, that which presides over each individual body.
25 Scil. with external objects.
26 I.e. the. 'contacts.'
27 The sense is this—there are two things apparently, the soul which is indestructible, and the feelings of pain &c. which 'come and go.' The true philosopher knows that the former only is real and exists; and that the latter is unreal and non-existent. He therefore does not mind the latter.
28 Scil. by those who are possessed of true knowledge.
29 Cf. Ka*th*a-upanishad, p. 104.
30 Ka*th*a-upanishad, pp. 103, 104.
31 'Eternal.' Nîlaka*nth*a explains this by 'unlimited by time, place,' &c. *S*an̲kara and others as 'uncreated,' 'without cause.' Stable = not assuming new forms; firm = not abandoning the original form. (*S*rîdhara.) The latter signifies a slight change; the former a total change.
32 Cf. the following from the Sutta Nipâta (Sir M. C. Swamy's translation), pp. 124, 125: 'There is, indeed, no means by which those born could be prevented from dying.' Even thus the world is afflicted with death and decay; therefore wise men, knowing the course of things in the world, do not give way to grief.
33 Cf. Sutta Nipâta, p. 125. 'In vain do you grieve, not knowing well the two ends of him whose manner either of coming or going you know not.'
34 I.e. the self spoken of above.
35 Ka*th*a-upanishad, p. 96.
36 One of the warrior caste.
37 Without any effort, that is to say, of one's own.
38 Sân̲khya is explained in different modes by the different commentators, but the resulting meaning here seems to be, that the doctrine stated is the doctrine of true knowledge and emancipation by its means. See infra, p. 52.
39 *Viz.* this mortal mundane life.
40 I.e. for those who enter on this 'path.'
41 I.e. of the supreme Being; Yoga meaning really the dedication of all acts to that Being.
42 See Sutta Nipâta, p. 4.
43 This is a merely temporary good, and not therefore deserving to be aspired to before final emancipation.
44 I.e. the whole course of worldly affairs. As to qualities, see chapter XIV.

45 Heat and cold, pain and pleasure, and so forth. Cf. Manu I, 26.
46 Cf. Sutta Nipâta, p. 17 and other places.
47 Keeping the mind from worldly objects.
48 The meaning here is not easily apprehended. I suggest the following explanation:—Having said that the Vedas are concerned with actions for special benefits, K*r*ish*n*a compares them to a reservoir which provides water for various special purposes, drinking, bathing, &c. The Vedas similarly prescribe particular rites and ceremonies for going to heaven, or destroying an enemy, &c. But, says K*r*ish*n*a, man's duty is merely to perform the actions prescribed for him among these, and not entertain desires for the special benefits named. The stanza occurs in the Sanatsu*g*âtîya, too.
49 Doing nothing at all.
50 Merit merely leads to heaven, as to which see note on last page. Cf. Sutta Nipâta, pp. 4, 136, 145 note.
51 Sutta Nipâta, pp. 3–7, &c.
52 Sutta Nipâta, p. 21.
53 This, according to Ânandagiri, means all writings other than those on the science of the soul.
54 I.e. about the means for the acquisition of various desired things.
55 I.e. of the soul (*S*an̲kara), of the supreme Being (*S*rîdhara). Substantially they both mean the same thing.
56 I.e. pleased, without regard to external objects, by self-contemplation alone.
57 Cf. Sutta Nipâta, p. 3.
58 The word *s*ubhâ*s*ubha in this sense also occurs in the Dhammapada, stanza 78, and in the Maitrî-upanishad, p. 34.
59 See on this, Wilson's Essays on Sanskrit Literature, vol. iii, p. 130.
60 I.e. when the desire is frustrated.
61 I.e. between right and wrong. Confusion of memory = forgetfulness of *S*âstras and rules prescribed in them.
62 Cf. Sutta Nipâta, p. 45.
63 Cf. Maitrî-upanishad, p. 134, where the commentator explains it to mean freedom from desires.
64 For a somewhat similar use of the word bhâvanâ in this sense, comp. Dhammapada, stanza 301.
65 Spiritual matters are dark as night to the common run of men, while they are wide awake in all worldly pursuits. With the sage the case is exactly the reverse.
66 Either pride or, better, the false notion mentioned infra, p. 55.
67 An almost identical expression occurs in the Dhammapada, stanza 367, and Maitrî-upanishad, p. 37.
68 The state of identification of oneself with the Brahman, which results from a correct knowledge of the Brahman.
69 Infra, p. 66.

DISCUSSION QUESTIONS

1. Explain how the Hindu views here in the *Bhagavad Gita* fit in with the views we saw earlier in the *Katha Upanishad*.

2. Krishna calls Arjuna a coward ("weak of heart" in our translation) at the beginning of Chapter 2 of the *Gita*. Based on Arjuna's speech in Chapter 1, do you think he is a coward? Why or why not? Explain.

3. One element of the ethic being advocated here is the idea of not paying attention to the result of an action when determining what to do. Why is this difficult to put into practice? Explain.

4. Another element of the ethic being advocated here is the idea of being in control of our emotions and not letting pleasure enter into our decision-making process. Why is this difficult to put into practice? Explain.

Akaranga Sutra

Edited and translated by Hermann Jacobi

The Akaranga Sutra *contains one of the most succinct versions of the concept of* ahimsa *(nonviolence) in Jain ethics. Jainism and Buddhism, as mentioned in Part I of* Four Fundamental Questions *are two of the views that came out of Hinduism as rejections of Buddhism around 2,500 years ago. The principal point here is to live your life in such a way that you do not increase the amount of violence in the world through your own thoughts and actions and you try to diminish the amount of violence by yourself and others. This is a wide-ranging view because it encompasses the nonhuman world, as well. As an ethic, this view both tells you what to do (practice* ahimsa*) and what kind of person to be (compassionate).*

BOOK I, LECTURE 1

SECOND LESSON

The (living) world is afflicted, miserable, difficult to instruct, and without discrimination. In this world full of pain, suffering by their different acts, see the benighted ones cause great pain. (1) See! there are beings individually embodied (in earth; not one all-soul). See! there are men who control themselves, (whilst others only) pretend to be houseless (i.e. monks, such as the Bauddhas, whose conduct differs not from that of householders), because one destroys this (earth-body) by bad and injurious doings, and many other beings, besides, which he hurts by means of earth, through his doing acts relating to earth. (2) About this the Revered One has taught the truth: for the sake of the splendour, honour, and glory of this life, for the sake of birth, death, and final liberation, for the removal of pain, man acts sinfully towards earth, or causes others to act so, or allows others to act so. This deprives him of happiness and perfect wisdom.

He who injures these (earth-bodies) does not comprehend and renounce the sinful acts; he who does not injure these, comprehends and renounces the sinful acts. Knowing them, a wise man should not act sinfully towards earth, nor cause others to act so, nor allow others to act so. H e who knows these causes of sin relating to earth, is called a reward-knowing sage. Thus I say. (6)

THIRD LESSON

(Thus I say): He who acts rightly, who does pious work, who practises no deceit, is called houseless. (1) One should, conquering the world, persevere in that (vigour of) faith which one had on the entrance in the order; the heroes (of faith), humbly bent, (should retain their belief in) the illustrious road (to final liberation) and in the world (of water-bodies); having rightly comprehended them through the instruction (of Mahâvîra), (they should retain) that which causes no danger (i.e. self-control). Thus I say. (2) A man should not (himself) deny the world of (water-bodies), nor should he deny the self. He who denies the world (of water-bodies), denies the self; and he who denies the self, denies the world of (water-bodies). (3)

See! there are men who control themselves; others pretend only to be houseless; for one destroys this (water-body) by bad, injurious doings, and many other beings, besides, which he hurts by means of water, through his doing acts relating to water. (4) About this the Revered One has taught the truth: for the sake of the splendour, honour, and glory of this life, for the sake of birth, death, and final liberation, for the removal of pain, man acts sinfully towards water, or causes others to act so, or allows others to act so. (5) This deprives him of happiness and perfect wisdom. About this he is informed when he has understood and heard from the Revered One, or from the monks, the faith to be coveted. There are some who, of a truth, know this (i.e. injuring) to be the bondage, the delusion, the death, the hell. For this a man is longing when he destroys this (water-body) by bad and injurious doings, and many other beings, besides, which he hurts by means of water, through his doing acts relating to water. Thus I say. (6)

There are beings living in water, many lives; of a truth, to the monks water has been declared to be living matter. See! considering the injuries (done to water-bodies), those acts (which are injuries, but must be done before the use of water, *eg.* straining) have been distinctly declared. Moreover he (who uses water which is not strained) takes away what has not been given (i.e. the bodies of water-lives). (A Bauddha will object): 'We have permission, we have permission to drink it, or (to take it) for toilet purposes.' Thus they destroy by various injuries (the water-bodies). But in this their doctrine is of no authority.

He who injures these (water-bodies) does not comprehend and renounce the sinful acts; he who does not injure these, comprehends and renounces the sinful acts. (7) Knowing them, a wise man should not act sinfully towards water, nor cause others to act so, nor allow others to act so. He who knows these causes of sin relating to water, is called a reward-knowing sage. Thus I say. (8)

FOURTH LESSON

(Thus I say): A man should not, of his own accord, deny the world (of fire-bodies), nor should he deny the self. He who denies the world (of fire-bodies), denies the self; and he who denies the self, denies the world (of fire-bodies). (1) He who knows that (*viz.* fire) through which injury is done to the long-living bodies (i.e. plants), knows also that which does no injury (i.e. control); and he who knows that which does no injury, knows also that through which no injury is done to the long-living bodies. (2) This has been seen by the heroes (of faith) who conquered ignorance; for they control themselves, always exert themselves, always mind their duty. He who is unmindful of duty, and desiring of the qualities (i.e. of the pleasure and profit which may be derived from the elements) is called the torment (of living beings). Knowing this, a wise man (resolves): 'Now (I shall do) no more what I used to do wantonly before.' (3) See! there are men who control themselves; others pretend only to be houseless; for one destroys this (fire-body) by bad and injurious doings, and many other beings, besides, which he hurts by means of fire, through his doing acts relating to fire. About this the Revered One has taught the truth: for the sake of the splendour, honour, and glory of this life, for the sake of birth, death, and final liberation, for the removal of pain, man acts sinfully towards fire, or causes others to act so, or allows others to act so. (4) This deprives him of happiness and perfect wisdom. About this he is informed when he has understood, or heard from the Revered One or from the monks, the faith to be coveted. There are some who, of a truth, know this (i.e. injuring) to be the bondage, the delusion, the death, the hell. For this a man is longing, when he destroys this (fire-body) by bad and injurious doings, and many other beings, besides, which he hurts by means of fire, through his doing acts relating to fire. Thus I say. (5)

There are beings living in the earth, living in grass, living on leaves, living in wood, living in cowdung, living in dust-heaps, jumping beings which coming near (fire) fall into it. Some, certainly, touched by fire, shrivel up; those which shrivel up there, lose their sense there; those which lose their sense there, die there. (6)

He who injures these (fire-bodies) does not comprehend and renounce the sinful acts; he who does not injure these, comprehends and renounces the sinful acts. Knowing them, a wise man should not act sinfully towards fire, nor cause others to act so, nor allow others to act so. He who knows the causes of sin relating to fire, is called a reward-knowing sage. Thus I say. (7)

FIFTH LESSON

'I shall not do (acts relating to plants) after having entered the order, having recognised (the truth about these acts), and having conceived that which is free from danger (i.e. control).'

He who does no acts (relating to plants), has ceased from works; he who has ceased from them is called 'houseless.' (1) Quality is the whirlpool (âva*tt*a = sa*m*sâra), and the whirlpool is quality. Looking up, down, aside, eastward, he sees colours, hearing he hears sounds; (2) longing upwards, down, aside, eastward, he becomes attached to colours and sounds. That is called the world; not guarded against it, not obeying the law (of the Tîrthakaras), relishing the qualities, conducting himself wrongly, he will wantonly live in a house (i.e. belong to the world). (3)

See! there are men who control themselves; others pretend only to be houseless, for one destroys this (body of a plant) by bad and injurious doings, and many other beings, besides, which he hurts by means of plants, through his doing acts relating to plants. (4) About this the Revered One has taught the truth: for the sake of the splendour, honour, and glory of this life, for the sake of birth, death, and final liberation, for the removal of pain, man acts sinfully towards plants, or causes others to act so, or allows others to act so. This deprives him of happiness and perfect wisdom. About this he is informed when he has understood, or heard from the Revered One or from the monks, the faith to be coveted. There are some who, of a truth, know this (i.e. injuring) to be the bondage, the delusion, the death, the hell. For this a man is longing when he destroys this (body of a plant) by bad and injurious doings, and many other beings, besides, which he hurts by means of plants, through his doing acts relating to plants. Thus I say. (5)

As the nature of this (i.e. men) is to be born and to grow old, so is the nature of that (i.e. plants) to be born and to grow old; as this has reason, so that has reason; as this falls sick when cut, so that falls sick when cut; as this needs food, so that needs food; as this will decay, so that will decay; as this is not eternal, so that is not eternal; as this takes increment, so that takes increment; as this is changing, so that is changing. (6) He who injures these (plants) does not comprehend and renounce the sinful acts; he who does not injure these, comprehends and renounces the sinful acts. Knowing them, a wise man should not act sinfully towards plants, nor cause others to act so, nor allow others to act so. He who knows these causes of sin relating to plants, is called a reward-knowing sage. Thus I say. (7)

SIXTH LESSON

Having well considered it, having well looked at it, I say thus: all beings, those with two, three, four senses, plants, those with five senses, and the rest of creation, (experience) individually pleasure or displeasure, pain, great terror, and unhappiness. Beings are filled with alarm from all directions and in all directions. See! there the benighted ones cause great pain. See! there are beings individually embodied. (2)

See! there are men who control themselves; others pretend only to be houseless, for one destroys this (body of an animal) by bad and injurious doings, and many other beings, besides, which he hurts by means of animals, through his doing acts relating to animals. (3) About this the Revered One has taught the truth: for the sake of the splendour, honour, and glory of this life, for the sake of birth, death, and final liberation, for the removal of pain, man acts sinfully towards animals, or causes others to act so, or allows others to act so. This deprives him of happiness and perfect wisdom. About this he is informed, when he has understood, or heard from the Revered One or from the monks, the faith to be coveted. There are some who, of a truth, know this (i.e. injuring) to be the bondage, the delusion, the death, the hell. For this a man is longing, when he injures this (body of an animal) by bad and injurious doings, and many other beings, besides, which he hurts by means of animals, through acts relating to animals. Thus I say. (4)

Some slay (animals) for sacrificial purposes, some kill (animals) for the sake of their skin, some kill (them) for the sake of their flesh, some kill them for the sake of their blood; thus for the sake of their heart, their bile, the feathers of their tail, their tail, their big or small horns, their teeth, their tusks, their nails, their sinews, their bones; with a purpose or without a purpose. Some kill animals because they have been wounded by them, or are wounded, or will be wounded. (5)

He who injures these (animals) does not comprehend and renounce the sinful acts; he who does not injure these, comprehends and renounces the sinful acts.

Knowing them, a wise man should not act sinfully towards animals, nor cause others to act so, nor allow others to act so. He who knows these causes of sin relating to animals, is called a reward-knowing sage. Thus I say. (6)

SEVENTH LESSON

He who is averse from (all actions relating to) wind, knows affliction. Knowing what is bad, he who knows it with regard to himself, knows it with regard to (the world) outside; and he who knows it with regard to (the world) outside, knows it with regard to himself: this reciprocity (between himself and) others (one should mind). Those who are appeased, who are free from passion, do not desire to live. (1)

See! there are men who control themselves; others pretend only to be houseless, for one destroys this (wind-body) by bad and injurious doings, and many other beings, besides, which he hurts by means of wind, through his doing acts relating to wind. (2) About this the Revered One has taught the truth: for the sake of the splendour, honour, and glory of this life, for the sake of birth, death, and final liberation, for the removal of pain, man acts sinfully towards wind, or causes others to act so, or allows others to act so. This deprives him of happiness and perfect wisdom. About this he is informed when he has understood, or heard from the Revered One or from the monks, the faith to be coveted. There are some who, of a truth, know this to be the bondage, the delusion, the death, the hell. For this a man is longing when he destroys this (wind-body) by bad and injurious acts, and many other beings, besides, which he hurts by means of wind, through his doing acts relating to wind. Thus I say. (3)

There are jumping beings which, coming near wind, fall into it. Some, certainly, touched by wind, shrivel up; those which shrivel up there, lose their sense there; those which lose their sense there, die there. (4)

He who injures these (wind-bodies) does not comprehend and renounce the sinful acts; he who does not injure these, comprehends and renounces the sinful acts. Knowing them, a wise man should not act sinfully towards wind, nor cause others to act so, nor allow others to act so. He who knows these causes of sin relating to wind, is called a reward-knowing sage. Thus I say. (5)

Be aware that about this (wind-body) too those are involved in sin who delight not in the right conduct, and, though doing acts, talk about religious discipline, who conducting themselves according to their own will, pursuing sensual pleasures, and engaging in acts, are addicted to worldliness. He who has the true knowledge about all things, will commit no sinful act, nor cause others to do so, &c. (6) Knowing them, a wise man should not act sinfully towards the aggregate of six (kinds of) lives, nor cause others to act so, nor allow others to act so. He who knows these causes of sin relating to the aggregate of the six (kinds of) lives, is called a reward-knowing sage. Thus I say. (7)

End of the First Lecture, called Knowledge of the Weapon.

DISCUSSION QUESTIONS

1. Contrast the view here with the one found in Hinduism. What are the main similarities and differences? Explain.

2. What would life be like for someone putting the idea of *ahimsa* into practice? Explain.

3. Mohandas Gandhi (1869–1948) advocated the use of *ahimsa* as the foundation for his idea of nonviolent civil disobedience. Why might *ahimsa* be an effective tactic? Explain.

The Beginning of Buddha's Preaching

Ed. by E.J. Thomas

The Buddhist way of describing what kind of person you should be can be found in the teaching called the Four Noble Truths, which can be found in many texts. Our selection is called "The Beginning of Buddha's Preaching." The focus in Buddhism is on relieving suffering. You need to think and act in a manner that both reduces the amount of suffering and minimizes the amount of new suffering that is created. The first three noble truths are self-explanatory. The fourth noble truth is also called the Eightfold Path. The eight requirements of the path are not fully explained in our excerpt; they are just listed. Here is the basic idea for each:

1. *Right views: the awareness of the first three noble truths*
2. *Right aspiration: the resolve to act in accordance with the noble truths*
3. *Right speech: to not cause suffering through your words—no lying, gossiping, abusive or belittling speech*
4. *Right action: to not cause suffering through your actions—no stealing, killing, or sexual misconduct*
5. *Right livelihood: to not cause suffering in the way you secure your livelihood (how you earn a living)—no business in weapons, slaving, sex-trade, intoxicants, poisons, the meat industry*
6. *Right effort ("endeavor" in our translation): the will to get rid of bad intentions, desires, and deeds*
7. *Right mindfulness ("watchfulness" in our translation): to stay alert to the things that can make you forget to do the right thing*
8. *Right concentration ("meditation" in our translation): to stay on the track of the noble truths by meditation and control of the body through breathing techniques*

The first discourse of the Buddha was given to the five disciples who had deserted him when he abandoned his austerities. It is given in the Vinaya in explaining the rules as to how the elder and younger brethren are to be addressed. The phrase "I have attained the immortal," used by Buddha, has nothing to do with immortal life. It refers to the permanent state of Nirvana, which does not pass away as do compound things. As the Vijaya Discourse puts it:

The bhikkhu, filled with wisdom here,
In lust, desire, delighting not,
He has attained immortal peace,
The unchangeable Nirvana-state.

The latter part of the following discourse, beginning with the words, "These two extremes," forms the Discourse of setting in motion the Wheel of the Doctrine. It teaches the middle path between the two extremes of self-indulgence and self-mortification. The statement is sometimes made that Buddha rejected asceticism. He certainly repudiated self-torture as a means of salvation, but not the asceticism which rejects all the lower desires in the pursuit of one highest goal. Compare the Ten Commandments below.

Now the Lord by gradual journeying came to Benares, to the deer-park Isipatana, where were the five brethren. The five brethren saw the Lord coming from afar, and on seeing him they decided among themselves, "This, friends, is the ascetic Gotama coming, who lives in abundance, has given up exertion, and turned to a life of abundance. We must not address him, nor rise to greet him, nor take his bowl and robe, but a seat shall be set for him. If he wishes he may sit down." But as the Lord approached the five brethren, so the five brethren did not abide by their agreement, but went to meet the Lord, and one took his bowl and robe, one arranged a seat, one set water for his feet, a footstool, and a cloth. The Lord sat on the appointed seat, and having sat down the Lord washed his feet. Then they addressed the Lord by name, and by the title of friend. When they spoke thus, the Lord said to the five brethren, "Brethren, do not address the Tathāgata by name, nor by the title of friend. The Tathāgata, brethren, is an arahat, and has obtained complete enlightenment. Give ear, brethren, I have attained the immortal, I instruct, I teach the doctrine. If you walk according to the teaching, for the sake of which noble youths go forth completely from a house to a houseless life, you will soon, on going forth yourselves, realize the transcendent faculties in this life, and will live in the attainment of the aim of the highest religious life." At these words the five brethren said to the Lord, "By that exercise, friend Gotama, by that course, that practice of penance, you have not attained supernatural excellence of most noble knowledge and insight. Will you, when you live in abundance, have given up exertion, and have turned to a life of abundance, now attain supernatural excellence of most noble knowledge and insight?" When they spoke thus, the Lord said to the five brethren, "Brethren, the Tathāgata does not live in abundance, he has not given up exertion, and has not turned to a life of abundance. The Tathāgata, brethren, is an arahat, and has attained complete enlightenment. Give ear, brethren, I have attained the immortal, I instruct, I teach the doctrine. If you walk according to the teaching, for the sake of which noble youths go forth completely from a house to a houseless life, you will soon, on going forth yourselves, realize the transcendent faculties in this life, and will live in the attainment of the aim of the highest religious life." [A second and third time the brethren asked the question, and the third time the Buddha replied:] "Do you perceive, brethren, that I have never spoken to you thus before now?" "Never thus, reverend sir." "The Tathāgata, brethren, is an arahat, and has attained complete enlightenment . . ." [etc., down to, "religious life "]. Then the Lord was able to convince the five brethren. They listened again to the Lord, gave ear, and fixed their minds on the knowledge.

Then the Lord addressed the five brethren: "These two extremes, brethren, are not to be practised by one who has given up the world. What are the two? The one, devotion to lusts and pleasures, base, sensual, vulgar, ignoble, and useless, and the other, devotion to self-mortification, painful, ignoble, and useless. By avoiding these two extremes, brethren, the Tathāgata has gained perfect knowledge of the middle path, which produces insight and knowledge, and conduces to tranquillity, to transcendent knowledge, to complete enlightenment, to Nirvana. What is this middle path, brethren? It is the Noble Eightfold Path, that is, right views, right aspiration, right speech, right action, right livelihood, right endeavour, right watchfulness, and right meditation. This, brethren, is the middle path, of which the Tathāgata has gained perfect knowledge, which produces insight and knowledge, and conduces to tranquillity, to supernatural faculty, to complete enlightenment, to Nirvana. This, brethren, is the noble truth of suffering: birth is suffering, old age is suffering, illness is suffering, death is suffering. Union with unpleasant things is suffering, separation from pleasant things is suffering, not obtaining what we wish is suffering, in short the fivefold clinging to existence is suffering. And this, brethren, is the noble truth of the cause of suffering: craving, which causes rebirth, accompanied by pleasure and lust, and rejoices at finding delight here and there, that is, craving for pleasure, craving for existence, and craving for prosperity. And this, brethren, is the noble truth of the destruction of suffering: which is the complete and trackless destruction of that thirst, its abandonment and relinquishment, liberation, and aversion. And this, brethren, is the noble truth of the path that leads to the destruction of suffering, that is, right views, right aspiration, right speech, right action, right livelihood, right endeavour, right watchfulness, and right meditation." (*Vin. Mahāv.* I. 6, 10 ff.)

DISCUSSION QUESTIONS

1. Contrast the view here with the one found in Hinduism. What are the main similarities and differences? Explain.

2. What would life be like for someone following the eightfold path? Explain.

3. The Buddha calls following the Four Noble Truths a middle path between two extremes. Explain this idea. Make sure to include an explanation of the two extremes.

The Doctrine of the Mean

By Confucius

Confucius (551–479 BCE, also known as K'ung-fu-tzu), is the Chinese philosopher who had the longest and most immediate impact on the history of China. From the second century BCE to the 19th century (more than 2,000 years) his works were required reading for civil service exams. He was also the first Chinese philosopher to be introduced to Europe, as the first translation into Latin was done in 1687. Like the examples from Taoists in Parts II and III of Four Fundamental Questions, *arguments are mostly analogical and metaphorical in Confucius' writing.*

The selection here is "The Doctrine of the Golden Mean." This work is a collection of sayings attributed to Confucius, though many put its authorship much later. The sayings point the way to becoming a "superior man." The Book of Poetry *mentioned here is a collection of songs and poems that may date as far back as 1000 BCE.*

What Heaven has conferred is called The Nature; an accordance with this nature is called The Path of duty; the regulation of this path is called Instruction.

The path may not be left for an instant. If it could be left, it would not be the path. On this account, the superior man does not wait till he sees things, to be cautious, nor till he hears things, to be apprehensive.

There is nothing more visible than what is secret, and nothing more manifest than what is minute. Therefore the superior man is watchful over himself, when he is alone.

While there are no stirrings of pleasure, anger, sorrow, or joy, the mind may be said to be in the state of Equilibrium. When those feelings have been stirred, and they act in their due degree, there ensues what may be called the state of Harmony. This Equilibrium is the great root from which grow all the human actings in the world, and this Harmony is the universal path which they all should pursue.

Let the states of equilibrium and harmony exist in perfection, and a happy order will prevail throughout heaven and earth, and all things will be nourished and flourish.

Chung-ni said, "The superior man embodies the course of the Mean; the mean man acts contrary to the course of the Mean."

"The superior man's embodying the course of the Mean is because he is a superior man, and so always maintains the Mean. The mean man's acting contrary to the course of the Mean is because he is a mean man, and has no caution."

The Master said, "Perfect is the virtue which is according to the Mean! Rare have they long been among the people, who could practice it! The Master said, "I know how it is that the path of the Mean is not walked in:—The knowing go beyond it, and the stupid do not come up to it. I know how it is that the path of the Mean is not understood:—The men of talents and virtue go beyond it, and the worthless do not come up to it.

The Master said, "Alas! How is the path of the Mean untrodden!"

The Master said, "There was Shun:—He indeed was greatly wise! Shun loved to question others, and to study their words, though they might be shallow. He concealed what was bad in them and displayed what was good. He took hold of their two extremes, determined the Mean, and employed it in his government of the people. It was by this that he was Shun!"

The Master said "Men all say, 'We are wise'; but being driven forward and taken in a net, a trap, or a pitfall, they know not how to escape. Men all say, 'We are wise'; but happening to choose the course of the Mean, they are not able to keep it for a round month."

The Master said "This was the manner of Hui:—he made choice of the Mean, and whenever he got hold of what was good, he clasped it firmly, as if wearing it on his breast, and did not lose it."

The Master said, "The kingdom, its states, and its families, maybe perfectly ruled; dignities and emoluments may be declined; naked weapons may be trampled under the feet; but the course of the Mean cannot be attained to."

Tsze-lu asked about energy.

The Master said, "Do you mean the energy of the South, the energy of the North, or the energy which you should cultivate yourself?"

"To show forbearance and gentleness in teaching others; and not to revenge unreasonable conduct:—this is the energy of southern regions, and the good man makes it his study.

"To lie under arms; and meet death without regret:—this is the energy of northern regions, and the forceful make it their study.

"Therefore, the superior man cultivates a friendly harmony, without being weak.—How firm is he in his energy! He stands erect in the middle, without inclining to either side.—How firm is he in his energy! When good principles prevail in the government of his country, he does not change from what he was in retirement. How firm is he in his energy! When bad principles prevail in the country, he maintains his course to death without changing.—How firm is he in his energy!"

The Master said, "To live in obscurity, and yet practice wonders, in order to be mentioned with honor in future ages:—this is what I do not do.

"The good man tries to proceed according to the right path, but when he has gone halfway, he abandons it:—I am not able so to stop.

"The superior man accords with the course of the Mean. Though he maybe all unknown, unregarded by the world, he feels no regret.—It is only the sage who is able for this."

The way which the superior man pursues, reaches wide and far, and yet is secret.

Common men and women, however ignorant, may intermeddle with the knowledge of it; yet in its utmost reaches, there is that which even the sage does not know. Common men and women, however much below the ordinary standard of character, can carry it into practice; yet in its utmost reaches, there is that which even the sage is not able to carry into practice. Great as heaven and earth are, men still find somethings in them with which to be dissatisfied. Thus it is that, were the superior man to speak of his way in all its greatness, nothing in the world would be found able to embrace it, and were he to speak of it in its minuteness, nothing in the world would be found able to split it.

The way of the superior man may be found, in its simple elements, in the intercourse of common men and women; but in its utmost reaches, it shines brightly through Heaven and earth.

The Master said "The path is not far from man. When men try to pursue a course, which is far from the common indications of consciousness, this course cannot be considered The Path."

"When one cultivates to the utmost the principles of his nature, and exercises them on the principle of reciprocity, he is not far from the path. What you do not like when done to yourself, do not do to others.

"In the way of the superior man there are four things, to not one of which have I as yet attained.—To serve my father, as I would require my son to serve me: to this I have not attained; to serve my prince as I would require my minister to serve me: to this I have not attained; to serve my elder brother as I would require my younger brother to serve me: to this I have not attained; to set the example in behaving to a friend, as I would require him to behave to me: to this I have not attained. Earnest in practicing the ordinary virtues, and careful in speaking about them, if, in his practice, he has anything defective, the superior man dares not but exert himself; and if, in his words, he has any excess, he dares not allow himself such license. Thus his words have respect to his actions, and his actions have respect to his words; is it not just an entire sincerity which marks the superior man?"

The superior man does what is proper to the station in which he is; he does not desire to go beyond this.

In a position of wealth and honor, he does what is proper to a position of wealth and honor. In a poor and low position, he does what is proper to a poor and low position. Situated among barbarous tribes, he does what is proper to a situation among barbarous tribes. In a position of sorrow and difficulty, he does what is proper to a position of sorrow and difficulty. The superior man can find himself in no situation in which he is not himself.

In a high situation, he does not treat with contempt his inferiors. In a low situation, he does not court the favor of his superiors. He rectifies himself, and seeks for nothing from others, so that he has no dissatisfactions. He does not murmur against Heaven, nor grumble against men.

Thus it is that the superior man is quiet and calm, waiting for the appointments of Heaven, while the mean man walks in dangerous paths, looking for lucky occurrences.

The Master said, "In archery we have something like the way of the superior man. When the archer misses the center of the target, he turns round and seeks for the cause of his failure in himself."

The way of the superior man may be compared to what takes place in traveling, when to go to a distance we must first traverse the space that is near, and in ascending a height, when we must begin from the lower ground.

The Master said, "How greatly filial was Shun! His virtue was that of a sage; his dignity was the throne; his riches were all within the four seas. He offered his sacrifices in his ancestral temple, and his descendants preserved the sacrifices to himself.

"Therefore having such great virtue, it could not but be that he should obtain the throne, that he should obtain those riches, that he should obtain his fame, that he should attain to his long life.

"Thus it is that Heaven, in the production of things, is sure to be bountiful to them, according to their qualities. Hence the tree that is flourishing, it nourishes, while that which is ready to fall, it overthrows.

"We may say therefore that he who is greatly virtuous will be sure to receive the appointment of Heaven."

The Master said, "It is only King Wan of whom it can be said that he had no cause for grief! His father was King Chi, and his son was King Wu. His father laid the foundations of his dignity, and his son transmitted it.

"King Wu continued the enterprise of King T'ai, King Chi, and King Wan. He once buckled on his armor, and got possession of the kingdom. He did not lose the distinguished personal reputation which he had throughout the kingdom. His dignity was the royal throne. His riches were the possession of all within the four seas. He offered his sacrifices in his ancestral temple, and his descendants maintained the sacrifices to himself.

"It was in his old age that King Wu received the appointment to the throne, and the duke of Chau completed the virtuous course of Wan and Wu. He carried up the title of king to T'ai and Chi, and sacrificed to all the former dukes above them with the royal ceremonies. And this rule he extended to the princes of the kingdom, the great officers, the scholars, and the common people. If the father were a great officer and the son a scholar, then the burial was that due to a great officer, and the sacrifice that due to a scholar. If the father were a scholar and the son a great officer, then the burial was that due to a scholar, and the sacrifice that due to a great officer. The one year's mourning was made to extend only to the great officers, but the three years' mourning extended to the Son of Heaven. In the mourning for a father or mother, he allowed no difference between the noble and the mean.

The Master said, "How far-extending was the filial piety of King Wu and the duke of Chau!

"Now filial piety is seen in the skillful carrying out of the wishes of our forefathers, and the skillful carrying forward of their undertakings.

"In spring and autumn, they repaired and beautified the temple halls of their fathers, set forth their ancestral vessels, displayed their various robes, and presented the offerings of the several seasons.

"By means of the ceremonies of the ancestral temple, they distinguished the royal kindred according to their order of descent. By ordering the parties present according to their rank, they distinguished the more noble and the less. By the arrangement of the services, they made a distinction of talents and worth. In the ceremony of general pledging, the inferiors presented the cup to their superiors, and thus something was given the lowest to do. At the concluding feast, places were given according to the hair, and thus was made the distinction of years.

"They occupied the places of their forefathers, practiced their ceremonies, and performed their music. They reverenced those whom they honored, and loved those whom they regarded with affection. Thus they served the dead as they would have served them alive; they served the departed as they would have served them had they been continued among them.

"By the ceremonies of the sacrifices to Heaven and Earth they served God, and by the ceremonies of the ancestral temple they sacrificed to their ancestors. He who understands the ceremonies of the sacrifices to Heaven and Earth, and the meaning of the several sacrifices to ancestors, would find the government of a kingdom as easy as to look into his palm!"

The Duke Ai asked about government.

The Master said, "The government of Wan and Wu is displayed in the records,—the tablets of wood and bamboo. Let there be the men and the government will flourish; but without the men, their government decays and ceases.

"With the right men the growth of government is rapid, just as vegetation is rapid in the earth; and, moreover, their government might be called an easily-growing rush.

"Therefore the administration of government lies in getting propermen. Such men are to be got by means of the ruler's own character. That character is to be cultivated by his treading in the ways of duty. And the treading those ways of duty is to be cultivated by the cherishing of benevolence.

"Benevolence is the characteristic element of humanity, and the great exercise of it is in loving relatives. Righteousness is the accordance of actions with what is right, and the great exercise of it is in honoring the worthy. The decreasing measures of the love due to relatives, and the steps in the honor due to the worthy, are produced by the principle of propriety.

"When those in inferior situations do not possess the confidence of their superiors, they cannot retain the government of the people.

"Hence the sovereign may not neglect the cultivation of his own character. Wishing to cultivate his character, he may not neglect to serve his parents. In order to serve his parents, he may not neglect to acquire knowledge of men. In order to know men, he may not dispense with a knowledge of Heaven.

"The duties of universal obligation are five and the virtues wherewith they are practiced are three. The duties are those between sovereign and minister, between father and son, between husband and wife, between elder brother and younger, and those belonging to the intercourse of friends. Those five are the duties of universal obligation. Knowledge, magnanimity, and energy, these three, are the virtues universally binding. And the means by which they carry the duties into practice is singleness.

"Some are born with the knowledge of those duties; some know them by study; and some acquire the knowledge after a painful feeling of their ignorance. But the knowledge being possessed, it comes to the same thing. Some practice them with a natural ease; some from a desire for their advantages; and some by strenuous effort. But the achievement being made, it comes to the same thing."

The Master said, "To be fond of learning is to be near to knowledge. To practice with vigor is to be near to magnanimity. To possess the feeling of shame is to be near to energy.

"He who knows these three things knows how to cultivate his own character. Knowing how to cultivate his own character, he knows how to govern other men. Knowing how to govern other men, he knows how to govern the kingdom with all its states and families.

"All who have the government of the kingdom with its states and families have nine standard rules to follow;—*viz.*, the cultivation of their own characters; the honoring of men of virtue and talents; affection towards their relatives; respect towards the great ministers; kind and considerate treatment of the whole body of officers; dealing with the mass of the people as children; encouraging the resort of all classes of artisans; indulgent treatment of men from a distance; and the kindly cherishing of the princes of the states.

"By the ruler's cultivation of his own character, the duties of universal obligation are set forth. By honoring men of virtue and talents, he is preserved from errors of judgment. By showing affection to his relatives, there is no grumbling nor resentment among his uncles and brethren. By respecting the great ministers, he is kept from errors in the practice of government. By kind and considerate treatment of the whole body of officers, they are led to make the most grateful return for his courtesies. By dealing with the mass of the people as his children, they are led to exhort one another to what is good. By encouraging the resort of an classes of artisans, his resources for expenditure are rendered ample. By indulgent treatment of men from a distance, they are brought to resort to him from all quarters. And by kindly cherishing the princes of the states, the whole kingdom is brought to revere him.

"Self-adjustment and purification, with careful regulation of his dress, and the not making a movement contrary to the rules of propriety this is the way for a ruler to cultivate his person. Discarding slanderers, and keeping himself from the seductions of beauty; making light of riches, and giving honor to virtue—this is the way for him to encourage men of worth and talents. Giving them places of honor and large emolument and sharing with them in their likes and dislikes—this is the way for him to encourage his relatives to love him. Giving them numerous officers to discharge their orders and commissions:—this is the way for him to encourage the great ministers. According to them a generous confidence, and making their emoluments large:—this is the way to encourage the body of officers. Employing them only at the proper times, and making the mposts light:—this is the way to encourage the people. By daily examinations and monthly trials, and by making their rations in accordance with their labors:—this is the way to encourage the classes of artisans. To escort them on their departure and meet them on their coming; to commend the good among them, and show compassion to the incompetent:—this is the way to treat indulgently men from a distance. To restore families whose line of succession has been broken, and to revive states that have been extinguished; to reduce to order states that are in confusion, and support those which are in peril; to have fixed times for their own reception at court, and the reception of their envoys; to send them away after liberal treatment, and welcome their coming with small contributions:—this is the way to cherish the princes of the states.

"All who have the government of the kingdom with its states and families have the above nine standard rules. And the means by which they are carried into practice is singleness.

"In all things success depends on previous preparation, and without such previous preparation there is sure to be failure. If what is to be spoken be previously determined, there will be no stumbling. If affairs be previously determined, there will be no difficulty with them. If one's actions have been previously determined, there will be no sorrow in connection with them. If principles of conduct have been previously determined, the practice of them will be inexhaustible.

"When those in inferior situations do not obtain the confidence of the sovereign, they cannot succeed in governing the people. There is away to obtain the confidence of the sovereign;—if one is not trusted by his friends, he will not get the confidence of his sovereign. There is a way to being trusted by one's friends;—if one is not obedient to his parents, he will not be true to friends. There is a way to being obedient to one's parents;—if one, on turning his thoughts in upon himself, finds a want of sincerity, he will not be obedient to his parents. There is a way to the attainment of sincerity in one's self;—if a man do not understand what is good, he will not attain sincerity in himself.

"Sincerity is the way of Heaven. The attainment of sincerity is the way of men. He who possesses sincerity is he who, without an effort, hits what is right, and apprehends, without the exercise of thought;—he is the sage who naturally and easily embodies the right way. He who attains to sincerity is he who chooses what is good, and firmly holds it fast.

"To this attainment there are requisite the extensive study of what is good, accurate inquiry about it, careful reflection on it, the clear discrimination of it, and the earnest practice of it.

"The superior man, while there is anything he has not studied, or while in what he has studied there is anything he cannot understand, Will not intermit his labor. While there is anything he has not inquired about, or anything in what he has inquired about which he does not know, he will not intermit his labor. While there is anything which he has not reflected on, or anything in what he has reflected on which he does not apprehend, he will not intermit his labor. While there is anything which he has not discriminated or his discrimination is not clear, he will not intermit his labor. If there be anything which he has not practiced, or his practice fails in earnestness, he will not intermit his labor. If another man succeed by one effort, he will use a hundred efforts. If another man succeed by ten efforts, he will use a thousand.

"Let a man proceed in this way, and, though dull, he will surely become intelligent; though weak, he will surely become strong."

When we have intelligence resulting from sincerity, this condition is to be ascribed to nature; when we have sincerity resulting from intelligence, this condition is to be ascribed to instruction. But given the sincerity, and there shall be the intelligence; given the intelligence, and there shall be the sincerity.

It is only he who is possessed of the most complete sincerity that can exist under heaven, who can give its fun development to his nature. Able to give its full development to his own nature, he can do the same to the nature of other men. Able to give its full development to the nature of other men, he can give their full development to the natures of animals and things. Able to give their full development to the natures of creatures and things, he can assist the transforming and nourishing powers of Heaven and Earth. Able to assist the transforming and nourishing powers of Heaven and Earth, he may with Heaven and Earth form a ternion.

Next to the above is he who cultivates to the utmost the shoots of goodness in him. From those he can attain to the possession of sincerity. This sincerity becomes apparent. From being apparent, it becomes manifest. From being manifest, it becomes brilliant. Brilliant, it affects others. Affecting others, they are changed by it. Changed by it, they are transformed. It is only he who is possessed of the most complete sincerity that can exist under heaven, who can transform.

It is characteristic of the most entire sincerity to be able to foreknow. When a nation or family is about to flourish, there are sure to be happy omens; and when it is about to perish, there are sure to be unlucky omens. Such events are seen in the milfoil and tortoise, and affect the movements of the four limbs. When calamity or happiness is about to come, the good shall certainly be foreknown by him, and the evil also. Therefore the individual possessed of the most complete sincerity is like a spirit.

Sincerity is that whereby self-completion is effected, and its way is that by which man must direct himself.

Sincerity is the end and beginning of things; without sincerity there would be nothing. On this account, the superior man regards the attainment of sincerity as the most excellent thing.

The possessor of sincerity does not merely accomplish the self-completion of himself. With this quality he completes other men and things also. The completing himself shows his perfect virtue. The completing other men and things shows his knowledge. But these are virtues belonging to the nature, and this is the way by which a union is effected of the external and internal. Therefore, whenever he—the entirely sincere man—employs them,—that is, these virtues, their action will be right.

Hence to entire sincerity there belongs ceaselessness.

Not ceasing, it continues long. Continuing long, it evidences itself.

Evidencing itself, it reaches far. Reaching far, it becomes large and substantial. Large and substantial, it becomes high and brilliant.

Large and substantial;—this is how it contains all things. High and brilliant;—this is how it overspreads all things. Reaching far and continuing long;—this is how it perfects all things.

So large and substantial, the individual possessing it is the co-equal of Earth. So high and brilliant, it makes him the co-equal of Heaven. So far-reaching and long-continuing, it makes him infinite.

Such being its nature, without any display, it becomes manifested; without any movement, it produces changes; and without any effort, it accomplishes its ends.

The way of Heaven and Earth may be completely declared in one sentence.—They are without any doubleness, and so they produce things in a manner that is unfathomable.

The way of Heaven and Earth is large and substantial, high and brilliant, far-reaching and long-enduring.

The Heaven now before us is only this bright shining spot; but when viewed in its inexhaustible extent, the sun, moon, stars, and constellations of the zodiac, are suspended in it, and all things are overspread by it. The earth before us is but a handful of soil; but when regarded in its breadth and thickness, it sustains mountains like the Hwa and the Yo, without feeling their weight, and contains the rivers and seas, without their leaking away. The mountain now before us appears only a stone; but when contemplated in all the vastness of its size, we see how the grass and trees are produced on it, and birds and beasts dwell on it, and precious things which men treasure up are found on it. The water now before us appears but a ladleful; yet extending our view to its unfathomable depths, the largest tortoises, iguanas, iguanodons, dragons, fishes, and turtles, are produced in it, articles of value and sources of wealth abound in it.

How great is the path proper to the Sage!

Like overflowing water, it sends forth and nourishes all things, and rises up to the height of heaven.

All-complete is its greatness! It embraces the three hundred rules of ceremony, and the three thousand rules of demeanor.

It waits for the proper man, and then it is trodden.

Hence it is said, "Only by perfect virtue can the perfect path, in all its courses, be made a fact."

Therefore, the superior man honors his virtuous nature, and maintains constant inquiry and study, seeking to carry it out to its breadth and greatness, so as to omit none of the more exquisite and minute points which it embraces, and to raise it to its greatest height and brilliancy, so as to pursue the course of the Mean. Hecherishes his old knowledge, and is continually acquiring new. Heexerts an honest, generous earnestness, in the esteem and practice of all propriety.

Thus, when occupying a high situation he is not proud, and in a low situation he is not insubordinate. When the kingdom is well governed, he is sure by his words to rise; and when it is illgoverned, he is sure by his silence to command forbearance to himself. Is not this what we find in the Book of Poetry,—"Intelligent is he and prudent, and so preserves his person?"

The Master said, Let a man who is ignorant be fond of using his own judgment; let a man without rank be fond of assuming a directing power to himself; let a man who is living in the present age go back to the ways of antiquity;—on the persons of all who act thus calamities will be sure to come.

To no one but the Son of Heaven does it belong to order ceremonies, to fix the measures, and to determine the written characters.

Now over the kingdom, carriages have all wheels of the same size; all writing is with the same characters; and for conduct there are the same rules.

One may occupy the throne, but if he have not the proper virtue, he may not dare to make ceremonies or music. One may have the virtue, but if he do not occupy the throne, he may not presume to make ceremonies or music.

The Master said, "I may describe the ceremonies of the Hsia dynasty, but Chi cannot sufficiently attest my words. I have learned the ceremonies of the Yin dynasty, and in Sung they still continue. I have learned the ceremonies of Chau, which are now used, and I follow Chau."

He who attains to the sovereignty of the kingdom, having those three important things, shall be able to effect that there shall be few errors under his government.

However excellent may have been the regulations of those of former times, they cannot be attested. Not being attested, they cannot command credence, and not being credited, the people would not follow them. However excellent might be the regulations made by one in an inferior situation, he is not in a position to be honored. Unhonored, he cannot command credence, and not being credited, the people would not follow his rules.

Therefore the institutions of the Ruler are rooted in his own character and conduct, and sufficient attestation of them is given by the masses of the people. He examines them by comparison with those of the three kings, and finds them without mistake. He sets them up before Heaven and Earth, and finds nothing in them contrary to their mode of operation. He presents himself with them before spiritual beings, and no doubts about them arise. He is prepared to wait for the rise of a sage a hundred ages after, and has no misgivings.

His presenting himself with his institutions before spiritual beings, without any doubts arising about them, shows that he knows Heaven. His being prepared, without any misgivings, to wait for the rise of a sage a hundred ages after, shows that he knows men.

Such being the case, the movements of such a ruler, illustrating his institutions, constitute an example to the world for ages. His acts are for ages a law to the kingdom. His words are for ages a lesson to the kingdom. Those who are far from him look longingly for him; and those who are near him are never wearied with him.

All things are nourished together without their injuring one another. The courses of the seasons, and of the sun and moon, are pursued without any collision among them. The smaller energies are like river currents; the greater energies are seen in mighty transformations. It is this which makes heaven and earth so great.

It is only he, possessed of all sagely qualities that can exist under heaven, who shows himself quick in apprehension, clear in discernment, of far-reaching intelligence, and all-embracing knowledge, fitted to exercise rule; magnanimous, generous, benign, and mild, fitted to exercise forbearance; impulsive, energetic, firm, and enduring, fitted to maintain a firm hold; self-adjusted, grave, never swerving from the Mean, and correct, fitted to command reverence; accomplished, distinctive, concentrative, and searching, fitted to exercise discrimination.

All-embracing is he and vast, deep and active as a fountain, sending forth in their due season his virtues.

All-embracing and vast, he is like Heaven. Deep and active as a fountain, he is like the abyss. He is seen, and the people all reverence him; he speaks, and the people all believe him; he acts, and the people all are pleased with him.

Therefore his fame overspreads the Middle Kingdom, and extends to all barbarous tribes. Wherever ships and carriages reach; wherever the strength of man penetrates; wherever the heavens overshadow and the earth sustains; wherever the sun and moon shine; wherever frosts and dews fall:—all who have blood and breath unfeignedly honor and love him. Hence it is said,—"He is the equal of Heaven."

It is only the individual possessed of the most entire sincerity that can exist under Heaven, who can adjust the great invariable relations of mankind, establish the great fundamental virtues of humanity, and know the transforming and nurturing operations of Heaven and Earth;—shall this individual have any being or anything beyond himself on which he depends?

Call him man in his ideal, how earnest is he! Call him an abyss, how deep is he! Call him Heaven, how vast is he!

Who can know him, but he who is indeed quick in apprehension, clear in discernment, of far-reaching intelligence, and all-embracing knowledge, possessing all Heavenly virtue?

DISCUSSION QUESTIONS

1. Compare the view here from Confucius with the ideas of Jainism and Buddhism. What are some of the similarities and differences? Explain.

2. How does Confucius' view differ from the Hindu view in the *Bhagavad Gita*? Explain.

3. Explain the nature of "harmony" and "equilibrium," as discussed at the beginning of "The Doctrine of the Mean."

4. Explain what the five duties of universal obligation are and the three virtues from the middle of the selection.

5. Why is sincerity such an important concept? Explain.

Euthyphro

By Plato
Translated by Benjamin Jowett

The Euthyphro *is one of Plato's early dialogues. Although the style of Socrates' manner of speaking is probably close to the real Socrates, there is no reason to think that the events portrayed here actually happened. The setting has Socrates on the way to his trial. Socrates encounters Euthyphro who asks Socrates what he's doing there. Socrates tells him that he is being prosecuted. Euthyphro assures Socrates that Socrates will be acquitted. This is an inside joke, as Plato, of course, knows that Socrates is not acquitted. This is a foreshadowing that Euthyphro knows not of what he speaks. Then we discover that Euthyphro is there to bring suit. It turns out that Euthyphro is prosecuting his father. Socrates says that Euthyphro must be an expert in piety (goodness), if he is going to prosecute his father. So, Socrates asks Euthyphro for instruction in the ways of piety. Like other early dialogues, the person Socrates is talking to attempts definitions, and Socrates points out deficiencies; the cycle continues until his interlocutor gives up and leaves. The reason his interlocutors have problems defining terms in the early dialogues is because they are trying to define abstract nouns (e.g., redness, five, love). In addition to the difficulties in defining the term, there is an interesting discussion of an ethical theory that later comes to be called the Divine Command theory. Euthyphro's third definition that the pious is what all the gods love and the impious is what all the gods hate, leads to a question. The question is this: Is it beloved because it is pious, or pious because it is beloved? As Socrates points out, if it is the first choice, then what's pious is independent of the gods, and if it is the second choice, then piety is arbitrary, depending on whatever the gods decide (and they could change their minds). Euthyphro chooses the first option, and Socrates points out that he hasn't defined piety then, he has only noted a quality of piety. There is also the knowledge question. How do you find out what the gods love?*

PERSONS OF THE DIALOGUE: Socrates, Euthyphro.

SCENE: The Porch of the King Archon.

EUTHYPHRO: Why have you left the Lyceum, Socrates? and what are you doing in the Porch of the King Archon? Surely you cannot be concerned in a suit before the King, like myself?

SOCRATES: Not in a suit, Euthyphro; impeachment is the word which the Athenians use.

EUTHYPHRO: What! I suppose that some one has been prosecuting you, for I cannot believe that you are the prosecutor of another.

SOCRATES: Certainly not.

EUTHYPHRO: Then some one else has been prosecuting you?

SOCRATES: Yes.

EUTHYPHRO: And who is he?

SOCRATES: A young man who is little known, Euthyphro; and I hardly know him: his name is Meletus, and he is of the deme of Pitthis. Perhaps you may remember his appearance; he has a beak, and long straight hair, and a beard which is ill grown.

EUTHYPHRO: No, I do not remember him, Socrates. But what is the charge which he brings against you?

SOCRATES: What is the charge? Well, a very serious charge, which shows a good deal of character in the young man, and for which he is certainly not to be despised. He says he knows how the youth are corrupted and who are their corruptors. I fancy that he must be a wise man, and seeing that I am the reverse of a wise man, he has found me out, and is going to accuse me of corrupting his young friends. And of this our mother the state is to be the judge. Of all our political men he is the only one who seems to me to begin in the right way, with the cultivation of virtue in youth; like a good husbandman, he makes the young shoots his first care, and clears away us who are the destroyers of them. This is only the first step; he will afterwards attend to the elder branches; and if he goes on as he has begun, he will be a very great public benefactor.

EUTHYPHRO: I hope that he may; but I rather fear, Socrates, that the opposite will turn out to be the truth. My opinion is that in attacking you he is simply aiming a blow at the foundation of the state. But in what way does he say that you corrupt the young?

SOCRATES: He brings a wonderful accusation against me, which at first hearing excites surprise: he says that I am a poet or maker of gods, and that I invent new gods and deny the existence of old ones; this is the ground of his indictment.

EUTHYPHRO: I understand, Socrates; he means to attack you about the familiar sign which occasionally, as you say, comes to you. He thinks that you are a neologian, and he is going to have you up before the court for this. He knows that such a charge is readily received by the world, as I myself know too well; for when I speak in the assembly about divine things, and foretell the future to them, they laugh at me and think me a madman. Yet every word that I say is true. But they are jealous of us all; and we must be brave and go at them.

SOCRATES: Their laughter, friend Euthyphro, is not a matter of much consequence. For a man may be thought wise; but the Athenians, I suspect, do not much trouble themselves about him until he begins to impart his wisdom to others, and then for some reason or other, perhaps, as you say, from jealousy, they are angry.

EUTHYPHRO: I am never likely to try their temper in this way.

SOCRATES: I dare say not, for you are reserved in your behaviour, and seldom impart your wisdom. But I have a benevolent habit of pouring out myself to everybody, and would even pay for a listener, and I am afraid that the Athenians may think me too talkative. Now if, as I was saying, they would only laugh at me, as you say that they laugh at you, the time might pass gaily enough in the court; but perhaps they may be in earnest, and then what the end will be you soothsayers only can predict.

EUTHYPHRO: I dare say that the affair will end in nothing, Socrates, and that you will win your cause; and I think that I shall win my own.

SOCRATES: And what is your suit, Euthyphro? are you the pursuer or the defendant?

EUTHYPHRO: I am the pursuer.

SOCRATES: Of whom?

EUTHYPHRO: You will think me mad when I tell you.

SOCRATES: Why, has the fugitive wings?

EUTHYPHRO: Nay, he is not very volatile at his time of life.

SOCRATES: Who is he?

EUTHYPHRO: My father.

SOCRATES: Your father! my good man?

EUTHYPHRO: Yes.

SOCRATES: And of what is he accused?

EUTHYPHRO: Of murder, Socrates.

SOCRATES: By the powers, Euthyphro! how little does the common herd know of the nature of right and truth. A man must be an extraordinary man, and have made great strides in wisdom, before he could have seen his way to bring such an action.

EUTHYPHRO: Indeed, Socrates, he must.

SOCRATES: I suppose that the man whom your father murdered was one of your relatives—clearly he was; for if he had been a stranger you would never have thought of prosecuting him.

EUTHYPHRO: I am amused, Socrates, at your making a distinction between one who is a relation and one who is not a relation; for surely the pollution is the same in either case, if you knowingly associate with the murderer when you ought to clear yourself and him by proceeding against him. The real question is whether the murdered man has been justly slain. If justly, then your duty is to let the matter alone; but if unjustly, then even if the murderer lives under the same roof with you and eats at the same table, proceed against him. Now the man who is dead was a poor dependant of mine who worked for us as a field labourer on our farm in Naxos, and one day in a fit of drunken passion he got into a quarrel with one of our domestic servants and slew him. My father bound him hand and foot and threw him into a ditch, and then sent to Athens to ask of a diviner what he should do with him. Meanwhile he never attended to him and took no care about him, for he regarded him as a murderer; and thought that no great harm would be done even if he did die. Now this was just what happened. For such was the effect of cold and hunger and chains upon him, that before the messenger returned from the diviner, he was dead. And my father and family are angry with me for taking the part of the murderer and prosecuting my father. They say that he did not kill him, and that if he did, the dead man was but a murderer, and

I ought not to take any notice, for that a son is impious who prosecutes a father. Which shows, Socrates, how little they know what the gods think about piety and impiety.

SOCRATES: Good heavens, Euthyphro! and is your knowledge of religion and of things pious and impious so very exact, that, supposing the circumstances to be as you state them, you are not afraid lest you too may be doing an impious thing in bringing an action against your father?

EUTHYPHRO: The best of Euthyphro, and that which distinguishes him, Socrates, from other men, is his exact knowledge of all such matters. What should I be good for without it?

SOCRATES: Rare friend! I think that I cannot do better than be your disciple. Then before the trial with Meletus comes on I shall challenge him, and say that I have always had a great interest in religious questions, and now, as he charges me with rash imaginations and innovations in religion, I have become your disciple. You, Meletus, as I shall say to him, acknowledge Euthyphro to be a great theologian, and sound in his opinions; and if you approve of him you ought to approve of me, and not have me into court; but if you disapprove, you should begin by indicting him who is my teacher, and who will be the ruin, not of the young, but of the old; that is to say, of myself whom he instructs, and of his old father whom he admonishes and chastises. And if Meletus refuses to listen to me, but will go on, and will not shift the indictment from me to you, I cannot do better than repeat this challenge in the court.

EUTHYPHRO: Yes, indeed, Socrates; and if he attempts to indict me I am mistaken if I do not find a flaw in him; the court shall have a great deal more to say to him than to me.

SOCRATES: And I, my dear friend, knowing this, am desirous of becoming your disciple. For I observe that no one appears to notice you—not even this Meletus; but his sharp eyes have found me out at once, and he has indicted me for impiety. And therefore, I adjure you to tell me the nature of piety and impiety, which you said that you knew so well, and of murder, and of other offences against the gods. What are they? Is not piety in every action always the same? and impiety, again—is it not always the opposite of piety, and also the same with itself, having, as impiety, one notion which includes whatever is impious?

EUTHYPHRO: To be sure, Socrates.

SOCRATES: And what is piety, and what is impiety?

EUTHYPHRO: Piety is doing as I am doing; that is to say, prosecuting any one who is guilty of murder, sacrilege, or of any similar crime—whether he be your father or mother, or whoever he may be—that makes no difference; and not to prosecute them is impiety. And please to consider, Socrates, what a notable proof I will give you of the truth of my words, a proof which I have already given to others:—of the principle, I mean, that the impious, whoever he may be, ought not to go unpunished. For do not men regard Zeus as the best and most righteous of the gods?—and yet they admit that he bound his father (Cronos) because he wickedly devoured his sons, and that he too had punished his own father (Uranus) for a similar reason, in a nameless manner. And yet when I proceed against my father, they are angry with me. So inconsistent are they in their way of talking when the gods are concerned, and when I am concerned.

SOCRATES: May not this be the reason, Euthyphro, why I am charged with impiety—that I cannot away with these stories about the gods? And therefore I suppose that people think me wrong. But, as you who are well informed about them approve of them, I cannot do better than assent to your superior wisdom. What else can I say, confessing as I do, that I know nothing about them? Tell me, for the love of Zeus, whether you really believe that they are true.

EUTHYPHRO: Yes, Socrates; and things more wonderful still, of which the world is in ignorance.

SOCRATES: And do you really believe that the gods fought with one another, and had dire quarrels, battles, and the like, as the poets say, and as you may see represented in the works of great artists? The temples are full of them; and notably the robe of Athene, which is carried up to the Acropolis at the great Panathenaea, is embroidered with them. Are all these tales of the gods true, Euthyphro?

EUTHYPHRO: Yes, Socrates; and, as I was saying, I can tell you, if you would like to hear them, many other things about the gods which would quite amaze you.

SOCRATES: I dare say; and you shall tell me them at some other time when I have leisure. But just at present I would rather hear from you a more precise answer, which you have not as yet given, my friend, to the question, What is 'piety'? When asked, you only replied, Doing as you do, charging your father with murder.

EUTHYPHRO: And what I said was true, Socrates.

SOCRATES: No doubt, Euthyphro; but you would admit that there are many other pious acts?

EUTHYPHRO: There are.

SOCRATES: Remember that I did not ask you to give me two or three examples of piety, but to explain the general idea which makes all pious things to be pious. Do you not recollect that there was one idea which made the impious impious, and the pious pious?

EUTHYPHRO: I remember.

SOCRATES: Tell me what is the nature of this idea, and then I shall have a standard to which I may look, and by which I may measure actions, whether yours or those of any one else, and then I shall be able to say that such and such an action is pious, such another impious.

EUTHYPHRO: I will tell you, if you like.

SOCRATES: I should very much like.

EUTHYPHRO: Piety, then, is that which is dear to the gods, and impiety is that which is not dear to them.

SOCRATES: Very good, Euthyphro; you have now given me the sort of answer which I wanted. But whether what you say is true or not I cannot as yet tell, although I make no doubt that you will prove the truth of your words.

EUTHYPHRO: Of course.

SOCRATES: Come, then, and let us examine what we are saying. That thing or person which is dear to the gods is pious, and that thing or person which is hateful to the gods is impious, these two being the extreme opposites of one another. Was not that said?

EUTHYPHRO: It was.

SOCRATES: And well said?

EUTHYPHRO: Yes, Socrates, I thought so; it was certainly said.

SOCRATES: And further, Euthyphro, the gods were admitted to have enmities and hatreds and differences?

EUTHYPHRO: Yes, that was also said.

SOCRATES: And what sort of difference creates enmity and anger? Suppose for example that you and I, my good friend, differ about a number; do differences of this sort make us enemies and set us at variance with one another? Do we not go at once to arithmetic, and put an end to them by a sum?

EUTHYPHRO: True.

SOCRATES: Or suppose that we differ about magnitudes, do we not quickly end the differences by measuring?

EUTHYPHRO: Very true.

SOCRATES: And we end a controversy about heavy and light by resorting to a weighing machine?

EUTHYPHRO: To be sure.

SOCRATES: But what differences are there which cannot be thus decided, and which therefore make us angry and set us at enmity with one another? I dare say the answer does not occur to you at the moment, and therefore I will suggest that these enmities arise when the matters of difference are the just and unjust, good and evil, honourable and dishonourable. Are not these the points about which men differ, and about which when we are unable satisfactorily to decide our differences, you and I and all of us quarrel, when we do quarrel? (Compare Alcib.)

EUTHYPHRO: Yes, Socrates, the nature of the differences about which we quarrel is such as you describe.

SOCRATES: And the quarrels of the gods, noble Euthyphro, when they occur, are of a like nature?

EUTHYPHRO: Certainly they are.

SOCRATES: They have differences of opinion, as you say, about good and evil, just and unjust, honourable and dishonourable: there would have been no quarrels among them, if there had been no such differences—would there now?

EUTHYPHRO: You are quite right.

SOCRATES: Does not every man love that which he deems noble and just and good, and hate the opposite of them?

EUTHYPHRO: Very true.

SOCRATES: But, as you say, people regard the same things, some as just and others as unjust,—about these they dispute; and so there arise wars and fightings among them.

EUTHYPHRO: Very true.

SOCRATES: Then the same things are hated by the gods and loved by the gods, and are both hateful and dear to them?

EUTHYPHRO: True.

SOCRATES: And upon this view the same things, Euthyphro, will be pious and also impious?

EUTHYPHRO: So I should suppose.

SOCRATES: Then, my friend, I remark with surprise that you have not answered the question which I asked. For I certainly did not ask you to tell me what action is both pious and impious: but now it would seem that what is loved by the gods is also hated by them. And therefore, Euthyphro, in thus chastising your father you may very likely be doing what is agreeable to Zeus but disagreeable to Cronos or Uranus, and what is acceptable to Hephaestus but unacceptable to Here, and there may be other gods who have similar differences of opinion.

EUTHYPHRO: But I believe, Socrates, that all the gods would be agreed as to the propriety of punishing a murderer: there would be no difference of opinion about that.

SOCRATES: Well, but speaking of men, Euthyphro, did you ever hear any one arguing that a murderer or any sort of evil-doer ought to be let off?

EUTHYPHRO: I should rather say that these are the questions which they are always arguing, especially in courts of law: they commit all sorts of crimes, and there is nothing which they will not do or say in their own defence.

SOCRATES: But do they admit their guilt, Euthyphro, and yet say that they ought not to be punished?

EUTHYPHRO: No; they do not.

SOCRATES: Then there are some things which they do not venture to say and do: for they do not venture to argue that the guilty are to be unpunished, but they deny their guilt, do they not?

EUTHYPHRO: Yes.

SOCRATES: Then they do not argue that the evil-doer should not be punished, but they argue about the fact of who the evil-doer is, and what he did and when?

EUTHYPHRO: True.

SOCRATES: And the gods are in the same case, if as you assert they quarrel about just and unjust, and some of them say while others deny that injustice is done among them. For surely neither God nor man will ever venture to say that the doer of injustice is not to be punished?

EUTHYPHRO: That is true, Socrates, in the main.

SOCRATES: But they join issue about the particulars—gods and men alike; and, if they dispute at all, they dispute about some act which is called in question, and which by some is affirmed to be just, by others to be unjust. Is not that true?

EUTHYPHRO: Quite true.

SOCRATES: Well then, my dear friend Euthyphro, do tell me, for my better instruction and information, what proof have you that in the opinion of all the gods a servant who is guilty of murder, and is put in chains by the master of the dead man, and dies because he is put in chains before he who bound him can learn from the interpreters of the gods what he ought to do with him, dies unjustly; and that on behalf of such an one a son ought to proceed against his father and accuse him of murder. How would you show that all the gods absolutely agree in approving of his act? Prove to me that they do, and I will applaud your wisdom as long as I live.

EUTHYPHRO: It will be a difficult task; but I could make the matter very clear indeed to you.

SOCRATES: I understand; you mean to say that I am not so quick of apprehension as the judges: for to them you will be sure to prove that the act is unjust, and hateful to the gods.

EUTHYPHRO: Yes indeed, Socrates; at least if they will listen to me.

SOCRATES: But they will be sure to listen if they find that you are a good speaker. There was a notion that came into my mind while you were speaking; I said to myself: 'Well, and what if Euthyphro does prove to me that all the gods regarded the death of the serf as unjust, how do I know anything more of the nature of piety and impiety? for granting that this action may be hateful to the gods, still piety and impiety are not adequately defined by these distinctions, for that which is hateful to the gods has been shown to be also pleasing and dear to them.' And therefore, Euthyphro, I do not ask you to prove this; I will suppose, if you like, that all the gods condemn and abominate such an action. But I will amend the definition so far as to say that what all the gods hate is impious, and what they love pious or holy; and what some of them love and others hate is both or neither. Shall this be our definition of piety and impiety?

EUTHYPHRO: Why not, Socrates?

SOCRATES: Why not! certainly, as far as I am concerned, Euthyphro, there is no reason why not. But whether this admission will greatly assist you in the task of instructing me as you promised, is a matter for you to consider.

EUTHYPHRO: Yes, I should say that what all the gods love is pious and holy, and the opposite which they all hate, impious.

SOCRATES: Ought we to enquire into the truth of this, Euthyphro, or simply to accept the mere statement on our own authority and that of others? What do you say?

EUTHYPHRO: We should enquire; and I believe that the statement will stand the test of enquiry.

SOCRATES: We shall know better, my good friend, in a little while. The point which I should first wish to understand is whether the pious or holy is beloved by the gods because it is holy, or holy because it is beloved of the gods.

EUTHYPHRO: I do not understand your meaning, Socrates.

SOCRATES: I will endeavour to explain: we, speak of carrying and we speak of being carried, of leading and being led, seeing and being seen. You know that in all such cases there is a difference, and you know also in what the difference lies?

EUTHYPHRO: I think that I understand.

SOCRATES: And is not that which is beloved distinct from that which loves?

EUTHYPHRO: Certainly.

SOCRATES: Well; and now tell me, is that which is carried in this state of carrying because it is carried, or for some other reason?

EUTHYPHRO: No; that is the reason.

SOCRATES: And the same is true of what is led and of what is seen?

EUTHYPHRO: True.

SOCRATES: And a thing is not seen because it is visible, but conversely, visible because it is seen; nor is a thing led because it is in the state of being led, or carried because it is in the state of being carried, but the converse of this. And now I think, Euthyphro, that my meaning will be intelligible; and my meaning is, that any state of action or passion implies previous action or passion. It does not become because it is becoming, but it is in a state of becoming because it becomes; neither does it suffer because it is in a state of suffering, but it is in a state of suffering because it suffers. Do you not agree?

EUTHYPHRO: Yes.

SOCRATES: Is not that which is loved in some state either of becoming or suffering?

EUTHYPHRO: Yes.

SOCRATES: And the same holds as in the previous instances; the state of being loved follows the act of being loved, and not the act the state.

EUTHYPHRO: Certainly.

SOCRATES: And what do you say of piety, Euthyphro: is not piety, according to your definition, loved by all the gods?

EUTHYPHRO: Yes.

SOCRATES: Because it is pious or holy, or for some other reason?

EUTHYPHRO: No, that is the reason.

SOCRATES: It is loved because it is holy, not holy because it is loved?

EUTHYPHRO: Yes.

SOCRATES: And that which is dear to the gods is loved by them, and is in a state to be loved of them because it is loved of them?

EUTHYPHRO: Certainly.

SOCRATES: Then that which is dear to the gods, Euthyphro, is not holy, nor is that which is holy loved of God, as you affirm; but they are two different things.

EUTHYPHRO: How do you mean, Socrates?

SOCRATES: I mean to say that the holy has been acknowledged by us to be loved of God because it is holy, not to be holy because it is loved.

EUTHYPHRO: Yes.

SOCRATES: But that which is dear to the gods is dear to them because it is loved by them, not loved by them because it is dear to them.

EUTHYPHRO: True.

SOCRATES: But, friend Euthyphro, if that which is holy is the same with that which is dear to God, and is loved because it is holy, then that which is dear to God would have been loved as being dear to God; but if that which is dear to God is dear to him because loved by him, then that which is holy would have been holy because loved by him. But now you see that the reverse is the case, and that they are quite different from one another. For one (*theophiles*) is of a kind to be loved cause it is loved, and the other (*osion*) is loved because it is of a kind to be loved. Thus you appear to me, Euthyphro, when I ask you what is the essence of holiness, to offer an attribute only, and not the essence—the attribute of being loved by all the gods. But you still refuse to explain to me the nature of holiness. And therefore, if you please, I will ask you not to hide your treasure, but to tell me once more what holiness or piety really is, whether dear to the gods or not (for that is a matter about which we will not quarrel); and what is impiety?

EUTHYPHRO: I really do not know, Socrates, how to express what I mean. For somehow or other our arguments, on whatever ground we rest them, seem to turn round and walk away from us.

SOCRATES: Your words, Euthyphro, are like the handiwork of my ancestor Daedalus; and if I were the sayer or propounder of them, you might say that my arguments walk away and will not remain fixed where they are placed because I am a descendant of his. But now, since these notions are your own, you must find some other gibe, for they certainly, as you yourself allow, show an inclination to be on the move.

EUTHYPHRO: Nay, Socrates, I shall still say that you are the Daedalus who sets arguments in motion; not I, certainly, but you make them move or go round, for they would never have stirred, as far as I am concerned.

SOCRATES: Then I must be a greater than Daedalus: for whereas he only made his own inventions to move, I move those of other people as well. And the beauty of it is, that I would rather not. For I would give the wisdom of Daedalus, and the wealth of Tantalus, to be able to detain them and keep them fixed. But enough of this. As I perceive that you are lazy, I will myself endeavour to show you how you might instruct me in the nature of piety; and I hope that you will not grudge your labour. Tell me, then—Is not that which is pious necessarily just?

EUTHYPHRO: Yes.

SOCRATES: And is, then, all which is just pious? or, is that which is pious all just, but that which is just, only in part and not all, pious?

EUTHYPHRO: I do not understand you, Socrates.

SOCRATES: And yet I know that you are as much wiser than I am, as you are younger. But, as I was saying, revered friend, the abundance of your wisdom makes you lazy. Please to exert yourself, for there is no real difficulty in understanding me. What I mean I may explain by an illustration of what I do not mean. The poet (Stasinus) sings—

'Of Zeus, the author and creator of all these things, You will not tell: for where there is fear there is also reverence.'

Now I disagree with this poet. Shall I tell you in what respect?

EUTHYPHRO: By all means.

SOCRATES: I should not say that where there is fear there is also reverence; for I am sure that many persons fear poverty and disease, and the like evils, but I do not perceive that they reverence the objects of their fear.

EUTHYPHRO: Very true.

SOCRATES: But where reverence is, there is fear; for he who has a feeling of reverence and shame about the commission of any action, fears and is afraid of an ill reputation.

EUTHYPHRO: No doubt.

SOCRATES: Then we are wrong in saying that where there is fear there is also reverence; and we should say, where there is reverence there is also fear. But there is not always reverence where there is fear; for fear is a more extended notion, and reverence is a part of fear, just as the odd is a part of number, and number is a more extended notion than the odd. I suppose that you follow me now?

EUTHYPHRO: Quite well.

SOCRATES: That was the sort of question which I meant to raise when I asked whether the just is always the pious, or the pious always the just; and whether there may not be justice where there is not piety; for justice is the more extended notion of which piety is only a part. Do you dissent?

EUTHYPHRO: No, I think that you are quite right.

SOCRATES: Then, if piety is a part of justice, I suppose that we should enquire what part? If you had pursued the enquiry in the previous cases; for instance, if you had asked me what is an even number, and what part of number the even is, I should have had no difficulty in replying, a number which represents a figure having two equal sides. Do you not agree?

EUTHYPHRO: Yes, I quite agree.

SOCRATES: In like manner, I want you to tell me what part of justice is piety or holiness, that I may be able to tell Meletus not to do me injustice, or indict me for impiety, as I am now adequately instructed by you in the nature of piety or holiness, and their opposites.

EUTHYPHRO: Piety or holiness, Socrates, appears to me to be that part of justice which attends to the gods, as there is the other part of justice which attends to men.

SOCRATES: That is good, Euthyphro; yet still there is a little point about which I should like to have further information, What is the meaning of 'attention'? For attention can hardly be used in the same sense when applied to the gods as when applied to other things. For instance, horses are said to require attention, and not every person is able to attend to them, but only a person skilled in horsemanship. Is it not so?

EUTHYPHRO: Certainly.

SOCRATES: I should suppose that the art of horsemanship is the art of attending to horses?

EUTHYPHRO: Yes.

SOCRATES: Nor is every one qualified to attend to dogs, but only the huntsman?

EUTHYPHRO: True.

SOCRATES: And I should also conceive that the art of the huntsman is the art of attending to dogs?

EUTHYPHRO: Yes.

SOCRATES: As the art of the oxherd is the art of attending to oxen?

EUTHYPHRO: Very true.

SOCRATES: In like manner holiness or piety is the art of attending to the gods?—that would be your meaning, Euthyphro?

EUTHYPHRO: Yes.

SOCRATES: And is not attention always designed for the good or benefit of that to which the attention is given? As in the case of horses, you may observe that when attended to by the horseman's art they are benefited and improved, are they not?

EUTHYPHRO: True.

SOCRATES: As the dogs are benefited by the huntsman's art, and the oxen by the art of the oxherd, and all other things are tended or attended for their good and not for their hurt?

EUTHYPHRO: Certainly, not for their hurt.

SOCRATES: But for their good?

EUTHYPHRO: Of course.

SOCRATES: And does piety or holiness, which has been defined to be the art of attending to the gods, benefit or improve them? Would you say that when you do a holy act you make any of the gods better?

EUTHYPHRO: No, no; that was certainly not what I meant.

SOCRATES: And I, Euthyphro, never supposed that you did. I asked you the question about the nature of the attention, because I thought that you did not.

EUTHYPHRO: You do me justice, Socrates; that is not the sort of attention which I mean.

SOCRATES: Good: but I must still ask what is this attention to the gods which is called piety?

EUTHYPHRO: It is such, Socrates, as servants show to their masters.

SOCRATES: I understand—a sort of ministration to the gods.

EUTHYPHRO: Exactly.

SOCRATES: Medicine is also a sort of ministration or service, having in view the attainment of some object—would you not say of health?

EUTHYPHRO: I should.

SOCRATES: Again, there is an art which ministers to the ship-builder with a view to the attainment of some result?

EUTHYPHRO: Yes, Socrates, with a view to the building of a ship.

SOCRATES: As there is an art which ministers to the house-builder with a view to the building of a house?

EUTHYPHRO: Yes.

SOCRATES: And now tell me, my good friend, about the art which ministers to the gods: what work does that help to accomplish? For you must surely know if, as you say, you are of all men living the one who is best instructed in religion.

EUTHYPHRO: And I speak the truth, Socrates.

SOCRATES: Tell me then, oh tell me—what is that fair work which the gods do by the help of our ministrations?

EUTHYPHRO: Many and fair, Socrates, are the works which they do.

SOCRATES: Why, my friend, and so are those of a general. But the chief of them is easily told. Would you not say that victory in war is the chief of them?

EUTHYPHRO: Certainly.

SOCRATES: Many and fair, too, are the works of the husbandman, if I am not mistaken; but his chief work is the production of food from the earth?

EUTHYPHRO: Exactly.

SOCRATES: And of the many and fair things done by the gods, which is the chief or principal one?

EUTHYPHRO: I have told you already, Socrates, that to learn all these things accurately will be very tiresome. Let me simply say that piety or holiness is learning how to please the gods in word and deed, by prayers and sacrifices. Such piety is the salvation of families and states, just as the impious, which is unpleasing to the gods, is their ruin and destruction.

SOCRATES: I think that you could have answered in much fewer words the chief question which I asked, Euthyphro, if you had chosen. But I see plainly that you are not disposed to instruct me—clearly not: else why, when we reached the point, did you turn aside? Had you only answered me I should have truly learned of you by this time the nature of piety. Now, as the asker of a question is necessarily dependent on the answerer, whither he leads I must follow; and can only ask again, what is the pious, and what is piety? Do you mean that they are a sort of science of praying and sacrificing?

EUTHYPHRO: Yes, I do.

SOCRATES: And sacrificing is giving to the gods, and prayer is asking of the gods?

EUTHYPHRO: Yes, Socrates.

SOCRATES: Upon this view, then, piety is a science of asking and giving?

EUTHYPHRO: You understand me capitally, Socrates.

SOCRATES: Yes, my friend; the reason is that I am a votary of your science, and give my mind to it, and therefore nothing which you say will be thrown away upon me. Please then to tell me, what is the nature of this service to the gods? Do you mean that we prefer requests and give gifts to them?

EUTHYPHRO: Yes, I do.

SOCRATES: Is not the right way of asking to ask of them what we want?

EUTHYPHRO: Certainly.

SOCRATES: And the right way of giving is to give to them in return what they want of us. There would be no meaning in an art which gives to any one that which he does not want.

EUTHYPHRO: Very true, Socrates.

SOCRATES: Then piety, Euthyphro, is an art which gods and men have of doing business with one another?

EUTHYPHRO: That is an expression which you may use, if you like.

SOCRATES: But I have no particular liking for anything but the truth. I wish, however, that you would tell me what benefit accrues to the gods from our gifts. There is no doubt about what they give to us; for there is no good thing which they do not give; but how we can give any good thing to them in return is far from being equally clear. If they give everything and we give nothing, that must be an affair of business in which we have very greatly the advantage of them.

EUTHYPHRO: And do you imagine, Socrates, that any benefit accrues to the gods from our gifts?

SOCRATES: But if not, Euthyphro, what is the meaning of gifts which are conferred by us upon the gods?

EUTHYPHRO: What else, but tributes of honour; and, as I was just now saying, what pleases them?

SOCRATES: Piety, then, is pleasing to the gods, but not beneficial or dear to them?

EUTHYPHRO: I should say that nothing could be dearer.

SOCRATES: Then once more the assertion is repeated that piety is dear to the gods?

EUTHYPHRO: Certainly.

SOCRATES: And when you say this, can you wonder at your words not standing firm, but walking away? Will you accuse me of being the Daedalus who makes them walk away, not perceiving that there is another and far greater artist than Daedalus who makes them go round in a circle, and he is yourself; for the argument, as you will perceive, comes round to the same point. Were we not saying that the holy or pious was not the same with that which is loved of the gods? Have you forgotten?

EUTHYPHRO: I quite remember.

SOCRATES: And are you not saying that what is loved of the gods is holy; and is not this the same as what is dear to them—do you see?

EUTHYPHRO: True.

SOCRATES: Then either we were wrong in our former assertion; or, if we were right then, we are wrong now.

EUTHYPHRO: One of the two must be true.

SOCRATES: Then we must begin again and ask, What is piety? That is an enquiry which I shall never be weary of pursuing as far as in me lies; and I entreat you not to scorn me, but to apply your mind to the utmost, and tell me the truth. For, if any man knows, you are he; and therefore I must detain you, like Proteus, until you tell. If you had not certainly known the nature of piety and impiety, I am confident that you would never, on behalf of a serf, have charged your aged father with murder. You would not have run such a risk of doing wrong in the sight of the gods, and you would have had too much respect for the opinions of men. I am sure, therefore, that you know the nature of piety and impiety. Speak out then, my dear Euthyphro, and do not hide your knowledge.

EUTHYPHRO: Another time, Socrates; for I am in a hurry, and must go now.

SOCRATES: Alas! my companion, and will you leave me in despair? I was hoping that you would instruct me in the nature of piety and impiety; and then I might have cleared myself of Meletus and his indictment. I would have told him that I had been enlightened by Euthyphro, and had given up rash innovations and speculations, in which I indulged only through ignorance, and that now I am about to lead a better life.

DISCUSSION QUESTIONS

1. Why does Socrates reject Euthyphro's first definition? Explain.

2. Why does Socrates reject Euthyphro's last definition? Explain.

3. Why is it so difficult to define abstract nouns such as piety? Explain.

Nicomachean Ethics

By Aristotle
Translated by W. D. Ross

Aristotle (384–322 BCE) studied philosophy with Plato for 20 years, until Plato's death. Most of Aristotle's works that were known in the ancient world have not survived. What we do have is still quite a lot. His impact on the history of ideas is at least as important as Plato's. For much of the medieval period, Aristotle was considered the authority on biology, psychology, physics, meteorology, rhetoric, zoology, and other topics, as well as philosophy. Thomas Aquinas (1225–1274) whose ideas (after an 1879 encyclical by Pope Leo XIII) became official Catholic doctrine, referred to Aristotle as "The Philosopher." The medieval Spanish Islamic philosopher Ibn-Rushd (1126–1198, also known by the Latin name Averröes) and the medieval Spanish Jewish philosopher Moshe ben Maimon (1135–1204, also known by the Latin name Maimonides) were also heavily shaped by Aristotelian ideas.

The Nicomachean Ethics *is a wide-ranging treatise on ethical topics in 10 books. Book I is an introduction to the topic and includes definitions of key terms. Books II–IV are about virtue. Justice is the subject of Book V. Book VI is about intellectual virtue and Book VII is about the difficulties in being virtuous. Friendship is the topic of Books VII–IX. The concluding book contains some summary and is also a segue to another of Aristotle's works, the* Politics*. To Aristotle, ethics and politics are two sides of the same coin. Our selection is from Books I–II. Aristotle starts by saying that happiness is the aim of human activity, as it is the only thing we aim at that it makes no sense to ask why we pursue it. All translators would at this point remind us that the word being translated as happiness,* eudaimonia*, does not mean happiness in the way the word is used in English. Better translations might include "well-being," "flourishing," or "good spiritedness." "Happy (*eudaimon*)" as an adjective can only be applied to a person after a full life. In his view, two conditions are necessary for happiness: virtue and minimum external goods. To achieve virtue, you need to develop the kind of character that can be depended on to make the right choices. The character is developed by habitually making the right choices. So, you get better at virtue the same way you become a better flute player or roofer. You make the right choices by looking for the mean between two extremes. For Aristotle, each virtue can be found between an excess and a deficiency. The mean is not mathematical, though. Six is the mean between two and ten, but courage may be closer to cowardice than to foolhardiness at one time, but the other way around next time. Ethics cannot meet with more precision than that for him. The fact that Aristotle's view aims at a goal makes this view teleological (end or goal-oriented), as opposed to deontological. His view is also called a virtue ethics, sometimes, because of its insistence that being virtuous is a necessary condition for happiness. Virtue is not a sufficient condition for happiness, because you may be lacking some of the minimum external goods.*

BOOK I

I

EVERY art and every inquiry, and similarly every action and pursuit, is thought to aim at some good; and for this reason the good has rightly been declared to be that at which all things aim. But a certain difference is found among ends; some are activities, others are products apart from the activities that produce them. Where there are ends apart from the actions, it is the nature of the products to be better than the activities. Now, as there are many actions, arts, and sciences, their ends also are many; the end of the medical art is health, that of shipbuilding a vessel, that of strategy victory, that of economics wealth. But where such arts fall under a single capacity—as bridle-making and the other arts concerned with the equipment of horses fall under the art of riding, and this and every military action under strategy, in the same way other arts fall under yet others—in all of these the ends of the master arts are to be preferred to all the subordinate ends; for it is for the sake of the former that the latter are pursued. It makes no difference whether the activities themselves are the ends of the actions, or something else apart from the activities, as in the case of the sciences just mentioned.

II

If, then, there is some end of the things we do, which we desire for its own sake (everything else being desired for the sake of this), and if we do not choose everything for the sake of something else (for at that rate the process would go on to infinity, so that our desire would be empty and vain), clearly this must be the good and the chief good. Will not the knowledge of it, then, have a great influence on life? Shall we not, like archers who have a mark to aim at, be more likely to hit upon what is right? If so, we must try, in outline at least, to determine what it is, and of which of the sciences or capacities it is the object. It would seem to belong to the most authoritative art and that which is most truly the master art. And politics appears to be of this nature; for it is this that ordains which of the sciences should be studied in a state, and which each class of citizens should learn and up to what point they should learn them; and we see even the most highly esteemed of capacities to fall under this, e.g. strategy, economics, rhetoric; now, since politics uses the rest of the sciences, and since, again, it legislates as to what we are to do and what we are to abstain from, the end of this science must include those of the others, so that this end must be the good for man. For even if the end is the same for a single man and for a state, that of the state seems at all events something greater and more complete whether to attain or to preserve; though it is worth while to attain the end merely for one man, it is finer and more godlike to attain it for a nation or for city-states. These, then, are the ends at which our inquiry aims, since it is political science, in one sense of that term.

III

Our discussion will be adequate if it has as much clearness as the subject-matter admits of, for precision is not to be sought for alike in all discussions, any more than in all the products of the crafts. Now fine and just actions, which political science investigates, admit of much variety and fluctuation of opinion, so that they may be thought to exist only by convention, and not by nature. And goods also give rise to a similar fluctuation because they bring harm to many people; for before now men have been undone by reason of their wealth, and others by reason of their courage. We must be content, then, in speaking of such subjects and with such premisses to indicate the truth roughly and in outline, and in speaking about things which are only for the most part true and with premisses of the same kind to reach conclusions that are no better. In the same spirit, therefore, should each type of statement be received; for it is the mark of an educated man to look for precision in each class of things just so far as the nature of the subject admits; it is evidently equally foolish to accept probable reasoning from a mathematician and to demand from a rhetorician scientific proofs.

Now each man judges well the things he knows, and of these he is a good judge. And so the man who has been educated in a subject is a good judge of that subject, and the man who has received an all-round education is a good judge in general. Hence a young man is not a proper hearer of lectures on political science; for he is inexperienced in the actions that occur in life, but its discussions start from these and are about these; and, further, since he tends to follow his passions, his study will be vain and unprofitable, because the end aimed at is not knowledge but action. And it makes no difference whether he is young in years or youthful in character; the defect does not depend on time, but on his living, and pursuing each successive object, as passion directs. For to such persons, as to the incontinent, knowledge brings no profit; but to those who desire and act in accordance with a rational principle knowledge about such matters will be of great benefit.

These remarks about the student, the sort of treatment to be expected, and the purpose of the inquiry, may be taken as our preface.

IV

Let us resume our inquiry and state, in view of the fact that all knowledge and every pursuit aims at some good, what it is that we say political science aims at and what is the highest of all goods achievable by action. Verbally there is very general agreement; for both the general run of men and people of superior refinement say that it is happiness, and identify living well and doing well with being happy; but with regard to what happiness is they differ, and the many do not give the same account as the wise. For the former think it is some plain and obvious thing, like pleasure, wealth, or honour; they differ, however, from one another—and often even the same man identifies it with different things, with health when he is ill, with wealth when he is poor; but, conscious of their ignorance, they admire those who proclaim some great ideal that is above their comprehension. Now some thought that apart from these many goods there is another which is self-subsistent and causes the goodness of all these as well. To examine all the opinions that have been held were perhaps somewhat fruitless; enough to examine those that are most prevalent or that seem to be arguable.

Let us not fail to notice, however, that there is a difference between arguments from and those to the first principles. For Plato, too, was right in raising this question and asking, as he used to do, 'are we on the way from or to the first principles?' There is a difference, as there is in a race-course between the course from the judges to the turning-point and the way back. For, while we must begin with what is known, things are objects of knowledge in two sensessome to us, some without qualification. Presumably, then, we must begin with things known to us. Hence any one who is to listen intelligently to lectures about what is noble and just, and generally, about the subjects of political science must have been brought up in good habits. For the fact is the starting-point, and if this is sufficiently plain to him, he will not at the start need the reason as well; and the man who has been well brought up has or can easily get startingpoints. And as for him who neither has nor can get them, let him hear the words of Hesiod:

Far best is he who knows all things himself;
Good, he that hearkens when men counsel right;
But he who neither knows, nor lays to heart
Another's wisdom, is a useless wight.

V

Let us, however, resume our discussion from the point at which we digressed. To judge from the lives that men lead, most men, and men of the most vulgar type, seem (not without some ground) to identify the good, or happiness, with pleasure; which is the reason why they love the life of enjoyment. For there are, we may say, three prominent types of life—that just mentioned, the political, and thirdly the contemplative life. Now the mass of mankind are evidently quite slavish in their tastes, preferring a life suitable to beasts, but they get some ground for their view from the fact that many of those in high places share the tastes of Sardanapallus. A consideration of the prominent types of life shows that people of superior refinement and of active disposition identify happiness with honour; for this is, roughly speaking, the end of the political life. But it seems too superficial to be what we are looking for, since it is thought to depend on those who bestow honour rather than on him who receives it, but the good we divine to be something proper to a man and not easily taken from him. Further, men seem to pursue honour in order that they may be assured of their goodness; at least it is by men of practical wisdom that they seek to be honoured, and among those who know them, and on the ground of their virtue; clearly, then, according to them, at any rate, virtue is better. And perhaps one might even suppose this to be, rather than honour, the end of the political life. But even this appears somewhat incomplete; for possession of virtue seems actually compatible with being asleep, or with lifelong inactivity, and, further, with the greatest sufferings and misfortunes; but a man who was living so no one would call happy, unless he were maintaining a thesis at all costs. But enough of this; for the subject has been sufficiently treated even in the current discussions. Third comes the contemplative life, which we shall consider later.

The life of money-making is one undertaken under compulsion, and wealth is evidently not the good we are seeking; for it is merely useful and for the sake of something else. And so one might rather take the aforenamed objects to be ends; for they are loved for themselves. But it is evident that not even these are ends; yet many arguments have been thrown away in support of them. Let us leave this subject, then.

• • •

VII

Let us again return to the good we are seeking, and ask what it can be. It seems different in different actions and arts; it is different in medicine, in strategy, and in the other arts likewise. What then is the good of each? Surely that for whose sake everything else is done. In medicine this is health, in strategy victory, in architecture a house, in any other sphere something else, and in every action and pursuit the end; for it is for the sake of this that all men do whatever else they do. Therefore, if there is an end for all that we do, this will be the good achievable by action, and if there are more than one, these will be the goods achievable by action.

So the argument has by a different course reached the same point; but we must try to state this even more clearly. Since there are evidently more than one end, and we choose some of these (e.g. wealth, flutes, and in general instruments) for the sake of something else, clearly not all ends are final ends; but the chief good is evidently something final. Therefore, if there is only one final end, this will be what we are seeking, and if there are more than one, the most final of these will be what we are seeking. Now we call that which is in itself worthy of pursuit more final than that which is worthy of pursuit for the sake of something else, and that which is never desirable for the sake of something else more final than the things that are desirable both in themselves and for the sake of that other thing, and therefore we call final without qualification that which is always desirable in itself and never for the sake of something else.

Now such a thing happiness, above all else, is held to be; for this we choose always for self and never for the sake of something else, but honour, pleasure, reason, and every virtue we choose indeed for themselves (for if nothing resulted from them we should still choose each of them), but we choose them also for the sake of happiness, judging that by means of them we shall be happy. Happiness, on the other hand, no one chooses for the sake of these, nor, in general, for anything other than itself.

From the point of view of self-sufficiency the same result seems to follow; for the final good is thought to be self-sufficient. Now by self-sufficient we do not mean that which is sufficient for a man by himself, for one who lives a solitary life, but also for parents, children, wife, and in general for his friends and fellow citizens, since man is born for citizenship. But some limit must be set to this; for if we extend our requirement to ancestors and descendants and friends' friends we are in for an infinite series. Let us examine this question, however, on another occasion; the self-sufficient we now define as that which when isolated makes life desirable and lacking in nothing; and such we think happiness to be; and further we think it most desirable of all things, without being counted as one good thing among others—if it were so counted it would clearly be made more desirable by the addition of even the least of goods; for that which is added becomes an excess of goods, and of goods the greater is always more desirable. Happiness, then, is something final and self-sufficient, and is the end of action.

Presumably, however, to say that happiness is the chief good seems a platitude, and a clearer account of what it is still desired. This might perhaps be given, if we could first ascertain the function of man. For just as for a flute-player, a sculptor, or an artist, and, in general, for all things that have a function or activity, the good and the 'well' is thought to reside in the function, so would it seem to be for man, if he has a function. Have the carpenter, then, and the tanner certain functions or activities, and has man none? Is he born without a function? Or as eye, hand, foot, and in general each of the parts evidently has a function, may one lay it down that man similarly has a function apart from all these? What then can this be? Life seems to be common even to plants, but we are seeking what is peculiar to man. Let us exclude, therefore, the life of nutrition and growth. Next there would be a life of perception, but it also seems to be common even to the horse, the ox, and every animal. There remains, then, an active life of the element that has a rational principle; of this, one part has such a principle in the sense of being obedient to one, the other in the sense of possessing one and exercising thought. And, as 'life of the rational element' also has two meanings, we must state that life in the sense of activity is what we mean; for this seems to be the more proper sense of the term. Now if the function of man is an activity of soul which follows or implies a rational principle, and if we say 'so-and-so-and 'a good so-and-so' have a function which is the same in kind, e.g. a lyre, and a good lyre-player, and so without qualification in all cases, eminence in respect of goodness being idded to the name of the function (for the function of a lyre-player is to play the lyre, and that of a good lyre-player is to do so well): if this is the case, and we state the function of man to be a certain kind of life, and this to be an activity or actions of the soul implying a rational principle, and the function of a good man to be the good and noble performance of these, and if any action is well performed when it is performed in accordance with the appropriate excellence: if this is the case, human good turns out to be activity of soul in accordance with virtue, and if there are more than one virtue, in accordance with the best and most complete.

But we must add 'in a complete life.' For one swallow does not make a summer, nor does one day; and so too one day, or a short time, does not make a man blessed and happy.

Let this serve as an outline of the good; for we must presumably first sketch it roughly, and then later fill in the details. But it would seem that any one is capable of carrying on and articulating what has once been well outlined, and that time is a good discoverer or partner in such a work; to which facts the advances of the arts are due; for any one can add what is lacking. And we must also remember what has been said before, and not look for precision in all things alike, but in each class of things such precision as accords with the subject-matter, and so much as is appropriate to the inquiry. For a carpenter and a geometer investigate the right angle in different ways; the former does so in so far as the right angle is useful for his work, while the latter inquires what it is or what sort of thing it is; for he is a spectator of the truth. We must act in the same way, then, in all other matters as well, that our main task may not be subordinated to minor questions. Nor must we demand the cause in all matters alike; it is enough in some cases that the fact be well established, as in the case of the first principles; the fact is the primary thing or first principle. Now of first principles we see some by induction, some by perception, some by a certain habituation, and others too in other ways. But each set of principles we must try to investigate in the natural way, and we must take pains to state them definitely, since they have a great influence on what follows. For the beginning is thought to be more than half of the whole, and many of the questions we ask are cleared up by it.

VIII

We must consider it, however, in the light not only of our conclusion and our premisses, but also of what is commonly said about it; for with a true view all the data harmonize, but with a false one the facts soon clash. Now goods have been divided into three classes, and some are described as external, others as relating to soul or to body; we call those that relate to soul most properly and truly goods, and psychical actions and activities we class as relating to soul. Therefore our account must be sound, at least according to this view, which is an old one and agreed on by philosophers. It is correct also in that we identify the end with certain actions and activities; for thus it falls among goods of the soul and not among external goods. Another belief which harmonizes with our account is that the happy man lives well and does well; for we have practically defined happiness as a sort of good life and good action. The characteristics that are looked for in happiness seem also, all of them, to belong to what we have defined happiness as being. For some identify happiness with virtue, some with practical wisdom, others with a kind of philosophic wisdom, others with these, or one of these, accompanied by pleasure or not without pleasure; while others include also external prosperity. Now some of these views have been held by many men and men of old, others by a few eminent persons; and it is not probable that either of these should be entirely mistaken, but rather that they should be right in at least some one respect or even in most respects.

With those who identify happiness with virtue or some one virtue our account is in harmony; for to virtue belongs virtuous activity. But it makes, perhaps, no small difference whether we place the chief good in possession or in use, in state of mind or in activity. For the state of mind may exist without producing any good result, as in a man who is asleep or in some other way quite inactive, but the activity cannot; for one who has the activity will of necessity be acting, and acting well. And as in the Olympic Games it is not the most beautiful and the strongest that are crowned but those who compete (for it is some of these that are victorious), so those who act win, and rightly win, the noble and good things in life.

Their life is also in itself pleasant. For pleasure is a state of soul, and to each man that which he is said to be a lover of is pleasant; e.g. not only is a horse pleasant to the lover of horses, and a spectacle to the lover of sights, but also in the same way just acts are pleasant to the lover of justice and in general virtuous acts to the lover of virtue. Now for most men their pleasures are in conflict with one another because these are not by nature pleasant, but the lovers of what is noble find pleasant the things that are by nature pleasant; and virtuous actions are such, so that these are pleasant for such men as well as in their own nature. Their life, therefore, has no further need of pleasure as a sort of adventitious charm, but has its pleasure in itself. For, besides what we have said, the man who does not rejoice in noble actions is not even good; since no one would call a man just who did not enjoy acting justly, nor any man liberal who did not enjoy liberal actions; and similarly in all other cases. If this is so, virtuous actions must be in themselves pleasant. But they are also good and noble, and have each of these attributes in the highest degree, since the good man judges well about these attributes; his judgement is such as we have described. Happiness then is the best, noblest, and most pleasant thing in the world, and these attributes are not severed as in the inscription at Delos.

Most noble is that which is justest, and best is health; But pleasantest is it to win what we love.

For all these properties belong to the best activities; and these, or one—the best—of these, we identify with happiness.

Yet evidently, as we said, it needs the external goods as well; for it is impossible, or not easy, to do noble acts without the proper equipment. In many actions we use friends and riches and political power as instruments; and there are some things the lack of which takes the lustre from happiness, as good birth, goodly children, beauty; for the man who is very ugly in appearance or ill-born or solitary and childless is not very likely to be happy, and perhaps a man would be still less likely if he had thoroughly bad children or friends or had lost good children or friends by death. As we said, then, happiness seems to need this sort of prosperity in addition; for which reason some identify happiness with good fortune, though others identify it with virtue.

IX

For this reason also the question is asked, whether happiness is to be acquired by learning or by habituation or some other sort of training, or comes in virtue of some divine providence or again by chance. Now if there is any gift of the gods to men, it is reasonable that happiness should be god-given, and most surely god-given of all human things inasmuch as it is the best. But this question would perhaps be more appropriate to another inquiry; happiness seems, however, even if it is not god-sent but comes as a result of virtue and some process of learning or training, to be among the most godlike things; for that which is the prize and end of virtue seems to be the best thing in the world, and something godlike and blessed.

It will also on this view be very generally shared; for all who are not maimed as regards their potentiality for virtue may win it by a certain kind of study and care.

But if it is better to be happy thus than by chance, it is reasonable that the facts should be so, since everything that depends on the action of nature is by nature as good as it can be, and similarly everything that depends on art or any rational cause, and especially if it depends on the best of all causes. To entrust to chance what is greatest and most noble would be a very defective arrangement.

The answer to the question we are asking is plain also from the definition of happiness; for it has been said to be a virtuous activity of soul, of a certain kind. Of the remaining goods, some must necessarily pre-exist as conditions of happiness, and others are naturally co-operative and useful as instruments. And this will be found to agree with what we said at the outset; for we stated the end of political science to be the best end, and political science spends most of its pains on making the citizens to be of a certain character, *viz.* good and capable of noble acts.

It is natural, then, that we call neither ox nor horse nor any other of the animals happy; for none of them is capable of sharing in such activity. For this reason also a boy is not happy; for he is not yet capable of such acts, owing to his age; and boys who are called happy are being congratulated by reason of the hopes we have for them. For there is required, as we said, not only complete virtue but also a complete life, since many changes occur in life, and all manner of chances, and the most prosperous may fall into great misfortunes in old age, as is told of Priam in the Trojan Cycle; and one who has experienced such chances and has ended wretchedly no one calls happy.

X

Must no one at all, then, be called happy while he lives; must we, as Solon says, see the end? Even if we are to lay down this doctrine, is it also the case that a man is happy when he is dead? Or is not this quite absurd, especially for us who say that happiness is an activity? But if we do not call the dead man happy, and if Solon does not mean this, but that one can then safely call a man blessed as being at last beyond evils and misfortunes, this also affords matter for discussion; for both evil and good are thought to exist for a dead man, as much as for one who is alive but not aware of them; e.g. honours and dishonours and the good or bad fortunes of children and in general of descendants. And this also presents a problem; for though a man has lived happily up to old age and has had a death worthy of his life, many reverses may befall his descendants—some of them may be good and attain the life they deserve, while with others the opposite may be the case; and clearly too the degrees of relationship between them and their ancestors may vary indefinitely. It would be odd, then, if the dead man were to share in these changes and become at one time happy, at another wretched; while it would also be odd if the fortunes of the descendants did not for some time have some effect on the happiness of their ancestors.

But we must return to our first difficulty; for perhaps by a consideration of it our present problem might be solved. Now if we must see the end and only then call a man happy, not as being happy but as having been so before, surely this is a paradox, that when he is happy the attribute that belongs to him is not to be truly predicated of him because we do not wish to call living men happy, on account of the changes that may befall them, and because we have assumed happiness to be something permanent and by no means easily changed, while a single man may suffer many turns of fortune's wheel. For clearly if we were to keep pace with his fortunes, we should often call the same man happy and again wretched, making the happy man out to be chameleon and insecurely based. Or is this keeping pace with his fortunes quite wrong? Success or failure in life does not depend on these, but human life, as we said, needs these as mere additions, while virtuous activities or their opposites are what constitute happiness or the reverse.

The question we have now discussed confirms our definition. For no function of man has so much permanence as virtuous activities (these are thought to be more durable even than knowledge of the sciences), and of these themselves the most valuable are more durable because those who are happy spend their life most readily and most continuously in these; for this seems to be the reason why we do not forget them. The attribute in question, then, will belong to the happy man, and he will be happy throughout his life; for always, or by preference to everything else, he will be engaged in virtuous action and contemplation, and he will bear the chances of life most nobly and altogether decorously, if he is 'truly good' and 'foursquare beyond reproach'.

Now many events happen by chance, and events differing in importance; small pieces of good fortune or of its opposite clearly do not weigh down the scales of life one way or the other, but a multitude of great events if they turn out well will make life happier (for not only are they themselves such as to add beauty to life, but the way a man deals with them may be noble and good), while if they turn out ill they crush and maim happiness; for they both bring pain with them and hinder many activities. Yet even in these nobility shines through, when a man bears with resignation many great misfortunes, not through insensibility to pain but through nobility and greatness of soul.

If activities are, as we said, what gives life its character, no happy man can become miserable; for he will never do the acts that are hateful and mean. For the man who is truly good and wise, we think, bears all the chances life becomingly and always makes the best of circumstances, as a good general makes the best military use of the army at his command and a good shoemaker makes the best shoes out of the hides that are given him; and so with all other craftsmen. And if this is the case, the happy man can never become miserable; though he will not reach blessedness, if he meet with fortunes like those of Priam.

Nor, again, is he many-coloured and changeable; for neither will he be moved from his happy state easily or by any ordinary misadventures, but only by many great ones, nor, if he has had many great misadventures, will he recover his happiness in a short time, but if at all, only in a long and complete one in which he has attained many splendid successes.

When then should we not say that he is happy who is active in accordance with complete virtue and is sufficiently equipped with external goods, not for some chance period but throughout a complete life? Or must we add 'and who is destined to live thus and die as befits his life'? Certainly the future is obscure to us, while happiness, we claim, is an end and something in every way final. If so, we shall call happy those among living men in whom these conditions are, and are to be, fulfilled—but happy men. So much for these questions.

XI

That the fortunes of descendants and of all a man's friends should not affect his happiness at all seems a very unfriendly doctrine, and one opposed to the opinions men hold; but since the events that happen are numerous and admit of all sorts of difference, and some come more near to us and others less so, it seems a long—nay, an infinite—task to discuss each in detail; a general outline will perhaps suffice. If, then, as some of a man's own misadventures have a certain weight and influence on life while others are, as it were, lighter, so too there are differences among the misadventures of our friends taken as a whole, and it makes a difference whether the various suffering befall the living or the dead (much more even than whether lawless and terrible deeds are presupposed in a tragedy or done on the stage), this difference also must be taken into account; or rather, perhaps, the fact that doubt is felt whether the dead share in any good or evil. For it seems, from these considerations, that even if anything whether good or evil penetrates to them, it must be something weak and negligible, either in itself or for them, or if not, at least it must be such in degree and kind as not to make happy those who are not happy nor to take away their blessedness from those who are. The good or bad fortunes of friends, then, seem to have some effects on the dead, but effects of such a kind and degree as neither to make the happy unhappy nor to produce any other change of the kind.

XII

These questions having been definitely answered, let us consider whether happiness is among the things that are praised or rather among the things that are prized; for clearly it is not to be placed among potentialities. Everything that is praised seems to be praised because it is of a certain kind and is related somehow to something else; for we praise the just or brave man and in general both the good man and virtue itself because of the actions and functions involved, and we praise the strong man, the good runner, and so on, because he is of a certain kind and is related in a certain way to something good and important. This is clear also from the praises of the gods; for it seems absurd that the gods should be referred to our standard, but this is done because praise involves a reference, to something else. But if praise is for things such as we have described, clearly what applies to the best things is not praise, but something greater and better, as is indeed obvious; for what we do to the gods and the most godlike of men is to call them blessed and happy. And so too with good things; no one praises happiness as he does justice, but rather calls it blessed, as being something more divine and better.

Eudoxus also seems to have been right in his method of advocating the supremacy of pleasure; he thought that the fact that, though a good, it is not praised indicated it to be better than the things that are praised, and that this is what God and the good are; for by reference to these all other things are judged. Praise is appropriate to virtue, for as a result of virtue men tend to do noble deeds, but encomia are bestowed on acts, whether of the body or of the soul. But perhaps nicety in these matters is more proper to those who have made a study of encomia; to us it is clear from what has been said that happiness is among the things that are prized and perfect. It seems to be so also from the fact that it is a first principle; for it is for the sake of this that we all do all that we do, and the first principle and cause of goods is, we claim, something prized and divine.

XIII

Since happiness is an activity of soul in accordance with perfect virtue, we must consider the nature of virtue; for perhaps we shall thus see better the nature of happiness. The true student of politics, too, is thought to have studied virtue above all things; for he wishes to make his fellow citizens good and obedient to the laws. As an example of this we have the lawgivers of the Cretans and the Spartans, and any others of the kind that there may have been. And if this inquiry belongs to political science, clearly the pursuit of it will be in accordance with our original plan. But clearly the virtue we must study is human virtue; for the good we were seeking was human good and the happiness human happiness. By human virtue we mean not that of the body but that of the soul; and happiness also we call an activity of soul. But if this is so, clearly the student of politics must know somehow the facts about soul, as the man who is to heal the eyes or the body as a whole must know about the eyes or the body; and all the more since politics is more prized and better than medicine; but even among doctors the best educated spend much labour on acquiring knowledge of the body. The student of politics, then, must study the soul, and must study it with these objects in view, and do so just to the extent which is sufficient for the questions we are discussing; for further precision is perhaps something more laborious than our purposes require.

Some things are said about it, adequately enough, even in the discussions outside our school, and we must use these; e.g. that one element in the soul is irrational and one has a rational principle. Whether these are separated as the parts of the body or of anything divisible are, or are distinct by definition but by nature inseparable, like convex and concave in the circumference of a circle, does not affect the present question.

Of the irrational element one division seems to be widely distributed, and vegetative in its nature, I mean that which causes nutrition and growth; for it is this kind of power of the soul that one must assign to all nurslings and to embryos, and this same power to fullgrown creatures; this is more reasonable than to assign some different power to them. Now the excellence of this seems to be common to all species and not specifically human; for this part or faculty seems to function most in sleep, while goodness and badness are least manifest in sleep (whence comes the saying that the happy are not better off than the wretched for half their lives; and this happens naturally enough, since sleep is an inactivity of the soul in that respect in which it is called good or bad), unless perhaps to a small extent some of the movements actually penetrate to the soul, and in this respect the dreams of good men are better than those of ordinary people. Enough of this subject, however; let us leave the nutritive faculty alone, since it has by its nature no share in human excellence.

There seems to be also another irrational element in the soul-one which in a sense, however, shares in a rational principle. For we praise the rational principle of the continent man and of the incontinent, and the part of their soul that has such a principle, since it urges them aright and towards the best objects; but there is found in them also another element naturally opposed to the rational principle, which fights against and resists that principle. For exactly as paralysed limbs when we intend to move them to the right turn on the contrary to the left, so is it with the soul; the impulses of incontinent people move in contrary directions. But while in the body we see that which moves astray, in the soul we do not. No doubt, however, we must none the less suppose that in the soul too there is something contrary to the rational principle, resisting and opposing it. In what sense it is distinct from the other elements does not concern us. Now even this seems to have a share in a rational principle, as we said; at any rate in the continent man it obeys the rational principle and presumably in the temperate and brave man it is still more obedient; for in him it speaks, on all matters, with the same voice as the rational principle.

Therefore the irrational element also appears to be two-fold. For the vegetative element in no way shares in a rational principle, but the appetitive and in general the desiring element in a sense shares in it, in so far as it listens to and obeys it; this is the sense in which we speak of 'taking account' of one's father or one's friends, not that in which we speak of 'accounting for a mathematical property. That the irrational element is in some sense persuaded by a rational principle is indicated also by the giving of advice and by all reproof and exhortation. And if this element also must be said to have a rational principle, that which has a rational principle (as well as that which has not) will be twofold, one subdivision having it in the strict sense and in itself, and the other having a tendency to obey as one does one's father.

Virtue too is distinguished into kinds in accordance with this difference; for we say that some of the virtues are intellectual and others moral, philosophic wisdom and understanding and practical wisdom being intellectual, liberality and temperance moral. For in speaking about a man's character we do not say that he is wise or has understanding but that he is good-tempered or temperate; yet we praise the wise man also with respect to his state of mind; and of states of mind we call those which merit praise virtues.

BOOK II

I

VIRTUE, then, being of two kinds, intellectual and moral, intellectual virtue in the main owes both its birth and its growth to teaching (for which reason it requires experience and time), while moral virtue comes about as a result of habit, whence also its name (ethike) is one that is formed by a slight variation from the word ethos (habit). From this it is also plain that none of the moral virtues arises in us by nature; for nothing that exists by nature can form a habit contrary to its nature. For instance the stone which by nature moves downwards cannot be habituated to move upwards, not even if one tries to train it by throwing it up ten thousand times; nor can fire be habituated to move downwards, nor can anything else that by nature behaves in one way be trained to behave in another. Neither by nature, then, nor contrary to nature do the virtues arise in us; rather we are adapted by nature to receive them, and are made perfect by habit.

Again, of all the things that come to us by nature we first acquire the potentiality and later exhibit the activity (this is plain in the case of the senses; for it was not by often seeing or often hearing that we got these senses, but on the contrary we had them before we used them, and did not come to have them by using them); but the virtues we get by first exercising them, as also happens in the case of the arts as well. For the things we have to learn before we can do them, we learn by doing them, e.g. men become builders by building and lyreplayers by playing the lyre; so too we become just by doing just acts, temperate by doing temperate acts, brave by doing brave acts.

This is confirmed by what happens in states; for legislators make the citizens good by forming habits in them, and this is the wish of every legislator, and those who do not effect it miss their mark, and it is in this that a good constitution differs from a bad one.

Again, it is from the same causes and by the same means that every virtue is both produced and destroyed, and similarly every art; for it is from playing the lyre that both good and bad lyre-players are produced. And the corresponding statement is true of builders and of all the rest; men will be good or bad builders as a result of building well or badly. For if this were not so, there would have been no need of a teacher, but all men would have been born good or bad at their craft. This, then, is the case with the virtues also; by doing the acts that we do in our transactions with other men we become just or unjust, and by doing the acts that we do in the presence of danger, and being habituated to feel fear or confidence, we become brave or cowardly. The same is true of appetites and feelings of anger; some men become temperate and good-tempered, others self-indulgent and irascible, by behaving in one way or the other in the appropriate circumstances. Thus, in one word, states of character arise out of like activities. This is why the activities we exhibit must be of a certain kind; it is because the states of character correspond to the differences between these. It makes no small difference, then, whether we form habits of one kind or of another from our very youth; it makes a very great difference, or rather all the difference.

II

Since, then, the present inquiry does not aim at theoretical knowledge like the others (for we are inquiring not in order to know what virtue is, but in order to become good, since otherwise our inquiry would have been of no use), we must examine the nature of actions, namely how we ought to do them; for these determine also the nature of the states of character that are produced, as we have said. Now, that we must act according to the right rule is a common principle and must be assumed-it will be discussed later, i.e. both what the right rule is, and how it is related to the other virtues. But this must be agreed upon beforehand, that the whole account of matters of conduct must be given in outline and not precisely, as we said at the very beginning that the accounts we demand must be in accordance with the subject-matter; matters concerned with conduct and questions of what is good for us have no fixity, any more than matters of health. The general account being of this nature, the account of particular cases is yet more lacking in exactness; for they do not fall under any art or precept but the agents themselves must in each case consider what is appropriate to the occasion, as happens also in the art of medicine or of navigation.

But though our present account is of this nature we must give what help we can. First, then, let us consider this, that it is the nature of such things to be destroyed by defect and excess, as we see in the case of strength and of health (for to gain light on things imperceptible we must use the evidence of sensible things); both excessive and defective exercise destroys the strength, and similarly drink or food which is above or below a certain amount destroys the health, while that which is proportionate both produces and increases and preserves it. So too is it, then, in the case of temperance and courage and the other virtues. For the man who flies from and fears everything and does not stand his ground against anything becomes a coward, and the man who fears nothing at all but goes to meet every danger becomes rash; and similarly the man who indulges in every pleasure and abstains from none becomes self-indulgent, while the man who shuns every pleasure, as boors do, becomes in a way insensible; temperance and courage, then, are destroyed by excess and defect, and preserved by the mean.

But not only are the sources and causes of their origination and growth the same as those of their destruction, but also the sphere of their actualization will be the same; for this is also true of the things which are more evident to sense, e.g. of strength; it is produced by taking much food and undergoing much exertion, and it is the strong man that will be most able to do these things. So too is it with the virtues; by abstaining from pleasures we become temperate, and it is when we have become so that we are most able to abstain from them; and similarly too in the case of courage; for by being habituated to despise things that are terrible and to stand our ground against them we become brave, and it is when we have become so that we shall be most able to stand our ground against them.

III

We must take as a sign of states of character the pleasure or pain that ensues on acts; for the man who abstains from bodily pleasures and delights in this very fact is temperate, while the man who is annoyed at it is self-indulgent, and he who stands his ground against things that are terrible and delights in this or at least is not pained is brave, while the man who is pained is a coward. For moral excellence is concerned with pleasures and pains; it is on account of the pleasure that we do bad things, and on account of the pain that we abstain from noble ones. Hence we ought to have been brought up in a particular way from our very youth, as Plato says, so as both to delight in and to be pained by the things that we ought; for this is the right education.

Again, if the virtues are concerned with actions and passions, and every passion and every action is accompanied by pleasure and pain, for this reason also virtue will be concerned with pleasures and pains. This is indicated also by the fact that punishment is inflicted by these means; for it is a kind of cure, and it is the nature of cures to be effected by contraries.

Again, as we said but lately, every state of soul has a nature relative to and concerned with the kind of things by which it tends to be made worse or better; but it is by reason of pleasures and pains that men become bad, by pursuing and avoiding these—either the pleasures and pains they ought not or when they ought not or as they ought not, or by going wrong in one of the other similar ways that may be distinguished. Hence men even define the virtues as certain states of impassivity and rest; not well, however, because they speak absolutely, and do not say 'as one ought' and 'as one ought not' and 'when one ought or ought not,' and the other things that may be added. We assume, then, that this kind of excellence tends to do what is best with regard to pleasures and pains, and vice does the contrary.

The following facts also may show us that virtue and vice are concerned with these same things. There being three objects of choice and three of avoidance, the noble, the advantageous, the pleasant, and their contraries, the base, the injurious, the painful, about all of these the good man tends to go right and the bad man to go wrong, and especially about pleasure; for this is common to the animals, and also it accompanies all objects of choice; for even the noble and the advantageous appear pleasant.

Again, it has grown up with us all from our infancy; this is why it is difficult to rub off this passion, engrained as it is in our life. And we measure even our actions, some of us more and others less, by the rule of pleasure and pain. For this reason, then, our whole inquiry must be about these; for to feel delight and pain rightly or wrongly has no small effect on our actions.

Again, it is harder to fight with pleasure than with anger, to use Heraclitus' phrase,' but both art and virtue are always concerned with what is harder; for even the good is better when it is harder. Therefore for this reason also the whole concern both of virtue and of political science is with pleasures and pains; for the man who uses these well will be good, he who uses them badly bad.

That virtue, then, is concerned with pleasures and pains, and that by the acts from which it arises it is both increased and, if they are done differently, destroyed, and that the acts from which it arose are those in which it actualizes itself—let this be taken as said.

IV

The question might be asked, what we mean by saying that we must become just by doing just acts, and temperate by doing temperate acts; for if men do just and temperate acts, they are already just and temperate, exactly as, if they do what is in accordance with the laws of grammar and of music, they are grammarians and musicians.

Or is this not true even of the arts? It is possible to do something that is in accordance with the laws of grammar, either by chance or at the suggestion of another. A man will be a grammarian, then, only when he has both done something grammatical and done it grammatically; and this means doing it in accordance with the grammatical knowledge in himself.

Again, the case of the arts and that of the virtues are not similar; for the products of the arts have their goodness in themselves, so that it is enough that they should have a certain character, but if the acts that are in accordance with the virtues have themselves a certain character it does not follow that they are done justly or temperately. The agent also must be in a certain condition when he does them; in the first place he must have knowledge, secondly he must choose the acts, and choose them for their own sakes, and thirdly his action must proceed from a firm and unchangeable character. These are not reckoned in as conditions of the possession of the arts, except the bare knowledge; but as a condition of the possession of the virtues knowledge has little or no weight, while the other conditions count not for a little but for everything, i.e. the very conditions which result from often doing just and temperate acts.

Actions, then, are called just and temperate when they are such as the just or the temperate man would do; but it is not the man who does these that is just and temperate, but the man who also does them as just and temperate men do them. It is well said, then, that it is by doing just acts that the just man is produced, and by doing temperate acts the temperate man; without doing these no one would have even a prospect of becoming good.

But most people do not do these, but take refuge in theory and think they are being philosophers and will become good in this way, behaving somewhat like patients who listen attentively to their doctors, but do none of the things they are ordered to do. As the latter will not be made well in body by such a course of treatment, the former will not be made well in soul by such a course of philosophy.

V

Next we must consider what virtue is. Since things that are found in the soul are of three kinds—passions, faculties, states of character, virtue must be one of these. By passions I mean appetite, anger, fear, confidence, envy, joy, friendly feeling, hatred, longing, emulation, pity, and in general the feelings that are accompanied by pleasure or pain; by faculties the things in virtue of which we are said to be capable of feeling these, e.g. of becoming angry or being pained or feeling pity; by states of character the things in virtue of which we stand well or badly with reference to the passions, e.g. with reference to anger we stand badly if we feel it violently or too weakly, and well if we feel it moderately; and similarly with reference to the other passions.

Now neither the virtues nor the vices are passions, because we are not called good or bad on the ground of our passions, but are so called on the ground of our virtues and our vices, and because we are neither praised nor blamed for our passions (for the man who feels fear or anger is not praised, nor is the man who simply feels anger blamed, but the man who feels it in a certain way), but for our virtues and our vices we are praised or blamed.

Again, we feel anger and fear without choice, but the virtues are modes of choice or involve choice. Further, in respect of the passions we are said to be moved, but in respect of the virtues and the vices we are said not to be moved but to be disposed in a particular way.

For these reasons also they are not faculties; for we are neither called good nor bad, nor praised nor blamed, for the simple capacity of feeling the passions; again, we have the faculties by nature, but we are not made good or bad by nature; we have spoken of this before. If, then, the virtues are neither passions nor faculties, all that remains is that they should be states of character.

Thus we have stated what virtue is in respect of its genus.

VI

We must, however, not only describe virtue as a state of character, but also say what sort of state it is. We may remark, then, that every virtue or excellence both brings into good condition the thing of which it is the excellence and makes the work of that thing be done well; e.g. the excellence of the eye makes both the eye and its work good; for it is by the excellence of the eye that we see well. Similarly the excellence of the horse makes a horse both good in itself and good at running and at carrying its rider and at awaiting the attack of the enemy. Therefore, if this is true in every case, the virtue of man also will be the state of character which makes a man good and which makes him do his own work well.

How this is to happen we have stated already, but it will be made plain also by the following consideration of the specific nature of virtue. In everything that is continuous and divisible it is possible to take more, less, or an equal amount, and that either in terms of the thing itself or relatively to us; and the equal is an intermediate between excess and defect. By the intermediate in the object I mean that which is equidistant from each of the extremes, which is one and the same for all men; by the intermediate relatively to us that which is neither too much nor too little—and this is not one, nor the same for all. For instance, if ten is many and two is few, six is the intermediate, taken in terms of the object; for it exceeds and is exceeded by an equal amount; this is intermediate according to arithmetical proportion. But the intermediate relatively to us is not to be taken so; if ten pounds are too much for a particular person to eat and two too little, it does not follow that the trainer will order six pounds; for this also is perhaps too much for the person who is to take it, or too little—too little for Milo, too much for the beginner in athletic exercises. The same is true of running and wrestling.

Thus a master of any art avoids excess and defect, but seeks the intermediate and chooses this—the intermediate not in the object but relatively to us.

If it is thus, then, that every art does its work well—by looking to the intermediate and judgling its works by this standard (so that we often say of good works of art that it is not possible either to take away or to add anything, implying that excess and defect destroy the goodness of works of art, while the mean preserves it; and good artists, as we say, look to this in their work), and if, further, virtue is more exact and better than any art, as nature also is, then virtue must have the quality of aiming at the intermediate. I mean moral virtue; for it is this that is concerned with passions and actions, and in these there is excess, defect, and the intermediate. For instance, both fear and confidence and appetite and anger and pity and in general pleasure and pain may be felt both too much and too little, and in both cases not well; but to feel them at the right times, with reference to the right objects, towards the right people, with the right motive, and in the right way, is what is both intermediate and best, and this is characteristic of virtue. Similarly with regard to actions also there is excess, defect, and the intermediate. Now virtue is concerned with passions and actions, in which excess is a form of failure, and so is defect, while the intermediate is praised and is a form of success; and being praised and being successful are both characteristics of virtue. Therefore virtue is a kind of mean, since, as we have seen, it aims at what is intermediate.

Again, it is possible to fail in many ways (for evil belongs to the class of the unlimited, as the Pythagoreans conjectured, and good to that of the limited), while to succeed is possible only in one way (for which reason also one is easy and the other difficult—to miss the mark easy, to hit it difficult); for these reasons also, then, excess and defect are characteristic of vice, and the mean of virtue;

For men are good in but one way, but bad in many.

Virtue, then, is a state of character concerned with choice, lying in a mean, i.e. the mean relative to us, this being determined by a rational principle, and by that principle by which the man of practical wisdom would determine it. Now it is a mean between two vices, that which depends on excess and that which depends on defect; and again it is a mean because the vices respectively fall short of or exceed what is right in both passions and actions, while virtue both finds and chooses that which is intermediate. Hence in respect of its substance and the definition which states its essence virtue is a mean, with regard to what is best and right an extreme.

But not every action nor every passion admits of a mean; for some have names that already imply badness, e.g. spite, shamelessness, envy, and in the case of actions adultery, theft, murder; for all of these and suchlike things imply by their names that they are themselves bad, and not the excesses or deficiencies of them. It is not possible, then, ever to be right with regard to them; one must always be wrong. Nor does goodness or badness with regard to such things depend on committing adultery with the right woman, at the right time, and in the right way, but simply to do any of them is to go wrong. It would be equally absurd, then, to expect that in unjust, cowardly, and voluptuous action there should be a mean, an excess, and a deficiency; for at that rate there would be a mean of excess and of deficiency, an excess of excess, and a deficiency of deficiency. But as there is no excess and deficiency of temperance and courage because what is intermediate is in a sense an extreme, so too of the actions we have mentioned there is no mean nor any excess and deficiency, but however they are done they are wrong; for in general there is neither a mean of excess and deficiency, nor excess and deficiency of a mean.

VII

We must, however, not only make this general statement, but also apply it to the individual facts. For among statements about conduct those which are general apply more widely, but those which are particular are more genuine, since conduct has to do with individual cases, and our statements must harmonize with the facts in these cases. We may take these cases from our table. With regard to feelings of fear and confidence courage is the mean; of the people who exceed, he who exceeds in fearlessness has no name (many of the states have no name), while the man who exceeds in confidence is rash, and he who exceeds in fear and falls short in confidence is a coward. With regard to pleasures and pains—not all of them, and not so much with regard to the pains—the mean is temperance, the excess self-indulgence. Persons deficient with regard to the pleasures are not often found; hence such persons also have received no name. But let us call them 'insensible.'

With regard to giving and taking of money the mean is liberality, the excess and the defect prodigality and meanness. In these actions people exceed and fall short in contrary ways; the prodigal exceeds in spending and falls short in taking, while the mean man exceeds in taking and falls short in spending. (At present we are giving a mere outline or summary, and are satisfied with this; later these states will be more exactly determined.) With regard to money there are also other dispositions—a mean, magnificence (for the magnificent man differs from the liberal man; the former deals with large sums, the latter with small ones), an excess, tastelessness and vulgarity, and a deficiency, niggardliness; these differ from the states opposed to liberality, and the mode of their difference will be stated later. With regard to honour and dishonour the mean is proper pride, the excess is known as a sort of 'empty vanity,' and the deficiency is undue humility; and as we said liberality was related to magnificence, differing from it by dealing with small sums, so there is a state similarly related to proper pride, being concerned with small honours while that is concerned with great. For it is possible to desire honour as one ought, and more than one ought, and less, and the man who exceeds in his desires is called ambitious, the man who falls short unambitious, while the intermediate person has no name. The dispositions also are nameless, except that of the ambitious man is called ambition. Hence the people who are at the extremes lay claim to the middle place; and we ourselves sometimes call the intermediate person ambitious and sometimes unambitious, and sometimes praise the ambitious man and sometimes the unambitious. The reason of our doing this will be stated in what follows; but now let us speak of the remaining states according to the method which has been indicated.

With regard to anger also there is an excess, a deficiency, and a mean. Although they can scarcely be said to have names, yet since we call the intermediate person good-tempered let us call the mean good temper; of the persons at the extremes let the one who exceeds be called irascible, and his vice irascibility, and the man who falls short an inirascible sort of person, and the deficiency inirascibility.

There are also three other means, which have a certain likeness to one another, but differ from one another: for they are all concerned with intercourse in words and actions, but differ in that one is concerned with truth in this sphere, the other two with pleasantness; and of this one kind is exhibited in giving amusement, the other in all the circumstances of life. We must therefore speak of these too, that we may the better see that in all things the mean is praise-worthy, and the extremes neither praiseworthy nor right, but worthy of blame. Now most of these states also have no names, but we must try, as in the other cases, to invent names ourselves so that we may be clear and easy to follow. With regard to truth, then, the intermediate is a truthful sort of person and the mean may be called truthfulness, while the pretence which exaggerates is boastfulness and the person characterized by it a boaster, and that which understates is mock modesty and the person characterized by it mock-modest. With regard to pleasantness in the giving of amusement the intermediate person is ready-witted and the disposition ready wit, the excess is buffoonery and the person characterized by it a buffoon, while the man who falls short is a sort of boor and his state is boorishness. With regard to the remaining kind of pleasantness, that which is exhibited in life in general, the man who is pleasant in the right way is friendly and the mean is friendliness, while the man who exceeds is an obsequious person if he has no end in view, a flatterer if he is aiming at his own advantage, and the man who falls short and is unpleasant in all circumstances is a quarrelsome and surly sort of person.

There are also means in the passions and concerned with the passions; since shame is not a virtue, and yet praise is extended to the modest man. For even in these matters one man is said to be intermediate, and another to exceed, as for instance the bashful man who is ashamed of everything; while he who falls short or is not ashamed of anything at all is shameless, and the intermediate person is modest. Righteous indignation is a mean between envy and spite, and these states are concerned with the pain and pleasure that are felt at the fortunes of our neighbours; the man who is characterized by righteous indignation is pained at undeserved good fortune, the envious man, going beyond him, is pained at all good fortune, and the spiteful man falls so far short of being pained that he even rejoices. But these states there will be an opportunity of describing elsewhere; with regard to justice, since it has not one simple meaning, we shall, after describing the other states, distinguish its two kinds and say how each of them is a mean; and similarly we shall treat also of the rational virtues.

VIII

There are three kinds of disposition, then, two of them vices, involving excess and deficiency respectively, and one a virtue, *viz.* the mean, and all are in a sense opposed to all; for the extreme states are contrary both to the intermediate state and to each other, and the intermediate to the extremes; as the equal is greater relatively to the less, less relatively to the greater, so the middle states are excessive relatively to the deficiencies, deficient relatively to the excesses, both in passions and in actions. For the brave man appears rash relatively to the coward, and cowardly relatively to the rash man; and similarly the temperate man appears self-indulgent relatively to the insensible man, insensible relatively to the self-indulgent, and the liberal man prodigal relatively to the mean man, mean relatively to the prodigal. Hence also the people at the extremes push the intermediate man each over to the other, and the brave man is called rash by the coward, cowardly by the rash man, and correspondingly in the other cases.

These states being thus opposed to one another, the greatest contrariety is that of the extremes to each other, rather than to the intermediate; for these are further from each other than from the intermediate, as the great is further from the small and the small from the great than both are from the equal. Again, to the intermediate some extremes show a certain likeness, as that of rashness to courage and that of prodigality to liberality; but the extremes show the greatest unlikeness to each other; now contraries are defined as the things that are furthest from each other, so that things that are further apart are more contrary.

To the mean in some cases the deficiency, in some the excess is more opposed; e.g. it is not rashness, which is an excess, but cowardice, which is a deficiency, that is more opposed to courage, and not insensibility, which is a deficiency, but self-indulgence, which is an excess, that is more opposed to temperance. This happens from two reasons, one being drawn from the thing itself; for because one extreme is nearer and liker to the intermediate, we oppose not this but rather its contrary to the intermediate. E.g. since rashness is thought liker and nearer to courage, and cowardice more unlike, we oppose rather the latter to courage; for things that are further from the intermediate are thought more contrary to it. This, then, is one cause, drawn from the thing itself; another is drawn from ourselves; for the things to which we ourselves more naturally tend seem more contrary to the intermediate. For instance, we ourselves tend more naturally to pleasures, and hence are more easily carried away towards self-indulgence than towards propriety. We describe as contrary to the mean, then, rather the directions in which we more often go to great lengths; and therefore self-indulgence, which is an excess, is the more contrary to temperance.

IX

That moral virtue is a mean, then, and in what sense it is so, and that it is a mean between two vices, the one involving excess, the other deficiency, and that it is such because its character is to aim at what is intermediate in passions and in actions, has been sufficiently stated. Hence also it is no easy task to be good. For in everything it is no easy task to find the middle, e.g. to find the middle of a circle is not for every one but for him who knows; so, too, any one can get angry—that is easy—or give or spend money; but to do this to the right person, to the right extent, at the right time, with the right motive, and in the right way, that is not for every one, nor is it easy; wherefore goodness is both rare and laudable and noble.

Hence he who aims at the intermediate must first depart from what is the more contrary to it, as Calypso advises.

Hold the ship out beyond that surf and spray.

For of the extremes one is more erroneous, one less so; therefore, since to hit the mean is hard in the extreme, we must as a second best, as people say, take the least of the evils; and this will be done best in the way we describe. But we must consider the things towards which we ourselves also are easily carried away; for some of us tend to one thing, some to another; and this will be recognizable from the pleasure and the pain we feel. We must drag ourselves away to the contrary extreme; for we shall get into the intermediate state by drawing well away from error, as people do in straightening sticks that are bent.

Now in everything the pleasant or pleasure is most to be guarded against; for we do not judge it impartially. We ought, then, to feel towards pleasure as the elders of the people felt towards Helen, and in all circumstances repeat their saying; for if we dismiss pleasure thus we are less likely to go astray. It is by doing this, then, (to sum the matter up) that we shall best be able to hit the mean.

But this is no doubt difficult, and especially in individual cases; for or is not easy to determine both how and with whom and on what provocation and how long one should be angry; for we too sometimes praise those who fall short and call them good-tempered, but sometimes we praise those who get angry and call them manly. The man, however, who deviates little from goodness is not blamed, whether he do so in the direction of the more or of the less, but only the man who deviates more widely; for he does not fail to be noticed. But up to what point and to what extent a man must deviate before he becomes blameworthy it is not easy to determine by reasoning, any more than anything else that is perceived by the senses; such things depend on particular facts, and the decision rests with perception. So much, then, is plain, that the intermediate state is in all things to be praised, but that we must incline sometimes towards the excess, sometimes towards the deficiency; for so shall we most easily hit the mean and what is right.

DISCUSSION QUESTIONS

1. Compare Aristotle's view to Confucius' "Doctrine of the Mean." What are some of the similarities and differences? Explain.

2. How does Aristotle's view differ from the three views from ancient India? Explain.

3. Explain the nature of the virtues discussed at the end of Book II.

Letter to Menoeceus

By Epicurus
Translated by Robert Drew Hicks

As mentioned in the discussion of Lucretius in Part II of Four Fundamental Questions, *Epicurus (341–270 BCE) was a Greek philosopher best known for his view on how to live a life worth living. The "Letter to Menoeceus" is a brief overview of Epicurean philosophy. He begins with the advice that it is never too late to start studying philosophy. Next, based on the atomic theory he accepts, he tells Menoeceus that death is nothing to us. There is a discussion of desires here as well. He makes a distinction between natural desires and groundless ones. Groundless desires are desires that cannot be realized, like the desire for immortality. There are two kinds of natural desires, necessary and unnecessary ones. Natural, but unnecessary desires are for things like sweets, luxurious food, and drinks. We should strive to satisfy our necessary, natural desires (seek simple desires) and try to avoid pain. For Epicurus a good life is a pleasant life, as "we cannot live pleasantly without living wisely, honorably, and justly; nor live wisely, honorably, and justly without living pleasantly."*

In this letter, Epicurus summarizes his ethical doctrines:

Epicurus to Menoeceus, greetings:

Let no one be slow to seek wisdom when he is young nor weary in the search of it when he has grown old. For no age is too early or too late for the health of the soul. And to say that the season for studying philosophy has not yet come, or that it is past and gone, is like saying that the season for happiness is not yet or that it is now no more. Therefore, both old and young alike ought to seek wisdom, the former in order that, as age comes over him, he may be young in good things because of the grace of what has been, and the latter in order that, while he is young, he may at the same time be old, because he has no fear of the things which are to come. So we must exercise ourselves in the things which bring happiness, since, if that be present, we have everything, and, if that be absent, all our actions are directed towards attaining it.

Those things which without ceasing I have declared unto you, do them, and exercise yourself in them, holding them to be the elements of right life. First believe that God is a living being immortal and blessed, according to the notion of a god indicated by the common sense of mankind; and so believing, you shall not affirm of him anything that is foreign to his immortality or that is repugnant to his blessedness. Believe about him whatever may uphold both his blessedness and his immortality. For there are gods, and the knowledge of them is manifest; but they are not such as the multitude believe, seeing that men do not steadfastly maintain the notions they form respecting them. Not the man who denies the gods worshipped by the multitude, but he who affirms of the gods what the multitude believes about them is truly impious. For the utterances of the multitude about the gods are not true preconceptions but false assumptions; hence it is that the greatest evils happen to the wicked and the greatest blessings happen to the good from the hand of the gods, seeing that they are always favorable to their own good qualities and take pleasure in men like themselves, but reject as alien whatever is not of their kind.

Accustom yourself to believing that death is nothing to us, for good and evil imply the capacity for sensation, and death is the privation of all sentience; therefore a correct understanding that death is nothing to us makes the mortality of life enjoyable, not by adding to life a limitless time, but by taking away the yearning after immortality. For life has no terrors for him who has thoroughly understood that there are no terrors for him in ceasing to live. Foolish, therefore, is the man who says that he fears death, not because it will pain when it comes, but because it pains in the prospect. Whatever causes no annoyance when it is present, causes only a groundless pain in the expectation. Death, therefore, the most awful of evils, is nothing to us, seeing that, when we are, death is not come, and, when death is come, we are not. It is nothing, then, either to the living or to the dead, for with the living it is not and the dead exist no longer.

But in the world, at one time men shun death as the greatest of all evils, and at another time choose it as a respite from the evils in life. The wise man does not deprecate life nor does he fear the cessation of life. The thought of life is no offense to him, nor is the cessation of life regarded as an evil. And even as men choose of food not merely and simply the larger portion, but the more pleasant, so the wise seek to enjoy the time which is most pleasant and not merely that which is longest. And he who admonishes the young to live well and the old to make a good end speaks foolishly, not merely because of the desirability of life, but because the same exercise at once teaches to live well and to die well. Much worse is he who says that it were good not to be born, but when once one is born to pass quickly through the gates of Hades. For if he truly believes this, why does he not depart from life? It would be easy for him to do so once he were firmly convinced. If he speaks only in jest, his words are foolishness as those who hear him do not believe.

We must remember that the future is neither wholly ours nor wholly not ours, so that neither must we count upon it as quite certain to come nor despair of it as quite certain not to come.

We must also reflect that of desires some are natural, others are groundless; and that of the natural some are necessary as well as natural, and some natural only. And of the necessary desires some are necessary if we are to be happy, some if the body is to be rid of uneasiness, some if we are even to live. He who has a clear and certain understanding of these things will direct every preference and aversion toward securing health of body and tranquillity of mind, seeing that this is the sum and end of a blessed life. For the end of all our actions is to be free from pain and fear, and, when once we have attained all this, the tempest of the soul is laid; seeing that the living creature has no need to go in search of something that is lacking, nor to look for anything else by which the good of the soul and of the body will be fulfilled. When we are pained because of the absence of pleasure, then, and then only, do we feel the need of pleasure. Wherefore we call pleasure the alpha and omega of a blessed life. Pleasure is our first and kindred good. It is the starting-point of every choice and of every aversion, and to it we come back, inasmuch as we make feeling the rule by which to judge of every good thing.

And since pleasure is our first and native good, for that reason we do not choose every pleasure whatsoever, but will often pass over many pleasures when a greater annoyance ensues from them. And often we consider pains superior to pleasures when submission to the pains for a long time brings us as a consequence a greater pleasure. While therefore all pleasure because it is naturally akin to us is good, not all pleasure is should be chosen, just as all pain is an evil and yet not all pain is to be shunned. It is, however, by measuring one against another, and by looking at the conveniences and inconveniences, that all these matters must be judged. Sometimes we treat the good as an evil, and the evil, on the contrary, as a good.

Again, we regard independence of outward things as a great good, not so as in all cases to use little, but so as to be contented with little if we have not much, being honestly persuaded that they have the sweetest enjoyment of luxury who stand least in need of it, and that whatever is natural is easily procured and only the vain and worthless hard to win. Plain fare gives as much pleasure as a costly diet, when once the pain of want has been removed, while bread and water confer the highest possible pleasure when they are brought to hungry lips. To habituate one's self, therefore, to simple and inexpensive diet supplies all that is needful for health, and enables a man to meet the necessary requirements of life without shrinking, and it places us in a better condition when we approach at intervals a costly fare and renders us fearless of fortune.

When we say, then, that pleasure is the end and aim, we do not mean the pleasures of the prodigal or the pleasures of sensuality, as we are understood to do by some through ignorance, prejudice, or willful misrepresentation. By pleasure we mean the absence of pain in the body and of trouble in the soul. It is not an unbroken succession of drinking-bouts and of revelry, not sexual lust, not the enjoyment of the fish and other delicacies of a luxurious table, which produce a pleasant life; it is sober reasoning, searching out the grounds of every choice and avoidance, and banishing those beliefs through which the greatest tumults take possession of the soul. Of all this the beginning and the greatest good is wisdom. Therefore wisdom is a more precious thing even than philosophy; from it spring all the other virtues, for it teaches that we cannot live pleasantly without living wisely, honorably, and justly; nor live wisely, honorably, and justly without living pleasantly. For the virtues have grown into one with a pleasant life, and a pleasant life is inseparable from them.

Who, then, is superior in your judgment to such a man? He holds a holy belief concerning the gods, and is altogether free from the fear of death. He has diligently considered the end fixed by nature, and understands how easily the limit of good things can be reached and attained, and how either the duration or the intensity of evils is but slight. Fate, which some introduce as sovereign over all things, he scorns, affirming rather that some things happen of necessity, others by chance, others through our own agency. For he sees that necessity destroys responsibility and that chance is inconstant; whereas our own actions are autonomous, and it is to them that praise and blame naturally attach. It were better, indeed, to accept the legends of the gods than to bow beneath that yoke of destiny which the natural philosophers have imposed. The one holds out some faint hope that we may escape if we honor the gods, while the necessity of the naturalists is deaf to all entreaties. Nor does he hold chance to be a god, as the world in general does, for in the acts of a god there is no disorder; nor to be a cause, though an uncertain one, for he believes that no good or evil is dispensed by chance to men so as to make life blessed, though it supplies the starting-point of great good and great evil. He believes that the misfortune of the wise is better than the prosperity of the fool. It is better, in short, that what is well judged in action should not owe its successful issue to the aid of chance.

Exercise yourself in these and related precepts day and night, both by yourself and with one who is like-minded; then never, either in waking or in dream, will you be disturbed, but will live as a god among men. For man loses all semblance of mortality by living in the midst of immortal blessings.

DISCUSSION QUESTIONS

1. Compare Epicurus' ideas to Aristotle's *Nicomachean Ethics*. What are some similarities and differences? Explain.

2. Which elements of Epicurus' advice to Menoeceus do you think are worth following? Why? Explain.

3. Explain Epicurus' position on death.

The Enchiridion

By Epictetus
Translated by George Long

Epictetus (ca. 55–135 CE), was a Roman philosopher who was a former slave. The philosophy he advocated is called stoicism. It has its origins with a philosopher named Zeno of Citium (334–262 BCE), who used to gather his friends on the porch (stoa) to discuss philosophy. Another stoic was Marcus Aurelius (121–180 CE) who was a Roman emperor. Stoics argue that you need to learn as much about the natural world as possible so that you will be prepared for whatever comes your way. The other main element of the stoic view of making life worth living is to not let the world affect you. A good popular culture representation of stoicism can be found in the portrayal of the Vulcans in Star Trek. *Our selection is from* The Enchiridion, *or handbook, which is a collection of sayings by Epictetus. The paragraphs do not link up in essay form—each one is a self-contained idea.*

CHAPTERS I-LI

I

Of things some are in our power, and others are not. In our power are opinion, movement toward a thing, desire, aversion (turning from a thing); and in a word, whatever are our own acts: not in our power are the body, property, reputation, offices (magisterial power), and in a word, whatever are not our own acts. And the things in our power are by nature free, not subject to restraint nor hindrance: but the things not in our power are weak, slavish, subject to restraint, in the power of others. Remember then that if you think the things which are by nature slavish to be free, and the things which are in the power of others to be your own, you will be hindered, you will lament, you will be disturbed, you will blame both gods and men: but if you think that only which is your own to be your own, and if you think that what is another's, as it really is, belongs to another, no man will ever compel you, no man will hinder you, you will never blame any man, you will accuse no man, you will do nothing involuntarily (against your will), no man will harm you, you will have no enemy, for you will not suffer any harm.

If then you desire (aim at) such great things, remember that you must not (attempt to) lay hold of them with a small effort; but you must leave alone some things entirely, and postpone others for the present. But if you wish for these things also (such great things), and power (office) and wealth, perhaps you will not gain even these very things (power and wealth) because you aim also at those former things (such great things): certainly you will fail in those things through which alone happiness and freedom are secured. Straightway, then, practice saying to every harsh appearance, You are an appearance, and in no manner what you appear to be. Then examine it by the rules which you possess, and by this first and chiefly, whether it relates to the things which are in our power or to the things which are not in our power: and if it relates to anything which is not in our power, be ready to say, that it does not concern you.

II

Remember that desire contains in it the profession (hope) of obtaining that which you desire; and the profession (hope) in aversion (turning from a thing) is that you will not fall into that which you attempt to avoid: and he who fails in his desire is unfortunate; and he who falls into that which he would avoid, is unhappy. If then you attempt to avoid only the things contrary to nature which are within your power, you will not be involved in any of the things which you would avoid. But if you attempt to avoid disease or death or poverty, you will be unhappy. Take away, then, aversion from all things which are not in our power, and transfer it to the things contrary to nature which are in our power. But destroy desire completely for the present. For if you desire anything which is not in our power, you must be unfortunate: but of the things in our power, and which it would be good to desire, nothing yet is before you. But employ only the power of moving toward an object and retiring from it; and these powers indeed only slightly and with exceptions and with remission.

III

In everything which pleases the soul, or supplies a want, or is loved, remember to add this to the (description, notion): What is the nature of each thing, beginning from the smallest? If you love an earthen vessel, say it is an earthen vessel which you love; for when it has been broken, you will not be disturbed. If you are kissing your child or wife, say that it is a human being whom you are kissing, for when the wife or child dies, you will not be disturbed.

IV

When you are going to take in hand any act, remind yourself what kind of an act it is. If you are going to bathe, place before yourself what happens in the bath: some splashing the water, others pushing against one another, others abusing one another, and some stealing: and thus with more safety you will undertake the matter, if you say to yourself, I now intend to bathe, and to maintain my will in a manner conformable to nature. And so you will do in every act: for thus if any hindrance to bathing shall happen, let this thought be ready; it was not this only that I intended, but I intended also to maintain my will in a way conformable to nature; but I shall not maintain it so, if I am vexed at what happens.

V

Men are disturbed not by the things which happen, but by the opinions about the things: for example, death is nothing terrible, for if it were, it would have seemed so to Socrates; for the opinion about death, that it is terrible, is the terrible thinghen, then, we are impeded or disturbed or grieved, let us never blame others, but ourselves, that is, our opinions. It is the act of an ill-instructed man to blame others for his own bad condition; it is the act of one who has begun to be instructed, to lay the blame on himself; and of one whose instruction is completed, neither to blame another, nor himself. beautiful, one might endure it. But when you are elated, and say, I have a beautiful horse, you must know that you are elated at having a good horse. What then is your own? The use of appearances. Consequently, when in the use of appearances you are conformable to nature, then be elated, for then you will be elated at something good which is your own.

VI

Be not elated at any advantage (excellence), which belongs to another. If a horse when he is elated should say, I am beautiful, one might endure it. But when you are elated, and say, I have a beautiful horse, you must know that you are elated at having a good horse. What then is your own? The use of appearances. Consequently, when in the use of appearances you are conformable to nature, then be elated, for then you will be elated at something good which is your own.

VII

As on a voyage when the vessel has reached a port, if you go out to get water, it is an amusement by the way to pick up a shellfish or some bulb, but your thoughts ought to be directed to the ship, and you ought to be constantly watching if the captain should call, and then you must throw away all those things, that you may not be bound and pitched into the ship like sheep: so in life also, if there be given to you instead of a little bulb and a shell a wife and child, there will be nothing to prevent (you from taking them). But if the captain should call, run to the ship, and leave all those things without regard to them. But if you are old, do not even go far from the ship, lest when you are called you make default.

VIII

Seek not that the things which happen should happen as you wish; but wish the things which happen to be as they are, and you will have a tranquil flow of life.

IX

Disease is an impediment to the body, but not to the will, unless the will itself chooses. Lameness is an impediment to the leg, but not to the will. And add this reflection on the occasion of everything that happens; for you will find it an impediment to something else, but not to yourself.

X

On the occasion of every accident (event) that befalls you, remember to turn to yourself and inquire what power you have for turning it to use. If you see a fair man or a fair woman, you will find that the power to resist is temperance (continence). If labor (pain) be presented to you, you will find that it is endurance. If it be abusive words, you will find it to be patience. And if you have been thus formed to the (proper) habit, the appearances will not carry you along with them.

XI

Never say about anything, I have lost it, but say I have restored it. Is your child dead? It has been restored. Is your wife dead? She has been restored. Has your estate been taken from you? Has not then this also been restored? But he who has taken it from me is a bad man. But what is it to you, by whose hands the giver demanded it back? So long as he may allow you, take care of it as a thing which belongs to another, as travelers do with their inn.

XII

If you intend to improve, throw away such thoughts as these: if I neglect my affairs, I shall not have the means of living: unless I chastise my slave, he will be bad. For it is better to die of hunger and so to be released from grief and fear than to live in abundance with perturbation; and it is better for your slave to be bad than for you to be unhappy. Begin then from little things. Is the oil spilled? Is a little wine stolen? Say on the occasion, at such price is sold freedom from perturbation; at such price is sold tranquility, but nothing is got for nothing. And when you call your slave, consider that it is possible that he does not hear; and if he does hear, that he will do nothing which you wish. But matters are not so well with him, but altogether well with you, that it should be in his power for you to be not disturbed.

XIII

If you would improve, submit to be considered without sense and foolish with respect to externals. Wish to be considered to know nothing: and if you shall seem to some to be a person of importance, distrust yourself. For you should know that it is not easy both to keep your will in a condition conformable to nature and (to secure) external things: but if a man is careful about the one, it is an absolute necessity that he will neglect the other.

XIV

If you would have your children and your wife and your friends to live forever, you are silly; for you would have the things which are not in your power to be in your power, and the things which belong to others to be yours. So if you would have your slave to be free from faults, you are a fool; for you would have badness not to be badness, but something else. But if you wish not to fail in your desires, you are able to do that. Practice, then, this which you are able to do. He is the master of every man who has the power over the things, which another person wishes or does not wish, the power to confer them on him or to take them away. Whoever then wishes to be free, let him neither wish for anything nor avoid anything which depends on others: if he does not observe this rule, he must be a slave.

XV

Remember that in life you ought to behave as at a banquet. Suppose that something is carried round and is opposite to you. Stretch out your hand and take a portion with decency. Suppose that it passes by you. Do not detain it. Suppose that it is not yet come to you. Do not send your desire forward to it, but wait till it is opposite to you. Do so with respect to children, so with respect to a wife, so with respect to magisterial offices, so with respect to wealth, and you will be some time a worthy partner of the banquets of the gods. But if you take none of the things which are set before you, and even despise them, then you will be not only a fellow banqueter with the gods, but also a partner with them in power. For by acting thus Diogenes and Heraclitus and those like them were deservedly divine, and were so called.

XVI

When you see a person weeping in sorrow either when a child goes abroad or when he is dead, or when the man has lost his property, take care that the appearance do not hurry you away with it, as if he were suffering in external things. But straightway make a distinction in your own mind, and be in readiness to say, it is not that which has happened that afflicts this man, for it does not afflict another, but it is the opinion about this thing which afflicts the man. So far as words, then, do not be unwilling to show him sympathy, and even if it happens so, to lament with him. But take care that you do not lament internally also.

XVII

Remember that thou art an actor in a play of such a kind as the teacher (author) may choose; if short, of a short one; if long, of a long one: if he wishes you to act the part of a poor man, see that you act the part naturally; if the part of a lame man, of a magistrate, of a private person, (do the same). For this is your duty, to act well the part that is given to you; but to select the part, belongs to another.

XVIII

When a raven has croaked inauspiciously, let not the appearance hurry you away with it; but straightaway make a distinction in your mind and say, None of these things is signified to me, but either to my poor body, or to my small property, or to my reputation, or to my children or to my wife: but to me all significations are auspicious if I choose. For whatever of these things results, it is in my power to derive benefit from it.

XIX

You can be invincible, if you enter into no contest in which it is not in your power to conquer. Take care, then, when you observe a man honored before others or possessed of great power or highly esteemed for any reason, not to suppose him happy, and be not carried away by the appearance. For if the nature of the good is in our power, neither envy nor jealousy will have a place in us. But you yourself will not wish to be a general or senator or consul, but a free man: and there is only one way to this, to despise (care not for) the things which are not in our power.

XX

Remember that it is not he who reviles you or strikes you, who insults you, but it is your opinion about these things as being insulting. When, then, a man irritates you, you must know that it is your own opinion which has irritated you. Therefore especially try not to be carried away by the appearance. For if you once gain time and delay, you will more easily master yourself.

XXI

Let death and exile and every other thing which appears dreadful be daily before your eyes; but most of all death: and you will never think of anything mean nor will you desire anything extravagantly.

XXII

If it should ever happen to you to be turned to externals in order to please some person, you must know that you have lost your purpose in life. Be satisfied, then, in everything with being a philosopher; and if you wish to seem also to any person to be a philosopher, appear so to yourself, and you will be able to do this.

XXIII

If you desire philosophy, prepare yourself from the beginning to be ridiculed, to expect that many will sneer at you, and say, He has all at once returned to us as a philosopher; and whence does he get this supercilious look for us? Do you not show a supercilious look; but hold on to the things which seem to you best as one appointed by God to this station. And remember that if you abide in the same principles, these men who first ridiculed will afterward admire you: but if you shall have been overpowered by them, you will bring on yourself double ridicule.

XXIV

If it should ever happen to you to be turned to externals in order to please some person, you must know that you have lost your purpose in life. Be satisfied, then, in everything with being a philosopher; and if you wish to seem also to any person to be a philosopher, appear so to yourself, and you will be able to do this.

XXV

Let not these thoughts afflict you, I shall live unhonored and be nobody nowhere. For if want of honor is an evil, you cannot be in evil through the means (fault) of another any more than you can be involved in anything base. Is it then your business to obtain the rank of a magistrate, or to be received at a banquet? By no means. How then can this be want of honor (dishonor)? And how will you be nobody nowhere, when you ought to be somebody in those things only which are in your power, in which indeed it is permitted to you to be a man of the greatest worth? But your friends will be without assistance! What do you mean by being without assistance? They will not receive money from you, nor will you make them Roman citizens. Who then told you that these are among the things which are in our power, and not in the power of others? And who can give to another what he has not himself? Acquire money then, your friends say, that we also may have something. If I can acquire money and also keep myself modest, and faithful and magnanimous, point out the way, and I will acquire it. But if you ask me to lose the things which are good and my own, in order that you may gain the things which are not good, see how unfair and silly you are. Besides, which would you rather have, money or a faithful and modest friend? For this end, then, rather help me to be such a man, and do not ask me to do this by which I shall lose that character. But my country, you say, as far as it depends on me, will be without my help. I ask again, what help do you mean? It will not have porticoes or baths through you. And what does this mean? For it is not furnished with shoes by means of a smith, nor with arms by means of a shoemaker. But it is enough if every man fully discharges the work that is his own: and if you provided it with another citizen faithful and modest, would you not be useful to it? Yes. Then you also cannot be useless to it. What place, then, you say, shall I hold in the city? Whatever you can, if you maintain at the same time your fidelity and modesty. But if when you wish to be useful to the state, you shall lose these qualities, what profit could you be to it, if you were made shameless and faithless?

XXVI

Has any man been preferred before you at a banquet, or in being saluted, or in being invited to a consultation? If these things are good, you ought to rejoice that he has obtained them: but if bad, be not grieved because you have not obtained them; and remember that you cannot, if you do not the same things in order to obtain what is not in our power, be considered worthy of the same (equal) things. For how can a man obtain an equal share with another when he does not visit a man's doors as that other man does, when he does not attend him when he goes abroad, as the other man does; when he does not praise (flatter) him as another does? You will be unjust, then, and insatiable, if you do not part with the price, in return for which those things are sold, and if you wish to obtain them for nothing. Well, what is the price of lettuces? An obolus perhaps. If, then, a man gives up the obolus, and receives the lettuces, and if you do not give up the obolus and do not obtain the lettuces, do not suppose that you receive less than he who has got the lettuces; for as he has the lettuces, so you have the obolus which you did not give. In the same way, then, in the other matter also you have not been invited to a man's feast, for you did not give to the host the price at which the supper is sold; but he sells it for praise (flattery), he sells it for personal attention. Give then the price, if it is for your interest, for which it is sold. But if you wish both not to give the price and to obtain the things, you are insatiable and silly. Have you nothing then in place of the supper? You have indeed, you have the not flattering of him, whom you did not choose to flatter; you have the not enduring of the man when he enters the room.

XXVII

We may learn the wish (will) of nature from the things in which we do not differ from one another; for instance, when your neighbor's slave has broken his cup, or anything else, we are ready to say forthwith, that it is one of the things which happen. You must know, then, that when your cup also is broken, you ought to think as you did when your neighbor's cup was broken. Transfer this reflection to greater things also. Is another man's child or wife dead? There is no one who would not say, this is an event incident to man. But when a man's own child or wife is dead, forthwith he calls out, Woe to me, how wretched I am. But we ought to remember how we feel when we hear that it has happened to others.

XXVIII

As a mark is not set up for the purpose of missing the aim, so neither does the nature of evil exist in the world.

XXIX

If any person was intending to put your body in the power of any man whom you fell in with on the way, you would be vexed: but that you put your understanding in the power of any man whom you meet, so that if he should revile you, it is disturbed and troubled, are you not ashamed at this?

XXX

In every act observe the things which come first, and those which follow it; and so proceed to the act. If you do not, at first you will approach it with alacrity, without having thought of the things which will follow; but afterward, when certain base (ugly) things have shown themselves, you will be ashamed. A man wishes to conquer at the Olympic games. I also wish indeed, for it is a fine thing. But observe both the things which come first, and the things which follow; and then begin the act. You must do everything according to rule, eat according to strict orders; abstain from delicacies; exercise yourself as you are bid at appointed times, in heat, in cold; you must not drink cold water, nor wine as you choose. In a word, you must deliver yourself up to the exercise master as you do to the physician, and then proceed to the contest. And sometimes you will strain the hand, put the ankle out of joint, swallow much dust, sometimes be flogged, and after all this be defeated. When you have considered all this, if you still choose, go to the contest: if you do not, you will behave like children, who at one time play at wrestlers, another time as flute players, again as gladiators, then as trumpeters, then as tragic actors: so you also will be at one time an athlete, at another a gladiator, then a rhetorician, then a philosopher, but with your whole soul you will be nothing at all; but like an ape you imitate everything that you see, and one thing after another pleases you. For you have not undertaken anything with consideration, nor have you surveyed it well; but carelessly and with cold desire.

Thus some who have seen a philosopher and having heard one speak, as Euphrates speaksâ€"and who can speak as he does? They wish to be philosophers themselves also.

My man, first of all consider what kind of thing it is: and then examine your own nature, if you are able to sustain the character. Do you wish to be a pentathlete or a wrestler? Look at your arms, your thighs, examine your loins. For different men are formed by nature for different things. Do you think that if you do these things, you can eat in the same manner, drink in the same manner, and in the same manner loathe certain things? You must pass sleepless nights; endure toil; go away from your kinsmen; be despised by a slave; in everything have the inferior part, in honor, in office, in the courts of justice, in every little matter. Consider these things, if you would exchange for them, freedom from passions, liberty, tranquility. If not, take care that, like little children, you be not now a philosopher, then a servant of the publicani,[] then a rhetorician, then a procurator (manager) for Caesar. These things are not consistent. You must be one man, either good or bad. You must either cultivate your own ruling faculty, or external things; you must either exercise your skill on internal things or on external things; that is, you must either maintain the position of a philosopher or that of a common person.

XXXI

Duties are universally measured by relations. Is a man a father? The precept is to take care of him, to yield to him in all things, to submit when he is reproachful, when he inflicts blows. But suppose that he is a bad father. Were you then by nature made akin to a good father? No; but to a father. Does a brother wrong you? Maintain then your own position toward him, and do not examine what he is doing, but what you must do that your will shall be conformable to nature. For another will not damage you, unless you choose: but you will be damaged then when you shall think that you are damaged. In this way, then, you will discover your duty from the relation of a neighbor, from that of a citizen, from that of a general, if you are accustomed to contemplate the relations.

XXXII

As to piety toward the gods you must know that this is the chief thing, to have right opinions about them, to think that they exist, and that they administer the All well and justly; and you must fix yourself in this principle (duty), to obey them, and yield to them in everything which happens, and voluntarily to follow it as being accomplished by the wisest intelligence. For if you do so, you will never either blame the gods, nor will you accuse them of neglecting you. And it is not possible for this to be done in any other way than by withdrawing from the things which are not in our power, and by placing the good and the evil only in those things which are in our power. For if you think that any of the things which are not in our power is good or bad, it is absolutely necessary that, when you do not obtain what you wish, and when you fall into those things which you do not wish, you will find fault and hate those who are the cause of them; for every animal is formed by nature to this, to fly from and to turn from the things which appear harmful and the things which are the cause of the harm, but to follow and admire the things which are useful and the causes of the useful.

It is impossible, then, for a person who thinks that he is harmed to be delighted with that which he thinks to be the cause of the harm, as it is also impossible to be pleased with the harm itself. For this reason also a father is reviled by his son, when he gives no part to his son of the things which are considered to be good: and it was this which made Polynices and Eteocles[] enemies, the opinion that royal power was a good. It is for this reason that the cultivator of the earth reviles the gods, for this reason the sailor does, and the merchant, and for this reason those who lose their wives and their children. For where the useful (your interest) is, there also piety is. Consequently, he who takes care to desire as he ought and to avoid as he ought, at the same time also cares after piety. But to make libations and to sacrifice and to offer first fruits according to the custom of our fathers, purely and not meanly nor carelessly nor scantily nor above our ability, is a thing which belongs to all to do.

XXXIII

When you have recourse to divination, remember that you do not know how it will turn out, but that you are come to inquire from the diviner. But of what kind it is, you know when you come, if indeed you are a philosopher. For if it is any of the things which are not in our power, it is absolutely necessary that it must be neither good nor bad. Do not then bring to the diviner desire or aversion: if you do, you will approach him with fear. But having determined in your mind that everything which shall turn out (result) is indifferent, and does not concern you, and whatever it may be, for it will be in your power to use it well, and no man will hinder this, come then with confidence to the gods as your advisers. And then, when any advice shall have been given, remember whom you have taken as advisers, and whom you will have neglected, if you do not obey them. And go to divination, as Socrates said that you ought, about those matters in which all the inquiry has reference to the result, and in which means are not given either by reason nor by any other art for knowing the thing which is the subject of the inquiry. Wherefore, when we ought to share a friend's danger or that of our country, you must not consult the diviner whether you ought to share it. For even if the diviner shall tell you that the signs of the victims are unlucky, it is plain that this is a token of death or mutilation of part of the body or of exile. But reason prevails that even with these risks we should share the dangers of our friend and of our country. Therefore attend to the greater diviner, the Pythian god, who ejected from the temple him who did not assist his friend when he was being murdered.

XXXIV

Immediately prescribe some character and some form to yourself, which you shall observe both when you are alone and when you meet with men. And let silence be the general rule, or let only what is necessary be said, and in few words. And rarely and when the occasion calls we shall say something; but about none of the common subjects, nor about gladiators, nor horse-races, nor about athletes, nor about eating or drinking, which are the usual subjects; and especially not about men, as blaming them or praising them, or comparing them. If then you are able, bring over by your conversation the conversation of your associates to that which is proper; but if you should happen to be confined to the company of strangers, be silent.

Let not your laughter be much, nor on many occasions, nor excessive.

Refuse altogether to take an oath, if it is possible: if it is not, refuse as far as you are able. Avoid banquets which are given by strangers and by ignorant persons. But if ever there is occasion to join in them, let your attention be carefully fixed, that you slip not into the manners of the vulgar (the uninstructed). For you must know, that if your companion be impure, he also who keeps company with him must become impure, thugh he should happen to be pure. Take (apply) the things which relate to the body as far as the bare use, as food, drink, clothing, house, and slaves: but exclude everything which is for show or luxury. As to pleasure with women, abstain as far as you can before marriage: but if you do indulge in it, do it in the way which is conformable to custom. Do not, however, be disagreeable to those who indulge in these pleasures, or reprove them; and do not often boast that you do not indulge in them yourself. If a man has reported to you, that a certain person speaks ill of you, do not make any defense (answer) to what has been told you: but reply, The man did not know the rest of my faults, for he would not have mentioned these only. It is not necessary to go to the theaters often: but if there is ever a proper occasion for going, do not show yourself as being a partisan of any man except yourself, that is, desire only that to be done which is done, and for him only to gain the prize who gains the prize; for in this way you will meet with no hindrance But abstain entirely from shouts and laughter at any (thing or person), or violent emotions. And when you are come away, do not talk much about what has passed on the stage, except about that which may lead to your own improvement. For it is plain, if you do talk much, that you admired the spectacle (more than you ought). Do not go to the hearing of certain persons' recitations nor visit them readily. But if you do attend, observe gravity and sedateness, and also avoid making yourself disagreeable.

When you are going to meet with any person, and particularly one of those who are considered to be in a superior condition, place before yourself what Socrates or Zeno would have done in such circumstances, and you will have no difficulty in making a proper use of the occasion.

When you are going to any of those who are in great power, place before yourself that you will not find the man at home, that you will be excluded, that the door will not be opened to you, that the man will not care about you. And if with all this it is your duty to visit him, bear what happens, and never say to yourself that it was not worth the trouble. For this is silly, and marks the character of a man who is offended by externals.

In company take care not to speak much and excessively about your own acts or dangers: for as it is pleasant to you to make mention of your dangers, it is not so pleasant to others to hear what has happened to you. Take care also not to provoke laughter; for this is a slippery way toward vulgar habits, and is also adapted to diminish the respect of your neighbors. It is a dangerous habit also to approach obscene talk. When, then, anything of this kind happens, if there is a good opportunity, rebuke the man who has proceeded to this talk: but if there is not an opportunity, by your silence at least, and blushing and expression of dissatisfaction by your countenance, show plainly that you are displeased at such talk.

XXXV

If you have received the impression of any pleasure, guard yourself against being carried away by it; but let the thing wait for you, and allow yourself a certain delay on your own part. Then think of both times, of the time when you will enjoy the pleasure, and of the time after the enjoyment of the pleasure when you will repent and will reproach yourself. And set against these things how you will rejoice if you have abstained from the pleasure, and how you will commend yourself. But if it seem to you seasonable to undertake (do) the thing, take care that the charm of it, and the pleasure, and the attraction of it shall not conquer you: but set on the other side the consideration how much better it is to be conscious that you have gained this victory.

XXXVI

When you have decided that a thing ought to be done and are doing it, never avoid being seen doing it, though the many shall form an unfavorable opinion about it. For if it is not right to do it, avoid doing the thing; but if it is right, why are you afraid of those who shall find fault wrongly?

XXXVII

As the proposition it is either day or it is night is of great importance for the disjunctive argument, but for the conjunctive is of no value, so in a symposium (entertainment) to select the larger share is of great value for the body, but for the maintenance of the social feeling is worth nothing. When then you are eating with another, remember to look not only to the value for the body of the things set before you, but also to the value of the behavior toward the host which ought to be observed.

XXXVIII

If you have assumed a character above your strength, you have both acted in this matter in an unbecoming way, and you have neglected that which you might have fulfilled.

XXXIX

In walking about as you take care not to step on a nail or to sprain your foot, so take care not to damage your own ruling faculty: and if we observe this rule in every act, we shall undertake the act with more security.

XL

The measure of possession (property) is to every man the body, as the foot is of the shoe. If then you stand on this rule (the demands of the body), you will maintain the measure: but if you pass beyond it, you must then of necessity be hurried as it were down a precipice. As also in the matter of the shoe, if you go beyond the (necessities of the) foot, the shoe is gilded, then of a purple color, then embroidered: for there is no limit to that which has once passed the true measure.

XLI

Women forthwith from the age of fourteen are called by the men mistresses (dominae). Therefore, since they see that there is nothing else that they can obtain, but only the power of lying with men, they begin to decorate themselves, and to place all their hopes in this. It is worth our while, then, to take care that they may know that they are valued (by men) for nothing else than appearing (being) decent and modest and discreet.

XLII

It is a mark of a mean capacity to spend much time on the things which concern the body, such as much exercise, much eating, much drinking, much easing of the body, much copulation. But these things should be done as subordinate things: and let all your care be directed to the mind.

XLIII

When any person treats you ill or speaks ill of, you, remember that he does this or says this because he thinks that it is his duty. It is not possible, then, for him to follow that which seems right to you, but that which seems right to himself. Accordingly, if he is wrong in his opinion, he is the person who is hurt, for he is the person who has been deceived; for if a man shall suppose the true conjunction to be false, it is not the conjunction which is hindered, but the man who has been deceived about it. If you proceed, then, from these opinions, you will be mild in temper to him who reviles you: for say on each occasion, It seemed so to him.

XLIV

Everything has two handles, the one by which it may be borne, the other by which it may not. If your brother acts unjustly, do not lay hold of the act by that handle wherein he acts unjustly, for this is the handle which cannot be borne; but lay hold of the other, that he is your brother, that he was nurtured with you, and you will lay hold of the thing by that handle by which it can be borne.

XLV

These reasonings do not cohere: I am richer than you, therefore I am better than you; I am more eloquent than you, therefore I am better than you. On the contrary these rather cohere, I am richer than you, therefore my possessions are greater than yours: I am more eloquent than you, therefore my speech is superior to yours. But you are neither possession nor speech.

XLVI

Does a man bathe quickly (early)? Do not say that he bathes badly, but that he bathes quickly. Does a man drink much wine? Do not say that he does this badly, but say that he drinks much. For before you shall have determined the opinion, how do you know whether he is acting wrong? Thus it will not happen to you to comprehend some appearances which are capable of being comprehended, but to assent to others.

XLVII

On no occasion call yourself a philosopher, and do not speak much among the uninstructed about theorems (philosophical rules, precepts): but do that which follows from them. For example, at a banquet do not say how a man ought to eat, but eat as you ought to eat. For remember that in this way Socrates also altogether avoided ostentation: persons used to come to him and ask to be recommended by him to philosophers, and he used to take them to philosophers: so easily did he submit to being overlooked. Accordingly, if any conversation should arise among uninstructed persons about any theorem, generally be silent; for there is great danger that you will immediately vomit up what you have not digested. And when a man shall say to you, that you know nothing, and you are not vexed, then be sure that you have begun the work (of philosophy). For even sheep do not vomit up their grass and show to the shepherds how much they have eaten; but when they have internally digested the pasture, they produce externally wool and milk. Do you also show not your theorems to the uninstructed, but show the acts which come from their digestion.

XLVIII

When at a small cost you are supplied with everything for the body, do not be proud of this; nor, if you drink water, say on every occasion, I drink water. But consider first how much more frugal the poor are than we, and how much more enduring of labor. And if you ever wish to exercise yourself in labor and endurance, do it for yourself, and not for others: do not embrace statues. But if you are ever very thirsty, take a draught of cold water, and spit it out, and tell no man.

XLIX

The condition and characteristic of an uninstructed person is this: he never expects from himself profit (advantage) nor harm, but from externals. The condition and characteristic of a philosopher is this: he expects all advantage and all harm from himself. The signs (marks) of one who is making progress are these: he censures no man, he praises no man, he blames no man, he accuses no man, he says nothing about himself as if he were somebody or knew something; when he is impeded at all or hindered, he blames himself: if a man praises him, he ridicules the praiser to himself: if a man censures him, he makes no defense: he goes about like weak persons, being careful not to move any of the things which are placed, before they are firmly fixed: he removes all desire from himself, and he transfers aversion to those things only of the things within our power which are contrary to nature: he employs a moderate movement toward everything: whether he is considered foolish or ignorant, he cares not: and in a word he watches himself as if he were an enemy and lying in ambush.

L

When a man is proud because he can understand and explain the writings of Chrysippus,[] say to yourself, If Chrysippus had not written obscurely, this man would have nothing to be proud of. But what is it that I wish? To understand Nature and to follow it. I inquire, therefore, who is the interpreter: and when I have heard that it is Chrysippus, I come to him (the interpreter). But I do not understand what is written, and therefore I seek the interpreter. And so far there is yet nothing to be proud of. But when I shall have found the interpreter, the thing that remains is to use the precepts (the lessons). This itself is the only thing to be proud of. But if I shall admire the exposition, what else have I been made unless a grammarian instead of a philosopher? except in one thing, that I am explaining Chrysippus instead of Homer. When, then, any man says to me, Read Chrysippus to me, I rather blush, when I cannot show my acts like to and consistent with his words.

LI

Whatever things (rules) are proposed to you [for the conduct of life] abide by them, as if they were laws, as if you would be guilty of impiety if you transgressed any of them. And whatever any man shall say about you, do not attend to it: for this is no affair of yours. How long will you then still defer thinking yourself worthy of the best things, and in no matter transgressing the distinctive reason? Have you accepted the theorems (rules), which it was your duty to agree to, and have you agreed to them?

What teacher, then, do you still expect that you defer to him the correction of yourself? You are no longer a youth, but already a full-grown man. If then you are negligent and slothful, and are continually making procrastination after procrastination, and proposal (intention) after proposal, and fixing day after day, after which you will attend to yourself, you will not know that you are not making improvement, but you will continue ignorant (uninstructed) both while you live and till you die. Immediately, then, think it right to live as a full-grown man, and one who is making proficiency, and let everything which appears to you to be the best be to you a law which must not be transgressed. And if anything laborious, or pleasant or glorious or inglorious be presented to you, remember that now is the contest, now are the Olympic games, and they cannot be deferred; and that it depends on one defeat and one giving way that progress is either lost or maintained. Socrates in this way becomes perfect, in all things improving himself, attending to nothing except to reason. But you, though you are not yet a Socrates, ought to live as one who wishes to be a Socrates.

DISCUSSION QUESTIONS

1. Compare Epictetus' ideas to those of Epicurus. Which thinker gives the best advice? Explain.

2. In what ways are the ideas of Epictetus similar to Aristotle? In what ways are they different? Explain.

3. Which five paragraphs offer what you think is the best advice? Explain why you think this.

The Good Brahmin

By Voltaire

Voltaire (1694–1778, real name: François-Marie Arouet), was a French philosopher, essayist, poet, playwright, and novelist. His works are considered among the most influential of the late Enlightenment period. He is probably best known for his short 1759 novel, Candide, or Optimism, *which is, in part, a satire on Leibniz's* Theodicy *(see Part II of* Four Fundamental Questions *for more on this). In the novel, every bad thing you can imagine happens to the main characters, but they persevere. One of the characters, Dr. Pangloss, continually asserts the Leibnizian position, in spite of the conditions he ends up in. Candide was made into an operetta by Leonard Bernstein in 1956. Our selection, though, is a short fiction, "The Good Brahmin," also from 1759. The issue that underlies the story is whether or not ignorance is bliss. If you could choose to stay intelligent and unsatisfied or trade places with a simpleton, but be happy, would you do it? The Brahmin says that he would not want to trade places. A Brahmin is someone who is a member of the priestly caste in Hinduism. This is why the Brahmin in the story is troubled—he doesn't have the answers to the deep metaphysical questions that the devotees of Hinduism might ask him. The narrator notes, at the end, that none of his learned friends would trade places, either.*

In my travels I once happened to meet with an aged Brahmin. This man had a great share of understanding and prudence, and was very learned. He was also very rich, and his riches added greatly to his popularity; for, wanting nothing that wealth could procure, he had no desire to defraud anyone. His family was admirably managed by three handsome wives, who always studied to please him; and when he was weary of their society, he had recourse to the study of philosophy.

Not far from his house, which was handsome, well-furnished and embellished with delightful gardens, dwelt an old Indian woman who was a great bigot, ignorant, and withal very poor.

"I wish," said the Brahmin to me one day, "I had never been born!"

"Why so?" said I.

"Because," replied he, "I have been studying these forty years, and I find it has been so much time lost. While I teach others I know nothing myself. The sense of my condition is so humiliating, it makes all things so distasteful to me, that life has become a burden. I have been born, and I exist in time, without knowing what time is. I am placed, as our wise men say, in the confines between two eternities, and yet I have no idea of eternity. I am composed of matter, I think, but have never been able to satisfy myself what it is that produces thought. I even am ignorant whether my understanding is a simple faculty I possess, like that of walking and digesting, or if

I think with my head in the same manner as I take hold of a thing with my hands. I am not only thus in the dark with relation to the principles of thought, but the principles of my motions are entirely unknown to me. I do not know why I exist, and yet I am applied to every day for a solution of the enigma. I must return an answer, but can say nothing satisfactory on the subject. I talk a great deal, and when I have done speaking remain confounded and ashamed of what I have said.

"I am in still greater perplexity when I am asked if Brahma was produced by Vishnu, or if they have both existed from eternity. God is my judge that I know nothing of the matter, as plainly appears by my answers. 'Reverend father,' says one, 'be pleased to inform me how evil is spread over the face of the earth.' I am as much at a loss as those who ask the question. Sometimes I tell them that every thing is for the best; but those who have the gout or the stone—those who have lost their fortunes or their limbs in the wars—believe as little of this assertion as I do myself. I retire to my own house full of curiosity, and endeavor to enlighten my ignorance by consulting the writings of our ancient sages, but they only serve to bewilder me the more. When I talk with my brethren upon this subject, some tell me we ought to make the most of life and laugh at the world. Others think they know something, and lose themselves in vain and chimerical hypotheses. Every effort I make to solve the mystery adds to the load I feel. Sometimes I am ready to fall into despair when I reflect that, after all my researches, I neither know from whence I came, what I am, whither I shall go, or what is to become of me."

The condition in which I saw this good man gave me real concern. No one could be more rational, no one more open and honest. It appeared to me that the force of his understanding and the sensibility of his heart were the causes of his misery.

The same day I had a conversation with the old woman, his neighbor. I asked her if she had ever been unhappy for not understanding how her soul was made? She did not even comprehend my question. She had not, for the briefest moment in her life, had a thought about these subjects with which the good Brahmin had so tormented himself. She believed from the bottom of her heart in the metamorphoses of her god Vishnu, and, provided she could get some of the sacred water of the Ganges in which to make her ablutions, she thought herself the happiest of women.

Struck with the happiness of this poor creature, I returned to my philosopher, whom I thus addressed:

"Are you not ashamed to be thus miserable when, not fifty yards from you, there is an old automaton who thinks of nothing and lives contented?"

"You are right," he replied. "I have said to myself a thousand times that I should be happy if I were but as ignorant as my old neighbor, and yet it is a happiness I do not desire."

This reply of the Brahmin made a greater impression on me than anything that had passed. I consulted my own heart and found that I myself should not wish to be happy on condition of being ignorant.

I submitted this matter to some philosophers, and they were all of my opinion: and yet, said I, there is something very contradictory in this manner of thinking; for, after all, what is the question? Is it not to be happy? What signifies it then whether we have understandings or whether we are fools? Besides, there is this to be said: those who are contented with their condition are sure of that content; while those who have the faculty of reasoning are not always sure of reasoning right. It is evident then, I continued, that we ought rather to wish not to have common sense, if that common sense contributes to our being either miserable or wicked.

They were all of my opinion, and yet not one of them could be found to accept of happiness on the terms of being ignorant. From hence I concluded, that although we may set a great value upon happiness, we set a still greater upon reason.

But after mature reflection upon this subject I still thought there was great madness in preferring reason to happiness. How is this contradiction to be explained? Like all other questions, a great deal may be said about it.

DISCUSSION QUESTIONS

1. Do you agree with the Brahmin and the narrator that we should not trade places? Why? Explain.

2. Reason is blamed here as the cause of his unhappiness. Does this make sense? Are there other causes we should be looking at? Explain.

3. How do the ideas here compare to the authors that precede Voltaire in Part IV of *Four Fundamental Questions*? Explain.

A Treatise of Human Nature

By David Hume

Our selection of Hume's view on ethics comes from Book II, Part III, section iii; and Book III, Part I, sections i–ii of Hume's Treatise on Human Nature *(for more on Hume and the* Treatise *see Part I of* Four Fundamental Questions. *In the first excerpt, from Book II, Hume explains his view on the relation of reason and passions (emotions), which he refers to as a combat. He argues for two positions here. First, reason cannot be a motive for action. Secondly, passion cannot be opposed by reason. Famously, he says, "[r]eason is, and ought only to be the slave of the passions, and can never pretend to any other office than to serve and obey them." Passions can only be opposed by other passions. What people call "listening to reason" would, for Hume, be a case of a calmer passion prevailing over a more violent passion. Reason can only "direct our judgment" and provide us information.*

His view on motivation and behavior is in the second excerpt, which is from Book III of the Treatise. *Part I, section I of Book III opens with Hume arguing for a position that follows from the Book II passage: reason cannot provide motive for morality or imply moral distinctions because reason cannot oppose passion. In section ii, he tells us where the motives do come from. They are natural tendencies of a moral sense. That which is pleasing to us or society, we denominate as good, and that which is not, not.*

BOOK II, PART III

SECT. III. OF THE INFLUENCING MOTIVES OF THE WILL

Nothing is more usual in philosophy, and even in common life, than to talk of the combat of passion and reason, to give the preference to reason, and assert that men are only so far virtuous as they conform themselves to its dictates. Every rational creature, it is said, is obliged to regulate his actions by reason; and if any other motive or principle challenge the direction of his conduct, he ought to oppose it, till it be entirely subdued, or at least brought to a conformity with that superior principle. On this method of thinking the greatest part of moral philosophy, antient and modern, seems to be founded; nor is there an ampler field, as well for metaphysical arguments, as popular declamations, than this supposed pre-eminence of reason above passion. The eternity, invariableness, and divine origin of the former have been displayed to the best advantage: The blindness, unconstancy, and deceitfulness of the latter have been as strongly insisted on. In order to shew the fallacy of all this philosophy, I shall endeavour to prove first, that reason alone can never be a motive to any action of the will; and secondly, that it can never oppose passion in the direction of the will.

The understanding exerts itself after two different ways, as it judges from demonstration or probability; as it regards the abstract relations of our ideas, or those relations of objects, of which experience only gives us information. I believe it scarce will be asserted, that the first species of reasoning alone is ever the cause of any action. As its proper province is the world of ideas, and as the will always places us in that of realities, demonstration and volition seem, upon that account, to be totally removed, from each other. Mathematics, indeed, are useful in all mechanical operations, and arithmetic in almost every art and profession: But it is not of themselves they have any influence: Mechanics are the art of regulating the motions of bodies to some designed end or purpose; and the reason why we employ arithmetic in fixing the proportions of numbers, is only that we may discover the proportions of their influence and operation. A merchant is desirous of knowing the sum total of his accounts with any person: Why? but that he may learn what sum will have the same effects in paying his debt, and going to market, as all the particular articles taken together. Abstract or demonstrative reasoning, therefore, never influences any of our actions, but only as it directs our judgment concerning causes and effects; which leads us to the second operation of the understanding.

It is obvious, that when we have the prospect of pain or pleasure from any object, we feel a consequent emotion of aversion or propensity, and are carryed to avoid or embrace what will give us this uneasines or satisfaction. It is also obvious, that this emotion rests not here, but making us cast our view on every side, comprehends whatever objects are connected with its original one by the relation of cause and effect. Here then reasoning takes place to discover this relation; and according as our reasoning varies, our actions receive a subsequent variation. But it is evident in this case that the impulse arises not from reason, but is only directed by it. It is from the prospect of pain or pleasure that the aversion or propensity arises towards any object: And these emotions extend themselves to the causes and effects of that object, as they are pointed out to us by reason and experience. It can never in the least concern us to know, that such objects are causes, and such others effects, if both the causes and effects be indifferent to us. Where the objects themselves do not affect us, their connexion can never give them any influence; and it is plain, that as reason is nothing but the discovery of this connexion, it cannot be by its means that the objects are able to affect us.

Since reason alone can never produce any action, or give rise to volition, I infer, that the same faculty is as incapable of preventing volition, or of disputing the preference with any passion or emotion. This consequence is necessary. It is impossible reason coued have the latter effect of preventing volition, but by giving an impulse in a contrary direction to our passion; and that impulse, had it operated alone, would have been able to produce volition. Nothing can oppose or retard the impulse of passion, but a contrary impulse; and if this contrary impulse ever arises from reason, that latter faculty must have an original influence on the will, and must be able to cause, as well as hinder any act of volition. But if reason has no original influence, it is impossible it can withstand any principle, which has such an efficacy, or ever keep the mind in suspence a moment. Thus it appears, that the principle, which opposes our passion, cannot be the same with reason, and is only called so in an improper sense. We speak not strictly and philosophically when we talk of the combat of passion and of reason. Reason is, and ought only to be the slave of the passions, and can never pretend to any other office than to serve and obey them. As this opinion may appear somewhat extraordinary, it may not be improper to confirm it by some other considerations.

A passion is an original existence, or, if you will, modification of existence, and contains not any representative quality, which renders it a copy of any other existence or modification. When I am angry, I am actually possest with the passion, and in that emotion have no more a reference to any other object, than when I am thirsty, or sick, or more than five foot high. It is impossible, therefore, that this passion can be opposed by, or be contradictory to truth and reason; since this contradiction consists in the disagreement of ideas, considered as copies, with those objects, which they represent.

What may at first occur on this head, is, that as nothing can be contrary to truth or reason, except what has a reference to it, and as the judgments of our understanding only have this reference, it must follow, that passions can be contrary to reason only so far as they are accompanyed with some judgment or opinion. According to this principle, which is so obvious and natural, it is only in two senses, that any affection can be called unreasonable. First, When a passion, such as hope or fear, grief or joy, despair or security, is founded on the supposition or the existence of objects, which really do not exist. Secondly, When in exerting any passion in action, we chuse means insufficient for the designed end, and deceive ourselves in our judgment of causes and effects. Where a passion is neither founded on false suppositions, nor chuses means insufficient for the end, the understanding can neither justify nor condemn it. It is not contrary to reason to prefer the destruction of the whole world to the scratching of my finger. It is not contrary to reason for me to chuse my total ruin, to prevent the least uneasiness of an Indian or person wholly unknown to me. It is as little contrary to reason to prefer even my own acknowledgeed lesser good to my greater, and have a more ardent affection for the former than the latter. A trivial good may, from certain circumstances, produce a desire superior to what arises from the greatest and most valuable enjoyment; nor is there any thing more extraordinary in this, than in mechanics to see one pound weight raise up a hundred by the advantage of its situation. In short, a passion must be accompanyed with some false judgment in order to its being unreasonable; and even then it is not the passion, properly speaking, which is unreasonable, but the judgment.

The consequences are evident. Since a passion can never, in any sense, be called unreasonable, but when founded on a false supposition, or when it chuses means insufficient for the designed end, it is impossible, that reason and passion can ever oppose each other, or dispute for the government of the will and actions. The moment we perceive the falshood of any supposition, or the insufficiency of any means our passions yield to our reason without any opposition. I may desire any fruit as of an excellent relish; but whenever you convince me of my mistake, my longing ceases. I may will the performance of certain actions as means of obtaining any desired good; but as my willing of these actions is only secondary, and founded on the supposition, that they are causes of the proposed effect; as soon as I discover the falshood of that supposition, they must become indifferent to me.

It is natural for one, that does not examine objects with a strict philosophic eye, to imagine, that those actions of the mind are entirely the same, which produce not a different sensation, and are not immediately distinguishable to the feeling and perception. Reason, for instance, exerts itself without producing any sensible emotion; and except in the more sublime disquisitions of philosophy, or in the frivolous subtilties of the school, scarce ever conveys any pleasure or uneasiness. Hence it proceeds, that every action of the mind, which operates with the same calmness and tranquillity, is confounded with reason by all those, who judge of things from the first view and appearance. Now it is certain, there are certain calm desires and tendencies, which, though they be real passions, produce little emotion in the mind, and are more known by their effects than by the immediate feeling or sensation. These desires are of two kinds; either certain instincts originally implanted in our natures, such as benevolence and resentment, the love of life, and kindness to children; or the general appetite to good, and aversion to evil, considered merely as such. When any of these passions are calm, and cause no disorder in the soul, they are very readily taken for the determinations of reason, and are supposed to proceed from the same faculty, with that, which judges of truth and falshood. Their nature and principles have been supposed the same, because their sensations are not evidently different.

Beside these calm passions, which often determine the will, there are certain violent emotions of the same kind, which have likewise a great influence on that faculty. When I receive any injury from another, I often feel a violent passion of resentment, which makes me desire his evil and punishment, independent of all considerations of pleasure and advantage to myself. When I am immediately threatened with any grievous ill, my fears, apprehensions, and aversions rise to a great height, and produce a sensible emotion.

The common error of metaphysicians has lain in ascribing the direction of the will entirely to one of these principles, and supposing the other to have no influence. Men often act knowingly against their interest: For which reason the view of the greatest possible good does not always influence them. Men often counter-act a violent passion in prosecution of their interests and designs: It is not therefore the present uneasiness alone, which determines them. In general we may observe, that both these principles operate on the will; and where they are contrary, that either of them prevails, according to the general character or present disposition of the person. What we call strength of mind, implies the prevalence of the calm passions above the violent; though we may easily observe, there is no man so constantly possessed of this virtue, as never on any occasion to yield to the sollicitations of passion and desire. From these variations of temper proceeds the great difficulty of deciding concerning the actions and resolutions of men, where there is any contrariety of motives and passions.

BOOK III, PART I

SECT. I. MORAL DISTINCTIONS NOT DERIVED FROM REASON

There is an inconvenience which attends all abstruse reasoning. that it may silence, without convincing an antagonist, and requires the same intense study to make us sensible of its force, that was at first requisite for its invention. When we leave our closet, and engage in the common affairs of life, its conclusions seem to vanish, like the phantoms of the night on the appearance of the morning; and it is difficult for us to retain even that conviction, which we had attained with difficulty. This is still more conspicuous in a long chain of reasoning, where we must preserve to the end the evidence of the first propositions, and where we often lose sight of ail the most received maxims, either of philosophy or common life. I am not, however, without hopes, that the present system of philosophy will acquire new force as it advances; and that our reasonings concerning morals will corroborate whatever has been said concerning the UNDERSTANDING and the PASSIONS. Morality is a subject that interests us above all others: We fancy the peace of society to be at stake in every decision concerning it; and it is evident, that this concern must make our speculations appear more real and solid, than where the subject is, in a great measure, indifferent to us. What affects us, we conclude can never be a chimera; and as our passion is engaged on the one side or the other, we naturally think that the question lies within human comprehension; which, in other cases of this nature, we are apt to entertain some doubt of. Without this advantage I never should have ventured upon a third volume of such abstruse philosophy, in an age, wherein the greatest part of men seem agreed to convert reading into an amusement, and to reject every thing that requires any considerable degree of attention to be comprehended.

It has been observed, that nothing is ever present to the mind but its perceptions; and that all the actions of seeing, hearing, judging, loving, hating, and thinking, fall under this denomination. The mind can never exert itself in any action, which we may not comprehend under the term of perception; and consequently that term is no less applicable to those judgments, by which we distinguish moral good and evil, than to every other operation of the mind. To approve of one character, to condemn another, are only so many different perceptions.

Now as perceptions resolve themselves into two kinds, *viz.* impressions and ideas, this distinction gives rise to a question, with which we shall open up our present enquiry concerning morals. WHETHER IT IS BY MEANS OF OUR IDEAS OR IMPRESSIONS WE DISTINGUISH BETWIXT VICE AND VIRTUE, AND PRONOUNCE AN ACTION BLAMEABLE OR PRAISEWORTHY? This will immediately cut off all loose discourses and declamations, and reduce us to something precise and exact on the present subject.

Those who affirm that virtue is nothing but a conformity to reason; that there are eternal fitnesses and unfitnesses of things, which are the same to every rational being that considers them; that the immutable measures of right and wrong impose an obligation, not only on human creatures, but also on the Deity himself: All these systems concur in the opinion, that morality, like truth, is discerned merely by ideas, and by their juxta-position and comparison. In order, therefore, to judge of these systems, we need only consider, whether it be possible, from reason alone, to distinguish betwixt moral good and evil, or whether there must concur some other principles to enable us to make that distinction.

If morality had naturally no influence on human passions and actions, it were in vain to take such pains to inculcate it; and nothing would be more fruitless than that multitude of rules and precepts, with which all moralists abound. Philosophy is commonly divided into speculative and practical; and as morality is always comprehended under the latter division, it is supposed to influence our passions and actions, and to go beyond the calm and indolent judgments of the understanding. And this is confirmed by common experience, which informs us, that men are often governed by their duties, and are detered from some actions by the opinion of injustice, and impelled to others by that of obligation.

Since morals, therefore, have an influence on the actions and affections, it follows, that they cannot be derived from reason; and that because reason alone, as we have already proved, can never have any such influence. Morals excite passions, and produce or prevent actions. Reason of itself is utterly impotent in this particular. The rules of morality, therefore, are not conclusions of our reason.

No one, I believe, will deny the justness of this inference; nor is there any other means of evading it, than by denying that principle, on which it is founded. As long as it is allowed, that reason has no influence on our passions and action, it is in vain to pretend, that morality is discovered only by a deduction of reason. An active principle can never be founded on an inactive; and if reason be inactive in itself, it must remain so in all its shapes and appearances, whether it exerts itself in natural or moral subjects, whether it considers the powers of external bodies, or the actions of rational beings.

• • •

Reason is the discovery of truth or falshood. Truth or falshood consists in an agreement or disagreement either to the real relations of ideas, or to real existence and matter of fact. Whatever, therefore, is not susceptible of this agreement or disagreement, is incapable of being true or false, and can never be an object of our reason. Now it is evident our passions, volitions, and actions, are not susceptible of any such agreement or disagreement; being original facts and realities, compleat in themselves, and implying no reference to other passions, volitions, and actions. It is impossible, therefore, they can be pronounced either true or false, and be either contrary or conformable to reason.

This argument is of double advantage to our present purpose. For it proves DIRECTLY, that actions do not derive their merit from a conformity to reason, nor their blame from a contrariety to it; and it proves the same truth more INDIRECTLY, by shewing us, that as reason can never immediately prevent or produce any action by contradicting or approving of it, it cannot be the source of moral good and evil, which are found to have that influence. Actions may be laudable or blameable; but they cannot be reasonable: Laudable or blameable, therefore, are not the same with reasonable or unreasonable. The merit and demerit of actions frequently contradict, and sometimes controul our natural propensities. But reason has no such influence. Moral distinctions, therefore, are not the offspring of reason. Reason is wholly inactive, and can never be the source of so active a principle as conscience, or a sense of morals.

But perhaps it may be said, that though no will or action can be immediately contradictory to reason, yet we may find such a contradiction in some of the attendants of the action, that is, in its causes or effects. The action may cause a judgment, or may be obliquely caused by one, when the judgment concurs with a passion; and by an abusive way of speaking, which philosophy will scarce allow of, the same contrariety may, upon that account, be ascribed to the action. How far this truth or faishood may be the source of morals, it will now be proper to consider.

It has been observed, that reason, in a strict and philosophical sense, can have influence on our conduct only after two ways: Either when it excites a passion by informing us of the existence of something which is a proper object of it; or when it discovers the connexion of causes and effects, so as to afford us means of exerting any passion. These are the only kinds of judgment, which can accompany our actions, or can be said to produce them in any manner; and it must be allowed, that these judgments may often be false and erroneous. A person may be affected with passion, by supposing a pain or pleasure to lie in an object, which has no tendency to produce either of these sensations, or which produces the contrary to what is imagined. A person may also take false measures for the attaining his end, and may retard, by his foolish conduct, instead of forwarding the execution of any project. These false judgments may be thought to affect the passions and actions, which are connected with them, and may be said to render them unreasonable, in a figurative and improper way of speaking. But though this be acknowledged, it is easy to observe, that these errors are so far from being the source of all immorality, that they are commonly very innocent, and draw no manner of guilt upon the person who is so unfortunate as to fail into them. They extend not beyond a mistake of fact, which moralists have not generally supposed criminal, as being perfectly involuntary. I am more to be lamented than blamed, if I am mistaken with regard to the influence of objects in producing pain or pleasure, or if I know not the proper means of satisfying my desires. No one can ever regard such errors as a defect in my moral character. A fruit, for instance, that is really disagreeable, appears to me at a distance, and through mistake

I fancy it to be pleasant and delicious. Here is one error. I choose certain means of reaching this fruit, which are not proper for my end. Here is a second error; nor is there any third one, which can ever possibly enter into our reasonings concerning actions. I ask, therefore, if a man, in this situation, and guilty of these two errors, is to be regarded as vicious and criminal, however unavoidable they might have been? Or if it be possible to imagine, that such errors are the sources of all immorality?

And here it may be proper to observe, that if moral distinctions be derived from the truth or falshood of those judgments, they must take place wherever we form the judgments; nor will there be any difference, whether the question be concerning an apple or a kingdom, or whether the error be avoidable or unavoidable. For as the very essence of morality is supposed to consist in an agreement or disagreement to reason, the other circumstances are entirely arbitrary, and can never either bestow on any action the character of virtuous or vicious, or deprive it of that character. To which we may add, that this agreement or disagreement, not admitting of degrees, all virtues and vices would of course be equal.

Should it be pretended, that though a mistake of fact be not criminal, yet a mistake of right often is; and that this may be the source of immorality: I would answer, that it is impossible such a mistake can ever be the original source of immorality, since it supposes a real right and wrong; that is, a real distinction in morals, independent of these judgments. A mistake, therefore, of right may become a species of immorality; but it is only a secondary one, and is founded on some other, antecedent to it.

As to those judgments which are the effects of our actions, and which, when false, give occasion to pronounce the actions contrary to truth and reason; we may observe, that our actions never cause any judgment, either true or false, in ourselves, and that it is only on others they have such an influence. It is certain, that an action, on many occasions, may give rise to false conclusions in others; and that a person, who through a window sees any lewd behaviour of mine with my neighbour's wife, may be so simple as to imagine she is certainly my own. In this respect my action resembles somewhat a lye or falshood; only with this difference, which is material, that I perform not the action with any intention of giving rise to a false judgment in another, but merely to satisfy my lust and passion. It causes, however, a mistake and false judgment by accident; and the falshood of its effects may be ascribed, by some odd figurative way of speaking, to the action itself. But still I can see no pretext of reason for asserting, that the tendency to cause such an error is the first spring or original source of all immorality.

One might think It were entirely superfluous to prove this, if a late author [William Wollaston, THE RELIGION OF NATURE DELINEATED (London 1722)], who has had the good fortune to obtain some reputation, had not seriously affirmed, that such a falshood is the foundation of all guilt and moral deformity. That we may discover the fallacy of his hypothesis, we need only consider, that a false conclusion is drawn from an action, only by means of an obscurity of natural principles, which makes a cause be secretly interrupted In its operation, by contrary causes, and renders the connexion betwixt two objects uncertain and variable. Now, as a like uncertainty and variety of causes take place, even in natural objects, and produce a like error in our judgment, if that tendency to produce error were the very essence of vice and immorality, it should follow, that even inanimate objects might be vicious and immoral.

It is in vain to urge, that inanimate objects act without liberty and choice. For as liberty and choice are not necessary to make an action produce in us an erroneous conclusion, they can be, in no respect, essential to morality; and I do not readily perceive, upon this system, how they can ever come to be regarded by it. If the tendency to cause error be the origin of immorality, that tendency and immorality would in every case be inseparable.

Add to this, that if I had used the precaution of shutting the windows, while I indulged myself in those liberties with my neighbour's wife, I should have been guilty of no immorality; and that because my action, being perfectly concealed, would have had no tendency to produce any false conclusion.

For the same reason, a thief, who steals In by a ladder at a window, and takes all imaginable care to cause no disturbance, is in no respect criminal. For either he will not be perceived, or if he be, it is impossible he can produce any error, nor will any one, from these circumstances, take him to be other than what he really is.

It is well known, that those who are squint-sighted, do very readily cause mistakes in others, and that we Imagine they salute or are talking to one person, while they address themselves to anther. Are they therefore, upon that account, immoral?

Besides, we may easily observe, that in all those arguments there is an evident reasoning in a circle. A person who takes possession of another's goods, and uses them as his own, in a manner declares them to be his own; and this falshood is the source of the immorality of injustice. But is property, or right, or obligation, intelligible, without an antecedent morality?

A man that is ungrateful to his benefactor, in a manner affirms, that he never received any favours from him. But in what manner? Is it because it is his duty to be grateful? But this supposes, that there is some antecedent rule of duty and morals. Is it because human nature is generally grateful, and makes us conclude, that a man who does any harm never received any favour from the person he harmed? But human nature is not so generally grateful, as to justify such a conclusion. Or if it were, is an exception to a general rule in every case criminal, for no other reason than because it is an exception?

But what may suffice entirely to destroy this whimsical system is, that it leaves us under the same difficulty to give a reason why truth is virtuous and falshood vicious, as to account for the merit or turpitude of any other action. I shall allow, if you please, that all immorality is derived from this supposed falshood in action, provided you can give me any plausible reason, why such a falshood is immoral. If you consider rightly of the matter, you will find yourself in the same difficulty as at the beginning.

This last argument is very conclusive; because, if there be not an evident merit or turpitude annexed to this species of truth or falahood, It can never have any influence upon our actions. For, who ever thought of forbearing any action, because others might possibly draw false conclusions from it? Or, who ever performed any, that he might give rise to true conclusions?

Thus upon the whole, it is impossible, that the distinction betwixt moral good and evil, can be made to reason; since that distinction has an influence upon our actions, of which reason alone is incapable. Reason and judgment may, indeed, be the mediate cause of an action, by prompting, or by directing a passion: But it is not pretended, that a judgment of this kind, either in its truth or falshood, is attended with virtue or vice. And as to the judgments, which are caused by our judgments, they can still less bestow those moral qualities on the actions, which are their causes.

But to be more particular, and to shew, that those eternal immutable fitnesses and unfitnesses of things cannot be defended by sound philosophy, we may weigh the following considerations.

If the thought and understanding were alone capable of fixing the boundaries of right and wrong, the character of virtuous and vicious either must lie in some relations of objects, or must be a matter of fact, which is discovered by our reasoning. This consequence is evident. As the operations of human understanding divide themselves into two kinds, the comparing of ideas, and the inferring of matter of fact; were virtue discovered by the understanding; it must be an object of one of these operations, nor is there any third operation of the understanding, which can discover it. There has been an opinion very industriously propagated by certain philosophers, that morality is susceptible of demonstration; and though no one has ever been able to advance a single step in those demonstrations; yet it is taken for granted, that this science may be brought to an equal certainty with geometry or algebra. Upon this supposition, vice and virtue must consist in some relations; since it is allowed on all hands, that no matter of fact is capable of being demonstrated. Let us, therefore, begin with examining this hypothesis, and endeavour, if possible, to fix those moral qualities, which have been so long the objects of our fruitless researches. Point out distinctly the relations, which constitute morality or obligation, that we may know wherein they consist, and after what manner we must judge of them.

If you assert, that vice and virtue consist in relations susceptible of certainty and demonstration, you must confine yourself to those four relations, which alone admit of that degree of evidence; and in that case you run into absurdities, from which you will never be able to extricate yourself. For as you make the very essence of morality to lie in the relations, and as there is no one of these relations but what is applicable, not only to an irrational, but also to an inanimate object; it follows, that even such objects must be susceptible of merit or demerit. RESEMBLANCE, CONTRARIETY, DEGREES IN QUALITY, and PROPORTIONS IN QUANTITY AND NUMBER; all these relations belong as properly to matter, as to our actions, passions, and volitions. It is unquestionable, therefore, that morality lies not in any of these relations, nor the sense of it in their discovery.

As a proof, how confused our way of thinking on this subject commonly is, we may observe, that those who assert, that morality is demonstrable, do not say, that morality lies in the relations, and that the relations are distinguishable by reason. They only say, that reason can discover such an action, In such relations, to be virtuous, and such another vicious. It seems they thought it sufficient, if they could bring the word, Relation, into the proposition, without troubling themselves whether it was to the purpose or not. But here, I think, is plain argument. Demonstrative reason discovers only relations. But that reason, according to this hypothesis, discovers also vice and virtue. These moral qualities, therefore, must be relations. When we blame any action, in any situation, the whole complicated object, of action and situation, must form certain relations, wherein the essence of vice consists. This hypothesis is not otherwise intelligible. For what does reason discover, when it pronounces any action vicious? Does it discover a relation or a matter of fact? These questions are decisive, and must not be eluded.

Should it be asserted, that the sense of morality consists in the discovery of some relation, distinct from these, and that our enumeration was not compleat, when we comprehended all demonstrable relations under four general heads: To this I know not what to reply, till some one be so good as to point out to me this new relation. It is impossible to refute a system, which has never yet been explained. In such a manner of fighting in the dark, a man loses his blows in the air, and often places them where the enemy is not present.

I must, therefore, on this occasion, rest contented with requiring the two following conditions of any one that would undertake to clear up this system. First, As moral good and evil belong only to the actions of the mind, and are derived from our situation with regard to external objects, the relations, from which these moral distinctions arise, must lie only betwixt internal actions, and external objects, and must not be applicable either to internal actions, compared among themselves, or to external objects, when placed in opposition to other external objects. For as morality is supposed to attend certain relations, if these relations coued belong to internal actions considered singly, it would follow, that we might be guilty of crimes in ourselves, and independent of our situation, with respect to the universe: And in like manner, if these moral relations coued be applied to external objects, it would follow, that even inanimate beings would be susceptible of moral beauty and deformity. Now it seems difficult to imagine, that any relation can be discovered betwixt our passions, volitions and actions, compared to external objects, which relation might not belong either to these passions and volitions, or to these external objects, compared among themselves. But it will be still more difficult to fulfil the second condition, requisite to justify this system. According to the principles of those who maintain an abstract rational difference betwixt moral good and evil, and a natural fitness and unfitness of things, it is not only supposed, that these relations, being eternal and immutable, are the same, when considered by every rational creature, but their effects are also supposed to be necessarily the same; and it is concluded they have no less, or rather a greater, influence in directing the will of the deity, than in governing the rational and virtuous of our own species. These two particulars are evidently distinct. It is one thing to know virtue, and another to conform the will to it. In order, therefore, to prove, that the measures of right and wrong are eternal laws, obligatory on every rational mind, it is not sufficient to shew the relations upon which they are founded: We must also point out the connexion betwixt the relation and the will; and must prove that this connexion is so necessary, that in every well-disposed mind, it must take place and have its influence; though the difference betwixt these minds be in other respects immense and infinite. Now besides what I have already proved, that even in human nature no relation can ever alone produce any action: besides this, I say, it has been shewn, in treating of the understanding, that there is no connexion of cause and effect, such as this is supposed to be, which is discoverable otherwise than by experience, and of which we can pretend to have any security by the simple consideration of the objects. All beings in the universe, considered in themselves, appear entirely loose and independent of each other. It is only by experience we learn their influence and connexion; and this influence we ought never to extend beyond experience.

Thus it will be impossible to fulfil the first condition required to the system of eternal measures of right and wrong; because it is impossible to shew those relations, upon which such a distinction may be founded: And it is as impossible to fulfil the second condition; because we cannot prove A PRIORI, that these relations, if they really existed and were perceived, would be universally forcible and obligatory.

But to make these general reflections more dear and convincing, we may illustrate them by some particular instances, wherein this character of moral good or evil is the most universally acknowledged. Of all crimes that human creatures are capable of committing, the most horrid and unnatural is ingratitude, especially when it is committed against parents, and appears in the more flagrant instances of wounds and death. This is acknowledged by all mankind, philosophers as well as the people; the question only arises among philosophers, whether the guilt or moral deformity of this action be discovered by demonstrative reasoning, or be felt by an internal sense, and by means of some sentiment, which the reflecting on such an action naturally occasions. This question will soon be decided against the former opinion, if we can shew the same relations in other objects, without the notion of any guilt or iniquity attending them. Reason or science is nothing but the comparing of ideas, and the discovery of their relations; and if the same relations have different characters, it must evidently follow, that those characters are not discovered merely by reason. To put the affair, therefore, to this trial, let us chuse any inanimate object, such as an oak or elm; and let us suppose, that by the dropping of its seed, it produces a sapling below it, which springing up by degrees, at last overtops and destroys the parent tree: I ask, if in this instance there be wanting any relation, which is discoverable in parricide or ingratitude? Is not the one tree the cause of the other's existence; and the latter the cause of the destruction of the former, in the same manner as when a child murders his parent? It is not sufficient to reply, that a choice or will is wanting. For in the case of parricide, a will does not give rise to any DIFFERENT relations, but is only the cause from which the action is derived; and consequently produces the same relations, that in the oak or elm arise from some other principles. It is a will or choice, that determines a man to kill his parent; and they are the laws of matter and motion, that determine a sapling to destroy the oak, from which it sprung. Here then the same relations have different causes; but still the relations are the same: And as their discovery is not in both cases attended with a notion of immorality, it follows, that that notion does not arise from such a discovery.

But to chuse an instance, still more resembling; I would fain ask any one, why incest in the human species is criminal, and why the very same action, and the same relations in animals have not the smallest moral turpitude and deformity? If it be answered, that this action is innocent in animals, because they have not reason sufficient to discover its turpitude; but that man, being endowed with that faculty which ought to restrain him to his duty, the same action instantly becomes criminal to him; should this be said, I would reply, that this is evidently arguing in a circle. For before reason can perceive this turpitude, the turpitude must exist; and consequently is independent of the decisions of our reason, and is their object more properly than their effect. According to this system, then, every animal, that has sense, and appetite, and will; that is, every animal must be susceptible of all the same virtues and vices, for which we ascribe praise and blame to human creatures. All the difference is, that our superior reason may serve to discover the vice or virtue, and by that means may augment the blame or praise: But still this discovery supposes a separate being in these moral distinctions, and a being, which depends only on the will and appetite, and which, both in thought and reality, may be distinguished from the reason. Animals are susceptible of the same relations, with respect to each other, as the human species, and therefore would also be susceptible of the same morality, if the essence of morality consisted in these relations. Their want of a sufficient degree of reason may hinder them from perceiving the duties and obligations of morality, but can never hinder these duties from existing; since they must antecedently exist, in order to their being perceived. Reason must find them, and can never produce them. This argument deserves to be weighed, as being, in my opinion, entirely decisive.

Nor does this reasoning only prove, that morality consists not in any relations, that are the objects of science; but if examined, will prove with equal certainty, that it consists not in any matter of fact, which can be discovered by the understanding. This is the second part of our argument; and if it can be made evident, we may conclude, that morality is not an object of reason. But can there be any difficulty in proving, that vice and virtue are not matters of fact, whose existence we can infer by reason? Take any action allowed to be vicious: Wilful murder, for instance. Examine it in all lights, and see if you can find that matter of fact, or real existence, which you call vice. In which-ever way you take it, you find only certain passions, motives, volitions and thoughts. There is no other matter of fact in the case. The vice entirely escapes you, as long as you consider the object. You never can find it, till you turn your reflection into your own breast, and find a sentiment of disapprobation, which arises in you, towards this action. Here is a matter of fact; but it is the object of feeling, not of reason. It lies in yourself, not in the object. So that when you pronounce any action or character to be vicious, you mean nothing, but that from the constitution of your nature you have a feeling or sentiment of blame from the contemplation of it. Vice and virtue, therefore, may be compared to sounds, colours, heat and cold, which, according to modern philosophy, are not qualities in objects, but perceptions in the mind: And this discovery in morals, like that other in physics, is to be regarded as a considerable advancement of the speculative sciences; though, like that too, it has little or no influence on practice. Nothing can be more real, or concern us more, than our own sentiments of pleasure and uneasiness; and if these be favourable to virtue, and unfavourable to vice, no more can be requisite to the regulation of our conduct and behaviour.

I cannot forbear adding to these reasonings an observation, which may, perhaps, be found of some importance. In every system of morality, which I have hitherto met with, I have always remarked, that the author proceeds for some time in the ordinary way of reasoning, and establishes the being of a God, or makes observations concerning human affairs; when of a sudden I am surprized to find, that instead of the usual copulations of propositions, is, and is not, I meet with no proposition that is not connected with an ought, or an ought not. This change is imperceptible; but is, however, of the last consequence. For as this ought, or ought not, expresses some new relation or affirmation, it is necessary that it should be observed and explained; and at the same time that a reason should be given, for what seems altogether inconceivable, how this new relation can be a deduction from others, which are entirely different from it. But as authors do not commonly use this precaution, I shall presume to recommend it to the readers; and am persuaded, that this small attention would subvert all the vulgar systems of morality, and let us see, that the distinction of vice and virtue is not founded merely on the relations of objects, nor is perceived by reason.

SECT. II. MORAL DISTINCTIONS DERIVED FROM A MORAL SENSE

Thus the course of the argument leads us to conclude, that since vice and virtue are not discoverable merely by reason, or the comparison of ideas, it must be by means of some impression or sentiment they occasion, that we are able to mark the difference betwixt them. Our decisions concerning moral rectitude and depravity are evidently perceptions; and as all perceptions are either impressions or ideas, the exclusion of the one is a convincing argument for the other. Morality, therefore, is more properly felt than judged of; though this feeling or sentiment is commonly so soft and gentle, that we are apt to confound it with an idea, according to our common custom of taking all things for the same, which have any near resemblance to each other.

The next question is, Of what nature are these impressions, and after what manner do they operate upon us? Here we cannot remain long in suspense, but must pronounce the impression arising from virtue, to be agreeable, and that proceding from vice to be uneasy. Every moments experience must convince us of this. There is no spectacle so fair and beautiful as a noble and generous action; nor any which gives us more abhorrence than one that is cruel and treacherous. No enjoyment equals the satisfaction we receive from the company of those we love and esteem; as the greatest of all punishments is to be obliged to pass our lives with those we hate or contemn. A very play or romance may afford us instances of this pleasure, which virtue conveys to us; and pain, which arises from vice.

Now since the distinguishing impressions, by which moral good or evil is known, are nothing but particular pains or pleasures; it follows, that in all enquiries concerning these moral distinctions, it will be sufficient to shew the principles, which make us feel a satisfaction or uneasiness from the survey of any character, in order to satisfy us why the character is laudable or blameable. An action, or sentiment, or character is virtuous or vicious; why? because its view causes a pleasure or uneasiness of a particular kind. In giving a reason, therefore, for the pleasure or uneasiness, we sufficiently explain the vice or virtue. To have the sense of virtue, is nothing but to feel a satisfaction of a particular kind from the contemplation of a character. The very feeling constitutes our praise or admiration. We go no farther; nor do we enquire into the cause of the satisfaction. We do not infer a character to be virtuous, because it pleases: But in feeling that it pleases after such a particular manner, we in effect feel that it is virtuous. The case is the same as in our judgments concerning all kinds of beauty, and tastes, and sensations. Our approbation is implyed in the immediate pleasure they convey to us.

I have objected to the system, which establishes eternal rational measures of right and wrong, that it is impossible to shew, in the actions of reasonable creatures, any relations, which are not found in external objects; and therefore, if morality always attended these relations, it were possible for inanimate matter to become virtuous or vicious. Now it may, in like manner, be objected to the present system, that if virtue and vice be determined by pleasure and pain, these qualities must, in every case, arise from the sensations; and consequently any object, whether animate or inanimate, rational or irrational, might become morally good or evil, provided it can excite a satisfaction or uneasiness. But though this objection seems to be the very same, it has by no means the same force, in the one case as in the other. For, first, tis evident, that under the term pleasure, we comprehend sensations, which are very different from each other, and which have only such a distant resemblance, as is requisite to make them be expressed by the same abstract term. A good composition of music and a bottle of good wine equally produce pleasure; and what is more, their goodness is determined merely by the pleasure. But shall we say upon that account, that the wine is harmonious, or the music of a good flavour? In like manner an inanimate object, and the character or sentiments of any person may, both of them, give satisfaction; but as the satisfaction is different, this keeps our sentiments concerning them from being confounded, and makes us ascribe virtue to the one, and not to the other. Nor is every sentiment of pleasure or pain, which arises from characters and actions, of that peculiar kind, which makes us praise or condemn. The good qualities of an enemy are hurtful to us; but may still command our esteem and respect. It is only when a character is considered in general, without reference to our particular interest, that it causes such a feeling or sentiment, as denominates it morally good or evil. It is true, those sentiments, from interest and morals, are apt to be confounded, and naturally run into one another. It seldom happens, that we do not think an enemy vicious, and can distinguish betwixt his opposition to our interest and real villainy or baseness. But this hinders not, but that the sentiments are, in themselves, distinct; and a man of temper and judgment may preserve himself from these illusions. In like manner, though it is certain a musical voice is nothing but one that naturally gives a particular kind of pleasure; yet it is difficult for a man to be sensible, that the voice of an enemy is agreeable, or to allow it to be musical. But a person of a fine ear, who has the command of himself, can separate these feelings, and give praise to what deserves it.

SECONDLY, We may call to remembrance the preceding system of the passions, in order to remark a still more considerable difference among our pains and pleasures. Pride and humility, love and hatred are excited, when there is any thing presented to us, that both bears a relation to the object of the passion, and produces a separate sensation related to the sensation of the passion. Now virtue and vice are attended with these circumstances. They must necessarily be placed either in ourselves or others, and excite either pleasure or uneasiness; and therefore must give rise to one of these four passions; which clearly distinguishes them from the pleasure and pain arising from inanimate objects, that often bear no relation to us: And this is, perhaps, the most considerable effect that virtue and vice have upon the human mind.

It may now be asked in general, concerning this pain or pleasure, that distinguishes moral good and evil, FROM WHAT PRINCIPLES IS IT DERIVED, AND WHENCE DOES IT ARISE IN THE HUMAN MIND? To this I reply, first, that it is absurd to imagine, that in every particular instance, these sentiments are produced by an original quality and primary constitution. For as the number of our duties is, in a manner, infinite, it is impossible that our original instincts should extend to each of them, and from our very first infancy impress on the human mind all that multitude of precepts, which are contained in the compleatest system of ethics. Such a method of proceeding is not conformable to the usual maxims, by which nature is conducted, where a few principles produce all that variety we observe in the universe, and every thing is carryed on in the easiest and most simple manner. It is necessary, therefore, to abridge these primary impulses, and find some more general principles, upon which all our notions of morals are founded.

But in the second place, should it be asked, Whether we ought to search for these principles in nature, or whether we must look for them in some other origin? I would reply, that our answer to this question depends upon the definition of the word, Nature, than which there is none more ambiguous and equivocal. If nature be opposed to miracles, not only the distinction betwixt vice and virtue is natural, but also every event, which has ever happened in the world, EXCEPTING THOSE MIRACLES, ON WHICH OUR RELIGION IS FOUNDED. In saying, then, that the sentiments of vice and virtue are natural in this sense, we make no very extraordinary discovery.

But nature may also be opposed to rare and unusual; and in this sense of the word, which is the common one, there may often arise disputes concerning what is natural or unnatural; and one may in general affirm, that we are not possessed of any very precise standard, by which these disputes can be decided. Frequent and rare depend upon the number of examples we have observed; and as this number may gradually encrease or diminish, it will be impossible to fix any exact boundaries betwixt them. We may only affirm on this head, that if ever there was any thing, which coued be called natural in this sense, the sentiments of morality certainly may; since there never was any nation of the world, nor any single person in any nation, who was utterly deprived of them, and who never, in any instance, shewed the least approbation or dislike of manners. These sentiments are so rooted in our constitution and temper, that without entirely confounding the human mind by disease or madness, it is impossible to extirpate and destroy them.

But nature may also be opposed to artifice, as well as to what is rare and unusual; and in this sense it may be disputed, whether the notions of virtue be natural or not. We readily forget, that the designs, and projects, and views of men are principles as necessary in their operation as heat and cold, moist and dry: But taking them to be free and entirely our own, it is usual for us to set them in opposition to the other principles of nature. Should it, therefore, be demanded, whether the sense of virtue be natural or artificial, I am of opinion, that it is impossible for me at present to give any precise answer to this question. Perhaps it will appear afterwards, that our sense of some virtues is artificial, and that of others natural. The discussion of this question will be more proper, when we enter upon an exact detail of each particular vice and virtue.

In the following discourse natural is also opposed sometimes to civil, sometimes to moral. The opposition will always discover the sense, in which it is taken.

Mean while it may not be amiss to observe from these definitions of natural and unnatural, that nothing can be more unphilosophical than those systems, which assert, that virtue is the same with what is natural, and vice with what is unnatural. For in the first sense of the word, Nature, as opposed to miracles, both vice and virtue are equally natural; and in the second sense, as opposed to what is unusual, perhaps virtue will be found to be the most unnatural. At least it must be owned, that heroic virtue, being as unusual, is as little natural as the most brutal barbarity. As to the third sense of the word, it is certain, that both vice and virtue are equally artificial, and out of nature. For however it may be disputed, whether the notion of a merit or demerit in certain actions be natural or artificial, it is evident, that the actions themselves are artificial, and are performed with a certain design and intention; otherwise they coued never be ranked under any of these denominations. It is impossible, therefore, that the character of natural and unnatural can ever, in any sense, mark the boundaries of vice and virtue.

Thus we are still brought back to our first position, that virtue is distinguished by the pleasure, and vice by the pain, that any action, sentiment or character gives us by the mere view and contemplation. This decision is very commodious; because it reduces us to this simple question, Why any action or sentiment upon the general view or survey, gives a certain satisfaction or uneasiness, in order to shew the origin of its moral rectitude or depravity, without looking for any incomprehensible relations and qualities, which never did exist in nature, nor even in our imagination, by any clear and distinct conception. I flatter myself I have executed a great part of my present design by a state of the question, which appears to me so free from ambiguity and obscurity.

DISCUSSION QUESTIONS

1. Do you agree with Hume that reason is a slave of the passions? Why or why not? Explain.

2. How does this selection fit in with his view of self and his view on knowledge? Explain.

3. Compare Hume's view on ethics with those of Aristotle and Epicurus. What are the main similarities and differences? Explain.

Fundamental Principles of the Metaphysic of Morals

By Immanuel Kant
Translated by Thomas Kingsmill Abbott

For Kant, reason is the source of morality and the means for choosing a motive to act on. Kant's discussion of knowledge can be found in Part III of Four Fundamental Questions. *Our selection is from his 1785 book,* The Fundamental Principles of the Metaphysic of Morals. *The section is called "Transition from the Common Rational Knowledge of Morality to the Philosophical." In this section, Kant explains how he thinks we should determine how to act. That is, he provides a decision procedure called "the categorical imperative." He begins by arguing that there is only one thing that is intrinsically good, except a good will. "Will" here means the part of the process of putting motive into action. Other things that are good could also be bad in certain circumstances, intelligence and wealth, for example, could be used as tools to plan a heist (like in so many action movies). A good will, though, is an unqualified good. He is not considering the result of the action because that is not part of the will, it is instead part of the empirical world. In Kant's ethics, it is the rational determination of the will that we judge in determining the moral worth (or lack thereof) of an action. This makes Kant's view deontological (duty-based). There are three propositions that define his ethics. First, an action must be done from duty, not just in accord with duty to have moral worth. The second one is "an action done from duty derives its moral worth, not from the purpose which is to be attained by it, but from the maxim by which it is determined." Third is this: "duty is the necessity of acting from respect for the law." The decision procedure is as follows. First you have to turn your proposed action into a maxim. A maxim, in this sense, is the generalized version of your proposed action. For example, you are considering whether to cross a grassy area despite the "Keep off the Grass" sign because you are in a hurry. Your maxim would be "whenever people are in a hurry, they can ignore the 'Keep off the Grass' sign." Next, we would need to know whether we could will our maxim to be a universal law of nature, like gravity. In our case, what would happen if our maxim were a universal law of nature? The result would be many more people walking on the grass and the grass dying. So, can we will it to be a universal law of nature? No, because the logical implication of our universalized maxim would make it impossible for our original proposed action to occur. So, it fails the test. An action that fails the test must not be performed. An action that passes the test may be performed.*

FIRST SECTION

TRANSITION FROM THE COMMON RATIONAL KNOWLEDGE OF MORALITY TO THE PHILOSOPHICAL

Nothing can possibly be conceived in the world, or even out of it, which can be called good, without qualification, except a good will. Intelligence, wit, judgement, and the other talents of the mind, however they may be named, or courage, resolution, perseverance, as qualities of temperament, are undoubtedly good and desirable in many respects; but these gifts of nature may also become extremely bad and mischievous if the will which is to make use of them, and which, therefore, constitutes what is called character, is not good. It is the same with the gifts of fortune. Power, riches, honour, even health, and the general well-being and contentment with one's condition which is called happiness, inspire pride, and often presumption, if there is not a good will to correct the influence of these on the mind, and with this also to rectify the whole principle of acting and adapt it to its end. The sight of a being who is not adorned with a single feature of a pure and good will, enjoying unbroken prosperity, can never give pleasure to an impartial rational spectator. Thus a good will appears to constitute the indispensable condition even of being worthy of happiness.

There are even some qualities which are of service to this good will itself and may facilitate its action, yet which have no intrinsic unconditional value, but always presuppose a good will, and this qualifies the esteem that we justly have for them and does not permit us to regard them as absolutely good. Moderation in the affections and passions, self-control, and calm deliberation are not only good in many respects, but even seem to constitute part of the intrinsic worth of the person; but they are far from deserving to be called good without qualification, although they have been so unconditionally praised by the ancients. For without the principles of a good will, they may become extremely bad, and the coolness of a villain not only makes him far more dangerous, but also directly makes him more abominable in our eyes than he would have been without it.

A good will is good not because of what it performs or effects, not by its aptness for the attainment of some proposed end, but simply by virtue of the volition; that is, it is good in itself, and considered by itself is to be esteemed much higher than all that can be brought about by it in favour of any inclination, nay even of the sum total of all inclinations. Even if it should happen that, owing to special disfavour of fortune, or the niggardly provision of a step-motherly nature, this will should wholly lack power to accomplish its purpose, if with its greatest efforts it should yet achieve nothing, and there should remain only the good will (not, to be sure, a mere wish, but the summoning of all means in our power), then, like a jewel, it would still shine by its own light, as a thing which has its whole value in itself. Its usefulness or fruitfulness can neither add nor take away anything from this value. It would be, as it were, only the setting to enable us to handle it the more conveniently in common commerce, or to attract to it the attention of those who are not yet connoisseurs, but not to recommend it to true connoisseurs, or to determine its value.

There is, however, something so strange in this idea of the absolute value of the mere will, in which no account is taken of its utility, that notwithstanding the thorough assent of even common reason to the idea, yet a suspicion must arise that it may perhaps really be the product of mere high-flown fancy, and that we may have misunderstood the purpose of nature in assigning reason as the governor of our will. Therefore we will examine this idea from this point of view.

In the physical constitution of an organized being, that is, a being adapted suitably to the purposes of life, we assume it as a fundamental principle that no organ for any purpose will be found but what is also the fittest and best adapted for that purpose. Now in a being which has reason and a will, if the proper object of nature were its conservation, its welfare, in a word, its happiness, then nature would have hit upon a very bad arrangement in selecting the reason of the creature to carry out this purpose. For all the actions which the creature has to perform with a view to this purpose, and the whole rule of its conduct, would be far more surely prescribed to it by instinct, and that end would have been attained thereby much more certainly than it ever can be by reason. Should reason have been communicated to this favoured creature over and above, it must only have served it to contemplate the happy constitution of its nature, to admire it, to congratulate itself thereon, and to feel thankful for it to the beneficent cause, but not that it should subject its desires to that weak and delusive guidance and meddle bunglingly with the purpose of nature. In a word, nature would have taken care that reason should not break forth into practical exercise, nor have the presumption, with its weak insight, to think out for itself the plan of happiness, and of the means of attaining it. Nature would not only have taken on herself the choice of the ends, but also of the means, and with wise foresight would have entrusted both to instinct.

And, in fact, we find that the more a cultivated reason applies itself with deliberate purpose to the enjoyment of life and happiness, so much the more does the man fail of true satisfaction. And from this circumstance there arises in many, if they are candid enough to confess it, a certain degree of misology, that is, hatred of reason, especially in the case of those who are most experienced in the use of it, because after calculating all the advantages they derive, I do not say from the invention of all the arts of common luxury, but even from the sciences (which seem to them to be after all only a luxury of the understanding), they find that they have, in fact, only brought more trouble on their shoulders, rather than gained in happiness; and they end by envying, rather than despising, the more common stamp of men who keep closer to the guidance of mere instinct and do not allow their reason much influence on their conduct. And this we must admit, that the judgement of those who would very much lower the lofty eulogies of the advantages which reason gives us in regard to the happiness and satisfaction of life, or who would even reduce them below zero, is by no means morose or ungrateful to the goodness with which the world is governed, but that there lies at the root of these judgements the idea that our existence has a different and far nobler end, for which, and not for happiness, reason is properly intended, and which must, therefore, be regarded as the supreme condition to which the private ends of man must, for the most part, be postponed.

For as reason is not competent to guide the will with certainty in regard to its objects and the satisfaction of all our wants (which it to some extent even multiplies), this being an end to which an implanted instinct would have led with much greater certainty; and since, nevertheless, reason is imparted to us as a practical faculty, i.e., as one which is to have influence on the will, therefore, admitting that nature generally in the distribution of her capacities has adapted the means to the end, its true destination must be to produce a will, not merely good as a means to something else, but good in itself, for which reason was absolutely necessary. This will then, though not indeed the sole and complete good, must be the supreme good and the condition of every other, even of the desire of happiness. Under these circumstances, there is nothing inconsistent with the wisdom of nature in the fact that the cultivation of the reason, which is requisite for the first and unconditional purpose, does in many ways interfere, at least in this life, with the attainment of the second, which is always conditional, namely, happiness. Nay, it may even reduce it to nothing, without nature thereby failing of her purpose. For reason recognizes the establishment of a good will as its highest practical destination, and in attaining this purpose is capable only of a satisfaction of its own proper kind, namely that from the attainment of an end, which end again is determined by reason only, notwithstanding that this may involve many a disappointment to the ends of inclination.

We have then to develop the notion of a will which deserves to be highly esteemed for itself and is good without a view to anything further, a notion which exists already in the sound natural understanding, requiring rather to be cleared up than to be taught, and which in estimating the value of our actions always takes the first place and constitutes the condition of all the rest. In order to do this, we will take the notion of duty, which includes that of a good will, although implying certain subjective restrictions and hindrances. These, however, far from concealing it, or rendering it unrecognizable, rather bring it out by contrast and make it shine forth so much the brighter.

I omit here all actions which are already recognized as inconsistent with duty, although they may be useful for this or that purpose, for with these the question whether they are done from duty cannot arise at all, since they even conflict with it. I also set aside those actions which really conform to duty, but to which men have no direct inclination, performing them because they are impelled thereto by some other inclination. For in this case we can readily distinguish whether the action which agrees with duty is done from duty, or from a selfish view. It is much harder to make this distinction when the action accords with duty and the subject has besides a direct inclination to it. For example, it is always a matter of duty that a dealer should not over charge an inexperienced purchaser; and wherever there is much commerce the prudent tradesman does not overcharge, but keeps a fixed price for everyone, so that a child buys of him as well as any other. Men are thus honestly served; but this is not enough to make us believe that the tradesman has so acted from duty and from principles of honesty: his own advantage required it; it is out of the question in this case to suppose that he might besides have a direct inclination in favour of the buyers, so that, as it were, from love he should give no advantage to one over another. Accordingly the action was done neither from duty nor from direct inclination, but merely with a selfish view.

On the other hand, it is a duty to maintain one's life; and, in addition, everyone has also a direct inclination to do so. But on this account the of anxious care which most men take for it has no intrinsic worth, and their maxim has no moral import. They preserve their life as duty requires, no doubt, but not because duty requires. On the other band, if adversity and hopeless sorrow have completely taken away the relish for life; if the unfortunate one, strong in mind, indignant at his fate rather than desponding or dejected, wishes for death, and yet preserves his life without loving it—not from inclination or fear, but from duty—then his maxim has a moral worth.

To be beneficent when we can is a duty; and besides this, there are many minds so sympathetically constituted that, without any other motive of vanity or self-interest, they find a pleasure in spreading joy around them and can take delight in the satisfaction of others so far as it is their own work. But I maintain that in such a case an action of this kind, however proper, however amiable it may be, bas nevertheless no true moral worth, but is on a level with other inclinations, e.g., the inclination to honour, which, if it is happily directed to that which is in fact of public utility and accordant with duty and consequently honourable, deserves praise and encouragement, but not esteem. For the maxim lacks the moral import, namely, that such actions be done from duty, not from inclination. Put the case that the mind of that philanthropist were clouded by sorrow of his own, extinguishing all sympathy with the lot of others, and that, while he still has the power to benefit others in distress, he is not touched by their trouble because he is absorbed with his own; and now suppose that he tears himself out of this dead insensibility, and performs the action without any inclination to it, but simply from duty, then first has his action its genuine moral worth. Further still; if nature bas put little sympathy in the heart of this or that man; if he, supposed to be an upright man, is by temperament cold and indifferent to the sufferings of others, perhaps because in respect of his own he is provided with the special gift of patience and fortitude and supposes, or even requires, that others should have the same—and such a man would certainly not be the meanest product of nature—but if nature had not specially framed him for a philanthropist, would he not still find in himself a source from whence to give himself a far higher worth than that of a good-natured temperament could be? Unquestionably. It is just in this that the moral worth of the character is brought out which is incomparably the highest of all, namely, that he is beneficent, not from inclination, but from duty.

To secure one's own happiness is a duty, at least indirectly; for discontent with one's condition, under a pressure of many anxieties and amidst unsatisfied wants, might easily become a great temptation to transgression of duty. But here again, without looking to duty, all men have already the strongest and most intimate inclination to happiness, because it is just in this idea that all inclinations are combined in one total. But the precept of happiness is often of such a sort that it greatly interferes with some inclinations, and yet a man cannot form any definite and certain conception of the sum of satisfaction of all of them which is called happiness. It is not then to be wondered at that a single inclination, definite both as to what it promises and as to the time within which it can be gratified, is often able to overcome such a fluctuating idea, and that a gouty patient, for instance, can choose to enjoy what he likes, and to suffer what he may, since, according to his calculation, on this occasion at least, be has not sacrificed the enjoyment of the present moment to a possibly mistaken expectation of a happiness which is supposed to be found in health. But even in this case, if the general desire for happiness did not influence his will, and supposing that in his particular case health was not a necessary element in this calculation, there yet remains in this, as in all other cases, this law, namely, that he should promote his happiness not from inclination but from duty, and by this would his conduct first acquire true moral worth.

It is in this manner, undoubtedly, that we are to understand those passages of Scripture also in which we are commanded to love our neighbour, even our enemy. For love, as an affection, cannot be commanded, but beneficence for duty's sake may; even though we are not impelled to it by any inclination—nay, are even repelled by a natural and unconquerable aversion. This is practical love and not pathological—a love which is seated in the will, and not in the propensions of sense—in principles of action and not of tender sympathy; and it is this love alone which can be commanded.

The second proposition is: That an action done from duty derives its moral worth, not from the purpose which is to be attained by it, but from the maxim by which it is determined, and therefore does not depend on the realization of the object of the action, but merely on the principle of volition by which the action has taken place, without regard to any object of desire. It is clear from what precedes that the purposes which we may have in view in our actions, or their effects regarded as ends and springs of the will, cannot give to actions any unconditional or moral worth. In what, then, can their worth lie, if it is not to consist in the will and in reference to its expected effect? It cannot lie anywhere but in the principle of the will without regard to the ends which can be attained by the action. For the will stands between its a priori principle, which is formal, and its a posteriori spring, which is material, as between two roads, and as it must be determined by something, it that it must be determined by the formal principle of volition when an action is done from duty, in which case every material principle has been withdrawn from it.

The third proposition, which is a consequence of the two preceding, I would express thus Duty is the necessity of acting from respect for the law. I may have inclination for an object as the effect of my proposed action, but I cannot have respect for it, just for this reason, that it is an effect and not an energy of will. Similarly I cannot have respect for inclination, whether my own or another's; I can at most, if my own, approve it; if another's, sometimes even love it; i.e., look on it as favourable to my own interest. It is only what is connected with my will as a principle, by no means as an effect—what does not subserve my inclination, but overpowers it, or at least in case of choice excludes it from its calculation—in other words, simply the law of itself, which can be an object of respect, and hence a command. Now an action done from duty must wholly exclude the influence of inclination and with it every object of the will, so that nothing remains which can determine the will except objectively the law, and subjectively pure respect for this practical law, and consequently the maxim* that I should follow this law even to the thwarting of all my inclinations.

A maxim is the subjective principle of volition. The objective principle (i.e., that which would also serve subjectively as a practical principle to all rational beings if reason had full power over the faculty of desire) is the practical law.

Thus the moral worth of an action does not lie in the effect expected from it, nor in any principle of action which requires to borrow its motive from this expected effect. For all these effects—agreeableness of one's condition and even the promotion of the happiness of others—could have been also brought about by other causes, so that for this there would have been no need of the will of a rational being; whereas it is in this alone that the supreme and unconditional good can be found. The pre-eminent good which we call moral can therefore consist in nothing else than the conception of law in itself, which certainly is only possible in a rational being, in so far as this conception, and not the expected effect, determines the will. This is a good which is already present in the person who acts accordingly, and we have not to wait for it to appear first in the result.

It might be here objected to me that I take refuge behind the word respect in an obscure feeling, instead of giving a distinct solution of the question by a concept of the reason. But although respect is a feeling, it is not a feeling received through influence, but is self-wrought by a rational concept, and, therefore, is specifically distinct from all feelings of the former kind, which may be referred either to inclination or fear, What I recognise immediately as a law for me, I recognise with respect. This merely signifies the consciousness that my will is subordinate to a law, without the intervention of other influences on my sense. The immediate determination of the will by the law, and the consciousness of this, is called respect, so that this is regarded as an effect of the law on the subject, and not as the cause of it. Respect is properly the conception of a worth which thwarts my self-love. Accordingly it is something which is considered neither as an object of inclination nor of fear, although it has something analogous to both. The object of respect is the law only, and that the law which we impose on ourselves and yet recognise as necessary in itself. As a law, we are subjected too it without consulting self-love; as imposed by us on ourselves, it is a result of our will. In the former aspect it has an analogy to fear, in the latter to inclination. Respect for a person is properly only respect for the law (of honesty, etc.) of which he gives us an example. Since we also look on the improvement of our talents as a duty, we consider that we see in a person of talents, as it were, the example of a law (*viz.*, to become like him in this by exercise), and this constitutes our respect. All so-called moral interest consists simply in respect for the law.

But what sort of law can that be, the conception of which must determine the will, even without paying any regard to the effect expected from it, in order that this will may be called good absolutely and without qualification? As I have deprived the will of every impulse which could arise to it from obedience to any law, there remains nothing but the universal conformity of its actions to law in general, which alone is to serve the will as a principle, i.e., I am never to act otherwise than so that I could also will that my maxim should become a universal law. Here, now, it is the simple conformity to law in general, without assuming any particular law applicable to certain actions, that serves the will as its principle and must so serve it, if duty is not to be a vain delusion and a chimerical notion. The common reason of men in its practical judgements perfectly coincides with this and always has in view the principle here suggested. Let the question be, for example: May I when in distress make a promise with the intention not to keep it? I readily distinguish here between the two significations which the question may have: Whether it is prudent, or whether it is right, to make a false promise? The former may undoubtedly of be the case. I see clearly indeed that it is not enough to extricate myself from a present difficulty by means of this subterfuge, but it must be well considered whether there may not hereafter spring from this lie much greater inconvenience than that from which I now free myself, and as, with all my supposed cunning, the consequences cannot be so easily foreseen but that credit once lost may be much more injurious to me than any mischief which I seek to avoid at present, it should be considered whether it would not be more prudent to act herein according to a universal maxim and to make it a habit to promise nothing except with the intention of keeping it. But it is soon clear to me that such a maxim will still only be based on the fear of consequences. Now it is a wholly different thing to be truthful from duty and to be so from apprehension of injurious consequences. In the first case, the very notion of the action already implies a law for me; in the second case, I must first look about elsewhere to see what results may be combined with it which would affect myself. For to deviate from the principle of duty is beyond all doubt wicked; but to be unfaithful to my maxim of prudence may often be very advantageous to me, although to abide by it is certainly safer. The shortest way, however, and an unerring one, to discover the answer to this question whether a lying promise is consistent with duty, is to ask myself, "Should I be content that my maxim (to extricate myself from difficulty by a false promise) should hold good as a universal law, for myself as well as for others? and should I be able to say to myself, "Every one may make a deceitful promise when he finds himself in a difficulty from which he cannot otherwise extricate himself?" Then I presently become aware that while I can will the lie, I can by no means will that lying should be a universal law. For with such a law there would be no promises at all, since it would be in vain to allege my intention in regard to my future actions to those who would not believe this allegation, or if they over hastily did so would pay me back in my own coin. Hence my maxim, as soon as it should be made a universal law, would necessarily destroy itself.

I do not, therefore, need any far-reaching penetration to discern what I have to do in order that my will may be morally good. Inexperienced in the course of the world, incapable of being prepared for all its contingencies, I only ask myself: Canst thou also will that thy maxim should be a universal law? If not, then it must be rejected, and that not because of a disadvantage accruing from it to myself or even to others, but because it cannot enter as a principle into a possible universal legislation, and reason extorts from me immediate respect for such legislation. I do not indeed as yet discern on what this respect is based (this the philosopher may inquire), but at least I understand this, that it is an estimation of the worth which far outweighs all worth of what is recommended by inclination, and that the necessity of acting from pure respect for the practical law is what constitutes duty, to which every other motive must give place, because it is the condition of a will being good in itself, and the worth of such a will is above everything.

Thus, then, without quitting the moral knowledge of common human reason, we have arrived at its principle. And although, no doubt, common men do not conceive it in such an abstract and universal form, yet they always have it really before their eyes and use it as the standard of their decision. Here it would be easy to show how, with this compass in hand, men are well able to distinguish, in every case that occurs, what is good, what bad, conformably to duty or inconsistent with it, if, without in the least teaching them anything new, we only, like Socrates, direct their attention to the principle they themselves employ; and that, therefore, we do not need science and philosophy to know what we should do to be honest and good, yea, even wise and virtuous. Indeed we might well have conjectured beforehand that the knowledge of what every man is bound to do, and therefore also to know, would be within the reach of every man, even the commonest. Here we cannot forbear admiration when we see how great an advantage the practical judgement has over the theoretical in the common understanding of men. In the latter, if common reason ventures to depart from the laws of experience and from the perceptions of the senses, it falls into mere inconceivabilities and self-contradictions, at least into a chaos of uncertainty, obscurity, and instability. But in the practical sphere it is just when the common understanding excludes all sensible springs from practical laws that its power of judgement begins to show itself to advantage. It then becomes even subtle, whether it be that it chicanes with its own conscience or with other claims respecting what is to be called right, or whether it desires for its own instruction to determine honestly the worth of actions; and, in the latter case, it may even have as good a hope of hitting the mark as any philosopher whatever can promise himself. Nay, it is almost more sure of doing so, because the philosopher cannot have any other principle, while he may easily perplex his judgement by a multitude of considerations foreign to the matter, and so turn aside from the right way. Would it not therefore be wiser in moral concerns to acquiesce in the judgement of common reason, or at most only to call in philosophy for the purpose of rendering the system of morals more complete and intelligible, and its rules more convenient for use (especially for disputation), but not so as to draw off the common understanding from its happy simplicity, or to bring it by means of philosophy into a new path of inquiry and instruction?

Innocence is indeed a glorious thing; only, on the other hand, it is very sad that it cannot well maintain itself and is easily seduced. On this account even wisdom—which otherwise consists more in conduct than in knowledge—yet has need of science, not in order to learn from it, but to secure for its precepts admission and permanence. Against all the commands of duty which reason represents to man as so deserving of respect, he feels in himself a powerful counterpoise in his wants and inclinations, the entire satisfaction of which he sums up under the name of happiness. Now reason issues its commands unyieldingly, without promising anything to the inclinations, and, as it were, with disregard and contempt for these claims, which are so impetuous, and at the same time so plausible, and which will not allow themselves to be suppressed by any command. Hence there arises a natural dialectic, i.e., a disposition, to argue against these strict laws of duty and to question their validity, or at least their purity and strictness; and, if possible, to make them more accordant with our wishes and inclinations, that is to say, to corrupt them at their very source, and entirely to destroy their worth—a thing which even common practical reason cannot ultimately call good.

Thus is the common reason of man compelled to go out of its sphere, and to take a step into the field of a practical philosophy, not to satisfy any speculative want (which never occurs to it as long as it is content to be mere sound reason), but even on practical grounds, in order to attain in it information and clear instruction respecting the source of its principle, and the correct determination of it in opposition to the maxims which are based on wants and inclinations, so that it may escape from the perplexity of opposite claims and not run the risk of losing all genuine moral principles through the equivocation into which it easily falls. Thus, when practical reason cultivates itself, there insensibly arises in it a dialetic which forces it to seek aid in philosophy, just as happens to it in its theoretic use; and in this case, therefore, as well as in the other, it will find rest nowhere but in a thorough critical examination of our reason.

DISCUSSION QUESTIONS

1. Compare the decision procedure here with the passage in Sartre's lecture where he describes how we choose for all people when we make a moral choice. Are these views compatible? Why or why not.

2. Kant's view is a deontological view, as is the position found in the *Bhagavad Gita*. What are the main similarities and differences between these two views? Explain.

3. Just as Kant's view on knowledge is a reaction to Hume, his view on ethics is, too. Explain how this is the case.

4. Kant says that your action has no moral worth if you have an inclination to do it and it happens to be the right thing to do. It only has moral worth if duty is the only motivation. Do you agree? Why or why not? Explain.

Utilitarianism

By John Stuart Mill

It is often said of John Stuart Mill (1806–1873) that he was the last person to know everything. Mill read and wrote on almost every major topic of discourse. He is most famous as a proponent of utilitarianism. Modern utilitarianism gets started with Mill's godfather Jeremy Bentham (1748–1832). The utilitarians were empiricists in the tradition of Hume on matters of knowledge. They were also advocates for social change and Mill had a seat in parliament from 1865–1868. Mill was one of the first men to argue for feminism in his book On the Subjection of Women *from 1869. Utilitarianism is primarily the moral, social, political, and legal philosophy that says the way to judge an action, policy, or law is by determining whether it produces the best consequences when compared to all other choices. This emphasis on consequences makes this a teleological view. The consequences it is most concerned with are happiness and/or pleasure. Bentham's version was purely quantitative, as he makes no distinction between kinds of pleasures. Mill, on the other hand, included qualitative distinctions, too. He noted a difference between higher and lower pleasures. Our selection is from the middle three chapters of Mill's short 1863 book,* Utilitarianism. *Chapter II is where Mill defines utilitarianism, Chapter III is his defense of the sanction of the principle, and Chapter IV discusses how to prove whether it is the best principle. Included in Chapter II is a famous passage where he defends his qualitative version of the principle. He introduces the idea of the competent judge. The one who is able to judge whether one kind of pleasure is superior to another is one who has understood both. He uses an analogy here about whether a pig can appreciate what a person can, and also whether a fool can appreciate what Socrates can.*

CHAPTER II
WHAT UTILITARIANISM IS

A passing remark is all that needs be given to the ignorant blunder of supposing that those who stand up for utility as the test of right and wrong, use the term in that restricted and merely colloquial sense in which utility is opposed to pleasure. An apology is due to the philosophical opponents of utilitarianism, for even the momentary appearance of confounding them with any one capable of so absurd a misconception; which is the more extraordinary, inasmuch as the contrary accusation, of referring everything to pleasure, and that too in its grossest form, is another of the common charges against utilitarianism: and, as has been pointedly remarked by an able writer, the same sort of persons, and often the very same persons, denounce the theory "as impracticably dry when the word utility precedes the word pleasure, and as too practicably voluptuous when the word pleasure precedes the word utility." Those who know anything about the matter are aware that every writer, from Epicurus to Bentham, who maintained the theory of utility, meant by it, not something to be contradistinguished from pleasure, but pleasure itself, together with exemption from pain; and instead of opposing the useful to the agreeable or the ornamental, have always declared that the useful means these, among other things. Yet the common herd, including the herd of writers, not only in newspapers and periodicals, but in books of weight and pretension, are perpetually falling into this shallow mistake. Having caught up the word utilitarian, while knowing nothing whatever about it but its sound, they habitually express by it the rejection, or the neglect, of pleasure in some of its forms; of beauty, of ornament, or of amusement. Nor is the term thus ignorantly misapplied solely in disparagement, but occasionally in compliment; as though it implied superiority to frivolity and the mere pleasures of the moment. And this perverted use is the only one in which the word is popularly known, and the one from which the new generation are acquiring their sole notion of its meaning. Those who introduced the word, but who had for many years discontinued it as a distinctive appellation, may well feel themselves called upon to resume it, if by doing so they can hope to contribute anything towards rescuing it from this utter degradation.[1]

The creed which accepts as the foundation of morals, Utility, or the Greatest Happiness Principle, holds that actions are right in proportion as they tend to promote happiness, wrong as they tend to produce the reverse of happiness. By happiness is intended pleasure, and the absence of pain; by unhappiness, pain, and the privation of pleasure. To give a clear view of the moral standard set up by the theory, much more requires to be said; in particular, what things it includes in the ideas of pain and pleasure; and to what extent this is left an open question. But these supplementary explanations do not affect the theory of life on which this theory of morality is grounded—namely, that pleasure, and freedom from pain, are the only things desirable as ends; and that all desirable things (which are as numerous in the utilitarian as in any other scheme) are desirable either for the pleasure inherent in themselves, or as means to the promotion of pleasure and the prevention of pain.

Now, such a theory of life excites in many minds, and among them in some of the most estimable in feeling and purpose, inveterate dislike. To suppose that life has (as they express it) no higher end than pleasure—no better and nobler object of desire and pursuit—they designate as utterly mean and grovelling; as a doctrine worthy only of swine, to whom the followers of Epicurus were, at a very early period, contemptuously likened; and modern holders of the doctrine are occasionally made the subject of equally polite comparisons by its German, French, and English assailants.

When thus attacked, the Epicureans have always answered, that it is not they, but their accusers, who represent human nature in a degrading light; since the accusation supposes human beings to be capable of no pleasures except those of which swine are capable. If this supposition were true, the charge could not be gainsaid, but would then be no longer an imputation; for if the sources of pleasure were precisely the same to human beings and to swine, the rule of life which is good enough for the one would be good enough for the other. The comparison of the Epicurean life to that of beasts is felt as degrading, precisely because a beast's pleasures do not satisfy a human being's conceptions of happiness. Human beings have faculties more elevated than the animal appetites, and when once made conscious of them, do not regard anything as happiness which does not include their gratification. I do not, indeed, consider the Epicureans to have been by any means faultless in drawing out their scheme of consequences from the utilitarian principle. To do this in any sufficient manner, many Stoic, as well as Christian elements require to be included. But there is no known Epicurean theory of life which does not assign to the pleasures of the intellect; of the feelings and imagination, and of the moral sentiments, a much higher value as pleasures than to those of mere sensation. It must be admitted, however, that utilitarian writers in general have placed the superiority of mental over bodily pleasures chiefly in the greater permanency, safety, uncostliness, &c., of the former—that is, in their circumstantial advantages rather than in their intrinsic nature. And on all these points utilitarians have fully proved their case; but they might have taken the other, and, as it may be called, higher ground, with entire consistency. It is quite compatible with the principle of utility to recognise the fact, that some *kinds* of pleasure are more desirable and more valuable than others. It would be absurd that while, in estimating all other things, quality is considered as well as quantity, the estimation of pleasures should be supposed to depend on quantity alone.

If I am asked, what I mean by difference of quality in pleasures, or what makes one pleasure more valuable than another, merely as a pleasure, except its being greater in amount, there is but one possible answer. Of two pleasures, if there be one to which all or almost all who have experience of both give a decided preference, irrespective of any feeling of moral obligation to prefer it, that is the more desirable pleasure. If one of the two is, by those who are competently acquainted with both, placed so far above the other that they prefer it, even though knowing it to be attended with a greater amount of discontent, and would not resign it for any quantity of the other pleasure which their nature is capable of, we are justified in ascribing to the preferred enjoyment a superiority in quality, so far outweighing quantity as to render it, in comparison, of small account.

Now it is an unquestionable fact that those who are equally acquainted with, and equally capable of appreciating and enjoying, both, do give a most marked preference to the manner of existence which employs their higher faculties. Few human creatures would consent to be changed into any of the lower animals, for a promise of the fullest allowance of a beast's pleasures; no intelligent human being would consent to be a fool, no instructed person would be an ignoramus, no person of feeling and conscience would be selfish and base, even though they should be persuaded that the fool, the dunce, or the rascal is better satisfied with his lot than they are with theirs. They would not resign what they possess more than he, for the most complete satisfaction of all the desires which they have in common with him. If they ever fancy they would, it is only in cases of unhappiness so extreme, that to escape from it they would exchange their lot for almost any other, however undesirable in their own eyes. A being of higher faculties requires more to make him happy, is capable probably of more acute suffering, and is certainly accessible to it at more points, than one of an inferior type; but in spite of these liabilities, he can never really wish to sink into what he feels to be a lower grade of existence. We may give what explanation we please of this unwillingness; we may attribute it to pride, a name which is given indiscriminately to some of the most and to some of the least estimable feelings of which mankind are capable; we may refer it to the love of liberty and personal independence, an appeal to which was with the Stoics one of the most effective means for the inculcation of it; to the love of power, or to the love of excitement, both of which do really enter into and contribute to it: but its most appropriate appellation is a sense of dignity, which all human beings possess in one form or other, and in some, though by no means in exact, proportion to their higher faculties, and which is so essential a part of the happiness of those in whom it is strong, that nothing which conflicts with it could be, otherwise than momentarily, an object of desire to them. Whoever supposes that this preference takes place at a sacrifice of happiness-that the superior being, in anything like equal circumstances, is not happier than the inferior-confounds the two very different ideas, of happiness, and content. It is indisputable that the being whose capacities of enjoyment are low, has the greatest chance of having them fully satisfied; and a highly-endowed being will always feel that any happiness which he can look for, as the world is constituted, is imperfect. But he can learn to bear its imperfections, if they are at all bearable; and they will not make him envy the being who is indeed unconscious of the imperfections, but only because he feels not at all the good which those imperfections qualify. It is better to be a human being dissatisfied than a pig satisfied; better to be Socrates dissatisfied than a fool satisfied. And if the fool, or the pig, is of a different opinion, it is because they only know their own side of the question. The other party to the comparison knows both sides.

It may be objected, that many who are capable of the higher pleasures, occasionally, under the influence of temptation, postpone them to the lower. But this is quite compatible with a full appreciation of the intrinsic superiority of the higher. Men often, from infirmity of character, make their election for the nearer good, though they know it to be the less valuable; and this no less when the choice is between two bodily pleasures, than when it is between bodily and mental. They pursue sensual indulgences to the injury of health, though perfectly aware that health is the greater good. It may be further objected, that many who begin with youthful enthusiasm for everything noble, as they advance in years sink into indolence and selfishness. But I do not believe that those who undergo this very common change, voluntarily choose the lower description of pleasures in preference to the higher. I believe that before they devote themselves exclusively to the one, they have already become incapable of the other. Capacity for the nobler feelings is in most natures a very tender plant, easily killed, not only by hostile influences, but by mere want of sustenance; and in the majority of young persons it speedily dies away if the occupations to which their position in life has devoted them, and the society into which it has thrown them, are not favourable to keeping that higher capacity in exercise. Men lose their high aspirations as they lose their intellectual tastes, because they have not time or opportunity for indulging them; and they addict themselves to inferior pleasures, not because they deliberately prefer them, but because they are either the only ones to which they have access, or the only ones which they are any longer capable of enjoying. It may be questioned whether any one who has remained equally susceptible to both classes of pleasures, ever knowingly and calmly preferred the lower; though many, in all ages, have broken down in an ineffectual attempt to combine both.

From this verdict of the only competent judges, I apprehend there can be no appeal. On a question which is the best worth having of two pleasures, or which of two modes of existence is the most grateful to the feelings, apart from its moral attributes and from its consequences, the judgment of those who are qualified by knowledge of both, or, if they differ, that of the majority among them, must be admitted as final. And there needs be the less hesitation to accept this judgment respecting the quality of pleasures, since there is no other tribunal to be referred to even on the question of quantity. What means are there of determining which is the acutest of two pains, or the intensest of two pleasurable sensations, except the general suffrage of those who are familiar with both? Neither pains nor pleasures are homogeneous, and pain is always heterogeneous with pleasure. What is there to decide whether a particular pleasure is worth purchasing at the cost of a particular pain, except the feelings and judgment of the experienced? When, therefore, those feelings and judgment declare the pleasures derived from the higher faculties to be preferable *in kind*, apart from the question of intensity, to those of which the animal nature, disjoined from the higher faculties, is susceptible, they are entitled on this subject to the same regard.

I have dwelt on this point, as being a necessary part of a perfectly just conception of Utility or Happiness, considered as the directive rule of human conduct. But it is by no means an indispensable condition to the acceptance of the utilitarian standard; for that standard is not the agent's own greatest happiness, but the greatest amount of happiness altogether; and if it may possibly be doubted whether a noble character is always the happier for its nobleness, there can be no doubt that it makes other people happier, and that the world in general is immensely a gainer by it. Utilitarianism, therefore, could only attain its end by the general cultivation of nobleness of character, even if each individual were only benefited by the nobleness of others, and his own, so far as happiness is concerned, were a sheer deduction from the benefit. But the bare enunciation of such an absurdity as this last, renders refutation superfluous.

According to the Greatest Happiness Principle, as above explained, the ultimate end, with reference to and for the sake of which all other things are desirable (whether we are considering our own good or that of other people), is an existence exempt as far as possible from pain, and as rich as possible in enjoyments, both in point of quantity and quality; the test of quality, and the rule for measuring it against quantity, being the preference felt by those who, in their opportunities of experience, to which must be added their habits of self-consciousness and self-observation, are best furnished with the means of comparison. This, being, according to the utilitarian opinion, the end of human action, is necessarily also the standard of morality; which may accordingly be defined, the rules and precepts for human conduct, by the observance of which an existence such as has been described might be, to the greatest extent possible, secured to all mankind; and not to them only, but, so far as the nature of things admits, to the whole sentient creation.

Against this doctrine, however, arises another class of objectors, who say that happiness, in any form, cannot be the rational purpose of human life and action; because, in the first place, it is unattainable: and they contemptuously ask, What right hast thou to be happy? a question which Mr. Carlyle clenches by the addition, What right, a short time ago, hadst thou even *to be*? Next, they say, that men can do *without* happiness; that all noble human beings have felt this, and could not have become noble but by learning the lesson of Entsagen, or renunciation; which lesson, thoroughly learnt and submitted to, they affirm to be the beginning and necessary condition of all virtue.

The first of these objections would go to the root of the matter were it well founded; for if no happiness is to be had at all by human beings, the attainment of it cannot be the end of morality, or of any rational conduct. Though, even in that case, something might still be said for the utilitarian theory; since utility includes not solely the pursuit of happiness, but the prevention or mitigation of unhappiness; and if the former aim be chimerical, there will be all the greater scope and more imperative need for the latter, so long at least as mankind think fit to live, and do not take refuge in the simultaneous act of suicide recommended under certain conditions by Novalis. When, however, it is thus positively asserted to be impossible that human life should be happy, the assertion, if not something like a verbal quibble, is at least an exaggeration. If by happiness be meant a continuity of highly pleasurable excitement, it is evident enough that this is impossible. A state of exalted pleasure lasts only moments, or in some cases, and with some intermissions, hours or days, and is the occasional brilliant flash of enjoyment, not its permanent and steady flame. Of this the philosophers who have taught that happiness is the end of life were as fully aware as those who taunt them. The happiness which they meant was not a life of rapture, but moments of such, in an existence made up of few and transitory pains, many and various pleasures, with a decided predominance of the active over the passive, and having as the foundation of the whole, not to expect more from life than it is capable of bestowing. A life thus composed, to those who have been fortunate enough to obtain it, has always appeared worthy of the name of happiness. And such an existence is even now the lot of many, during some considerable portion of their lives. The present wretched education, and wretched social arrangements, are the only real hindrance to its being attainable by almost all.

The objectors perhaps may doubt whether human beings, if taught to consider happiness as the end of life, would be satisfied with such a moderate share of it. But great numbers of mankind have been satisfied with much less. The main constituents of a satisfied life appear to be two, either of which by itself is often found sufficient for the purpose: tranquillity, and excitement. With much tranquillity, many find that they can be content with very little pleasure: with much excitement, many can reconcile themselves to a considerable quantity of pain. There is assuredly no inherent impossibility in enabling even the mass of mankind to unite both; since the two are so far from being incompatible that they are in natural alliance, the prolongation of either being a preparation for, and exciting a wish for, the other. It is only those in whom indolence amounts to a vice, that do not desire excitement after an interval of repose; it is only those in whom the need of excitement is a disease, that feel the tranquillity which follows excitement dull and insipid, instead of pleasurable in direct proportion to the excitement which preceded it. When people who are tolerably fortunate in their outward lot do not find in life sufficient enjoyment to make it valuable to them, the cause generally is, caring for nobody but themselves. To those who have neither public nor private affections, the excitements of life are much curtailed, and in any case dwindle in value as the time approaches when all selfish interests must be terminated by death: while those who leave after them objects of personal affection, and especially those who have also cultivated a fellow-feeling with the collective interests of mankind, retain as lively an interest in life on the eve of death as in the vigour of youth and health. Next to selfishness, the principal cause which makes life unsatisfactory, is want of mental cultivation. A cultivated mind—I do not mean that of a philosopher, but any mind to which the fountains of knowledge have been opened, and which has been taught, in any tolerable degree, to exercise its faculties—finds sources of inexhaustible interest in all that surrounds it; in the objects of nature, the achievements of art, the imaginations of poetry, the incidents of history, the ways of mankind past and present, and their prospects in the future. It is possible, indeed, to become indifferent to all this, and that too without having exhausted a thousandth part of it; but only when one has had from the beginning no moral or human interest in these things, and has sought in them only the gratification of curiosity.

Now there is absolutely no reason in the nature of things why an amount of mental culture sufficient to give an intelligent interest in these objects of contemplation, should not be the inheritance of every one born in a civilized country. As little is there an inherent necessity that any human being should be a selfish egotist, devoid of every feeling or care but those which centre in his own miserable individuality. Something far superior to this is sufficiently common even now, to give ample earnest of what the human species may be made. Genuine private affections, and a sincere interest in the public good, are possible, though in unequal degrees, to every rightly brought-up human being. In a world in which there is so much to interest, so much to enjoy, and so much also to correct and improve, every one who has this moderate amount of moral and intellectual requisites is capable of an existence which may be called enviable; and unless such a person, through bad laws, or subjection to the will of others, is denied the liberty to use the sources of happiness within his reach, he will not fail to find this enviable existence, if he escape the positive evils of life, the great sources of physical and mental suffering—such as indigence, disease, and the unkindness, worthlessness, or premature loss of objects of affection. The main stress of the problem lies, therefore, in the contest with these calamities, from which it is a rare good fortune entirely to escape; which, as things now are, cannot be obviated, and often cannot be in any material degree mitigated. Yet no one whose opinion deserves a moment's consideration can doubt that most of the great positive evils of the world are in themselves removable, and will, if human affairs continue to improve, be in the end reduced within narrow limits. Poverty, in any sense implying suffering, may be completely extinguished by the wisdom of society, combined with the good sense and providence of individuals. Even that most intractable of enemies, disease, may be indefinitely reduced in dimensions by good physical and moral education, and proper control of noxious influences; while the progress of science holds out a promise for the future of still more direct conquests over this detestable foe. And every advance in that direction relieves us from some, not only of the chances which cut short our own lives, but, what concerns us still more, which deprive us of those in whom our happiness is wrapt up. As for vicissitudes of fortune, and other disappointments connected with worldly circumstances, these are principally the effect either of gross imprudence, of ill-regulated desires, or of bad or imperfect social institutions. All the grand sources, in short, of human suffering are in a great degree, many of them almost entirely, conquerable by human care and effort; and though their removal is grievously slow—though a long succession of generations will perish in the breach before the conquest is completed, and this world becomes all that, if will and knowledge were not wanting, it might easily be made—yet every mind sufficiently intelligent and generous to bear a part, however small and unconspicuous, in the endeavour, will draw a noble enjoyment from the contest itself, which he would not for any bribe in the form of selfish indulgence consent to be without.

And this leads to the true estimation of what is said by the objectors concerning the possibility, and the obligation, of learning to do without happiness. Unquestionably it is possible to do without happiness; it is done involuntarily by nineteen-twentieths of mankind, even in those parts of our present world which are least deep in barbarism; and it often has to be done voluntarily by the hero or the martyr, for the sake of something which he prizes more than his individual happiness. But this something, what is it, unless the happiness of others, or some of the requisites of happiness? It is noble to be capable of resigning entirely one's own portion of happiness, or chances of it: but, after all, this self-sacrifice must be for some end; it is not its own end; and if we are told that its end is not happiness, but virtue, which is better than happiness, I ask, would the sacrifice be made if the hero or martyr did not believe that it would earn for others immunity from similar sacrifices? Would it be made, if he thought that his renunciation of happiness for himself would produce no fruit for any of his fellow creatures, but to make their lot like his, and place them also in the condition of persons who have renounced happiness? All honour to those who can abnegate for themselves the personal enjoyment of life, when by such renunciation they contribute worthily to increase the amount of happiness in the world; but he who does it, or professes to do it, for any other purpose, is no more deserving of admiration than the ascetic mounted on his pillar. He may be an inspiriting proof of what men *can* do, but assuredly not an example of what they *should*.

Though it is only in a very imperfect state of the world's arrangements that any one can best serve the happiness of others by the absolute sacrifice of his own, yet so long as the world is in that imperfect state, I fully acknowledge that the readiness to make such a sacrifice is the highest virtue which can be found in man. I will add, that in this condition of the world, paradoxical as the assertion may be, the conscious ability to do without happiness gives the best prospect of realizing such happiness as is attainable. For nothing except that consciousness can raise a person above the chances of life, by making him feel that, let fate and fortune do their worst, they have not power to subdue him: which, once felt, frees him from excess of anxiety concerning the evils of life, and enables him, like many a Stoic in the worst times of the Roman Empire, to cultivate in tranquillity the sources of satisfaction accessible to him, without concerning himself about the uncertainty of their duration, any more than about their inevitable end.

Meanwhile, let utilitarians never cease to claim the morality of self-devotion as a possession which belongs by as good a right to them, as either to the Stoic or to the Transcendentalist. The utilitarian morality does recognise in human beings the power of sacrificing their own greatest good for the good of others. It only refuses to admit that the sacrifice is itself a good. A sacrifice which does not increase, or tend to increase, the sum total of happiness, it considers as wasted. The only self-renunciation which it applauds, is devotion to the happiness, or to some of the means of happiness, of others; either of mankind collectively, or of individuals within the limits imposed by the collective interests of mankind.

I must again repeat, what the assailants of utilitarianism seldom have the justice to acknowledge, that the happiness which forms the utilitarian standard of what is right in conduct, is not the agent's own happiness, but that of all concerned. As between his own happiness and that of others, utilitarianism requires him to be as strictly impartial as a disinterested and benevolent spectator. In the golden rule of Jesus of Nazareth, we read the complete spirit of the ethics of utility. To do as one would be done by, and to love one's neighbour as oneself, constitute the ideal perfection of utilitarian morality. As the means of making the nearest approach to this ideal, utility would enjoin, first, that laws and social arrangements should place the happiness, or (as speaking practically it may be called) the interest, of every individual, as nearly as possible in harmony with the interest of the whole; and secondly, that education and opinion, which have so vast a power over human character, should so use that power as to establish in the mind of every individual an indissoluble association between his own happiness and the good of the whole; especially between his own happiness and the practice of such modes of conduct, negative and positive, as regard for the universal happiness prescribes: so that not only he may be unable to conceive the possibility of happiness to himself, consistently with conduct opposed to the general good, but also that a direct impulse to promote the general good may be in every individual one of the habitual motives of action, and the sentiments connected therewith may fill a large and prominent place in every human being's sentient existence. If the impugners of the utilitarian morality represented it to their own minds in this its true character, I know not what recommendation possessed by any other morality they could possibly affirm to be wanting to it: what more beautiful or more exalted developments of human nature any other ethical system can be supposed to foster, or what springs of action, not accessible to the utilitarian, such systems rely on for giving effect to their mandates.

The objectors to utilitarianism cannot always be charged with representing it in a discreditable light. On the contrary, those among them who entertain anything like a just idea of its disinterested character, sometimes find fault with its standard as being too high for humanity. They say it is exacting too much to require that people shall always act from the inducement of promoting the general interests of society. But this is to mistake the very meaning of a standard of morals, and to confound the rule of action with the motive of it. It is the business of ethics to tell us what are our duties, or by what test we may know them; but no system of ethics requires that the sole motive of all we do shall be a feeling of duty; on the contrary, ninety-nine hundredths of all our actions are done from other motives, and rightly so done, if the rule of duty does not condemn them. It is the more unjust to utilitarianism that this particular misapprehension should be made a ground of objection to it, inasmuch as utilitarian moralists have gone beyond almost all others in affirming that the motive has nothing to do with the morality of the action, though much with the worth of the agent. He who saves a fellow creature from drowning does what is morally right, whether his motive be duty, or the hope of being paid for his trouble: he who betrays the friend that trusts him, is guilty of a crime, even if his object be to serve another friend to whom he is under greater obligations.[2] But to speak only of actions done from the motive of duty, and in direct obedience to principle: it is a misapprehension of the utilitarian mode of thought, to conceive it as implying that people should fix their minds upon so wide a generality as the world, or society at large. The great majority of good actions are intended, not for the benefit of the world, but for that of individuals, of which the good of the world is made up; and the thoughts of the most virtuous man need not on these occasions travel beyond the particular persons concerned, except so far as is necessary to assure himself that in benefiting them he is not violating the rights—that is, the legitimate and authorized expectations—of any one else. The multiplication of happiness is, according to the utilitarian ethics, the object of virtue: the occasions on which any person (except one in a thousand) has it in his power to do this on an extended scale, in other words, to be a public benefactor, are but exceptional; and on these occasions alone is he called on to consider public utility; in every other case, private utility, the interest or happiness of some few persons, is all he has to attend to. Those alone the influence of whose actions extends to society in general, need concern themselves habitually about so large an object. In the case of abstinences indeed—of things which people forbear to do, from moral considerations, though the consequences in the particular case might be beneficial—it would be unworthy of an intelligent agent not to be consciously aware that the action is of a class which, if practised generally, would be generally injurious, and that this is the ground of the obligation to abstain from it. The amount of regard for the public interest implied in this recognition, is no greater than is demanded by every system of morals; for they all enjoin to abstain from whatever is manifestly pernicious to society.

The same considerations dispose of another reproach against the doctrine of utility, founded on a still grosser misconception of the purpose of a standard of morality, and of the very meaning of the words right and wrong. It is often affirmed that utilitarianism renders men cold and unsympathizing; that it chills their moral feelings towards individuals; that it makes them regard only the dry and hard consideration of the consequences of actions, not taking into their moral estimate the qualities from which those actions emanate. If the assertion means that they do not allow their judgment respecting the rightness or wrongness of an action to be influenced by their opinion of the qualities of the person who does it, this is a complaint not against utilitarianism, but against having any standard of morality at all; for certainly no known ethical standard decides an action to be good or bad because it is done by a good or a bad man, still less because done by an amiable, a brave, or a benevolent man or the contrary. These considerations are relevant, not to the estimation of actions, but of persons; and there is nothing in the utilitarian theory inconsistent with the fact that there are other things which interest us in persons besides the rightness and wrongness of their actions. The Stoics, indeed, with the paradoxical misuse of language which was part of their system, and by which they strove to raise themselves above all concern about anything but virtue, were fond of saying that he who has that has everything; that he, and only he, is rich, is beautiful, is a king. But no claim of this description is made for the virtuous man by the utilitarian doctrine. Utilitarians are quite aware that there are other desirable possessions and qualities besides virtue, and are perfectly willing to allow to all of them their full worth. They are also aware that a right action does not necessarily indicate a virtuous character, and that actions which are blameable often proceed from qualities entitled to praise. When this is apparent in any particular case, it modifies their estimation, not certainly of the act, but of the agent. I grant that they are, notwithstanding, of opinion, that in the long run the best proof of a good character is good actions; and resolutely refuse to consider any mental disposition as good, of which the predominant tendency is to produce bad conduct. This makes them unpopular with many people; but it is an unpopularity which they must share with every one who regards the distinction between right and wrong in a serious light; and the reproach is not one which a conscientious utilitarian need be anxious to repel.

If no more be meant by the objection than that many utilitarians look on the morality of actions, as measured by the utilitarian standard, with too exclusive a regard, and do not lay sufficient stress upon the other beauties of character which go towards making a human being loveable or admirable, this may be admitted. Utilitarians who have cultivated their moral feelings, but not their sympathies nor their artistic perceptions, do fall into this mistake; and so do all other moralists under the same conditions. What can be said in excuse for other moralists is equally available for them, namely, that if there is to be any error, it is better that it should be on that side. As a matter of fact, we may affirm that among utilitarians as among adherents of other systems, there is every imaginable degree of rigidity and of laxity in the application of their standard: some are even puritanically rigorous, while others are as indulgent as can possibly be desired by sinner or by sentimentalist. But on the whole, a doctrine which brings prominently forward the interest that mankind have in the repression and prevention of conduct which violates the moral law, is likely to be inferior to no other in turning the sanctions of opinion against such violations. It is true, the question, What does violate the moral law? is one on which those who recognise different standards of morality are likely now and then to differ. But difference of opinion on moral questions was not first introduced into the world by utilitarianism, while that doctrine does supply, if not always an easy, at all events a tangible and intelligible mode of deciding such differences.

It may not be superfluous to notice a few more of the common misapprehensions of utilitarian ethics, even those which are so obvious and gross that it might appear impossible for any person of candour and intelligence to fall into them: since persons, even of considerable mental endowments, often give themselves so little trouble to understand the bearings of any opinion against which they entertain a prejudice, and men are in general so little conscious of this voluntary ignorance as a defect, that the vulgarest misunderstandings of ethical doctrines are continually met with in the deliberate writings of persons of the greatest pretensions both to high principle and to philosophy. We not uncommonly hear the doctrine of utility inveighed against as a *godless* doctrine. If it be necessary to say anything at all against so mere an assumption, we may say that the question depends upon what idea we have formed of the moral character of the Deity. If it be a true belief that God desires, above all things, the happiness of his creatures, and that this was his purpose in their creation, utility is not only not a godless doctrine, but more profoundly religious than any other. If it be meant that utilitarianism does not recognise the revealed will of God as the supreme law of morals, I answer, that an utilitarian who believes in the perfect goodness and wisdom of God, necessarily believes that whatever God has thought fit to reveal on the subject of morals, must fulfil the requirements of utility in a supreme degree. But others besides utilitarians have been of opinion that the Christian revelation was intended, and is fitted, to inform the hearts and minds of mankind with a spirit which should enable them to find for themselves what is right, and incline them to do it when found, rather than to tell them, except in a very general way, what it is: and that we need a doctrine of ethics, carefully followed out, to *interpret* to us the will of God. Whether this opinion is correct or not, it is superfluous here to discuss; since whatever aid religion, either natural or revealed, can afford to ethical investigation, is as open to the utilitarian moralist as to any other. He can use it as the testimony of God to the usefulness or hurtfulness of any given course of action, by as good a right as others can use it for the indication of a transcendental law, having no connexion with usefulness or with happiness.

Again, Utility is often summarily stigmatized as an immoral doctrine by giving it the name of Expediency, and taking advantage of the popular use of that term to contrast it with Principle. But the Expedient, in the sense in which it is opposed to the Right, generally means that which is expedient for the particular interest of the agent himself: as when a minister sacrifices the interest of his country to keep himself in place. When it means anything better than this, it means that which is expedient for some immediate object, some temporary purpose, but which violates a rule whose observance is expedient in a much higher degree. The Expedient, in this sense, instead of being the same thing with the useful, is a branch of the hurtful. Thus, it would often be expedient, for the purpose of getting over some momentary embarrassment, or attaining some object immediately useful to ourselves or others, to tell a lie. But inasmuch as the cultivation in ourselves of a sensitive feeling on the subject of veracity, is one of the most useful, and the enfeeblement of that feeling one of the most hurtful, things to which our conduct can be instrumental; and inasmuch as any, even unintentional, deviation from truth, does that much towards weakening the trustworthiness of human assertion, which is not only the principal support of all present social well-being, but the insufficiency of which does more than any one thing that can be named to keep back civilisation, virtue, everything on which human happiness on the largest scale depends; we feel that the violation, for a present advantage, of a rule of such transcendent expediency, is not expedient, and that he who, for the sake of a convenience to himself or to some other individual, does what depends on him to deprive mankind of the good, and inflict upon them the evil, involved in the greater or less reliance which they can place in each other's word, acts the part of one of their worst enemies. Yet that even this rule, sacred as it is, admits of possible exceptions, is acknowledged by all moralists; the chief of which is when the withholding of some fact (as of information from a male-factor, or of bad news from a person dangerously ill) would preserve some one (especially a person other than oneself) from great and unmerited evil, and when the withholding can only be effected by denial. But in order that the exception may not extend itself beyond the need, and may have the least possible effect in weakening reliance on veracity, it ought to be recognized, and, if possible, its limits defined; and if the principle of utility is good for anything, it must be good for weighing these conflicting utilities against one another, and marking out the region within which one or the other preponderates.

Again, defenders of utility often find themselves called upon to reply to such objections as this—that there is not time, previous to action, for calculating and weighing the effects of any line of conduct on the general happiness. This is exactly as if any one were to say that it is impossible to guide our conduct by Christianity, because there is not time, on every occasion on which anything has to be done, to read through the Old and New Testaments. The answer to the objection is, that there has been ample time, namely, the whole past duration of the human species. During all that time mankind have been learning by experience the tendencies of actions; on which experience all the prudence, as well as all the morality of life, is dependent. People talk as if the commencement of this course of experience had hitherto been put off, and as if, at the moment when some man feels tempted to meddle with the property or life of another, he had to begin considering for the first time whether murder and theft are injurious to human happiness. Even then I do not think that he would find the question very puzzling; but, at all events, the matter is now done to his hand. It is truly a whimsical supposition, that if mankind were agreed in considering utility to be the test of morality, they would remain without any agreement as to what is useful, and would take no measures for having their notions on the subject taught to the young, and enforced by law and opinion. There is no difficulty in proving any ethical standard whatever to work ill, if we suppose universal idiocy to be conjoined with it, but on any hypothesis short of that, mankind must by this time have acquired positive beliefs as to the effects of some actions on their happiness; and the beliefs which have thus come down are the rules of morality for the multitude, and for the philosopher until he has succeeded in finding better. That philosophers might easily do this, even now, on many subjects; that the received code of ethics is by no means of divine right; and that mankind have still much to learn as to the effects of actions on the general happiness, I admit, or rather, earnestly maintain. The corollaries from the principle of utility, like the precepts of every practical art, admit of indefinite improvement, and, in a progressive state of the human mind, their improvement is perpetually going on. But to consider the rules of morality as improvable, is one thing; to pass over the intermediate generalizations entirely, and endeavour to test each individual action directly by the first principle, is another. It is a strange notion that the acknowledgment of a first principle is inconsistent with the admission of secondary ones. To inform a traveller respecting the place of his ultimate destination, is not to forbid the use of landmarks and direction-posts on the way. The proposition that happiness is the end and aim of morality, does not mean that no road ought to be laid down to that goal, or that persons going thither should not be advised to take one direction rather than another. Men really ought to leave off talking a kind of nonsense on this subject, which they would neither talk nor listen to on other matters of practical concernment. Nobody argues that the art of navigation is not founded on astronomy, because sailors cannot wait to calculate the Nautical Almanack. Being rational creatures, they go to sea with it ready calculated; and all rational creatures go out upon the sea of life with their minds made up on the common questions of right and wrong, as well as on many of the far more difficult questions of wise and foolish. And this, as long as foresight is a human quality, it is to be presumed they will continue to do. Whatever we adopt as the fundamental principle of morality, we require subordinate principles to apply it by: the impossibility of doing without them, being common to all systems, can afford no argument against any one in particular: but gravely to argue as if no such secondary principles could be had, and as if mankind had remained till now, and always must remain, without drawing any general conclusions from the experience of human life, is as high a pitch, I think, as absurdity has ever reached in philosophical controversy.

The remainder of the stock arguments against utilitarianism mostly consist in laying to its charge the common infirmities of human nature, and the general difficulties which embarrass conscientious persons in shaping their course through life. We are told that an utilitarian will be apt to make his own particular case an exception to moral rules, and, when under temptation, will see an utility in the breach of a rule, greater than he will see in its observance. But is utility the only creed which is able to furnish us with excuses for evil doing, and means of cheating our own conscience? They are afforded in abundance by all doctrines which recognise as a fact in morals the existence of conflicting considerations; which all doctrines do, that have been believed by sane persons. It is not the fault of any creed, but of the complicated nature of human affairs, that rules of conduct cannot be so framed as to require no exceptions, and that hardly any kind of action can safely be laid down as either always obligatory or always condemnable. There is no ethical creed which does not temper the rigidity of its laws, by giving a certain latitude, under the moral responsibility of the agent, for accommodation to peculiarities of circumstances; and under every creed, at the opening thus made, self-deception and dishonest casuistry get in. There exists no moral system under which there do not arise unequivocal cases of conflicting obligation. These are the real difficulties, the knotty points both in the theory of ethics, and in the conscientious guidance of personal conduct. They are overcome practically with greater or with less success according to the intellect and virtue of the individual; but it can hardly be pretended that any one will be the less qualified for dealing with them, from possessing an ultimate standard to which conflicting rights and duties can be referred. If utility is the ultimate source of moral obligations, utility may be invoked to decide between them when their demands are incompatible. Though the application of the standard may be difficult, it is better than none at all: while in other systems, the moral laws all claiming independent authority, there is no common umpire entitled to interfere between them; their claims to precedence one over another rest on little better than sophistry, and unless determined, as they generally are, by the unacknowledged influence of considerations of utility, afford a free scope for the action of personal desires and partialities. We must remember that only in these cases of conflict between secondary principles is it requisite that first principles should be appealed to. There is no case of moral obligation in which some secondary principle is not involved; and if only one, there can seldom be any real doubt which one it is, in the mind of any person by whom the principle itself is recognized.

CHAPTER III
OF THE ULTIMATE SANCTION OF THE PRINCIPLE OF UTILITY

The question is often asked, and properly so, in regard to any supposed moral standard—What is its sanction? what are the motives to obey it? or more specifically, what is the source of its obligation? whence does it derive its binding force? It is a necessary part of moral philosophy to provide the answer to this question; which, though frequently assuming the shape of an objection to the utilitarian morality, as if it had some special applicability to that above others, really arises in regard to all standards. It arises, in fact, whenever a person is called on to adopt a standard or refer morality to any basis on which he has not been accustomed to rest it. For the customary morality, that which education and opinion have consecrated, is the only one which presents itself to the mind with the feeling of being *in itself* obligatory; and when a person is asked to believe that this morality *derives* its obligation from some general principle round which custom has not thrown the same halo, the assertion is to him a paradox; the supposed corollaries seem to have a more binding force than the original theorem; the superstructure seems to stand better without, than with, what is represented as its foundation. He says to himself, I feel that I am bound not to rob or murder, betray or deceive; but why am I bound to promote the general happiness? If my own happiness lies in something else, why may I not give that the preference?

• • •

The principle of utility either has, or there is no reason why it might not have, all the sanctions which belong to any other system of morals. Those sanctions are either external or internal. Of the external sanctions it is not necessary to speak at any length. They are, the hope of favour and the fear of displeasure from our fellow creatures or from the Ruler of the Universe, along with whatever we may have of sympathy or affection for them or of love and awe of Him, inclining us to do His will independently of selfish consequences. There is evidently no reason why all these motives for observance should not attach themselves to the utilitarian morality, as completely and as powerfully as to any other. Indeed, those of them which refer to our fellow creatures are sure to do so, in proportion to the amount of general intelligence; for whether there be any other ground of moral obligation than the general happiness or not, men do desire happiness; and however imperfect may be their own practice, they desire and commend all conduct in others towards themselves, by which they think their happiness is promoted. With regard to the religious motive, if men believe, as most profess to do, in the goodness of God, those who think that conduciveness to the general happiness is the essence, or even only the criterion, of good, must necessarily believe that it is also that which God approves. The whole force therefore of external reward and punishment, whether physical or moral, and whether proceeding from God or from our fellow men, together with all that the capacities of human nature admit, of disinterested devotion to either, become available to enforce the utilitarian morality, in proportion as that morality is recognized; and the more powerfully, the more the appliances of education and general cultivation are bent to the purpose.

So far as to external sanctions. The internal sanction of duty, whatever our standard of duty may be, is one and the same—a feeling in our own mind; a pain, more or less intense, attendant on violation of duty, which in properly cultivated moral natures rises, in the more serious cases, into shrinking from it as an impossibility. This feeling, when disinterested, and connecting itself with the pure idea of duty, and not with some particular form of it, or with any of the merely accessory circumstances, is the essence of Conscience; though in that complex phenomenon as it actually exists, the simple fact is in general all encrusted over with collateral associations, derived from sympathy, from love, and still more from fear; from all the forms of religious feeling; from the recollections of childhood and of all our past life; from self-esteem, desire of the esteem of others, and occasionally even self-abasement. This extreme complication is, I apprehend, the origin of the sort of mystical character which, by a tendency of the human mind of which there are many other examples, is apt to be attributed to the idea of moral obligation, and which leads people to believe that the idea cannot possibly attach itself to any other objects than those which, by a supposed mysterious law, are found in our present experience to excite it. Its binding force, however, consists in the existence of a mass of feeling which must be broken through in order to do what violates our standard of right, and which, if we do nevertheless violate that standard, will probably have to be encountered afterwards in the form of remorse. Whatever theory we have of the nature or origin of conscience, this is what essentially constitutes it.

The ultimate sanction, therefore, of all morality (external motives apart) being a subjective feeling in our own minds, I see nothing embarrassing to those whose standard is utility, in the question, what is the sanction of that particular standard? We may answer, the same as of all other moral standards—the conscientious feelings of mankind. Undoubtedly this sanction has no binding efficacy on those who do not possess the feelings it appeals to; but neither will these persons be more obedient to any other moral principle than to the utilitarian one. On them morality of any kind has no hold but through the external sanctions. Meanwhile the feelings exist, a feet in human nature, the reality of which, and the great power with which they are capable of acting on those in whom they have been duly cultivated, are proved by experience. No reason has ever been shown why they may not be cultivated to as great intensity in connection with the utilitarian, as with any other rule of morals.

There is, I am aware, a disposition to believe that a person who sees in moral obligation a transcendental fact, an objective reality belonging to the province of "Things in themselves," is likely to be more obedient to it than one who believes it to be entirely subjective, having its seat in human consciousness only. But whatever a person's opinion may be on this point of Ontology, the force he is really urged by is his own subjective feeling, and is exactly measured by its strength. No one's belief that Duty is an objective reality is stronger than the belief that God is so; yet the belief in God, apart from the expectation of actual reward and punishment, only operates on conduct through, and in proportion to, the subjective religious feeling. The sanction, so far as it is disinterested, is always in the mind itself; and the notion, therefore, of the transcendental moralists must be, that this sanction will not exist *in* the mind unless it is believed to have its root out of the mind; and that if a person is able to say to himself, That which is restraining me, and which is called my conscience, is only a feeling in my own mind, he may possibly draw the conclusion that when the feeling ceases the obligation ceases, and that if he find the feeling inconvenient, he may disregard it, and endeavour to get rid of it. But is this danger confined to the utilitarian morality? Does the belief that moral obligation has its seat outside the mind make the feeling of it too strong to be got rid of? The fact is so far otherwise, that all moralists admit and lament the ease with which, in the generality of minds, conscience can be silenced or stifled. The question, Need I obey my conscience? is quite as often put to themselves by persons who never heard of the principle of utility, as by its adherents. Those whose conscientious feelings are so weak as to allow of their asking this question, if they answer it affirmatively, will not do so because they believe in the transcendental theory, but because of the external sanctions.

It is not necessary, for the present purpose, to decide whether the feeling of duty is innate or implanted. Assuming it to be innate, it is an open question to what objects it naturally attaches itself; for the philosophic supporters of that theory are now agreed that the intuitive perception is of principles of morality, and not of the details. If there be anything innate in the matter, I see no reason why the feeling which is innate should not be that of regard to the pleasures and pains of others. If there is any principle of morals which is intuitively obligatory, I should say it must be that. If so, the intuitive ethics would coincide with the utilitarian, and there would be no further quarrel between them. Even as it is, the intuitive moralists, though they believe that there are other intuitive moral obligations, do already believe this to be one; for they unanimously hold that a large portion of morality turns upon the consideration due to the interests of our fellow creatures. Therefore, if the belief in the transcendental origin of moral obligation gives any additional efficacy to the internal sanction, it appears to me that the utilitarian principle has already the benefit of it.

On the other hand, if, as is my own belief, the moral feelings are not innate, but acquired, they are not for that reason the less natural. It is natural to man to speak, to reason, to build cities, to cultivate the ground, though these are acquired faculties. The moral feelings are not indeed a part of our nature, in the sense of being hi any perceptible degree present in all of us; but this, unhappily, is a fact admitted by those who believe the most strenuously in their transcendental origin. Like the other acquired capacities above referred to, the moral faculty, if not a part of our nature, is a natural outgrowth from it; capable, like them, in a certain small degree, of springing up spontaneously; and susceptible of being brought by cultivation to a high degree of development. Unhappily it is also susceptible, by a sufficient use of the external sanctions and of the force of early impressions, of being cultivated in almost any direction: so that there is hardly anything so absurd or so mischievous that it may not, by means of these influences, be made to act on the human mind with all the authority of conscience. To doubt that the same potency might be given by the same means to the principle of utility, even if it had no foundation in human nature, would be flying in the face of all experience.

But moral associations which are wholly of artificial creation, when intellectual culture goes on, yield by degrees to the dissolving force of analysis: and if the feeling of duty, when associated with utility, would appear equally arbitrary; if there were no leading department of our nature, no powerful class of sentiments, with which that association would harmonize, which would make us feel it congenial, and incline us not only to foster it in others (for which we have abundant interested motives), but also to cherish it in ourselves; if there were not, in short, a natural basis of sentiment for utilitarian morality, it might well happen that this association also, even after it had been implanted by education, might be analysed away.

But there is this basis of powerful natural sentiment; and this it is which, when once the general happiness is recognized as the ethical standard, will constitute the strength of the utilitarian morality. This firm foundation is that of the social feelings of mankind; the desire to be in unity with our fellow creatures, which is already a powerful principle in human nature, and happily one of those which tend to become stronger, even without express inculcation, from the influences of advancing civilization. The social state is at once so natural, so necessary, and so habitual to man, that, except in some unusual circumstances or by an effort of voluntary abstraction, he never conceives himself otherwise than as a member of a body; and this association is riveted more and more, as mankind are further removed from the state of savage independence. Any condition, therefore, which is essential to a state of society, becomes more and more an inseparable part of every person's conception of the state of things which he is born into, and which is the destiny of a human being. Now, society between human beings, except in the relation of master and slave, is manifestly impossible on any other footing than that the interests of all are to be consulted. Society between equals can only exist on the understanding that the interests of all are to be regarded equally. And since in all states of civilization, every person, except an absolute monarch, has equals, every one is obliged to live on these terms with somebody; and in every age some advance is made towards a state in which it will be impossible to live permanently on other terms with anybody. In this way people grow up unable to conceive as possible to them a state of total disregard of other people's interests. They are under a necessity of conceiving themselves as at least abstaining from all the grosser injuries, and (if only for their own protection.) living in a state of constant protest against them. They are also familiar with the fact of co-operating with others, and proposing to themselves a collective, not an individual, interest, as the aim (at least for the time being) of their actions. So long as they are co-operating, their ends are identified with those of others; there is at least a temporary feeling that the interests of others are their own interests. Not only does all strengthening of social ties, and all healthy growth of society, give to each individual a stronger personal interest in practically consulting the welfare of others; it also leads him to identify his feelings more and more with their good, or at least with an ever greater degree of practical consideration for it. He comes, as though instinctively, to be conscious of himself as a being who *of course* pays regard to others. The good of others becomes to him a thing naturally and necessarily to be attended to, like any of the physical conditions of our existence. Now, whatever amount of this feeling a person has, he is urged by the strongest motives both of interest and of sympathy to demonstrate it, and to the utmost of his power encourage it in others; and even if he has none of it himself, he is as greatly interested as any one else that others should have it. Consequently, the smallest germs of the feeling are laid hold of and nourished by the contagion of sympathy and the influences of education; and a complete web of corroborative association is woven round it, by the powerful agency of the external sanctions. This mode of conceiving ourselves and human life, as civilization goes on, is felt to be more and more natural. Every step in political improvement renders it more so, by removing the sources of opposition of interest, and levelling those inequalities of legal privilege between individuals or classes, owing to which there are large portions of mankind whose happiness it is still practicable to disregard. In an improving state of the human mind, the influences are constantly on the increase, which tend to generate in each individual a feeling of unity with all the rest; which feeling, if perfect, would make him never think of, or desire, any beneficial condition for himself, in the benefits of which they are not included. If we now suppose this feeling of unity to be taught as a religion, and the whole force of education, of institutions, and of opinion, directed, as it once was in the case of religion, to make every person grow up from infancy surrounded on all sides both by the profession and by the practice of it, I think that no one, who can realize this conception, will feel any misgiving about the sufficiency of the ultimate sanction for the Happiness morality. To any ethical student who finds the realization difficult, I recommend, as a means of facilitating it, the second of M. Comte's two principal works, the *Système de Politique Positive.* I entertain the strongest objections to the system of politics and morals set forth in that treatise; but I think it has superabundantly shown the possibility of giving to the service of humanity, even without the aid of belief in a Providence, both the physical power and the social efficacy of a religion; making it take hold of human life, and colour all thought, feeling, and action, in a manner of which the greatest ascendency ever exercised by any religion may be but a type and foretaste; and of which the danger is, not that it should be insufficient, but that it should be so excessive as to interfere unduly with human freedom and individuality.

Neither is it necessary to the feeling which constitutes the binding force of the utilitarian morality on those who recognize it, to wait for those social influences which would make its obligation felt by mankind at large. In the comparatively early state of human advancement in which we now live, a person cannot indeed feel that entireness of sympathy with all others, which would make any real discordance in the general direction of their conduct in life impossible; but already a person in whom the social feeling is at all developed, cannot bring himself to think of the rest of his fellow creatures as struggling rivals with him for the means of happiness, whom he must desire to see defeated in their object in order that he may succeed in his. The deeply-rooted conception which every individual even now has of himself as a social being, tends to make him feel it one of his natural wants that there should be harmony between his feelings and aims and those of his fellow creatures. If differences of opinion and of mental culture make it impossible for him to share many of their actual feelings-perhaps make him denounce and defy those feelings-he still needs to be conscious that his real aim and theirs do not conflict; that he is not opposing himself to what they really wish for, namely, their own good, but is, on the contrary, promoting it. This feeling in most individuals is much inferior in strength to their selfish feelings, and is often wanting altogether. But to those who have it, it possesses all the characters of a natural feeling. It does not present itself to their minds as a superstition of education, or a law despotically imposed by the power of society, but as an attribute which it would not be well for them to be without. This conviction is the ultimate sanction of the greatest-happiness morality. This it is which makes any mind, of well-developed feelings, work with, and not against, the outward motives to care for others, afforded by what I have called the external sanctions; and when those sanctions are wanting, or act in an opposite direction, constitutes in itself a powerful internal binding force, in proportion to the sensitiveness and thoughtfulness of the character; since few but those whose mind is a moral blank, could bear to lay out their course of life on the plan of paying no regard to others except so far as their own private interest compels.

CHAPTER IV
OF WHAT SORT OF PROOF THE PRINCIPLE OF UTILITY IS SUSCEPTIBLE

It has already been remarked, that questions of ultimate ends do not admit of proof, in the ordinary acceptation of the term. To be incapable of proof by reasoning is common to all first principles; to the first premises of our knowledge, as well as to those of our conduct. But the former, being matters of fact, may be the subject of a direct appeal to the faculties which judge of fact—namely, our senses, and our internal consciousness. Can an appeal be made to the same faculties on questions of practical ends? Or by what other faculty is cognizance taken of them?

Questions about ends are, in other words, questions what things are desirable. The utilitarian doctrine is, that happiness is desirable, and the only thing desirable, as an end; all other things being only desirable as means to that end. What ought to be required of this doctrine—what conditions is it requisite that the doctrine should fulfil—to make good its claim to be believed?

The only proof capable of being given that an object is visible, is that people actually see it. The only proof that a sound is audible, is that people hear it: and so of the other sources of our experience. In like manner, I apprehend, the sole evidence it is possible to produce that anything is desirable, is that people do actually desire it. If the end which the utilitarian doctrine proposes to itself were not, in theory and in practice, acknowledged to be an end, nothing could ever convince any person that it was so. No reason can be given why the general happiness is desirable, except that each person, so far as he believes it to be attainable, desires his own happiness. This, however, being a fact, we have not only all the proof which the case admits of, but all which it is possible to require, that happiness is a good: that each person's happiness is a good to that person, and the general happiness, therefore, a good to the aggregate of all persons. Happiness has made out its title as *one* of the ends of conduct, and consequently one of the criteria of morality.

But it has not, by this alone, proved itself to be the sole criterion. To do that, it would seem, by the same rule, necessary to show, not only that people desire happiness, but that they never desire anything else. Now it is palpable that they do desire things which, in common language, are decidedly distinguished from happiness. They desire, for example, virtue, and the absence of vice, no less really than pleasure and the absence of pain. The desire of virtue is not as universal, but it is as authentic a fact, as the desire of happiness. And hence the opponents of the utilitarian standard deem that they have a right to infer that there are other ends of human action besides happiness, and that happiness is not the standard of approbation and disapprobation.

But does the utilitarian doctrine deny that people desire virtue, or maintain that virtue is not a thing to be desired? The very reverse. It maintains not only that virtue is to be desired, but that it is to be desired disinterestedly, for itself. Whatever may be the opinion of utilitarian moralists as to the original conditions by which virtue is made virtue; however they may believe (as they do) that actions and dispositions are only virtuous because they promote another end than virtue; yet this being granted, and it having been decided, from considerations of this description, what *is* virtuous, they not only place virtue at the very head of the things which are good as means to the ultimate end, but they also recognise as a psychological fact the possibility of its being, to the individual, a good in itself, without looking to any end beyond it; and hold, that the mind is not in a right state, not in a state conformable to Utility, not in the state most conducive to the general happiness, unless it does love virtue in this manner—as a thing desirable in itself, even although, in the individual instance, it should not produce those other desirable consequences which it tends to produce, and on account of which it is held to be virtue. This opinion is not, in the smallest degree, a departure from the Happiness principle. The ingredients of happiness are very various, and each of them is desirable in itself, and not merely when considered as swelling an aggregate. The principle of utility does not mean that any given pleasure, as music, for instance, or any given exemption from pain, as for example health, are to be looked upon as means to a collective something termed happiness, and to be desired on that account. They are desired and desirable in and for themselves; besides being means, they are a part of the end. Virtue, according to the utilitarian doctrine, is not naturally and originally part of the end, but it is capable of becoming so; and in those who love it disinterestedly it has become so, and is desired and cherished, not as a means to happiness, but as a part of their happiness.

To illustrate this farther, we may remember that virtue is not the only thing, originally a means, and which if it were not a means to anything else, would be and remain indifferent, but which by association with what it is a means to, comes to be desired for itself, and that too with the utmost intensity. What, for example, shall we say of the love of money? There is nothing originally more desirable about money than about any heap of glittering pebbles. Its worth is solely that of the things which it will buy; the desires for other things than itself, which it is a means of gratifying. Yet the love of money is not only one of the strongest moving forces of human life, but money is, in many cases, desired in and for itself; the desire to possess it is often stronger than the desire to use it, and goes on increasing when all the desires which point to ends beyond it, to be compassed by it, are falling off. It may be then said truly, that money is desired not for the sake of an end, but as part of the end. From being a means to happiness, it has come to be itself a principal ingredient of the individual's conception of happiness. The same may be said of the majority of the great objects of human life—power, for example, or fame; except that to each of these there is a certain amount of immediate pleasure annexed, which has at least the semblance of being naturally inherent in them; a thing which cannot be said of money. Still, however, the strongest natural attraction, both of power and of fame, is the immense aid they give to the attainment of our other wishes; and it is the strong association thus generated between them and all our objects of desire, which gives to the direct desire of them the intensity it often assumes, so as in some characters to surpass in strength all other desires. In these cases the means have become a part of the end, and a more important part of it than any of the things which they are means to. What was once desired as an instrument for the attainment of happiness, has come to be desired for its own sake. In being desired for its own sake it is, however, desired as part of happiness. The person is made, or thinks he would be made, happy by its mere possession; and is made unhappy by failure to obtain it. The desire of it is not a different thing from the desire of happiness, any more than the love of music, or the desire of health. They are included in happiness. They are some of the elements of which the desire of happiness is made up. Happiness is not an abstract idea, but a concrete whole; and these are some of its parts. And the utilitarian standard sanctions and approves their being so. Life would be a poor thing, very ill provided with sources of happiness, if there were not this provision of nature, by which things originally indifferent, but conducive to, or otherwise associated with, the satisfaction of our primitive desires, become in themselves sources of pleasure more valuable than the primitive pleasures, both in permanency, in the space of human existence that they are capable of covering, and even in intensity. Virtue, according to the utilitarian conception, is a good of this description. There was no original desire of it, or motive to it, save its conduciveness to pleasure, and especially to protection from pain. But through the association thus formed, it may be felt a good in itself, and desired as such with as great intensity as any other good; and with this difference between it and the love of money, of power, or of fame, that all of these may, and often do, render the individual noxious to the other members of the society to which he belongs, whereas there is nothing which makes him so much a blessing to them as the cultivation of the disinterested, love of virtue. And consequently, the utilitarian standard, while it tolerates and approves those other acquired desires, up to the point beyond which they would be more injurious to the general happiness than promotive of it, enjoins and requires the cultivation of the love of virtue up to the greatest strength possible, as being above all things important to the general happiness.

It results from the preceding considerations, that there is in reality nothing desired except happiness. Whatever is desired otherwise than as a means to some end beyond itself, and ultimately to happiness, is desired as itself a part of happiness, and is not desired for itself until it has become so. Those who desire virtue for its own sake, desire it either because the consciousness of it is a pleasure, or because the consciousness of being without it is a pain, or for both reasons united; as in truth the pleasure and pain seldom exist separately, but almost always together, the same person feeling pleasure in the degree of virtue attained, and pain in not having attained more. If one of these gave him no pleasure, and the other no pain, he would not love or desire virtue, or would desire it only for the other benefits which it might produce to himself or to persons whom he cared for.

• • •

And now to decide whether this is really so; whether mankind do desire nothing for itself but that which is a pleasure to them, or of which the absence is a pain; we have evidently arrived at a question of fact and experience, dependent, like all similar questions, upon evidence. It can only be determined by practised self-consciousness and self-observation, assisted by observation of others. I believe that these sources of evidence, impartially consulted, will declare that desiring a thing and finding it pleasant, aversion to it and thinking of it as painful, are phenomena entirely inseparable, or rather two parts of the same phenomenon; in strictness of language, two different modes of naming the same psychological fact: that to think of an object as desirable (unless for the sake of its consequences), and to think of it as pleasant, are one and the same thing; and that to desire anything, except in proportion as the idea of it is pleasant, is a physical and metaphysical impossibility.

So obvious does this appear to me, that I expect it will hardly be disputed: and the objection made will be, not that desire can possibly be directed to anything ultimately except pleasure and exemption from pain, but that the will is a different thing from desire; that a person of confirmed virtue, or any other person whose purposes are fixed, carries out his purposes without any thought of the pleasure he has in contemplating them, or expects to derive from their fulfilment; and persists in acting on them, even though these pleasures are much diminished, by changes in his character or decay of his passive sensibilities, or are outweighed by the pains which the pursuit of the purposes may bring upon him. All this I fully admit, and have stated it elsewhere, as positively and emphatically as any one. Will, the active phenomenon, is a different thing from desire, the state of passive sensibility, and though originally an offshoot from it, may in time take root and detach itself from the parent stock; so much so, that in the case of an habitual purpose, instead of willing the thing because we desire it, we often desire it only because we will it. This, however, is but an instance of that familiar fact, the power of habit, and is nowise confined to the case of virtuous actions. Many indifferent things, which men originally did from a motive of some sort, they continue to do from habit. Sometimes this is done unconsciously, the consciousness coming only after the action: at other times with conscious volition, but volition which has become habitual, and is put into operation by the force of habit, in opposition perhaps to the deliberate preference, as often happens with those who have contracted habits of vicious or hurtful indulgence. Third and last comes the case in which the habitual act of will in the individual instance is not in contradiction to the general intention prevailing at other times, but in fulfilment of it; as in the case of the person of confirmed virtue, and of all who pursue deliberately and consistently any determinate end. The distinction between will and desire thus understood, is an authentic and highly important psychological fact; but the fact consists solely in this—that will, like all other parts of our constitution, is amenable to habit, and that we may will from habit what we no longer desire for itself, or desire only because we will it. It is not the less true that will, in the beginning, is entirely produced by desire; including in that term the repelling influence of pain as well as the attractive one of pleasure. Let us take into consideration, no longer the person who has a confirmed will to do right, but him in whom that virtuous will is still feeble, conquerable by temptation, and not to be fully relied on; by what means can it be strengthened? How can the will to be virtuous, where it does not exist in sufficient force, be implanted or awakened? Only by making the person *desire* virtue—by making him think of it in a pleasurable light, or of its absence in a painful one. It is by associating the doing right with pleasure, or the doing wrong with pain, or by eliciting and impressing and bringing home to the person's experience the pleasure naturally involved in the one or the pain in the other, that it is possible to call forth that will to be virtuous, which, when confirmed, acts without any thought of either pleasure or pain. Will is the child of desire, and passes out of the dominion of its parent only to come under that of habit. That which is the result of habit affords no presumption of being intrinsically good; and there would be no reason for wishing that the purpose of virtue should become independent of pleasure and pain, were it not that the influence of the pleasurable and painful associations which prompt to virtue is not sufficiently to be depended on for unerring constancy of action until it has acquired the support of habit. Both in feeling and in conduct, habit is the only thing which imparts certainty; and it is because of the importance to others of being able to rely absolutely on one's feelings and conduct, and to oneself of being able to rely on one's own, that the will to do right ought to be cultivated into this habitual independence. In other words, this state of the will is a means to good, not intrinsically a good; and does not contradict the doctrine that nothing is a good to human beings but in so far as it is either itself pleasurable, or a means of attaining pleasure or averting pain.

But if this doctrine be true, the principle of utility is proved. Whether it is so or not, must now be left to the consideration of the thoughtful reader.

ENDNOTES

1 The author of this essay has reason for believing himself to be the first person who brought the word utilitarian into use. He did not invent it, but adopted it from a passing expression in Mr. Galt's *Annals of the Parish*. After using it as a

designation for several years, he and others abandoned it from a growing dislike to anything resembling a badge or watchword of sectarian distinction. But as a name for one single opinion, not a set of opinions—to denote the recognition of utility as a standard, not any particular way of applying it—the term supplies a want in the language, and offers, in many cases, a convenient mode of avoiding tiresome circumlocution.

2 An opponent, whose intellectual and moral fairness it is a pleasure to acknowledge (the Rev. J. Llewellyn Davis), has objected to this passage, saying, "Surely the rightness or wrongness of saving a man from drowning does depend very much upon the motive with which it is done. Suppose that a tyrant, when his enemy jumped into the sea to escape from him, saved him from drowning simply in order that he might inflict upon him more exquisite tortures, would it tend to clearness to speak of that rescue as 'a morally right action?' Or suppose again, according to one of the stock illustrations of ethical inquiries, that a man betrayed a trust received from a friend, because the discharge of it would fatally injure that friend himself or some one belonging to him, would utilitarianism compel one to call the betrayal 'a crime' as much as if it had been done from the meanest motive?"

I submit, that he who saves another from drowning in order to kill him by torture afterwards, does not differ only in motive from him who does the same thing from duty or benevolence; the act itself is different. The rescue of the man is, in the case supposed, only the necessary first step of an act far more atrocious than leaving him to drown would have been. Had Mr. Davis said, "The rightness or wrongness of saving a man from drowning does depend very much"—not upon the motive, but—"upon the *intention*" no utilitarian would have differed from him. Mr. Davis, by an oversight too common not to be quite venial, has in this case confounded the very different ideas of Motive and Intention. There is no point which utilitarian thinkers (and Bentham pre-eminently) have taken more pains to illustrate than this. The morality of the action depends entirely upon the intention—that is, upon what the agent *wills to do*. But the motive, that is, the feeling which makes him will so to do, when it makes no difference in the act, makes none in the morality: though it makes a great difference in our moral estimation of the agent, especially if it indicates a good or a bad habitual *disposition*—a bent of character from which useful, or from which hurtful actions are likely to arise.

DISCUSSION QUESTIONS

1. Compare the idea of the competent judge to Voltaire's story "The Good Brahmin."

2. Mill's teleological decision procedure is the polar opposite to Kant's deontological one. Which approach to making moral decisions do you think is more on the right track? Why? Explain.

3. Chapter IV of *Utilitarianism* talks about the difficulties in proving fundamental principles. What are the primary reasons it is hard to defend a moral principle? Explain.

4. What are the main similarities between Mill's view and the one proposed by Epicurus? Explain.

5. Compare Mill's view to Hume's. What are the significant similarities and differences? Explain.

Beyond Good and Evil

By Friedrich Nietzsche

In Beyond Good and Evil: Prelude to a Philosophy of the Future *(1886), Friedrich Nietzsche develops a view of ethics that rejects the views of both deontological views like Kant's and consequentialist (teleological) views like Mill's. As we saw in Part II of Four Fundamental Questions, Nietzsche rejects views that focus on the denial of life. Instead, he advocates us making our own values and affirming life. Like our earlier selection from* The Gay Science, Beyond Good and Evil *is aphoristic in style.*

Here we have Part IX, "What is Noble?" In §259 we see a discussion of his view on the affirmation of life. In §§260–261, he introduces the distinction between master morality and slave morality. In a master morality, you choose your own values. In a slave morality, your will is directed by something outside yourself, like another person, a book, or an institution. This distinction is one of his most famous ideas. Many of the rest of the paragraphs draw out the implications of his view of the master morality as one of nobility.

CHAPTER IX
WHAT IS NOBLE?

Every elevation of the type "man," has hitherto been the work of an aristocratic society and so it will always be—a society believing in a long scale of gradations of rank and differences of worth among human beings, and requiring slavery in some form or other. Without the PATHOS OF DISTANCE, such as grows out of the incarnated difference of classes, out of the constant out-looking and down-looking of the ruling caste on subordinates and instruments, and out of their equally constant practice of obeying and commanding, of keeping down and keeping at a distance—that other more mysterious pathos could never have arisen, the longing for an ever new widening of distance within the soul itself, the formation of ever higher, rarer, further, more extended, more comprehensive states, in short, just the elevation of the type "man," the continued "self-surmounting of man," to use a moral formula in a supermoral sense. To be sure, one must not resign oneself to any humanitarian illusions about the history of the origin of an aristocratic society (that is to say, of the preliminary condition for the elevation of the type "man"): the truth is hard. Let us acknowledge unprejudicedly how every higher civilization hitherto has ORIGINATED! Men with a still natural nature, barbarians in every terrible sense of the word, men of prey, still in possession of unbroken strength of will and desire for power, threw themselves upon weaker, more moral, more peaceful races (perhaps trading or cattle-rearing communities), or upon old mellow civilizations in which the final vital force was flickering out in brilliant fireworks of wit and depravity. At the commencement, the noble caste was always the barbarian caste: their superiority did not consist first of all in their physical, but in their psychical power—they were more COMPLETE men (which at every point also implies the same as "more complete beasts").

Corruption—as the indication that anarchy threatens to break out among the instincts, and that the foundation of the emotions, called "life," is convulsed—is something radically different according to the organization in which it manifests itself. When, for instance, an aristocracy like that of France at the beginning of the Revolution, flung away its privileges with sublime disgust and sacrificed itself to an excess of its moral sentiments, it was corruption:—it was really only the closing act of the corruption which had existed for centuries, by virtue of which that aristocracy had abdicated step by step its lordly prerogatives and lowered itself to a FUNCTION of royalty (in the end even to its decoration and parade-dress). The essential thing, however, in a good and healthy aristocracy is that it should not regard itself as a function either of the kingship or the commonwealth, but as the SIGNIFICANCE and highest justification thereof—that it should therefore accept with a good conscience the sacrifice of a legion of individuals, who, FOR ITS SAKE, must be suppressed and reduced to imperfect men, to slaves and instruments. Its fundamental belief must be precisely that society is NOT allowed to exist for its own sake, but only as a foundation and scaffolding, by means of which a select class of beings may be able to elevate themselves to their higher duties, and in general to a higher EXISTENCE: like those sun-seeking climbing plants in Java—they are called Sipo Matador,—which encircle an oak so long and so often with their arms, until at last, high above it, but supported by it, they can unfold their tops in the open light, and exhibit their happiness.

To refrain mutually from injury, from violence, from exploitation, and put one's will on a par with that of others: this may result in a certain rough sense in good conduct among individuals when the necessary conditions are given (namely, the actual similarity of the individuals in amount of force and degree of worth, and their co-relation within one organization). As soon, however, as one wished to take this principle more generally, and if possible even as the FUNDAMENTAL PRINCIPLE OF SOCIETY, it would immediately disclose what it really is—namely, a Will to the DENIAL of life, a principle of dissolution and decay. Here one must think profoundly to the very basis and resist all sentimental weakness: life itself is ESSENTIALLY appropriation, injury, conquest of the strange and weak, suppression, severity, obtrusion of peculiar forms, incorporation, and at the least, putting it mildest, exploitation;—but why should one for ever use precisely these words on which for ages a disparaging purpose has been stamped? Even the organization within which, as was previously supposed, the individuals treat each other as equal—it takes place in every healthy aristocracy—must itself, if it be a living and not a dying organization, do all that towards other bodies, which the individuals within it refrain from doing to each other it will have to be the incarnated Will to Power, it will endeavour to grow, to gain ground, attract to itself and acquire ascendancy—not owing to any morality or immorality, but because it LIVES, and because life is precisely Will to Power. On no point, however, is the ordinary consciousness of Europeans more unwilling to be corrected than on this matter, people now rave everywhere, even under the guise of science, about coming conditions of society in which "the exploiting character" is to be absent—that sounds to my ears as if they promised to invent a mode of life which should refrain from all organic functions. "Exploitation" does not belong to a depraved, or imperfect and primitive society it belongs to the nature of the living being as a primary organic function, it is a consequence of the intrinsic Will to Power, which is precisely the Will to Life—Granting that as a theory this is a novelty—as a reality it is the FUNDAMENTAL FACT of all history let us be so far honest towards ourselves!

In a tour through the many finer and coarser moralities which have hitherto prevailed or still prevail on the earth, I found certain traits recurring regularly together, and connected with one another, until finally two primary types revealed themselves to me, and a radical distinction was brought to light. There is MASTER-MORALITY and SLAVE-MORALITY,—I would at once add, however, that in all higher and mixed civilizations, there are also attempts at the reconciliation of the two moralities, but one finds still oftener the confusion and mutual misunderstanding of them, indeed sometimes their close juxtaposition—even in the same man, within one soul. The distinctions of moral values have either originated in a ruling caste, pleasantly conscious of being different from the ruled—or among the ruled class, the slaves and dependents of all sorts. In the first case, when it is the rulers who determine the conception "good," it is the exalted, proud disposition which is regarded as the distinguishing feature, and that which determines the order of rank. The noble type of man separates from himself the beings in whom the opposite of this exalted, proud disposition displays itself he despises them. Let it at once be noted that in this first kind of morality the antithesis "good" and "bad" means practically the same as "noble" and "despicable,"—the antithesis "good" and "EVIL" is of a different origin. The cowardly, the timid, the insignificant, and those thinking merely of narrow utility are despised; moreover, also, the distrustful, with their constrained glances, the self-abasing, the dog-like kind of men who let themselves be abused, the mendicant flatterers, and above all the liars:—it is a fundamental belief of all aristocrats that the common people are untruthful. "We truthful ones"—the nobility in ancient Greece called themselves. It is obvious that everywhere the designations of moral value were at first applied to MEN; and were only derivatively and at a later period applied to ACTIONS; it is a gross mistake, therefore, when historians of morals start with questions like, "Why have sympathetic actions been praised?" The noble type of man regards HIMSELF as a determiner of values; he does not require to be approved of; he passes the judgment: "What is injurious to me is injurious in itself;" he knows that it is he himself only who confers honour on things; he is a CREATOR OF VALUES. He honours whatever he recognizes in himself: such morality equals self-glorification. In the foreground there is the feeling of plenitude, of power, which seeks to overflow, the happiness of high tension, the consciousness of a wealth which would fain give and bestow:—the noble man also helps the unfortunate, but not—or scarcely—out of pity, but rather from an impulse generated by the super-abundance of power. The noble man honours in himself the powerful one, him also who has power over himself, who knows how to speak and how to keep silence, who takes pleasure in subjecting himself to severity and hardness, and has reverence for all that is severe and hard. "Wotan placed a hard heart in my breast," says an old Scandinavian Saga: it is thus rightly expressed from the soul of a proud Viking. Such a type of man is even proud of not being made for sympathy; the hero of the Saga therefore adds warningly: "He who has not a hard heart when young, will never have one." The noble and brave who think thus are the furthest removed from the morality which sees precisely in sympathy, or in acting for the good of others, or in DESINTERESSEMENT, the characteristic of the moral; faith in oneself, pride in oneself, a radical enmity and irony towards "selflessness," belong as definitely to noble morality, as do a careless scorn and precaution in presence of sympathy and the "warm heart."—It is the powerful who KNOW how to honour, it is their art, their domain for invention. The profound reverence for age and for tradition—all law rests on this double reverence,—the belief and prejudice in favour of ancestors and unfavourable to newcomers, is typical in the morality of the powerful; and if, reversely, men of "modern ideas" believe almost instinctively in "progress" and the "future," and are more and more lacking in respect for old age, the ignoble origin of these "ideas" has complacently betrayed itself thereby. A morality of the ruling class, however, is more especially foreign and irritating to present-day taste in the sternness of its principle that one has duties only to one's equals; that one may act towards beings of a lower rank, towards all that is foreign, just as seems good to one, or "as the heart desires," and in any case "beyond good and evil": it is here that sympathy and similar sentiments can have a place. The ability and obligation to exercise prolonged gratitude and prolonged revenge—both only within the circle of equals,—artfulness in retaliation, RAFFINEMENT of the idea in friendship, a certain necessity to have enemies (as outlets for the emotions of envy, quarrelsomeness, arrogance—in fact, in order to be a good FRIEND): all these are typical characteristics of the noble morality, which, as has been pointed out, is not the morality of "modern ideas," and is therefore at present difficult to realize, and also to unearth and disclose.—It is otherwise with the second type of morality, SLAVE-MORALITY. Supposing that the abused, the oppressed, the suffering, the unemancipated, the weary, and those uncertain of themselves should moralize, what will be the common element in their moral estimates? Probably a pessimistic suspicion with regard to the entire situation of man will find expression, perhaps a condemnation of man, together with his situation. The slave has an unfavourable eye for the virtues of the powerful; he has a skepticism and distrust, a REFINEMENT of distrust of everything "good" that is there honoured—he would fain persuade himself that the very happiness there is not genuine. On the other hand, those qualities which serve to alleviate the existence of sufferers are brought into prominence and flooded with light; it is here that sympathy, the kind, helping hand, the warm heart, patience, diligence, humility, and friendliness attain to honour; for here these are the most useful qualities, and almost the only means of supporting the burden of existence. Slave-morality is essentially the morality of utility. Here is the seat of the origin of the famous antithesis "good" and "evil":—power and dangerousness are assumed to reside in the evil, a certain dreadfulness, subtlety, and strength, which do not admit of being despised. According to slave-morality, therefore, the "evil" man arouses fear; according to master-morality, it is precisely the "good" man who arouses fear and seeks to arouse it, while the bad man is regarded as the despicable being. The contrast attains its maximum when, in accordance with the logical consequences of slave-morality, a shade of depreciation—it may be slight and well-intentioned—at last attaches itself to the "good" man of this morality; because, according to the servile mode of thought, the good man must in any case be the SAFE man: he is good-natured, easily deceived, perhaps a little stupid, un bonhomme. Everywhere that slave-morality gains the ascendancy, language shows a tendency to approximate the significations of the words "good" and "stupid."—A last fundamental difference: the desire for FREEDOM, the instinct for happiness and the refinements of the feeling of liberty belong as necessarily to slave-morals and morality, as artifice and enthusiasm in reverence and devotion are the regular symptoms of an aristocratic mode of thinking and estimating.—Hence we can understand without further detail why love AS A PASSION—it is our European specialty—must absolutely be of noble origin; as is well known, its invention is due to the Provencal poet-cavaliers, those brilliant, ingenious men of the "gai saber," to whom Europe owes so much, and almost owes itself.

Vanity is one of the things which are perhaps most difficult for a noble man to understand: he will be tempted to deny it, where another kind of man thinks he sees it self-evidently. The problem for him is to represent to his mind beings who seek to arouse a good opinion of themselves which they themselves do not possess—and consequently also do not "deserve,"—and who yet BELIEVE in this good opinion afterwards. This seems to him on the one hand such bad taste and so self-disrespectful, and on the other hand so grotesquely unreasonable, that he would like to consider vanity an exception, and is doubtful about it in most cases when it is spoken of. He will say, for instance: "I may be mistaken about my value, and on the other hand may nevertheless demand that my value should be acknowledged by others precisely as I rate it:—that, however, is not vanity (but self-conceit, or, in most cases, that which is called 'humility,' and also 'modesty')." Or he will even say: "For many reasons I can delight in the good opinion of others, perhaps because I love and honour them, and rejoice in all their joys, perhaps also because their good opinion endorses and strengthens my belief in my own good opinion, perhaps because the good opinion of others, even in cases where I do not share it, is useful to me, or gives promise of usefulness:—all this, however, is not vanity." The man of noble character must first bring it home forcibly to his mind, especially with the aid of history, that, from time immemorial, in all social strata in any way dependent, the ordinary man was only that which he PASSED FOR:—not being at all accustomed to fix values, he did not assign even to himself any other value than that which his master assigned to him (it is the peculiar RIGHT OF MASTERS to create values). It may be looked upon as the result of an extraordinary atavism, that the ordinary man, even at present, is still always WAITING for an opinion about himself, and then instinctively submitting himself to it; yet by no means only to a "good" opinion, but also to a bad and unjust one (think, for instance, of the greater part of the self-appreciations and self-depreciations which believing women learn from their confessors, and which in general the believing Christian learns from his Church). In fact, conformably to the slow rise of the democratic social order (and its cause, the blending of the blood of masters and slaves), the originally noble and rare impulse of the masters to assign a value to themselves and to "think well" of themselves, will now be more and more encouraged and extended; but it has at all times an older, ampler, and more radically ingrained propensity opposed to it—and in the phenomenon of "vanity" this older propensity overmasters the younger. The vain person rejoices over EVERY good opinion which he hears about himself (quite apart from the point of view of its usefulness, and equally regardless of its truth or falsehood), just as he suffers from every bad opinion: for he subjects himself to both, he feels himself subjected to both, by that oldest instinct of subjection which breaks forth in him.—It is "the slave" in the vain man's blood, the remains of the slave's craftiness—and how much of the "slave" is still left in woman, for instance!—which seeks to SEDUCE to good opinions of itself; it is the slave, too, who immediately afterwards falls prostrate himself before these opinions, as though he had not called them forth.—And to repeat it again: vanity is an atavism.

A SPECIES originates, and a type becomes established and strong in the long struggle with essentially constant UNFAVOURABLE conditions. On the other hand, it is known by the experience of breeders that species which receive super-abundant nourishment, and in general a surplus of protection and care, immediately tend in the most marked way to develop variations, and are fertile in prodigies and monstrosities (also in monstrous vices). Now look at an aristocratic commonwealth, say an ancient Greek polis, or Venice, as a voluntary or involuntary contrivance for the purpose of REARING human beings; there are there men beside one another, thrown upon their own resources, who want to make their species prevail, chiefly because they MUST prevail, or else run the terrible danger of being exterminated. The favour, the super-abundance, the protection are there lacking under which variations are fostered; the species needs itself as species, as something which, precisely by virtue of its hardness, its uniformity, and simplicity of structure, can in general prevail and make itself permanent in constant struggle with its neighbours, or with rebellious or rebellion-threatening vassals. The most varied experience teaches it what are the qualities to which it principally owes the fact that it still exists, in spite of all Gods and men, and has hitherto been victorious: these qualities it calls virtues, and these virtues alone it develops to maturity. It does so with severity, indeed it desires severity; every aristocratic morality is intolerant in the education of youth, in the control of women, in the marriage customs, in the relations of old and young, in the penal laws (which have an eye only for the degenerating): it counts intolerance itself among the virtues, under the name of "justice." A type with few, but very marked features, a species of severe, warlike, wisely silent, reserved, and reticent men (and as such, with the most delicate sensibility for the charm and nuances of society) is thus established, unaffected by the vicissitudes of generations; the constant struggle with uniform UNFAVOURABLE conditions is, as already remarked, the cause of a type becoming stable and hard. Finally, however, a happy state of things results, the enormous tension is relaxed; there are perhaps no more enemies among the neighbouring peoples, and the means of life, even of the enjoyment of life, are present in superabundance. With one stroke the bond and constraint of the old discipline severs: it is no longer regarded as necessary, as a condition of existence—if it would continue, it can only do so as a form of LUXURY, as an archaizing TASTE. Variations, whether they be deviations (into the higher, finer, and rarer), or deteriorations and monstrosities, appear suddenly on the scene in the greatest exuberance and splendour; the individual dares to be individual and detach himself. At this turning-point of history there manifest themselves, side by side, and often mixed and entangled together, a magnificent, manifold, virgin-forest-like up-growth and up-striving, a kind of TROPICAL TEMPO in the rivalry of growth, and an extraordinary decay and self-destruction, owing to the savagely opposing and seemingly exploding egoisms, which strive with one another "for sun and light," and can no longer assign any limit, restraint, or forbearance for themselves by means of the hitherto existing morality. It was this morality itself which piled up the strength so enormously, which bent the bow in so threatening a manner:—it is now "out of date," it is getting "out of date." The dangerous and disquieting point has been reached when the greater, more manifold, more comprehensive life is LIVED BEYOND the old morality; the "individual" stands out, and is obliged to have recourse to his own law-giving, his own arts and artifices for self-preservation, self-elevation, and self-deliverance. Nothing but new "Whys," nothing but new "Hows," no common formulas any longer, misunderstanding and disregard in league with each other, decay, deterioration, and the loftiest desires frightfully entangled, the genius of the race overflowing from all the cornucopias of good and bad, a portentous simultaneousness of Spring and Autumn, full of new charms and mysteries peculiar to the fresh, still inexhausted, still unwearied corruption. Danger is again present, the mother of morality, great danger; this time shifted into the individual, into the neighbour and friend, into the street, into their own child, into their own heart, into all the most personal and secret recesses of their desires and volitions. What will the moral philosophers who appear at this time have to preach? They discover, these sharp onlookers and loafers, that the end is quickly approaching, that everything around them decays and produces decay, that nothing will endure until the day after tomorrow, except one species of man, the incurably MEDIOCRE. The mediocre alone have a prospect of continuing and propagating themselves—they will be the men of the future, the sole survivors; "be like them! become mediocre!" is now the only morality which has still a significance, which still obtains a hearing.—But it is difficult to preach this morality of mediocrity! it can never avow what it is and what it desires! it has to talk of moderation and dignity and duty and brotherly love—it will have difficulty IN CONCEALING ITS IRONY!

There is an INSTINCT FOR RANK, which more than anything else is already the sign of a HIGH rank; there is a DELIGHT in the NUANCES of reverence which leads one to infer noble origin and habits. The refinement, goodness, and loftiness of a soul are put to a perilous test when something passes by that is of the highest rank, but is not yet protected by the awe of authority from obtrusive touches and incivilities: something that goes its way like a living touchstone, undistinguished, undiscovered, and tentative, perhaps voluntarily veiled and disguised. He whose task and practice it is to investigate souls, will avail himself of many varieties of this very art to determine the ultimate value of a soul, the unalterable, innate order of rank to which it belongs: he will test it by its INSTINCT FOR REVERENCE. DIFFERENCE ENGENDRE HAINE: the vulgarity of many a nature spurts up suddenly like dirty water, when any holy vessel, any jewel from closed shrines, any book bearing the marks of great destiny, is brought before it; while on the other hand, there is an involuntary silence, a hesitation of the eye, a cessation of all gestures, by which it is indicated that a soul FEELS the nearness of what is worthiest of respect. The way in which, on the whole, the reverence for the BIBLE has hitherto been maintained in Europe, is perhaps the best example of discipline and refinement of manners which Europe owes to Christianity: books of such profoundness and supreme significance require for their protection an external tyranny of authority, in order to acquire the PERIOD of thousands of years which is necessary to exhaust and unriddle them. Much has been achieved when the sentiment has been at last instilled into the masses (the shallow-pates and the boobies of every kind) that they are not allowed to touch everything, that there are holy experiences before which they must take off their shoes and keep away the unclean hand—it is almost their highest advance towards humanity. On the contrary, in the so-called cultured classes, the believers in "modern ideas," nothing is perhaps so repulsive as their lack of shame, the easy insolence of eye and hand with which they touch, taste, and finger everything; and it is possible that even yet there is more RELATIVE nobility of taste, and more tact for reverence among the people, among the lower classes of the people, especially among peasants, than among the newspaper-reading DEMIMONDE of intellect, the cultured class.

It cannot be effaced from a man's soul what his ancestors have preferably and most constantly done: whether they were perhaps diligent economizers attached to a desk and a cash-box, modest and citizen-like in their desires, modest also in their virtues; or whether they were accustomed to commanding from morning till night, fond of rude pleasures and probably of still ruder duties and responsibilities; or whether, finally, at one time or another, they have sacrificed old privileges of birth and possession, in order to live wholly for their faith—for their "God,"—as men of an inexorable and sensitive conscience, which blushes at every compromise. It is quite impossible for a man NOT to have the qualities and predilections of his parents and ancestors in his constitution, whatever appearances may suggest to the contrary. This is the problem of race. Granted that one knows something of the parents, it is admissible to draw a conclusion about the child: any kind of offensive incontinence, any kind of sordid envy, or of clumsy self-vaunting—the three things which together have constituted the genuine plebeian type in all times—such must pass over to the child, as surely as bad blood; and with the help of the best education and culture one will only succeed in DECEIVING with regard to such heredity.—And what else does education and culture try to do nowadays! In our very democratic, or rather, very plebeian age, "education" and "culture" MUST be essentially the art of deceiving—deceiving with regard to origin, with regard to the inherited plebeianism in body and soul. An educator who nowadays preached truthfulness above everything else, and called out constantly to his pupils: "Be true! Be natural! Show yourselves as you are!"—even such a virtuous and sincere ass would learn in a short time to have recourse to the FURCA of Horace, NATURAM EXPELLERE: with what results? "Plebeianism" USQUE RECURRET[1].

At the risk of displeasing innocent ears, I submit that egoism belongs to the essence of a noble soul, I mean the unalterable belief that to a being such as "we," other beings must naturally be in subjection, and have to sacrifice themselves. The noble soul accepts the fact of his egoism without question, and also without consciousness of harshness, constraint, or arbitrariness therein, but rather as something that may have its basis in the primary law of things:—if he sought a designation for it he would say: "It is justice itself." He acknowledges under certain circumstances, which made him hesitate at first, that there are other equally privileged ones; as soon as he has settled this question of rank, he moves among those equals and equally privileged ones with the same assurance, as regards modesty and delicate respect, which he enjoys in intercourse with himself—in accordance with an innate heavenly mechanism which all the stars understand. It is an ADDITIONAL instance of his egoism, this artfulness and self-limitation in intercourse with his equals—every star is a similar egoist; he honours HIMSELF in them, and in the rights which he concedes to them, he has no doubt that the exchange of honours and rights, as the ESSENCE of all intercourse, belongs also to the natural condition of things. The noble soul gives as he takes, prompted by the passionate and sensitive instinct of requital, which is at the root of his nature. The notion of "favour" has, INTER PARES, neither significance nor good repute; there may be a sublime way of letting gifts as it were light upon one from above, and of drinking them thirstily like dew-drops; but for those arts and displays the noble soul has no aptitude. His egoism hinders him here: in general, he looks "aloft" unwillingly—he looks either FORWARD, horizontally and deliberately, or downwards—HE KNOWS THAT HE IS ON A HEIGHT.

"One can only truly esteem him who does not LOOK OUT FOR himself."—Goethe to Rath Schlosser.

The Chinese have a proverb which mothers even teach their children: "SIAO-SIN" ("MAKE THY HEART SMALL"). This is the essentially fundamental tendency in latter-day civilizations. I have no doubt that an ancient Greek, also, would first of all remark the self-dwarfing in us Europeans of today—in this respect alone we should immediately be "distasteful" to him.

What, after all, is ignobleness?—Words are vocal symbols for ideas; ideas, however, are more or less definite mental symbols for frequently returning and concurring sensations, for groups of sensations. It is not sufficient to use the same words in order to understand one another: we must also employ the same words for the same kind of internal experiences, we must in the end have experiences IN COMMON. On this account the people of one nation understand one another better than those belonging to different nations, even when they use the same language; or rather, when people have lived long together under similar conditions (of climate, soil, danger, requirement, toil) there ORIGINATES there from an entity that "understands itself"—namely, a nation. In all souls a like number of frequently recurring experiences have gained the upper hand over those occurring more rarely: about these matters people understand one another rapidly and always more rapidly—the history of language is the history of a process of abbreviation; on the basis of this quick comprehension people always unite closer and closer. The greater the danger, the greater is the need of agreeing quickly and readily about what is necessary; not to misunderstand one another in danger—that is what cannot at all be dispensed with in intercourse. Also in all loves and friendships one has the experience that nothing of the kind continues when the discovery has been made that in using the same words, one of the two parties has feelings, thoughts, intuitions, wishes, or fears different from those of the other. (The fear of the "eternal misunderstanding": that is the good genius which so often keeps persons of different sexes from too hasty attachments, to which sense and heart prompt them—and NOT some Schopenhauerian "genius of the species!") Whichever groups of sensations within a soul awaken most readily, begin to speak, and give the word of command—these decide as to the general order of rank of its values, and determine ultimately its list of desirable things. A man's estimates of value betray something of the STRUCTURE of his soul, and wherein it sees its conditions of life, its intrinsic needs. Supposing now that necessity has from all time drawn together only such men as could express similar requirements and similar experiences by similar symbols, it results on the whole that the easy COMMUNICABILITY of need, which implies ultimately the undergoing only of average and COMMON experiences, must have been the most potent of all the forces which have hitherto operated upon mankind. The more similar, the more ordinary people, have always had and are still having the advantage; the more select, more refined, more unique, and difficultly comprehensible, are liable to stand alone; they succumb to accidents in their isolation, and seldom propagate themselves. One must appeal to immense opposing forces, in order to thwart this natural, all-too-natural PROGRESSUS IN SIMILE, the evolution of man to the similar, the ordinary, the average, the gregarious—to the IGNOBLE!

The more a psychologist—a born, an unavoidable psychologist and soul-diviner—turns his attention to the more select cases and individuals, the greater is his danger of being suffocated by sympathy: he NEEDS sternness and cheerfulness more than any other man. For the corruption, the ruination of higher men, of the more unusually constituted souls, is in fact, the rule: it is dreadful to have such a rule always before one's eyes. The manifold torment of the psychologist who has discovered this ruination, who discovers once, and then discovers ALMOST repeatedly throughout all history, this universal inner "desperateness" of higher men, this eternal "too late!" in every sense—may perhaps one day be the cause of his turning with bitterness against his own lot, and of his making an attempt at self-destruction—of his "going to ruin" himself. One may perceive in almost every psychologist a tell-tale inclination for delightful intercourse with commonplace and well-ordered men; the fact is thereby disclosed that he always requires healing, that he needs a sort of flight and forgetfulness, away from what his insight and incisiveness—from what his "business"—has laid upon his conscience. The fear of his memory is peculiar to him. He is easily silenced by the judgment of others; he hears with unmoved countenance how people honour, admire, love, and glorify, where he has PERCEIVED—or he even conceals his silence by expressly assenting to some plausible opinion. Perhaps the paradox of his situation becomes so dreadful that, precisely where he has learnt GREAT SYMPATHY, together with great CONTEMPT, the multitude, the educated, and the visionaries, have on their part learnt great reverence—reverence for "great men" and marvelous animals, for the sake of whom one blesses and honours the fatherland, the earth, the dignity of mankind, and one's own self, to whom one points the young, and in view of whom one educates them. And who knows but in all great instances hitherto just the same happened: that the multitude worshipped a God, and that the "God" was only a poor sacrificial animal! SUCCESS has always been the greatest liar—and the "work" itself is a success; the great statesman, the conqueror, the discoverer, are disguised in their creations until they are unrecognizable; the "work" of the artist, of the philosopher, only invents him who has created it, is REPUTED to have created it; the "great men," as they are reverenced, are poor little fictions composed afterwards; in the world of historical values spurious coinage PREVAILS. Those great poets, for example, such as Byron, Musset, Poe, Leopardi, Kleist, Gogol (I do not venture to mention much greater names, but I have them in my mind), as they now appear, and were perhaps obliged to be: men of the moment, enthusiastic, sensuous, and childish, light-minded and impulsive in their trust and distrust; with souls in which usually some flaw has to be concealed; often taking revenge with their works for an internal defilement, often seeking forgetfulness in their soaring from a too true memory, often lost in the mud and almost in love with it, until they become like the Will-o'-the-Wisps around the swamps, and PRETEND TO BE stars—the people then call them idealists,—often struggling with protracted disgust, with an ever-reappearing phantom of disbelief, which makes them cold, and obliges them to languish for GLORIA and devour "faith as it is" out of the hands of intoxicated adulators:—what a TORMENT these great artists are and the so-called higher men in general, to him who has once found them out! It is thus conceivable that it is just from woman—who is clairvoyant in the world of suffering, and also unfortunately eager to help and save to an extent far beyond her powers—that they have learnt so readily those outbreaks of boundless devoted SYMPATHY, which the multitude, above all the reverent multitude, do not understand, and overwhelm with prying and self-gratifying interpretations. This sympathizing invariably deceives itself as to its power; woman would like to believe that love can do EVERYTHING—it is the SUPERSTITION peculiar to her. Alas, he who knows the heart finds out how poor, helpless, pretentious, and blundering even the best and deepest love is—he finds that it rather DESTROYS than saves!—It is possible that under the holy fable and travesty of the life of Jesus there is hidden one of the most painful cases of the martyrdom of KNOWLEDGE ABOUT LOVE: the martyrdom of the most innocent and most craving heart, that never had enough of any human love, that DEMANDED love, that demanded inexorably and frantically to be loved and nothing else, with terrible outbursts against those who refused him their love; the story of a poor soul insatiated and insatiable in love, that had to invent hell to send thither those who WOULD NOT love him—and that at last, enlightened about human love, had to invent a God who is entire love, entire CAPACITY for love—who takes pity on human love, because it is so paltry, so ignorant! He who has such sentiments, he who has such KNOWLEDGE about love—SEEKS for death!—But why should one deal with such painful matters? Provided, of course, that one is not obliged to do so.

The intellectual haughtiness and loathing of every man who has suffered deeply—it almost determines the order of rank HOW deeply men can suffer—the chilling certainty, with which he is thoroughly imbued and coloured, that by virtue of his suffering he KNOWS MORE than the shrewdest and wisest can ever know, that he has been familiar with, and "at home" in, many distant, dreadful worlds of which "YOU know nothing!"—this silent intellectual haughtiness of the sufferer, this pride of the elect of knowledge, of the "initiated," of the almost sacrificed, finds all forms of disguise necessary to protect itself from contact with officious and sympathizing hands, and in general from all that is not its equal in suffering. Profound suffering makes noble: it separates.—One of the most refined forms of disguise is Epicurism, along with a certain ostentatious boldness of taste, which takes suffering lightly, and puts itself on the defensive against all that is sorrowful and profound. They are "gay men" who make use of gaiety, because they are misunderstood on account of it—they WISH to be misunderstood. There are "scientific minds" who make use of science, because it gives a gay appearance, and because scientificness leads to the conclusion that a person is superficial—they WISH to mislead to a false conclusion. There are free insolent minds which would fain conceal and deny that they are broken, proud, incurable hearts (the cynicism of Hamlet—the case of Galiani); and occasionally folly itself is the mask of an unfortunate OVER-ASSURED knowledge.—From which it follows that it is the part of a more refined humanity to have reverence "for the mask," and not to make use of psychology and curiosity in the wrong place.

That which separates two men most profoundly is a different sense and grade of purity. What does it matter about all their honesty and reciprocal usefulness, what does it matter about all their mutual good-will: the fact still remains—they "cannot smell each other!" The highest instinct for purity places him who is affected with it in the most extraordinary and dangerous isolation, as a saint: for it is just holiness—the highest spiritualization of the instinct in question. Any kind of cognizance of an indescribable excess in the joy of the bath, any kind of ardour or thirst which perpetually impels the soul out of night into the morning, and out of gloom, out of "affliction" into clearness, brightness, depth, and refinement:—just as much as such a tendency DISTINGUISHES—it is a noble tendency—it also SEPARATES.—The pity of the saint is pity for the FILTH of the human, all-too-human. And there are grades and heights where pity itself is regarded by him as impurity, as filth.

Signs of nobility: never to think of lowering our duties to the rank of duties for everybody; to be unwilling to renounce or to share our responsibilities; to count our prerogatives, and the exercise of them, among our DUTIES.

A man who strives after great things, looks upon every one whom he encounters on his way either as a means of advance, or a delay and hindrance—or as a temporary resting-place. His peculiar lofty BOUNTY to his fellow-men is only possible when he attains his elevation and dominates. Impatience, and the consciousness of being always condemned to comedy up to that time—for even strife is a comedy, and conceals the end, as every means does—spoil all intercourse for him; this kind of man is acquainted with solitude, and what is most poisonous in it.

THE PROBLEM OF THOSE WHO WAIT.—Happy chances are necessary, and many incalculable elements, in order that a higher man in whom the solution of a problem is dormant, may yet take action, or "break forth," as one might say—at the right moment. On an average it DOES NOT happen; and in all corners of the earth there are waiting ones sitting who hardly know to what extent they are waiting, and still less that they wait in vain. Occasionally, too, the waking call comes too late—the chance which gives "permission" to take action—when their best youth, and strength for action have been used up in sitting still; and how many a one, just as he "sprang up," has found with horror that his limbs are benumbed and his spirits are now too heavy! "It is too late," he has said to himself—and has become self-distrustful and henceforth for ever useless.—In the domain of genius, may not the "Raphael without hands" (taking the expression in its widest sense) perhaps not be the exception, but the rule?—Perhaps genius is by no means so rare: but rather the five hundred HANDS which it requires in order to tyrannize over the "the right time"—in order to take chance by the forelock!

He who does not WISH to see the height of a man, looks all the more sharply at what is low in him, and in the foreground—and thereby betrays himself.

In all kinds of injury and loss the lower and coarser soul is better off than the nobler soul: the dangers of the latter must be greater, the probability that it will come to grief and perish is in fact immense, considering the multiplicity of the conditions of its existence.—In a lizard a finger grows again which has been lost; not so in man.—

It is too bad! Always the old story! When a man has finished building his house, he finds that he has learnt unawares something which he OUGHT absolutely to have known before he—began to build. The eternal, fatal "Too late!" The melancholia of everything COMPLETED!

Wanderer, who art thou? I see the follow thy path without scorn, without love, with unfathomable eyes, wet and sad as a plummet which has returned to the light insatiated out of every depth—what did it seek down there?—with a bosom that never sighs, with lips that conceal their loathing, with a hand which only slowly grasps: who art thou? what hast thou done? Rest thee here: this place has hospitality for every one—refresh thyself! And whoever thou art, what is it that now pleases thee? What will serve to refresh thee? Only name it, whatever I have I offer thee! "To refresh me? To refresh me? Oh, thou prying one, what sayest thou! But give me, I pray thee—" What? what? Speak out! "Another mask! A second mask!"

Men of profound sadness betray themselves when they are happy: they have a mode of seizing upon happiness as though they would choke and strangle it, out of jealousy—ah, they know only too well that it will flee from them!

"Bad! Bad! What? Does he not—go back?" Yes! But you misunderstand him when you complain about it. He goes back like every one who is about to make a great spring.

"Will people believe it of me? But I insist that they believe it of me: I have always thought very unsatisfactorily of myself and about myself, only in very rare cases, only compulsorily, always without delight in 'the subject,' ready to digress from 'myself,' and always without faith in the result, owing to an unconquerable distrust of the POSSIBILITY of self-knowledge, which has led me so far as to feel a CONTRADICTIO IN ADJECTO even in the idea of 'direct knowledge' which theorists allow themselves:—this matter of fact is almost the most certain thing I know about myself. There must be a sort of repugnance in me to BELIEVE anything definite about myself.—Is there perhaps some enigma therein? Probably; but fortunately nothing for my own teeth.—Perhaps it betrays the species to which I belong?—but not to myself, as is sufficiently agreeable to me."

"But what has happened to you?"—"I do not know," he said, hesitatingly; "perhaps the Harpies have flown over my table."—It sometimes happens nowadays that a gentle, sober, retiring man becomes suddenly mad, breaks the plates, upsets the table, shrieks, raves, and shocks everybody—and finally withdraws, ashamed, and raging at himself—whither? for what purpose? To famish apart? To suffocate with his memories?—To him who has the desires of a lofty and dainty soul, and only seldom finds his table laid and his food prepared, the danger will always be great—nowadays, however, it is extraordinarily so. Thrown into the midst of a noisy and plebeian age, with which he does not like to eat out of the same dish, he may readily perish of hunger and thirst—or, should he nevertheless finally "fall to," of sudden nausea.—We have probably all sat at tables to which we did not belong; and precisely the most spiritual of us, who are most difficult to nourish, know the dangerous DYSPEPSIA which originates from a sudden insight and disillusionment about our food and our messmates—the AFTER-DINNER NAUSEA.

If one wishes to praise at all, it is a delicate and at the same time a noble self-control, to praise only where one DOES NOT agree—otherwise in fact one would praise oneself, which is contrary to good taste:—a self-control, to be sure, which offers excellent opportunity and provocation to constant MISUNDERSTANDING. To be able to allow oneself this veritable luxury of taste and morality, one must not live among intellectual imbeciles, but rather among men whose misunderstandings and mistakes amuse by their refinement—or one will have to pay dearly for it!—"He praises me, THEREFORE he acknowledges me to be right"—this asinine method of inference spoils half of the life of us recluses, for it brings the asses into our neighbourhood and friendship.

To live in a vast and proud tranquility; always beyond . . . To have, or not to have, one's emotions, one's For and Against, according to choice; to lower oneself to them for hours; to SEAT oneself on them as upon horses, and often as upon asses:—for one must know how to make use of their stupidity as well as of their fire. To conserve one's three hundred foregrounds; also one's black spectacles: for there are circumstances when nobody must look into our eyes, still less into our "motives." And to choose for company that roguish and cheerful vice, politeness. And to remain master of one's four virtues, courage, insight, sympathy, and solitude. For solitude is a virtue with us, as a sublime bent and bias to purity, which divines that in the contact of man and man—"in society"—it must be unavoidably impure. All society makes one somehow, somewhere, or sometime—"commonplace."

The greatest events and thoughts—the greatest thoughts, however, are the greatest events—are longest in being comprehended: the generations which are contemporary with them do not EXPERIENCE such events—they live past them. Something happens there as in the realm of stars. The light of the furthest stars is longest in reaching man; and before it has arrived man DENIES—that there are stars there. "How many centuries does a mind require to be understood?"—that is also a standard, one also makes a gradation of rank and an etiquette therewith, such as is necessary for mind and for star.

"Here is the prospect free, the mind exalted[2]."—But there is a reverse kind of man, who is also upon a height, and has also a free prospect—but looks DOWNWARDS.

What is noble? What does the word "noble" still mean for us nowadays? How does the noble man betray himself, how is he recognized under this heavy overcast sky of the commencing plebeianism, by which everything is rendered opaque and leaden?—It is not his actions which establish his claim—actions are always ambiguous, always inscrutable; neither is it his "works." One finds nowadays among artists and scholars plenty of those who betray by their works that a profound longing for nobleness impels them; but this very NEED of nobleness is radically different from the needs of the noble soul itself, and is in fact the eloquent and dangerous sign of the lack thereof. It is not the works, but the BELIEF which is here decisive and determines the order of rank—to employ once more an old religious formula with a new and deeper meaning—it is some fundamental certainty which a noble soul has about itself, something which is not to be sought, is not to be found, and perhaps, also, is not to be lost.—THE NOBLE SOUL HAS REVERENCE FOR ITSELF.—

There are men who are unavoidably intellectual, let them turn and twist themselves as they will, and hold their hands before their treacherous eyes—as though the hand were not a betrayer; it always comes out at last that they have something which they hide—namely, intellect. One of the subtlest means of deceiving, at least as long as possible, and of successfully representing oneself to be stupider than one really is—which in everyday life is often as desirable as an umbrella,—is called ENTHUSIASM, including what belongs to it, for instance, virtue. For as Galiani said, who was obliged to know it: VERTU EST ENTHOUSIASME.

In the writings of a recluse one always hears something of the echo of the wilderness, something of the murmuring tones and timid vigilance of solitude; in his strongest words, even in his cry itself, there sounds a new and more dangerous kind of silence, of concealment. He who has sat day and night, from year's end to year's end, alone with his soul in familiar discord and discourse, he who has become a cave-bear, or a treasure-seeker, or a treasure-guardian and dragon in his cave—it may be a labyrinth, but can also be a gold-mine—his ideas themselves eventually acquire a twilight-colour of their own, and an odour, as much of the depth as of the mould, something uncommunicative and repulsive, which blows chilly upon every passer-by. The recluse does not believe that a philosopher—supposing that a philosopher has always in the first place been a recluse—ever expressed his actual and ultimate opinions in books: are not books written precisely to hide what is in us?—indeed, he will doubt whether a philosopher can have "ultimate and actual" opinions at all; whether behind every cave in him there is not, and must necessarily be, a still deeper cave: an ampler, stranger, richer world beyond the surface, an abyss behind every bottom, beneath every "foundation." Every philosophy is a foreground philosophy—this is a recluse's verdict: "There is something arbitrary in the fact that the PHILOSOPHER came to a stand here, took a retrospect, and looked around; that he HERE laid his spade aside and did not dig any deeper—there is also something suspicious in it." Every philosophy also CONCEALS a philosophy; every opinion is also a LURKING-PLACE, every word is also a MASK.

Every deep thinker is more afraid of being understood than of being misunderstood. The latter perhaps wounds his vanity; but the former wounds his heart, his sympathy, which always says: "Ah, why would you also have as hard a time of it as I have?"

Man, a COMPLEX, mendacious, artful, and inscrutable animal, uncanny to the other animals by his artifice and sagacity, rather than by his strength, has invented the good conscience in order finally to enjoy his soul as something SIMPLE; and the whole of morality is a long, audacious falsification, by virtue of which generally enjoyment at the sight of the soul becomes possible. From this point of view there is perhaps much more in the conception of "art" than is generally believed.

A philosopher: that is a man who constantly experiences, sees, hears, suspects, hopes, and dreams extraordinary things; who is struck by his own thoughts as if they came from the outside, from above and below, as a species of events and lightning-flashes PECULIAR TO HIM; who is perhaps himself a storm pregnant with new lightnings; a portentous man, around whom there is always rumbling and mumbling and gaping and something uncanny going on. A philosopher: alas, a being who often runs away from himself, is often afraid of himself—but whose curiosity always makes him "come to himself" again.

A man who says: "I like that, I take it for my own, and mean to guard and protect it from every one"; a man who can conduct a case, carry out a resolution, remain true to an opinion, keep hold of a woman, punish and overthrow insolence; a man who has his indignation and his sword, and to whom the weak, the suffering, the oppressed, and even the animals willingly submit and naturally belong; in short, a man who is a MASTER by nature—when such a man has sympathy, well! THAT sympathy has value! But of what account is the sympathy of those who suffer! Or of those even who preach sympathy! There is nowadays, throughout almost the whole of Europe, a sickly irritability and sensitiveness towards pain, and also a repulsive irrestrainableness in complaining, an effeminizing, which, with the aid of religion and philosophical nonsense, seeks to deck itself out as something superior—there is a regular cult of suffering. The UNMANLINESS of that which is called "sympathy" by such groups of visionaries, is always, I believe, the first thing that strikes the eye.—One must resolutely and radically taboo this latest form of bad taste; and finally I wish people to put the good amulet, "GAI SABER" ("gay science," in ordinary language), on heart and neck, as a protection against it.

THE OLYMPIAN VICE.—Despite the philosopher who, as a genuine Englishman, tried to bring laughter into bad repute in all thinking minds—"Laughing is a bad infirmity of human nature, which every thinking mind will strive to overcome" (Hobbes),—I would even allow myself to rank philosophers according to the quality of their laughing—up to those who are capable of GOLDEN laughter. And supposing that Gods also philosophize, which I am strongly inclined to believe, owing to many reasons—I have no doubt that they also know how to laugh thereby in an overman-like and new fashion—and at the expense of all serious things! Gods are fond of ridicule: it seems that they cannot refrain from laughter even in holy matters.

The genius of the heart, as that great mysterious one possesses it, the tempter-god and born rat-catcher of consciences, whose voice can descend into the nether-world of every soul, who neither speaks a word nor casts a glance in which there may not be some motive or touch of allurement, to whose perfection it pertains that he knows how to appear,—not as he is, but in a guise which acts as an ADDITIONAL constraint on his followers to press ever closer to him, to follow him more cordially and thoroughly;—the genius of the heart, which imposes silence and attention on everything loud and self-conceited, which smoothes rough souls and makes them taste a new longing—to lie placid as a mirror, that the deep heavens may be reflected in them;—the genius of the heart, which teaches the clumsy and too hasty hand to hesitate, and to grasp more delicately; which scents the hidden and forgotten treasure, the drop of goodness and sweet spirituality under thick dark ice, and is a divining-rod for every grain of gold, long buried and imprisoned in mud and sand; the genius of the heart, from contact with which every one goes away richer; not favoured or surprised, not as though gratified and oppressed by the good things of others; but richer in himself, newer than before, broken up, blown upon, and sounded by a thawing wind; more uncertain, perhaps, more delicate, more fragile, more bruised, but full of hopes which as yet lack names, full of a new will and current, full of a new ill-will and counter-current . . . but what am I doing, my friends? Of whom am I talking to you? Have I forgotten myself so far that I have not even told you his name? Unless it be that you have already divined of your own accord who this questionable God and spirit is, that wishes to be PRAISED in such a manner? For, as it happens to every one who from childhood onward has always been on his legs, and in foreign lands, I have also encountered on my path many strange and dangerous spirits; above all, however, and again and again, the one of whom I have just spoken: in fact, no less a personage than the God DIONYSUS, the great equivocator and tempter, to whom, as you know, I once offered in all secrecy and reverence my first-fruits—the last, as it seems to me, who has offered a SACRIFICE to him, for I have found no one who could understand what I was then doing. In the meantime, however, I have learned much, far too much, about the philosophy of this God, and, as I said, from mouth to mouth—I, the last disciple and initiate of the God Dionysus: and perhaps I might at last begin to give you, my friends, as far as I am allowed, a little taste of this philosophy? In a hushed voice, as is but seemly: for it has to do with much that is secret, new, strange, wonderful, and uncanny. The very fact that Dionysus is a philosopher, and that therefore Gods also philosophize, seems to me a novelty which is not unensnaring, and might perhaps arouse suspicion precisely among philosophers;—among you, my friends, there is less to be said against it, except that it comes too late and not at the right time; for, as it has been disclosed to me, you are loth nowadays to believe in God and gods. It may happen, too, that in the frankness of my story I must go further than is agreeable to the strict usages of your ears? Certainly the God in question went further, very much further, in such dialogues, and was always many paces ahead of me...Indeed, if it were allowed, I should have to give him, according to human usage, fine ceremonious tides of lustre and merit, I should have to extol his courage as investigator and discoverer, his fearless honesty, truthfulness, and love of wisdom. But such a God does not know what to do with all that respectable trumpery and pomp. "Keep that," he would say, "for thyself and those like thee, and whoever else require it! I—have no reason to cover my nakedness!" One suspects that this kind of divinity and philosopher perhaps lacks shame?—He once said: "Under certain circumstances I love mankind"—and referred thereby to Ariadne, who was present; "in my opinion man is an agreeable, brave, inventive animal, that has not his equal upon earth, he makes his way even through all labyrinths. I like man, and often think how I can still further advance him, and make him stronger, more evil, and more profound."—"Stronger, more evil, and more profound?" I asked in horror. "Yes," he said again, "stronger, more evil, and more profound; also more beautiful"—and thereby the tempter-god smiled with his halcyon smile, as though he had just paid some charming compliment. One here sees at once that it is not only shame that this divinity lacks;—and in general there are good grounds for supposing that in some things the Gods could all of them come to us men for instruction. We men are—more human.—

Alas! what are you, after all, my written and painted thoughts! Not long ago you were so variegated, young and malicious, so full of thorns and secret spices, that you made me sneeze and laugh—and now? You have already doffed your novelty, and some of you, I fear, are ready to become truths, so immortal do they look, so pathetically honest, so tedious! And was it ever otherwise? What then do we write and paint, we mandarins with Chinese brush, we immortalisers of things which LEND themselves to writing, what are we alone capable of painting? Alas, only that which is just about to fade and begins to lose its odour! Alas, only exhausted and departing storms and belated yellow sentiments! Alas, only birds strayed and fatigued by flight, which now let themselves be captured with the hand—with OUR hand! We immortalize what cannot live and fly much longer, things only which are exhausted and mellow! And it is only for your AFTERNOON, you, my written and painted thoughts, for which alone I have colours, many colours, perhaps, many variegated softenings, and fifty yellows and browns and greens and reds;—but nobody will divine thereby how ye looked in your morning, you sudden sparks and marvels of my solitude, you, my old, beloved—EVIL thoughts!

ENDNOTES

1 Horace's "Epistles," I. x. 24.
2 Goethe's "Faust," Part II, Act V. The words of Dr. Marianus.

DISCUSSION QUESTIONS

1. Explain the distinction between master morality and slave morality and its implications.

2. Nietzsche mentions happiness in a few of these paragraphs. What is Nietzsche's view? Explain.

3. How do the ideas of *amor fati* and eternal recurrence from the Part II Nietzsche selection fit in with the ideas in the selection here? Explain.

4. What are the main differences between Nietzsche's approach and the ones seen in the selections from Kant and Mill? Explain.

The Ideal Types of Care and Justice

By Grace Clement

In 1982, Carol Gilligan (b. 1936) published her groundbreaking work in psychology, In a Different Voice. *The book is, in part, a criticism of the view of moral development put forth by Lawrence Kohlberg (1927–1987), who was a colleague of Gilligan's at Harvard. Kohlberg's model was influenced by the work of Swiss developmental psychologist Jean Piaget (1896–1980), who studied how children acquired concepts like space, time, number, geometry, and causality. Kohlberg determined in his 1958 doctoral dissertation that there are six stages of moral development. Gilligan's book noted that in numerous tests which asked young people to give their responses to moral dilemmas, girls scored lower on Kohlberg's scale than boys did. Gilligan argues Kohlberg based his model primarily on studying boys. Girls, she says, seem to be speaking in a different voice (hence the title of the book). She argues that it is not a lower developmental stage, but rather a different approach to the problem. In the years after this book, the two voices have come to be called justice and care. Philosophers and psychologists have been studying the topics ever since.*

One such philosopher is Grace Clement, who is Associate Professor of Philosophy at Salisbury University in Maryland. Her 1996 book, Care, Autonomy, and Justice: Feminism and the Ethic of Care, *analyzes the justice/care distinction in a new light. Our selection is Chapter 1 of her book, "The Ideal Types of Care and Justice." Her goal in this chapter is to explore the ideal forms of each of the types of ethic. She notes that the focus on picking sides between the two views has prevented us from thinking more clearly about whether there are better or worse versions of these perspectives.*

The recent and ongoing care/justice debate has focused on questions about the relationship between predominant approaches to ethics, especially Kantian ethics, labeled the ethic of justice, and the newly articulated ethic of care. The answers to these questions have depended on what I will call the ideal types of the ethic of care and the ethic of justice. These ideal types are rarely defended in the extreme forms I present. My purpose is not to claim that any individual has defended these accounts of care or justice but to clarify the ideal types that underlie and motivate much of the recent discussion of care and justice. In the rest of the book I examine and challenge both these assumptions and the resulting conclusions. Although I maintain that justice and care are different ethics, I also show that they are not always different in the ways indicated by their ideal types.

The most important feature of the ideal types of care and justice is that the two ethics are defined as alternatives to one another. They are understood as conflicting ethics, each with its own ontology, method, and priorities, committed to mutually exclusive values and best suited to different kinds of situations. The two ethics are generally distinguished in three ways: (1) the ethic of justice takes an abstract approach, while the ethic of care takes a contextual approach, (2) the ethic of justice begins with an assumption of human separateness, while the ethic of care begins with an assumption of human connectedness, and (3) the ethic of justice has some form of equality as a priority, while the ethic of care has the maintenance of relationships as a priority. These features in turn are generally taken to result in conflicting evaluations of autonomy and a division of labor between the two ethics along public/private lines.

I will illustrate these standard differences between the ethic of justice and the ethic of care by referring to the Heinz dilemma:

> *In Europe, a woman was near death from cancer. One drug might save her, a rare form of radium that a druggist in the same town had discovered. The druggist was charging $2000, ten times what the drug cost him to make. The sick woman's husband, Heinz, went to everyone he knew to borrow the money, but he could only get together about half of what it cost. He told the druggist that his wife was dying, and asked him to sell it cheaper or let him pay later. But the druggist said, "No." The husband got desperate and broke into the man's store to steal the drug for his wife. Should the husband have done that? Why? (Kohlberg 1969, 379)*

Both Lawrence Kohlberg and Carol Gilligan used this hypothetical situation to elicit individuals' styles and levels of moral reasoning. Gilligan discerned in subjects' responses to this dilemma features of the ethic of care and the ethic of justice that have become the bases of the ideal types of the two ethics.

The first standard distinction drawn between the two moral orientations is their relative abstractness or concreteness. The primary focus of an ethic of justice is a set of abstract principles. In order to act justly in a particular situation we must abstract from the particular features of that situation to see how it comes under a general rule. For instance, we must abstract from individuals' distinguishing features. As Seyla Benhabib puts it, this requires taking the "standpoint of the generalized other," in which we "abstract from the individuality and concrete identity of the other," because "moral dignity is based on what we have in common, not in what differentiates us" (Benhabib 1987, 163–4). In contrast, the ethic of care has as its primary focus the unique and particular features of a situation. For example, rather than abstracting from a person's individuating features, using the ethic of care, we make moral decisions *on the basis of* these features. In Benhabib's language, we take the "standpoint of the concrete other"; "we view every individual as an individual with a concrete history, identity, and affective emotional constitution" (Benhabib 1987, 163–4).

This difference between these approaches can be seen in their responses to the Heinz dilemma. First, however, it is important to note that as it is written the dilemma already abstracts from most of the particular features of its characters, and in this way it is biased toward the ethic of justice. For instance, the dilemma does not reveal anything about the relationship between Heinz and his wife, or about the druggist's motivations in charging Heinz so much for the drug, or about Heinz's wife's wishes. From the justice perspective, it can be argued that these sorts of details are unnecessary: We can tell from the limited information presented that this dilemma represents a conflict between the right to life and the right to property. As one respondent in Gilligan's study put it, the situation can be understood as "a math problem with humans" (Gilligan 1982, 26). Those who approach this dilemma from the justice perspective reach differing conclusions about whether Heinz is justified in stealing the drug, but they are likely to accept the dilemma as presented and to resolve it by fitting the situation under a general rule.

In contrast, those who approach the Heinz dilemma using an ethic of care are generally frustrated by its lack of detail. They are likely to resist the dilemma's attempt to close off all options for getting the drug short of stealing it. Surely, they insist, Heinz could reason with the druggist about the situation. Or he could find a way to borrow more money from friends and family. Or he could hold a bake sale to raise money. Those approaching the dilemma from a care perspective are also likely to worry about whether Heinz will be imprisoned for stealing the drug, thereby abandoning his wife when she needs him most, or whether the drug will really work, or whether Heinz's wife even wants to go on living. From a justice perspective, such questions would reveal an inability to identify the *real* moral issue in the Heinz dilemma but from a care perspective such questions are essential to understanding the situation, and thus to resolving it.

Allied to this abstract/concrete distinction is a distinction between reason and emotion. From the justice perspective, feelings are seen as threatening the universality demanded of moral judgment, and thus we should seek to abstract from our particular feelings and focus on universal principles to be properly moral. As its extreme, in Kant's ethics, an action motivated by feelings, however right it is, has no moral worth. In contrast, from a care perspective, feelings are regarded as morally central. As Emmett Barcalow writes, caring people "rely on their feelings, emotions, natural impulses rather than on rules and principles in deciding what is the right thing to do" (Barcalow 1994, 203). Thus an action motivated by principle, however right it is, has less moral worth than an action arising out of the appropriate feelings of care.

The second standard distinction between the ethic of justice and the ethic of care is based on their different conceptions of the self. The ethic of justice begins with an assumption of human separateness, so that in order to be obligated to others, we must in some sense consent to those obligations.[1] Thus the ethic of justice emphasizes notions of choice and will in understanding our moral obligations. In contrast, the ethic of care begins with an assumption of human connectedness, the result of which is that to a large extent we recognize rather than choose our obligations to others. In other words, the ethic of justice takes freedom as its starting point, while the ethic of care takes obligation as its starting point. This means that the general challenge of the ethic of justice is to show how one's obligations to others arise without violating one's individual autonomy, while the general challenge of the ethic of care is to show how one can achieve individual freedom without violating one's moral obligations to others.

An example might be helpful to show the plausibility of the idea that we have obligations to which we have not consented. Nancy Hirschmann illustrates and defends the view that our obligations are not necessarily grounded in consent by referring to the case of a couple who decide to have child. This voluntary decision would seem to ground the couple's obligations toward the child they create. But suppose the child is born with severe mental or physical disabilities. Assuming that the parents have some obligations toward their disabled child, Hirschmann argues that these obligations should not be understood in terms of consent, as the parents never consented to the situation in which they have found themselves. Rather, the parents *recognize* an obligation that they have not explicitly chosen (Hirschmann 1992, 235).

The different starting points of the two ethics are reflected in two different ways of constructing the problem in the Heinz dilemma. Those using the ethic of justice assume the important question is whether Heinz should steal the drug *as opposed to not stealing it.* Heinz and his wife are, first and foremost, separate individuals, and the question is whether Heinz has this particular obligation to his wife or not. In contrast, those using an ethic of care assume the important question is whether Heinz should steal the drug, *as opposed to getting the drug in some other way*. From this perspective, Heinz and his wife are understood as importantly connected to one another and thus responsible for one another. Thus it is assumed that Heinz has an obligation to help his wife; the question is not *whether* Heinz should help his wife but *how* he should do so. The proposed action of stealing the drug seems irresponsible from the care perspective because it involves severing more connections, when the problem arose in the first place because the druggist severed his connections to the Heinzes by refusing to help them. That is, according to the care perspective, severing connections tends to cause rather than solve moral problems.

This brings me to the third standard distinction between the ethic of care and the ethic of justice, the distinction between their priorities. The ethic of care has two interrelated priorities: maintaining one's relationships and meeting the needs of those to whom one is connected. In contrast, the ethic of justice takes some form of equality as a priority. To be sure, equality is interpreted in different ways in different theories of justice; for example, a libertarian would argue for the equal right to use one's resources as one chooses; a socialist would argue for the equal right to have one's basic needs met; an Aristotelian would argue for returns in proportion to contributions. Libertarians focus on a set of negative rights, socialists on a set of positive rights, and Aristotelians not on rights but duties. Still, all derive these truths from some conception of equality.

These different priorities of care and justice are reflected in different responses to the Heinz dilemma. Those who approach the dilemma using an ethic of justice seek to promote equality as they understand it: some argue that Heinz's actions are wrong because they deprive the druggist of his equal right to use his property as he chooses, while others argue that Heinz's actions are justified because they are necessary to fulfill Heinz's wife's equal right to medical treatment. Conversely, those who interpret the dilemma using the ethic of care hold that Heinz should meet his wife's need for medical treatment but are wary of the solution of stealing the drug because doing so would sever Heinz's relationship to the druggist, and possibly his relationship to his wife as well, if he is caught and imprisoned for his action. Instead, those with a care perspective suggest ways that Heinz might meet his obligation to his wife by drawing upon rather than severing his relationships to others. As the dilemma was constructed, however, Heinz's relations to others would not allow him to provide his wife with the drug she needs, and thus the dilemma rules out the possibility of meeting the priorities of an ethic of care.

So far I have discussed three ways in which the ethic of justice and the ethic of care are usually distinguished. These three distinctions are generally thought to justify two further differences between the ethics that are the source of much of the controversy surrounding the ethics. First, while the ethic of justice is understood to take the concept of autonomy as central, the ethic of care is understood to be opposed to the concept of autonomy on the grounds that it is excessively individualistic. Second, it is typically held that the ethic of justice applies to the public sphere of politics and civil society, while the ethic of care applies to the private sphere of family and friends. I will show how the above three features of the two ethics are thought to result in these characterizations.

First, I will focus on the role of autonomy in the ideal types of care and justice. I will offer an extensive account and defense of an unconventional concept of autonomy in Chapter 2, but here I will refer to a standard notion of autonomy that is typically at issue in the care/justice debate. A general and uncontroversial definition of autonomy is self-determination, or doing what one as an individual has decided to do. Thus an autonomous individual is self-defining, choosing projects and life plans without the interference of outside influences or other people. Autonomous actions are ones that can be said to be truly the agent's own.

Based on their differing assumptions about the role of social relations in constituting an individual's identity, the ethic of justice and the ethic of care reach differing conclusions about autonomy. According to Carol Gilligan, the different images of the self embedded in the two ethics result in different ways of organizing "the basic elements of moral judgment: self, others, and the relationship between them" (Gilligan 1987, 22). Gilligan characterizes these different ways of organizing experience as alternative gestalts, with shifting figures and grounds. From the justice perspective, individual selves are the figures, and moral judgments evaluate the ground—that is, the relationships between individuals—based on the moral ideal of equality. However, from the care perspective, the relationship becomes the figure, while self and other become the ground that is defined by the figure, and moral judgments call for individual response based on the moral ideal of attachment. Whereas the justice perspective takes inequality as its primary cause for moral concern, the care perspective takes detachment as its primary cause for moral concern. From the care perspective, one is able to avoid detachment, or sustain relationships, by recognizing and responding to individuals' needs. In general, then, whereas the justice orientation takes individual identities as fundamental and develops moral injunctions to protect those identities, the care orientation takes relationships as fundamental and develops moral injunctions to protect those relationships.

The ethic of justice's focus on individual identities translates into an emphasis on autonomy. As long as individuals do not interfere with the autonomy of others, they ought to be allowed to define themselves freely. However, the ethic of care's focus on relationships between individuals leads its advocates to be skeptical of the desirability and even the possibility of autonomy. For instance, Gilligan writes that "since the reality of interconnection as experienced by women is given rather than freely contracted, they arrive at an understanding of life that reflects the *limits of autonomy* and control" (Gilligan 1982, 172). She also writes that the ethic of care has "a view of action as responsive and, therefore, as arising in relationship *rather than the view of action as emanating from within the self and, therefore, self-governed*" (Gilligan 1987, 24). That is, since one's identity is to a large degree socially constituted, it would be unrealistic to believe that one could freely define one's own identity.

Although Gilligan believes that the ethic of care does not allow for autonomy, she does not take this to be an indictment of the care orientation; on the contrary, she takes it to be an indictment of the concept of autonomy. For instance, she writes: "Illuminating life as a web rather than a succession of relationships, women portray autonomy rather than attachment as the illusory and dangerous quest" (Gilligan 1982, 48). From a care perspective, autonomy is dangerous because it is maximized through isolation from others, as others represent potential threats to our ability to define ourselves freely. But the more isolated we are, the less we are able to do what the ethic of care values, to create and maintain relationships with particular others. Thus, autonomy is a central value for an ethic of justice while it is generally regarded as illusory or as a negative value by advocates of the ethic of care.

The public/private boundaries of justice and care are more often taken for granted than explicitly defended. But all three standard distinctions between care and justice are understood as implying a division of labor between the two ethics along public/private lines. Those defending the conventional boundaries of justice and care argue that because of the features of the ethic of care, it would be impossible, immoral, or unhelpful to use the ethic in the public sphere.

First, the contextuality of care seems to limit it to situations about which we can know extensive details. We do not know the details of the lives of individuals on the other side of the world, so it would seem impossible for us to care for them. Nel Noddings argues that this is the case. She holds that the contextuality of care means that caring requires real encounters with and responses from individuals. Thus we cannot care for starving children in Africa (if we don't know them), and we cannot care for all humankind. "Caring itself is reduced to mere talk about caring when we attempt to do so" (Noddings 1984, 86). According to Noddings, real caring requires that we not just "care about" but "care for."

> *Caring is not simply a matter of feeling favorably disposed toward humankind in general, of being concerned about people with whom we have no concrete connections. There is a fundamental difference between the kind of care a mother has for her child and the kind of 'care' a well-fed American adult has for a starving Somali child s/he has never met. Real care requires actual encounters with specific individuals. (Tong 1993, 110)*

According to Noddings, then, the essence of caring—its attention to the uniqueness of the individual cared for—is present only in personal relationships, so "caring" for distant peoples is care in name only.

If, as Noddings argues, we cannot care for people we do not know, it follows that *either* we have no moral obligations toward them *or* our moral obligations toward them are based on something other than care. Critics have argued that Noddings's account of care results in the conclusion that we have *no* obligations to distant peoples. This is because Noddings not only delimits caring to personal relations but defends caring as an alternative to, not merely a complement to justice. As Claudia Card writes, "Resting all of ethics on caring threatens to exclude as ethically insignificant our relationships with most people in the world, because we do not know them and never will" (Card 1990a, 102). Obviously, this is a morally unacceptable conclusion.

In responding to the criticisms of Card and others on this point, Noddings has insisted that she did not mean to suggest that we have no moral obligations to people we do not know. But she has seemed unsure of how to account for these obligations. At times she suggests that her account of caring might be somehow extended to include obligations toward distant people. She offers, for instance, that we might "construct ever-widening circles of care," such that I care for people I meet, who in turn care for people they meet, and so on, until, presumably, everyone is cared for (Noddings 1991, 97). Moreover, recognizing the importance of personal contact in caring, we might press those nearby the distant needy to care for them. In short, at times it looks like Noddings would like her account of caring to be comprehensive but not at the expense of diluting caring so that it does not require personal contact.

At other times, Noddings seems willing to acknowledge that justice is necessary for a comprehensive account of morality. For instance, she writes, "Reducing everything in moral theory to caring is indeed likely to be an error—as are most reductionist attempts—and I did not intend to do this. However, I am not ready to say exactly how justice and care should be combined" (Noddings 1990, 120). Noddings may not be willing to draw the obvious conclusion, but others are: If care is restricted to personal relationships, then all moral obligations beyond personal relations must be based on justice. John Broughton defends Kohlberg against advocates of the ethic of care in writing that justice is "intended as the abstract form that caring takes when respect is maintained and responsibility assumed for people whom one does not know personally and may never come to know" (Broughton 1983, 614).[2] Our moral obligations toward starving children in Africa must be based on abstract principles of justice, according to which, for example, all human beings have a right to have their basic subsistence needs met. The individuating details of these people's lives are both unavailable and irrelevant when we make this judgment: The point is, they are starving and should be fed.

Thus, it has been argued that the first feature of care I have emphasized—its contextuality—requires that care be a personal ethic. Again, this argument holds that because it is impossible to take a contextual perspective in nonpersonal contexts, we must take an abstract perspective. The second feature of care is also thought to rule out the possibility of the ethic of care in non-personal contexts. The ethic of care presupposes the ontological view that the self is socially constituted or defined through its relationships to others. According to this view, *all* individuals, not just those who accept the ethic of care, are socially constituted. Those who accept the ethic of care tend to *experience* themselves as socially constituted and because of this experience, feel an obligation to care for those to whom they feel connected. Yet this experience of social connection is thought to have a limited scope. The recipients of one's care may be one's friends, one's family, or possibly even one's community or nation, but it is hard to imagine that one could experience oneself as connected to all human beings. As Owen Flanagan and Kathryn Jackson argue, citing Hume, it is part of our basic psychological makeup that we have great difficulty widening our "fellow feeling" indefinitely (Flanagan and Jackson 1987, 625). Thus the sense of social connection thought to underlie the ethic of care seems to limit the ethic's scope. According to this argument, since justice does not rely on this social sense,[3] we must turn to rationally grounded theories of justice to ground our moral obligations to those distant and different from us.

Others have allowed that it may be *possible* to use an ethic of care in nonpersonal contexts but have argued that it is nevertheless *unjust* to do so. They have agreed with the above critics that the sense of social connection underlying the ethic of care is limited and have envisioned a public ethic of care based on that sense of social connection. Such an ethic of care would express partiality toward our friends and family members. As Friedman points out, "The infamous 'boss' of Chicago's old-time Democratic machine, Mayor Richard J. Daley, was legendary for his nepotism and political partisanship, he cared extravagantly for his relatives, friends, and political cronies" (Friedman 1987a, 103). Such critics argue that because the ethic of care involves favoritism toward those one is related to, it must be restricted to the sphere of personal relations, where such favoritism is appropriate. To use the Bernard Williams's famous example, a man is allowed (or even required) to save his drowning wife before he saves a drowning stranger (Williams 1981). But, at least in many businesses, it would be morally wrong for that man to *hire* his wife simply because she was his wife. In favoring those close to us, a public ethic of care would be unfair to those outside one's sphere of personal relations.

Others have argued that a political ethic of care would involve partiality toward those we do not know personally, but whom we experience as "like" ourselves in other senses. Joan Tronto writes: "We care more for those who are emotionally, physically, and even culturally closer to us. Thus an ethic of care could become a defense of caring only for one's own family, friends, group, nation. From this perspective, caring could become a justification for any set of conventional relationships" (Tronto 1987, 659). In other words, public versions of the ethic of care, based on a sense of social connection, would seem to endorse clear injustices such as racism or sexism. Therefore we must appeal to the ethic of justice, and its commitment to impartiality, to account for our moral obligations to those we understand as different from us. Rosemarie Tong makes the same point in terms of the abstract/concrete distinction between the two ethics:

> *Given the fact that so many social groups knowingly or negligently, willfully or unintentionally, fail to care about those whose sex, race, ethnicity, religion differ from our own, justice must be treasured. Justice often is correctly blind to particulars in order to prevent details of sex, race, and creed from determining whether we care for someone or not (Tong 1993, 126).*

The ethic of care's attention to individual particularities, including the particular relationship between the carer and the person cared for, seem to make it inappropriate as a moral theory for the public sphere. Only an ethic that abstracts from such particularities can avoid unjust favoritism in public decisionmaking.

Finally, some arguments for the restriction of the ethic of care to personal relations focus on the ethic's distinctive priorities: meeting individuals' needs and maintaining one's relationships to others. Critics have argued that such priorities would fail to meet the moral demands of the public sphere, specifically the resolution of conflicting claims, whereas the ethic of justice is specifically designed to address such conflicts. Kohlberg writes that the "ethic of care is, in and of itself, not well-adapted to resolve . . . problems which require principles to resolve conflicting claims among persons, all of whom in some sense should be cared about" (Kohlberg, 1984, 20–21). The ethic of care asks us to meet everyone's needs, but the fact of conflicts over the division of scarce resources, which are the conflicts characteristic of the public sphere, means that not everyone's needs *can* be met. A comprehensive moral theory must offer us fair ways to settle such conflicts, and the ethic of care, with its "warm, mushy and wholly impossible politics of universal love," cannot do so (Ferguson 1984, 172). Broughton also makes this argument: "A principle of help or care does not work in situations where helping one agent harms another. Even in the Heinz dilemma this is a problem; shouldn't Heinz 'care' for the druggist too?" (Broughton 1993, 123). According to Broughton, since it is impossible for

Heinz to care for both his wife and the druggist, he must dispense with an ethic of care and make use of an ethic of justice that ranks his wife's right to life against the druggist's right to property.

To summarize, the commonly cited distinguishing features of the ethic of care—its concreteness, its social conception of the self, and its priorities—seem to characterize it as an ethic of personal relations. In some ways, it would be *impossible* to expand the ethic's application beyond personal relations; in other ways it would be *morally wrong* to do so; and in still other ways, it would be *morally unhelpful* to do so.

Although I will not focus on them, corresponding arguments can be made about the role of an ethic of justice in personal or familial contexts. That is, the defining features of the family seem to rule out features of the ethic of justice: the intimacy of family members makes an abstract approach inappropriate; the extent to which our identities are defined by our families makes an individualistic conception of the self inappropriate; and the inherent hierarchy of the family makes the goal of equality inappropriate. The family, it is thought, is beyond justice, and any attempt to reduce the family to justice can only detract from the emotional ties and the common purposes that make the family morally important and unique.[4]

In this chapter I have presented the ideal types of the ethic of care and the ethic of justice. The fact that the two ethics are understood as mutually exclusive of one another has led commentators to focus on particular kinds of questions, such as *which* ethic is better, either in general, or in a particular situation such as the Heinz dilemma. However, as I will argue, it has discouraged commentators from addressing the most important questions surrounding the two ethics, such as how we can distinguish between better and worse versions of each ethic, and how the two ethics are related to one another. In the following chapters, I show some of the limitations and consequences of these ideal types, as well as how we might move beyond them.

ENDNOTES

1 Individual theorists who might be understood as defending an ethic of justice would not accept this view. For example, Kant's "will" is not choice, and "consent" is what any rational being *could* will, Kant agrees that we recognize rather than choose our obligations to others. Nevertheless, contractual thinking is an important element in many versions of the ethic of justice, including those of some neo-Kantians such as Rawls. See Held 1987b.

2 I will not examine the claim that this *is* Kohlberg's view but instead the claim that one *could* have such a theory of justice.

3 In Chapter 4, I will argue that it *does*. We apply principles of justice to humans but not usually to non-humans because we experience ourselves as more connected to humans than to nonhumans.

4 See Sandel 1982 for the view that justice is inappropriate in the family.

DISCUSSION QUESTIONS

1. Clement offers Kant as an example of an ethic of justice. Explain in what ways this is so.

2. One early advocate of an ethic of care that Clement mentions is Nel Noddings (b. 1929). Explain the discussion of Noddings's work that occurs in Clement's chapter.

3. Discuss Clement's consideration of Gilligan and Kohlberg in the course of the chapter.

4. Some argue that Hume was an early advocate of something like an ethic of care. Is there anything in the passages we considered from Hume's ethics that might support this interpretation of Hume? Explain.